STERLING
Test Prep

GRE

Physics

Practice Questions

4th edition

www.Sterling-Prep.com

Copyright © 2019 Sterling Test Prep

4 3 2 1

ISBN-13: 978-1-9475564-7-8

Sterling Test Prep products are available at special quantity discounts for sales, promotions, academic counseling offices and other educational purposes.

For more information contact our Sales Department at:

Sterling Test Prep
6 Liberty Square #11
Boston, MA 02109
info@sterling-prep.com

© 2019 Sterling Test Prep

Published by Sterling Test Prep

Congratulations on choosing this book as part of your GRE Physics preparation!

Scoring well on the GRE Physics is important for admission to graduate school. To achieve a high score, you need to develop skills to properly apply the knowledge you have and quickly choose the correct answer. You must solve numerous practice questions that represent the style and content of GRE Physics questions. Understanding key physical relationships and formulas is more valuable for the test than memorizing terms.

This book provides over 1,335 physics practice questions that test your knowledge of GRE Physics topics. The book contains six Diagnostic Tests to help you identify the topics you are not well prepared for. It also contain six sections of topical practice questions, so you can selectively work with the topic you want to study and master. In the second part of the book, you will find the answer keys and detailed step-by-step solutions to the problems in the diagnostic tests and topical practice questions.

To extract the maximum benefit from this book, we recommend that you start by doing the first two Diagnostic Tests and using the answer keys to identify the topics you need to spend more time on. Spend some time going through the explanations to these Diagnostic Tests. Review them all, not only those that you got right. After this, practice with the topical questions for those topics you identified as your weak areas; take your time and master those questions. Now take another two Diagnostic Tests. At this point, you should see a dramatic improvement in your performance on the topics that you practiced. Analyze your performance on the second set of diagnostic tests and find new topics that you can improve on. Work with the corresponding topical practice questions. Finally, take the last two of the six Diagnostic Tests. At this point, you should be very strong on all topics. If you still find weaknesses, spend extra time going through the solutions and do more practice.

Your goal should be to complete all six Diagnostic Tests, all topical practice questions and go through all the explanations. These explanations provide step-by-step solutions for quantitative questions and detailed explanations for conceptual questions. The explanations include the foundations and details of important science topics needed to answer related questions on the GRE Physics. By reading these explanations carefully and understanding how they apply to solving the question, you will learn important physical concepts and the relationships between them. This will prepare you for the GRE Physics test and you will significantly increase your score.

We wish you great success in your future academic achievements and look forward to being an important part of your successful preparation for GRE Physics!

Sterling Test Prep Team   180628gdx

Our Commitment to the Environment

Sterling Test Prep is committed to protecting our planet's resources by supporting environmental organizations with proven track records of conservation, environmental research and education and preservation of vital natural resources. A portion of our profits is donated to support these organizations so they can continue their important missions. These organizations include:

 For over 40 years, Ocean Conservancy has been advocating for a healthy ocean by supporting sustainable solutions based on science and cleanup efforts. Among many environmental achievements, Ocean Conservancy laid the groundwork for an international moratorium on commercial whaling, played an instrumental role in protecting fur seals from overhunting and banning the international trade of sea turtles. The organization created national marine sanctuaries and served as the lead non-governmental organization in the designation of 10 of the 13 marine sanctuaries.

 For 25 years, Rainforest Trust has been saving critical lands for conservation through land purchases and protected area designations. Rainforest Trust has played a central role in the creation of 73 new protected areas in 17 countries, including Falkland Islands, Costa Rica and Peru. Nearly 8 million acres have been saved thanks to Rainforest Trust's support of in-country partners across Latin America, with over 500,000 acres of critical lands purchased outright for reserves.

 Since 1980, Pacific Whale Foundation has been saving whales from extinction and protecting our oceans through science and advocacy. As an international organization, with ongoing research projects in Hawaii, Australia and Ecuador, PWF is an active participant in global efforts to address threats to whales and other marine life. A pioneer in non-invasive whale research, PWF was an early leader in educating the public, from a scientific perspective, about whales and the need for ocean conservation.

Thank you for choosing our products to achieve your educational goals.

With your purchase you support environmental causes around the world.

Table of Contents

Table of Contents (*continued*)

Test-Taking Strategies For GRE Physics

The best way to do well on GRE Physics is to be really good at physics. There is no way around that. Prepare for the test as much as you can, so you can answer with confidence as many questions as possible. With that being said, for multiple choice questions the only thing that matters is how many questions were answered correctly, not how much work you did to come up with those answers. A lucky guess will get you the same points as an answer you knew with confidence.

Below are some test-taking strategies to help you maximize your score. Many of these strategies you already know and they may seem like common sense. However, when a student is feeling the pressure of a timed test, these common sense strategies might be forgotten.

Mental Attitude

If you psych yourself out, chances are you will do poorly on the test. To do well, particularly in physics, which calls for cool, systemic thinking, you must remain calm. If you start to panic, your mind will not be able to find correct solutions to the questions. Many steps can be taken before the test to increase your confidence level. Buying this book is a good start because you can begin to practice, learn the information you need to know to master the topics and get used to answering physics questions. However, there are other things you should keep in mind:

Study in advance. The information will be more manageable, and you will feel more confident if you've studied at regular intervals during the weeks leading up to the test. Cramming the night before is not a successful tactic.

Be well rested. If you are up late the night before the test, chances are you will have a difficult time concentrating and focusing on the day of the test, as you will not feel fresh and alert.

Come up for air. The best way to take this long test is not to keep your head down, concentrating the full 170 minutes. Even though you have only a short time to answer each question and there is no time to waste, it is recommended to take a few seconds between the questions to take a deep breath and relax your muscles.

Time Management

Aside from good preparation, time management is the most important strategy that you should know how to use on any test. You have an average time of 1 minute 42 seconds for each question. You will breeze through some in fifteen seconds, and others you may be stuck on for two minutes.

Do not dwell on any one question for too long. You should aim to look at every question on the test. It would be unfortunate to not earn the points for a question you could have easily answered just because you did not get a chance to look at it. If you are still in the first half of the test and find yourself spending more than a minute on one question and not getting closer to solving it, it is better to move on. It will be more productive if you come back to this question with a fresh mind at the end of the test. You do not want to lose points because you were stuck on one or few questions and did not get a chance to work with other questions that are easy for you.

Nail the easy questions quickly. On GRE physics tests, you get as many points for answering easy questions as you do for answering difficult questions. This means that you get a lot more points for five quickly answered questions than for one hard-earned victory. The questions do increase in difficulty as you progress throughout the test. However, each student has their strong and weak areas, and you might be a master on a certain type of questions that are normally considered difficult. Skip the questions you are struggling with and nail the easy ones.

Skip the unfamiliar. If you come across a question that is totally unfamiliar to you, skip it. Do not try to figure out what is going on or what they are trying to ask. At the end of the test, you can go back to these questions if you have time. If you are encountering a question that you have no clue about, most likely you won't be able to answer it through analysis. The better strategy is to leave such questions to the end and use the guessing strategy on them at the end of the test.

Set a Target Score

The task of pacing yourself will become easier if you are aware of the number of questions you need to answer to reach the score you want to get. Always strive for the highest score, but also be realistic about your level of preparation. It may be helpful if you research what counts as a good score for the programs you are applying to. You can talk to admissions offices at schools, research guidebooks or specific schools' websites. Find the average score received by students that were admitted to the graduate schools of your choice and set your target score higher than the average.

If the average score on GRE Physics for the school you are interested in is 700, set your target at about 750. To achieve that score, you need to get about 54 questions right. Therefore, you can leave a number of questions blank, get some wrong, and still achieve 750. If you have an idea of how many questions you need to answer correctly, you can pace yourself accordingly. Keep in mind that you will likely get some questions wrong.

Understanding the Question

It is important that you know what the question is asking before you select your answer choice. This seems obvious, but it is surprising how many students don't read a question carefully because they rush through the test and select a wrong answer choice.

A successful student will not just read the question, but will take a moment to understand the question before even looking at the answer choices. This student will be able to separate the important information from distracters and will not get confused on the questions that are asking to identify a false statement (which is the correct answer). Once you've identified what you're dealing with and what is being asked, you should be able to spend less time on picking the right answer. If the question is asking for a general concept, try to answer the question before looking at the answer choices, then look at the choices. If you see a choice that matches the answer you thought of, most likely it is the correct choice.

Correct Way to Guess

Random guessing will not help you on the test, but educated guessing is the strategy you should use in certain situations if you can eliminate at least one (or even two) of the five possible choices.

If you just randomly entered responses for the first 20 questions, there is a 20% chance of guessing correctly on any given question. Therefore, the odds are you would guess right on 4 questions and wrong on 16 questions. However, if for each of the 20 questions you can eliminate one answer choice because you know it to be wrong, you will have a 25% chance of being right. Therefore, your odds would move to 5 questions right and 15 questions wrong.

Guessing is not cheating and should not be viewed that way. Rather, it is a form of "partial credit" because while you might not be sure of the correct answer, you do have relevant knowledge to identify one or two choices that are wrong.

GRE Physics Tips

Tip 1: Know the formulas

Since 70–80% of the test requires that you know how to use the formulas, it is imperative that you memorize and understand when to use each one. It is not permitted to bring any papers with notes to the test. Therefore, you must memorize all the formulas you will need to solve the questions on the test, and there is no way around it.

As you work with this book, you will learn the application of all the important physical formulas and will use them in many different question types. If you are feeling nervous about having a lot of formulas in your head and worry that it will affect your problem-solving skills, look over the formulas right before you go into the testing space and write them down before you start the test. This way, you don't have to worry about remembering the formulas throughout the test. When you need to use them, you can refer back to where you wrote them down earlier.

Tip 2: Know how to manipulate the formulas

You must know how to apply the formulas in addition to just memorizing them. Questions will be worded in ways unfamiliar to you in order to test whether you can manipulate equations that you know to calculate the correct answer. Knowing that $F = ma$ is not helpful without understanding that $a = F/m$, because it is very unlikely that a question will ask to calculate the force acting on an object with a given mass and acceleration. Rather, you will be asked to calculate the acceleration of an object of a given mass with the force acting on it.

Tip 3: Estimating

This tip is only helpful for quantitative questions. For example, estimating can help you choose the correct answer if you have a general sense of the order of magnitude. This is especially applicable to questions where all answer choices have different orders of magnitude and you can save time that you would have to spend on actual calculations.

Tip 4: Draw the question

Do not hesitate to write, draw or graph your thought process once you have read and understood the question. This can help you determine what kind of information you are dealing with. Draw the force and velocity vectors, ray/wave paths, or anything else that may be helpful. Even if a question does not require a graphic answer, drawing a graph (for example, a sketch of a particle's velocity) can allow a solution to become obvious.

Tip 5: Eliminating wrong answers

This tip utilizes the strategy of educated guessing. You can usually eliminate one or two answer choices right away in most questions. In addition, there are certain types of questions for which you can use a particular elimination method.

By using logical estimations for qualitative questions, you can eliminate the answer choices that are unreasonably high or unreasonably low.

Roman numeral questions are the type of multiple-choice questions that list a few possible answers with five different combinations of these answers. Supposing that you know that one of the Roman numeral choices is wrong, you can eliminate all answer choices that include it. These questions are usually difficult for most test takers because they tend to present more than one potentially correct statement which is often included in more than one answer choice. However, they have a certain upside if you can eliminate at least one wrong statement.

Last helpful tip: fill in your answers carefully

This seems like a simple thing, but it is extremely important. Many test takers make mistakes when filling in answers, regardless of whether it is a paper test or computer-based test. Make sure you pay attention and check off the answer choice you actually chose as correct.

COMMON PHYSICS FORMULAS & CONVERSIONS

Constants and Conversion Factors

1 unified atomic mass unit	$1\ u = 1.66 \times 10^{-27}$ kg
	$1\ u = 931$ MeV/c^2
Proton mass	$m_p = 1.67 \times 10^{-27}$ kg
Neutron mass	$m_n = 1.67 \times 10^{-27}$ kg
Electron mass	$m_e = 9.11 \times 10^{-31}$ kg
Electron charge magnitude	$e = 1.60 \times 10^{-19}$ C
Avogadro's number	$N_0 = 6.02 \times 10^{23}$ mol^{-1}
Universal gas constant	$R = 8.31$ J/(mol·K)
Boltzmann's constant	$k_B = 1.38 \times 10^{-23}$ J/K
Speed of light	$c = 3.00 \times 10^8$ m/s
Planck's constant	$h = 6.63 \times 10^{-34}$ J·s
	$h = 4.14 \times 10^{-15}$ eV·s
	$hc = 1.99 \times 10^{-25}$ J·m
	$hc = 1.24 \times 10^3$ eV·nm
Vacuum permittivity	$\varepsilon_0 = 8.85 \times 10^{-12}$ C^2/N·m^2
Coulomb's law constant	$k = 1/4\pi\varepsilon_0 = 9.0 \times 10^9$ N·m^2/C^2
Vacuum permeability	$\mu_0 = 4\pi \times 10^{-7}$ (T·m)/A
Magnetic constant	$k' = \mu_0/4\pi = 10^{-7}$ (T·m)/A
Universal gravitational constant	$G = 6.67 \times 10^{-11}$ m^3/kg·s^2
Acceleration due to gravity at Earth's surface	$g = 9.8$ m/s^2
1 atmosphere pressure	$1\ atm = 1.0 \times 10^5$ N/m^2
	$1\ atm = 1.0 \times 10^5$ Pa
1 electron volt	$1\ eV = 1.60 \times 10^{-19}$ J
Balmer constant	$B = 3.645 \times 10^{-7}$ m
Rydberg constant	$R = 1.097 \times 10^7$ m^{-1}
Stefan constant	$\sigma = 5.67 \times 10^{-8}$ W/m^{2}K^4

Units			Prefixes	
Name	**Symbol**	**Factor**	**Prefix**	**Symbol**
meter	m	10^{12}	tera	T
kilogram	kg	10^{9}	giga	G
second	s	10^{6}	mega	M
ampere	A	10^{3}	kilo	k
kelvin	K	10^{-2}	centi	c
mole	mol	10^{-3}	mili	m
hertz	Hz	10^{-6}	micro	μ
newton	N	10^{-9}	nano	n
pascal	Pa	10^{-12}	pico	p
joule	J			
watt	W			
coulomb	C			
volt	V			
ohm	Ω			
henry	H			
farad	F			
tesla	T			
degree Celsius	°C			
electronvolt	eV			

Values of Trigonometric Functions for Common Angles

θ	$\sin \theta$	$\cos \theta$	$\tan \theta$
0°	0	1	0
30°	1/2	$\sqrt{3}/2$	$\sqrt{3}/3$
37°	3/5	4/5	3/4
45°	$\sqrt{2}/2$	$\sqrt{2}/2$	1
53°	4/5	3/5	4/3
60°	$\sqrt{3}/2$	1/2	$\sqrt{3}$
90°	1	0	∞

Newtonian Mechanics

Translational Motion	$v = v_0 + a\Delta t$ $x = x_0 + v_0\Delta t + \frac{1}{2}a\Delta t^2$ $v^2 = v_0^2 + 2a\Delta x$ $\vec{a} = \frac{\sum \vec{F}}{m} = \frac{\vec{F}_{net}}{m}$	a = acceleration A = amplitude E = energy F = force f = frequency h = height
Rotational Motion	$\omega = \omega_0 + \alpha t$ $\theta = \theta_0 + \omega_0 t + \frac{1}{2}\alpha t^2$ $\omega^2 = \omega_0^2 + 2\alpha\Delta\theta$ $\vec{\alpha} = \frac{\sum \vec{\tau}}{I} = \frac{\vec{\tau}_{net}}{I}$	I = rotational inertia J = impulse K = kinetic energy k = spring constant ℓ = length
Force of Friction	$|\vec{F}_f| \leq \mu|\vec{F}_n|$	m = mass N = normal force
Centripetal Acceleration	$a_c = \frac{v^2}{r}$	P = power p = momentum
Torque	$\tau = r_\perp F = rF\sin\theta$	L = angular momentum r = radius of distance
Momentum	$\vec{p} = m\vec{v}$	T = period
Impulse	$\vec{J} = \Delta\vec{p} = \vec{F}\Delta t$	t = time U = potential energy
Kinetic Energy	$K = \frac{1}{2}mv^2$	v = velocity or speed W = work done on a
Potential Energy	$\Delta U_g = mg\Delta y$	system
Work	$\Delta E = W = F_\parallel d = Fd\cos\theta$	x = position
Power	$P = \frac{\Delta E}{\Delta t} = \frac{\Delta W}{\Delta t}$	y = height

Simple Harmonic Motion	$x = A\cos(\omega t) = A\cos(2\pi f t)$	α = angular acceleration
Center of Mass	$x_{cm} = \dfrac{\sum m_i x_i}{\sum m_i}$	
Angular Momentum	$L = I\omega$	μ = coefficient of friction
Angular Impulse	$\Delta L = \tau \Delta t$	θ = angle
		τ = torque
Angular Kinetic Energy	$K = \dfrac{1}{2} I \omega^2$	ω = angular speed
Work	$W = F\Delta r \cos\theta$	
Power	$P = F\upsilon \cos\theta$	
Spring Force	$\left|\vec{F}_s\right| = k\left|\vec{x}\right|$	
Spring Potential Energy	$U_s = \dfrac{1}{2}kx^2$	
Period of Spring Oscillator	$T_s = 2\pi\sqrt{m/k}$	
Period of Simple Pendulum	$T_p = 2\pi\sqrt{\ell/g}$	
Period	$T = \dfrac{2\pi}{\omega} = \dfrac{1}{f}$	
Gravitational Body Force	$\left|\vec{F}_g\right| = G\dfrac{m_1 m_2}{r^2}$	
Gravitational Potential Energy of Two Masses	$U_G = -\dfrac{G m_1 m_2}{r}$	

Electricity and Magnetism

Electric Field
$$\vec{E} = \frac{\vec{F}_E}{q}$$

Electric Field Strength
$$|\vec{E}| = \frac{1}{4\pi\varepsilon_0}\frac{|q|}{r^2}$$

Electric Field Strength
$$|\vec{E}| = \frac{|\Delta V|}{|\Delta r|}$$

Electrostatic Force Between Charged Particles
$$|\vec{F}_E| = \frac{1}{4\pi\varepsilon_0}\frac{|q_1 q_2|}{r^2}$$

Electric Potential Energy
$$\Delta U_E = q\Delta V$$

Electrostatic Potential due to a Charge
$$V = \frac{1}{4\pi\varepsilon_0}\frac{q}{r}$$

Capacitor Voltage
$$V = \frac{Q}{C}$$

Capacitance of a Parallel Plate Capacitor
$$C = \kappa\varepsilon_0\frac{A}{d}$$

Electric Field Inside a Parallel Plate Capacitor
$$E = \frac{Q}{\varepsilon_0 A}$$

Capacitor Potential Energy
$$U_C = \frac{1}{2}Q\Delta V = \frac{1}{2}C(\Delta V)^2$$

Current
$$I = \frac{\Delta Q}{\Delta t}$$

Resistance
$$R = \frac{\rho l}{A}$$

Power
$$P = I\Delta V$$

A = area
B = magnetic field
C = capacitance
d = distance
E = electric field
ϵ = emf
F = force
I = current
l = length
P = power
Q = charge
q = point charge
R = resistance
r = separation
t = time
U = potential energy
V = electric potential
v = speed
κ = dielectric constant
ρ = resistivity
θ = angle
Φ = flux

Current	$I = \dfrac{\Delta V}{R}$
Resistors in Series	$R_s = \displaystyle\sum_i R_i$
Resistors in Parallel	$\dfrac{1}{R_p} = \displaystyle\sum_i \dfrac{1}{R_i}$
Capacitors in Parallel	$C_p = \displaystyle\sum_i C_i$
Capacitors in Series	$\dfrac{1}{C_s} = \displaystyle\sum_i \dfrac{1}{C_i}$
Magnetic Field Strength (from a long straight current-carrying wire)	$B = \dfrac{\mu_0 I}{2\pi r}$
Magnetic Force	$\vec{F}_M = q\vec{v} \times \vec{B}$ $\vec{F}_M = \lvert q\vec{v} \rvert \lvert \sin\theta \rvert \lvert \vec{B} \rvert$ $\vec{F}_M = I\vec{l} \times \vec{B}$ $\vec{F}_M = \lvert I\vec{l} \rvert \lvert \sin\theta \rvert \lvert \vec{B} \rvert$
Magnetic Flux	$\Phi_B = \vec{B} \cdot \vec{A}$ $\Phi_B = \lvert \vec{B} \rvert \cos\theta \lvert \vec{A} \rvert$
Electromagnetic Induction	$\epsilon = \dfrac{-\Delta\Phi_B}{\Delta t}$ $\epsilon = Blv$

Fluid Mechanics and Thermal Physics

Density	$\rho = \dfrac{m}{V}$	A = area
Pressure	$P = \dfrac{F}{A}$	c = specific heat
Absolute Pressure	$P = P_0 + \rho g h$	d = thickness
Buoyant Force	$F_b = \rho V g$	e = emissivity
Fluid Continuity Equation	$A_1 v_1 = A_2 v_2$	F = force
Bernoulli's Equation	$P_1 + \rho g y_1 + \dfrac{1}{2}\rho v_1^2 = P_2 + \rho g y_2 + \dfrac{1}{2}\rho v_2^2$	h = depth
Heat Conduction	$\dfrac{Q}{\Delta t} = \dfrac{kA\Delta T}{d}$	k = thermal conductivity
Thermal Radiation	$P = e\sigma A(T^4 - T_C^4)$	K = kinetic energy
Ideal Gas Law	$PV = nRT = Nk_BT$	l = length
Average Energy	$K = \dfrac{3}{2}k_BT$	L = latent heat
Work	$W = -P\Delta V$	m = mass
Conservation of Energy	$\Delta E = Q + W$	n = number of moles
Linear Expansion	$\Delta l = \alpha l_o \Delta T$	n_c = efficiency
Heat Engine Efficiency	$n_c = |W/Q_H|$	N = number of molecules
Carnot Heat Engine Efficiency	$n_c = \dfrac{T_H - T_C}{T_H}$	P = pressure or power
Energy of Temperature Change	$Q = mc\Delta T$	Q = energy transferred to a system by heating
Energy of Phase Change	$Q = mL$	T = temperature

t = time

E = internal energy

V = volume

v = speed

W = work done on a system

y = height

σ = Stefan constant

α = coefficient of linear expansion

ρ = density

Optics

d = separation

Wavelength to Frequency	$\lambda = \dfrac{v}{f}$	

f = frequency or focal length

h = height

| Index of Refraction | $n = \dfrac{c}{v}$ | |

L = distance

M = magnification

| Snell's Law | $n_1 \sin \theta_1 = n_2 \sin \theta_2$ | |

m = an integer

| Thin Lens Equation | $\dfrac{1}{s_i} + \dfrac{1}{s_0} = \dfrac{1}{f}$ | |

n = index of refraction

R = radius of curvature

| Magnification Equation | $|M| = \left|\dfrac{h_i}{h_o}\right| = \left|\dfrac{s_i}{s_o}\right|$ | |

s = distance

v = speed

| Double Slit Diffraction | $d \sin \theta = m\lambda$ | |
| | $\Delta L = m\lambda$ | |

x = position

λ = wavelength

θ = angle

| Critical Angle | $\sin \theta_c = \dfrac{n_2}{n_1}$ | |

| Focal Length of Spherical Mirror | $f = \dfrac{R}{2}$ | |

Acoustics

		$f = frequency$
Standing Wave/ Open Pipe Harmonics	$\lambda = \dfrac{2L}{n}$	$L = length$
		$m = mass$
Closed Pipe Harmonics	$\lambda = \dfrac{4L}{n}$	$M = molecular$
		$mass$
Harmonic Frequencies	$f_n = nf_1$	$n = harmonic$
Speed of Sound in Ideal Gas	$v_{sound} = \sqrt{\dfrac{yRT}{M}}$	$number$
		$R = gas\ constant$
		$T = tension$
Speed of Wave Through Wire	$v = \sqrt{\dfrac{T}{m/L}}$	$v = velocity$
		$y = adiabatic$
Doppler Effect (Approaching Stationary Observer)	$f_{observed} = \left(\dfrac{v}{v - v_{source}}\right)f_{source}$	$constant$
		$\lambda = wavelength$
Doppler Effect (Receding Stationary Observer)	$f_{observed} = \left(\dfrac{v}{v + v_{source}}\right)f_{source}$	
Doppler Effect (Observer Moving towards Source)	$f_{observed} = \left(1 + \dfrac{v_{observer}}{v}\right)f_{source}$	
Doppler Effect (Observer Moving away from Source)	$f_{observed} = \left(1 - \dfrac{v_{observer}}{v}\right)f_{source}$	

Modern Physics

Photon Energy	$E = hf$	B = Balmer constant
		c = speed of light
Photoelectric Electron Energy	$K_{max} = hf - \phi$	E = energy
		f = frequency
Electron Wavelength	$\lambda = \dfrac{h}{p}$	K = kinetic energy
		m = mass
Energy Mass Relationship	$E = mc^2$	p = momentum
Rydberg Formula	$\dfrac{1}{\lambda} = R(\dfrac{1}{n_f^2} - \dfrac{1}{n_i^2})$	R = Rydberg constant
		v = velocity
Balmer Formula	$\lambda = B(\dfrac{n^2}{n^2 - 2^2})$	λ = wavelength
		ϕ = work function
Lorentz Factor	$\gamma = \dfrac{1}{\sqrt{1 - \dfrac{v^2}{c^2}}}$	γ = Lorentz factor

Geometry and Trigonometry

Rectangle	$A = bh$	$A = area$
		$C = circumference$
Triangle	$A = \dfrac{1}{2}bh$	$V = volume$
		$S = surface\ area$
Circle	$A = \pi r^2$	$b = base$
	$C = 2\pi r$	$h = height$
Rectangular Solid	$V = lwh$	$l = length$
		$w = width$
Cylinder	$V = \pi r^2 l$	$r = radius$
	$S = 2\pi rl + 2\pi r^2$	$\theta = angle$
Sphere	$V = \dfrac{4}{3}\pi r^3$	
	$S = 4\pi r^2$	
Right Triangle	$a^2 + b^2 = c^2$	
	$\sin\theta = \dfrac{a}{c}$	
	$\cos\theta = \dfrac{b}{c}$	
	$\tan\theta = \dfrac{a}{b}$	

Our guarantee – the highest quality preparation materials.

We expect our books to have the highest quality content and be error-free.

Be the first to report an error, typo or inaccuracy and receive a
$10 reward for a content error or
$5 reward for a typo or grammatical mistake.

info@sterling-prep.com

Diagnostic Test #1

Answer Sheet

#	Answer:					Mark for review	#	Answer:					Mark for review
1:	A	B	C	D	E	___	31:	A	B	C	D	E	___
2:	A	B	C	D	E	___	32:	A	B	C	D	E	___
3:	A	B	C	D	E	___	33:	A	B	C	D	E	___
4:	A	B	C	D	E	___	34:	A	B	C	D	E	___
5:	A	B	C	D	E	___	35:	A	B	C	D	E	___
6:	A	B	C	D	E	___	36:	A	B	C	D	E	___
7:	A	B	C	D	E	___	37:	A	B	C	D	E	___
8:	A	B	C	D	E	___	38:	A	B	C	D	E	___
9:	A	B	C	D	E	___	39:	A	B	C	D	E	___
10:	A	B	C	D	E	___	40:	A	B	C	D	E	___
11:	A	B	C	D	E	___	41:	A	B	C	D	E	___
12:	A	B	C	D	E	___	42:	A	B	C	D	E	___
13:	A	B	C	D	E	___	43:	A	B	C	D	E	___
14:	A	B	C	D	E	___	44:	A	B	C	D	E	___
15:	A	B	C	D	E	___	45:	A	B	C	D	E	___
16:	A	B	C	D	E	___	46:	A	B	C	D	E	___
17:	A	B	C	D	E	___	47:	A	B	C	D	E	___
18:	A	B	C	D	E	___	48:	A	B	C	D	E	___
19:	A	B	C	D	E	___	49:	A	B	C	D	E	___
20:	A	B	C	D	E	___	50:	A	B	C	D	E	___
21:	A	B	C	D	E	___	51:	A	B	C	D	E	___
22:	A	B	C	D	E	___	52:	A	B	C	D	E	___
23:	A	B	C	D	E	___	53:	A	B	C	D	E	___
24:	A	B	C	D	E	___	54:	A	B	C	D	E	___
25:	A	B	C	D	E	___	55:	A	B	C	D	E	___
26:	A	B	C	D	E	___	56:	A	B	C	D	E	___
27:	A	B	C	D	E	___	57:	A	B	C	D	E	___
28:	A	B	C	D	E	___	58:	A	B	C	D	E	___
29:	A	B	C	D	E	___	59:	A	B	C	D	E	___
30:	A	B	C	D	E	___	60:	A	B	C	D	E	___

#	Answer:					Mark for review	#	Answer:					Mark for review
61:	A	B	C	D	E	___	81:	A	B	C	D	E	___
62:	A	B	C	D	E	___	82:	A	B	C	D	E	___
63:	A	B	C	D	E	___	83:	A	B	C	D	E	___
64:	A	B	C	D	E	___	84:	A	B	C	D	E	___
65:	A	B	C	D	E	___	85:	A	B	C	D	E	___
66:	A	B	C	D	E	___	86:	A	B	C	D	E	___
67:	A	B	C	D	E	___	87:	A	B	C	D	E	___
68:	A	B	C	D	E	___	88:	A	B	C	D	E	___
69:	A	B	C	D	E	___	89:	A	B	C	D	E	___
70:	A	B	C	D	E	___	90:	A	B	C	D	E	___
71:	A	B	C	D	E	___	91:	A	B	C	D	E	___
72:	A	B	C	D	E	___	92:	A	B	C	D	E	___
73:	A	B	C	D	E	___	93:	A	B	C	D	E	___
74:	A	B	C	D	E	___	94:	A	B	C	D	E	___
75:	A	B	C	D	E	___	95:	A	B	C	D	E	___
76:	A	B	C	D	E	___	96:	A	B	C	D	E	___
77:	A	B	C	D	E	___	97:	A	B	C	D	E	___
78:	A	B	C	D	E	___	98:	A	B	C	D	E	___
79:	A	B	C	D	E	___	99:	A	B	C	D	E	___
80:	A	B	C	D	E	___	100:	A	B	C	D	E	___

> This Diagnostic Test is designed for you to assess your proficiency on each topic. Use your test results and identify areas of your strength and weakness to adjust your study plan and enhance your fundamental knowledge.

1. What property of matter determines an object's resistance to change in its state of motion?

   I. mass   II. density   III. volume

   A. I only   **B.** II only   **C.** III only   **D.** I and II only   **E.** I and III only

2. Two forces of equal magnitude act on an object. If each force is 4.6 N and the angle between them is 40°, what is the magnitude and direction of a third force for the object to be in equilibrium?

   A. 2.3 N, to the right
   B. 4.3 N, to the right

   C. 6.5 N, to the right
   D. 0.6 N, to the right
   E. 8.6 N, to the right

3. A thermally-isolated system is made up of a hot piece of aluminum and a cold piece of copper, with the aluminum and copper in thermal contact. The specific heat capacity of aluminum is more than double that of copper. Which object experiences the greater magnitude of gain or loss of heat during the time the system takes to reach thermal equilibrium?

   A. Aluminum
   B. Copper
   C. Neither, because both undergo the same magnitude of gain or loss of heat
   D. Requires knowing the masses
   E. Requires knowing the volumes

4. In the absence of friction, how much work would a boy do while pulling a 10 kg sled a distance of 3.5 m with a 20 N force?

   A. 57 J   **B.** 70 J   **C.** 1.8 J   **D.** 85 J   **E.** 280 J

5. Total constructive interference is observed when two waves with the same frequency and wavelength are at a:

   A. 45° phase difference
   B. 90° phase difference

   C. 180° phase difference
   D. –90° phase difference   **E.** 0° phase difference

6. The Doppler shift occurs when the source of waves and a detector are moving relative to each other. There is an increase in the detected frequency when the source and detector are approaching each other, and a decrease in the detected frequency when they are moving away from each other. A commuter train is moving rapidly at 50 m/s towards Kevin who is standing still. The train sounds its horn at 420 Hz. The speed of sound is 350 m/s at a temperature of 29 °C. What frequency does Kevin hear after the train passes?

   A. 335 Hz   **B.** 368 Hz   **C.** 424 Hz   **D.** 446 Hz   **E.** 295 Hz

7. As a lead weight drops into water of uniform density and continues to sink deeper, what happens to the buoyant force on the lead weight from its origin above the surface of the water?

    A. First increases, then remains constant   **C.** Increases steadily
    B. First decreases, then remains constant   **D.** First decreases, then increases steadily
                                      E. First increases, then decreases steadily

8. A charged particle that is moving in a uniform static magnetic field:

    A. may experience a magnetic force, but its speed does not change
    B. may experience a magnetic force, but its direction of motion does not change
    C. always experiences a magnetic force, and its direction of motion does change
    D. always experiences a magnetic force, and its speed does not change
    E. always experiences a magnetic force, and its direction of motion does not change

9. Two objects, I and II, have equal charge and mass. Because of equal gravitational and electrostatic forces between them, neither body is in motion. If the mass of object I is halved, equilibrium is maintained if which change occurs for object II:

    A. mass is quadrupled   **C.** charge is doubled
    B. mass is halved   **D.** charge is halved   **E.** charge is increased by $\sqrt{2}$

10. What is the focal length of a lens if a candle is placed at a distance of 4 m from the lens and the image is 2 m from the other side of the lens?

    A. –2 m   **B.** –4/3 m   **C.** 3/4 m   **D.** 2 m   **E.** 4/3 m

11. When a nucleus captures a β^- particle, the atomic number of the nucleus:

    A. increases by two   **C.** increases by one
    B. decreases by one   **D.** remains the same   **E.** decreases by two

12. How far from the heavier end must the fulcrum of a massless 10 m seesaw be if an 800 N father on one side is to balance his 200 N son at the other end?

    A. 0.5 m   **B.** 2 m   **C.** 1 m   **D.** 8 m   **E.** 6 m

13. A ball bounces on the floor three times, whereby it loses 20% of its energy with each bounce due to heating. How high is the third bounce, provided the ball was released 250 cm from the floor?

    A. 115 cm   **B.** 150 cm   **C.** 75 cm   **D.** 180 cm   **E.** 128 cm

14. What is the period of a wave if its frequency is 10 Hz?

    A. 0.1 s   **B.** 1 s   **C.** 100 s   **D.** 10 s   **E.** 0.01 s

15. What is the frequency of a pressure wave with a wavelength of 2.5 m that is traveling at 1,600 m/s?

A. 640 Hz   **B.** 5.6 kHz   **C.** 0.64 Hz   **D.** 4 kHz   **E.** 64 Hz

16. How long does it take for a rotating object to speed up from 15.0 rad/s to 33.3 rad/s if it has a uniform angular acceleration of 3.45 rad/s^2?

A. 3.45 s   **C.** 8.35 s
B. 5.30 s   **D.** 14.60 s   **E.** 20.80 s

17. Which characteristic is required for a mass spectrometer?

   A. Perpendicular electric and gravitational fields
   B. Perpendicular gravitational and magnetic fields
   C. Perpendicular magnetic and electric fields
   D. Collinear magnetic and electric fields
   E. Collinear gravitational and magnetic fields

18. What is the rms current for a 26 μF capacitor connected across a 120 V$_{rms}$ 60 Hz source?

   A. 1.2 A   **B.** 7.3 A   **C.** 2.7 A   **D.** 0 A   **E.** 0.13 A

19. A light ray in glass arrives at the glass-water interface at an angle of $\theta = 48°$ with respect to the normal. The refracted ray in the water makes an angle of $\phi = 61°$ with respect to the normal. If the angle of incidence changes to $\theta = 25°$, what is the new angle of refraction ϕ in the water? (Use index of refraction of water = 1.33)

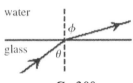

   A. 16°   **B.** 54°   **C.** 30°   **D.** 24°   **E.** 38°

20. An organ pipe is a cylindrical tube open at both ends. The air column is set to vibrate by air flowing through the lower portion of the pipe. The length of the pipe is 0.1 m and the diameter is 0.2 m. What is the frequency of the fundamental? (Use the velocity of sound $v = $ 340 m/s)

   A. 300 Hz   **B.** 600 Hz   **C.** 1,700 Hz   **D.** 800 Hz   **E.** 1,200 Hz

21. As a solid goes through a phase change to a liquid, heat is absorbed and the temperature:

   A. fluctuates   **C.** decreases
   B. remains the same   **D.** increases   **E.** depends on the heat absorbed

22. Which of the following statements is TRUE regarding the acceleration experienced by a block moving down a frictionless plane that is inclined at a 20° angle?

A. It decreases as the block moves down the plane
B. It increases as the block moves down the plane
C. It increases at a rate proportional to the incline
D. It decreases at a rate proportional to the incline
E. It remains constant

23. Which of the following statements is FALSE?

A. Waves from a vibrating string are transverse waves
B. Sound travels much slower than light
C. Sound waves are longitudinal pressure waves
D. Sound can travel through a vacuum
E. In music, pitch and frequency have approximately the same meaning

24. In a given medium with fixed boundaries, the longest wavelength that produces a standing wave is 4 m. What is the lowest possible frequency associated with a standing wave within this medium, if waves propagate through the medium at 8 m/s?

A. 0.5 Hz   B. 1 Hz   C. 2 Hz   D. 6 Hz   E. 8 Hz

25. Two charges, $Q_1 = 3.4 \times 10^{-10}$ C and $Q_2 = 6.8 \times 10^{-9}$ C, are separated by a distance of 1 cm. Let F_1 be the magnitude of the electrostatic force felt by Q_1 due to Q_2 and let F_2 be the magnitude of the electrostatic force felt by Q_2 due to Q_1. What is the ratio of F_1 / F_2?

A. 2   B. 1   C. 16   D. 8   E. 4

26. The electric power of a lamp that carries 2 A at 120 V is:

A. 24 W   B. 2 W   C. 60 W   D. 120 W   E. 240 W

27. What happens to an atom when it absorbs energy?

A. The atom re-emits the energy as light
B. The atom stores the energy as potential energy
C. The average distance between the electron and nucleus is reduced
D. The atom stores the energy as kinetic energy
E. The atom re-emits the energy as alpha particles

28. What is the de Broglie wavelength of a 1.30 kg missile moving at 28.10 m/s. (Use $h = 6.626 \times 10^{-34}$ J·s)

A. 1.85×10^{-37} m   C. 1.81×10^{-35} m
B. 2.40×10^{-36} m   D. 3.37×10^{-35} m   E. 6.43×10^{-35} m

$\frac{1}{2}(-9.8)t^2 + 42 = 0$

29. Ignoring air resistance, how long does it take a coin to reach the ground when it is dropped from a 42 m building? Use $g = 10$ m/s²

    A. 1.4 s   **B.** 2.9 s   **C.** 3.6 s   **D.** 5.4 s   **E.** 4.7 s

30. A box that weighs 40 N is on a rough horizontal surface. An external force F is applied horizontally to the box. A normal force and a friction force are also present. When force F equals 8.8 N, the box is in motion at a constant velocity. The box decelerates when force F is removed. What is the magnitude of the acceleration of the box? (Use acceleration due to gravity $g = 10$ m/s²)

    A. 0.55 m/s²   **B.** 1.1 m/s²   **C.** 4.4 m/s²   **D.** 2.2 m/s²   **E.** 0 m/s²

31. A bullet shot from a gun with a longer barrel has a greater muzzle velocity because the bullet receives a greater:

        I. force   II. impulse   III. acceleration

    A. I only   **B.** II only   **C.** III only   **D.** I and II only   **E.** II and III only

32. A 1,000 kg car is traveling at 30 m/s on a level road when the driver slams on the brakes, bringing the car to a stop. What is the change in kinetic energy during the braking, if the skid marks are 35 m long?

    A. -4.5×10^5 J   **B.** 0 J   **C.** -9×10^{10} J   **D.** 4.2×10^5 J   **E.** 9×10^{10} J

33. The graph shows the position (x) as a function of time (t) for a system undergoing simple harmonic motion. Which of the following graphs represents the acceleration of this system as a function of time?

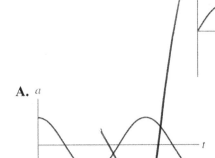

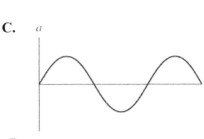

    E. None of the above

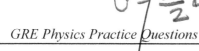
$\bar{U} = \frac{3}{2} kT$

34. What is the average kinetic energy of a molecule in an ideal gas at 740 K? (Use Boltzmann's constant $k = 1.38 \times 10^{-23}$ J/K)

    A. 3.9×10^{-19} J   **C.** 5.8×10^{-21} J

    B. 2.4×10^{-17} J   **D.** 1.5×10^{-20} J   **E.** 4.5×10^{-22} J

35. If two converging lenses with focal lengths of 10 cm and 20 cm are placed in contact, what is the power of the combination?

    A. 10 D   **B.** 15 D   **C.** 20 D   **D.** 30 D   **E.** 25 D

36. What is the capacitance of a capacitor having an impedance of 4 kΩ when operating at 0.6 kHz?

    A. 96 μF   **B.** 2.4 μF   **C.** 0.15 μF   **D.** 0.024 μF   **E.** 0.066 μF

37. A 3 Ω and a 1.5 Ω resistor are connected in parallel within a circuit. If the voltage drop across the 3 Ω resistor is 2 V, what is the sum of the currents through these two resistors?

$V = IR$

    A. 4/3 amps   **B.** 3/2 amps   **C.** 2 amps   **D.** 2/3 amps   **E.** 3/4 amps

38. The density of the material at the center of a neutron star is about 1×10^{18} kg/m³. Calculate the approximate mass of a cube of this material that is 1.76 microns on each side. 1 micron = 1×10^{-6} m.

    A. 5.5 kg   **B.** 4.8 kg   **C.** 7.8 kg   **D.** 6.4 kg   **E.** 3.6 kg

39. An adiabatic and isothermal process are shown on the pressure vs. volume diagram. Which is the isothermal process?

    I. Process A
    II. Process B
    III. Requires knowing if the gas is monatomic or diatomic

    A. I only   **C.** III only

    B. II only   **D.** I and II only   **E.** None are correct

40. Crests of an ocean wave pass a pier every 10 s. What is the wavelength of the ocean waves if the waves are moving at 4.6 m/s?

    A. 4.4 m   **B.** 0.46 m   **C.** 4.6 m   **D.** 2.2 m   **E.** 46 m

41. How much work is done on a crate if it is pushed 2 m with a force of 20 N?

    A. 10 J   **B.** 20 J   **C.** 30 J   **D.** 40 J   **E.** 50 J

42. Two friends are standing on opposite ends of a canoe which is initially at rest with respect to the lake. Steve is on the right when he throws a very massive ball to the left, and Mike, on the left, catches it. Ignoring friction between the canoe and the water, after the ball is caught, the canoe:

    A. moves to the right before reversing direction   **C.** remains stationary
    B. moves to the left before reversing direction   **D.** moves to the right
    E. moves to the left

43. At age 21, Joseph sets out for a star that is 50 light-years from Earth. How fast would his spaceship have to travel in order to reach that star when he is 61 years old? One light-year is the distance light travels in one year.

    A. $0.58c$ **B.** $0.68c$ **C.** $0.78c$ **D.** $0.88c$ **E.** $0.96c$

44. A massless, ideal spring is projected horizontally from a wall and is connected to a 0.3 kg mass. The mass is oscillating in one dimension, such that it moves 0.5 m from one end of its oscillation to the other. What is the frequency of the oscillation if it undergoes 10 complete oscillations in 60 s?

    A. 0.17 Hz   **B.** 3.9 Hz   **C.** 3.1 Hz   **D.** 11.2 Hz   **E.** 17.6 Hz

45. Aluminum has a positive coefficient of thermal expansion. Consider a round hole that has been drilled in a large sheet of aluminum. As the temperature increases and the surrounding metal expands, the diameter of the hole:

    A. either increases or decreases, depending on how much metal surrounds the hole
    B. remains constant
    C. decreases
    D. increases
    E. either increases or decreases, depending on the total change in temperature

46. Which statement is correct when a flower pot of mass m falls from rest to the ground for a distance h below?

    A. The speed of the pot when it hits the ground is proportional to m
    B. The KE of the pot when it hits the ground does not depend on h
    C. The KE of the pot when it hits the ground is proportional to h
    D. The speed of the pot when it hits the ground is proportional to h
    E. The speed of the pot when it hits the ground is inversely proportional to h

$$\tfrac{1}{2}mv^2 = mgh$$

$$v = \sqrt{2gh}$$

47. Two speakers placed 3 m apart are producing in-phase sound waves with a wavelength of 1 m. A microphone is placed between the speakers to determine the intensity of the sound at various points. What kind of point exists exactly 0.5 m to the left of the speaker on the right? (Use speed of sound $v = 340$ m/s)

    A. Node   **C.** Node and antinode
    B. Antinode   **D.** Destructive interference   **E.** None of the above

48. What causes an object to become electrostatically charged?

    A. Charge is created

    B. Protons are transferred

    C. Electrons are transferred

    D. Protons and electrons are transferred

    E. Charge is destroyed

49. A 12-liter volume of oil is subjected to pressure which produces a volume strain of -3×10^{-4}. The bulk modulus of the oil is 6.3×10^9 Pa and is independent of the pressure. What is the change in the pressure of the oil? (Use 1 atm = 10^5 Pa)

    A. 26 atm   **B.** 4 atm   **C.** 7 atm   **D.** 19 atm   **E.** 13 atm

50. A small boat is moving at a velocity of 3.35 m/s when it is accelerated by a river current perpendicular to the initial direction of motion. Relative to the initial direction of motion, what is the new velocity of the boat after 33.5 s if the current acceleration is 0.75 m/s²?

    A. 62 m/s at 7.6°

    B. 62 m/s at 82.4°

    C. 25 m/s at 7.6°

    D. 25 m/s at 82.4°

    E. 40 m/s at 82.4°

51. A machinist turns the power on for a stationary grinding wheel at time $t = 0$ s. The wheel accelerates uniformly for 10 s and reaches the operating angular velocity of 58 radians/s. The wheel is run at that angular velocity for 30 s before the power is shut off. The wheel slows down uniformly at 1.4 radians/s² until it stops. What is the approximate total number of revolutions for the wheel?

    A. 460   **B.** 320   **C.** 380   **D.** 510   **E.** 720

52. A light ray in glass arrives at the glass-water interface at an angle of $\theta = 48°$ with the normal. The refracted ray in water makes an angle of $\phi = 72°$ with respect to the normal. What is the new angle of refraction ϕ in the water if the angle of incidence is changed to $\theta = 37°$? (Use index of refraction for water n = 1.33)

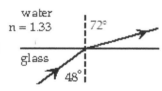

    A. 43°   **B.** 55°   **C.** 37°   **D.** 59°   **E.** 50°

53. With a total of four tuning forks, what is the greatest number of different beat frequencies that can be heard by striking the forks one pair at a time?

    A. 2   **B.** 4   **C.** 6   **D.** 8   **E.** 10

54. Initially, for the circuit shown, the switch S is open and the capacitor voltage is 80 V. The switch S is closed at time $t = 0$. What is the charge on the capacitor when the current in the circuit is 33 µA?

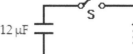

    A. 2,200 µC   **B.** 2,600 µC   **C.** 3,000 µC   **D.** 1,800 µC   **E.** 3,400 µC

55. A solid uniform sphere of mass 120.0 kg and radius 1.7 m starts from rest and rolls without slipping down an inclined plane of vertical height 5.3 m; the sphere started at the top of the ramp. What is the angular speed of the sphere at the bottom of the inclined plane? The moment of inertia of a solid sphere is $(2/5)mR^2$.

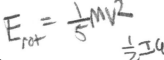

A. 0.81 rad/s   **C.** 2.9 rad/s
B. 1.7 rad/s   **D.** 4.3 rad/s   **E.** 5.1 rad/s

56. Which of the following is a TRUE statement?

A. It is impossible to convert work entirely into heat
B. It is impossible to transfer heat from a cooler to a hotter body
C. The second law of thermodynamics is a consequence of the first law of thermodynamics
D. It is possible for heat to flow spontaneously from a hot body to a cold one or vice versa, depending on whether the process is reversible or irreversible
E. All of these statements are false

57. Ignoring air resistance, what is the speed of a rock as it hits the ground if it was dropped from a 50 m cliff? (Use acceleration due to gravity $g = 10$ m/s^2)

A. 21 m/s   **B.** 14 m/s   **C.** 32 m/s   **D.** 42 m/s   **E.** 9 m/s

58. A 15 kg block on a table is connected by a string to a 60 kg mass, which is hanging over the edge of the table. Ignoring the frictional force, what is acceleration of the 15 kg block when the 60 kg block is released? (Use acceleration due to gravity $g = 10$ m/s^2)

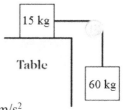

A. 9.5 m/s^2 **C.** 10.5 m/s^2
B. 7.5 m/s^2 **D.** 8 m/s^2 **E.** 6 m/s^2

59. Suppose a van de Graaff generator builds a negative static charge, and a grounded conductor is placed near enough to it so that 9 μC of negative charge arcs to the conductor. What is the number of electrons that are transferred? (Use Coulomb's constant $k = 9 \times 10^9$ N·m^2/C^2 and charge of an electron $= 1.6 \times 10^{-19}$ C)

A. 1.6×10^{18} electrons   **C.** 5.6×10^{13} electrons
B. 43.8×10^{12} electrons   **D.** 7 electrons
                                                E. 4.1×10^{20} electrons

60. What type of radioactive decay produces a daughter nuclide that is the same element as the parent nuclide?

I. Alpha   II. Gamma   III. Beta
A. I only   **B.** II only   **C.** III only   **D.** I and II only   **E.** I and III only

---

61. Two charged objects attract each other with a certain force. If the charges on both objects are doubled with no change in separation, what is the force between them?

A. Quadruples   C. Doubles   E. Requires knowing the distance between them
B. Halves   D. Becomes zero

62. A potted plant of mass M is resting on a flat board. One end of the board is lifted slowly until the potted plant begins to slide. What does the angle θ that the board must make for sliding to occur depend on?

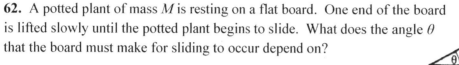

A. M
B. μ_s, static friction
C. μ_k, kinetic friction
D. g, acceleration due to gravity   E. all of the above

63. Objects 1 and 2 are heated from the same initial temperature (T_i) to the same final temperature (T_f). Object 1 has three times the specific heat capacity of Object 2 and four times the mass. If Object 1 absorbs heat Q during this process, what is the amount of heat absorbed by Object 2?

A. $(4/3)Q$ B. $(3/4)Q$ C. $6Q$ D. $12Q$ E. $(1/12)Q$

64. A 20 kg object is dropped from a height of 100 m. Ignoring air resistance, how much gravitational PE has the object lost when its speed is 30 m/s?

A. 2,050 J   B. 2,850 J   C. 9,000 J   D. 5,550 J   E. 6,750 J

65. What is the approximate wavelength of a wave that has a speed of 360 m/s and a period of 4.2 s?

A. 85.7 m   B. 1.86 m   C. 1,512 m   D. 288.6 m   E. 422.1 m

66. What is the effect on a system's mechanical energy if only the amplitude of a vibrating mass-and-spring system is doubled?

A. Increases by a factor of 2   C. Increases by a factor of 3
B. Increases by a factor of 4   D. Remains the same
     E. Increases by a factor of $\sqrt{2}$

67. When an 8.8 kg mass is suspended from a 4.4 m long wire with 1.6 mm diameter, the wire stretches by 3.3 mm. What is the Young's modulus for the wire? (Use acceleration due to gravity $g = 9.8$ m/s^2)

A. 2.4×10^{10} N/m^2 C. 5.7×10^{10} N/m^2
B. 3.6×10^{11} N/m^2 D. 7.1×10^{12} N/m^2 E. 6.9×10^{11} N/m^2

68. If the distance between two electrostatic charges is doubled, how is the force between them affected?

A. Increases by 2   C. Decreases by $\sqrt{2}$
B. Increases by 4   D. Decreases by 4   E. Remains the same

69. When fully charged, a particular battery provides 1 mW of power at 9 V. What is the current that it delivers?

    A. 0.13 kA   **B.** 9 kA   **C.** 0.11 mA   **D.** 18 mA   **E.** 0.55 mA

70. A girl of height *h* stands in front of a plane mirror. What must the minimum length of the mirror be, so she can view her entire body?

    A. ¼*h*   **C.** ½*h*
    B. 2*h*   **D.** *h*   **E.** Depends on her distance from the mirror

71. The fission of an atom that has a larger atomic number (e.g. uranium) can be induced by bombarding the atom with:

    A. electrons   **B.** positrons   **C.** neutrons   **D.** protons   **E.** gamma rays

72. A 1 kg chunk of putty moving at 1 m/s collides and sticks to a stationary 6 kg box. What is the total momentum of the box and putty? (Assume the box rests on a frictionless surface)

    A. 0 kg·m/s   **B.** 1 kg·m/s   **C.** 2 kg·m/s   **D.** 3 kg·m/s   **E.** 5 kg·m/s

73. Which statement correctly describes the situation when a 6 kg mass moving at 2 m/s and a 3 kg mass moving at 4 m/s are gliding over a horizontal frictionless surface? A horizontal force *F*, which directly opposes their motion, results in the objects coming to rest.

    A. The 6 kg mass travels twice the distance of the 3 kg mass before stopping
    B. The 3 kg mass travels farther, but less than twice the distance of the 6 kg mass before stopping
    C. The 3 kg mass travels twice the distance of the 6 kg mass before stopping
    D. The 6 kg mass loses four times more KE than the 3 kg mass before stopping
    E. The 6 kg mass loses two times more KE than the 3 kg mass before stopping

74. Which statement is correct for the separation between adjacent maxima in a double-slit interference pattern for monochromatic light?

    A. Greatest for red light   **C.** Greatest for yellow light
    B. Greatest for violet light   **D.** Greatest for blue light
                                    E. The same for all colors of light

75. If a 25 cm violin string is vibrating at its fundamental frequency of 860 Hz, what is the speed of transverse waves on the string?

    A. 220 m/s   **B.** 430 m/s   **C.** 880 m/s   **D.** 1,680 m/s   **E.** 2,260 m/s

76. A pipe with a 3 cm radius carries water at a velocity of 4 m/s. What is the volume flow rate?

    A. 1.1×10^{-2} m³/s   **C.** 7.5×10^{-3} m³/s
    B. 48 m³/s   **D.** 2.7×10^{2} m³/s   **E.** 4.3 m³/s

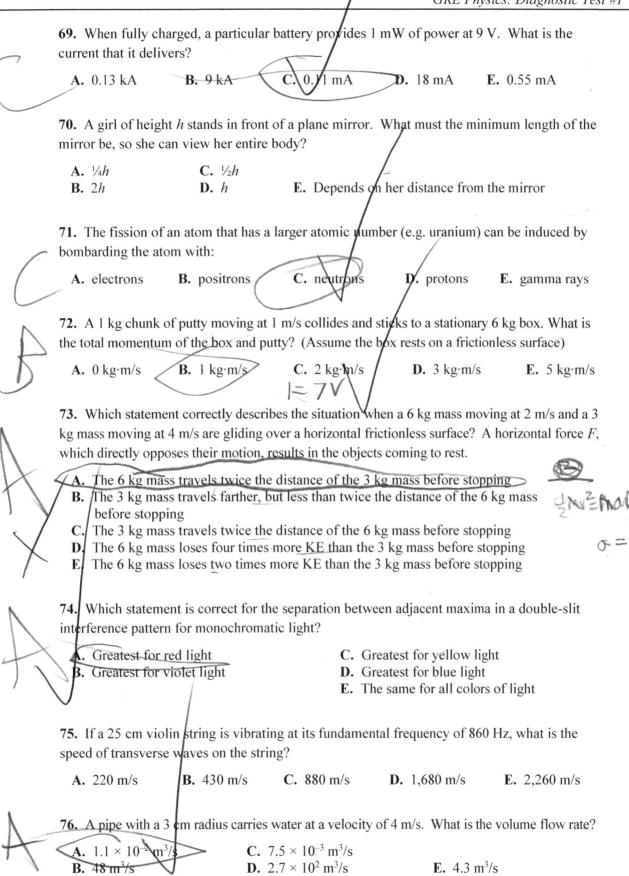

77. A conductor differs from an insulator in that a conductor has:

A. slower moving molecules   C. more protons than electrons
B. tightly-bound outer electrons   D. more electrons than protons
                                       E. none of the above

78. Which statement is true for two conductors that are joined by a long copper wire?

A. One conductor must have a lower potential than the other conductor
B. Shortening the wire increases the potential of both conductors
C. Each conductor must have the same potential
D. The potential on the wire is the sum of the potentials of each conductor
E. The potential on the wire is the average of the potentials of each conductor

79. Two antennas 130 m apart on a North-South line radiate in phase at a frequency of 3.6 MHz, and all radio measurements are recorded far away from the antennas. What is the smallest angle, East of North from the antennas, for constructive interference of the two radio waves? (Use speed of light $c = 3 \times 10^8$ m/s)

A. 45°   B. 60°   C. 50°   D. 30°   E. 90°

80. According to the quantum mechanical model of the He atom, if the orbital angular momentum quantum number is ℓ, how many magnetic quantum numbers are possible?

A. $2\ell + 1$ B. $2\ell - 1$ C. 2ℓ D. $\ell/2$ E. 3ℓ

81. The closest star to our solar system is Alpha Centauri, which is 4.367 light-years away. A spaceship with a constant speed of $0.800c$ relative to Earth travels toward the star. How many years would elapse on a clock on the earth before the spaceship reaches Alpha Centauri?

A. 0.32   B. 0.97   C. 3.56   D. 5.49   E. 7.32

82. A stable nucleus has many positively-charged protons packed very close to each other. Why do the protons not move apart due to mutual Coulomb repulsion?

A. The neutrons in the nucleus shield the protons from each other's positive charge
B. The Coulomb force cannot operate within small nuclei
C. An attractive nuclear force in the nucleus counteracts the Coulomb force
D. There are an equal number of electrons in the nucleus, which neutralize the protons
E. The gravitational force on the protons and neutrons overcome their repulsion at such close distances

83. The intensity of a sound wave is directly proportional to the:

A. Doppler shift   C. decibel level
B. power   D. wavelength   E. frequency

84. What force needs to be applied to a 6 cm diameter piston to lift a 12,000 N container with a hydraulic piston that has a diameter of 25 cm?

    A. 26 N   **B.** 360 N   **C.** 1,040 N   **D.** 2,080 N   **E.** 691 N

85. Two parallel metal plates, separated by a 0.05 m distance, are charged to produce a uniform electric field between them that points down. What is the magnitude of the force experienced by a proton between the two plates? (Use acceleration due to gravity $g = 10$ m/s^2, charge of a proton $= 1.6 \times 10^{-19}$ C and uniform electric field $= 4 \times 10^4$ N/C)

    A. 6.4×10^{-10} N   **C.** 3.2×10^{-15} N
    B. 3.2×10^{-10} N   **D.** 6.4×10^{-15} N   **E.** 2.5×10^{-5} N

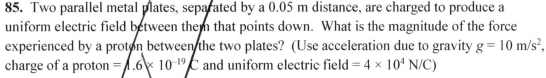

86. 200 kcal of heat raises the temperature of 3 kg of material by 90 °C. What is the material's specific heat capacity?

    A. 0.74 kcal/kg·°C   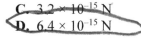   **C.** 1.42 kcal/kg·°C
    B. 0.33 kcal/kg·°C   **D.** 1.13 kcal/kg·°C   **E.** 0.14 kcal/kg·°C

87. Optical density is proportional to:

    A. index of refraction   **C.** mass density
    B. index of reflection   **D.** light speed   **E.** wavelength

88. Which radiation type penetrates about 1 cm of human tissue and requires a minimum protective shielding made of wood or aluminum?

    A. Gamma   **C.** Alpha
    B. Beta   **D.** Nuclide
                   E. None of the above

89. Reynold's number is given by Re $= L\rho v / \mu$, where L is some characteristic length related to the path that the fluid travels (e.g., the length or diameter of the pipe), ρ is the density of the fluid, v is the velocity of the fluid, and μ is the viscosity. A larger Reynold's number for a given flow indicates the increased likelihood of developing turbulence. For water flowing in a pipe, which might reduce the likelihood of turbulent flow?

    A. Raising the temperature   **C.** Increasing the flow rate
    B. Increasing the radius of the pipe   **D.** Increasing the viscosity
                                     E. None of the above

90. What is the tension in a cable that pulls a 900 kg object straight upward at an acceleration of 0.6 m/s^2? (Use acceleration due to gravity $g = 9.8$ m/s^2)

    A. 8,280 N   **B.** 980 N   **C.** 9,800 N   **D.** 9,360 N   **E.** 930 N

$$T - 9000 = 0.6(900)$$

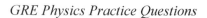

91. The masses of the blocks and the velocities before and after a collision are:

In this example, the collision is:

A. completely inelastic
B. completely elastic
C. characterized by an increase in KE
D. characterized by a decrease in momentum
E. characterized by an increase in PE

92. What is Amanda's mass, if Steve does 174 J of work while pulling her backwards on a swing that has a 5.1 m chain until the swing makes an angle of 32° with the vertical? (Use acceleration due to gravity $g = 9.8$ m/s^2)

A. 17.4 kg   **B.** 21.0 kg   **C.** 29.8 kg   **D.** 37.8 kg   **E.** 14.4 kg

93. For an object that exhibits simple harmonic motion (SHM), what is the frequency of the motion, if the shortest time interval between the two extremes of the object's displacement from its equilibrium position is 2 s?

A. 0.25 cycle/s   **C.** 2.5 cycles/s
B. 0.5 cycle/s   **D.** 5 cycles/s   **E.** 1 cycle/s

94. A few 10 cm long aluminum rods and 8 cm long steel rods are at 5 °C temperature and are joined together to form a 60 cm long rod. What is the increase in the length of the joined rod when the temperature is raised to 80 °C? (Use coefficient of linear expansion for aluminum = 2.4×10^{-5} K^{-1} and coefficient of linear expansion for steel = 1.2×10^{-5} K^{-1})

A. 0.3 mm   **B.** 0.5 mm   **C.** 1.8 mm   **D.** 0.72 mm **E.** 1.4 mm

95. Relative to the mirror, where is the resulting image when a light source is placed 12 m in front of a diverging mirror that has a focal length of 6 m?

A. 2 m in front   **C.** 4 m in front
B. 2 m behind   **D.** 4 m behind   **E.** 0.5 m in front

96. A beam of light falling on a metal surface is causing electrons to be ejected from the surface. If the frequency of the light now doubles, which of the following statements is always true?

A. The number of electrons ejected per second doubles
B. Twice as many photons hit the metal surface as before
C. The kinetic energy of the ejected electrons doubles
D. The speed of the ejected electrons doubles
E. None of the above statements is always true

97. What is the efficiency of a heat engine that receives 8,500 J of heat and loses 4,500 J in each cycle?

   A. 57%   **B.** 47%   **C.** 33%   **D.** 16%   **E.** 29%

98. A marble cube is lowered at a steady rate into the ocean by a crane, while its top and bottom surfaces remain parallel with the water's surface. Which graph describes the buoyant force (*B*) on this cube as a function of time (*t*), if the cube enters the water at time *t* = 0 s and is lowered until its top surface is well below the water?

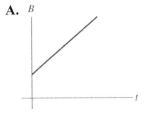

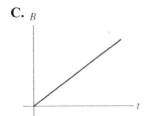

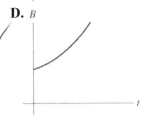

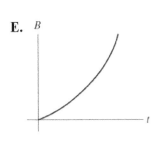

99. A commuter train is moving at a speed of 50 m/s directly toward Daud, who is whistling at 420 Hz while standing. If a passenger on the train hears him, what frequency would she hear? (Use the speed of sound *v* = 350 m/s)

   A. 300 Hz   **B.** 360 Hz   **C.** 480 Hz   **D.** 500 Hz   **E.** 520 Hz

100. Both constructive and destructive interference are necessary to produce the sound phenomena:

    beats   II. resonance   III. refraction

   A. I only   **B.** II only   **C.** III only   **D.** I and II only   **E.** I and III only

---

Check your answers using the answer key. Then, go to the explanations section and review the explanations in detail, paying particular attention to questions you didn't answer correctly or marked for review. Note the topic that those questions belong to.

We recommend that you do this BEFORE taking the next Diagnostic Test.

Diagnostic Test #2

Answer Sheet

#	Answer:					Mark for review	#	Answer:					Mark for review
1:	A	B	C	D	E	___	31:	A	B	C	D	E	___
2:	A	B	C	D	E	___	32:	A	B	C	D	E	___
3:	A	B	C	D	E	___	33:	A	B	C	D	E	___
4:	A	B	C	D	E	___	34:	A	B	C	D	E	___
5:	A	B	C	D	E	___	35:	A	B	C	D	E	___
6:	A	B	C	D	E	___	36:	A	B	C	D	E	___
7:	A	B	C	D	E	___	37:	A	B	C	D	E	___
8:	A	B	C	D	E	___	38:	A	B	C	D	E	___
9:	A	B	C	D	E	___	39:	A	B	C	D	E	___
10:	A	B	C	D	E	___	40:	A	B	C	D	E	___
11:	A	B	C	D	E	___	41:	A	B	C	D	E	___
12:	A	B	C	D	E	___	42:	A	B	C	D	E	___
13:	A	B	C	D	E	___	43:	A	B	C	D	E	___
14:	A	B	C	D	E	___	44:	A	B	C	D	E	___
15:	A	B	C	D	E	___	45:	A	B	C	D	E	___
16:	A	B	C	D	E	___	46:	A	B	C	D	E	___
17:	A	B	C	D	E	___	47:	A	B	C	D	E	___
18:	A	B	C	D	E	___	48:	A	B	C	D	E	___
19:	A	B	C	D	E	___	49:	A	B	C	D	E	___
20:	A	B	C	D	E	___	50:	A	B	C	D	E	___
21:	A	B	C	D	E	___	51:	A	B	C	D	E	___
22:	A	B	C	D	E	___	52:	A	B	C	D	E	___
23:	A	B	C	D	E	___	53:	A	B	C	D	E	___
24:	A	B	C	D	E	___	54:	A	B	C	D	E	___
25:	A	B	C	D	E	___	55:	A	B	C	D	E	___
26:	A	B	C	D	E	___	56:	A	B	C	D	E	___
27:	A	B	C	D	E	___	57:	A	B	C	D	E	___
28:	A	B	C	D	E	___	58:	A	B	C	D	E	___
29:	A	B	C	D	E	___	59:	A	B	C	D	E	___
30:	A	B	C	D	E	___	60:	A	B	C	D	E	___

#	Answer:					Mark for review	#	Answer:					Mark for review
61:	A	B	C	D	E	___	**81:**	A	B	C	D	E	___
62:	A	B	C	D	E	___	**82:**	A	B	C	D	E	___
63:	A	B	C	D	E	___	**83:**	A	B	C	D	E	___
64:	A	B	C	D	E	___	**84:**	A	B	C	D	E	___
65:	A	B	C	D	E	___	**85:**	A	B	C	D	E	___
66:	A	B	C	D	E	___	**86:**	A	B	C	D	E	___
67:	A	B	C	D	E	___	**87:**	A	B	C	D	E	___
68:	A	B	C	D	E	___	**88:**	A	B	C	D	E	___
69:	A	B	C	D	E	___	**89:**	A	B	C	D	E	___
70:	A	B	C	D	E	___	**90:**	A	B	C	D	E	___
71:	A	B	C	D	E	___	**91:**	A	B	C	D	E	___
72:	A	B	C	D	E	___	**92:**	A	B	C	D	E	___
73:	A	B	C	D	E	___	**93:**	A	B	C	D	E	___
74:	A	B	C	D	E	___	**94:**	A	B	C	D	E	___
75:	A	B	C	D	E	___	**95:**	A	B	C	D	E	___
76:	A	B	C	D	E	___	**96:**	A	B	C	D	E	___
77:	A	B	C	D	E	___	**97:**	A	B	C	D	E	___
78:	A	B	C	D	E	___	**98:**	A	B	C	D	E	___
79:	A	B	C	D	E	___	**99:**	A	B	C	D	E	___
80:	A	B	C	D	E	___	**100:**	A	B	C	D	E	___

This Diagnostic Test is designed for you to assess your proficiency on each topic. Use your test results and identify areas of your strength and weakness to adjust your study plan and enhance your fundamental knowledge.

1. Determine the resting length of a spring if one end of the spring (spring constant $k = 40$ N/m) is fixed at point P, while the other end is connected to a 7 kg mass. The fixed end and the mass sit on a horizontal frictionless surface, and the mass and the spring are able to rotate about P. The mass moves in a circle with $r = 2$ m and the force on the mass is 12 N.

    A. 0.1 m   **B.** 1.7 m   **C.** 0.8 m   **D.** 2.3 m   **E.** 3.8 m

2. An electrical motor spins at a constant 2,640 rpm. What is the acceleration of the edge of the motor if the armature radius is 7.2 cm?

    A. 87 m/s^2 **B.** 1,690 m/s^2 **C.** 8,432 m/s^2 **D.** 2,420 m/s^2 **E.** 5,451 m/s^2

3. As in the figure, when a 100 kg block is released from rest from a height of 1 m, it takes 0.51 s to hit the floor. Assuming no friction and that the pulley is massless, what is the mass of the block on the other end? (Use acceleration due to gravity $g = 9.8$ m/s^2)

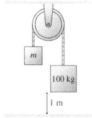

    A. 9 kg   **C.** 16 kg
    B. 23 kg   **D.** 12 kg   **E.** 19 kg

4. A rock from a volcanic eruption is propelled straight up into the air. Ignoring air resistance, which of the statements is correct about the rock while it is in the air? (Take the positive axis to point up)

    A. Throughout its motion, the acceleration is always negative
    B. Throughout its motion, the acceleration is always negative and the velocity is always increasing
    C. On the way up, its velocity is increasing and its acceleration is positive
    D. On the way down, its velocity is increasing and its acceleration is negative
    E. At the highest point, both its velocity and acceleration are zero

5. Three solid, uniform, cylindrically shaped flywheels, each of mass 65.0 kg and radius 1.47 m, rotate independently around a common axis. Two of the flywheels rotate in one direction at 3.83 rad/s; the other rotates in the opposite direction at 3.42 rad/s. What is the magnitude of the net angular momentum of the system?

    A. 168.0 kg·m^2/s   **C.** 456.0 kg·m^2/s
    B. 298.0 kg·m^2/s   **D.** 622.0 kg·m^2/s   **E.** 882.0 kg·m^2/s

6. An object weighing 50 N is traveling vertically upward from the Earth without air resistance at a constant velocity of 10 m/s. What is the power required to keep the object in motion?

    A. 0 W   **B.** 10 W   **C.** 50 W   **D.** 100 W   **E.** 500 W

7. Which statement is correct for a pipe with a length of L, that is closed at one end, and is resonating at its fundamental frequency?

    A. The wavelength is $2L$ and there is a displacement node at the pipe's closed end
    B. The wavelength is $2L$ and there is a displacement antinode at the pipe's open end
    C. The wavelength is $4L$ and there is a displacement antinode at the pipe's closed end
    D. The wavelength is $4L$ and there is a displacement antinode at the pipe's open end
    E. The wavelength is $4L$ and there is a displacement node at the pipe's open end

8. Which statement regarding the electric charge is NOT correct if the electric charge is conserved?

    A. Will not interact with neighboring electric charges
    B. Can neither be created nor destroyed
    C. Is a whole-number multiple of the charge of one electron
    D. May occur in an infinite variety of quantities
    E. Can only occur in restricted (i.e. allowable) quantities

9. Which of the graphs illustrates Hooke's Law?

A. 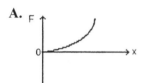   **C.**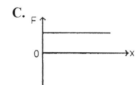

B. 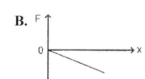   **D.** 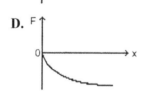   **E.** None of the above

10. The area under the curve in a velocity vs. time graph determines:

    A. position   **B.** displacement   **C.** velocity   **D.** acceleration   **E.** time

11. Which statement is correct if two hockey pucks, each with a nonzero velocity, undergo an elastic collision as they slide toward each other on a surface of frictionless ice and collide head on?

    A. Both momentum and KE are doubled
    B. Neither momentum nor KE is conserved
    C. Momentum is conserved but KE is not conserved
    D. Momentum is not conserved but KE is conserved
    E. Both momentum and KE are conserved

12. A gamma ray is a pulse of electromagnetic energy with a frequency of 2.4×10^{20} Hz. What is the ratio of its wavelength to the radius of the nucleus which produced it? (Use speed of light $c = 3 \times 10^8$ m/s and radius of the nucleus $= 5 \times 10^{-13}$ cm)

    A. 0.028   **B.** 1.33×10^7 **C.** 38.2   **D.** 250   **E.** 2.58×10^{-7}

13. A water tank open to the atmosphere is elevated above the ground by 25 m and is filled to a depth of 12 m. What is the approximate water pressure in a hose with a 2 cm diameter at ground level? (Use acceleration due to gravity $g = 9.8$ m/s^2, density of water $\rho = 1,000$ kg/m^3 and atmospheric pressure P = 1 atm or 101,325 N/m^2)

A. 8.4 N/m^2

B. 3.2×10^5 N/m^2

C. 4.6×10^5 N/m^2

D. 5.6 N/m^2

E. Requires the cross-sectional area of the tank

14. Which of the following diagrams is correct for a circuit with a battery connected to four resistors, R_1, R_2, R_3, and R_4? Resistors R_1 and R_2 are connected in parallel, resistors R_3 and R_4 are connected in parallel, and both parallel sets of resistors are connected in series across the battery.

A.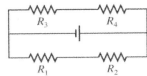

C.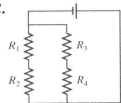

B.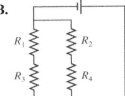

D.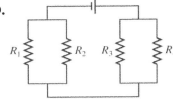

E. None of the above

15. Monochromatic light is incident on a metal surface and electrons are ejected. How do the ejection rate and maximum energy of the electrons change if the intensity of the light is increased?

A. Same rate; same maximum energy

B. Greater rate; greater maximum energy

C. Same rate; lower maximum energy

D. Greater rate; same maximum energy

E. Greater rate; lower maximum energy

16. Which is an important feature of the Carnot cycle?

A. Efficiency is determined only by the properties of the working substance used

B. It is an irreversible process that can be analyzed exactly without approximations

C. Efficiency can be 100%

D. Efficiency depends only on the absolute temperature of the hot reservoir used

E. It is the most efficient engine operating between two temperatures

17. An object travels along the *x*-axis at a constant speed of 3 m/s in the –*x* direction. If the object is on *x* = 4 m at *t* = 0, where is it at time *t* = 4 s?

    A. *x* = –16 m
    B. *x* = –12 m
    C. *x* = –8 m
    D. *x* = –6 m
    E. *x* = –2 m

18. In an air-free chamber, a pebble is thrown horizontally and, at the same instant, a second pebble is dropped from the same height. Compare the time it took for the two pebbles to hit the ground:

    A. They hit at the same time
    B. Requires values for the initial velocities of both pebbles
    C. The thrown pebble hits first
    D. The dropped pebble hits first
    E. Requires the height from which they were released

19. Cart 1 (2 kg) and Cart 2 (2.5 kg) run along a frictionless, level, one-dimensional track. Cart 2 is initially at rest, and Cart 1 is traveling 0.6 m/s toward the right when it encounters Cart 2. After the collision, Cart 1 is at rest. What is the efficiency of the collision with respect to kinetic energy?

    A. 16%   **B.** 65%   **C.** 80%   **D.** 25%   **E.** 53%

20. The two strongest forces that act between protons in a nucleus are the:

    A. electrostatic and gravitational forces
    B. strong nuclear and electrostatic forces
    C. weak nuclear and electrostatic forces
    D. strong nuclear and gravitational forces
    E. weak nuclear and gravitational forces

21. A projectile is fired at time *t* = 0 s from point O of a ledge. It has initial velocity components of v_{ox} = 30 m/s and v_{oy} = 300 m/s with a time in flight of 75 s. The projectile lands at point P. What is the horizontal distance that the projectile travels?

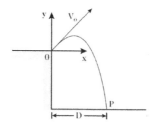

    A. 3,020 m   **B.** 2,880 m   **C.** 2,420 m   **D.** 2,250 m   **E.** 3,360 m

22. A car of mass m is traveling along the roadway up a slight incline of angle θ to the horizontal when the driver sees a deer and suddenly applies the brakes. The car skids before coming to rest. Which expression gives the force of friction on the car if the coefficient of static friction between the tires and the road is μ_s, and the coefficient of kinetic friction is μ_k?

   A. $\mu_k N$ **B.** $\mu_s N$ **C.** mg **D.** $mg \sin \theta$ **E.** $(\mu_s - \mu_k)N$

23. Once a steady-state heat flow is established, the thickness of a wall built from solid uniform material is doubled. Relative to the original value, what is the result for the rate of heat loss for a given temperature difference across the wall?

   A. $1 / \sqrt{2}$ **B.** ¼   **C.** 2 times   **D.** ½   **E.** 4 times

24. Energy is the:

    I. ability to do work
    II. work that can be done by an object with potential or kinetic energy
    III. work needed to generate potential or kinetic energy

   A. I only   **B.** II only   **C.** III only   **D.** I and III only   **E.** I, II and III

25. The displacement of a vibrating tuning fork and the resulting sound wave is related to:

   A. period   **C.** resonance
   B. wavelength   **D.** frequency   **E.** amplitude

26. The decibel level of sound is related to its:

   A. velocity   **B.** frequency   **C.** wavelength   **D.** intensity   **E.** pitch

27. A tank of water has a hose, filled with water, projecting from the top. The system acts as a siphon as the other end of the hose is below the tank. The end of the hose outside the tank is at height $h = 0$ m. The bottom of the tank is at height h_1, the end of the hose inside the tank is at height h_2, and the top of the water is at height h_3. Assuming that the flow is without viscosity, which is the best expression for the pressure at the bottom of the tank?

   A. $P_{atm} + \rho g(h_3 + h_1)$ **C.** $P_{atm} + \rho g(h_3 - h_1)$
   B. $P_{atm} - \rho g(h_3 + h_1)$ **D.** $P_{atm} - \rho g(h_3 - h_1)$ **E.** $P_{atm} \times \rho g(h_3 - h_1)$

28. Which statement(s) is/are correct?

    I. Current results in voltage
    II. Current flows through a circuit
    III. Voltage flows through a circuit

   A. I only   **B.** II only   **C.** III only   **D.** I and II only   **E.** I and III only

29. At what speed is a moving clock traveling if it is observed by a stationary observer as running at one-half its normal rate?

    A. $0.402c$ **C.** $0.682c$

    B. $0.536c$ **D.** $0.866c$ **E.** $1.090c$

30. Which of the following types of electromagnetic radiation has the highest energy per photon?

    I. Microwave   II. Infrared   III. Ultraviolet

    A. I only   **B.** II only   **C.** III only   **D.** I and II only   **E.** I and III only

31. This is an example of what type of nuclear reaction: $^{126}_{50}\text{Sn} \rightarrow {}^{126}_{51}\text{Sb}$?

    A. Transmutation   **C.** Fusion

    B. Gamma particle   **D.** Fission   **E.** Beta emission

32. A torque of 14 N·m is applied to a solid, uniform disk with a radius of 0.6 m. What is the mass of the disk if it accelerates at 5.3 rad/s^2?

    A. 7.6 kg   **B.** 4.2 kg   **C.** 14.7 kg   **D.** 21.4 kg   **E.** 13.8 kg

33. Marshall drops a water balloon from the top of a building onto Peter on the sidewalk below. Ignoring air resistance, how tall is the building if the balloon is traveling at 29 m/s when it strikes Peter's head? (Use acceleration due to gravity $g = 10$ m/s^2 and the distance of Peter's head above the ground = 1 m)

    A. 50.5 m   **B.** 37.5 m   **C.** 43 m   **D.** 26 m   **E.** 33 m

34. Assuming no change in the system's mass m, increasing the spring constant k of a spring system causes what kind of change in the resonant frequency of the system?

    A. No change   **C.** Decrease only if the ratio k/m is > 1

    B. Increase   **D.** Increase only if the ratio k/m is ≥ 1

                           E. Decrease

35. Assuming that all other factors remain constant, what happens to the velocity of sound as the temperature of the air increases?

    A. Does not change because it is dependent only on the state of the substance

    B. Increases when atmospheric pressure is high and decreases when the pressure is low

    C. Increases

    D. Decreases

    E. Decreases when atmospheric pressure is high and increases when the pressure is low

36. A 0.1 m cube consists of six aluminum plates that are insulated from each other. Plates A and D are opposite and maintained at 750 V. Plates B and E are opposite and maintained at 0 V. Plates C and F are opposite and maintained at –750 V. A force moves a charge of 10^{-14} C at constant speed straight across from the center of plate A to the center of plate D. What is the total work done by this force? (Use the elementary charge = 1.6×10^{-19} C)

A. 7.5×10^{-12} J   **C.** 5.1×10^{-14} J

B. 0 J   **D.** 7.5×10^{-14} J   **E.** 2.3×10^{5} J

37. A likely cause for the existence of Earth's magnetic field is:

    I. moving charges in the liquid part of Earth's core
    II. convection currents in the liquid part of Earth's core
    III. great numbers of very slow moving charges in the Earth

A. I only   **B.** II only   **C.** III only   **D.** I and III only   **E.** I, II and III

38. How often does the polarity of the voltage reverse in a 60 Hz circuit?

A. 60 times/s   **C.** 90 times/s

B. 120 times/s   **D.** 1/60 times/s   **E.** 30 times/s

39. A blue object appears black when illuminated with which color of light?

A. Green   **B.** Yellow   **C.** Cyan   **D.** Blue   **E.** None of the above

40. What type of radiation is released when $^{220}_{86}\text{Rn} \rightarrow \, ^{216}_{84}\text{Po}$?

    I. Gamma   II. Beta   III. Alpha

A. I only   **B.** II only   **C.** III only   **D.** I and II only   **E.** I and III only

41. According to the laws of thermodynamics:

A. entropy decreases as more energy is consumed
B. heat flows naturally from a region of lower to a region of higher temperature
C. mechanical energy cannot be completely converted into heat
D. at constant temperature, entropy increases as heat is extracted from a system
E. heat energy cannot be completely converted into mechanical energy

42. What is the net force on a 1,200 kg Alfa Romeo that is moving at a constant speed of 3.5 m/s and turning to the left on a curve of the road that has an effective radius of 4 m?

A. 1,550 N   **B.** 2,160 N   **C.** 3,675 N   **D.** 8,465 N   **E.** 5,830 N

43. A guitar has a 14 cm string and sounds a 440 Hz musical note when played without fingering. How far from the end of the string should Samantha place her fingers to play a 520 Hz note?

A. 5.8 cm   **B.** 0.8 cm   **C.** 1.6 cm   **D.** 2.2 cm   **E.** 3.4 cm

44. In Egypt, the Aswan Dam on the Nile River is 110 m high. Assuming the density of water is 1,000 kg/m^3, what is the gauge pressure of the water at the foot of the dam? (Use acceleration due to gravity $g = 10$ m/s^2)

    A. 2.1×10^5 Pa   **C.** 1.8×10^7 Pa

    B. 2.9×10^3 Pa   **D.** 1.1×10^6 Pa   **E.** 0.8×10^2 Pa

45. Consider two current-carrying circular loops. Both are made from one strand of wire each and both carry the same amount of current, but one has double the radius. Compared to the magnetic moment of the smaller loop, the magnetic moment of the larger loop is:

    A. √2 times stronger   **C.** √2 times weaker

    B. 4 times stronger   **D.** 2 times stronger   **E.** 3 times stronger

46. What is the equivalent resistance of the circuits if each has a resistance of 600 Ω?

    A. 60 Ω   **C.** 600 Ω

    B. 1,200 Ω   **D.** 175 Ω   **E.** 350 Ω

47. A simple compound microscope normally uses a:

    A. long focal length objective and a longer focal length eyepiece

    B. long focal length objective and a short focal length eyepiece

    C. focal length objective and focal length eyepiece of the same length

    D. short focal length objective and a shorter focal length eyepiece

    E. short focal length objective and a long focal length eyepiece

48. What happens to the de Broglie wavelength for a particle as it increases its velocity?

    A. Increases   **C.** Remains constant

    B. Decreases   **D** Increases by $\sqrt{\Delta v}$ **E.** Increases by Δv^2

49. What is the longest wavelength of a photon that can be emitted by a hydrogen atom, for which the initial state is n = 3?

    A. 486 nm   **B.** 510 nm   **C.** 540 nm   **D.** 610 nm   **E.** 656 nm

50. What is the reaction force if, as a ball falls, the action force is the pull of the Earth's mass on the ball?

    A. None present   **C.** The downward acceleration due to gravity

    B. The pull of the ball's mass on Earth   **D.** The air resistance acting against the ball

                                                     E. Less than the action force

51. An irregularly-shaped object 10 m long is placed with each end on two nearby scales. If the scale on the right reads 94 N and the scale on the left reads 69 N, how far from the left is the object's center of gravity? (Use acceleration due to gravity $g = 9.8$ m/s^2)

    A. 6.8 m   **B.** 6.3 m   **C.** 7.7 m   **D.** 8.1 m   **E.** 5.8 m

52. Is it possible for a system to have negative potential energy?

   A. Yes, because the choice of the zero for potential energy is arbitrary
   B. No, because this has no physical meaning
   C. Yes, if the kinetic energy is positive
   D. Yes, if the total energy is positive
   E. No, because the kinetic energy of a system must be equal to its potential energy

53. What is the speed of 2 m long water waves as they pass by a floating piece of cork that bobs up and down for one complete cycle each second?

   A. 8 m/s   **B.** 0.5 m/s   **C.** 1 m/s   **D.** 2 m/s   **E.** 4 m/s

54. When 110 J of heat is added to a system that performs 40 J of work, the total thermal energy change of the system is:

   A. 2.8 J   **B.** 40 J   **C.** 70 J   **D.** 0 J   **E.** 150 J

55. The image of a real object from a plane mirror has the following characteristics:

   A. real, erect, with magnification = 1   **C.** real, erect, with magnification > 1
   B. real, inverted, with magnification = 1   **D.** virtual, erect, with magnification = 1
                                      E. virtual, erect, with magnification < 1

56. What is the current through the 2 Ω resistor if the current through the 8 Ω resistor is 0.8 A?

   A. 15.2 A
   B. 18.7 A
   C. 1.5 A
   D. 6.6 A
   E. 8.8 A

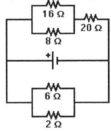

57. A proton is traveling to the right and encounters region Y that contains an electric field where the proton speeds up. In what direction does the electric field in region Y point?

   A. To the left   **C.** Down into the page
   B. To the right   **D.** Up from the page   **E.** To the left and into the page

58. An over-taut violin string was tuned with a tuning fork that produced an accurate pitch of 340 Hz. What is the period of vibration of the violin string if a beat frequency of 4 Hz is produced when the string and the fork are sounded together?

   A. 1/336 sec   **B.** 1/321 sec   **C.** 1/340 sec   **D.** 1/327 sec   **E.** 1/344 sec

59. Simple harmonic motion (SMH) is characterized by acceleration that:

A. is proportional to displacement
B. is proportional to velocity
C. decreases linearly
D. is inversely proportional to displacement
E. is inversely proportional to velocity

60. A simple pendulum has a bob of mass M and a period T. If M is doubled, what is the new period?

A. $T/\sqrt{2}$ B. T   C. $T\sqrt{2}$ D. 2T   E. T/2

61. Susan pulls on a wagon with a force of 70 N. What is the average power generated by Susan if the wagon moves a total of 45 m in 3 min?

A. 18 W   B. 27 W   C. 14 W   D. 21 W   E. 28 W

62. Shawn, with a mass of 105 kg, sits 5.5 m to the left of the center of a seesaw. Mark and John, each with a mass of 20 kg, are seated on the right side of the seesaw. If Mark sits 10 m to the right of the center, how far to the right from the center should John sit to balance the seesaw? (Use acceleration due to gravity $g = 10$ m/s^2)

A. 5 m   B. 10 m   C. 19 m   D. 20 m   E. 25 m

63. A cylinder and a sphere are released simultaneously at the top of an inclined plane. Which reaches the bottom first if they roll down the incline plane without slipping?

A. The one of smallest diameter
B. The one of greatest mass
C. The disk
D. The sphere
E. They reach the bottom at the same time

64. How long does it take for a rock to reach the maximum height of its trajectory if a boy throws it with an initial velocity of 3.13 m/s at 30° above the horizontal? (Use acceleration due to gravity $g = 9.8$ m/s^2)

A. 0.16 s   B. 0.28 s   C. 0.333 s   D. 0.446 s   E. 0.84 s

65. If Susan stands in front of a concave mirror, at the same distance from it as its focal length:

A. her image appears larger and upright
B. no image is formed
C. her image appears larger, but upside down
D. her image appears the same size as her and upright
E. her image appears the same size as her, but upside down

66. A hammer of mass *m* is dropped from a roof and falls a distance *h* before striking the ground. How does the maximum velocity of the hammer, just before it hits the ground, change if *h* is doubled? Assume no air resistance.

A. It is multiplied by √2   **C.** It is increased by 200%
B. It is multiplied by 2   **D.** It is multiplied by 4   **E.** It remains constant

67. Color always depends on what characteristics of light?

     I. frequency   II. wavelength   III. amplitude

A. I only   **B.** II only   **C.** III only   **D.** I and II only   **E.** I and III only

68. The water fountain pump recirculates water from a pool and pumps it up to a trough, where it flows along the trough and passes through a hole in the bottom of it. As the water falls back into the pool, it turns a water wheel. What aspect of this water fountain is analogous to an electric current within an electric circuit?

A. Volume flow rate   **C.** Density of water
B. Height of water   **D.** Flow velocity   **E.** Volume of the trough

69. A 25-year-old astronaut goes off on a long-term mission in a spacecraft that travels at speeds close to that of light. The mission lasts exactly 15 years as measured on Earth. With respect to biology, at the end of the mission, the astronaut's age would be:

A. exactly 25 years   **C.** exactly 40 years
B. less than 40 years   **D.** more than 40 years   **E.** exactly 10 years

70. What is the shape of the line on a position vs. time graph for constant linear acceleration?

A. curve   **C.** sinusoidal graph
B. sloped line   **D.** horizontal line   **E.** vertical line

71. A steel ball A is thrown in the air with a speed of 4 m/s at an angle of 60° from the horizontal. It drops onto steel ball B which is 1.4 times the mass of A. If ball A comes to rest after the collision and ball B bounces, what is the horizontal component of ball B's velocity?

A. 0.4 m/s   **B.** 0.6 m/s   **C.** 1.4 m/s   **D.** 1.8 m/s   **E.** 1.1 m/s

72. Which of the following always increases if the brightness of a beam of light is increased without changing its color?

    I. the speed of the photons
    II. the average energy of each photon
    III. the number of photons

A. I only   **C.** III only
B. II only   **D.** I and II only   **E.** I, II and III

73. A pump uses a piston with a 20 cm diameter that moves at 3 cm/s to push a liquid through a pipe. Assuming that the liquid is ideal and incompressible, what is the speed of the liquid when it enters a portion of the pipe that is 4 mm in diameter?

    A. 5 m/s   **B.** 60 cm/s   **C.** 22 m/s   **D.** 38 cm/s   **E.** 75 m/s

74. Which statement is accurate?

    A. The magnetic force on a moving charge does not change its energy
    B. The magnetic force on a current-carrying wire is minimal when the wire is perpendicular to the magnetic field
    C. All magnetic fields originate from the North and South poles
    D. By definition, a magnetic field line is tangent to the direction of the magnetic force on a moving charge at a given point in space
    E. A current-carrying loop of wire tends to line up with its plane parallel to an external magnetic field in which it is positioned

75. In β⁻ decay, the number of protons in the nucleus:

    A. increases by 2   **C.** decreases by 2
    B. increases by 1   **D.** decreases by 1   **E.** remains unchanged

76. If 60 g of material at 100 °C is mixed with 200 g of water at 0 °C, the final temperature is 40 °C. What is the specific heat of the material?

    A. 2.2 kcal/kg·°C   **C.** 0.4 kcal/kg·°C
    B. 6.3 kcal/kg·°C   **D.** 4.6 kcal/kg·°C   **E.** 1.6 kcal/kg·°C

77. A ball is projected horizontally with an initial speed of 5 m/s from an initial height of 50 m. Ignoring air resistance, how far has the ball traveled horizontally from its original position when it lands? (Use acceleration due to gravity $g = 10$ m/s^2)

    A. 11 m   **B.** 16 m   **C.** 20 m   **D.** 7 m   **E.** 27 m

78. A 200 g hockey puck slides up a metal ramp that is inclined at a 30° angle. The coefficients of static and kinetic friction between the hockey puck and the metal ramp are $\mu_s = 0.4$ and $\mu_k = 0.3$, respectively. The initial speed of the hockey puck is 14 m/s. What vertical height does the puck reach above its starting point? (Use acceleration due to gravity $g = 9.8$ m/s^2)

    A. 11 m   **B.** 4.8 m   **C.** 6.6 m   **D.** 14 m   **E.** 14.3 m

79. A 6.5 g bullet was fired horizontally into a 2 kg wooden block that is suspended on a 1.5 m string. The bullet becomes embedded in the block of wood, and immediately after that, the block and the bullet move at 2 m/s. The suspended wooden block with embedded bullet swings upward by height h. How high does the block with bullet swing before it comes to rest? (Use acceleration due to gravity $g = 9.8$ m/s^2)

    A. 5.5 cm   **B.** 20 cm   **C.** 12 cm   **D.** 44 cm   **E.** 56 cm

80. In a transition from one vibrational state to another, a molecule emits a photon of wavelength 6.5 μm. What is the energy difference between these two states? (Use speed of light $c = 3 \times 10^8$ m/s and Planck's constant $h = 4.136 \times 10^{-15}$ eV·s)

A. 11.1 eV   **B.** 11.1 MeV   **C.** 0.28 MeV   **D.** 2.6 MeV   **E.** 0.19 eV

81. An object starting from rest accelerates uniformly along a straight line until its final velocity is *v*, while traveling a distance *d*. What would be the distance traveled if the object accelerated uniformly from rest until its final velocity was 4*v*?

A. 2*d*   **B.** 4*d*   **C.** 6*d*   **D.** 12*d*   **E.** 16*d*

82. Satellite #1 has mass *M*, which takes time T to orbit Earth. If satellite #2 has twice the mass, how long does it take for satellite #2 to orbit Earth?

A. T/2   **B.** T   **C.** 2T   **D.** 4T   **E.** T/4

83. An engineer is studying the rate of heat loss, $\Delta Q / \Delta t$ through a sheet of insulating material as a function of the thickness of the sheet. Assuming fixed temperatures on the two faces of the sheet and steady-state heat flow, which of the graphs best represents the rate of heat transfer as a function of the thickness of the insulating sheet?

A.
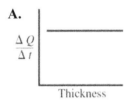

C.
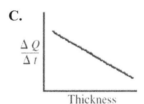

B.
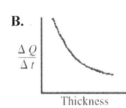

D.
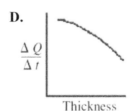

E.
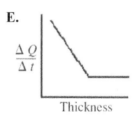

84. Two identical arrows, one with twice the kinetic energy, are fired into a hay bale. Compared to the slower arrow, the faster arrow penetrates:

A. the same distance   **C.** four times as far   **E.** less than twice as far
B. twice as far   **D.** more than four times as far

85. On the Moon, the acceleration of gravity is *g* / 6. If a pendulum has a period T on Earth, what will be the period on the Moon?

A. 6T   **B.** T/6   **C.** T/√6   **D.** T/3   **E.** T√6

86. What is the decibel level of a sound with an intensity of 10^{-7} W/m²?

A. 10 dB   **B.** 20 dB   **C.** 30 dB   **D.** 50 dB   **E.** 70 dB

87. What would be the apparent mass of a 2 in × 4 in × 6 in lead brick if it was placed in oil? (Use acceleration due to gravity $g = 9.8$ m/s², density of oil $\rho = 0.92$ g/cm³, density of lead $\rho = 11.4$ g/cm³ and 1 in³ = 16.4 cm³)

A. 8.2 kg   **B.** 6 kg   **C.** 0.3 kg   **D.** 1.8 kg   **E.** 3.4 kg

88. A positive charge Q is held fixed at the origin. A positive charge z is let go from point p on the positive x-axis. Ignoring friction, which statement describes the velocity of z after it is released?

A. Increases indefinitely   **C.** Increases, then decreases, but never reaches zero
B. Decreases to zero   **D.** Increases, but never exceeds a certain limit
                                       E. Increases, then decreases forever to zero

89. A 9 V battery is connected to two resistors in a series. One resistance is 5 ohms and the other is 10 ohms. Which is true about the current for the locations (A, B, C, D) marked along the circuit?

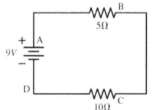

A. Current at A > current at B > current at C > current at D
B. Current at A > current at B = current at C = current at D
C. Current at A = current at B = current at C = current at D
D. Current at A = current at B = current at C > current at D
E. Current at A = current at B > current at C = current at D

90. Which expression describes the critical angle for the interface of water with air? (Use index of refraction for water n = 1.33 and index of refraction for air n = 1)

A. $\sin^{-1}(1/3)$ **B.** $\sin^{-1}(3/4)$ **C.** $\sin^{-1}(2/3)$ **D.** $\sin^{-1}(4/3)$ **E.** $\sin^{-1}(3/2)$

91. What is the amount of energy required to ionize a hydrogen atom from the ground state? (Use Rydberg formula where $E_0 = -13.6$ eV)

A. 4.1 eV   **B.** 9.8 eV   **C.** 13.6 eV   **D.** 22.3 eV   **E.** ∞

92. Sonja is sitting on the outer edge of a carousel that is 18 m in diameter. What is the velocity of Sonja in m/s if the carousel makes 5 rev/min?

A. 3.3 m/s   **B.** 0.8 m/s   **C.** 8.8 m/s   **D.** 4.7 m/s   **E.** 3.2 m/s

93. A projectile weighing 120 N is traveling horizontally with respect to the surface of the Earth at a constant velocity of 6 m/s. Ignoring air resistance, what is the power required to maintain this motion?

A. 0 W   **B.** 20 W   **C.** 120 W   **D.** 2 W   **E.** 12 W

94. A 0.4 kg mass is attached to a massless spring. The mass oscillates and has a total energy of 10 J. What is the oscillation frequency if the oscillation amplitude is 20 cm? (Use 1 J = 1 N·m)

A. 3 Hz   **B.** 4.3 Hz   **C.** 2.1 Hz   **D.** 5.6 Hz   **E.** 9.9 Hz

95. Electromagnetic waves consist of:

    A. particles of heat energy
    B. high-frequency gravitational waves
    C. compressions and rarefactions of electromagnetic pulses
    D. low-frequency gravitational waves
    E. oscillating electric and magnetic fields

96. Jack is breathing through a snorkel as he swims in the Caribbean Sea. He experiences difficulty breathing when his chest is submerged about 1 meter under water. Which expression gives the force that his muscles must exert to expand his chest?

    A. (atmospheric pressure) × (area of his chest)
    B. (atmospheric pressure) × (area of snorkel hole + area of his chest)
    C. (gauge pressure of the water) × (area of his chest)
    D. (gauge pressure of the water) × (area of snorkel hole)
    E. (gauge pressure of the water) × (area of his chest + area of snorkel hole)

97. Two solenoids are close to each other with the switch S open. In which direction does the induced current flow through the galvanometer in the left-hand solenoid when the switch is closed?

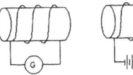

    A. From left to right
    B. From right to left
    C. There will be no induced current through the galvanometer
    D. It depends on the amount of the induced current
    E. Closing the switch has no effect on the left-hand solenoid because they are independent

98. If the length and cross-sectional diameter of a wire are both doubled, the resistance is:

    A. halved
    C. doubled
    B. increased fourfold
    D. decreased by one fourth
    E. unchanged

99. Using a mirror with a focal length of 10 m, an object is viewed at various distances. What is its magnification and orientation when the object is 5 m in front of the mirror?

    A. Twice as large and upright
    C. Half as large and upright
    B. Twice as large and inverted
    D. Same size and inverted
    E. Same size and upright

100. Which energy source provides most of a person's annual exposure to radiation?

    A. Cell phones and hand-held electronic devices
    C. Background radiation
    B. Televisions (i.e. cathode ray tubes)
    D. Sunlight and UV rays
    E. Dental and medical X rays

Diagnostic Test #3

Answer Sheet

#	Answer:					Mark for review	#	Answer:					Mark for review
1:	A	B	C	D	E	___	31:	A	B	C	D	E	___
2:	A	B	C	D	E	___	32:	A	B	C	D	E	___
3:	A	B	C	D	E	___	33:	A	B	C	D	E	___
4:	A	B	C	D	E	___	34:	A	B	C	D	E	___
5:	A	B	C	D	E	___	35:	A	B	C	D	E	___
6:	A	B	C	D	E	___	36:	A	B	C	D	E	___
7:	A	B	C	D	E	___	37:	A	B	C	D	E	___
8:	A	B	C	D	E	___	38:	A	B	C	D	E	___
9:	A	B	C	D	E	___	39:	A	B	C	D	E	___
10:	A	B	C	D	E	___	40:	A	B	C	D	E	___
11:	A	B	C	D	E	___	41:	A	B	C	D	E	___
12:	A	B	C	D	E	___	42:	A	B	C	D	E	___
13:	A	B	C	D	E	___	43:	A	B	C	D	E	___
14:	A	B	C	D	E	___	44:	A	B	C	D	E	___
15:	A	B	C	D	E	___	45:	A	B	C	D	E	___
16:	A	B	C	D	E	___	46:	A	B	C	D	E	___
17:	A	B	C	D	E	___	47:	A	B	C	D	E	___
18:	A	B	C	D	E	___	48:	A	B	C	D	E	___
19:	A	B	C	D	E	___	49:	A	B	C	D	E	___
20:	A	B	C	D	E	___	50:	A	B	C	D	E	___
21:	A	B	C	D	E	___	51:	A	B	C	D	E	___
22:	A	B	C	D	E	___	52:	A	B	C	D	E	___
23:	A	B	C	D	E	___	53:	A	B	C	D	E	___
24:	A	B	C	D	E	___	54:	A	B	C	D	E	___
25:	A	B	C	D	E	___	55:	A	B	C	D	E	___
26:	A	B	C	D	E	___	56:	A	B	C	D	E	___
27:	A	B	C	D	E	___	57:	A	B	C	D	E	___
28:	A	B	C	D	E	___	58:	A	B	C	D	E	___
29:	A	B	C	D	E	___	59:	A	B	C	D	E	___
30:	A	B	C	D	E	___	60:	A	B	C	D	E	___

	Answer:					Mark for review		Answer:					Mark for review
#							**#**						
61:	A	B	C	D	E	___	**81:**	A	B	C	D	E	___
62:	A	B	C	D	E	___	**82:**	A	B	C	D	E	___
63:	A	B	C	D	E	___	**83:**	A	B	C	D	E	___
64:	A	B	C	D	E	___	**84:**	A	B	C	D	E	___
65:	A	B	C	D	E	___	**85:**	A	B	C	D	E	___
66:	A	B	C	D	E	___	**86:**	A	B	C	D	E	___
67:	A	B	C	D	E	___	**87:**	A	B	C	D	E	___
68:	A	B	C	D	E	___	**88:**	A	B	C	D	E	___
69:	A	B	C	D	E	___	**89:**	A	B	C	D	E	___
70:	A	B	C	D	E	___	**90:**	A	B	C	D	E	___
71:	A	B	C	D	E	___	**91:**	A	B	C	D	E	___
72:	A	B	C	D	E	___	**92:**	A	B	C	D	E	___
73:	A	B	C	D	E	___	**93:**	A	B	C	D	E	___
74:	A	B	C	D	E	___	**94:**	A	B	C	D	E	___
75:	A	B	C	D	E	___	**95:**	A	B	C	D	E	___
76:	A	B	C	D	E	___	**96:**	A	B	C	D	E	___
77:	A	B	C	D	E	___	**97:**	A	B	C	D	E	___
78:	A	B	C	D	E	___	**98:**	A	B	C	D	E	___
79:	A	B	C	D	E	___	**99:**	A	B	C	D	E	___
80:	A	B	C	D	E	___	**100:**	A	B	C	D	E	___

This Diagnostic Test is designed for you to assess your proficiency on each topic. Use your test results and identify areas of your strength and weakness to adjust your study plan and enhance your fundamental knowledge.

1. A charged parallel-plate capacitor has an electric field E_0 between its plates. A stationary proton and an electron are both between the plates. Ignoring the force of gravity, how does the magnitude of the acceleration of the proton a_p compare with the magnitude of the acceleration of the electron a_e? (Use the mass of an electron = 9×10^{-31} kg, the mass of a proton = 1.67×10^{-27} kg and the charge of a proton = 1.6×10^{-19} C)

A. $a_p = (1,850)^2 a_e$ C. $a_p = a_e$
B. $a_p = 1,850 a_e$ D. $a_p = (1 / 1,850) a_e$ E. $a_p = (1 / 1,850)^2 a_e$

2. A 5.5 kg box slides down an inclined plane that makes an angle of 40° with the horizontal. At what rate does the box accelerate down the slope if the coefficient of kinetic friction μ_k is 0.19? (Use acceleration due to gravity $g = 9.8$ m/s²)

A. 7.5 m/s²   B. 6.4 m/s²   C. 4.9 m/s²   D. 5.9 m/s²   E. 6.5 m/s²

3. Assume that the sound level of a whisper is 20 dB and a shout is 90 dB. How many times greater is the intensity of a shout than a whisper, given that the decibel level of a sound wave is related to the intensity I of the wave by:

$$dB = 10 \log(I / I_0), \text{ where } I_0 = 10^{-12} \text{ W/m}^2$$

A. Seven   C. Seventy million
B. Seventy thousand   D. Seven million   E. Ten million

4. What is the mass of a cylindrical rod with a length of 14 cm and a diameter of 2 cm that just barely floats in water? (Use density of water $\rho = 1,000$ kg/m³)

A. 44 g   B. 70 g   C. 140 g   D. 28 g   E. 90 g

5. What is the angular speed of a flywheel turning at 813.0 rpm?

A. 8.33 rad/s   C. 33.84 rad/s
B. 56.23 rad/s   D. 85.14 rad/s   E. 116.48 rad/s

6. Which quantity is expressed in units of Ω·m?

A. Flow   B. Capacitance   C. Resistivity   D. Potential   E. Current

7. A candle is viewed through a converging lens. What is the magnification of the image when the candle is 6 m from the lens, and the image is 3 m from the lens on the other side?

A. Twice as large and upright   C. Half as large and upright
B. Same size and inverted   D. Half as large and inverted
                                    E. Same size and upright

8. Uranium has an atomic number of 92, but often contains 146 or more neutrons and undergoes radioactive decay. Which statement describes why this occurs?

      I. The electromagnetic repulsion overcomes the strong nuclear force
      II. Excess neutrons increase the electromagnetic repulsion
      III. The strong nuclear force has a limited range

    A. I only   **B.** II only   **C.** III only   **D.** I and III only   **E.** I, II and III

9. The captain of a yacht intends to travel due north. He checks his navigation gear and discovers that due to ocean currents, the yacht is travelling NE at a constant 10.7 m/s. To correct the yacht's bearing, the captain turns the vessel to point north-west and accelerates. How long does it take for the yacht to correct the bearing and achieve a due north bearing, given the engine delivers a constant acceleration of 4.4 m/s^2?

    A. 1.3 s   **B.** 1.8 s   **C.** 3.3 s   **D.** 3.6 s   **E.** 2.4 s

10. A 100 kg lion sees an antelope and, from rest, accelerates uniformly to 20 m/s in 10 s. How much distance does the lion cover in 10 s?

    A. 100 m   **B.** 200 m   **C.** 180 m   **D.** 50 m   **E.** 150 m

11. An object is released from rest at a height h above the surface of the Earth, where h is much smaller than the radius of the Earth. The object's speed is v as it strikes the ground. Ignoring air resistance, at what height should the object be released from rest for it to strike the ground with a speed of $2v$? (Use g = acceleration due to gravity)

    A. $4gh$ **B.** $4h$ **C.** $2gh$ **D.** $2h$ **E.** h

12. A 4 kg ball is attached to one end of a 1.4 m light rod, while the other end is loosely affixed at a frictionless pivot. The rod is raised until it is vertical, with the ball above the pivot. The ball moves in a circle when the rod is released. What is the tension in the rod as the ball moves through the bottom of the circle? (Use acceleration due to gravity $g = 9.8$ m/s^2)

    A. 30.0 N   **B.** 84.8 N   **C.** 46.6 N   **D.** 120.0 N   **E.** 196.0 N

13. The crests of ocean waves pass a pier every 12 s. What is the wavelength of the ocean waves if the waves are moving at 4.5 m/s?

    A. 84 m   **B.** 66 m   **C.** 54 m   **D.** 38 m   **E.** 47 m

14. Compared to a giant iceberg, a hot cup of coffee has:

    A. a higher temperature, but more thermal energy
    B. a greater specific heat and more thermal energy
    C. a higher temperature, but less thermal energy
    D. more thermal energy and lower temperature
    E. a higher temperature and the same amount of thermal energy

15. What is the focal length of the mirror if, when an object is 24 cm in front of a concave spherical mirror, the image is formed 3 cm in front of the mirror?

   A. 1.5 cm   **B.** 2.7 cm   **C.** 5 cm   **D.** 6.3 cm   **E.** 7.4 cm

16. Which of the following correctly balances the decay reaction when $^{230}_{90}Th \rightarrow {}^{0}_{-1}e + \_\_$?

   A. $^{230}_{91}Pa$ **B.** $^{233}_{89}Ac$ **C.** $^{230}_{89}Ac$ **D.** $^{230}_{91}Th$ **E.** $^{231}_{90}Th$

17. By what magnitude does a magnetic field produced by a wire decrease when the distance from a long current-carrying wire is doubled?

   A. $1/\sqrt{2}$ **B.** ½   **C.** ¼   **D.** 1/6   **E.** $\sqrt{(½)}$

18. A pipe with a circular cross section has water flowing from point I to point II. The radius of the pipe is 6 cm at point I, while the radius at point II is 3 cm. At the end of point I, the flow rate is 0.04 m³/s. What is the velocity of the water at point I?

   A. 3.5 m/s   **B.** 22 m/s   **C.** 18.5 m/s   **D.** 6 m/s   **E.** 9 m/s

19. If the intensity of sound increases by a factor of 100, the decibel level increases by:

   A. 20   **B.** 1,000   **C.** $\log_{100}$ **D.** 100   **E.** 0.1

20. What is the tension on an aluminum wire with a diameter of 4.4 mm and a density of 2,600 kg/m³ when transverse waves propagate at 42 m/s?

   A. 15 N   **B.** 24 N   **C.** 46 N   **D.** 70 N   **E.** 76 N

21. A 5 kg box of books slides 10 m down a ramp inclined at 30° from the horizontal. What is the work done by gravity if the box slides at a constant velocity of 4 m/s? (Use acceleration due to gravity $g = 9.8$ m/s²)

   A. 0 J   **B.** −32 J   **C.** 245 J   **D.** 32 J   **E.** 133 J

22. What is the average momentum of a 65 kg runner who travels 400 m in 50 s?

   A. 19 kg·m/s   **B.** 63 kg·m/s   **C.** 520 kg·m/s   **D.** 112 kg·m/s   **E.** 386 kg·m/s

23. Michael is moving at a speed $2/3c$ toward Susan when she shines a light toward Michael. At what speed does Michael see the light approaching him?

   A. $1/3c$ **B.** $3/5c$ **C.** $4/3c$ **D.** c **E.** $2/3c$

24. An object is traveling uniformly at a v of 5 m/s. What is its final velocity if it experiences a uniform acceleration of 2 m/s² for 6 s?

   A. 12 m/s   **B.** 28 m/s   **C.** 24 m/s   **D.** 32 m/s   **E.** 17 m/s

25. A 830 g meteor impacts the Earth at a speed of 1,250 m/s. If its kinetic energy is entirely converted to heat of the meteorite, by what temperature does it increase? (Use specific heat for the meteor = 108 cal/kg·°C and 1 cal = 4.186 Joules)

    A. 1,728 °C   **B.** 1,346 °C   **C.** 2,628 °C   **D.** 7,142 °C   **E.** 4,286 °C

26. Mary and Brittany throw identical balls vertically upward. Mary throws her ball with an initial speed of twice Brittany's ball. The maximum height of Mary's ball will be:

    A. higher than Brittany's ball, but less than two times as high
    B. equal to the maximum height of Brittany's ball
    C. two times higher than the maximum height of Brittany's ball
    D. four times higher than the maximum height of Brittany's ball
    E. higher than twice Brittany's ball, but less than four times as high

27. An organ pipe is a cylindrical tube open at both ends. The air column is set to vibrate by air flowing through the pipe. The length of the pipe is 0.2 m and the diameter is 0.04 m. What is the wavelength of the fundamental? (Use *v* of sound at 23 °C = 340 m/s)

    A. 0.1 m   **B.** 2 m   **C.** 1 m   **D.** 0.4 m   **E.** 0.8 m

28. A proton, moving in a uniform magnetic field, moves in a circle perpendicular to the field. If the proton's speed is tripled, what happens to the time needed to complete a circular path?

    A. Increases   **C.** Decreases
    B. Remains constant   **D.** Doubles   **E.** Triples

29. A sodium emission tube produces a light of frequency 4.9×10^{14} Hz. Which is true of the image if it is placed 6 m from a converging lens of focal length 2 m?

    A. Inverted and virtual   **C.** Upright and virtual
    B. Inverted and real   **D.** Upright and real   **E.** Same as if it were 1 m away

30. How much heat must be added to a 10 kg block of ice at –8 °C to change it to water at 14 °C? (Use specific heat of ice = 0.5 kcal/kg·°C, latent heat of fusion L_f = 80 kcal/kg and specific heat of water = 1 kcal/kg·°C)

    A. 840 kcal   **B.** 280 kcal   **C.** 440 kcal   **D.** 980 kcal   **E.** 744 kcal

31. A 6 kg ball collides head on with a stationary 8 kg ball. Which statement is true if the collision between the balls is inelastic? Assume there are no external forces acting on the balls.

    A. Δp that the 6 kg ball experiences is greater than the Δp of the 8 kg ball
    B. Δv that the 6 kg ball experiences is equal to the Δv of the 8 kg ball
    C. Δv that the 6 kg ball experiences is greater than the Δv of the 8 kg ball
    D. Δv that the 6 kg ball experiences is less than the Δv of the 8 kg ball
    E. Δp that the 6 kg ball experiences is less than the Δp of the 8 kg ball

32. A pendulum of length L is suspended from the ceiling of an elevator. When the elevator is at rest, the period of the pendulum is T. How does the period of the pendulum change when the elevator moves upward with constant acceleration?

    A. Remains the same
    B. Decreases
    C. Increases
    D. Decreases only if the upward acceleration is less than $g / 2$
    E. Increases only if the upward acceleration is greater than $g / 2$

33. A small aircraft is traveling at a constant speed in a circular path with a radius of 200 m parallel to the ground. The center of the circular path is 400 m above an air traffic control tower. Its engine is the source of audible sound waves of a fixed frequency. To a stationary observer in the tower, how would the detected frequency (f_d) of the engine differ from that of the source (f_s) while the aircraft circled above?

    A. Remains constant and equal to f_s
    B. Higher than f_s during one orbit, and lower during each subsequent orbit
    C. Higher than f_s during half the orbit, and lower during each subsequent half-orbit
    D. Remains constant, but is lower than f_s
    E. Remains constant, but is higher than f_s

34. Which of the following is an accurate statement?

    A. The magnetic force on a current-carrying wire is smallest when the wire is perpendicular to the magnetic field
    B. The magnetic force on a moving charge does not change its energy
    C. A magnetic field line is, by definition, tangent to the direction of the magnetic force on a moving charge at a given point in space
    D. All magnetic fields have North and South poles as their sources
    E. A current-carrying loop of wire tends to line up with its plane parallel to an external magnetic field in which it is positioned

35. The isotope $^{238}_{92}\text{U}$ is most likely to emit:

    A. a γ ray
    B. a β particle
    C. an α particle
    D. both an α and β particle
    E. both a β particle and a γ ray

36. An auto mechanic needs to remove a tight-fitting pin of material X from a hole in a block made of material Y. The mechanic heats both the pin and the block to the same high temperature and removes the pin easily. What statement relates the coefficient of thermal expansion of material X to that of material Y?

    A. Material Y has a negative coefficient of expansion and material X has a positive coefficient of expansion
    B. Material Y has the same coefficient of expansion as material X
    C. The situation is not possible, heating material Y shrinks the hole in the material as the material expands with increasing temperature
    D. Material Y has a greater coefficient of expansion than material X
    E. Material X has a greater coefficient of expansion than material Y

37. A change in the state of motion is evidence of:

    I. a force that is wearing down
    II. an applied force that is unbalanced
    III. an increase in total force

    A. I only   **B.** II only   **C.** III only   **D.** I and II only   **E.** I and III only

38. The reason an astronaut in one of Earth's satellites feels weightless is because:

    A. gravity does not affect the astronaut because there is no atmospheric pressure
    B. the forces acting on the astronaut are negative
    C. the astronaut is beyond the range of the Earth's gravity
    D. the astronaut is in free fall
    E. the astronaut's acceleration is zero

39. A child throws a ball over a fence that is 2 m high at an angle of 40° above the horizontal. The ball leaves her hand 1 m above the ground. How far is the child from the fence, if the ball just clears the fence at the peak of its arc and experiences no significant air resistance? (Use acceleration due to gravity $g = 9.8$ m/s^2)

    A. 1.6 m   **B.** 2.4 m   **C.** 3.9 m   **D.** 4.6 m   **E.** 8.8 m

40. A β⁻ decay occurs in an unstable nucleus when a neutron is converted to a:

    A. beta particle by the weak force
    B. positron by the weak force
    C. neutron by the strong force
    D. proton by the strong force
    E. proton by the weak force

41. In a particular case of Compton scattering, a photon collides with a free electron and scatters backwards. The wavelength after the collision is exactly double the wavelength before the collision. What is the wavelength of the incident photon? (Use $m_{electron} = 9.11 \times 10^{-31}$ kg, $c = 3.00 \times 10^8$ m/s and $h = 6.626 \times 10^{-34}$ J·s)

    A. 3.4×10^{-12} m
    B. 4.8×10^{-12} m
    C. 5.6×10^{-12} m
    D. 6.8×10^{-12} m
    E. 8.8×10^{-12} m

42. Which statement must be true for an object moving with constant nonzero velocity?

    A. The net force on the object is zero
    B. The net force on the object is positive
    C. A constant force is being applied to the object in the direction opposite of motion
    D. A constant force is being applied to the object in the direction of motion
    E. Its acceleration is equal to its velocity

43. A solid cylindrical bar conducts heat at a rate of 30 W from a hot to a cold reservoir under steady-state conditions. What is the rate at which it conducts heat between these reservoirs if both the diameter and length and of the bar are doubled? Assume heat transfer is lengthwise and sides of bar are perfectly insulated.

    A. 30 W   **B.** 60 W   **C.** 15 W **D.** 120 W   **E.** 7.5 W

44. An ideal, massless spring with a spring constant of 3 N/m has a 0.9 kg mass attached to one end and the other end is attached to a beam. If the system is initially at equilibrium and the mass is then down 18 cm below the equilibrium length and released, what is the magnitude of the net force on the mass just after its release? (Use acceleration due to gravity is $g = 10$ m/s^2)

    A. 0.54 N   **B.** 0.75 N   **C.** 6 N   **D.** 0.35 N   **E.** 3.5 N

45. A 30.0 N block is attached to the free end of an anchored spring and is allowed to slide back and forth on a frictionless table. Determine the frequency of motion, if the spring constant $k = 40.0$ N/m. (Use the acceleration due to gravity $g = 9.8$ m/s^2)

    A. 0.30 Hz   **B.** 0.58 Hz   **C.** 2.3 Hz   **D.** 3.6 Hz   **E.** 5.4 Hz

46. A piano is tuned so that the frequency of the third harmonic of one string is 786.3 Hz. If the fundamental frequency of another string is 785.8 Hz then what is the beat frequency between the notes?

    A. 0 Hz   **B.** 1 Hz   **C.** 785.8 Hz   **D.** 786.3 Hz   **E.** 0.5 Hz

47. A 600 N weight sits on the small piston of a hydraulic machine. The small piston has an area of 5 cm^2. If the large piston has an area of 50 cm^2, how much force can the large piston support?

    A. 200 N   **B.** 300 N   **C.** 3,000 N   **D.** 6,000 N   **E.** 10,000 N

48. A cube with 0.1 m sides is constructed of six insulated metal plates. Plates I and IV are opposite to each other and are maintained at 500 V. Plates II and V are opposite to each other and are maintained at 0 V. Plates III and VI are opposite to each other and are maintained at – 500 V. What is the change in potential energy, if an electron is transferred from plate I to plate III? (Use charge of $e = 1.6 \times 10^{-19}$ C)

    A. -3.2×10^{-14} J   **C.** 3.2×10^{-12} J
    B. -1.6×10^{-15} J   **D.** 1.6×10^{-16} J   **E.** -1.6×10^{-17} J

49. What quantity does the slope of this graph represent if the graph shows the power dissipated in a resistor as a function of the resistance?

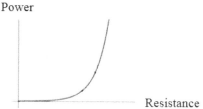

A. Maximum power transferred across the resistor
B. Square of the current across resistor
C. Current across the resistor
D. Potential difference across the resistor
E. Voltage across the resistor

50. What color light allows the investigator to see with the greatest resolution in a light microscope?

A. Red light because it is refracted less than other colors by the objective lens
B. Blue light because it has a shorter wavelength
C. Violet light because it has a longer wavelength
D. Blue light because it is brighter
E. The color of light makes no difference for relative resolution

51. A blue laser beam is incident on a metallic surface, causing electrons to be ejected from the metal. What is the effect on the rate of ejected electrons if the frequency of the laser beam is increased, while the intensity of the beam is held fixed?

A. Remains the same, but the maximum kinetic energy decreases
B. Decreases and the maximum kinetic energy decreases
C. Decreases, but the maximum kinetic energy remains the same
D. Decreases, but the maximum kinetic energy increases
E. Remains the same, but the maximum kinetic energy increases

52. A 3 kg stone is dropped from a height of 5 m. Ignoring air resistance, what is its momentum on impact? (Use acceleration due to gravity $g = 10$ m/s^2)

A. 7.5 kg·m/s   B. 5 kg·m/s   C. 30 kg·m/s   D. 45 kg·m/s   E. 15 kg·m/s

53. A 1,500 kg car moving at 45 km/h locks its brakes and skids 30 m. How far does the same car skid if it is traveling at 150 km/h?

A. 230 m   B. 160 m   C. 445 m   D. 90 m   E. 333 m

54. How does the frequency of vibration relate to the time it takes to complete one cycle?

A. Inversely with the time
B. Inversely with the amplitude
C. Directly with the time
D. Directly with the amplitude
E. Directly with the wavelength

55. A 12 L volume of oil is subjected to pressure that produces a volume strain of -3×10^{-4}. The bulk modulus of the oil is 6×10^9 Pa and is independent of the pressure. What is the reduction in the volume of the oil?

A. 1.8 ml   B. 2.6 ml   C. 4.4 ml   D. 3.1 ml   E. 3.6 ml

56. How many grams of ethanol should be added to 5 grams of chloroform for the resulting mixture to have a specific gravity of 1.2? (Use specific gravity of ethanol = 0.8, specific gravity of chloroform = 1.5 and conversion factor of 1 mL = 1 g)

    A. 1.5 g   **B.** 2.6 g   **C.** 3.8 g   **D.** 1.0 g   **E.** 2.0 g

57. Four 8 V batteries (A + B + C + D) are connected in series to power lights A and B. The resistance of light A is 45 Ω and the resistance of light B is 25 Ω. What is the current through the wire at a point between battery C and D?

    A. 0.46 A   **B.** 0.31 A   **C.** 0.17 A   **D.** 0.84 A   **E.** 1.2 A

58. Which statement is correct about the equivalent resistance when four unequal resistors are connected in parallel?

    A. It is the average of the largest and smallest resistance
    B. It is less than the smallest resistance
    C. It is more than the largest resistance
    D. It is the average of the four resistances
    E. It is ¼ the largest resistance

59. What is the distance between a lens and a screen so that when the screen and the converging lens of focal length f are arranged, an image of the Moon falls on the screen? Assume that the Moon is infinity ∞ away from the lens.

    A. $f/2$ **B.** $2f$ **C.** f **D.** infinity   **E.** f^2

60. A machinist turns on the power on to a grinding wheel at time $t = 0$ s. The wheel accelerates uniformly from rest for 10.0 s and reaches the operating angular speed of 96.0 rad/s. The wheel is run at that angular velocity for 40.0 s and then power is shut off. The wheel slows down uniformly at 1.5 rad/s^2 until the wheel stops. For how long after the power is shut off does it take the wheel to stop?

    A. 56.0 s   **B.** 64.0 s   **C.** 72.0 s   **D.** 82.0 s   **E.** 90.0 s

61. Bombarding ^{23}Na with protons produces nuclide Y and a neutron. What is nuclide Y?

    A. ^{24}Na   **B.** ^{21}Ne   **C.** ^{24}Mg   **D.** ^{23}Mg   **E.** ^{22}Na

62. Why does it take more force to start moving a heavy bookcase across the carpet than to keep it moving?

    A. For objects in motion, kinetic friction is a force in the same direction as the motion
    B. The coefficient of static friction is greater than the forces of movement
    C. The coefficient of static friction is greater than the coefficient of kinetic friction
    D. The coefficient of kinetic friction is greater than the coefficient of static friction
    E. The cumulative forces acting on it are negative

63. What is the wavelength of the standing wave when a 12 m string, fixed at both ends, is resonating at a frequency that produces 4 nodes?

    A. 6 m   **B.** 8 m   **C.** 4 m   **D.** 24 m   **E.** 12 m

64. A silver necklace that has a mass of 60 grams and a volume of 5.7 cm^3 is lowered into a container of water and is tied to a string connected to a force meter. What is the reading on the force meter? (Use density of water = 1 g/cm^3 and acceleration due to gravity g = 9.8 m/s^2)

    A. 0.53 N   **C.** 0.62 N

    B. 0.22 N   **D.** 0.38 N   **E.** Requires more information

65. A charged particle is traveling in a circular path of radius r in a uniform magnetic field. The plane of the circular path is perpendicular to the magnetic field. What is the radius of the circular path if the particle travels twice as fast?

    A. $\sqrt{2}r$ **B.** $r/2$ **C.** $4r$ **D.** $2r$ **E.** $r/4$

66. In which direction is the magnetic field if a positive charge is moving to the right and experiences a vertical (upward) magnetic force?

    A. Out of the page   **C.** To the left

    B. Upward   **D.** To the right   **E.** Into the page

67. What is the result for temperature, measured in Kelvin, if both the pressure and volume of a given sample of an ideal gas double?

    A. Decreases to one-fourth original value   **C.** Decreases to one-half original value

    B. Quadruples original value   **D.** Doubles original value

                                   E. Remains the same

68. An electron is initially moving to the right when it enters a uniform electric field that is directed upwards. Which trajectory represents the path of the electron?

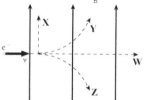

    A. W   **C.** Y

    B. X   **D.** Z   **E.** More than one

69. The graph shows the position of an object as a function of time. At which moment in time is the speed of the object equal to zero?

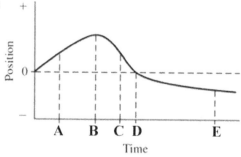

    A. A

    B. B

    C. C

    D. D

    E. E

70. Michelle takes off down a 50 m high, 10° slope on her jet-powered skis. The skis have a thrust of 260 N. The combined mass of the skis and Michelle is 50 kg. Michelle's speed at the bottom of the slope is 40 m/s. Assuming the mass of the fuel is negligible, what is the coefficient of kinetic friction of her skis on the snow? (Use acceleration due to gravity $g = 9.8$ m/s^2)

    A. 0.23   **B.** 0.53   **C.** 0.68   **D.** 0.42   **E.** 0.36

71. A 1 kg chunk of putty moving at 1 m/s collides with and sticks to a 7 kg box that is initially at rest. What is the speed that the box and putty are then set in motion? (Assume the box rests on a frictionless surface)

    A. 1/8 m/s   **C.** 1/4 m/s

    B. 1/6 m/s   **D.** 1/7 m/s   **E.** requires more information

72. A 4 kg mass is affixed to the end of a vertical spring with a spring constant of 10 N/m. When the mass comes to rest, how much has the spring stretched?

    A. 1 m   **B.** 4 m   **C.** 5 m   **D.** 0.1 m   **E.** 0.2 m

73. In music, the 3rd harmonic corresponds to which overtone?

    A. 1st   **B.** 2nd   **C.** 3rd   **D.** 4th   **E.** 5th

74. A spaceship traveling at constant velocity passes by Earth and later passes by Mars. In which frame of reference is the amount of time separating these two events the proper time?

    A. Any inertial frame of reference   **C.** The Mars frame of reference

    B. The spaceship frame of reference   **D.** The Earth frame of reference

                                           E. Any frame of reference, inertial or not

75. What is the orientation and magnification of the image of a light bulb if the light bulb is placed 2 m in front of a mirror and the image is 6 m behind the mirror?

    A. Upright and × 3   **C.** Upright and × 0.5

    B. Inverted and × 3   **D.** Inverted and × 1.5   **E.** Upright and × 1

76. A series circuit has a 50 Hz AC source, a 0.4 H inductor, a 50 μF capacitor and a 30 Ω resistor. If the rms current in the circuit is 1.8 A, what is the voltage of the source?

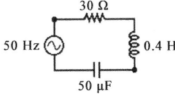

    A. 142 V   **B.** 124 V   **C.** 75.5 V   **D.** 96.7 V   **F.** 41.9 V

77. Two particles of like charge and equal mass are separated by a fixed distance. What is the effect on the repulsive force between the particles if the mass of one particle is doubled?

- **A.** Doubles
- **B.** Quadruples
- **C.** Increases by ½
- **D.** Remains the same
- **E.** Increases by $\sqrt{2}$

78. A water tank is filled to a depth of 6 m, and the bottom of the tank is 22 m above ground. A water-filled hose that is 2 cm in diameter extends from the bottom of the tank to the ground, but no water is flowing in the hose. What is the gauge water pressure at ground level in the hose? (Use density of water $\rho = 1,000$ kg/m^3 and acceleration due to gravity $g = 9.8$ m/s^2)

- **A.** 2.7×10^5 N/m^2
- **B.** 5.3×10^4 N/m^2
- **C.** 8.7 N/m^2
- **D.** Requires the cross-sectional area of the tank
- **E.** Requires the water pressure at tank level

79. The tension in each of two strings is adjusted so that both vibrate at exactly 822 Hz. The tension in one string is then increased slightly. Five beats per second are then heard when both strings vibrate. What is a new frequency of the string that was tightened?

- **A.** 824 Hz
- **B.** 816 Hz
- **C.** 827 Hz
- **D.** 818 Hz
- **E.** 837 Hz

80. When a light ray traveling in glass strikes an air boundary, which type of phase change occurs in the reflected ray?

- **A.** 45° phase change
- **B.** 180° phase change
- **C.** −45° phase change
- **D.** 90° phase change
- **E.** No phase change

81. A stone of mass m is dropped from a height h toward the ground. Ignoring air resistance, which statement is true about the stone as it hits the ground?

- **A.** Its KE is proportional to h
- **B.** Its KE is proportional to h^2
- **C.** Its speed is proportional to h
- **D.** Its speed is inversely proportional to h^2
- **E.** Its speed is inversely proportional to h

82. Johnny is sitting on the outer edge of a carousel that is 18 m in diameter. What is the velocity of Johnny if the carousel makes 5.3 rev/min?

- **A.** 4.2 m/s
- **B.** 5 m/s
- **C.** 3.1 m/s
- **D.** 9.8 m/s
- **E.** 6.2 m/s

83. A 40 kg runner is running around a track. The curved portions of the track are arcs of a circle that has a radius of 16 m. The runner is running at a constant speed of 4 m/s. What is the net force on the runner on the curved portion of the track?

- **A.** 150 N
- **B.** 5 N
- **C.** 40 N
- **D.** 100 N
- **E.** 10 N

84. If an object is accelerating, which values must change?

      I. Speed   II. Velocity   III. Direction

- **A.** I only
- **B.** II only
- **C.** III only
- **D.** I and II only
- **E.** I and III only

85. A 1,140 g empty iron kettle is on a hot stove. How much heat must it absorb to raise its temperature from 18 °C to 90 °C? (Use specific heat for iron = 113 cal/kg·°C and 1 cal = 4.186 J)

    A. 8,230 J   **B.** 20,340 J   **C.** 38,825 J   **D.** 41,650 J   **E.** 17,300 J

86. A 1.2 kg bowling ball is dropped from a height of 6 m. During its fall, it is constantly acted upon by air resistance, with a force of 3.4 N. Accounting for air resistance, what is the speed of the bowling ball as it hits the ground? (Use acceleration due to gravity $g = 10$ m/s^2)

    A. 9.2 m/s   **B.** 10.6 m/s   **C.** 11.3 m/s   **D.** 13.4 m/s   **E.** 7.6 m/s

87. Sound intensity is defined as:

    A. power per unit time
    B. power passing through a unit of area per unit time
    C. energy passing through a unit of volume per unit time
    D. energy passing through a unit of area
    E. energy passing through a unit of area per unit time

88. A kilowatt-hour is a unit of:

    A. work   **B.** current   **C.** power   **D.** charge   **E.** force

89. The index of refraction of the core of a piece of fiber optic cable is 1.6. If the index of the surrounding cladding is 1.3, what is the critical angle for total internal reflection of a light ray in the core, incident on the core-cladding interface?

    A. 82°   **B.** 40°   **C.** 34°   **D.** 54°   **E.** 69°

90. Consider the group of charges in the figure. All three charges have $Q = 6.2$ nC. What is their electric potential energy? (Use Coulomb's constant $k = 9 \times 10^9$ Nm^2/C^2).

    A. 5.2×10^{-5} J   **C.** 1.9×10^{-5} J   **E.** 6.4×10^{-5} J
    B. 5.9×10^{-5} J   **D.** 6.1×10^{-5} J

91. A solid cylinder with an 80 cm radius is positioned on a frictionless plane inclined at 30° above the horizontal. A force (F) is exerted by a string wrapped around the cylinder. The center of mass of the cylinder does not move when F has a certain critical value. What is the angular acceleration of the spool when F is at this critical value? (The moment of inertia of a solid cylinder is I = ½mr^2; use acceleration due to gravity $g = 10$ m/s^2)

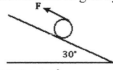

    A. 15.8 rad/s^2 **C.** 12.5 rad/s^2
    B. 23 rad/s^2 **D.** 18.6 rad/s^2 **E.** 8.2 rad/s^2

92. As a water wave passes, a floating leaf oscillates up and down completely for two cycles in 1 s. What is the wave's speed, if the wave's wavelength is 12 m?

    A. 1 m/s   **B.** 10 m/s   **C.** 24 m/s   **D.** 6 m/s   **E.** 12 m/s

93. When a dam began to leak, Mike placed his finger in the hole to stop the flow. The dam is 20 m high and 100 km long and sits on top of a lake which is another 980 m deep, 100 km wide, and 100 km long. The hole that Mike blocked is a square 0.01 m by 0.01 m located 1 m below the surface of the water. Assuming that the viscosity of the water is negligible, what force does Mike have to exert to prevent water from leaking? (Use atmospheric pressure $P_{atm} = 10^5$ Pa, density of water $\rho = 10^3$ kg/m^3 and acceleration due to gravity $g = 10$ m/s^2)

    A. 10 N   **B.** 100 N   **C.** 1,000 N   **D.** 0.1 N   **E.** 1 N

94. For a graph of potential vs. power, what does the slope represent for a DC circuit?

    A. 1 / resistance
    B. current
    C. 1 / current
    D. resistance
    E. resistivity

95. What is the amount of energy required to ionize a hydrogen atom from the ground state? (Use Rydberg formula where $E_0 = -13.6$ eV)

    A. 4.1 eV   **B.** 9.8 eV   **C.** 13.6 eV   **D.** 22.3 eV   **E.** ∞

96. How much heat is needed to melt a 70 kg sample of ice that is at 0 °C? (Use latent heat of fusion for water $L_f = 334,000$ J/kg and heat of vaporization for water $L_v = 2.3 \times 10^6$ J/kg)

    A. 1.3×10^5 kJ   **C.** 4.0×10^6 kJ
    B. 5.7×10^4 kJ   **D.** 2.3×10^4 kJ   **E.** 1.4×10^3 kJ

97. A car and a truck are initially alongside each other at time $t = 0$. Their motions along a straight road are represented by the velocity vs. time graph. At time T, which statement is true for the vehicles?

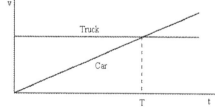

    A. The car traveled farther than the truck
    B. The truck traveled farther than the car
    C. They traveled the same distance
    D. The truck had a greater acceleration than the car
    E. The car's velocity remained constant

98. Two sources emit beams of microwaves. The microwaves from source A have a frequency of 15 GHz, and the microwaves from source B have a frequency of 30 GHz. This is all the information available for the two beams. Which of the following statements about these microwave beams must be correct?

    A. The intensity of beam B is twice as great as the intensity of beam A
    B. A photon in beam B has the same energy as a photon in beam A
    C. Beam B carries twice as many photons per second as beam A
    D. A photon in beam B has twice the energy of a photon in beam A
    E. None of the above statements is true

99. A motor can provide a maximum of 120 N·m of torque. If all of this torque is used to accelerate a solid, uniform flywheel of mass 12 kg and radius 4 m, what is the time necessary for the flywheel to accelerate from rest to 7.35 rad/s?

    A. 4.4 s   **B.** 3.9 s   **C.** 1.1 s   **D.** 1.9 s   **E.** 5.9 s

100. The image shows three beams of radiation passing between two electrically-charged plates. Which of the beams is due to a high-energy electron?

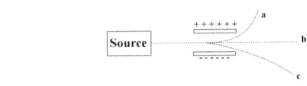

    I. a   II. b   III. c

  A. I only   **B.** II only   **C.** III only   **D.** I and II only   **E.** I and III only

Diagnostic Test #4

Answer Sheet

#	Answer:					Mark for review	#	Answer:					Mark for review
1:	A	B	C	D	E	___	31:	A	B	C	D	E	___
2:	A	B	C	D	E	___	32:	A	B	C	D	E	___
3:	A	B	C	D	E	___	33:	A	B	C	D	E	___
4:	A	B	C	D	E	___	34:	A	B	C	D	E	___
5:	A	B	C	D	E	___	35:	A	B	C	D	E	___
6:	A	B	C	D	E	___	36:	A	B	C	D	E	___
7:	A	B	C	D	E	___	37:	A	B	C	D	E	___
8:	A	B	C	D	E	___	38:	A	B	C	D	E	___
9:	A	B	C	D	E	___	39:	A	B	C	D	E	___
10:	A	B	C	D	E	___	40:	A	B	C	D	E	___
11:	A	B	C	D	E	___	41:	A	B	C	D	E	___
12:	A	B	C	D	E	___	42:	A	B	C	D	E	___
13:	A	B	C	D	E	___	43:	A	B	C	D	E	___
14:	A	B	C	D	E	___	44:	A	B	C	D	E	___
15:	A	B	C	D	E	___	45:	A	B	C	D	E	___
16:	A	B	C	D	E	___	46:	A	B	C	D	E	___
17:	A	B	C	D	E	___	47:	A	B	C	D	E	___
18:	A	B	C	D	E	___	48:	A	B	C	D	E	___
19:	A	B	C	D	E	___	49:	A	B	C	D	E	___
20:	A	B	C	D	E	___	50:	A	B	C	D	E	___
21:	A	B	C	D	E	___	51:	A	B	C	D	E	___
22:	A	B	C	D	E	___	52:	A	B	C	D	E	___
23:	A	B	C	D	E	___	53:	A	B	C	D	E	___
24:	A	B	C	D	E	___	54:	A	B	C	D	E	___
25:	A	B	C	D	E	___	55:	A	B	C	D	E	___
26:	A	B	C	D	E	___	56:	A	B	C	D	E	___
27:	A	B	C	D	E	___	57:	A	B	C	D	E	___
28:	A	B	C	D	E	___	58:	A	B	C	D	E	___
29:	A	B	C	D	E	___	59:	A	B	C	D	E	___
30:	A	B	C	D	E	___	60:	A	B	C	D	E	___

#	Answer:					Mark for review	#	Answer:					Mark for review
61:	A	B	C	D	E	___	**81:**	A	B	C	D	E	___
62:	A	B	C	D	E	___	**82:**	A	B	C	D	E	___
63:	A	B	C	D	E	___	**83:**	A	B	C	D	E	___
64:	A	B	C	D	E	___	**84:**	A	B	C	D	E	___
65:	A	B	C	D	E	___	**85:**	A	B	C	D	E	___
66:	A	B	C	D	E	___	**86:**	A	B	C	D	E	___
67:	A	B	C	D	E	___	**87:**	A	B	C	D	E	___
68:	A	B	C	D	E	___	**88:**	A	B	C	D	E	___
69:	A	B	C	D	E	___	**89:**	A	B	C	D	E	___
70:	A	B	C	D	E	___	**90:**	A	B	C	D	E	___
71:	A	B	C	D	E	___	**91:**	A	B	C	D	E	___
72:	A	B	C	D	E	___	**92:**	A	B	C	D	E	___
73:	A	B	C	D	E	___	**93:**	A	B	C	D	E	___
74:	A	B	C	D	E	___	**94:**	A	B	C	D	E	___
75:	A	B	C	D	E	___	**95:**	A	B	C	D	E	___
76:	A	B	C	D	E	___	**96:**	A	B	C	D	E	___
77:	A	B	C	D	E	___	**97:**	A	B	C	D	E	___
78:	A	B	C	D	E	___	**98:**	A	B	C	D	E	___
79:	A	B	C	D	E	___	**99:**	A	B	C	D	E	___
80:	A	B	C	D	E	___	**100:**	A	B	C	D	E	___

This Diagnostic Test is designed for you to assess your proficiency on each topic. Use your test results and identify areas of your strength and weakness to adjust your study plan and enhance your fundamental knowledge.

1. When an object moves with constant acceleration, can its velocity change direction?

  A. Yes, a car that starts from rest, speeds up, slows to a stop, and then backs up is an example
  B. No, because it is always slowing down
  C. No, because it is always speeding up
  D. Yes, a Frisbee thrown straight up is an example
  E. No, because a constant acceleration means the speed, and therefore the velocity, is also constant

2. A car of mass m is driving up a road with a slight incline θ above the horizontal. The driver sees a road closure and skids to a stop. The coefficient of static friction between the tires and the road is μ_s, and the coefficient of kinetic friction is μ_k. What is the magnitude of the gravity component of the force parallel to the surface of the road?

  A. $mg \sin \theta$ **C.** mg
  B. $mg \tan \theta$ **D.** $mg \cos \theta$ **E.** $m / (g \sin \theta)$

3. A change in which of the following will affect the buoyant force experienced by an object that is completely submerged in an incompressible liquid?

  I. Density of the liquid
  II. Density of the object
  III. Depth of the object

  A. I only   **B.** III only   **C.** I and III only   **D.** I and II only   **E.** I, II and III

4. What is the power output necessary for a 54 kg person to run at constant velocity up a 10 m hillside in 4 s, if the hillside is inclined at 30° above the horizontal? (Use acceleration due to gravity $g = 9.8$ m/s^2 and 1 hp = 745 W)

  A. 1.92 hp   **B.** 1.12 hp   **C.** 0.89 hp   **D.** 3.94 hp   **E.** 2.46 hp

5. Some of a wave's energy dissipates as heat. In time, this reduces the wave's:

  A. amplitude   **B.** frequency   **C.** speed   **D.** wavelength **E.** period

6. A piano tuned with the frequency of the third harmonic of the C$_3$ string is 783 Hz. What is the frequency of the C$_3$ fundamental?

  A. 473 Hz   **B.** 261 Hz   **C.** 387 Hz   **D.** 185 Hz   **E.** 127 Hz

7. What is the density of an object if it weighs 7.86 N when it is in air and 6.92 N when it is immersed in water? (Use acceleration due to gravity $g = 9.8$ m/s^2 and density of water $\rho = 1,000$ kg/m^3)

  A. 6,042 kg/m^3 **C.** 8,333 kg/m^3
  B. 7,286 kg/m^3 **D.** 9,240 kg/m^3 **E.** 11,868 kg/m^3

8. A water fountain pump recirculates water from a pool and pumps it up to a trough, where it flows along the trough and passes through a hole in the bottom of it. As the water falls back into the pool, it turns a water wheel. What aspect of this water fountain is analogous to an electric potential within an electric circuit?

A. Height of water   **C.** Flow velocity

B. Volume flow rate   **D.** Mass of water   **E.** Trough

9. If a sheet of copper is quickly passed through a strong permanent magnet with the plane of the sheet perpendicular to the magnetic field, which statement is true?

A. There is no movement because there is no magnetic force
B. The force experienced by the sheet of copper is due mainly to lead impurities in the copper, since copper is not magnetic
C. There is a magnetic force opposing the motion of the sheet
D. There is a magnetic force assisting the motion of the sheet
E. Both B and C are true

10. A light ray in water passes into air where the angle of incidence in the water is 42°. What is the angle of refraction in the air? (Use index of refraction of air $n = 1$ and index of refraction of water = 1.33)

A. 32°   **B.** 18°   **C.** 46°   **D.** 74°   **E.** 63°

11. ^{3}Hydrogen can be used as a chemical tracer. What is the half-life of the radionuclide if 3,200 µg decays to 800 µg after 24.6 years?

A. 6.1 years   **B.** 12.3 years   **C.** 24.6 years   **D.** 49.2 years   **E.** 98.4 years

12. An object with a mass of 60 kg moves across a level surface with a constant speed of 13.5 m/s. If there is a frictional force, and the coefficient of kinetic friction is 0.8, which must be true about the forces acting on the object?

A. There must be an unbalanced amount of vertical force acting on the object allowing it to move
B. No forces are doing work on the object
C. There must be some other horizontal force acting on the object
D. The force exerted on the object by kinetic friction is negligible
E. The total force exerted on the object is not balanced

13. The total mechanical energy of a system is:

A. either all kinetic energy or all potential energy, at any one instant
B. constant if there are only conservative forces acting
C. found through the product of potential energy and kinetic energy
D. equally divided between kinetic energy and potential energy in every instance
E. never a constant value; it always changes depending on the conditions

14. A 340 nm thick oil film floats on the surface of water. The surface of the oil is illuminated from above at normal incidence with white light. What are the two wavelengths of light that are in the 400 nm to 800 nm wavelength band, which are most strongly reflected? (Use the index of refraction for oil n = 1.5 and index of refraction for water n = 1.33)

A. 420 nm and 750 nm   C. 410 nm and 760 nm

B. 406 nm and 706 nm   D. 408 nm and 680 nm   E. 484 nm and 792 nm

15. A 1 m string is fixed at both ends and plucked. What is the wavelength corresponding to the fourth harmonic if the speed of the waves on this string is 4.2×10^4 m/s?

A. 1 m   B. 0.5 m   C. 4/3 m   D. 3/2 m   E. 2 m

16. Which statement is accurate?

A. Tensile stress is measured in N·m
B. Stress has a meaning similar to work
C. Strain has a meaning similar to force
D. The elastic modulus is the stress/strain ratio
E. Tensile strain is measured in Joules

17. Two point charges of +18 μC and –6 μC are separated by a distance of 15 cm. What is the electric field E midway between the two charges? (Coulomb's constant $k = 9 \times 10^9$ N·m^2·C^{-2})

A. 28.8×10^6 N/C toward the positive charge
B. 28.8×10^6 N/C toward the negative charge
C. 38.4×10^6 N/C toward the positive charge
D. 38.4×10^6 N/C toward the negative charge
E. 38.4×10^4 N/C toward the negative charge

18. When the current through a resistor is increased by a factor of 4, by what factor does the power dissipated by the resistor change?

A. Increases by 16   C. Decreases by 4

B. Increases by 4   D. Decreases by 16   E. Increases by 2

19. The image of an object placed outside the focal point of a concave mirror is:

A. virtual and inverted
B. virtual and upright
C. real and inverted
D. real and upright
E. real, but the object can be inverted or upright

20. A futuristic design for a car is to have a large disk-like flywheel within the car storing kinetic energy. The flywheel has mass 370.0 kg with a radius of 0.500 m and can rotate up to 200.0 rev/s. Assuming all of this stored kinetic energy could be transferred to the linear velocity of the 1500.0-kg car, what is the maximum attainable speed of the car?

   A. 29.6 m/s   **B.** 88.4 m/s   **C.** 162 m/s   **D.** 221 m/s   **E.** 318 m/s

21. A 500 g empty iron pot is put on a stove. How much heat must it absorb to raise its temperature from 20 °C to 70 °C? (Use specific heat c of iron = 92 cal/kg·°C and 1 cal = 4.186 J)

   A. 8,110 J   **B.** 9,628 J   **C.** 20,100 J   **D.** 12,500 J   **E.** 14,400 J

22. In a binary star system, two stars revolve about their combined center of mass and are attracted to each other by the force of gravity. The force of gravity between the stars (masses M_1 and M_2) is F. If the mass of one of the stars is decreased by a factor of 2, how would this affect the force between them?

   A. Remains the same   **C.** Decreases by a factor of 4
   B. Increases by a factor of 2   **D.** Increases by a factor of 4
                             E. Decreases by a factor of 2

23. In motion pictures, when a character falls off a cliff, he screams. If portrayed correctly, from the vantage point of an observer at the top of the cliff, the pitch of the scream the observer hears is:

   A. higher than the actual pitch and increasing as he falls
   B. lower than the actual pitch and decreasing as he falls
   C. higher than the actual pitch and constant
   D. lower than the actual pitch and increasing as he falls
   E. higher than the actual pitch and decreasing as he falls

24. As a cubical block of marble is lowered at a steady rate into the ocean by a crane, the top and bottom faces are kept horizontal. Which graph depicts the total pressure (P) on the bottom of the block as a function of time (t) as the block just enters the water at $t = 0$ s?

A.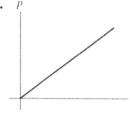

B.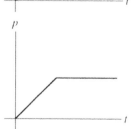

C.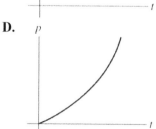

D.

E.

25. Two parallel metal plates separated by a distance of 0.03 m are charged to create a uniform electric field (4×10^4 N/C) between them, which points down. How does the force exerted on an α particle between the plates compare with the force exerted on a proton between the plates? (Use acceleration due to gravity $g = 10$ m/s^2 and the charge on a proton = 1.6×10^{-19} C)

    A. Twice as large and in the same direction
    B. Four times as large and in the same direction
    C. The same magnitude, but in the opposite direction
    D. The same magnitude and in the same direction
    E. Twice as large, but in the opposite direction

26. How much current flows through a 57 m length of copper wire with a radius of 5.7 mm if it is connected to a source supplying 70 V? (Use resistivity of copper = 1.68×10^{-8} Ω·m)

    A. 180 nA   **B.** 3,600 A   **C.** 7,447 A   **D.** 3.7×10^8 A   **E.** 8,200 A

27. Which statement about images is correct?

    A. A real image is always upright
    B. A virtual image cannot be photographed
    C. A virtual image cannot be seen by the unaided eye
    D. A virtual image cannot be formed on a screen
    E. Mirrors always produce real images because they reflect light

28. When a β$^+$ particle is emitted from an unstable nucleus, the atomic number of the nucleus:

    A. decreases by 2   **C.** decreases by 1
    B. increases by 2   **D.** increases by 1   **E.** does not change

29. Which answer is correct when the first law of thermodynamics, $Q = \Delta U - W$, is applied to an ideal gas that is taken through an isothermal process?

    A. $Q = 0$ **B.** $\Delta P = 0$ **C.** $\Delta U = 0$ **D.** $W = 0$ **E.** None are correct

30. Consider three galaxies, Alpha, Beta and Gamma. An observer on Gamma sees the other two galaxies each moving away from him in opposite directions at speed $0.7c$. At what speed would an observer in Alpha see the galaxy Gamma moving?

    A. $0.64c$ **C.** $0.88c$
    B. $0.70c$ **D.** $0.28c$ **E.** $0.53c$

31. For projectile motion with no air resistance, the vertical component of a projectile's acceleration:

    A. is always positive   **C.** continuously increases
    B. remains a nonzero constant   **D.** continuously decreases
    E. first increases and then decreases

32. A motor is connected to a power supply that supplies 5 A of current with a 25 V potential difference. The motor has a 30% efficiency rating and is used to lift a 50 kg box. How far does the motor lift the box in 60 s? (Use acceleration due to gravity $g = 10$ m/s^2)

A. 4.5 m **B.** 7.4 m **C.** 1.8 m **D.** 18 m **E.** 3.2 m

33. If the height that a pendulum reaches is doubled, what happens to its velocity as it passes its equilibrium position?

A. Remains the same
B. Increases by a factor of 4
C. Increases by a factor of 2
D. Increases by a factor of $\sqrt{2}$
E. Decreases by a factor of 2

34. Two metal rods are made of the same material and have the same cross-sectional area. The two rods differ only in their lengths of L and $3L$. The two rods are heated from the same initial temperature to the same final temperature. The short rod expands its length by an amount of ΔL. What is the amount by which the length of the long rod increases?

A. $\sqrt{3}\Delta L$ **B.** $3\Delta L$ **C.** ΔL **D.** $3/2\Delta L$ **E.** $9\Delta L$

35. If n_1 is the index of refraction for the incident medium, and n_2 is the index of the refracting medium, what conditions are necessary for the critical angle to exist?

A. $n_1 = n_2$ **B.** $n_1 < n_2$ **C.** $n_1 < 2n_2$ **D.** $n_1 < \frac{1}{2}n_2$ **E.** $n_1 > n_2$

36. Which graph is representative for a semiconductor material? R = resistivity, T = temperature.

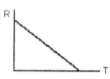

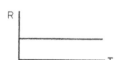

E. None of the graphs

37. Three capacitors C_1, C_2 and C_3 have equal capacitance and are connected to a battery as shown. Which capacitor stores the most potential energy?

A. C_3
B. C_1
C. C_2
D. C_2 or C_3
E. All three capacitors store the same amount of energy

38. A spherical inflated balloon is submerged in a swimming pool. How is the buoyant force affected if the balloon is inflated to double its radius?

A. 6 times larger   **C.** 4 times larger
B. 2 times larger   **D.** 2 times smaller   **E.** 8 times larger

39. An atom of He is twice as massive as a molecule of H. How much faster is the speed of sound in H compared to the speed of sound in He?

A. 4 times faster   **C.** 1.41 times faster
B. 8 times faster   **D.** 2 times faster   **E.** $1/\sqrt{2}$ times faster

40. If the energy that starts a vibration increases, this increases the:

A. number of cycles/sec   **C.** frequency
B. wavelength   **D.** amplitude   **E.** period

41. The potential energy of a box on a shelf, relative to the floor, is a measure of the:

     I. work done putting the box on the shelf from the floor
     II. energy the box has because of its position above the floor
     III. weight of the box × the distance above the floor

A. I only   **B.** II only   **C.** III only   **D.** I and III only   **E.** I, II and III

42. Block m has a mass of 3.3 kg. It is moving on a frictionless surface with a speed (v_i) of 8.5 m/s when it makes a perfectly elastic collision with a stationary block M, which has a mass of 6.5 kg. After the collision, block m recoils with a speed (v_f) of 3 m/s. What is the speed of block M after the collision?

A. 5.8 m/s   **C.** 3.6 m/s
B. 7.2 m/s   **D.** 9.4 m/s   **E.** 12 m/s

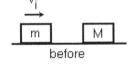
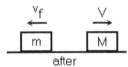

43. A 10 kg block is connected by a massless string to a 70 kg mass, which hangs over the edge of the table. Ignoring friction, what is the acceleration of the 10 kg block when the other block is released? (Use acceleration due to gravity $g = 10$ m/s^2)

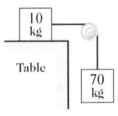

A. 5.5 m/s^2 **C.** 8.8 m/s^2
B. 10.5 m/s^2 **D.** 7.3 m/s^2 **E.** 16.3 m/s^2

44. An object with an initial velocity of 4 m/s moves along the *x*-axis with constant acceleration. How far did it travel in 2 s, if its final velocity is 16 m/s?

A. 9 m   **B.** 13 m   **C.** 32 m   **D.** 26 m   **E.** 20 m

45. When grinding a culinary knife, the 70 g of metal becomes heated to 450 °C. What is the minimum amount of 25 °C water needed if the water is to remain liquid and not rise above 100 °C when the hot knife is cooled in it? (Use specific heat of the knife = 0.11 cal/g·°C and specific heat of water = 1 cal/g·°C)

    A. 36 g   **B.** 28 g   **C.** 47 g   **D.** 18 g   **E.** 54 g

46. A horizontal spring-mass system oscillates on a frictionless table. If the ratio of the mass to the spring constant is 0.031 kg·m/N, and the maximum speed of the mass is 30 m/s, what is the maximum extension of the spring?

    A. 0.67 m   **B.** 460 cm   **C.** 5.3 m   **D.** 2.6 cm   **E.** 4.2 m

47. What is the shortest wavelength of a photon that can be emitted by a hydrogen atom, for which the initial state is n = 3?

    A. 102.6 nm   **B.** 97.3 nm   **C.** 820.0 nm   **D.** 121.6 nm   **E.** 91.2 nm

48. The H nucleus, which has a charge of e^+, is situated to the left of a C nucleus, which has a charge of $6\,e^+$. Which is true regarding the direction and magnitude of the electrical force experienced by the H nucleus?

    A. To the right and equal to the force exerted on the C nucleus.
    B. To the left and less than the force exerted on the C nucleus.
    C. To the right and greater than the force exerted on the C nucleus.
    D. To the left and equal to the force exerted on the C nucleus.
    E. To the right and less than the force exerted on the C nucleus.

49. An object is viewed at various distances using a concave mirror with a focal length of 10 m. Where is the image relative to the mirror when the object is 20 m away from the mirror?

    A. 20 m behind   **C.** 10 m behind
    B. 20 m in front   **D.** 10 m in front   **E.** 5 m behind

50. The electric field at point P due to a point charge Q a distance R away has magnitude E. What change would double the magnitude of the field at P?

    A. Reduce the distance to $R/2$
    B. Reduce the distance to $R/4$
    C. Double the charge to $2Q$
    D. Double the distance to $2R$
    E. Double the charge to $2Q$ and at the same time reduce the distance to $R/2$

51. A 9 g bullet is shot into a stationary 4 kg block lying on a frictionless horizontal surface. The bullet remains lodged in the block and, together, they push into a spring and compress it by 3.4 cm. What is the initial velocity of the bullet? (Use the spring constant $k = 2{,}400$ N/m)

    A. 664 m/s   **B.** 383 m/s   **C.** 370 m/s   **D.** 588 m/s   **E.** 274 m/s

52. By what factor does the time required to complete one full cycle increase for a simple pendulum when the length is tripled?

A. 1/3   **B.** 3   **C.** 1/9   **D.** 9   **E.** $\sqrt{3}$

53. A water tank is 30 m above ground and is filled to a depth of 15 m. What is the gauge pressure at ground level in a 3 cm diameter hose? (Use acceleration due to gravity $g = 9.8$ m/s^2 and density of water $\rho = 1,000$ kg/m^3)

A. 7.2×10^3 N/m^2
B. 6.1×10^1 N/m^2
C. 1.4×10^4 N/m^2
D. 4.4×10^5 N/m^2
E. Requires the cross-sectional area of the tank

54. Consider two copper wires of equal length. How do the resistances of these two wires compare if one wire has twice the cross-sectional area?

A. The thicker wire has one-half the resistance of the thinner wire
B. The thicker wire has four times the resistance of the thinner wire
C. The thicker wire has twice the resistance of the thinner wire
D. The thicker wire has eight times the resistance of the thinner wire
E. The thicker wire has one-fourth the resistance of the thinner wire

55. For a given value of the principal quantum number n, what are the allowable orbital angular momentum quantum numbers?

A. $\ell = 1, 2, 3, \ldots, n$
B. $\ell = 0, 1, 2, \ldots, (n-1)$
C. $\ell = 0, 1, 2, \ldots, n$
D. $\ell = 1, 2, 3, \ldots, (n-1)$ **E.** $\ell = 1, 2, 3, \ldots, (n+1)$

56. It is necessary to determine the specific heat of a 185 g object. It is determined experimentally that it takes 14 J to raise the temperature 10° C. What is the specific heat of the object?

A. 343 J/kg·K   **B.** 1.6 J/kg·K   **C.** 25.9 J/kg·K   **D.** 7.6 J/kg·K   **E.** 13.4 J/kg·K

57. A ball is projected upward at time $t = 0$ s from a point on a roof 50 m above the ground. The ball rises, then falls and strikes the ground. The initial velocity of the ball is 24 m/s. Consider all quantities as positive in the upward direction. At time $t = 3.8$ s, the acceleration of the ball is:

A. 10 m/s^2 **B.** −5 m/s^2 **C.** zero   **D.** 24 m/s^2 **E.** −10 m/s^2

58. Two astronauts conducted an experiment where a 3,500 kg spacecraft was connected with an orbiting rocket. The rocket thrusters were fired to provide 900 N for 8 s. What was the mass of the rocket, if the change in velocity of the spacecraft and rocket was 0.9 m/s?

A. 3,100 kg   **B.** 4,500 kg   **C.** 10,820 kg   **D.** 2,430 kg   **E.** 7,304 kg

59. A 0.3 kg ball hits a wall and rebounds. Initially the ball is going 7 m/s, but after the rebound it is going 5 m/s. What is the impulse imparted to the ball by the wall?

A. 0.6 kg·m/s   **B.** 1.8 kg·m/s   **C.** 2.1 kg·m/s   **D.** 3.6 kg·m/s   **E.** 0.9 kg·m/s

60. The Bohr model of the hydrogen atom was not able to explain:

A. the wavelengths of the emission lines in the infrared range
B. the wavelengths of the emission lines in the ultraviolet range
C. the observation that the atom does not lose energy to radiation as the electron orbits
D. the Bohr model explained the exact characteristics of a hydrogen atom
E. why some emission lines were brighter than other emission lines

61. An object is at height h above the surface of the Earth, where h is much smaller than the radius of the Earth. It takes t seconds to fall to the ground. Ignoring air resistance, at what height would this object need to be released in order to take $2t$ s to fall?

A. $4h$ B. $4gh$ C. $2h$ D. $2gh$ E. $2g$

62. Two 1 kg blocks are connected by rope 1. Rope 2 hangs beneath the block B. Each rope has a mass of 350 g. The entire assembly is accelerated upward at 5.5 m/s² by a force F. What is the tension at the bottom end of rope 1? (Use acceleration due to gravity $g = 9.8$ m/s²)

A. 7.9 N   B. 31.5 N   C. 23 N   D. 20.6 N   E. 13 N

63. A fluid in an insulated, flexible bottle is heated by a high-resistance wire and expands. If 9 kJ of heat is applied to the system and the system does 5 kJ of work, how much does the internal energy change?

A. –4 kJ   B. 32 kJ   C. 4 kJ   D. 12 kJ   E. 52 kJ

64. One end of a spring, with a spring constant 50 N/m, is fixed at point A, while the other end is connected to a 5 kg mass. The fixed end and the mass sit on a horizontal frictionless surface, so that the mass and the spring rotate about point A. The mass moves in a circle with $r = 4$ m, and the force on the mass is 20 N. How long does it take for the mass to make one complete revolution around point A?

A. 5.7 s   B. 6.3 s   C. 4.4 s   D. 3.2 s   E. 8.6 s

65. All of the following are true statements, EXCEPT:

A. Waves transport energy and matter from one region to another
B. The speed of a wave and the speed of the vibrating particles of the wave are not the same entities
C. A wave that is being reflected at the same frequency as it is being produced is referred to as a standing wave
D. For a transverse wave, the motion of the particles is perpendicular to the velocity vector of the wave
E. A wave in which particles move back and forth in the same direction that the wave is moving is referred to as a longitudinal wave

66. What are the wavelengths of the three lowest tones produced by an open pipe of length L?

A. $2L, L, 2L/3$

B. $4L, 4L/3, 4L/5$

C. $4L, 2L, L$

D. $2L, L, L/2$

E. $2L, L/2, L/8$

67. A 4.2 m steel wire has a diameter of 1.8 mm. The wire stretches 1.8 mm when it bears a load. What is the mass of the load? (Use Young's modulus for steel $= 2 \times 10^{11}$ N/m^2 and acceleration due to gravity $g = 9.8$ m/s^2)

A. 22 kg   **B.** 26 kg   **C.** 30 kg   **D.** 16 kg   **E.** 10 kg

68. A circular loop of wire is positioned in a region of a changing magnetic field; the direction of the field remains constant, but the magnitude is fluctuating. What must the orientation of the loop's area vector be in relation to the magnetic field direction in order to create the maximum induced emf?

A. An angle of 45° to the magnetic field
B. An angle of −45° to the magnetic field
C. An angle of 90° to the magnetic field
D. Parallel to the magnetic field
E. Perpendicular to the magnetic field

69. A charged, parallel-plate capacitor has an electric field E_0 between its plates. The bare nuclei of ^{1}H and of ^{3}H, both at rest, are placed between the plates. Ignoring the force of gravity, how does the force, F_1, of the light ^{1}H nucleus compare with the force, F_3, of the heavy ^{3}H nucleus?

A. $F_3 = 3F_1$ **B.** $F_3 = \sqrt{2}F_1$ **C.** $F_3 = F_1$ **D.** $F_3 = (1/3)F_1$ **E.** $F_3 = \frac{1}{2}F_1$

70. Which statement about thin, single lenses is correct?

A. A diverging lens can only sometimes produce a virtual erect image
B. A diverging lens always produces a virtual erect image
C. A converging lens always produces a real inverted image
D. A diverging lens always produces a real inverted image
E. A diverging lens produces a virtual erect image only if the object is located within the focal point

71. During β^+ decay:

A. a proton is transformed to a neutron
B. an electron is released from its orbit

C. a neutron is transformed to a positron
D. a neutron is transformed to a proton
E. the number of nucleons decreases

72. Consider objects that slide friction-free along a horizontal air track. Glider A, which has a mass of 2 kg and a speed of 2 m/s, collides with glider B of 5 kg, which is at rest. If they stick together, what is their speed after the collision?

A. 0.25 m/s   **B.** 0.33 m/s   **C.** 1.2 m/s   **D.** 1 m/s   **E.** 0.6 m/s

73. A child, while pulling a box from the ground up to his tree house with a rope, does 400 J of work. What is the mass of the box if the tree house is 4 m above the ground? (Use acceleration due to gravity $g = 9.8$ m/s^2)

    A. 13.2 kg   **B.** 6.6 kg   **C.** 5.2 kg   **D.** 10.2 kg   **E.** 8.6 kg

74. An electrical motor spins at a constant 2,695.0 rpm. If the rotor radius is 7.165 cm what is the linear acceleration of the edge of the rotor?

    A. 707.0 m/s^2 **C.** 3,272 m/s^2
    B. 1,280 m/s^2 **D.** 4,028 m/s^2 **E.** 5,707 m/s^2

75. Some wave fronts are emitted by a source S. This diagram illustrates why:

    A. beats are heard
    B. sonar works
    C. a sound appears louder as the observer moves closer to the source
    D. the siren on a fire engine truck changes its pitch as it passes the observer
    E. a sound appears softer as the observer moves further from the source

76. A plastic container in the shape of a cube with 0.2 m sides is suspended in a vacuum. The container is filled to 3 atm with 10 g of N_2 gas. What is the force that the N_2 gas exerts on one face of the cube? (Use ideal gas constant $R = 0.0821$ L atm/K mol and 1 atm $= 1.01 \times 10^5$ Pa)

    A. 2.1×10^3 N   **C.** 3.7×10^5 N
    B. 5.6×10^4 N   **D.** 4.2×10^4 N   **E.** 1.2×10^4 N

77. What is the maximum magnetic field for a wave if an electromagnetic wave is traveling in a vacuum that has a maximum electric field of 1,200 V/m? (Use speed of light c in a vacuum $= 3 \times 10^8$ m/s)

    A. 4×10^{-6} T   **C.** 3.3×10^{-4} T
    B. 2×10^{-5} T   **D.** 8×10^{-6} T   **E.** 12×10^{-6} T

78. An alternating voltage, oscillating at 60 Hz, has a maximum value of 200 V during each cycle. What would be the reading if an rms (root mean square) voltmeter is connected to the circuit?

    A. 142 V   **B.** 100 V   **C.** 35 V   **D.** 284 V   **E.** 71 V

79. Where is the resulting image if a candle 21 cm tall is placed 4 m away from a diverging lens with a focal length of 3 m?

    A. 12/7 m from the lens on the opposite side from the object
    B. 12 m from the lens on the opposite side from the object
    C. 12/7 m from the lens on the same side as the object
    D. 12 m from the lens on the same side as the object
    E. 4 m from the lens on the same side as the object

80. An energy level diagram of a certain atom is shown below whereby the energy difference between levels 1 and 2 is twice the energy difference between levels 2 and 3. A wavelength λ is emitted when an electron makes a transition from level 3 to 2. What possible radiation λ might be produced by other transitions between the three energy levels?

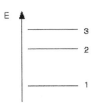

A. 2λ only

B. both 2λ and 3λ

C. ½λ only

D. both ½λ and λ/3

E. both λ/√2 and λ/√3

81. A person running in place on an exercise machine for 10 min expends 19 kcal. Another person exercises by repeatedly lifting two 3 kg weights a distance of 50 cm. How many repetitions of this exercise are equivalent to 10 minutes of running in place? Assume that the person uses negligible energy in letting down the weights after each lift. (Use acceleration due to gravity $g = 9.8$ m/s^2 and 1 kcal = 1,000 cal and 1 cal = 4.186 J)

A. 2,300 repetitions

B. 1,800 repetitions

C. 1,360 repetitions

D. 3,940 repetitions

E. 2,705 repetitions

82. A 18 kg block is on a ramp that is inclined at 20° above the horizontal and is connected by a string to a 21 kg mass that hangs over the edge of the ramp. Ignoring frictional forces, what is the acceleration of the 21 kg block? (Use acceleration due to gravity $g = 9.8$ m/s^2)

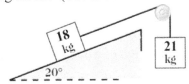

A. 3.2 m/s^2 **B.** 2.6 m/s^2 **C.** 3.7 m/s^2 **D.** 5.3 m/s^2 **E.** 7.6 m/s^2

83. A transverse wave in a string, with a wavelength of 8 m, is travelling at 4 m/s. At $t = 0$, a point on the string has a displacement of $+x$, where x is the amplitude of the wave. At what value of t is the same point on the string at a displacement of $-x$?

A. 1 s   **B.** 2 s   **C.** ¼ s   **D.** ½ s   **E.** 5 s

84. If the amount of fluid flowing through a tube remains constant, by what factor does the speed of the fluid change when the radius of the tube decreases from 16 cm to 4 cm?

A. Increases by √2

B. Increases by 16

C. Decreases by 16

D. Decreases by 4

E. Remains the same

85. Two identically-charged balls are a certain distance apart as shown in the vector diagram.

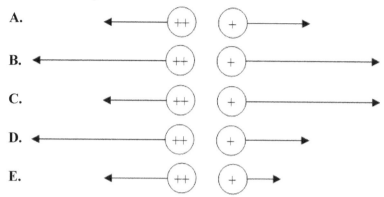

If the charge of the ball on the left is doubled (represented by ++), which diagram represents the forces now acting on the two balls?

A.

B.

C.

D.

E.

86. If Mario were in a spaceship traveling close to the speed of light with respect to Earth, he would notice that:

    A. his pulse rate was greater than normal
    B. his mass was greater than normal
    C. his mass was less than normal
    D. some of his physical dimensions were smaller than normal
    E. none of the above effects occur

87. Which statement is true if the magnification of a mirror or lens is negative?

    A. Object is closer to the mirror or lens than to the image
    B. Image is inverted
    C. Image is erect and smaller than the object
    D. Image is smaller than the object
    E. Image is erect and larger than the object

88. The masses of all isotopes are based on a comparison to the mass of which isotope?

    A. Uranium-232   **C.** Carbon-12
    B. Carbon-13   **D.** Hydrogen-1   **E.** Helium-10

89. Ignoring air resistance, a 30 kg and a 60 kg rock are thrown upward with the same initial speed (v_i). If the 30 kg rock reaches a maximum height h, what maximum height does the 60 kg ball reach?

    A. $2h$ **B.** h **C.** $h/2$ **D.** $h/4$ **E.** $4h$

90. A hockey puck is set in motion across a frozen pond. Ignoring the friction of ice and air resistance, what is the force required to keep the puck sliding at constant velocity?

    A. mass of the puck × 9.8 m/s²   **C.** weight of the puck   **E.** 0 N
    B. weight of the puck / mass of the puck   **D.** √mass of the puck

91. A 0.24 kg piece of clay is thrown at a wall with an initial velocity of 16 m/s. What is the average force experienced by the clay if it stops after 91 milliseconds?

    A. 84 N   **B.** 32 N   **C.** 24 N   **D.** 42 N   **E.** 64 N

92. A car drives 5 km North, then 7.3 km East, then 3.4 km Northeast, all at a constant speed. What was the magnitude of the average frictional force on the car if it performed 2.6×10^6 J of work during this trip?

    A. 1.7×10^2 N   **C.** 7×10^1 N

    B. 4.2×10^2 N   **D.** 5.7×10^2 N   **E.** 6.9×10^2 N

93. A red shift for light indicates that the light source moves:

    I. at right angles to the observer
    II. towards the observer
    III. away from the observer

    A. I only   **C.** III only

    B. II only   **D.** I and II only   **E.** I and III only

94. An object having an emissivity 0.867 radiates heat at a rate of 15 W when it is at a temperature T. If its temperature is doubled, what is the rate at which it radiates heat?

    A. 30 W   **B.** 60 W   **C.** 80 W   **D.** 240 W   **E.** 120 W

95. A lens of focal length 50 mm is used as a magnifier to view a 6.4 mm object that is positioned at the focal point of the lens. The user of the magnifier has a near point at 25 cm. What is the angular magnification of the magnifier?

    A. 7.6   **B.** 6.9   **C.** 5.8   **D.** 8.1   **E.** 5

96. In Experiment 1, a magnet was moved toward the end of a solenoid and a voltage was induced between the two ends of the solenoid wire. In Experiment 2, a higher voltage was observed. What might have changed between the two experiments?

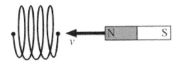

    I. The bar magnet was replaced by a stronger magnet
    II. The solenoid was replaced by one with more loops but the same length
    III. The speed of the magnet increased

    A. I only   **B.** II only   **C.** III only   **D.** I and III only   **E.** I, II and III

97. A car of mass m is driving up a shallow incline of angle θ with the horizontal when the driver sees a deer and quickly steps on the brakes and the tires lock up (the tires skid along the surface of the road rather than gripping it smoothly). The coefficient of static friction between the tires and the road is μ_s, and the coefficient of kinetic friction is μ_k. What is the magnitude of the net force on the car during the skid?

A. $mg\,(\mu_s \cos \theta - \sin \theta)$

C. $mg\,\mu_s \cos \theta$

B. $mg\,(\mu_s \cos \theta + \sin \theta)$

D. $mg\,(\mu_k \cos \theta + \sin \theta)$

E. $mg\,(\mu_k \cos \theta + \sin \theta)$

98. The radius of a typical nucleus is about 5.0×10^{-15} m. Assuming this to be the uncertainty in the position of a proton in the nucleus, what is the uncertainty in the proton's energy? (Use 1.67×10^{-27} kg as the proton mass)

A. 0.06 MeV

C. 0.4 MeV

B. 0.25 MeV

D. 0.8 MeV

E. 1.2 MeV

99. A 0.2 m long string vibrates in the $n = 5$ harmonic. What is the distance between a node and an adjacent antinode? (Use speed of sound in air $v = 340$ m/s)

A. 30 mm   **B.** 60 mm   **C.** 7.5 mm   **D.** 20 mm   **E.** 120 mm

100. The graph shows position x as a function of time t for a system undergoing simple harmonic motion. Which graph represents the velocity of this system as a function of time?

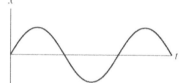

A.
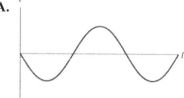

C.
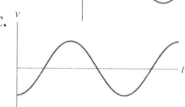

B.
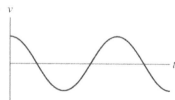

D.
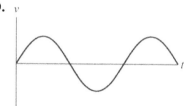

E. None of the above

Check your answers using the answer key. Then, go to the explanations section and review the explanations in detail, paying particular attention to questions you didn't answer correctly or marked for review. Note the topic that those questions belong to.

We recommend that you do this BEFORE taking the next Diagnostic Test.

Diagnostic Test #5

Answer Sheet

#	Answer:					Mark for review	#	Answer:					Mark for review
1:	A	B	C	D	E	___	**31:**	A	B	C	D	E	___
2:	A	B	C	D	E	___	**32:**	A	B	C	D	E	___
3:	A	B	C	D	E	___	**33:**	A	B	C	D	E	___
4:	A	B	C	D	E	___	**34:**	A	B	C	D	E	___
5:	A	B	C	D	E	___	**35:**	A	B	C	D	E	___
6:	A	B	C	D	E	___	**36:**	A	B	C	D	E	___
7:	A	B	C	D	E	___	**37:**	A	B	C	D	E	___
8:	A	B	C	D	E	___	**38:**	A	B	C	D	E	___
9:	A	B	C	D	E	___	**39:**	A	B	C	D	E	___
10:	A	B	C	D	E	___	**40:**	A	B	C	D	E	___
11:	A	B	C	D	E	___	**41:**	A	B	C	D	E	___
12:	A	B	C	D	E	___	**42:**	A	B	C	D	E	___
13:	A	B	C	D	E	___	**43:**	A	B	C	D	E	___
14:	A	B	C	D	E	___	**44:**	A	B	C	D	E	___
15:	A	B	C	D	E	___	**45:**	A	B	C	D	E	___
16:	A	B	C	D	E	___	**46:**	A	B	C	D	E	___
17:	A	B	C	D	E	___	**47:**	A	B	C	D	E	___
18:	A	B	C	D	E	___	**48:**	A	B	C	D	E	___
19:	A	B	C	D	E	___	**49:**	A	B	C	D	E	___
20:	A	B	C	D	E	___	**50:**	A	B	C	D	E	___
21:	A	B	C	D	E	___	**51:**	A	B	C	D	E	___
22:	A	B	C	D	E	___	**52:**	A	B	C	D	E	___
23:	A	B	C	D	E	___	**53:**	A	B	C	D	E	___
24:	A	B	C	D	E	___	**54:**	A	B	C	D	E	___
25:	A	B	C	D	E	___	**55:**	A	B	C	D	E	___
26:	A	B	C	D	E	___	**56:**	A	B	C	D	E	___
27:	A	B	C	D	E	___	**57:**	A	B	C	D	E	___
28:	A	B	C	D	E	___	**58:**	A	B	C	D	E	___
29:	A	B	C	D	E	___	**59:**	A	B	C	D	E	___
30:	A	B	C	D	E	___	**60:**	A	B	C	D	E	___

	Mark for review			Mark for review

#	Answer:	Mark for review	#	Answer:	Mark for review
61:	A B C D E	___	**81:**	A B C D E	___
62:	A B C D E	___	**82:**	A B C D E	___
63:	A B C D E	___	**83:**	A B C D E	___
64:	A B C D E	___	**84:**	A B C D E	___
65:	A B C D E	___	**85:**	A B C D E	___
66:	A B C D E	___	**86:**	A B C D E	___
67:	A B C D E	___	**87:**	A B C D E	___
68:	A B C D E	___	**88:**	A B C D E	___
69:	A B C D E	___	**89:**	A B C D E	___
70:	A B C D E	___	**90:**	A B C D E	___
71:	A B C D E	___	**91:**	A B C D E	___
72:	A B C D E	___	**92:**	A B C D E	___
73:	A B C D E	___	**93:**	A B C D E	___
74:	A B C D E	___	**94:**	A B C D E	___
75:	A B C D E	___	**95:**	A B C D E	___
76:	A B C D E	___	**96:**	A B C D E	___
77:	A B C D E	___	**97:**	A B C D E	___
78:	A B C D E	___	**98:**	A B C D E	___
79:	A B C D E	___	**99:**	A B C D E	___
80:	A B C D E	___	**100:**	A B C D E	___

This Diagnostic Test is designed for you to assess your proficiency on each topic. Use your test results and identify areas of your strength and weakness to adjust your study plan and enhance your fundamental knowledge.

The length of the Diagnostic Tests is proven to be optimal for a single study session.

1. What is the potential energy with respect to the ground for a 2 kg mass that is held 4 m above the ground? (Use acceleration due to gravity $g = 9.8$ m/s^2)

  A. 20 J   **B.** 40 J   **C.** 60 J   **D.** 80 J   **E.** 120 J

2. Which point on the graph represents the maximum momentum for a diver as she leaps from a platform?

  A. A
  B. B
  C. C
  D. D
  E. A and C

3. To drive a typical car at 40.0 mph on a level road for one hour requires about 3.2×10^7 J of energy. Suppose one tried to store this much energy in a spinning solid cylindrical flywheel which was then coupled to the wheels of the car. What angular speed would be required to store 3.2×10^7 J if the flywheel has of radius 0.60 m and mass 400.0 kg?

  A. 943.0 rad/s   **C.** 1,822.4 rad/s
  B. 1,384.2 rad/s   **D.** 2,584.5 rad/s   **E.** 5,360.8 rad/s

4. A box is being dragged to the right at constant velocity along a level floor by a string which is horizontal with tension T. The magnitude of the frictional force is F, the gravitational force is G, and the normal force is N. Which relationship is true?

  A. $T + F = G + N$ **B.** $T > F$ **C.** $T + F = G - N$ **D.** $T < F$ **E.** $T = F$

5. A gas is confined to a rigid container that cannot expand as heat energy is added to it. This process is referred to as:

  A. isokinetic   **C.** isothermal
  B. isentropic   **D.** isometric   **E.** adiabatic

6. Which of the following expressions is equal to a watt?

  A. kg·m^2/s^3 **B.** kg^2·m^2·s^2 **C.** kg·m/s^3 **D.** kg·m/s   **E.** kg·m^2/s^2

7. An organ pipe is a cylindrical tube that opens at both ends whereby the air column vibrates from air flowing through the lower portion of the pipe. On an 8 °C day, the speed of sound is 3% slower than on a 20 °C day. How is the f affected?

  A. Remains the same   **C.** Decreases by 9%
  B. Increases by $\sqrt{3}$%   **D.** Decreases by 3%   **E.** Decreases by $\sqrt{3}$%

8. Three particles travel through a region of space where the magnetic field is pointing out of the page. What are the signs of the charges of these three particles?

A. 1 is negative, 2 is positive and 3 is neutral
B. 1 is positive, 2 is negative and 3 is neutral
C. 1 is positive, 2 is neutral and 3 is negative
D. 1 is neutral, 2 is positive and 3 is negative
E. 1 is negative, 2 is neutral and 3 is positive

9. Which form of electromagnetic radiation has the lowest frequency?

A. X-rays
B. γ rays
C. Radio waves
D. Microwaves
E. Infrared radiation

10. Ignoring air resistance, a purple marble is thrown upwards from a cliff with an initial speed of v_0. A grey marble is thrown downwards with the same initial speed. When the marbles reach the ground, the:

A. two marbles travel at a speed proportional to their mass
B. two marbles have the same speed
C. grey marble moves faster than the purple marble
D. purple marble moves faster than the grey marble
E. two marbles travel at a speed inversely proportional to their mass

11. A solid cylinder and a thin loop have the same mass and radius. Which statement is true about their moment of inertia about an axis through the exact center of the flat surfaces?

A. Both the solid cylinder and thin loop have the same moment of inertia
B. The solid cylinder has the greater moment of inertia
C. The thin loop has the greater moment of inertia
D. The moment of inertia cannot be determined because the volume of each is unknown
E. None of the above

12. What is the speed of transverse waves on a steel cable that lifts a 2,500 kg mass where the cable has a mass per unit length of 0.65 kg/m? (Use acceleration due to gravity $g = 9.8$ m/s^2)

A. 410 m/s   B. 920 m/s   C. 668 m/s   D. 470 m/s   E. 194 m/s

13. A viscous oil flows through a narrow pipe at constant velocity. By what factor does the flow rate increase if the diameter of the pipe is doubled?

A. 4   B. $\sqrt{2}$ C. 6   D. 8   E. 12

14. Ignoring air resistance, two objects are thrown from the top of a tall building. With the same initial speed, one is thrown upward and the other is thrown downward. What is the relationship between their speeds when they hit the street?

    A. It is impossible to determine because the height of the building is unknown
    B. They are traveling at the same speed
    C. The object thrown downward is traveling faster
    D. The object thrown upward is traveling faster
    E. It is impossible to determine because their initial velocities are unknown

15. Which forces hold the protons in a nucleus together?

    A. dipole–dipole   **C.** nuclear
    B. gravitational   **D.** electrostatic attraction   **E.** electromagnetic

16. How much heat is required to raise the temperature of a 300 g lead ball from 20 °C to 30 °C? The specific heat of lead is 128 J/kg·K.

    A. 224 J   **B.** 168 J   **C.** 576 J   **D.** 725 J   **E.** 384 J

17. Calculate the speed at which a 0.723 kg object has the same momentum as a 1.30 kg object that is moving $0.515c$:

    A. $0.548c$ **B.** $0.621c$ **C.** $0.734c$ **D.** $0.916c$ **E.** $0.416c$

18. A photocathode has a work function of 2.4 eV. The photocathode is illuminated with monochromatic radiation and electrons are emitted with a stopping potential of 1.1 volt. What is the wavelength of the illuminating radiation? (Use $c = 3.00 \times 10^8$ m/s, $h = 6.626 \times 10^{-34}$ J·s and 1 eV $= 1.60 \times 10^{-19}$ J)

    A. 300 nm   **C.** 390 nm
    B. 350 nm   **D.** 420 nm   **E.** 480 nm

19. A 0.01 kg bullet is moving horizontally when it strikes a 1.5 kg block of wood that is suspended on a pendulum with a 2 m string. The bullet imbeds into the wood, and together they swing upward a distance of 0.4 m. What was the velocity of the bullet just before it struck the wooden block? (Use acceleration due to gravity $g = 9.8$ m/s²)

    A. 423 m/s   **B.** 225 m/s   **C.** 168 m/s   **D.** 326 m/s   **E.** 526 m/s

20. Why do heavy nuclei contain more neutrons than protons?

    A. Neutrons are heavier than protons
    B. Neutrons and heavy nuclei are not radioactive
    C. Neutrons reduce the electric repulsion of the protons
    D. Neutrons are lighter than protons
    E. Neutrons amplify the electric repulsion of the protons

21. How far will an object have traveled after 3 s if it starts from rest and undergoes uniform acceleration given that it reaches 5 m/s after 1 s?

    A. 5 m   **B.** 10 m   **C.** 18 m   **D.** 22.5 m   **E.** 40 m

22. A block is at rest on the surface of an inclined plane as the angle of elevation is gradually increased. Which statement is true about the normal force exerted by the plane on the block?

    A. It is independent of the angle of elevation
    B. It is inversely dependent on the coefficient of static friction between the block and plane
    C. It increases as the angle of elevation increases
    D. It is independent of the total amount of forces acting upon it
    E. It decreases as the angle of elevation increases

23. An aluminum rod 10 cm long and a steel rod 80 cm long are joined end-to-end. Both rods are at a temperature of 15 °C and have the same diameter. What is the increase in the length of the joined rod when the temperature is raised to 90 °C? (Use the coefficient of linear expansion α for aluminum = 2.4×10^{-5} K^{-1} and α for steel = 1.2×10^{-5} K^{-1})

    A. 0.7 mm   **B.** 1.1 mm   **C.** 0.9 mm   **D.** 0.8 mm **E.** 1 mm

24. Which quantity is conserved when a falling object strikes the ground?

    I. Momentum of the object   II. KE of the object   III. Total energy

    A. I only   **B.** III only   **C.** I and III only   **D.** II and III only   **E.** I, II and III

25. If the frequency of the motion of a simple harmonic oscillator is doubled, by what factor does the maximum speed of the oscillator change?

    A. ½   **B.** √2   **C.** 4   **D.** 2   **E.** ¼

26. A standing wave of the third overtone is induced in a 1.2 m pipe that is open at one end and closed at the other. What is the number of antinodes in the standing wave? (Use the speed of sound = 340 m/s)

    A. 3   **B.** 4   **C.** 5   **D.** 6   **E.** 7

27. A wire circle and solid circle of the same diameter are resting on the surface of the water. Which one can have the larger maximum mass without sinking?

    A. The solid circle, by a factor of 2   **C.** The wire circle, by a factor of 2
    B. The solid circle, by a factor of 4   **D.** They have the same maximum mass
                                    E. The wire circle, by a factor of 4

28. Which statement applies to the 120 V circuit shown?

    A. 120 J of energy are given to each Coulomb of charge making up the current in the circuit
    B. 120 J of energy are equally shared among all Coulombs in the circuit at any instant
    C. 120 C of charge flow through the lamp every second
    D. 120 C of energy are converted to heat and light in the circuit every second
    E. 120 J of energy are unequally shared among the Coulombs in the circuit, depending on location

29. How many electrons pass a given point in a minute for a wire that has a current of 6 mA? (Use charge of an electron = 1.602×10^{-19} C)

    A. 5.3×10^{14} electrons   **C.** 2.3×10^{18} electrons
    B. 5.4×10^{-15} electrons   **D.** 3.7×10^{12} electrons   **E.** 720 electrons

30. How does an image appear if an object is placed in front of a convex mirror at a distance larger than twice the magnitude of the focal length of the mirror?

    A. upright and smaller   **C.** inverted and smaller
    B. inverted and larger   **D.** inverted and the same size
                            E. upright and the same size

31. According to the de Broglie hypothesis, the idea of matter waves describes the wavelike behavior of:

    I. Positively-charged stationary particles
    II. Negatively-charged stationary particles
    III. Particles that are moving

    A. I only   **B.** II only   **C.** III only   **D.** I and II   **E.** I, II and III

32. Block I and block II slide on a frictionless level surface in one dimension and stick together when they make contact. Block II is also connected to a massless, ideal spring that extends horizontally and is connected to a wall. Initially, block II is at rest, and block I approaches from the right. The two blocks move before oscillating. Take the system to be the two blocks and the spring. Which statement is true?

    I. Momentum is conserved
    II. The sum of the spring PE and KE is conserved
    III. KE is conserved

    A. I only   **B.** II only   **C.** I and II only   **D.** II and III only   **E.** I, II and III

33. Ignoring air resistance, when a pebble is thrown straight upward with an initial speed *v*, it reaches a maximum height *h*. At what speed should the pebble be thrown upward vertically for it to go twice as high?

    A. 16*v*   **B.** 8*v*   **C.** 4*v*   **D.** 2*v*   **E.** $\sqrt{2}v$

34. If the mass and the length of a simple pendulum are doubled, the period:

A. increases by a factor of 4
B. increases by a factor of $\sqrt{2}$

C. remains the same
D. increases by a factor of 2
E. decreases by a factor of 2

35. Which type of organ pipe can produce only odd harmonics?

I. open   II. long   III. closed

A. I only   C. III only
B. II only   D. II and III only   E. None of the above

36. Determine the speed at which water exits a tank through a very small hole in the bottom of the tank that is 20 cm in diameter and filled with water to a height of 50 cm. (Use acceleration due to gravity $g = 9.8$ m/s^2)

A. 8.8 m/s   B. 17.8 m/s   C. 31.2 m/s   D. 21.6 m/s   E. 3.1 m/s

37. While being pulled apart, the plates of a parallel-plate capacitor are maintained with constant voltage by a battery. What happens to the strength of the electric field between the plates during this process?

A. Remains constant
B. Decreases

C. Increases by the $\sqrt{\text{voltage}}$
D. Increases by the (distance)^2
E. Increases by the $\sqrt{\text{distance}}$

38. An electron and a deuteron (^{2}H nucleus) are placed in an electric field (E_0) between the plates of a charged parallel-plate capacitor. Ignoring the force of gravity, how does the magnitude of the force on an electron F_{elec} compare with the force on the deuteron F_d? (Use mass of proton $m_{proton} \approx 1{,}850 \times m_{electron}$)

A. $F_{elec} = \frac{1}{2}F_d$
B. $F_{elec} = 1{,}850\ F_d$

C. $F_{elec} = F_d$
D. $F_{elec} = 3{,}700\ F_d$ E. $F_{elec} = 925\ F_d$

39. A 1.8×10^{14} Hz electromagnetic wave propagates in CCl$_4$ with a speed of 2.43×10^8 m/s. The wave then leaves the CCl$_4$ and enters a vacuum. What is the wavelength of the wave in the vacuum? (Use speed of light in a vacuum $c = 3 \times 10^8$ m/s)

A. 2,260 nm   B. 1,280 nm   C. 1,040 nm   D. 1,667 nm   E. 1,840 nm

40. How much energy does a photon of wavelength 580 nm have? (Use Planck's constant $h = 6.626 \times 10^{-34}$ J·s and speed of light $c = 3 \times 10^8$ m/s)

A. 6.4×10^{-32} J
B. 8.8 eV

C. 2.6×10^{-38} J
D. 1.3×10^{-19} eV   E. 3.4×10^{-19} J

41. At constant pressure and temperature, Graham's Law states that the diffusion rate for a gas molecule is:

A. inversely proportional to $\sqrt{mass}$

B. inversely proportional to mass

C. proportional to the log of the mass

D. proportional to mass

E. proportional to $\sqrt{mass}$

42. A skier falls while skiing, and one ski, with weight w, loosens and slides down an icy slope which makes an angle θ with the horizontal. Ignoring friction, what is the force that pushes the ski down the hill?

A. $w^2 \cos \theta$ B. $w \sin \theta$ C. w D. $w \cos \theta$ E. $\sqrt{w} \tan \theta$

43. By what factor does the velocity of sound in a gas change when the absolute temperature of that gas is doubled?

A. It increases by 4

B. It increases by $\sqrt{2}$

C. It remains the same

D. It increases by 2

E. It increases by $1/\sqrt{2}$

44. A pipe with a circular cross-section has water flowing within it from point I to point II. The radius of the pipe at point I is 12 cm, while the radius at point II is 6 cm. If at the end of point I the flow rate is 0.09 m³/s, what is the flow rate at the end of point II?

A. 0.6 m³/s

B. 0.09 m³/s

C. 0.15 m³/s

D. 1.2 m³/s

E. 2.4 m³/s

45. What is the path for an electron moving on the page toward the right when subjected to a magnetic field pointing out of the page?

A. Curves upward (path X)

B. Continues straight ahead (path Y)

C. Curves downward (path Z)

D. Decelerates

E. Accelerates

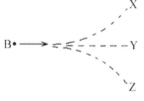

46. A positively-charged particle is traveling on a path parallel to a straight wire that contains a current. Which change increases the magnetic field at a point along the particle's path?

A. Increasing the speed of the particle

B. Increasing the distance of the particle from the wire

C. Decreasing the distance of the particle from the wire

D. Decreasing the current in the wire

E. Increasing the charge of the particle

47. If parallel light rays were incident on a lens of power 4 D, which statement is true for the rays on the other side of the lens?

    A. The rays diverge as if from a point 4 m behind the lens
    B. The rays diverge as if from a point ¼ m in front of the lens
    C. The rays converge with a focal length of ¼ m
    D. The rays converge with a focal length of 4 m
    E. The rays either diverge or converge, but more information is needed

48. The α particle has twice the electric charge of the β particle but deflects less than the β in a magnetic field because it:

    A. is smaller   **C.** moves slower
    B. has less inertia   **D.** is larger   **E.** has more inertia

49. Which statement explains why a sponge ball of the same size as a marble ball takes a longer time to reach the ground?

    A. Air resistance is more significant for the sponge ball than for the marble
    B. There is a stronger gravitational force between the marble ball and the ground
    C. The force of gravity only acts on the marble ball
    D. The force of gravity on the sponge ball is less than that on the marble ball
    E. None of the above is a good explanation

50. The Moon and the Earth are attracted by the force of gravity. The Earth's radius is 3.7 times that of the Moon, and the Earth's mass is 80 times that of the Moon. The acceleration due to gravity on the surface of the Moon is one sixth the acceleration due to gravity on the Earth's surface. How does the Earth's gravitational pull on the Moon differ from the Moon's pull on the Earth?

    A. 80 times greater   **C.** 3.7 times greater
    B. 6 times greater   **D.** Identical   **E.** 6 times smaller

51. A uniform 16 kg board of length L is positioned horizontally, with its two ends supported by scales. A 4 kg package is positioned at a distance of $L / 3$ from the left end. What is the weight reading for the scale on the right? (Use acceleration due to gravity $g = 9.8$ m/s^2 and assume mass is centered in the middle of the board)

    A. 53.1 N   **B.** 91.5 N   **C.** 81.9 N   **D.** 43.3 N   **E.** 62 N

52. The brakes of a car are applied abruptly whereby the car skids a certain distance on a straight, level road. If the car had been traveling twice as fast, what is the distance that the car would have skidded, under the same conditions?

    A. $\sqrt{2}$ times farther   **C.** 4 times farther
    B. Half as far   **D.** Twice as far   **E.** Unable to determine

53. A pair of narrow slits, separated by 1.8 mm, is illuminated by a monochromatic light source. Light waves arrive at the two slits in phase. A fringe pattern is observed on a screen 4.8 m from the slits. There are 5 bright fringes per cm on the screen. What is the λ of the monochromatic light?

    A. 550 nm   **B.** 600 nm   **C.** 650 nm   **D.** 700 nm   **E.** 750 nm

54. A 0.4 kg ice cube at 0 °C has sufficient heat added to it to cause total melting, and the resulting water is heated to 60 °C. How much heat is added? (Use latent heat of fusion for water L_f = 334,000 J/kg, latent heat of vaporization for water L_v = 2.256 × 10^6 J/kg and specific heat c = 4.186 × 10^3 J/kg·°C)

    A. 56 kJ   **B.** 84 kJ   **C.** 470 kJ   **D.** 234 kJ   **E.** 310 kJ

55. A concave spherical mirror has a focal length of 20 cm. Where, relative to the mirror, is the image located if an object is placed 10 cm in front of the mirror?

    A. 7.5 cm in front   **C.** 20 cm in front
    B. 7.5 cm behind   **D.** 20 cm behind   **E.** 10 cm behind

56. For a DC circuit, what physical quantity does the slope of the graph represent?

    A. potential   **C.** 1 / resistance
    B. (potential)^2 **D.** resistance   **E.** 1 / potential

57. Two identical metal balls, each with a radius of 0.15 m, are located 4 m apart, are neutral and have an electrical potential of zero. Electrons are transferred as an isolated system from ball I to II. After the transfer, ball I has acquired a potential of 8,000 V and ball II a potential of –8,000 V. How much work is required to transfer 10^{-10} C from ball I to ball II?

    A. –1.6 × 10^{-6} J   **C.** 7.1 × 10^{-5} J
    B. –4.7 × 10^{-7} J   **D.** 3.3 × 10^{-6} J   **E.** 5.7 × 10^{-5} J

58. Which answer best describes what happens to a spherical lead ball with a density of 11.3 g/cm^3 when it is placed in a tub of mercury with a density of 13.6 g/cm^3?

    A. It sinks slowly to the bottom of the mercury
    B. It floats with about 17% of its volume above the surface of the mercury
    C. It floats with its top exactly even with the surface of the mercury
    D. It floats with about 83% of its volume above the surface of the mercury
    E. It floats somewhere within the mercury, but it is impossible to determine where

59. An ambulance is moving directly towards a police station at 50 m/s. The ambulance emits a siren at 420 Hz. What is the frequency of the signal heard by police at the station? (Use speed of sound v_s = 350 m/s)

    A. 280 Hz   **B.** 330 Hz   **C.** 420 Hz   **D.** 490 Hz   **E.** 540 Hz

60. A simple pendulum has a period of 3 s on Earth. If it is taken to the Moon, where the acceleration due to gravity is 1/6 of that on Earth, what is its period on the Moon?

    A. 0.5 s   **B.** 3.7 s   **C.** 7.3 s   **D.** 5 s   **E.** 12.4 s

61. An ideal, massless spring with a spring constant of 3 N/m has a resting length 0.25 m. The spring is hanging from the ceiling when a 1.2 kg block is added to the bottom end of the spring. What is the length of the spring at static equilibrium? (Use acceleration due to gravity $g = 10$ m/s^2)

    A. 2.35 m   **B.** 1.45 m   **C.** 4.96 m   **D.** 4.25 m   **E.** 5.5 m

62. A boy jumps with a velocity of 20 m/s at an angle of 25° above the horizontal. What is the horizontal component of the boy's velocity?

    A. 8.7 m/s   **B.** 14.6 m/s   **C.** 18.1 m/s   **D.** 14.9 m/s   **E.** 23.3 m/s

63. Which of the following is true about the force due to friction when a block is sliding down the surface of an inclined plane while the elevation angle is gradually decreased?

    A. Increases and the weight of the block remains constant
    B. Increases and the weight of the block increases
    C. Increases and the weight of the block decreases
    D. Decreases and the weight of the block remains constant
    E. Decreases and the weight of the block increases

64. The average velocity of an object is equal to the instantaneous velocity only when the velocity is:

    I. increasing at a constant rate
    II. constant
    III. decreasing at a constant rate

    A. I only   **B.** II only   **C.** III only   **D.** I and II only   **E.** II and III only

65. A sphere of surface area 1.25 m^2 and emissivity 1 is at a temperature of 100 °C. What is the rate at which it radiates heat into empty space? (Use the Stefan-Boltzmann constant $\sigma = 5.67 \times 10^{-8}$ W/m^{2}K^4)

    A. 1.4 kW   **B.** 7.6 kW   **C.** 27.3 kW   **D.** 0.63 kW   **E.** 3.1 kW

66. A projectile is fired at time $t = 0$ s, from point 0 at the edge of a cliff. It has initial velocity components of $v_x = 50$ m/s and $v_y = 240$ m/s with a time in flight of 60 s. The projectile lands at point P. What is the y coordinate of the projectile when its x coordinate is 1,000 m? (Use acceleration due to gravity $g = 9.8$ m/s^2)

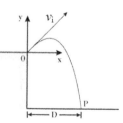

    A. −160 m   **B.** 1,240 m   **C.** 2,840 m   **D.** 850 m   **E.** 1,600 m

67. A uniform, solid, cylindrical flywheel of radius 1.4 m and mass 15.0 kg rotates at 2.7 rad/s about an axis through its circular faces. What is the magnitude of the flywheel's angular momentum?

    A. 22 kg·m²/s
    C. 64 kg·m²/s
    B. 40 kg·m²/s
    D. 80 kg·m²/s
    E. 140 kg·m²/s

68. Two particles of like charge are separated by a given distance. What is the resulting force between the particles if the charge on each particle and the distance between the two particles are doubled?

    A. 4 × original
    C. equal to the original
    B. 2 × original
    D. √2 × original
    E. ¼ × original

69. If an object is placed inside the focal point of a diverging lens, the image is:

    A. virtual, inverted and enlarged
    C. real, inverted and enlarged
    B. real, upright and enlarged
    D. virtual, upright and reduced
    E. real, upright and reduced

70. A heat engine takes 4 moles of an ideal gas through the reversible cycle *abca*, on the pressure vs. volume diagram, as shown. The path *bc* is an isothermal process. The temperature at *c* is 650 K, and the volumes at *a* and *c* are 0.025 m³ and 0.33 m³, respectively. What is the work done by the gas for the path *bc*? (Use molar heat capacity at constant volume of the gas = 18 J/mol·K and universal gas constant R = 8.134 J/mol·K)

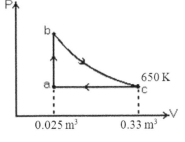

    A. −56 kJ
    C. 56 kJ
    B. −82 kJ
    D. 82 kJ
    E. 0 kJ

71. Three objects are moving along a straight line. If the positive direction is to the right, what is the total momentum of this system?

    A. 86 kg·m/s
    C. −14 kg·m/s
    B. −86 kg·m/s
    D. 14 kg·m/s
    E. 0 kg·m/s

72. In which medium do sound waves travel the fastest?

    A. Cool air   **B.** Warm air   **C.** A vacuum   **D.** Icy cold air   **E.** Moving air

73. The Bernoulli Equation is described by: $P_1 + \frac{1}{2}\rho v_1^2 + \rho g h_1 = P_2 + \frac{1}{2}\rho v_2^2 + \rho g h_2$. What is the origin of the relation within this expression?

    A. the conservation of energy for a moving fluid
    B. the continuity principle for moving particles
    C. the conservation of linear momentum across an uneven surface
    D. Newton's Third Law that relates equal action and reaction
    E. $F = ma$, as applied to a fluid

74. How do the resistances of two copper wires compare where one has twice the length and twice the cross-sectional area?

    A. The longer wire has one fourth the resistance of the shorter wire
    B. The shorter wire has $\sqrt{2}$ times the resistance of the longer wire
    C. The shorter wire has twice the resistance of the longer wire
    D. Both wires have the same resistance
    E. The shorter wire has one half the resistance of the longer wire

75. Which type of emission from the reactant nucleus causes the transformation: $^{15}_{8}O \rightarrow {}^{15}_{7}N$?

    A. Neutron emission   **C.** Electron
    B. Alpha particle   **D.** Proton emission   **E.** Positron emission

76. Which is an example of a reversible process?

    A. Hooke's cycle   **C.** Swinn cycle
    B. Carnot cycle   **D.** Boltzmann's cycle   **E.** Calvin cycle

77. A vehicle is driving in reverse at 6 m/s. After 10 s of uniform acceleration, the vehicle is going forward at 12 m/s. What is the acceleration?

    A. 1 m/s^2 **B.** 2.5 m/s^2 **C.** 3 m/s^2 **D.** 4.5 m/s^2 **E.** 1.8 m/s^2

78. A 10 kg brick and a 1 kg book are dropped in a vacuum. What is the force of gravity on the 10 kg brick? (Use acceleration due to gravity $g = 9.8$ m/s^2)

    A. Zero
    B. Twice the force on the 1 kg book
    C. The same force on the 1 kg book
    D. 9.8 times the force on the 1 kg book
    E. Ten times the force on the 1 kg book

79. A 0.06 kg golf ball is at rest on a tee. The ball has a velocity of 106 m/s immediately after being struck. If the club and ball were in contact for 0.85 ms, what is the average force exerted on the ball?

    A. 4200 N   **B.** 5600 N   **C.** 3600 N   **D.** 7500 N   **E.** 6900 N

80. What happens to the atomic mass number of a nucleus when a β⁻ particle is emitted from an unstable nucleus?

A. Decreases by 2   **C.** Decreases by 1
B. Increases by 2   **D.** Increases by 1   **E.** Remains the same

81. A chipmunk is running along a wire with constant acceleration. If it has an initial velocity of 0.4 m/s and a final velocity of 1.8 m/s after 4 s, how far does the chipmunk run in that time?

A. 2.3 m   **B.** 4.4 m   **C.** 6.7 m   **D.** 9.9 m   **E.** 7.2 m

82. An object is moving to the right in a straight line. What happens to the object if the net force acting on the object is also directed to the right, but the magnitude of the force decreases with time?

A. It continues moving to the right with a constant speed
B. It stops and then begins moving to the left with increasing speed
C. It continues moving to the right with increasing speed
D. It continues moving to the right with decreasing speed
E. It moves to the left with increasing speed

83. What is the specific heat capacity of a material if 150 kcal of heat raises the temperature of 3 kg of the material by 200 °C?

A. 0.35 kcal/kg·°C   **C.** 0.75 kcal/kg·°C
B. 0.5 kcal/kg·°C   **D.** 1.15 kcal/kg·°C   **E.** 0.25 kcal/kg·°C

84. It takes 40 J of work to push a large suitcase 4 m across a floor. Assuming the suitcase is being pushed in the same direction as it moves, what is the magnitude of the force on the suitcase?

A. 10 N   **B.** 4 N   **C.** 16 N   **D.** 26 N   **E.** 34 N

85. A simple pendulum with a length of 58 cm has a period of 2.5 s on Mars. What is the acceleration g due to gravity on Mars?

A. 0.7 m/s²   **B.** 3.7 m/s²   **C.** 6.8 m/s²   **D.** 9.8 m/s²   **E.** 17.2 m/s²

86. What is the source of all electromagnetic waves?

A. Crystalline fluctuations   **C.** Accelerating electric charges
B. Vibrating nuclei   **D.** Changes in atomic energy levels
                                      E. All of the above

87. How far does a wave front of an acoustical wave travel in 1 s if it has an f of 800 Hz and a λ of 0.5 m?

A. 400 m   **B.** 150 m   **C.** 75 m   **D.** 300 m   **E.** 600 m

88. Elena is a passenger on a spaceship. After the speed of the spaceship has increased, she observes:

    A. no change in the length of the spaceship
    B. the length of the spaceship is zero
    C. the length of the spaceship got longer
    D. the length of the spaceship got shorter
    E. cannot be determined from the information provided

89. What is the result of connecting two identical storage batteries in parallel in a circuit?

    A. Half the voltage and half the total charge compared to a circuit from a single battery
    B. Half the voltage, but the same total charge compared to a circuit from a single battery
    C. The same voltage and the same total charge compared to a circuit from a single battery
    D. The same voltage, but half the total charge compared to a circuit from a single battery
    E. The same voltage, but twice the total charge compared to a circuit from a single battery

90. What is the power of the combination for 5 D and 3 D thin lenses that are positioned near each other?

    A. 1/8 D   **B.** 5/3 D   **C.** 3/5 D   **D.** 8 D   **E.** 8/3 D

91. Is it possible for a hydrogen nucleus to emit an α particle?

    A. Yes, it usually emits α particles
    B. No, because it does not contain enough nucleons
    C. Yes, because α particles are the simplest form of radiation
    D. No, because it would require nuclear fission of hydrogen, which is impossible
    E. Yes, but hydrogen generally emits β particles instead

92. A 1,450 kg cannon fires a 90 kg cannonball at 30 m/s. Assuming that frictional forces are negligible and the cannonball is fired horizontally, what is the recoil velocity of the cannon?

    A. 5.1 m/s   **B.** 1.2 m/s   **C.** 3.4 m/s   **D.** 1.9 m/s   **E.** 2.8 m/s

93. An engineer expends 900 J to lift a block to a height h. He then repeats the task using a simple non-motorized pulley system that reduces the input force by half. Using the pulley system, how much work must the engineer perform in order to lift the block to height h?

    A. 100 J   **B.** 225 J   **C.** 900 J   **D.** 450 J   **E.** 1,400 J

94. A massless, ideal spring projects horizontally from a wall and connects to a 0.1 kg mass. The mass is oscillating in one dimension, such that it moves 0.4 m from one end of its oscillation to the other. What is the amplitude of the oscillation if it experiences 20 complete oscillations in 60 s?

    A. 0.2 m   **B.** 0.4 m   **C.** 0.8 m   **D.** $\sqrt{0.4}$ m   **E.** 4 m

95. What is the wave speed of the standing wave shown, if it is oscillating at 900 Hz on a string?

    A. 280 m/s   **C.** 360 m/s

    B. 170 m/s   **D.** 570 m/s   **E.** 420 m/s

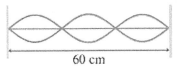

60 cm

96. What is the density of water?

    A. 1×10^3 kg/cm^3 **C.** 1×10^2 kg/m^3

    B. 1×10^1 kg/cm^3 **D.** 1×10^{-3} g/m^3 **E.** 1×10^3 kg/m^3

97. Two stationary positive charges of $Q = 10^{-10}$ C are fixed and separated by a distance of $d = 4$ cm. What is the net electrostatic force on a charge $q = -10^{-9}$ C that is placed at a distance of $d / 2$ from each of the charges?

    A. 5×10^{-10} N   **B.** 1.5×10^{-9} N   **C.** 0 N   **D.** 2.5×10^{-10} N   **E.** 1×10^{-9} N

98. A capacitor, initially having a charge of Q on the left plate and a charge of $-Q$ on the right plate, is connected to a switch and an inductor. Assuming that the resistance of the circuit is zero, which statement is true when the switch is closed?

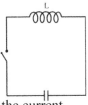

    A. Current flows back and forth through the inductor, with the magnitude of the current steadily decreasing and eventually becoming zero

    B. Current flows until the left plate of the capacitor has a charge $-Q$, and then current flows in the opposite direction, reversing again when the left plate has a charge of $+Q$. The cycle repeats

    C. Charge flows out of the capacitor until the left plate is no longer charged, and then all current ceases

    D. Because the switch is closed, the current flows clockwise with a constant magnitude.

    E. Current flows back and forth through the inductor, with the magnitude of the current increasing at a constant rate

99. The Compton effect directly demonstrated which property of electromagnetic radiation?

    I. energy content
    II. particle nature
    III. momenta

    A. I only   **C.** I and II only

    B. II only   **D.** II and III only   **E.** I, II and III

100. How many $2d$ electron states are possible for an atom?

    A. 0   **B.** 8   **C.** 6   **D.** 18   **E.** 10

Diagnostic Test #6

Answer Sheet

#	Answer:					Mark for review	#	Answer:					Mark for review
1:	A	B	C	D	E	___	31:	A	B	C	D	E	___
2:	A	B	C	D	E	___	32:	A	B	C	D	E	___
3:	A	B	C	D	E	___	33:	A	B	C	D	E	___
4:	A	B	C	D	E	___	34:	A	B	C	D	E	___
5:	A	B	C	D	E	___	35:	A	B	C	D	E	___
6:	A	B	C	D	E	___	36:	A	B	C	D	E	___
7:	A	B	C	D	E	___	37:	A	B	C	D	E	___
8:	A	B	C	D	E	___	38:	A	B	C	D	E	___
9:	A	B	C	D	E	___	39:	A	B	C	D	E	___
10:	A	B	C	D	E	___	40:	A	B	C	D	E	___
11:	A	B	C	D	E	___	41:	A	B	C	D	E	___
12:	A	B	C	D	E	___	42:	A	B	C	D	E	___
13:	A	B	C	D	E	___	43:	A	B	C	D	E	___
14:	A	B	C	D	E	___	44:	A	B	C	D	E	___
15:	A	B	C	D	E	___	45:	A	B	C	D	E	___
16:	A	B	C	D	E	___	46:	A	B	C	D	E	___
17:	A	B	C	D	E	___	47:	A	B	C	D	E	___
18:	A	B	C	D	E	___	48:	A	B	C	D	E	___
19:	A	B	C	D	E	___	49:	A	B	C	D	E	___
20:	A	B	C	D	E	___	50:	A	B	C	D	E	___
21:	A	B	C	D	E	___	51:	A	B	C	D	E	___
22:	A	B	C	D	E	___	52:	A	B	C	D	E	___
23:	A	B	C	D	E	___	53:	A	B	C	D	E	___
24:	A	B	C	D	E	___	54:	A	B	C	D	E	___
25:	A	B	C	D	E	___	55:	A	B	C	D	E	___
26:	A	B	C	D	E	___	56:	A	B	C	D	E	___
27:	A	B	C	D	E	___	57:	A	B	C	D	E	___
28:	A	B	C	D	E	___	58:	A	B	C	D	E	___
29:	A	B	C	D	E	___	59:	A	B	C	D	E	___
30:	A	B	C	D	E	___	60:	A	B	C	D	E	___

#	Answer:					Mark for review	#	Answer:					Mark for review
61:	A	B	C	D	E	___	**81:**	A	B	C	D	E	___
62:	A	B	C	D	E	___	**82:**	A	B	C	D	E	___
63:	A	B	C	D	E	___	**83:**	A	B	C	D	E	___
64:	A	B	C	D	E	___	**84:**	A	B	C	D	E	___
65:	A	B	C	D	E	___	**85:**	A	B	C	D	E	___
66:	A	B	C	D	E	___	**86:**	A	B	C	D	E	___
67:	A	B	C	D	E	___	**87:**	A	B	C	D	E	___
68:	A	B	C	D	E	___	**88:**	A	B	C	D	E	___
69:	A	B	C	D	E	___	**89:**	A	B	C	D	E	___
70:	A	B	C	D	E	___	**90:**	A	B	C	D	E	___
71:	A	B	C	D	E	___	**91:**	A	B	C	D	E	___
72:	A	B	C	D	E	___	**92:**	A	B	C	D	E	___
73:	A	B	C	D	E	___	**93:**	A	B	C	D	E	___
74:	A	B	C	D	E	___	**94:**	A	B	C	D	E	___
75:	A	B	C	D	E	___	**95:**	A	B	C	D	E	___
76:	A	B	C	D	E	___	**96:**	A	B	C	D	E	___
77:	A	B	C	D	E	___	**97:**	A	B	C	D	E	___
78:	A	B	C	D	E	___	**98:**	A	B	C	D	E	___
79:	A	B	C	D	E	___	**99:**	A	B	C	D	E	___
80:	A	B	C	D	E	___	**100:**	A	B	C	D	E	___

This Diagnostic Test is designed for you to assess your proficiency on each topic. Use your test results and identify areas of your strength and weakness to adjust your study plan and enhance your fundamental knowledge.

1. A heat engine performs the reversible cycle *abca* with 9 moles of an ideal gas. Path *ca* is an adiabatic process. The temperatures at points *a* and *b* are 300 K and 500 K, respectively. The volume at point *c* is 0.2 m³. The adiabatic constant of the gas is 1.6. What is the heat absorbed by the gas in path *ca*?

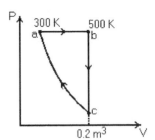

    A. −10 kJ   **C.** 10 kJ

    B. 16 kJ   **D.** 0 kJ   **E.** −16 kJ

2. Forces A, B and C act on a body. A fourth force, *F*, keeps the body in equilibrium. What is the *x* component of the force *F*?

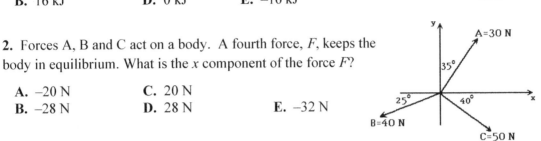

    A. −20 N   **C.** 20 N

    B. −28 N   **D.** 28 N   **E.** −32 N

3. In an organ pipe (cylindrical 0.2 m long tube 0.02 m in diameter, open at both ends), what is the λ of the 4th harmonic?

    A. 0.08 m   **B.** 0.1 m   **C.** 0.05 m   **D.** 0.2 m   **E.** 0.8 m

4. What is the velocity of a fluid in a tube with the diameter 3 mm for a pump that has a piston of 15 cm in diameter that moves 2 cm/s?

    A. 50 m/s   **B.** 21 cm/s   **C.** 25 m/s   **D.** 50 cm/s   **E.** 5 cm/s

5. What is the essential difference between microwaves and blue light?

    A. One is a form of radiation while the other is not
    B. Blue light is a beam of photons and microwaves are positrons
    C. One has a positive charge while the other does not
    D. One undergoes refraction while the other does not
    E. There is no essential difference other than frequency and wavelength

6. The resistance of a variable resistor can be adjusted. A battery is connected to a variable resistor. The potential difference across the resistor and the current through it are recorded at variable resistance. Assume that the battery is an ideal potential source in series with an internal resistor. Under which circumstances is it valid to ignore the internal resistance of the battery?

    I. small external resistance   II. large external resistance   III. low total current

    A. I only   **B.** II only   **C.** III only   **D.** I and III only   **E.** II and III only

7. Which type of mirror produces an image that is always virtual, erect the same height as the object?

    A. concave   **C.** plane
    B. convex   **D.** spherical   **E.** none of above

8. Which nuclear radiation particles have the greatest mass?

    A. Neutrons   **C.** Beta particles

    B. Gamma radiation photons   **D.** Alpha particles   **E.** Protons

9. A particular motor can provide a maximum torque of 110.0 N·m. Assuming that all of this torque is used to accelerate a solid, uniform, cylindrical flywheel of mass 10.0 kg and radius 3.00 m, how long will it take for the flywheel to accelerate from rest to 8.13 rad/s?

    A. 2.13 s   **C.** 4.65 s

    B. 3.33 s   **D.** 5.46 s   **E.** 6.80 s

10. A spaceship is moving away from an asteroid with a speed of $0.80c$ relative to the asteroid. The spaceship then fires a missile with a speed of $0.50c$ relative to the spaceship. What is the speed of the missile measured by astronauts on the asteroid if the missile is fired toward the asteroid?

    A. $0.32c$ **B.** $0.50c$ **C.** $0.92c$ **D.** $1.6c$ **E.** $0.68c$

11. Compared to falling on a wooden floor, a wine glass may not break when it falls on a carpeted floor because of the:

    I. lesser impulse in stopping

    II. longer time to stop

    III. decreased acceleration due to gravity

    A. I only   **B.** II only   **C.** III only   **D.** I and II only   **E.** I and III only

12. A 6.5 kg bag of groceries is carried 1.1 m above the ground at constant velocity across a 3.8 m room. How much work was done on the bag in this process?

    A. 183 J   **B.** 155 J   **C.** 0 J   **D.** 84 J   **E.** 22.7 J

13. A wave that has a lower frequency has a:

    A. higher amplitude   **C.** slower velocity

    B. shorter period   **D.** shorter wavelength   **E.** longer wavelength

14. A rod has a length 2.0000 m at 20 °C. The length of the rod increases to 2.0005 m when the temperature increases to 40 °C. What is the coefficient of thermal expansion α of the material for the rod?

    A. 1.25×10^{-5}/K   **B.** 5×10^{-3}/K   **C.** 0.75×10^{-5}/K   **D.** 2.5×10^{-5}/K   **E.** 0.75×10^{-3}/K

15. An object is viewed at various distances using a concave mirror with focal length of 12 m. Relative to the mirror, where is the image when the object is 6 m in front of the mirror?

    A. 12 m behind   **B.** 12 m in front   **C.** 6 m behind   **D.** 6 m in front   **E.** 24 m behind

16. What effect does the addition of resistors in parallel have on a circuit?

A. Decreases the current
B. Increases the current

C. Decreases the voltage
D. Increases the voltage

E. No change in the current

17. The electric field at point P due to a point charge of Q a distance R away has a magnitude of E. Which statement is true to double the magnitude of the field at P?

A. Reduce the charge to $Q/2$
B. Reduce the distance to R/2
C. Double the distance to 2R while reducing the charge to $Q/2$
D. Double the charge to $2Q$
E. Double the charge to $2Q$ while reducing the distance to R/2

18. If 20% of the volume of a floating buoy is above the surface of a liquid, then the density of the buoy is what percent of the density of the surrounding liquid?

A. 40%   B. 90%   C. 60%   D. 70%   E. 80%

19. A pipe of length L that is open at both ends is resonating at its fundamental frequency. Which statement about the sound is correct?

A. The λ is $L/2$, and there is a displacement node at the midpoint of the pipe
B. The λ is $L/2$, and there is a displacement antinode at the midpoint of the pipe
C. The λ is $2L$, and there is a displacement node at the midpoint of the pipe
D. The λ is $2L$, and there is a displacement antinode at the midpoint of the pipe
E. The λ is $4L$, and there is a displacement node at the midpoint of the pipe

20. Wave interference occurs for:

    I. sound waves   II. water waves   III. light waves

A. I only   B. II only   C. III only   D. I and III only   E. I, II and III

21. What is the value of the spring constant if a force of 30 N stretches a spring 0.75 m from equilibrium?

A. 85 N/m   B. 25 N/m   C. 35 N/m   D. 40 N/m   E. 30 N/m

22. In a perfectly inelastic collision, two moving objects of unequal mass (A and B) collide and immediately come to rest. Before colliding, object A was traveling at a speed 5 times that of object B. Which is the ratio of the mass of object A to that of object B?

A. 50 : 1   B. 5 : 1   C. 1 : 5   D. 1 : 50   E. $\sqrt{5}$: 1

23. What is the wavelength of the matter wave associated with an electron moving with a speed of 2.5×10^7 m/s? (Use $m_{electron} = 9.11 \times 10^{-31}$ kg and $h = 6.626 \times 10^{-34}$ J·s)

A. 17 pm
B. 29 pm

C. 39 pm
D. 51 pm

E. 76 pm

24. A chestnut falls straight down from a chestnut tree growing on a 20° slope. What is the component of the chestnut's impact velocity parallel to the ground if it hits the ground with a speed of 16 m/s?

    A. 5.5 m/s   **B.** 8.6 m/s   **C.** 4.1 m/s   **D.** 11.4 m/s   **E.** 10.6 m/s

25. In a given reversible process, the temperature of an ideal gas is kept constant as the gas is compressed to a smaller volume. Which statement is correct?

    A. The process is adiabatic   **C.** The gas releases heat to its surroundings
    B. The pressure remains constant   **D.** The gas absorbs heat from its surroundings
                                      E. None of the above

26. A heavy pile driver starting from rest smashes into a pile with a force that depends on the:

        I. distance the pile driver falls
        II. initial potential energy of the driver
        III. initial height of the driver

A. I only   **B.** II only   **C.** III only   **D.** I and III only   **E.** I, II and III

27. Which of the following is an accurate statement?

    A. The fundamental frequency is the highest frequency at which a system naturally vibrates
    B. The air in an organ pipe can vibrate at an infinite number of frequencies
    C. A system, like a vibrating string, has only one possible frequency
    D. For a singer to break a wine glass by singing, the amplitude of sound must be greater than the amplitude of vibration for a wine glass
    E. None of the above

28. A satellite is in a circular orbit around a planet. What is the satellite's orbital speed if the orbital radius is 34.0 km and the gravitational acceleration at that height is 2.3 m/s^2?

    A. 26 m/s   **B.** 150 m/s   **C.** 280 m/s   **D.** 310 m/s   **E.** 390 m/s

29. A myopic girl wears eyeglasses that allow her to have clear distant vision. The power of the lenses of her eyeglasses is –3 diopters. Without eyeglasses, the far point of the girl is:

    A. 0.32 m   **B.** 0.17 m   **C.** 0.75 m   **D.** 0.33 m   **E.** 0.50 m

30. A woman starts her car from rest and accelerates at a constant 2.5 m/s^2 for 8 s to get to her cruising speed. What is her velocity 8 s after beginning her trip?

    A. 1.8 m/s   **B.** 5.5 m/s **C.** 12.5 m/s   **D.** 7.5 m/s   **E.** 20 m/s

31. What is the velocity of the cars immediately after impact for a perfectly inelastic collision between a 2,500 kg car moving North at 7 m/s and a 2,000 kg car moving South at 14 m/s?

    A. 2.3 m/s S   **B.** 9.4 m/s S   **C.** 5.4 m/s N   **D.** 9.4 m/s N   **E.** 11 m/s N

32. Grandfather clocks are designed so they can be adjusted by moving the weight at the bottom of the pendulum up or down. Suppose a grandfather clock is running slow. Which of the following adjustments of the weight would make it more accurate?

    A. Move weight down   **C.** Remove half the mass from the weight
    B. Move weight up   **D.** Add double the mass to the weight
                              E. Increase the amplitude of swing by a significant amount

33. Why does the paper rise when air is blown above a paper strip?

    A. Air above the paper moves slower, while the pressure remains constant
    B. Air above the paper moves slower and the pressure is higher
    C. Air above the paper moves faster, while the pressure remains constant
    D. Air above the paper moves slower and the pressure is lower
    E. Air above the paper moves faster and the pressure is lower

34. If the internal resistance of the battery is 20 Ω, what current flows in a 4 V battery if the circuit is shorted?

    A. 5 A   **B.** 3.2 A   **C.** 80 A   **D.** 0.2 A   **E.** 7.3 A

35. One becquerel equals:

    A. a mole of disintegrations/sec   **C.** 1 disintegration/sec   **E.** 1 rem
    B. 100 rads   **D.** 3.7×10^{10} disintegrations/sec

36. A glass flask has a volume of 450 ml at a temperature of 22 °C. The flask contains 442 ml of mercury at an equilibrium temperature 22 °C. The temperature is raised until the mercury reaches the 450 ml reference mark. What is the temperature at which this occurs? (Use coefficients of volume expansion α of mercury $= 18 \times 10^{-5}$ K^{-1} and α of glass $= 2 \times 10^{-5}$ K^{-1})

    A. 103 °C   **B.** 152 °C   **C.** 92 °C   **D.** 135 °C   **E.** 116 °C

37. Which graph represents a constant positive acceleration?

  I.    II. v   III.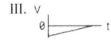

    A. I only   **B.** II only   **C.** III only   **D.** II and III only   **E.** I, II and III

38. In formulating the special theory of relativity, Einstein postulated that the laws of physics are the same in reference frames that:

    A. are stationary, but not in moving frames
    B. oscillate
    C. move at constant velocity with respect to an inertial frame
    D. accelerate
    E. none of the above

39. What happens to an object if a constant net torque is applied?

   A. Rotates with increasing angular acceleration
   B. Rotates with constant angular acceleration
   C. Rotates with constant angular velocity
   D. Rotates with increasing linear velocity
   E. Increases its moment of inertia

40. Researchers who work around radioactivity wear dosimeter badges on their clothing to monitor their radiation exposure. These badges consist of small pieces of photographic film enclosed in a holder that protects the film against light exposure. What kind of radiation do these devices monitor?

      I. alpha radiation   II. beta radiation   III. gamma radiation

   A. I only   **B.** II only   **C.** III only   **D.** I and II only   **E.** I and III only

41. Ignoring air resistance, if it takes 16 s for a package to strike the ground, how high above the ground was the package when it was thrown upward from a stationary helicopter at 15 m/s? (Use acceleration due to gravity $g = 10$ m/s^2)

   A. 920 m   **B.** 740 m   **C.** 1,400 m   **D.** 1,040 m   **E.** 1,800 m

42. What is the mass of the car if a tow truck exerts a force of 3,000 N on a car and accelerates it at 2 m/s^2?

   A. 500 kg   **B.** 1,000 kg   **C.** 1,500 kg   **D.** 2,000 kg   **E.** None of the above

43. A bimetallic strip, consisting of metal A on the top and metal B on the bottom, is rigidly attached to a wall at the left, as shown. The coefficient of linear thermal expansion of metal A is greater than that of metal B. Which statement is true if the strip is heated uniformly?

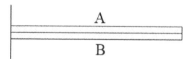

   A. remains horizontal, but increases in length   **C.** curves upward
   B. remains horizontal, but decreases in length   **D.** curves downward
                                                            E. bends in the middle

44. A massless, ideal spring has a spring constant of 4,600 N/m as it hangs from the ceiling. By how much does its potential energy increase if a 30 kg mass is attached to it? (Use acceleration due to gravity $g = 10$ m/s^2)

   A. 9.8 J   **B.** 6.3 J   **C.** 19.4 J   **D.** 12.4 J   **E.** 4.3 J

45. What is the speed of a water wave if a floating object oscillates up and down two complete cycles in 1 s as the water wave with a wavelength of 6 m passes?

   A. 1 m/s   **B.** 0.17 m/s   **C.** 12 m/s   **D.** 18 m/s   **E.** 3 m/s

46. By what value does the sound level of a wave decrease if the intensity of the sound wave decreases by a factor of 10?

A. 0.1 dB   **B.** 10 dB   **C.** 1 dB   **D.** 100 dB   **E.** 0.01 dB

47. A piece of wood is floating in a bathtub. A second piece of wood sits on top of the first piece, and does not touch the water. If the top piece is taken off and placed in the water, what happens to the water level in the tub?

A. It remains the same   **C.** It increases
B. It decreases   **D.** Requires the volumes of the two pieces of wood
                                E. Requires the densities of the two pieces of wood

48. A point charge Q_1 has a charge of -1 μC. What is the number of excess electrons in charge Q_1? (Use charge of an electron $e = -1.60 \times 10^{-19}$ C)

A. 2×10^{11} **B.** 2×10^{12} **C.** 6.3×10^{12} **D.** 6.3×10^{13} **E.** 2×10^{13}

49. The capacitance of a capacitor depends on its:

     I. energy stored   II. charge   III. potential difference across it

A. I only   **C.** II and III only
B. II only   **D.** I and III only   **E.** none of the above

50. What is the radius of curvature for a flat plane mirror?

A. Imaginary   **B.** Zero   **C.** Infinite   **D.** Negative   **E.** Undefined

51. During a nuclear fusion reaction, it is possible to produce neutrons with 12.5 MeV and a speed of approximately 54,300 km/s. At this speed, what is the mass of a neutron? (Use rest mass of a neutron $m_0 = 1.675 \times 10^{-24}$ g, speed of light $c = 3.8 \times 10^8$ m/s and 1 eV $= 1.602 \times 10^{-19}$ J)

A. 4.3×10^{-34} g   **C.** 2.8×10^{-23} g
B. 6.4×10^{-21} g   **D.** 5.1×10^{-17} g   **E.** 1.7×10^{-24} g

52. Consider two uniform solid spheres where both have the same diameter, but one has twice the mass of the other. What is the ratio of the larger moment of inertia to the smaller?

A. $\sqrt{2} : 1$ **B.** 4 : 1   **C.** 10 : 1   **D.** 2 : 1   **E.** 16 : 1

53. Using 1,000 J of work, an elevator is raised from the ground to the second floor in 40 s. How much power does the elevator use?

A. 100 W   **B.** 25 W   **C.** 50 W   **D.** 1,000 W   **E.** 200 W

54. A ball is attached to an ideal spring and oscillates with a period T. What is the new period that is produced if the mass of the ball is doubled?

    A. T√2   **B.** T   **C.** T/2   **D.** 2T   **E.** T/√2

55. Larry drops a mailing tube to the floor and the tube produces a musical note. The mailing tube is 1.5 m long with a cylindrical cross-sectional diameter of 3.5 cm. It is sealed at one end and open at the other. What is the wavelength of the third harmonic? (Use speed of sound in air $v = 340$ m/s)

    A. 1.5 m   **B.** 2 m   **C.** 3.5 m   **D.** 4 m   **E.** 7.5 m

56. A compressed gas with a total mass of 115 kg is stored in a spherical container that has a radius of 0.6 m. What is the density of the compressed gas?

    A. 147 kg/m^3 **B.** 183 kg/m^3 **C.** 151 kg/m^3 **D.** 127 kg/m^3 **E.** 267 kg/m^3

57. Electrons are made to flow in a wire when there is:

    I. a potential difference across its ends
    II. an imbalance between positive and negative charges in the wire
    III. more final kinetic energy than initial kinetic energy in the wire

    A. I only   **B.** II only   **C.** III only   **D.** I and II only   **E.** I and III only

58. A Coulomb per second is the same as a(n):

    A. Newton   **C.** ampere
    B. volt-second   **D.** watt   **E.** volt per second

59. What is observed when an object is placed exactly at its center of curvature in front of a concave mirror?

    A. The image is not seen because it is focused at a different distance
    B. The image is seen, but it appears smaller
    C. The image is seen, but it appears larger
    D. The image is seen as the same size and it is upright
    E. The image is seen as the same size, but it is inverted

60. Which type of radiation cannot penetrate human skin and requires only heavy paper or clothing as minimum protective shielding?

    A. α   **B.** γ   **C.** β   **D.** Nuclide   **E.** X ray

61. The process shown on the pressure vs. volume diagram represents which type of expansion?

    A. Isobaric   **C.** Isothermal
    B. Isometric   **D.** Adiabatic   **E.** Isochoric

62. A block is on a frictionless table on Earth. The block accelerates at 4 m/s² when a 20 N horizontal force is applied to it. The block and table are then set up on the Moon where the acceleration due to gravity is 1.62 m/s². What is the weight of the block on the Moon?

    A. 11 N   **B.** 9.7 N   **C.** 5.6 N   **D.** 6.2 N   **E.** 8.1 N

63. In the figure, the frequency is:

    A. 2 Hz
    B. 4 Hz
    C. 0.5 Hz
    D. 1 Hz
    E. 1.5 Hz

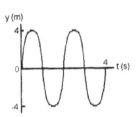

64. Consider a very small hole in the bottom of a tank that is 18 cm in diameter and is filled with water to a height of 80 cm. What is the speed at which the water exits the tank through the hole? (Use acceleration due to gravity g = 9.8 m/s²)

    A. 4 m/s   **B.** 17 m/s   **C.** 42 m/s   **D.** 36 m/s   **E.** 7 m/s

65. A coil of wire containing N turns is in an external magnetic field that is perpendicular to the plane of the coil. The magnetic field is steadily changing and an emf (V) is induced in the coil. With other values constant, if the magnetic flux and the number of turns in the coil are doubled, by what factor does the induced emf increase or decrease?

    A. V/4   **B.** 4V   **C.** V/2   **D.** 2V   **E.** V

66. A component with an 18 Ω resistor is rated for use at power levels not exceeding 16 W. How much current can safely flow through the component?

    A. 0.12 A   **B.** 2.8 A   **C.** 1.31 A   **D.** 0.94 A   **E.** 12.1 A

67. How are wavelength and frequency of light related?

    A. Wavelength increases as the frequency increases
    B. Wavelength increases as the frequency decreases
    C. Wavelength is one-fourth of the frequency
    D. Wavelength is four times the frequency
    E. Wavelength is not related to the frequency

68. Which of the following has the highest ionizing power?

    A. β particle   **B.** positron   **C.** α particle   **D.** γ particle   **E.** All are equal

69. A merry-go-round is 18 m in diameter with a child sitting on the outer edge. If the merry-go-round makes 8.3 rev/min, what is the velocity of the child?

    A. 1.9 m/s   **B.** 7.8 m/s   **C.** 3.9 m/s   **D.** 14.6 m/s   **E.** 18.3 m/s

70. What is the magnitude of the instantaneous force with which a ball hits a bat if a batter hits a ball pitched with a 1,700 N instantaneous force?

A. Greater than 1,700 N   **C.** Equal to $\sqrt{1,700}$ N
B. Zero   **D.** Less than 1,700 N   **E.** Equal to 1,700 N

71. A 2.8 kg block, moving on a frictionless surface with a speed (v_i) of 8.5 m/s, makes a perfectly elastic collision with a block of mass m at rest. After the collision, the 2.8 kg block recoils with a speed (v_f) of 1.1 m/s. What is the mass of block m?

A. 22.8 kg   **B.** 14.4 kg   **C.** 17.8 kg   **D.** 3.6 kg   **E.** 12.2 kg

72. If the height of a frictionless incline is h, determine the work done by the force due to gravity F as the crate of mass m slides down the incline.

A. $mgh \sin^2$ **B.** mgh **C.** $mgh \cos^2$ **D.** $mgh \sin$ **E.** $mgh \tan$

73. What is the speed of a wave if it has a wavelength of 25 cm and a frequency of 1.6 kHz?

A. 400 m/s   **B.** 1,400 m/s   **C.** 0.4 m/s   **D.** 14 m/s   **E.** 28 m/s

74. A glass beaker of unknown mass contains 60 ml of water. The system absorbs 2,200 cal of heat and the temperature rises 25 °C as a result. What is the mass of the beaker? (Use specific heat for glass = 0.18 cal/g·°C and specific heat for water = 1.0 cal/g·°C)

A. 675 g   **B.** 540 g   **C.** 460 g   **D.** 370 g   **E.** 156 g

75. What is the radius of curvature for a concave mirror with a focal length of 20 cm?

A. 20 cm   **B.** –40 cm   **C.** 40 cm   **D.** 10 cm   **E.** –20 cm

76. What is the power dissipated in the 2 Ω resistor in the circuit?

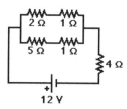

A. 6.3 W   **C.** 3.5 W
B. 5.7 W   **D.** 7.8 W   **E.** 8.5 W

77. When a charged particle moves with a velocity perpendicular to a magnetic field, the field acts to change the particle's:

A. v **B.** KE   **C.** m **D.** ρ **E.** q

78. What is the gauge pressure 10 m below the surface of the ocean? (Use acceleration due to gravity g = 9.8 m/s², density of water ρ = 10^3 kg/m³ and P_{atm} = 1.01 × 10^5 Pa)

A. 1.4 × 10^5 Pa   **C.** 9.8 × 10^4 Pa
B. 2.3 × 10^5 Pa   **D.** 6.5 × 10^4 Pa   **E.** 5 × 10^6 Pa

79. If a 75 cm string, which is fixed at both ends between two adjacent nodes, supports a standing wave, what is the wavelength λ?

    A. 15 cm   **B.** 300 cm   **C.** 7.5 cm   **D.** 200 cm   **E.** 150 cm

80. The speed of sound in steel is 4,900 m/s. What is the wavelength of a sound wave in steel of frequency 640 Hz?

    A. 1.3 m   **B.** 0.83 m   **C.** 7.7 m   **D.** 4.2 m   **E.** 2.6 m

81. Ignoring the force of friction, what is the work done by Stacey when she carries a 15 kg mass and walks along the *x*-axis for a distance of 100 m with a constant velocity of 2.5 m/s?

    A. 0 J   **B.** 5 J   **C.** 30 J   **D.** 50 J   **E.** 450 J

82. Hannah is in karate and delivers a swift blow to sever a cement block in two with her bare hand. The magnitude is the same for the:

    I. time of impact on both the block and Hannah's hand
    II. force on both the block and Hannah's hand
    III. impulse on both the block and Hannah's hand

    A. I only   **B.** II only   **C.** III only   **D.** I and III only   **E.** I, II and III

83. Karen is driving a car along a road when she realizes, almost too late, that she needs to make a left-hand turn. Karen quickly turns the car's steering wheel, and the textbooks that were in the passenger seat go crashing against the passenger door. Which of the following statements are true?

    I. The textbooks were pushed against the door by a centrifugal force
    II. The textbooks were pushed against the door by a centripetal force
    III. The forces acting on the textbooks when they crashed against the door were gravity, the normal force and a force toward the right

    A. I and III only   **C.** III only
    B. II and III only   **D.** I, II and III   **E.** None of the above

84. How far does a car travel while accelerating if it accelerates from 5 m/s to 21 m/s at a rate of 4 m/s^2?

    A. 112 m   **B.** 35 m   **C.** 71 m   **D.** 52 m   **E.** 153 m

85. The coefficient of linear expansion of lead is 30×10^{-6} K^{-1}. What change in temperature causes a 10 m long lead bar to change in length by 3 mm?

    A. 7.5 K   **B.** 20 K   **C.** 10 K   **D.** 5 K   **E.** 40 K

86. A constant force of 10 N is applied horizontally for 15 s on a 2 kg toy cart, so that the cart begins to move along the level frictionless floor. What is the kinetic energy of the cart just after the 15 s?

A. 1,540 J   **B.** 2,300 J   **C.** 3,450 J   **D.** 2,985 J   **E.** 5,625 J

87. Mary has tuned the B string of a guitar to the fundamental frequency of an E (680 Hz). The E string is left untuned. When she plucks the B string and the untuned E string together, she hears a note that changes from loud to soft to loud twice per second. What is an allowable fundamental f on the untuned E string?

A. 2 Hz   **B.** 340 Hz   **C.** 680 Hz   **D.** 682 Hz   **E.** 1,360 Hz

88. A positive reaction charge Q is held fixed at the origin. A positive charge q is on the positive x-axis and released. Assuming no friction, which statement describes the theoretical acceleration of q after its release?

- **A.** Decreases and then increases
- **B.** Remains constant for a while and then decreases, eventually reaching zero
- **C.** Decreases and eventually reaches zero
- **D.** Decreases forever, but never reaches zero
- **E.** Acceleration remains unchanged

89. Which statement about a single thin lens is correct?

- **A.** A diverging lens always produces a virtual upright image
- **B.** A converging lens sometimes produces a real upright image
- **C.** A diverging lens sometimes produces a virtual upright image
- **D.** A converging lens always produces a real upright image
- **E.** A diverging lens produces a virtual upright image only if the object is located between the lens and its focal point

90. What is the magnitude and direction of the combined vectors A and B if vector A has a length of 5 units and is directed to the North (N) while vector B has a length of 11 units and is directed to the South (S)?

A. 16 units, S   **B.** 16 units, N   **C.** 6 units, N   **D.** 6 units, S   **E.** 2.2 units, N

91. A laser produces a beam of 4000 nm light. A shutter allows a pulse of light for 30.0 ps to pass. What is the uncertainty in the energy of a photon in the pulse? ($h = 6.626 \times 10^{-34}$ J·s and 1 eV $= 1.60 \times 10^{-19}$ J)

A. 2.6×10^{-2} eV   **C.** 6.8×10^{-4} eV

B. 4.2×10^{-3} eV   **D.** 2.2×10^{-5} eV   **E.** 2.4×10^{-6} eV

92. At which point in a swinging pendulum's arc does it have the most energy?

I. At its lowest point, it has the most potential energy
II. The energy is the same at all points of the arc
III. At its highest point, it has the most kinetic energy

A. I only   **B.** II only   **C.** III only   **D.** I and II only   **E.** I and III only

93. If the amount of fluid flowing through a tube remains constant, how does the speed of the fluid change if the diameter of the tube increases from 3 cm to 8 cm?

  A. Increases by a factor of 5   **C.** Decreases by a factor of 5
  B. Increases by a factor of 9   **D.** Decreases by a factor of 7
                                          E. Remains the same

94. Voltage can be induced in a wire by:

    I. changing the current in a nearby wire
    II. moving a magnet near the wire
    III. moving the wire near a magnet

  A. I only   **B.** II only   **C.** III only   **D.** II and III only   **E.** I, II and III

95. Ionizing radiation is dangerous to living tissue because it:

  A. causes electrons to be absorbed by the cell's nucleus
  B. alters the chemical structure of atoms or molecules
  C. causes a large release of heat energy
  D. binds protons and neutrons together
  E. has a penetrating power that varies with its source

96. A container of ideal gas at standard temperature and pressure undergoes an isothermal expansion. How much work does it do if its entropy changes by 2.6 J/K? (Use standard temperature = 273 K and pressure = 1 atm)

  A. 1.4×10^3 J   **B.** -1×10^3 J   **C.** 7.1×10^2 J   **D.** 0 J   **E.** -1.4×10^3 J

97. Jack stands on a bridge and throws a rock straight down. The rock leaves Jack's hand at $t = 0$. Which of the graphs represents the velocity of the stone as a function of time?

A.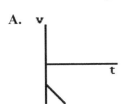

C.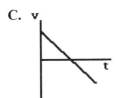

B.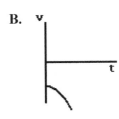

D.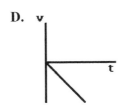

E.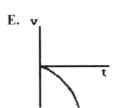

98. A 100 g ball of clay is thrown horizontally with a speed of 50 m/s toward a 900 g block resting on a frictionless surface. It hits the block and sticks. The clay exerts a constant force on the block during the 10 ms it takes for the clay to come to rest relative to the block. After 10 ms, the block and the clay are sliding along the surface as a single system. What is the force of the clay on the block during the collision?

A. 500 N   **B.** 2,250 N   **C.** 5,400 N   **D.** 4,500 N   **E.** 450 N

99. Cart A (2 kg) and Cart B (2.5 kg) run along a frictionless, level, one-dimensional track. Cart B is initially at rest, and Cart A is traveling 0.6 m/s toward the right when it encounters Cart B. After the collision, Cart A is at rest. What is the final velocity of Cart B?

A. 0.48 m/s   **B.** 0.36 m/s   **C.** 0.75 m/s   **D.** 0.64 m/s   **E.** 1.1 m/s

100. What is the name of the unit used to measure the amount of radiation absorbed per gram of tissue?

A. Becquerel   **B.** Rad   **C.** Curie   **D.** Roentgen

Check your answers using the answer key. Then, go to the explanations section and review the explanations in detail, paying particular attention to questions you didn't answer correctly or marked for review. Note the topic that those questions belong to.

Topical
Practice Questions

Our guarantee – the highest quality preparation materials.

We expect our books to have the highest quality content and be error-free.

Be the first to report an error, typo or inaccuracy and receive a
$10 reward for a content error or
$5 reward for a typo or grammatical mistake.

info@sterling-prep.com

Kinematics and Dynamics

1. Starting from rest, how long does it take for a sports car to reach 60 mi/h, if it has an average acceleration of 13.1 mi/h·s?

    A. 6.6 s   **B.** 3.1 s   **C.** 4.5 s   **D.** 4.6 s   **E.** 13.1 s

2. A cannon ball is fired with an initial speed of 20 m/s at a 30° angle with the horizontal. Ignoring air resistance, how long does it take the cannon ball to reach the top of its trajectory? (Use acceleration due to gravity $g = 10$ m/s^2)

    A. 0.5 s   **B.** 1 s   **C.** 1.5 s   **D.** 2 s   **E.** 2.5 s

3. Darlene starts her car from rest and accelerates at a constant 2.5 m/s^2 for 9 s to get to her cruising speed. She then drives for 15 minutes at constant speed. She arrives at her destination, which is a straight-line distance of 31.5 km away, exactly 1.25 hours later. What is her average velocity during the interval of 1.25 hours?

    A. 3 m/s   **B.** 7 m/s   **C.** 18 m/s   **D.** 22.5 m/s   **E.** 2.5 m/s

4. Which of the following cannot be negative?

    A. Instantaneous speed   **C.** Acceleration of gravity
    B. Instantaneous acceleration   **D.** Displacement   **E.** Position

5. How far does a car travel while accelerating from 5 m/s to 21 m/s at a rate of 3 m/s^2?

    A. 15 m   **B.** 21 m   **C.** 69 m   **D.** 105 m   **E.** 210 m

6. Acceleration is sometimes expressed in multiples of g, where g is the acceleration due to gravity. How many g are experienced, on average, by the driver in a car crash if the car's velocity changes from 30 m/s to 0 m/s in 0.15 s? (Use acceleration due to gravity $g = 9.8$ m/s^2)

    A. 22 g **B.** 28 g **C.** 16 g **D.** 14 g **E.** 20 g

7. Ignoring air resistance, how many forces are acting on a bullet fired horizontally after it leaves the rifle?

    A. Two (one from the gunpowder explosion and one from gravity)
    B. One (from the motion of the bullet)
    C. One (from the gunpowder explosion)
    D. One (from the pull of gravity)
    E. None; it is in freefall and unaffected by any forces

8. Suppose that a car traveling to the East begins to slow down as it approaches a traffic light. Which of the following statements about its acceleration is correct?

    A. The acceleration is towards the East
    B. The acceleration is towards the West
    C. Since the car is slowing, its acceleration is positive
    D. The acceleration is zero
    E. Since the car is slowing, its acceleration cannot be determined

9. On a planet where the acceleration due to gravity is 20 m/s^2, a freely falling object increases its speed each second by about:

    A. 20 m/s   **B.** 10 m/s   **C.** 30 m/s   **D.** 40 m/s   **E.** depends on its initial speed

10. A projectile is fired at time $t = 0$ s from point 0 at the edge of a cliff with initial velocity components of $v_{0x} = 80$ m/s and $v_{0y} = 800$ m/s. The projectile rises, then falls into the sea at point P. The time of flight of the projectile is 200 s. What is the height of the cliff? (Use acceleration due to gravity $g = 10$ m/s^2)

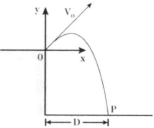

    A. 30,000 m   **C.** 47,500 m
    B. 45,000 m   **D.** 35,000 m   **E.** 40,000 m

11. If the fastest a person can drive is 65 mi/h, what is the longest time she can stop for lunch if she wants to travel 540 mi in 9.8 h?

    A. 1 h   **B.** 2.4 h   **C.** 1.5 h   **D.** 2 h   **E.** 0.5 h

12. What is a racecar's average velocity if it completes one lap around a 500 m track in 10 s?

    A. 10 m/s   **B.** 0 m/s   **C.** 5 m/s **D.** 20 m/s   **E.** 15 m/s

13. What is a ball's net displacement after 5 s if it is initially rolling up a slight incline at 0.2 m/s and decelerates uniformly at 0.05 m/s^2?

    A. 0.38 m   **B.** 0.6 m   **C.** 0.9 m   **D.** 1.2 m   **E.** 2.4 m

14. How much farther would an intoxicated driver's car travel before he hits the brakes than a sober driver's car if both cars are initially traveling at 49 mi/h, and the sober driver takes 0.33 s to hit the brakes while the intoxicated driver takes 1 s to hit the brakes?

    A. 38 ft   **B.** 52 ft   **C.** 32 ft   **D.** 48 ft   **E.** 60 ft

15. An airplane needs to reach a speed of 210.0 km/h to take off. On a 1,800.0 m runway, what is the minimum acceleration necessary for the plane to reach this speed, assuming acceleration is constant?

    A. 0.78 m/s^2 **B.** 0.95 m/s^2 **C.** 1.47 m/s^2 **D.** 1.1 m/s^2 **E.** 2.5 m/s^2

16. A test rocket is fired straight up from rest with a net acceleration of 22 m/s². What maximum elevation does the rocket reach if the motor turns off after 4 s, but the rocket continues to coast upward? (Use acceleration due to gravity $g = 10$ m/s²)

    A. 408 m   **B.** 320 m   **C.** 357 m   **D.** 563 m   **E.** 260 m

17. If a cat jumps at a 60° angle off the ground with an initial velocity of 2.74 m/s, what is the highest point of the cat's trajectory? (Use acceleration due to gravity $g = 9.8$ m/s²)

    A. 9.46 m   **B.** 0.69 m   **C.** 5.75 m   **D.** 1.55 m   **E.** 0.29 m

18. Ignoring air resistance, a 10 kg rock and a 20 kg rock are dropped at the same time. If the 10 kg rock falls with acceleration a, what is the acceleration of the 20 kg rock?

    A. $a/2$ **B.** a **C.** $2a$ **D.** $4a$ **E.** $a/4$

19. As an object falls freely, its magnitude of:

    I. velocity increases   II. acceleration increases   III. displacement increases

    A. I only   **B.** I and II only   **C.** II and III only   **D.** I and III only   **E.** I, II and III

20. A man stands in an elevator that is ascending at constant velocity. What forces are being exerted on the man, and which direction does the net force point?

    A. Gravity pointing downward, normal force from the floor pointing upward, and tension force from the elevator cable pointing upward; net force points upward
    B. Gravity pointing downward and the normal force from the floor pointing upward; net force points upward
    C. Gravity pointing downward and normal force from the floor pointing upward; net force is 0
    D. Gravity pointing downward; net force is zero
    E. Gravity pointing downward, normal force from the floor pointing upward, and tension force from the elevator cable pointing upward; net force is 0

21. A football kicker is attempting a field goal from 44 m away, and the ball just clears the lower bar with a time of flight of 2.9 s. What was the initial speed of the ball if the angle of the kick was 45° with the horizontal?

    A. 37 m/s   **B.** 2.5 m/s   **C.** 18.3 m/s   **D.** 7.2 m/s   **E.** 21.4 m/s

22. Ignoring air resistance, if a rock, starting at rest, is dropped from a cliff and strikes the ground with an impact velocity of 14 m/s, from what height was it dropped? (Use acceleration due to gravity $g = 10$ m/s²)

    A. 10 m   **B.** 30 m   **C.** 45 m   **D.** 70 m   **E.** 90 m

23. An SUV is traveling at 20 m/s. Then Joseph steps on the accelerator pedal, accelerating at a constant 1.4 m/s² for 7 s. How far does he travel during these 7 s?

    A. 205 m   **B.** 174 m   **C.** 143 m   **D.** 158 m   **E.** 115 m

24. Which of the following is NOT a scalar?

    A. temperature   **B.** distance   **C.** mass   **D.** force   **E.** time

25. Two identical balls (A and B) fall from rest from different heights to the ground. Ignoring air resistance, what is the ratio of the heights from which A and B fall if ball B takes twice as long as ball A to reach the ground?

    A. $1 : \sqrt{2}$ **B.** $1 : 4$ **C.** $1 : 2$ **D.** $1 : 8$ **E.** $1 : 9$

26. How far does a car travel in 10 s when it accelerates uniformly in one direction from 5 m/s to 30 m/s?

    A. 65 m   **B.** 25 m   **C.** 250 m   **D.** 650 m   **E.** 175 m

27. A train starts from rest and accelerates uniformly, until it has traveled 5.6 km and has acquired a velocity of 42 m/s. The train then moves at a constant velocity of 42 m/s for 420 s. The train then slows down uniformly at 0.065 m/s², until it stops moving. What is the acceleration during the first 5.6 km of travel?

    A. 0.29 m/s²   **B.** 0.23 m/s²   **C.** 0.16 m/s²   **D.** 0.12 m/s²   **E.** 0.20 m/s²

28. Doubling the distance between an orbiting satellite and the Earth results in what change in the gravitational attraction between the two?

    A. Twice as much   **C.** One half as much   **E.** Remains the same
    B. Four times as much   **D.** One fourth as much

29. An object is moving in a straight line. Consider its motion during some interval of time: under what conditions is it possible for the instantaneous velocity of the object at some point during the interval to be equal to the average velocity over the interval?

    I. When velocity is constant during the interval
    II. When velocity is increasing at a constant rate during the interval
    III. When velocity is increasing at an irregular rate during the interval

    A. II only   **C.** II and III only
    B. I and III only   **D.** I, II and III   **E.** I and II only

30. A car travels 95 km North at 70 km/h, then turns around and travels 21.9 km at 80 km/h. What is the difference between the average speed and the average velocity on this trip?

    A. 58 km/h   **B.** 37 km/h   **C.** 19 km/h   **D.** 27 km/h   **E.** 44 km/h

31. A truck travels a certain distance at a constant velocity v for time t. If the truck travels three times as fast, covering the same distance, then by what factor does the time of travel in relation to t change?

    A. Increases by 3   **C.** Decreases by $\sqrt{3}$
    B. Decreases by 3   **D.** Increases by 9   **E.** Decreases by 1/9

32. Assuming equal rates of acceleration, how much farther would Steve travel if he braked from 59 mi/h to rest than from 29 mi/h to rest?

    A. 2 times farther   **C.** 4 times farther

    B. 16 times farther   **D.** 3.2 times farther   **E.** 1.5 times farther

33. How long does it take a ball to fall if it is dropped from a height of 10 m to the ground and experiences a constant downward acceleration of 9.8 m/s²?

    A. 1.1 s   **B.** 1.4 s   **C.** 2.4 s   **D.** 3.1 s   **E.** 1.9 s

34. What was a car's initial velocity if the car is traveling up a slight slope while decelerating at 0.1 m/s² and comes to a stop after 5 s?

    A. 0.02 m/s   **B.** 0.25 m/s   **C.** 2 m/s   **D.** 1.5 m/s   **E.** 0.5 m/s

35. Average velocity equals the average of an object's initial and final velocity when acceleration is:

    A. constantly decreasing   **C.** constant

    B. constantly increasing   **D.** equal to zero

    E. equal to the reciprocal of the initial velocity

36. Ignoring air resistance, compared to a rock dropped from the same point, how much earlier does a thrown rock strike the ground, if it is thrown downward with an initial velocity of 10 m/s from the top of a 300 m building? (Use acceleration due to gravity $g = 9.8$ m/s²)

    A. 0.75 s   **B.** 0.33 s   **C.** 0.66 s   **D.** 0 s   **E.** 0.95 s

37. With all other factors equal, what happens to the acceleration if the unbalanced force on an object of a given mass is doubled?

    A. Increased by one fourth   **C.** Increased fourfold

    B. Increased by one half   **D.** Doubled   **E.** Remains the same

38. How far does a car travel if it starts from rest and accelerates at a constant 2 m/s² for 10 s, then travels with the constant speed it has achieved for another 10 s and finally slows to a stop with constant deceleration of magnitude 2 m/s²?

    A. 150 m   **B.** 200 m   **C.** 350 m   **D.** 400 m   **E.** 500 m

39. Which statement concerning a car's acceleration must be correct if a car traveling to the North (+y direction) begins to slow down as it approaches a stop sign?

    A. Acceleration is positive   **C.** Cannot be determined from the data provided

    B. Acceleration is zero   **D.** Acceleration decreases in magnitude as the car slows

    E. Acceleration is negative

40. For the velocity vs. time graph of a basketball player traveling up and down the court in a straight-line path, what is the total distance run by the player in the 10 s?

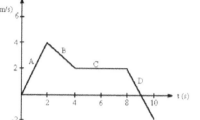

A. 24 m   C. 14 m
B. 22 m   D. 18 m   E. 20 m

41. At the same time that a bullet is dropped into a river from a high bridge, another bullet is fired from a gun, straight down towards the water. Ignoring air resistance, the acceleration just before striking the water:

A. is greater for the dropped bullet
B. is greater for the fired bullet
C. is the same for each bullet
D. depends on how high the bullets started
E. depends on the mass of the bullets

42. Sarah starts her car from rest and accelerates at a constant 2.5 m/s² for 9 s to get to her cruising speed. What was her final velocity?

A. 22.5 m/s   B. 12.3 m/s   C. 4.6 m/s   D. 8.5 m/s   E. 1.25 m/s

43. A bat hits a baseball, and the baseball's direction is completely reversed and its speed is doubled. If the actual time of contact with the bat is 0.45 s, what is the ratio of the acceleration to the original velocity?

A. $-2.5 \text{ s}^{-1} : 1$ B. $-0.15 \text{ s}^{-1} : 1$ C. $-9.8 \text{ s}^{-1} : 1$ D. $-4.1 \text{ s}^{-1} : 1$ E. $-6.7 \text{ s}^{-1} : 1$

44. A 2 kg weight is thrown vertically upward from the surface of the Moon at a speed of 3.2 m/s and it returns to its starting point in 4 s. What is the magnitude of acceleration due to gravity on the Moon?

A. 0.8 m/s²   B. 1.6 m/s²   C. 3.7 m/s²   D. 8.4 m/s²   E. 12.8 m/s²

45. What is the change in velocity for a bird that is cruising at 1.5 m/s and then accelerates at a constant 0.3 m/s² for 3 s?

A. 0.9 m/s   B. 0.6 m/s   C. 1.6 m/s   D. 0.3 m/s   E. 1.9 m/s

46. A car is traveling North at 17.7 m/s. After 12 s, its velocity is 14.1 m/s in the same direction. What is the magnitude and direction of the car's average acceleration?

A. 0.3 m/s², North
B. 2.7 m/s², North
C. 0.3 m/s², South
D. 3.6 m/s², South
E. 2.5 m/s², South

Questions **47-49** are based on the following:

A toy rocket is launched vertically from ground level where $y = 0$ m, at time $t = 0$ s. The rocket engine provides constant upward acceleration during the burn phase. At the instant of engine burnout, the rocket has risen to 64 m and acquired a velocity of 60 m/s. The rocket continues to rise in unpowered flight, reaches maximum height and then falls back to the ground. (Use acceleration due to gravity $g = 9.8$ m/s^2)

47. What is the maximum height reached by the rocket?

    A. 274 m   **B.** 205 m   **C.** 223 m   **D.** 120 m   **E.** 248 m

48. What is the upward acceleration of the rocket during the burn phase?

    A. 9.9 m/s^2 **B.** 4.8 m/s^2 **C.** 28 m/s^2 **D.** 11.8 m/s^2 **E.** 8.6 m/s^2

49. What is the time interval during which the rocket engine provides upward acceleration?

    A. 1.5 s   **B.** 1.9 s   **C.** 2.3 s   **D.** 2.1 s   **E.** 2.6 s

50. A car accelerates uniformly from rest along a straight track that has markers spaced at equal distances along it. As it passes Marker 2, the car reaches a speed of 140 km/h. Where on the track is the car when it is traveling at 70 km/h?

    Start   Marker 1   Marker 2

    A. Close to Marker 2   **C.** At Marker 1
    B. Between Marker 1 and Marker 2   **D.** Close to the starting point
                                         E. Before Marker 1

Force, Motion, Gravitation

1. A boy attaches a weight to a string, which he swings counter-clockwise in a horizontal circle. Which path does the weight follow when the string breaks at point P?

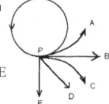

   A. path A   **B.** path B   **C.** path C   **D.** path D   **E.** path E

2. A garment bag hangs from a clothesline. The tension in the clothesline is 10 N on the right side of the garment bag and 10 N on the left side of the garment bag. The clothesline makes an angle of 60° from vertical. What is the mass of the garment bag? (Use the acceleration due to gravity g = 10.0 m/s²)

   A. 0.5 kg   **B.** 8 kg   **C.** 4 kg   **D.** 10 kg   **E.** 1 kg

3. A sheet of paper can be withdrawn from under a milk carton without toppling the carton if the paper is jerked away quickly. This demonstrates:

   A. the inertia of the milk carton
   B. that gravity tends to hold the milk carton secure
   C. there is an action-reaction pair of forces
   D. that the milk carton has no acceleration
   E. none of the above

4. A car of mass m is going up a shallow slope with an angle θ to the horizontal when the driver suddenly applies the brakes. The car skids as it comes to a stop. The coefficient of static friction between the tires and the road is μ_s, and the coefficient of kinetic friction is μ_k. Which expression represents the normal force on the car?

   A. $mg \tan \theta$ **B.** $mg \sin \theta$ **C.** $mg \cos \theta$ **D.** mg **E.** $mg \sec \theta$

5. Two forces of equal magnitude are acting on an object as shown. If the magnitude of each force is 2.3 N and the angle between them is 40°, which third force causes the object to be in equilibrium?

   A. 1.8 N pointing to the right   **C.** 3.5 N pointing to the right
   B. 2.2 N pointing to the right   **D.** 6.6 N pointing to the right
   E. 4.3 N pointing to the right

6. How are two identical masses moving if they are attached by a light string that passes over a small pulley? Assume that the table and the pulley are frictionless.

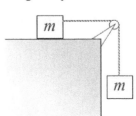

   A. With an acceleration equal to g
   B. With an acceleration greater than g
   C. At a constant speed
   D. With an acceleration less than g
   E. Not moving because the masses are equal

7. An object is moving to the right in a straight line. The net force acting on the object is also directed to the right, but the magnitude of the force is decreasing with time. What happens to the object?

    A. Continues to move to the right with its speed increasing with time
    B. Continues to move to the right with a constant speed
    C. Continues to move to the right with its speed decreasing with time
    D. Continues to move to the right, slowing quickly to a stop
    E. Stops and then begins moving to the left with its speed decreasing with time

8. A crate is sliding down an inclined ramp at a constant speed of 0.55 m/s. Where does the vector sum of all the forces acting on this crate point?

    A. Perpendicular to the ramp
    C. Vertically upward
    B. Vertically downward
    D. Across the ramp
    E. None of the above

9. Consider an inclined plane that makes an angle θ with the horizontal. What is the relationship between the length of the ramp L and the vertical height of the ramp h?

    A. $h = L \sin \theta$
    C. $L = h \sin \theta$
    B. $h = L \tan \theta$
    D. $h = L \cos \theta$
    E. $L = h \cos \theta$

10. Why is it just as difficult to accelerate a car on the Moon as it is to accelerate the same car on Earth?

    I. Moon and Earth have the same gravity
    II. weight of the car is independent of gravity
    III. mass of the car is independent of gravity

    A. I only   **B.** II only   **C.** III only   **D.** I and II only   **E.** I and III only

11. Sean is pulling his son in a toy wagon. His son and the wagon together are 60 kg. For 3 s Sean exerts a force which uniformly accelerates the wagon from 1.5 m/s to 3.5 m/s. What is the acceleration of the wagon with his son?

    A. 0.67 m/s²   **B.** 0.84 m/s²   **C.** 1.66 m/s²   **D.** 15.32 m/s²   **E.** 20.84 m/s²

12. When an object moves in uniform circular motion, the direction of its acceleration is:

    A. directed away from the center of its circular path
    B. dependent on its speed
    C. in the opposite direction of its velocity vector
    D. in the same direction as its velocity vector
    E. directed toward the center of its circular path

13. What happens to a moving object in the absence of an external force?

    A. Gradually accelerates until it reaches its terminal velocity, at which point it continues at a constant velocity

    B. Moves with constant velocity

    C. Stops immediately

    D. Slows and eventually stops

    E. Moves with a constant speed in a circular orbit

14. What are the readings on the spring scales when a 17 kg fish is weighed with two spring scales, if each scale has negligible weight?

    A. The top scale reads 17 kg, and the bottom scale reads 0 kg

    B. Each scale reads greater than 0 kg and less than 17 kg, but the sum of the scales is 17 kg

    C. The bottom scale reads 17 kg, and the top scale reads 0 kg

    D. The sum of the two scales is 34 kg

    E. Each scale reads 8.5 kg

15. Which of the following statements is true about an object in two-dimensional projectile motion with no air resistance?

    A. The acceleration of the object is zero at its highest point

    B. The horizontal acceleration is always positive, regardless of the vertical acceleration

    C. The velocity is always in the same direction as the acceleration

    D. The acceleration of the object is $+g$ when the object is rising and $-g$ when it is falling

    E. The horizontal acceleration is always zero, and the vertical acceleration is always a nonzero constant downward

16. A can of paint with a mass of 10 kg hangs from a rope. If the can is to be pulled up to a rooftop with a constant velocity of 0.5 m/s, what must the tension on the rope be? (Use acceleration due to gravity $g = 10$ m/s²)

    A. 100 N   **B.** 40 N   **C.** 0 N   **D.** 120 N   **E.** 160 N

17. Two forces acting on an object have magnitudes $F_1 = -6.6$ N and $F_2 = 2.2$ N. Which third force causes the object to be in equilibrium?

    A. 4.4 N at 162° counterclockwise from F_1

    B. 4.4 N at 108° counterclockwise from F_1

    C. 7 N at 162° counterclockwise from F_1

    D. 7 N at 108° counterclockwise from F_1

    E. 3.3 N at 162° counterclockwise from F_1

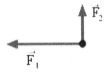

18. A 1,300 kg car is driven at a constant speed of 4 m/s and turns to the right on a curve on the road, which has an effective radius of 4 m. What is the acceleration of the car?

    A. 0 m/s²   **B.** 3 m/s²   **C.** 4 m/s²   **D.** 9.8 m/s²   **E.** 8 m/s²

19. A block of mass m is resting on a 20° slope. The block has coefficients of friction $\mu_s = 0.55$ and $\mu_k = 0.45$ with the surface. Block m is connected via a massless string over a massless, frictionless pulley to a hanging 2 kg block. What is the minimum mass of block m so that it does not slip? (Use acceleration due to gravity $g = 9.8$ m/s²)

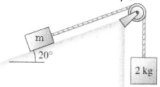
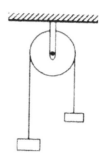

    A. 0.8 kg   **B.** 1.3 kg   **C.** 3.7 kg   **D.** 4.1 kg   **E.** 2.3 kg

20. As shown in the figure to the right, two identical masses, attached by a light cord passing over a massless, frictionless pulley on an Atwood's machine, are hanging at different heights. If the two masses are suddenly released, then the:

    A. lower mass moves down   **C.** higher mass moves down
    B. masses remain stationary   **D.** motion is unpredictable
                                      E. masses oscillate uniformly

21. When Victoria jumps up in the air, which of the following statements is the most accurate?

    A. The ground cannot exert the upward force necessary to lift her into the air, because the ground is stationary. Rather, Victoria is propelled into the air by the internal force of her muscles acting on her body
    B. When Victoria pushes down on the Earth with a force greater than her weight, the Earth pushes back with the same magnitude force and propels her into the air
    C. Victoria is propelled up by the upward force exerted by the ground, but this force cannot be greater than her weight
    D. The Earth exerts an upward force on Victoria that is stronger than the downward force she exerts on the Earth, therefore Victoria is able to spring up
    E. Because gravity is what keeps her on the ground, the internal force of her muscles acting on her body needs to be greater than the force of gravity in order to propel her into the air

22. If a feather is pounded with a hammer, which experiences a greater force?

    A. The magnitude of the force is always the same on both
    B. If the feather moves, then it felt the greater force
    C. Depends on the force with which the hammer strikes the feather
    D. Always the hammer
    E. Always the feather

23. A block is moving down a slope of a frictionless inclined plane. Compared to the weight of the block, what is the force parallel to the surface of the plane experienced by the block?

    A. Greater   **C.** Less than
    B. Unrelated   **D.** Equal   **E.** Requires more information

24. A package falls off a truck that is moving at 30 m/s. Ignoring air resistance, the horizontal speed of the package just before it hits the ground is:

    A. 0 m/s   **B.** 15 m/s   **C.** $\sqrt{60}$ m/s   **D.** $\sqrt{30}$ m/s   **E.** 30 m/s

25. A carousel with the radius r is turning counterclockwise at a frequency f. How does the velocity of a seat on the carousel change when f is doubled?

   A. Increases by a factor of $2r$
   B. Increases by a factor of r

   C. Remains unchanged
   D. Doubles
   E. It depends on the mass of the chair

26. The Earth and the Moon attract each other with the force of gravity. The Earth's radius is 3.7 times that of the Moon, and the Earth's mass is 80 times greater than the Moon's. The acceleration due to gravity on the surface of the Moon is 1/6 the acceleration due to gravity on the Earth's surface. If the distance between the Earth and the Moon decreases by a factor of 4, how would the force of gravity between the Earth and the Moon change?

   A. Remain the same
   B. Increase by a factor of 16

   C. Decrease by a factor of 16
   D. Decrease by a factor of 4
   E. Increase by a factor of $1/\sqrt{4}$

27. Steve is standing facing forward in a moving bus. What force causes Steve to suddenly move forward when the bus comes to an abrupt stop?

   A. Force due to the air pressure inside the previously moving bus
   B. Force due to kinetic friction between Steve and the floor of the bus
   C. Force due to stored kinetic energy
   D. Force of gravity
   E. No forces were responsible for Steve's movement

28. A plastic ball in a liquid is acted upon by its weight and a buoyant force. The weight of the ball is 4.4 N. The buoyant force of 8.4 N acts vertically upward. An external force acting on the ball maintains it in a state of rest. What is the magnitude and direction of the external force?

   A. 4 N, upward
   B. 8.4 N, downward

   C. 4.4 N, upward
   D. 4 N, downward

   E. 2 N, downward

29. A passenger on a train traveling in the forward direction notices that a piece of luggage starts to slide directly toward the front of the train. From this, it can be concluded that the train is:

   A. slowing down
   B. speeding up

   C. moving at a constant velocity forward
   D. changing direction
   E. moving at a constant velocity in the reverse direction

30. An object has a mass of 36 kg and weighs 360 N at the surface of the Earth. If this object is transported to an altitude that is twice the Earth's radius, what is the object's mass and weight, respectively?

   A. 9 kg and 90 N
   B. 36 kg and 90 N

   C. 4 kg and 90 N
   D. 36 kg and 40 N

   E. 9 kg and 40 N

31. A truck is moving at constant velocity. Inside the storage compartment, a rock is dropped from the midpoint of the ceiling and strikes the floor below. The rock hits the floor:

A. just behind the midpoint of the ceiling
B. exactly halfway between the midpoint and the front of the truck
C. exactly below the midpoint of the ceiling
D. just ahead of the midpoint of the ceiling
E. exactly halfway between the midpoint and the rear of the truck

32. Jason takes off across level water on his jet-powered skis. The combined mass of Jason and his skis is 75 kg (the mass of the fuel is negligible). The skis have a thrust of 200 N and a coefficient of kinetic friction on water of 0.1. If the skis run out of fuel after only 67 s, how far has Jason traveled before he stops?

A. 5,428 m   **B.** 3,793 m   **C.** 8,224 m   **D.** 7,642 m   **E.** 10,331 m

33. A 200 g hockey puck is launched up a metal ramp that is inclined at a 30° angle. The puck's initial speed is 63 m/s. What vertical height does the puck reach above its starting point? (Use acceleration due to gravity $g = 9.8$ m/s^2, the coefficient of static friction $\mu_s = 0.40$ and kinetic friction $\mu_k = 0.30$ between the hockey puck and the metal ramp)

A. 66 m   **B.** 200 m   **C.** 170 m   **D.** 130 m   **E.** 48 m

34. When a 4 kg mass and a 10 kg mass are pushed from rest with equal force:

A. 4 kg mass accelerates 2.5 times faster than the 10 kg mass
B. 10 kg mass accelerates 10 times faster than the 4 kg mass
C. 4 kg mass accelerates at the same rate as the 10 kg mass
D. 10 kg mass accelerates 2.5 times faster than the 4 kg mass
E. 4 kg mass accelerates 10 times faster than the 10 kg mass

35. Assume the strings and pulleys in the diagram below have negligible masses and the coefficient of kinetic friction between the 2 kg block and the table is 0.25. What is the acceleration of the 2 kg block? (Use acceleration due to gravity $g = 9.8$ m/s^2)

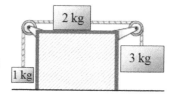

A. 3.2 m/s^2 **B.** 4 m/s^2 **C.** 0.3 m/s^2 **D.** 1.7 m/s^2 **E.** 2.5 m/s^2

36. Which of the following statements must be true when a 20 ton truck collides with a 1,500 lb car?

A. During the collision, the force on the truck is equal to the force on the car
B. The truck did not slow down during the collision, but the car did
C. During the collision, the force on the truck is greater than the force on the car
D. During the collision, the force on the truck is smaller than the force on the car
E. The car did not slow down during the collision, but the truck did

37. A block is on a frictionless table on Earth. The block accelerates at 3 m/s^2 when a 20 N horizontal force is applied to it. The block and table are then transported to the Moon. What is the weight of the block on the Moon? (Use acceleration due to gravity at the surface of the Moon = 1.62 m/s^2)

    A. 5.8 N   **B.** 14.2 N   **C.** 8.5 N   **D.** 11 N   **E.** 17.5 N

38. A 500 kg rocket ship is firing two jets at once. The two jets are at right angles to each other with one firing with a force of 500 N and the other with a force of 1,200 N. What is the magnitude of the acceleration of the rocket ship?

    A. 1.4 m/s^2 **B.** 2.6 m/s^2 **C.** 3.4 m/s^2 **D.** 5.6 m/s^2 **E.** 4.2 m/s^2

39. Car A starts from rest and accelerates uniformly for time t to travel a distance of d. Car B, which has four times the mass of car A, starts from rest and also accelerates uniformly. If the magnitudes of the forces accelerating car A and car B are the same, how long does it take car B to travel the same distance d?

    A. t **B.** $2t$ **C.** $t/2$ **D.** $16t$ **E.** $4t$

40. A 1,100 kg vehicle is traveling at 27 m/s when it starts to decelerate. What is the average braking force acting on the vehicle, if after 578 m it comes to a complete stop?

    A. –440 N   **B.** –740 N   **C.** –690 N   **D.** –540 N   **E.** –880 N

41. An ornament of mass M, is suspended by a string from the ceiling inside an elevator. What is the tension in the string holding the ornament when the elevator is traveling upward with a constant speed?

    A. Equal to Mg **C.** Greater than Mg
    B. Less than Mg **D.** Equal to M/g **E.** Less than M/g

42. An object that weighs 75 N is pulled on a horizontal surface by a force of 50 N to the right. The friction force on this object is 30 N to the left. What is the acceleration of the object? (Use acceleration due to gravity $g = 9.8$ m/s^2)

    A. 0.46 m/s^2 **B.** 1.7 m/s^2 **C.** 2.6 m/s^2 **D.** 10.3 m/s^2 **E.** 12.1 m/s^2

43. While flying horizontally in an airplane, a string attached from the overhead luggage compartment hangs at rest 15° away from the vertical toward the front of the plane. From this observation, it can be concluded that the airplane is:

    A. accelerating forward   **C.** accelerating upward at 15° from horizontal
    B. accelerating backward   **D.** moving backward
                             E. not moving

44. An object slides down an inclined ramp with a constant speed. If the ramp's incline angle is θ, what is the coefficient of kinetic friction (μ_k) between the object and the ramp?

A. $\mu_k = 1$

B. $\mu_k = \cos \theta / \sin \theta$

C. $\mu_k = \sin \theta / \cos \theta$

D. $\mu_k = \sin \theta$

E. $\mu_k = \cos \theta$

45. What is the magnitude of the net force on a 1 N apple when it is in free fall?

A. 1 N   **B.** 0.1 N   **C.** 0.01 N   **D.** 10 N   **E.** 100 N

46. A person who normally weighs 600 N is standing on a scale in an elevator. The elevator is initially moving upwards at a constant speed of 8 m/s and starts to slow down at a rate of 6 m/s^2. What is the reading of the person's weight on the scale in the elevator during the slowdown? (Use acceleration due to gravity $g = 9.8$ m/s^2)

A. 600 N   **B.** 588 N   **C.** 98 N   **D.** 233 N   **E.** 61 N

47. Yania tries to pull an object by tugging on a rope attached to the object with a force of F. If the object does not move, what does this imply?

A. The object has reached its natural state of rest and can no longer be set into motion

B. The rope is not transmitting the force to the object

C. There are no other forces acting on the object

D. The inertia of the object prevents it from accelerating

E. There are one or more other forces that act on the object with a sum of $-F$

48. If a force F is exerted on an object, the force which the object exerts back:

A. depends on the mass of the object

B. depends on the density of the object

C. depends on if the object is moving

D. depends on if the object is stationary

E. equals $-F$

49. What is the net force acting at the top of the path for an arrow that is shot upwards?

A. Greater than its weight

B. Equal to its weight

C. Instantaneously equal to zero

D. Greater than zero, but less than its weight

E. Horizontal

50. Sarah and her father Bob (who weighs four times as much) are standing on identical skateboards (with frictionless ball bearings), both initially at rest. For a short time, Bob pushes Sarah on the skateboard. When Bob stops pushing:

A. Sarah and Bob move away from each other, and Sarah's speed is four times that of Bob's

B. Sarah and Bob move away from each other, and Sarah's speed is one fourth of Bob's

C. Sarah and Bob move away from each other with equal speeds

D. Sarah moves away from Bob, and Bob is stationary

E. Sarah and Bob move away from each other and Bob's speed is less than one fourth that of Sarah's

Equilibrium and Momentum

1. When is the angular momentum of a system constant?

  A. When no net external torque acts on the system
  B. When the linear momentum and the energy are constant
  C. When no net external force acts on the system
  D. When the total kinetic energy is positive
  E. When the moment of inertia is positive

2. When a rock rolls down a mountainside at 7 m/s, the horizontal component of its velocity vector is 1.8 m/s. What was the angle of the mountain surface above the horizontal?

  A. 15°   **B.** 63°   **C.** 40°   **D.** 75°   **E.** 9.5°

3. A 200 N sled slides down a frictionless hill at an angle of 37° to the horizontal. What is the magnitude of the force that the hill exerts on the sled parallel to the surface of the hill?

  A. 170 N   **B.** 200 N   **C.** 74 N   **D.** 37 N   **E.** 0 N

4. Water causes a water wheel to turn as it passes by. The force of the water is 300 N, and the radius of the wheel is 10 m. What is the torque around the center of the wheel?

  A. 0 N·m
  B. 300 N·m
  C. 3,000 N·m
  D. 3 N·m
  E. 30 N·m

5. Through what angle, in degrees, does a 33 rpm record turn in 0.32 s?

  A. 44°   **B.** 94°   **C.** 113°   **D.** 32°   **E.** 63°

6. A 2.2 kg block of mass m is moving on frictionless surface with a speed of $v_i = 9.2$ m/s, and it makes a perfectly elastic collision with a stationary block of mass M. After the collision, the 2.2 kg block recoils with a speed of $v_f = 2.5$ m/s. What is the mass of M?

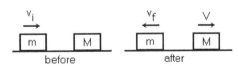

  A. 5.4 kg   **B.** 8.4 kg   **C.** 2.9 kg   **D.** 12.8 kg   **E.** 3.8 kg

---

Questions **7-9** are based on the following:

Three carts run along a level, frictionless one-dimensional track. Furthest to the left is a 1 kg cart I, moving at 0.5 m/s to the right. In the middle is a 1.5 kg cart II moving at 0.3 m/s to the left. Furthest to the right is a 3.5 kg cart III moving at 0.5 m/s to the left. The carts collide in sequence, sticking together. (Assume the direction to the right is the positive direction)

7. What is the total momentum of the system before the collision?

A. −2.6 kg·m/s   **C.** 0.6 kg·m/s
B. 1.4 kg·m/s   **D.** −1.7 kg·m/s   **E.** 1.1 kg·m/s

8. Assuming cart I and cart II collide first and cart III is still independent, what is the total momentum of the system just after cart I and cart II collide?

A. −1.7 kg·m/s   **C.** 0.9 kg·m/s
B. 0.1 kg·m/s   **D.** −0.9 kg·m/s   **E.** −0.11 kg·m/s

9. What is the final velocity of the three carts?

A. −0.35 m/s   **C.** −0.87 m/s
B. −0.28 m/s   **D.** 0.35 m/s   **E.** 0.15 m/s

10. A 480 kg car is moving at 14.4 m/s when it collides with another car that is moving at 13.3 m/s in the same direction. If the second car has a mass of 570 kg and a new velocity of 17.9 m/s after the collision, what is the velocity of the first car after the collision?

A. 19 m/s   **B.** −9 m/s   **C.** 9 m/s   **D.** 14 m/s   **E.** −14 m/s

11. An 8 g bullet is shot into a 4 kg block at rest on a frictionless horizontal surface. The bullet remains lodged in the block. The block moves into a spring and compresses it by 8.9 cm. After the block comes to a stop, the spring fully decompresses and sends the block in the opposite direction. What is the magnitude of the impulse of the block (including the bullet), due to the spring, during the entire time interval in which the block and spring are in contact? (Use the spring constant = 1,400 N/m)

A. 11 N·s   **B.** 8.3 N·s   **C.** 6.4 N·s   **D.** 12 N·s   **E.** 13 N·s

12. An ice skater performs a fast spin by pulling in her outstretched arms close to her body. What happens to her rotational kinetic energy about the axis of rotation?

A. Decreases   **C.** Increases
B. Remains the same   **D.** It changes, but it depends on her body mass
                                E. It decreases in proportion to $\sqrt{\text{length of her arms}}$

13. A toy car is traveling in a circular path. The force required to maintain this motion is F. If the velocity of the object is doubled, what is the force required to maintain its motion?

A. $2F$ **B.** F **C.** $\frac{1}{2}F$ **D.** $4F$ **E.** $\sqrt{2}F$

14. Which of the following is units of momentum?

A. $kg \cdot m/s^2$ B. $J \cdot s/m$ C. $N \cdot m$ D. $kg \cdot s$ E. $kg \cdot m^2/s^2$

15. The impulse on an apple hitting the ground depends on:

I. the speed of the apple just before it hits
II. whether or not the apple bounces
III. the time of impact with the ground

A. I only   B. II only   C. III only   D. I and III only   E. I, II and III

16. A 55 kg girl throws a 0.8 kg ball against a wall. The ball strikes the wall horizontally with a speed of 25 m/s and bounces back with the same speed. The ball is in contact with the wall for 0.05 s. What is the average force exerted on the wall by the ball?

A. 27,500 N   B. 55,000 N   C. 400 N   D. 800 N   E. 13,750 N

17. Three objects are moving along a straight line as shown. If the positive direction is to the right, what is the total momentum of this system?

A. -70 kg·m/s   C. $+86$ kg·m/s
B. $+70$ kg·m/s   D. -86 kg·m/s   E. 0 kg·m/s

6 m/s   3 m/s   2 m/s
•——→   •——→   ←——•
7 kg   12 kg   4 kg

Questions **18-19** are based on the following:

Two ice skaters, Vladimir (60 kg) and Olga (40 kg) collide in midair. Just before the collision, Vladimir was going North at 0.5 m/s and Olga was going West at 1 m/s. Right after the collision and well before they land on the ground, they stick together. Assume they have no vertical velocity.

18. What is the magnitude of their velocity just after the collision?

A. 0.1 m/s   B. 1.8 m/s   C. 0.9 m/s   D. 1.5 m/s   E. 0.5 m/s

19. What is the magnitude of the total momentum just after the collision?

A. 25 kg·m/s   B. 50 kg·m/s   C. 65 kg·m/s   D. 80 kg·m/s   E. 40 kg·m/s

20. A horse is running in a straight line. If both the mass and the speed of the horse are doubled, by what factor does its momentum increase?

A. $\sqrt{2}$ B. 2   C. 4   D. 8   E. 16

21. The mass of box P is greater than the mass of box Q. Both boxes are on a frictionless horizontal surface and connected by a light cord. A horizontal force F is applied to box Q, accelerating the boxes to the right. What is the magnitude of the force exerted by the connecting cord on box P?

A. equal to F **B.** equal to $2F$ **C.** zero   **D.** less than F but > 0 **E.** equal to $3F$

22. Which of the following is true when Melissa and her friend Samantha are riding on a merry-go-round, as viewed from above?

    A. They have the same speed, but different angular velocity
    B. They have different speeds, but the same angular velocity
    C. They have the same speed and the same angular velocity
    D. They have different speeds and different angular velocities
    E. Requires the radius of the merry-go-round

23. The relationship between impulse and impact force involves the:

    A. time the force acts
    B. distance the force acts
    C. difference between acceleration and velocity
    D. mass and its effect on resisting a change in velocity
    E. difference between acceleration and speed

24. Angular momentum cannot be conserved if the:

    A. moment of inertia changes
    B. system is experiencing a net force
    C. angular velocity changes
    D. angular displacement changes
    E. system has a net torque

25. A 6.8 kg block of mass m is moving on a frictionless surface with a speed of $v_i = 5.4$ m/s and makes a perfectly elastic collision with a stationary block of mass M. After the collision, the 6.8 kg block recoils with a speed of $v_f = 3.2$ m/s. What is the magnitude of the average force on the 6.8 kg block while the two blocks are in contact for 2 s?

    A. 4.4 N   **B.** 47.6 N   **C.** 32.6 N   **D.** 29.2 N   **E.** 18.4 N

> Questions **26-27** are based on the following:

A 4 kg rifle imparts a high velocity to a small 10 g bullet by exploding a charge that causes the bullet to leave the barrel at 300 m/s. Take the system as the combination of the rifle and bullet. Normally, the rifle is fired with the butt of the gun pressed against the shooter's shoulder. Ignore the force of the shoulder on the rifle.

26. What is the momentum of the system just after the bullet leaves the barrel?

    A. 0 kg·m/s   **B.** 3 kg·m/s   **C.** 9 kg·m/s   **D.** 30 kg·m/s   **E.** 120 kg·m/s

27. What is the recoil velocity of the rifle (i.e. the velocity of the rifle just after firing)?

    A. 23 m/s   **B.** 1.5 m/s   **C.** 5.6 m/s   **D.** 12.4 m/s   **E.** 0.75 m/s

28. A ball thrown horizontally from a point 24 m above the ground strikes the ground after traveling horizontally a distance of 18 m. With what speed was it thrown, assuming negligible air resistance? (Use acceleration due to gravity $g = 9.8$ m/s^2)

    A. 6.8 m/s   **B.** 7.5 m/s   **C.** 8.1 m/s   **D.** 8.6 m/s   **E.** 9.7 m/s

29. A 3.3 kg object moving at 6.9 m/s makes a perfectly inelastic collision with a 3.6 kg object that is initially at rest. What percentage of the initial kinetic energy of the system is lost during the collision?

    A. 66%   **B.** 59%   **C.** 71%   **D.** 52%   **E.** 83%

30. Impulse is equal to the:

    I. force multiplied by the distance over which the force acts
    II. change in momentum
    III. momentum

    A. I only   **B.** II only   **C.** III only   **D.** I and II only   **E.** I and III only

31. A 4 kg object is at a height of 10 m above the Earth's surface. Ignoring air resistance, what is its kinetic energy immediately before impacting the ground if it is thrown straight downward with an initial speed of 20 m/s? (Use acceleration due to gravity $g = 10$ m/s^2)

    A. 150 J   **B.** 300 J   **C.** 1,200 J   **D.** 900 J   **E.** 600 J

32. A car traveling along the highway needs a certain amount of force exerted on it to stop. More stopping force may be required when the car has:

    I. less stopping distance   II. more momentum   III. more mass

    A. I only   **B.** II only   **C.** III only   **D.** I and III only   **E.** I, II and III

33. A table tennis ball moving East at a speed of 4 m/s collides with a stationary bowling ball. The table tennis ball bounces back to the West, and the bowling ball moves very slowly to the East. Which ball experiences the greater magnitude of impulse during the collision?

    A. Bowling ball
    B. Table tennis ball
    C. Neither because both experience the same magnitude of impulse
    D. It is not possible to determine since the velocities after the collision are unknown
    E. It is not possible to determine since the masses of the objects are unknown

34. Assume that a massless bar of 5 m is suspended from a rope and that the rope is attached to the bar at a distance x from the bar's left end. If a 30 kg mass hangs from the right side of the bar and a 6 kg mass hangs from the left side of the bar, what value of x results in equilibrium? (Use acceleration due to gravity $g = 9.8$ m/s^2)

    A. 2.8 m   **B.** 4.2 m   **C.** 3.2 m   **D.** 1.6 m   **E.** 4.5 m

35. A block of mass _m_ sits at rest on a rough inclined ramp that makes an angle _θ_ with the horizontal. What must be true about the force of static friction (_f_) on the block?

A. $f > mg \sin \theta$

B. $f = mg \cos \theta$

C. $f = mg$

D. $f < mg \cos \theta$

E. $f = mg \sin \theta$

36. A 30 kg block is pushed in a straight line across a horizontal surface. What is the coefficient of kinetic friction μ_k between the block and the surface if a constant force of 45 N must be applied to the block in order to maintain a constant velocity of 3 m/s? (Use acceleration due to gravity $g = 10$ m/s^2)

A. 0.1   **B.** 0.33   **C.** 0.15   **D.** 0.5   **E.** 0.66

37. The impulse-momentum relationship is a direct result of:

     I. Newton's First Law   II. Newton's Second Law   III. Newton's Third Law

A. I only   **B.** II only   **C.** III only **D.** I and II only **E.** I and III only

Questions **38-40** are based on the following:

A 0.5 m by 0.6 m rectangular piece of metal is hinged (⊗) (as shown) in the upper left corner, hanging so that the long edge is vertical. A 25 N force (Y) acts to the left at the lower left corner. A 15 N force (X) acts down at the lower right corner. A 30 N force (Z) acts to the right at the upper right corner. Each force vector is in the plane of the metal. Use counterclockwise as the positive direction.

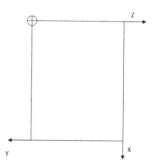

38. What is the torque of force X about the pivot?

A. 5 N·m   **B.** 3 N·m   **C.** −7.5 N·m   **D.** 0 N·m **E.** −5 N·m

39. What is the torque of force Z about the pivot?

A. −10 N·m   **B.** −4.5 N·m   **C.** 4.5 N·m   **D.** 10 N·m **E.** 0 N·m

40. What is the torque of force Y about the pivot?

A. −15 N·m   **B.** −3 N·m   **C.** 0 N·m   **D.** 3 N·m   **E.** 7.5 N·m

41. A 50 g weight is tied to the end of a string and whirled at 20 m/s in a horizontal circle with a radius of 2 m. Ignoring the force of gravity, what is the tension in the string?

A. 5 N   **B.** 10 N   **C.** 50 N   **D.** 150 N **E.** 20 N

42. A small car collides with a large truck in a head-on collision. Which of the following statements concerning the magnitude of the average force during the collision is correct?

- **A.** The small car and the truck experience the same average force
- **B.** The force experienced by each one is inversely proportional to its velocity
- **C.** The truck experiences the greater average force
- **D.** The small car experiences the greater average force
- **E.** The force experienced by each one is directly proportional to its velocity

43. A 10 kg bar that is 2 m long extends perpendicularly from a vertical wall. The free end of the bar is attached to a point on the wall by a light cable, which makes an angle of 30° with the bar. What is the tension in the cable? (Use acceleration due to gravity $g = 10$ m/s^2)

- **A.** 75 N
- **B.** 150 N
- **C.** 100 N
- **D.** 125 N
- **E.** 50 N

44. Object A has the same size and shape as object B, but is twice as heavy. When objects A and B are dropped simultaneously from a tower, they reach the ground at the same time. Object A has greater:

I. speed   II. momentum   III. acceleration

- **A.** I only
- **B.** II only
- **C.** III only
- **D.** I and II only
- **E.** I and III only

45. Two vehicles approach a right angle intersection and then collide. After the collision, they become entangled. If their mass ratio was 1 : 4 and their respective speeds as they approached were both 12 m/s, what is the magnitude of the velocity immediately following the collision?

- **A.** 16.4 m/s
- **B.** 11.9 m/s
- **C.** 13.4 m/s
- **D.** 9.9 m/s
- **E.** 8.5 m/s

46. A skater stands stationary on frictionless ice. She throws a heavy ball to the right at an angle of 5° above the horizontal. With respect to the ice, if the ball weighs one-third as much as the skater and she is measured to be moving with a speed of 2.9 m/s to the left after the throw, how fast did she throw the ball?

- **A.** 10.2 m/s
- **B.** 7.2 m/s
- **C.** 8.73 m/s
- **D.** 9.8 m/s
- **E.** 8.1 m/s

47. Ignoring the forces of friction, what horizontal force must be applied to an object with a weight of 98 N to give it a horizontal acceleration of 10 m/s^2? (Use acceleration due to gravity $g = 9.8$ m/s^2)

- **A.** 9.8 N
- **B.** 100 N
- **C.** 79 N
- **D.** 125 N
- **E.** 4.9 N

48. Consider a winch that pulls a cart at constant speed up an incline. Point A is at the bottom of the incline and point B is at the top. Which of the following statements is/are true from point A to B?

        I. The KE of the cart is constant
        II. The PE of the cart is constant
        III. The sum of the KE and PE of the cart is constant

    A. I only   **B.** II only   **C.** III only   **D.** I and II only   **E.** I, II and III

49. A high speed dart is shot from ground level with a speed of 140 m/s at an angle of 35° above the horizontal. What is the vertical component of its velocity after 4 s if air resistance is ignored? (Use acceleration due to gravity $g = 9.8$ m/s^2)

    A. 59 m/s   **B.** 75 m/s   **C.** 34 m/s   **D.** 41 m/s   **E.** 38 m/s

50. What does the area under the curve of a force vs. time graph represent for a diver as she leaves the platform during her approach to the water below?

    A. Work   **B.** Momentum   **C.** Impulse   **D.** Displacement   **E.** Force

Rotational Motion

1. Suppose a uniform solid sphere of mass M and radius R rolls without slipping down an inclined plane starting from rest. The linear velocity of the sphere at the bottom of the incline depends on:

A. the radius of the sphere
B. the mass of the sphere
C. both the mass and the radius of the sphere
D. neither the mass nor the radius of the sphere
E. both the mass and the square root of the radius of the sphere

2. A solid, uniform sphere of mass 2.0 kg and radius 1.7 m rolls from rest without slipping down an inclined plane of height 5.3 m. What is the angular velocity of the sphere at the bottom of the inclined plane?

A. 3.7 rad/s   **C.** 6.7 rad/s
B. 5.1 rad/s   **D.** 8.3 rad/s   **E.** 11.9 rad/s

3. A solid uniform ball with a mass of 125.0 g is rolling without slipping along the horizontal surface of a table with a speed of 4.5 m/s when it rolls off the edge and falls towards the floor, 1.1 m below. What is the rotational kinetic energy of the ball just before it hits the floor?

A. 0.51 J   **C.** 1.03 J
B. 0.87 J   **D.** 2.26 J   **E.** Requires the radius of the ball

4. David swings a 0.38 kg ball in a circle on a string that is 1.3 m long. What is the magnitude of the ball's angular momentum, if the ball makes 1.2 rev/s?

A. 0.6 kg·m^2/s   **C.** 3.6 kg·m^2/s
B. 2.2 kg·m^2/s   **D.** 4.8 kg·m^2/s   **E.** 6.2 kg·m^2/s

5. An ice skater has a moment of inertia of 5.0 kg·m^2 when her arms are outstretched, and at this time she is spinning at 3.0 rev/s. If she pulls in her arms and decreases her moment of inertia to 2.0 kg·m^2, how fast will she be spinning?

A. 1.8 rev/s   **C.** 7.5 rev/s
B. 4.5 rev/s   **D.** 10.5 rev/s   **E.** 12.5 rev/s

6. The angular momentum of a system remains constant when:

A. its total kinetic energy is constant
B. the moment of inertia is constant
C. no net external torque acts on the system
D. no net external force acts on the system
E. the linear momentum and the energy are constant

---

7. A bicycle has wheels that are 60.0 cm in diameter. What is the angular speed of these wheels when it is moving at 4.0 m/s?

    A. 0.28 rad/s   **C.** 3.4 rad/s
    B. 1.6 rad/s   **D.** 6.7 rad/s   **E.** 13.3 rad/s

8. What is the kinetic energy of a thin uniform rod of length 120.0 cm with a mass of 450.0 g that is rotating about its center along the short axis at 3.60 rad/s? (The short axis is perpendicular to the axis of the rod. Imagine spinning the rod like an airplane propeller.)

    A. 0.350 J   **C.** 2.70 J
    B. 1.30 J   **D.** 4.96 J   **E.** 6.10 J

9. A rope is wrapped around a wheel of radius R = 2.0 meters. The wheel is mounted with frictionless bearings on an axle through its center. A block of mass 14.0 kg is suspended from the end of the rope. When the system is released from rest it is observed that the block descends 10.0 meters in 2.0 seconds. What is the moment of inertia of the wheel?

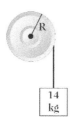

    A. 300.0 kg·m^2 **C.** 53.8 kg·m^2
    B. 185.0 kg·m^2 **D.** 521.0 kg·m^2 **E.** 88.5 kg·m^2

10. A string is wrapped tightly around a fixed frictionless pulley that has a moment of inertia of 0.0352 kg·m^2 and a radius of 12.5 cm. The string is pulled away from the pulley with a constant force of 5.00 N, causing the pulley to rotate. If the string does not slip on the pulley, what is the speed of the string after it has unwound 1.25 m? Consider the string to be massless.

    A. 0.69 m/s   **C.** 3.62 m/s
    B. 2.36 m/s   **D.** 4.90 m/s   **E.** 6.12 m/s

11. When a rigid object rotates about a fixed axis, what is true about all the points in the object?

    I. They all have the same angular acceleration
    II. They all have the same tangential acceleration
    III. They all have the same radial acceleration

    A. I only   **C.** III only
    B. II only   **D.** I and II only   **E.** I, II and III

12. A small mass is placed on a record turntable that is rotating at 33.33 rpm. The linear velocity of the mass is:

   A. zero
   B. directed parallel to the line joining the mass and the center of rotation
   C. independent (in magnitude) of the position of the mass on the turntable
   D. greater the closer the mass is to the center
   E. greater the farther the mass is from the center

13. To drive a midsize car at 40.0 mph on a level road for one hour requires about 3.2×10^7 J of energy. Suppose this much energy were attempted to be stored in a spinning, solid, uniform, cylindrical flywheel. If a flywheel with a diameter 1.2 m and mass 400.0 kg were used, what angular speed would be required to store 3.2×10^7 J?

   A. 380 rad/s   **C.** 940 rad/s
   B. 620 rad/s   **D.** 1,450 rad/s   **E.** 2,860 rad/s

14. A wheel having a moment of inertia of 5.0 kg·m² starts from rest and accelerates for 8.0 s under a constant torque of 3.0 N·m. What is the wheel's rotational kinetic energy at the end of 8.0 s?

   A. 29 J   **C.** 83 J
   B. 58 J   **D.** 112 J   **E.** 146 J

15. When a rigid object rotates about a fixed axis, what is true about all the points in the object?

     I. They have the same angular speed
     II. They have the same tangential speed
     III. They have the same angular acceleration

   A. I only   **C.** III only
   B. II only   **D.** I and III only   **E.** I, II and III

16. A uniform, solid cylindrical flywheel of radius 1.4 m and mass 15.0 kg rotates at 2.4 rad/s. What is the magnitude of the flywheel's angular momentum?

   A. 11 kg·m²/s   **C.** 25 kg·m²/s
   B. 18 kg·m²/s   **D.** 35 kg·m²/s   **E.** 64 kg·m²/s

17. A uniform solid disk is released from rest and rolls without slipping down an inclined plane that makes an angle of 25° with the horizontal. What is the forward speed of the disk after it has rolled 3.0 m, measured along the plane?

   A. 0.8 m/s   **C.** 2.9 m/s
   B. 1.8 m/s   **D.** 3.5 m/s   **E.** 4.1 m/s

18. A tire is rolling along a road, without slipping, with a center-of-mass velocity v. A piece of tape is attached to the tire. When the tape is opposite the road (at the top of the tire), what is its velocity with respect to the road?

A. $2v$ **C.** $1.5v$

B. v **D.** $\sqrt{v}$ **E.** The velocity depends on the radius of the tire

19. A string is wound tightly around a fixed pulley having a radius of 5.0 cm. As the string is pulled, the pulley rotates without any slipping of the string. What is the angular speed of the pulley when the string is moving at 5.0 m/s?

A. 10.0 rad/s   **C.** 75.0 rad/s

B. 25.0 rad/s   **D.** 100.0 rad/s   **E.** 150.0 rad/s

20. A 1.4 kg object at $x = 2.00$ m, $y = 3.10$ m moves at 4.62 m/s at an angle 45° north of east. What is the magnitude of the object's angular momentum about the origin?

A. 1.2 kg·m²/s   **C.** 3.8 kg·m²/s

B. 2.6 kg·m²/s   **D.** 5.0 kg·m²/s   **E.** 8.4 kg·m²/s

21. When a fan is turned off, its angular speed decreases from 10.0 rad/s to 6.3 rad/s in 5.0 s. What is the magnitude of the average angular acceleration of the fan?

A. 0.46 rad/s²   **C.** 1.86 rad/s²

B. 0.74 rad/s²   **D.** 2.80 rad/s²   **E.** 3.62 rad/s²

22. At time $t = 0$ s, a wheel has an angular displacement of 0 radians and an angular velocity of +26.0 rad/s. The wheel has a constant acceleration of –0.43 rad/s². In this situation, what is the time t (after $t = 0$ s), at which the kinetic energy of the wheel is twice the initial value?

A. 48 s   **B.** 86 s   **C.** 115 s   **D.** 146 s   **E.** 185 s

23. A solid uniform disk of diameter 3.20 m and mass 42.0 kg rolls without slipping to the bottom of a hill, starting from rest. If the angular speed of the disk is 4.27 rad/s at the bottom, how high vertically did it start on the hill above the bottom?

A. 2.46 m   **B.** 3.57 m   **C.** 4.85 m   **D.** 6.24 m   **E.** 8.44 m

24. When Steve rides a bicycle, in what direction is the angular velocity of the wheels?

A. to his left   **C.** forwards

B. to his right   **D.** backwards   **E.** up

25. A rolling wheel of diameter of 68.0 cm slows down uniformly from 8.4 m/s to rest over a distance of 115.0 m. What is the magnitude of its angular acceleration if there was no slipping?

A. 0.90 rad/s²   **C.** 4.2 rad/s²

B. 1.6 rad/s²   **D.** 7.8 rad/s²   **E.** 11.4 rad/s²

26. A uniform solid cylinder with a radius of 10.0 cm and a mass of 3.0 kg is rotating about its center axis with an angular speed of 33.4 rpm. What is the kinetic energy of the uniform solid cylinder?

    A. 0.091 J   **C.** 0.66 J

    B. 0.19 J   **D.** 1.14 J   **E.** 2.46 J

27. A uniform 135.0-g meter stick rotates about an axis perpendicular to the stick passing through its center with an angular speed of 3.50 rad/s. What is the magnitude of the angular momentum of the stick?

    A. 0.0394 kg·m^2/s   **C.** 0.286 kg·m^2/s

    B. 0.0848 kg·m^2/s   **D.** 0.458 kg·m^2/s   **E.** 0.826 kg·m^2/s

28. A 23.0 kg mass is connected to a nail on a frictionless table by a massless string of length 1.3 m. If the tension in the string is 51.0 N while the mass moves in a uniform circle on the table, how long does it take for the mass to make one complete revolution?

    A. 2.8 s   **C.** 4.8 s

    B. 3.6 s   **D.** 5.4 s   **E.** 6.2 s

29. A machinist turns on the power to a grinding wheel at time $t = 0$ s. The wheel accelerates uniformly from rest for 10.0 s and reaches the operating angular speed of 38.0 rad/s. The wheel is run at that angular speed for 30.0 s and then power is shut off. The wheel slows down uniformly at 2.1 rad/s^2 until the wheel stops. What is the angular acceleration of the wheel between $t = 0$ s and $t = 10.0$ s?

    A. 1.21 rad/s^2 **C.** 3.80 rad/s^2

    B. 2.63 rad/s^2 **D.** 5.40 rad/s^2 **E.** 6.81 rad/s^2

30. A force of 17.0 N is applied to the end of a 0.63 m long torque wrench at an angle 45° from a line joining the pivot point to the handle. What is the magnitude of the torque generated about the pivot point?

    A. 4.3 N·m   **C.** 7.6 N·m

    B. 8.2 N·m   **D.** 11.8 N·m   **E.** 14.0 N·m

31. A solid disk of radius 1.60 m and mass 2.30 kg rolls from rest without slipping to the bottom of an inclined plane. If the angular velocity of the disk is 4.27 rad/s at the bottom, what is the height of the inclined plane?

    A. 0.57 m   **C.** 2.84 m

    B. 1.08 m   **D.** 3.57 m   **E.** 5.66 m

32. A merry-go-round spins freely when Paul moves quickly to the center along a radius of the merry-go-round. As he does this, the moment of inertia of the system:

    A. increases and the angular speed increases
    B. decreases and the angular speed remains the same
    C. decreases and the angular speed decreases
    D. decreases and the angular speed increases
    E. increases and the angular speed decreases

33. What is the angular speed of a compact disc that, at a certain instant, is rotating at 210.0 rpm?

    A. 8.5 rad/s   **C.** 36.4 rad/s
    B. 22.0 rad/s   **D.** 52.6 rad/s   **E.** 68.2 rad/s

34. A solid uniform sphere is rolling without slipping along a horizontal surface with a speed of 5.5 m/s when it starts up a ramp that makes an angle of 25° with the horizontal. What is the speed of the sphere after it has rolled 3.0 m up as measured along the surface of the ramp?

    A. 0.8 m/s   **B.** 1.6 m/s   **C.** 3.5 m/s   **D.** 4.8 m/s   **E.** 6.4 m/s

35. A force of 16.88 N is applied tangentially to a wheel of radius 0.340 m and gives rise to an angular acceleration of 1.20 rad/s². What is the rotational inertia of the wheel?

    A. 1.48 kg·m²   **C.** 3.48 kg·m²
    B. 2.26 kg·m²   **D.** 4.78 kg·m²   **E.** 6.42 kg·m²

36. A machine does 3.9 kJ of work on a spinning flywheel to bring it from 500.0 rpm to rest. This flywheel is in the shape of a solid uniform disk of radius 1.2 m. What is the mass of this flywheel?

    A. 2.6 kg   **C.** 5.2 kg
    B. 4.0 kg   **D.** 6.4 kg   **E.** 8.6 kg

37. A rectangular billboard with $h = 20.0$ cm high and $w = 11.0$ cm wide loses three of its four support bolts and rotates into the position as shown, with P_1 directly over P_3. It is supported by P_2, which is so tight it holds the billboard from further rotation. What is the gravitational torque about P_2, if the mass of the billboard is 5.0 kg?

    A. 1.2 Nm   **C.** 4.7 Nm
    B. 2.5 Nm   **D.** 6.8 Nm   **E.** 8.2 Nm

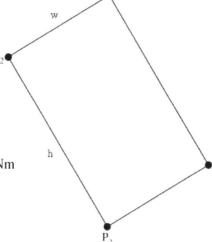

38. A disk, a hoop, and a solid sphere are released at the same time at the top of an inclined plane. In which order do they reach the bottom if each is uniform and rolls without slipping?

A. sphere, hoop, disk   C. hoop, sphere, disk
B. sphere, disk, hoop   D. disk, hoop, sphere   E. hoop, disk, sphere

39. A uniform disk is attached at the rim to a vertical shaft and is used as a cam. A side view and top view of the disk and shaft are shown.

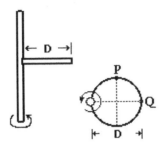

The disk has a diameter of 80.0 cm. The moment of inertia of the disk about the axis of the shaft is 6.0×10^{-3} kg·m². What is the kinetic energy of the disk as the shaft rotates uniformly about its axis at 96.0 rpm?

A. 0.18 J   C. 0.49 J
B. 0.30 J   D. 0.57 J   E. 1.0 J

40. A scooter has wheels with a diameter of 240.0 mm. What is the angular speed of the wheels when the scooter is moving forward at 6.00 m/s?

A. 128.6 rpm   C. 472.0 rpm
B. 248.2 rpm   D. 478.0 rpm   E. 1,260.6 rpm

41. A spinning ice skater on frictionless ice is able to control the rate at which she rotates by pulling in her arms. Which of the following statements are true about the skater during this process?

    I. Her kinetic energy remains constant
    II. Her moment of inertia remains constant
    III. Her angular momentum remains constant

A. I only   C. III only
B. II only   D. I and II only   E. I, II and III

42. Tanya is riding a merry-go-round that has an instantaneous angular speed of 1.25 rad/s and an angular acceleration of 0.745 rad/s². Tanya is standing 4.65 m from the center of the merry-go-round. What is the magnitude of the linear acceleration of Tanya?

A. 2.45 m/s²   C. 6.82 m/s²
B. 4.20 m/s²   D. 8.05 m/s²   E. 12.10 m/s²

43. Through how many degrees does a 33.0 rpm turntable rotate in 0.32 s?

   A. 31°   **B.** 42°   **C.** 63°   **D.** 76°   **E.** 85°

44. A 50.0 kg uniform ladder, length $L = 5.00$ m long, is placed against a smooth wall at a height of $h = 3.70$ m. The base of the ladder rests on a rough horizontal surface whose coefficient of static friction $\mu = 0.750$. An 80.0 kg block is suspended from the top rung of the ladder, just at the wall. What is the approximate magnitude of the force exerted on the base of the ladder, due to contact with the rough horizontal surface?

   A. 1,370 N   **C.** 1,580 N

   B. 1,460 N   **D.** 1,640 N   **E.** 1,760 N

45. At time $t = 0$ s, a wheel has an angular displacement of zero radians and an angular velocity of +29.0 rad/s. The wheel has a constant acceleration of –0.52 rad/s². In this situation, what is the maximum value of the angular displacement?

   A. +467 rad   **C.** +1,110 rad

   B. +809 rad   **D.** +1,460 rad   **E.** +1,840 rad

46. A disk lies in the *xz*-plane with its center at the origin. When viewed from the positive *y*-axis (i.e., above the disk), the direction of rotation appears clockwise. In what direction does the angular velocity of the disk point?

   A. to her right   **C.** down

   B. to her left   **D.** up   **E.** forwards

Work and Energy

1. Consider the following ways that a girl might throw a stone from a bridge. The speed of the stone as it leaves her hand is the same in each of the three cases.

     I. Thrown straight up
     II. Thrown straight down
     III. Thrown straight out horizontally

Ignoring air resistance, in which case is the vertical speed of the stone the greatest when it hits the water below?

    A. I only
    B. II only
    C. III only
    D. I and II only
    E. II and III only

2. A package is being pulled along the ground by a 5 N force F directed 45° above the horizontal. Approximately how much work is done by the force when it pulls the package 10 m?

    A. 14 J
    B. 35 J
    C. 70 J
    D. 46 J
    E. 64 J

3. Which quantity has the greatest influence on the amount of kinetic energy that a large truck has while moving down the highway?

    A. Velocity
    B. Mass
    C. Density
    D. Direction
    E. Acceleration

4. No work is done by gravity on a bowling ball that rolls along the floor of a bowling alley because:

    A. no potential energy is being converted to kinetic energy
    B. the force on the ball is at a right angle to the ball's motion
    C. its velocity is constant
    D. the total force on the ball is zero
    E. its kinetic energy remains constant

5. A tennis ball bounces on the floor. During each bounce, it loses 31% of its energy due to heating. How high does the ball reach after the third bounce, if it is initially released 4 m from the floor?

    A. 55 cm
    B. 171 mm
    C. 106 cm
    D. 131 cm
    E. 87 cm

6. A tree house is 8 m above the ground. If Peter does 360 J of work while pulling a box from the ground up to his tree house with a rope, what is the mass of a box? (Use acceleration due to gravity $g = 10$ m/s²)

    A. 4.5 kg
    B. 3.5 kg
    C. 5.8 kg
    D. 2.5 kg
    E. 1.4 kg

7. For an ideal elastic spring, what does the slope of the curve represent for a displacement (x) vs. applied force (F) graph?

A. The acceleration of gravity

B. The square root of the spring constant

C. The spring constant

D. The reciprocal of the spring constant

E. The square of the spring constant

8. A spring with a spring constant of 22 N/m is stretched from equilibrium to 3 m. How much work is done in the process?

A. 33 J   B. 66 J   C. 99 J   D. 198 J   E. 242 J

9. A baseball is thrown straight up. Compare the sign of the work done by gravity while the ball goes up with the sign of the work done by gravity while it goes down:

A. negative on the way up and positive on the way down

B. negative on the way up and negative on the way down

C. positive on the way up and positive on the way down

D. positive on the way up and negative on the way down

E. requires information about the mass of the baseball

10. Let A_1 represent the magnitude of the work done by gravity as mass A's gravitational energy increases by 400 J. Let B_1 represent the total amount of work necessary to increase mass B's kinetic energy by 400 J. How do A_1 and B_1 compare?

A. $A_1 > B_1$

B. $A_1 = B_1$

C. $A_1 < B_1$

D. $A_1 = 400\ B_1$

E. $400\ A_1 = B_1$

11. According to the definition of work, pushing on a rock accomplishes no work unless there is:

A. an applied force equal to the rock's weight

B. movement perpendicular to the force

C. an applied force greater than the rock's weight

D. movement parallel to the force

E. force perpendicular to the movement

12. A job is done slowly, while an identical job is done quickly. Both jobs require the same amount of work, but different amounts of:

I. energy   II. power   III. torque

A. I only   B. II only   C. I and II only   D. I and III only   E. none are true

13. On a force (F) vs. distance (d) graph, what represents the work done by the force F?

A. The area under the curve

B. A line connecting two points on the curve

C. The slope of the curve

D. The length of the curve

E. The maximum F × the maximum d

14. A helicopter with a single landing gear, descends vertically to land with a speed of 4.5 m/s. The helicopter's shock absorbers have an initial length of 0.60 m. They compress to 77% of their original length and the air in the tires absorbs 23% of the initial energy as heat. What is the ratio of the spring constant to the helicopter's mass?

A. 0.11 kN/kg·m   **C.** 0.82 kN/kg·m

B. 1.1 N/kg·m   **D.** 11 N/kg·m   **E.** 0.11 N/kg·m

15. A book is resting on a plank of wood. Jackie pushes the plank and accelerates it in such a way that the book is stationary with respect to the plank. The work done by static friction is:

A. zero   **C.** negative

B. positive   **D.** parallel to the surface   **E.** perpendicular to the surface

16. 4.5×10^5 J of work are done on a 1,150 kg car while it accelerates from 10 m/s to some final velocity. What is this final velocity? (Use acceleration due to gravity $g = 10$ m/s^2)

A. 30 m/s   **B.** 37 m/s   **C.** 12 m/s   **D.** 19 m/s   **E.** 43 m/s

17. A lightweight object and a very heavy object are sliding with equal speeds along a level, frictionless surface. They both slide up the same frictionless hill with no air resistance. Which object rises to a greater height?

A. The lightweight object, because the force of gravity on it is less
B. The heavy object, because it has more kinetic energy to carry it up the hill
C. The heavy object, because it has greater potential energy
D. The lightweight object, because it has more kinetic energy to carry it up the hill
E. They both slide to exactly the same height

18. If Investigator II does 3 times the work of Investigator I in one third the time, the power output of Investigator II is:

A. 9 times greater   **C.** 1/3 times greater

B. 3 times greater   **D.** the same   **E.** √3 times greater

19. A diver who weighs 450 N steps off a diving board that is 9 m above the water. What is the kinetic energy when the diver strikes the water? (Use acceleration due to gravity $g = 10$ m/s^2)

A. 160 J   **B.** 540 J   **C.** 45 J   **D.** 4,050 J   **E.** 5,400 J

20. A vertical, hanging spring stretches by 23 cm when a 160 N object is attached. What is the weight of a hanging plant that stretches the spring by 34 cm?

A. 237 N   **B.** 167 N   **C.** 158 N   **D.** 309 N   **E.** 249 N

21. A mule pulls with a horizontal force F on a covered wagon of mass M. The mule and covered wagon are traveling at a constant speed v on level ground. How much work is done by the mule on the covered wagon during time Δt? (Use acceleration due to gravity $g = 10$ m/s^2)

A. $-Fv\Delta t$ **B.** $Fv\Delta t$ **C.** 0 J **D.** $-F\sqrt{v}\Delta t$ **E.** $-Fv / \Delta t$

22. Jane pulls on the strap of a sled at an angle of 32° above the horizontal. If 540 J of work are done by the strap while moving the sled a horizontal distance of 18 m, what is the tension in the strap?

A. 86 N **B.** 112 N **C.** 24 N **D.** 35 N **E.** 69 N

23. A vertical spring stretches 6 cm from equilibrium when a 120 g mass is attached to the bottom. If an additional 120 g mass is added to the spring, how does the potential energy of the spring change?

A. the same
B. 4 times greater
C. 2 times greater
D. $\sqrt{2}$ times greater
E. 3 times greater

24. A Ferrari, Maserati and Lamborghini are moving with the same speed and each driver slams on his brakes. The most massive is the Ferrari, and the least massive is the Lamborghini. If the tires of all three cars have identical coefficients of friction with the road surface, which car experiences the greatest amount of work done by friction?

A. Maserati
B. Lamborghini
C. Ferrari
D. The amount is the same
E. Requires more information

25. A hammer does the work of driving a nail into a wooden board. Compared to the moment before the hammer strikes the nail, after it impacts the nail, the hammer's mechanical energy is:

A. the same
B. less, because work has been done on the hammer
C. greater, because the hammer has done work
D. greater, because work has been done on the hammer
E. less, because the hammer has done work

26. A 1,500 kg car is traveling at 25 m/s on a level road and the driver slams on the brakes. The skid marks are 10 m long. What is the work done by the road on the car?

A. -4.7×10^5 J
B. 0 J
C. 2×10^5 J
D. 3.5×10^5 J
E. -3.5×10^5 J

27. A 1,000 kg car is traveling at 4.72 m/s. If a 2,000 kg truck has 20 times the kinetic energy of the car, how fast is the truck traveling?

A. 23.6 m/s **B.** 47.2 m/s **C.** 94.4 m/s **D.** 14.9 m/s **E.** 9.71 m/s

28. A 1,500 kg car is traveling at 25 m/s on a level road and the driver slams on the brakes. The skid marks are 30 m long. What forces are acting on the car while it is coming to a stop?

   A. Gravity down, normal force up, and a frictional force forwards
   B. Gravity down, normal force up, and the engine force forwards
   C. Gravity down, normal force forward, and a frictional force backwards
   D. Gravity down, normal force forward, and the engine force backwards
   E. Gravity down, normal force up, and a frictional force backwards

29. A 6,000 N piano is being raised via a pulley. For every 1 m that the rope is pulled down, the piano rises 0.15 m. In this pulley system, what is the force needed to lift the piano?

   A. 60 N   **B.** 900 N   **C.** 600 N   **D.** 300 N   **E.** 6 N

30. What does the area under the curve on a force vs. position graph represent?

   A. Kinetic energy   **B.** Momentum   **C.** Work   **D.** Displacement   **E.** Friction

31. What is the form in which most energy comes to and leaves the Earth?

   A. Kinetic   **B.** Radiant   **C.** Chemical   **D.** Light   **E.** Heat

32. A driver abruptly slams on the brakes in her car, and the car skids a certain distance on a straight level road. If she had been traveling twice as fast, what distance would the car have skid, under the same conditions?

   A. 1.4 times farther   **C.** 4 times farther
   B. ½ as far   **D.** 2 times farther   **E.** 8 times farther

33. A crane hoists an object weighing 2,000 N to the top of a building. The crane raises the object straight upward at a constant rate. Ignoring the forces of friction, at what rate is energy consumed by the electric motor of the crane if it takes 60 s to lift the mass 320 m?

   A. 2.5 kW   **B.** 6.9 kW   **C.** 3.50 kW   **D.** 10.7 kW   **E.** 16.3 kW

34. A barbell with a mass of 25 kg is raised 3.0 m in 3.0 s before it reaches constant velocity. What is the net power expended by all forces in raising the barbell? (Use acceleration due to gravity $g = 9.8$ m/s^2 and the acceleration of the barbell is constant)

   A. 138 W   **B.** 34 W   **C.** 67 W   **D.** 98 W   **E.** 17 W

35. Susan carried a 6.5 kg bag of groceries 1.4 m above the ground at constant velocity for 2.4 m across the kitchen. How much work did Susan do on the bag in the process? (Use acceleration due to gravity $g = 10$ m/s^2)

   A. 52 J   **B.** 0 J   **C.** 164 J   **D.** 138 J   **E.** 172 J

36. A 1,000 kg car experiences a net force of 9,600 N while decelerating from 30 m/s to 22 m/s. How far does it travel while slowing down?

    A. 17 m   **B.** 22 m   **C.** 12 m   **D.** 34 m   **E.** 26 m

37. A 1,320 kg car climbs a 5° slope at a constant velocity of 70 km/h. Ignoring air resistance, at what rate must the engine deliver energy to drive the car? (Use acceleration due to gravity $g = 9.8$ m/s^2)

    A. 45.1 kW   **B.** 12.7 kW   **C.** 6.3 kW   **D.** 22.6 kW   **E.** 32.2 kW

38. If a ball is released from a cliff ledge 58 m above the ground, how fast is the ball traveling when it reaches the ground? (Use acceleration due to gravity $g = 10$ m/s^2)

    A. 68 m/s   **B.** 16 m/s   **C.** 44 m/s   **D.** 34 m/s   **E.** 53 m/s

39. A stone is held at a height h above the ground. A second stone with four times the mass is held at the same height. What is the gravitational potential energy of the second stone compared to that of the first stone?

    A. Twice as much   **C.** One fourth as much
    B. The same   **D.** One half as much   **E.** Four times as much

40. A 1.3 kg coconut falls off a coconut tree, landing on the ground 600 cm below. How much work is done on the coconut by the gravitational force? (Use acceleration due to gravity $g = 10$ m/s^2)

    A. 6 J   **B.** 78 J   **C.** 168 J   **D.** 340 J   **E.** 236 J

41. The potential energy of a pair of interacting objects is related to their:

    A. relative position   **B.** momentum **C.** acceleration   **D.** kinetic energy   **E.** velocity

42. A spring has a spring constant of 65 N/m. One end of the spring is fixed at point P, while the other end is connected to a 7 kg mass m. The fixed end and the mass sit on a horizontal, frictionless surface, so that the mass and the spring are able to rotate about P. The mass moves in a circle of radius $r = 4$ m, and the centripetal force of the mass is 15 N. What is the potential energy stored in the spring?

    A. 1.7 J   **B.** 2.8 J   **C.** 3.7 J   **D.** 7.5 J   **E.** 11.2 J

43. If electricity costs 8.16 cents/kW·h, how much would it cost you to run a 120 W stereo system 3.5 hours per day for 5 weeks?

    A. $1.11   **B.** $1.46   **C.** $1.20   **D.** $0.34   **E.** $0.49

44. A boy does 120 J of work to pull his sister back on a swing that has a 5.1 m chain, until the swing makes an angle of 32° with the vertical. What is the mass of his sister? (Use acceleration due to gravity $g = 9.8$ m/s^2)

    A. 18 kg   **B.** 16.4 kg   **C.** 13.6 kg   **D.** 11.8 kg   **E.** 15.8 kg

45. What is the value of the spring constant if 111 J of work are needed to stretch a spring from 1.4 to 2.9 m, if the spring's equilibrium position is at 0.0 m?

    A. 58 N/m   **B.** 53 N/m   **C.** 67 N/m   **D.** 34 N/m   **E.** 41 N/m

46. The metric unit of a joule (J) is a unit of:

    I. potential energy   II. kinetic energy   III. work

    A. I only   **B.** II only   **C.** III only   **D.** I and III only   **E.** I, II and III

47. A horizontal spring-mass system oscillates on a frictionless table. Find the maximum extension of the spring if the ratio of the mass to the spring constant is 0.038 kg·m/N, and the maximum speed of the mass is 18 m/s?

    A. 3.5 m   **B.** 0.67 m   **C.** 3.4 cm   **D.** 67 cm   **E.** 34 cm

48. A truck weighs twice as much as a car, and is moving at twice the speed of the car. Which statement is true about the truck's kinetic energy compared to that of the car?

    A. The truck has 8 times the KE   **C.** The truck has $\sqrt{2}$ times the KE
    B. The truck has twice the KE   **D.** The truck has 4 times the KE
                                                    E. The truck has $\sqrt{8}$ times the KE

49. When a car brakes to a stop, its kinetic energy is transformed into:

    A. energy of rest   **C.** potential energy
    B. energy of momentum   **D.** stopping energy   **E.** heat

50. A 30 kg block hangs from a spring with a spring constant of 900 N/m. How far does the spring stretch from its equilibrium position? (Use acceleration due to gravity $g = 10$ m/s^2)

    A. 12 cm   **B.** 33 cm   **C.** 50 cm   **D.** 0.5 cm   **E.** 5 cm

Waves and Periodic Motion

1. A simple harmonic oscillator oscillates with frequency f when its amplitude is A. What is the new frequency if the amplitude is doubled to 2A?

    A. $f/2$ **B.** f **C.** $4f$ **D.** $2f$ **E.** $f/4$

2. Springs A and B are attached in series with the free end of spring B attached to a wall. The free end of spring A is pulled, and both springs expand from their equilibrium lengths. The length of spring A increases by L_A, and the length of spring B increases by L_B. What is the expression for the spring constant k_B of spring B?

    A. L_B/k_A **B.** k_A^2 **C.** $k_A L_B$ **D.** $(k_A L_A)/L_B$ **E.** $2k_A$

3. Particles of a material that move back and forth in the same direction the wave is moving are in what type of wave?

    A. Standing   **C.** Transverse
    B. Torsional   **D.** Longitudinal
                                  E. Diffusion

4. After a rain, one sometimes sees brightly colored oil slicks on the road. These are due to:

    A. selective absorption of different λ by oil   **C.** polarization effects
    B. diffraction effects   **D.** interference effects
                                        E. birefringence

5. The total stored energy in a system undergoing simple harmonic motion (SHM) is proportional to the:

    A. (amplitude)^2 **C.** (spring constant)^2
    B. wavelength   **D.** amplitude   **E.** $\sqrt{\lambda}$

6. A 11 kg mass m is attached to a spring and allowed to hang in the Earth's gravitational field. The spring stretches 3 cm before reaching its equilibrium position. If the spring were allowed to oscillate, what would be its frequency? (Use acceleration due to gravity $g = 9.8$ m/s^2)

    A. 0.7 Hz   **B.** 1.8 Hz   **C.** 4.1 Hz   **D.** 0.6×10^{-3} Hz   **E.** 2.9 Hz

7. For an object undergoing simple harmonic motion, the:

    A. maximum potential energy is larger than the maximum kinetic energy
    B. acceleration is greatest when the displacement is greatest
    C. displacement is greatest when the speed is greatest
    D. acceleration is greatest when the speed is greatest
    E. total object energy oscillates at frequency $f = \frac{1}{2}\pi(\sqrt{k/m})$

8. A pendulum of length L is suspended from the ceiling of an elevator. When the elevator is at rest, the period of the pendulum is T. How does T change when the elevator moves upward with a constant velocity?

    A. Decreases only if the upward acceleration is less than $\frac{1}{2}g$
    B. Decreases
    C. Increases
    D. Remains the same
    E. Increases only if the upward acceleration is more than $\frac{1}{2}g$

9. A simple pendulum that has a bob of mass M has a period T. What is the effect on the period if M is doubled while all other factors remain unchanged?

    A. T/2   **B.** $T/\sqrt{2}$ **C.** 2T   **D.** $\sqrt{2}T$ **E.** T

10. Two radio antennae are located on a seacoast 10 km apart on a North-South axis. The antennas broadcast identical in-phase AM radio waves at a frequency of 4.7 MHz. 200 km offshore, a steamship travels North at 15 km/h passing East of the antennae with a radio tuned to the broadcast frequency. From the moment of the maximum reception of the radio signal on the ship, what is the time interval until the next occurrence of maximum reception? (Use the speed of radio waves equals the speed of light $c = 3 \times 10^8$ m/s and the path difference = 1 λ)

    A. 7.7 min   **B.** 6.4 min   **C.** 3.8 min   **D.** 8.9 min   **E.** 5.1 min

11. A 2.31 kg rope is stretched between supports 10.4 m apart. If one end of the rope is tweaked, how long will it take for the resulting disturbance to reach the other end? Assume that the tension in the rope is 74.4 N.

    A. 0.33 s   **B.** 0.74 s   **C.** 0.65 s   **D.** 0.57 s   **E.** 0.42 s

12. Simple pendulum A swings back and forth at twice the frequency of simple pendulum B. Which statement is correct?

    A. Pendulum A is ¼ as long as B   **C.** Pendulum A is ½ as long as B
    B. Pendulum A is twice as massive as B   **D.** Pendulum B is twice as massive as A
                                           E. Pendulum B is ¼ as long as A

13. A weight attached to the free end of an anchored spring is allowed to slide back and forth in simple harmonic motion on a frictionless table. How many times greater is the spring's restoring force at $x = 5$ cm compared to $x = 1$ cm (measured from equilibrium)?

    A. 2.5   **B.** 5   **C.** 7.5   **D.** 15   **E.** $\sqrt{2.5}$

14. A massless, ideal spring projects horizontally from a wall and is connected to a 1 kg mass. The mass is oscillating in one dimension, such that it moves 0.5 m from one end of its oscillation to the other. It undergoes 10 complete oscillations in 60 s. What is the period of the oscillation?

    A. 9 s   **B.** 3 s   **C.** 6 s   **D.** 12 s   **E.** 0.6 s

15. The total mechanical energy of a simple harmonic oscillating system is:

    A. always zero, which is why it is oscillating
    B. maximum when it reaches the maximum displacement
    C. zero when it reaches the maximum displacement
    D. zero as it passes the equilibrium point
    E. a nonzero constant

16. What is the frequency of the oscillations when a vibrating spring moves from its position of maximum elongation to its position of maximum compression in 1 s?

    A. 0.75 Hz   **B.** 0.5 Hz   **C.** 1 Hz   **D.** 2.5 Hz   **E.** 4 Hz

17. Which of the following is not a transverse wave?

    I. Radio   II. Light   III. Sound

    A. I only   **B.** II only   **C.** III only   **D.** I and II only   **E.** I and III only

18. If a wave has a speed of 362 m/s and a period of 4 ms, its wavelength is closest to:

    A. 8.6 m   **B.** 5.2 m   **C.** 0.86 m   **D.** 15 m   **E.** 1.5 m

19. Simple harmonic motion is characterized by:

    A. acceleration that is proportional to negative displacement
    B. acceleration that is proportional to velocity
    C. constant positive acceleration
    D. acceleration that is inversely proportional to negative displacement
    E. acceleration that is inversely proportional to velocity

20. If the frequency of a harmonic oscillator doubles, by what factor does the maximum value of acceleration change?

    A. $2/\pi$ **B.** $\sqrt{2}$ **C.** 2   **D.** 4   **E.** ½

21. An object that hangs from the ceiling of a stationary elevator by an ideal spring oscillates with a period T. If the elevator were to accelerate upwards with an acceleration of 2g, what is the period of oscillation of the object?

    A. T/2   **B.** T   **C.** 2T   **D.** 4T   **E.** T/4

22. Which of the following changes made to a transverse wave must result in an increase in wavelength?

    A. An increase in frequency and a decrease in speed
    B. The wavelength is only affected by a change in amplitude
    C. An increase in frequency and an increase in speed
    D. A decrease in frequency and a decrease in speed
    E. A decrease in frequency and an increase in speed

23. If a wave travels 30 m in 1 s, making 60 vibrations per second, what are its frequency and speed, respectively?

A. 30 Hz and 60 m/s

C. 30 Hz and 30 m/s

B. 60 Hz and 30 m/s

D. 60 Hz and 15 m/s

E. 15 Hz and 30 m/s

24. Transverse waves propagate at 40 m/s in a string that is subjected to a tension of 60 N. If the string is 16 m long, what is its mass?

A. 0.6 kg   **B.** 0.9 kg   **C.** 0.2 kg   **D.** 9 kg   **E.** 2 kg

25. Doubling only the amplitude of a vibrating mass-on-spring system, changes the system frequency by what factor?

A. Increases by 3

C. Increases by 5

B. Increases by 2

D. Increases by 4

E. Remains the same

26. Increasing the mass m of a mass-and-spring system causes what kind of change on the resonant frequency f of the system?

A. The f decreases

C. The f decreases only if the ratio k / m is < 1

B. There is no change in the f

D. The f increases

E. The f decreases only if the ratio k / m is > 1

27. Particles of a material that move up and down perpendicular to the direction that the wave is moving are in what type of wave?

A. Torsional

C. Longitudinal

B. Mechanical

D. Transverse

E. Surface

28. The figure shows a graph of the velocity v as a function of time t for a system undergoing simple harmonic motion. Which one of the following graphs represents the acceleration of this system as a function of time?

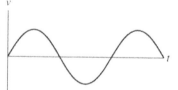

A.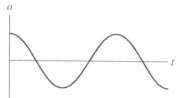

C.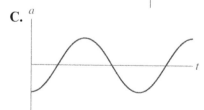

B.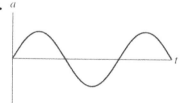

D.

E. None of these

29. When compared, a transverse wave and a longitudinal wave are found to have amplitudes of equal magnitude. Which statement is true about their speeds?

A. The waves have the same speeds
B. The transverse wave has exactly twice the speed of the longitudinal wave
C. The transverse wave has a slower speed
D. The longitudinal wave has a slower speed
E. The speeds of the two waves are unrelated to their amplitudes

30. A simple pendulum and a mass oscillating on an ideal spring both have period T in an elevator at rest. If the elevator now accelerates downward uniformly at 2 m/s², what is true about the periods of these two systems?

A. The period of the pendulum increases, but the period of the spring remains the same
B. The period of the pendulum increases and the period of the spring decreases
C. The period of the pendulum decreases, but the period of the spring remains the same
D. The periods of the pendulum and of the spring both increase
E. The periods of the pendulum and of the spring both decrease

31. The velocity of a given longitudinal sound wave in an ideal gas is $v = 340$ m/s at constant pressure and constant volume. Assuming an ideal gas, what is the wavelength for a 2,100 Hz sound wave?

A. 0.08 m   **B.** 0.16 m   **C.** 1.6 m   **D.** 7.3 m   **E.** 0.73 m

32. When the mass of a simple pendulum is quadrupled, how does the time *t* required for one complete oscillation change?

A. Decreases to ¼*t*   **C.** Increases to 4*t*
B. Decreases to ¾*t*   **D.** Remains the same   **E.** Decreases to ½*t*

33. An object undergoing simple harmonic motion has an amplitude of 2.5 m. If the maximum velocity of the object is 15 m/s, what is the object's angular frequency (ω)?

A. 0.17 rad/s   **B.** 3.6 rad/s   **C.** 37.5 rad/s   **D.** 8.8 rad/s   **E.** 6.0 rad/s

34. Unpolarized light is incident upon two polarization filters that do not have their transmission axes aligned. If 14% of the light passes through, what is the measure of the angle between the transmission axes of the filters?

A. 73°   **B.** 81°   **C.** 43°   **D.** 58°   **E.** 64°

35. A mass on a spring undergoes simple harmonic motion. Which of the statements is true when the mass is at its maximum distance from the equilibrium position?

A. KE is nonzero   **C.** Speed is zero
B. Acceleration is at a minimum   **D.** Speed is maximum
     E. Total mechanical energy = KE

36. All of the following is true of a pendulum that has swung to the top of its arc and has not yet reversed its direction, EXCEPT:

A. The PE of the pendulum is at a maximum
B. The displacement of the pendulum from its equilibrium position is at a maximum
C. The KE of the pendulum equals zero
D. The velocity of the pendulum equals zero
E. The acceleration of the pendulum equals zero

37. Unlike a transverse wave, a longitudinal wave has no:

A. wavelength
B. crests or troughs

C. amplitude
D. frequency

E. all of the above

38. The density of aluminum is 2,700 kg/m³. If transverse waves propagate at 36 m/s in a 9.2 mm diameter aluminum wire, what is the tension in the wire?

A. 43 N   B. 68 N   C. 233 N   D. 350 N   E. 72 N

39. When a wave obliquely crosses a boundary into another medium, it is:

A. always slowed down
B. reflected

C. diffracted
D. refracted

E. always sped up

40. The Doppler effect occurs when a source of sound moves:

I. toward the observer
II. away from the observer
III. with the observer

A. I only   B. II only   C. III only   D. I and II only   E. I and III only

41. A higher pitch for a sound wave means the wave has a greater:

A. frequency
B. wavelength

C. amplitude
D. period

E. acceleration

42. An object is attached to a vertical spring and bobs up and down between points A and B. Where is the object located when its kinetic energy is at a maximum?

A. One fourth of the way between A and B
B. One third of the way between A and B

C. Midway between A and B
D. At either A or B
E. At none of the above points

43. A pendulum consists of a 0.5 kg mass attached to the end of a 1 m rod of negligible mass. What is the magnitude of the torque τ about the pivot when the rod makes an angle θ of 60° with the vertical? (Use acceleration due to gravity g = 10 m/s²)

A. 2.7 N·m   B. 4.4 N·m   C. 5.2 N·m   D. 10.6 N·m   E. 12.7 N·m

44. The Doppler effect is characteristic of:

     I. light waves   II. sound waves   III. water waves

     A. I only   **B.** II only   **C.** III only   **D.** I and III only   **E.** I, II and III

45. A crane lifts a 2,500 kg cement block using a steel cable which has a mass per unit length of 0.65 kg/m. What is the speed of the transverse waves on this cable? (Use acceleration due to gravity $g = 10$ m/s^2)

     A. 196 m/s   **B.** 1,162 m/s   **C.** 322 m/s   **D.** 558 m/s   **E.** 1,420 m/s

46. A simple pendulum consists of a mass M attached to a weightless string of length L. Which statement about the frequency f is accurate for this system when it experiences small oscillations?

     A. The f is directly proportional to the period
     B. The f is independent of the mass M
     C. The f is inversely proportional to the amplitude
     D. The f is independent of the length L
     E. The f is dependent on the mass M

47. A child on a swing set swings back and forth. If the length of the supporting cables for the swing is 3.3 m, what is the period of oscillation? (Use acceleration due to gravity $g = 10$ m/s^2)

     A. 3.6 s   **B.** 5.9 s   **C.** 4.3 s   **D.** 2.7 s   **E.** 5 s

48. A massless, ideal spring projects horizontally from a wall and is connected to a 0.3 kg mass. The mass is oscillating in one dimension, such that it moves 0.4 m from one end of its oscillation to the other. It undergoes 15 complete oscillations in 60 s. How does the frequency change if the spring constant is increased by a factor of 2?

     A. Increases by 200%   **C.** Increases by 41%
     B. Decreases by 59%   **D.** Decreases by 41%   **E.** Increases by 59%

49. A ball swinging at the end of a massless string undergoes simple harmonic motion. At what point(s) is the instantaneous acceleration of the ball the greatest?

     A. A   **C.** C   **E.** B and C
     B. B   **D.** A and D

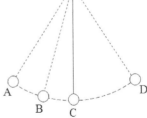

50. A simple pendulum, consisting of a 2 kg weight connected to a 10 m massless rod, is brought to an angle of 90° from the vertical, and then released. What is the speed of the weight at its lowest point? (Use acceleration due to gravity $g = 10$ m/s^2)

     A. 14 m/s   **B.** 10 m/s   **C.** 20 m/s   **D.** 25 m/s   **E.** 7 m/s

Sound

1. A 20 decibel (dB) noise is heard from a cricket 30 m away. How loud would it sound if the cricket were 3 m away?

    A. 30 dB   **B.** 40 dB   **C.** $20 \times \sqrt{2}$ dB   **D.** 80 dB   **E.** 60 dB

2. Two tuning forks are struck simultaneously and beats are heard every 500 ms. What is the frequency of the sound wave produced by one tuning fork, if the other produces a sound wave of 490 Hz frequency?

    A. 490 Hz   **B.** 498 Hz   **C.** 492 Hz   **D.** 506 Hz   **E.** 510 Hz

3. Enrico Caruso, a famous opera singer, is said to have made a crystal chandelier shatter with his voice. This is a demonstration of:

    A. ideal frequency   **C.** a standing wave
    B. resonance   **D.** sound refraction   **E.** interference

4. A taut 2 m string is fixed at both ends and plucked. What is the wavelength corresponding to the third harmonic?

    A. 2/3 m   **B.** 1 m   **C.** 4/3 m   **D.** 3 m   **E.** 4 m

5. A standing wave is oscillating at 670 Hz on a string, as shown in the figure. What is the wave speed?

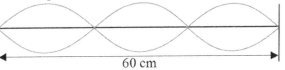

    A. 212 m/s   **B.** 178 m/s   **C.** 268 m/s   **D.** 404 m/s   **E.** 360 m/s

6. A light ray in air strikes a medium whose index of refraction is 1.5. If the angle of incidence is 60°, which of the following expressions gives the angle of refraction? (Use $n_{air} = 1$)

    A. $\sin^{-1}(1.5 \sin 60°)$ **C.** $\sin^{-1}(1.5 \sin 30°)$
    B. $\sin^{-1}(1.5 \cos 60°)$ **D.** $\sin^{-1}(0.67 \sin 30°)$ **E.** $\sin^{-1}(0.67 \sin 60°)$

7. A string, 2 m in length, is fixed at both ends and tightened until the wave speed is 92 m/s. What is the frequency of the standing wave shown?

    A. 46 Hz   **B.** 33 Hz   **C.** 240 Hz   **D.** 138 Hz   **E.** 184 Hz

8. A 0.6 m uniform bar of metal, with a diameter of 2 cm, has a mass of 2.5 kg. A 1.5 MHz longitudinal wave is propagated along the length of the bar. A wave compression traverses the length of the bar in 0.14 ms. What is the wavelength of the longitudinal wave in the metal?

A. 2.9 mm   **B.** 1.8 mm   **C.** 3.2 mm   **D.** 4.6 mm   **E.** 3.8 mm

> Questions **9-12** are based on the following:

The velocity of a wave on a wire or string is not dependent (to a close approximation) on frequency or amplitude and is given by $v^2 = T / \rho_L$. T is the tension is the wire. The linear mass density ρ_L (rho) is the mass per unit length of wire. Therefore ρ_L is the product of the mass density and the cross-sectional area (A).

A sine wave is traveling to the right with frequency 250 Hz. Wire A is composed of steel and has a circular cross-section diameter of 0.6 mm and a tension of 2,000 N. Wire B is under the same tension and is made of the same material as wire A, but has a circular cross-section diameter of 0.3 mm. Wire C has the same tension as wire A and is made of a composite material. (Use density of steel wire $\rho = 7$ g/cm³ and density of the composite material $\rho = 3$ g/cm³)

9. By how much does the tension need to be increased to increase the wave velocity on a wire by 30%?

A. 37%   **B.** 60%   **C.** 69%   **D.** 81%   **E.** 74%

10. What is the linear mass density of wire B compared to wire A?

A. √2 times   **B.** 2 times   **C.** 1/8   **D.** 1/4   **E.** 4 times

11. What must the diameter of wire C be to have the same wave velocity as wire A?

A. 0.41 mm   **B.** 0.92 mm   **C.** 0.83 mm   **D.** 3.2 mm   **E.** 0.2 mm

12. How does the cross-sectional area change if the diameter increases by a factor of 4?

A. Increases by a factor of 16   **C.** Increases by a factor of 2
B. Increases by a factor of 4   **D.** Decreases by a factor of 4
     E. Increases by a factor of √2

13. A bird, emitting sounds with a frequency of 60 kHz, is moving at a speed of 10 m/s toward a stationary observer. What is the frequency of the sound waves detected by the observer? (Use speed of sound in air $v = 340$ m/s)

A. 55 kHz   **B.** 46 kHz   **C.** 68 kHz   **D.** 76 kHz   **E.** 62 kHz

14. What is observed for a frequency heard by a stationary person when a sound source is approaching?

A. Equal to zero   **C.** Higher than the source   **E.** Requires more information
B. The same as the source   **D.** Lower than the source

15. Which of the following is a false statement?

   A. The transverse waves on a vibrating string are different from sound waves
   B. Sound travels much slower than light
   C. Sound waves are longitudinal pressure waves
   D. Sound can travel through a vacuum
   E. Perceived musical pitch is correlated with frequency

16. Which of the following is a real-life example of the Doppler effect?

   A. London police whistle, which uses two short pipes to produce a three-note sound
   B. Radio signal transmission
   C. Sound becomes quieter as the observer moves away from the source
   D. Human hearing is most acute at 2,500 Hz
   E. Changing pitch of the siren as an ambulance passes by the observer

17. Two sound waves have the same frequency and amplitudes of 0.4 Pa and 0.6 Pa, respectively. When they arrive at point X, what is the range of possible amplitudes for sound at point X?

   A. $0 - 0.4$ Pa   **B.** $0.4 - 0.6$ Pa   **C.** $0.2 - 1.0$ Pa   **D.** $0.4 - 0.8$ Pa   **E.** $0.2 - 0.6$ Pa

18. The intensity of the waves from a point source at a distance d from the source is I. What is the intensity at a distance $2d$ from the source?

   A. I/2   **B.** I/4   **C.** 4I   **D.** 2I   **E.** $I/\sqrt{2}$

19. Sound would be expected to travel most slowly in a medium that exhibited:

   A. low resistance to compression and high density
   B. high resistance to compression and low density
   C. low resistance to compression and low density
   D. high resistance to compression and high density
   E. equal resistance to compression and density

20. Which is true for a resonating pipe that is open at both ends?

   A. Displacement node at one end and a displacement antinode at the other end
   B. Displacement antinodes at each end
   C. Displacement nodes at each end
   D. Displacement node at one end and a one-fourth antinode at the other end
   E. Displacement antinode at one end and a one-fourth node at the other end

21. In a pipe of length L that is open at both ends, the lowest tone to resonate is 200 Hz. Which of the following frequencies does not resonate in this pipe?

   A. 400 Hz   **B.** 600 Hz   **C.** 1,200 Hz   **D.** 800 Hz   **E.** 500 Hz

22. In general, sound is conducted fastest through:

   A. vacuum   **B.** gases   **C.** liquids   **D.** solids   **E.** warm air

23. If an electric charge is shaken up and down:

A. electron excitation occurs   **C.** sound is emitted

B. a magnetic field is created   **D.** its charge changes   **E.** its mass decreases

24. A speaker is producing a total of 10 W of sound, and Rahul hears the music at 20 dB. His roommate turns up the power to 100 W. What level of sound does Rahul now hear?

A. 15 dB   **B.** 30 dB   **C.** 40 dB   **D.** 100 dB   **E.** 120 dB

25. If the sound from a constant sound source is radiating equally in all directions, as the distance doubles, by what amount is the intensity of the sound reduced?

A. 1/8   **B.** 1/16   **C.** $1/\sqrt{2}$ **D.** ½   **E.** ¼

26. Why does the intensity of waves from a sound source decrease with the square of the distance from the source?

A. The medium through which the waves travel absorbs the energy of the waves

B. The waves speed up as they travel away from the source

C. The waves lose energy as they travel

D. The waves spread out as they travel

E. The frequency of the waves decreases as they get farther from the source

Questions **27-30** are based on the following:

Steven is preparing a mailing tube that is 1.5 m long and 4 cm in diameter. The tube is open at one end and sealed at the other. Before he inserted his documents, the mailing tube fell to the floor and produced a note. (Use the speed of sound in air $v = 340$ m/s)

27. What is the wavelength of the fundamental?

A. 0.04 m   **B.** 6 m   **C.** 0.75 m   **D.** 1.5 m   **E.** 9 m

28. If the tube was filled with helium, in which sound travels at 960 m/s, what would be the frequency of the fundamental?

A. 160 Hz   **B.** 320 Hz   **C.** 80 Hz   **D.** 640 Hz   **E.** 590 Hz

29. What is the wavelength of the fifth harmonic?

A. 3.2 m   **B.** 0.6 m   **C.** 2.4 m   **D.** 1.5 m   **E.** 1.2 m

30. What is the frequency of the note that Steven heard?

A. 57 Hz   **B.** 85 Hz   **C.** 30 Hz   **D.** 120 Hz   **E.** 25 Hz

31. A 4 g string, 0.34 m long, is under tension. The string vibrates in the third harmonic. What is the wavelength of the standing wave in the string? (Use the speed of sound in air = 344 m/s)

    A. 0.56 m   **B.** 0.33 m   **C.** 0.23 m   **D.** 0.61 m   **E.** 0.87 m

32. Two pure tones are sounded together and a particular beat frequency is heard. What happens to the beat frequency if the frequency of one of the tones is increased?

    A. Increases   **C.** Remains the same
    B. Decreases   **D.** Either increase or decrease
                            E. Increases logarithmically

33. Consider a closed pipe of length L. What are the wavelengths of the three lowest tones produced by this pipe?

    A. $4L, 4/3L, 4/5L$ **C.** $2L, L, \frac{1}{2}L$
    B. $2L, L, 2/3L$ **D.** $4L, 2L, L$ **E.** $4L, 4/3L, L$

34. Mary hears the barely perceptible buzz of a mosquito one meter away from her ear in a quiet room. How much energy does a mosquito produce in 200 s? (Note: an almost inaudible sound has a threshold value of 9.8×10^{-12} W/m^2)

    A. 6.1×10^{-8} J   **C.** 6.4×10^{-10} J
    B. 1.3×10^{-8} J   **D.** 3.6×10^{-10} J   **E.** 2.5×10^{-8} J

35. How long does it take for a light wave to travel 1 km through water with a refractive index of 1.33? (Use the speed of light $c = 3 \times 10^8$ m/s)

    A. 4.4×10^{-6} s   **C.** 2.8×10^{-9} s
    B. 4.4×10^{-9} s   **D.** 2.8×10^{-12} s   **E.** 3.4×10^{-9} s

36. In designing a music hall, an acoustical engineer deals mainly with:

    A. beats   **C.** forced vibrations
    B. resonance   **D.** modulation   **E.** wave interference

37. Which curve in the figure represents the variation of wave speed (v) as a function of tension (T) for transverse waves on a stretched string?

    A. A
    B. B
    C. C
    D. D
    E. E

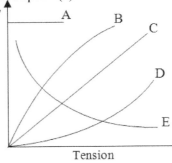

38. A string, 4 meters in length, is fixed at both ends and tightened until the wave speed is 20 m/s. What is the frequency of the standing wave shown?

    A. 13 Hz   **B.** 8.1 Hz   **C.** 5.4 Hz   **D.** 15.4 Hz   **E.** 7.8 Hz

39. Compared to the velocity of a 600 Hz sound, the velocity of a 300 Hz sound through air is:

    A. one-half as great   **C.** twice as great
    B. one-fourth as great   **D.** four times as great   **E.** the same

40. Consider a string having linear mass density of 0.40 g/m stretched to a length of 0.50 m by a tension of 75 N, vibrating at the 6th harmonic. It excites an open pipe into the second overtone. What is the length of the pipe?

    A. 0.25 m   **B.** 0.1 m   **C.** 0.20 m   **D.** 0.6 m   **E.** 0.32 m

41. A string of length L is under tension, and the speed of a wave in the string is v. What is the speed of a wave in a string of the same mass under the same tension but twice as long?

    A. $v\sqrt{2}$ **B.** $2v$ **C.** $v/2$ **D.** $v/\sqrt{2}$ **E.** $4v$

42. If a guitar string has a fundamental frequency of 500 Hz, which one of the following frequencies can set the string into resonant vibration?

    A. 450 Hz   **B.** 760 Hz   **C.** 1,500 Hz   **D.** 2,250 Hz   **E.** 1,250 Hz

43. When a light wave is passing from a medium with lower refractive index to a medium with higher refractive index, some of the incident light is refracted, while some is reflected. What is the angle of refraction?

    A. Greater than the angle of incidence and less than the angle of reflection
    B. Less than the angle of incidence and greater than the angle of reflection
    C. Greater than the angles of incidence and reflection
    D. Less than the angles of incidence and reflection
    E. Equal to the angles of incidence and reflection

44. The speed of a sound wave in air depends on:

    I. the air temperature   II. its wavelength   III. its frequency

    A. I only   **B.** II only   **C.** III only   **D.** I and II only   **E.** I and III only

45. Which of the following statements is false?

    A. The speed of a wave and the speed of the vibrating particles that constitute the wave are different entities

    B. Waves transport energy and matter from one region to another

    C. In a transverse wave, the particle motion is perpendicular to the velocity vector of the wave

    D. Not all waves are mechanical in nature

    E. A wave in which particles move back and forth in the same direction that the wave is moving is referred to as a longitudinal wave

46. A violin with string length 36 cm and string density 3.8 g/cm resonates with the first overtone of an organ pipe with one end closed. The pipe length is 3 m. What is the tension in the string so that the sound wave resonates at its fundamental frequency? (Use the speed of sound $v = 340$ m/s)

    A. 1,390 N   **B.** 1,946 N   **C.** 1,414 N   **D.** 987 N   **E.** 1,216 N

47. Suppose that a source of sound is emitting waves uniformly in all directions. If an observer moves to a point twice as far away from the source, what is the frequency of the sound?

    A. $\sqrt{2}$ as large   **C.** Unchanged

    B. Twice as large   **D.** Half as large   **E.** One-fourth as large

48. A 2.5 kg rope is stretched between supports 8 m apart. If one end of the rope is tweaked, how long will it take for the resulting disturbance to reach the other end? Assume that the tension in the rope is 40 N.

    A. 0.71 s   **B.** 0.62 s   **C.** 0.58 s   **D.** 0.47 s   **E.** 0.84 s

49. An office machine is making a rattling sound with an intensity of 10^{-5} W/m² when perceived by an office worker that is sitting 3 m away. What is the sound level in decibels for the sound of the machine? (Use threshold of hearing $I_0 = 10^{-12}$ W/m²)

    A. 10 dB   **B.** 35 dB   **C.** 70 dB   **D.** 95 dB   **E.** 45 dB

50. A taut 1 m string is plucked. Point B is midway between both ends and a finger is placed on point B such that a waveform exists with a node at B. What is the lowest frequency that can be heard? (Use the speed of waves on the string $v = 3.8 \times 10^4$ m/s)

    A. 4.8×10^5 Hz   **C.** 9.7×10^3 Hz

    B. 2.3×10^4 Hz   **D.** 7.4×10^3 Hz   **E.** 3.8×10^4 Hz

Fluids and Solids

Questions **1-3** are based on the following:

A container has a vertical tube with an inner radius of 20 mm that is connected to the container at its side. An unknown liquid reaches level A in the container and level B in the tube. Level A is 5 cm higher than level B. The liquid supports a 20 cm high column of oil between levels B and C that has a density of 850 kg/m³. (Use acceleration due to gravity $g = 9.8$ m/s²)

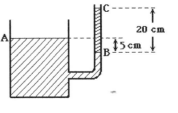

1. What is the density of the unknown liquid?

   A. 2,800 kg/m³   **B.** 2,100 kg/m³   **C.** 3,400 kg/m³   **D.** 3,850 kg/m³   **E.** 1,800 kg/m³

2. The gauge pressure at level B is closest to:

   A. 1,250 Pa   **B.** 1,830 Pa   **C.** 340 Pa   **D.** 1,666 Pa   **E.** 920 Pa

3. What is the mass of the oil?

   A. 210 g   **B.** 453 g   **C.** 620 g   **D.** 847 g   **E.** 344 g

4. A cubical block of stone is lowered at a steady rate into the ocean by a crane, always keeping the top and bottom faces horizontal. Which of the following graphs best describes the gauge pressure P on the bottom of this block as a function of time t if the block just enters the water at time $t = 0$ s?

A.    **C.**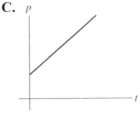

B. 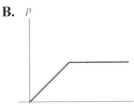   **D.**    **E.**

5. Consider a very small hole in the bottom of a tank that is 19 cm in diameter and is filled with water to a height of 80 cm. What is the speed at which the water exits the tank through the hole? (Use acceleration due to gravity $g = 9.8$ m/s²)

   A. 8.6 m/s   **B.** 12 m/s   **C.** 14.8 m/s   **D.** 8.4 m/s   **E.** 4 m/s

6. An ideal gas at standard temperature and pressure is compressed until its volume is half the initial volume, and then it is allowed to expand until its pressure is half the initial pressure. This is achieved while holding the temperature constant. If the initial internal energy of the gas is U, the final internal energy of the gas is:

    A. U/2   **B.** U/3   **C.** U   **D.** 2U   **E.** U/4

7. When 9.5 kg mass is suspended from a 4.5 m long wire with 1.2 mm diameter, the wire stretches by 4 mm. What is the effective spring constant for the wire? (Use acceleration due to gravity $g = 9.8$ m/s^2)

    A. 5.6×10^4 N/m   **C.** 3.7×10^5 N/m
    B. 2.3×10^4 N/m   **D.** 7.2×10^3 N/m   **E.** 9.2×10^4 N/m

8. An object is sinking in a fluid. What is the weight of the fluid displaced by the sinking object when the object is completely submerged?

    A. Dependent on the viscosity of the liquid   **C.** Greater than the weight of the object
    B. Equal to the weight of the object   **D.** Zero
        E. Less than the weight of the object

9. A submarine in neutral buoyancy is 100 m below the surface of the water. For the submarine to surface, how much air pressure must be supplied to remove water from the ballast tanks? (Use acceleration due to gravity $g = 9.8$ m/s^2 and density of water $\rho = 10^3$ kg/m^3)

    A. 9.8×10^5 N/m^2 **C.** 7.6×10^5 N/m^2
    B. 4.7×10^5 N/m^2 **D.** 5.6×10^5 N/m^2
        E. Requires the cross-sectional area of the tank

10. When atmospheric pressure increases, what happens to the absolute pressure at the bottom of a pool?

    A. It does not change   **C.** It increases by the same amount
    B. It increases by double the amount   **D.** It increases by half the amount
        E. It depends on the depth of the pool

11. When soup gets cold, it often tastes greasy because oil spreads out on the surface of the soup, instead of staying in small globules. This is explained in terms of the:

    A. increase in the surface tension of water with decreasing temperature
    B. Archimedes' principle
    C. decrease in the surface tension of water with decreasing temperature
    D. Joule-Thomson effect
    E. Braggs' law

12. For a wire of diameter d and fixed length L, the weight that causes the wire to stretch a given distance is:

    A. directly proportional to d^2 of the wire

    B. inversely proportional to d^2 of the wire

    C. proportional to d of the wire

    D. independent of d of the wire

    E. independent of L of the wire

13. An object whose weight is 60 N is floating at the surface of a container of water. How much of the object's volume is submerged? (Use acceleration due to gravity $g = 10$ m/s^2)

    A. 0.006 m^3 **B.** 0.06 m^3 **C.** 0.6 m^3 **D.** 6%   **E.** 60%

14. What is the volume flow rate of a fluid, if it flows at 2.5 m/s through a pipe of diameter 3 cm?

    A. 0.9 m^3/s

    B. 4.7 m^3/s

    C. 5.7×10^{-4} m^3/s

    D. 5.7×10^{-3} m^3/s

    E. 1.8×10^{-3} m^3/s

15. What is the specific gravity of a cork that floats with three quarters of its volume in and one quarter of its volume out of the water?

    A. 0.25   **B.** 0.5   **C.** 0.75   **D.** 2   **E.** 1

16. A particular grade of motor oil, which has a viscosity of 0.3 N·s/m^2, is flowing through a 1 m long tube with a radius of 3.2 mm. What is the average speed of the oil, if the drop in pressure over the length of the tube is 225 kPa?

    A. 0.82 m/s   **B.** 0.96 m/s   **C.** 1.2 m/s   **D.** 1.4 m/s   **E.** 1.7 m/s

17. The kinetic theory of a monatomic gas suggests the average kinetic energy per molecule is:

    A. $1/3\, k_B T$ **B.** $2\, k_B T$ **C.** $3/2\, k_B T$ **D.** $2/3\, k_B T$ **E.** $\sqrt{2} k_B T$

18. An object is weighed in air, and it is also weighed while totally submerged in water. If it weighs 150 N less when submerged, find the volume of the object. (Use acceleration due to gravity $g = 10$ m/s^2 and density of water $\rho = 1{,}000$ kg/m^3)

    A. 0.0015 m^3 **B.** 0.015 m^3 **C.** 0.15 m^3 **D.** 1 m^3 **E.** 1.5 m^3

19. When a container of water is placed on a laboratory scale, the scale reads 140 g. Now a 30 g piece of copper is suspended from a thread and lowered into the water without making contact with the bottom of the container. What does the scale read? (Use acceleration due to gravity $g = 9.8$ m/s^2, density of water $\rho = 1$ g/cm^3 and density of copper $\rho = 8.9$ g/cm^3)

    A. 122 g   **B.** 168 g   **C.** 143 g   **D.** 110 g   **E.** 94 g

20. An ideal, incompressible fluid flows through a 6 cm diameter pipe at 1 m/s. There is a 3 cm decrease in diameter within the pipe. What is the speed of the fluid in this constriction?

    A. 3 m/s   **B.** 1.5 m/s   **C.** 8 m/s   **D.** 4 m/s   **E.** 2.5 m/s

21. Two blocks are submerged in a fluid. Block A has dimensions 2 cm high × 3 cm wide × 4 cm long and Block B is 2 cm × 3 cm × 8 cm. Both blocks are submerged with their large faces pointing up and down (i.e., the blocks are horizontal), and they are submerged to the same depth. Compared to the fluid pressure on the bottom of Block A, the bottom of Block B experiences:

    A. pressure that depends on density of the objects
    B. greater fluid pressure
    C. exactly double the fluid pressure
    D. less fluid pressure
    E. equal fluid pressure

22. A piece of thread of diameter d is in the shape of a rectangle (length l, width w) and is lying on the surface of water in a beaker. If A is the surface tension of the water, what is the maximum weight that the thread can have without sinking?

    A. $Ad(l + w) / \pi$ **C.** $4A(l + w)$
    B. $A(l + w)$ **D.** $A(l + w) / 2$ **E.** $Ad(l + w)$

23. What is the difference between the pressure inside and outside a tire called?

    A. Absolute pressure   **C.** Atmospheric pressure
    B. Fluid pressure   **D.** Gauge pressure   **E.** N/m^2

24. Which of the following is NOT a unit of pressure?

    A. atm   **B.** psi   **C.** inches of mercury   **D.** Pascal   **E.** $N \cdot m^2$

25. Which of the following is a dimensionless number?

    I. Reynolds number   II. specific gravity   III. sheer stress

    A. I only   **B.** II only   **C.** III only   **D.** I and II only   **E.** I and III only

26. Water flows out of a large reservoir through a 5 cm diameter pipe. The pipe connects to a 3 cm diameter pipe that is open to the atmosphere, as shown. What is the speed of the water in the 5 cm pipe? Treat the water as an ideal incompressible fluid. (Use acceleration due to gravity $g = 9.8$ m/s^2)

    A. 2.6 m/s   **C.** 4.8 m/s
    B. 3.2 m/s   **D.** 8.9 m/s   **E.** 6.7 m/s

4.0 m

27. If the pressure acting on an ideal gas at constant temperature is tripled, what is the resulting volume of the ideal gas?

A. Increased by a factor of two   **C.** Reduced to one-half
B. Remains the same   **D.** Increased by a factor of three
                                  E. Reduced to one-third

28. A circular plate with an area of 1 m^2 covers a drain-hole at the bottom of a tank of water that is 1 m deep. Approximately how much force is required to lift the cover if it weighs 1,500 N? (Use acceleration due to gravity $g = 10$ m/s^2)

A. 4,250 N   **B.** 9,550 N   **C.** 16,000 N   **D.** 11,500 N   **E.** 14,000 N

29. A bowling ball that weighs 80 N is dropped into a swimming pool filled with water. If the buoyant force on the bowling ball is 20 N when the ball is 1 m below the surface (and sinking), what is the normal force exerted by the bottom of the pool on the ball when it comes to rest there, 4 m below the surface?

A. 0 N   **B.** 60 N   **C.** 50 N   **D.** 70 N   **E.** 40 N

30. A block of an unknown material is floating in a fluid, half-submerged. If the specific gravity of the fluid is 1.6, what is the block's density? (Use specific gravity = $\rho_{fluid} / \rho_{water}$ and density of water $\rho = 1,000$ kg/m^3)

A. 350 kg/m^3 **C.** 900 kg/m^3
B. 800 kg/m^3 **D.** 1,250 kg/m^3 **E.** 1,600 kg/m^3

31. Three equal mass Styrofoam balls, of radii R, 2R and 3R, are released simultaneously from a tall tower. Which reaches the ground last?

A. The smallest Styrofoam ball
B. The middle size Styrofoam ball
C. The largest Styrofoam ball
D. All three reach the ground simultaneously
E. The result will depend on the atmospheric pressure

32. In a closed container of fluid, object A is submerged at 6 m from the bottom and object B is submerged at 12 m from the bottom. Compared to object A, object B experiences:

A. less fluid pressure   **C.** equal fluid pressure   **E.** one fifth the fluid pressure
B. double the fluid pressure   **D.** triple the fluid pressure

33. Ideal, incompressible water flows at 14 m/s in a horizontal pipe with a pressure of 3.5×10^4 Pa. If the pipe widens to twice its original radius, what is the pressure in the wider section? (Use density of water $\rho = 1,000$ kg/m^3)

A. 7.6×10^4 Pa   **C.** 2×10^5 Pa
B. 12.7×10^4 Pa   **D.** 11.1×10^3 Pa   **E.** 6.3×10^4 Pa

34. Two kilometers above the surface of the Earth, the atmospheric pressure is:

A. unrelated to the atmospheric pressure at the surface
B. twice the atmospheric pressure at the surface
C. triple the atmospheric pressure at the surface
D. less than the atmospheric pressure at the surface
E. requires more information

35. A 80 kg man would weigh 784 N if there were no atmosphere. By how much does the buoyancy due to air reduce the man's weight? (Use density of the man = 1 g/cm^3, density of the air = 1.2×10^{-3} g/cm^3, m = 80 kg and acceleration due to gravity g = 9.8 m/s^2)

A. 0.58 N   B. 0.32 N   C. 0.94 N   D. 2.8 N   E. 1.2 N

36. Diffusion is described by which law?

A. Dulong's   C. Kepler's
B. Faraday's   D. Graham's   E. Archimedes'

37. As a metal rod is stretched, which condition is reached first?

A. Elastic limit   C. Breaking point
B. Proportional limit   D. Fracture point   E. Elastic modulus

38. A pump uses a piston 12 cm in diameter that moves 3 cm/s. What is the fluid velocity in a tube that is 2 mm in diameter?

A. 218 cm/s   B. 88 cm/s   C. 136 cm/s   D. 108 m/s   E. 52 m/s

39. What is its specific gravity of an object floating with one tenth of its volume out of the water?

A. 0.3   B. 0.9   C. 1.3   D. 2.1   E. 2.9

40. If each of the factors listed below was changed by 15%, which would have the greatest effect on the flow rate?

A. Fluid density   C. Length of the pipe
B. Pressure difference   D. Fluid viscosity   E. Radius of the pipe

41. A 680 g steel hammer (m_h) is tied to a string that is hung from a force meter. A 5 kg container of water (m_w) sits on a scale. The hammer is lowered completely into the water, but above the bottom. What does the force meter read? (Use density of steel ρ = 7.9 g/cm^3, density of water ρ = 1 g/cm^3 and acceleration due to gravity g = 10 m/s^2)

A. 5.9 N   C. 10.7 N
B. 8.4 N   D. 5.2 N   E. 11.2 N

42. Two horizontal pipes (A and B) are the same length, but pipe B has twice the diameter of pipe A. Water undergoes viscous flow in both pipes, subject to the same pressure difference across the lengths of the pipes. If the flow rate in pipe A is Q, what is the flow rate in pipe B?

   A. 2Q   **B.** 4Q   **C.** 8Q   **D.** 16Q   **E.** $\sqrt{2}$Q

43. A submarine rests on the bottom of the sea. What is the normal force exerted upon the submarine by the sea floor equal to?

   A. weight of the submarine
   B. weight of the submarine minus the weight of the displaced water
   C. buoyant force minus the atmospheric pressure acting on the submarine
   D. weight of the submarine plus the weight of the displaced water
   E. buoyant force plus the atmospheric pressure acting on the submarine

44. Consider a brick that is totally immersed in water, with the long edge of the brick vertical. Which statement describes the pressure on the brick?

   A. Greatest on the sides of the brick   **C.** Smallest on the sides with largest area
   B. Greatest on the top of the brick   **D.** Same on all surfaces of the brick
                                         E. Greatest on the bottom of the brick

45. Water is flowing in a drainage channel of a rectangular cross section. The width of the channel is 14 m, the depth of water is 7 m, and the speed of the flow is 3 m/s. What is the mass flow rate of the water? (Use density of water $\rho = 1{,}000$ kg/m^3)

   A. 2.9×10^5 kg/s   **C.** 6.2×10^5 kg/s
   B. 4.8×10^4 kg/s   **D.** 9.3×10^4 kg/s   **E.** 4.3×10^2 kg/s

46. What is the magnitude of the buoyant force if a 3 kg object floats motionlessly in a fluid of specific gravity 0.8? (Use acceleration due to gravity $g = 10$ m/s^2)

   A. 15 N   **B.** 7.5 N   **C.** 30 N   **D.** 45 N   **E.** 0 N

47. What is the pressure 6 m below the surface of the ocean? (Use density of water $\rho = 10^3$ kg/m^3, atmospheric pressure $P_{atm} = 1.01 \times 10^5$ Pa and acceleration due to gravity $g = 10$ m/s^2)

   A. 1.6×10^5 Pa   **C.** 2.7×10^4 Pa
   B. 0.8×10^5 Pa   **D.** 3.3×10^4 Pa   **E.** 4.8×10^4 Pa

48. What is the wall thickness of a hollow steel ball of diameter 3 m that barely floats in water? (Use density of steel $\rho_{steel} = 7.87$ g/cm^3 and density of water $\rho_{water} = 10^3$ kg/m^3)

   A. 3 cm   **B.** 18 cm   **C.** 7 cm   **D.** 26 cm   **E.** 34 cm

49. Which of the following would be expected to have the smallest bulk modulus?

A. Solid plutonium   **C.** Solid lead

B. Liquid water   **D.** Liquid mercury   **E.** Helium vapor

50. When an 8 kg object is suspended from a steel wire that is 2.7 m long and 0.8 mm in diameter, by how much does the wire stretch? (Use acceleration due to gravity $g = 9.8$ m/s^2 and Young's modulus $= 20 \times 10^{10}$ N/m^2)

A. 2.8 mm   **B.** 3.2 mm   **C.** 0.8 mm   **D.** 2.1 mm   **E.** 1.1 mm

Electrostatics and Electromagnetism

1. How many excess electrons are present for an object that has a charge of -1 Coulomb? (Use Coulomb's constant $k = 9 \times 10^9$ N·m^2/C^2 and charge of an electron $e = -1.6 \times 10^{-19}$ C)

    A. 3.1×10^{19} electrons   **C.** 6.3×10^{18} electrons

    B. 6.3×10^{19} electrons   **D.** 1.6×10^{19} electrons   **E.** 6.5×10^{17} electrons

2. A flat disk 1 m in diameter is oriented so that the area vector of the disk makes an angle of $\pi/6$ radians with a uniform electric field. What is the electric flux through the surface if the field strength is 740 N/C?

    A. 196π N·m^2/C   **C.** 644π N·m^2/C

    B. $250/\pi$ N·m^2/C   **D.** 160π N·m^2/C   **E.** $10/\pi$ N·m^2/C

3. A positive charge $Q = 1.3 \times 10^{-9}$ C is located along the x-axis at $x = -10^{-3}$ m, and a negative charge of the same magnitude is located at the origin. What is the magnitude and direction of the electric field at the point along the x-axis where $x = 10^{-3}$ m? (Use Coulomb's constant $k = 9 \times 10^9$ N·m^2/C^2 and to the right as the positive direction)

    A. 8.8×10^6 N/C to the left   **C.** 5.5×10^7 N/C to the right

    B. 3.25×10^7 N/C to the right   **D.** 2.75×10^6 N/C to the right   **E.** 8.5×10^7 N/C to the left

4. Two charges $Q_1 = 2.4 \times 10^{-10}$ C and $Q_2 = 9.2 \times 10^{-10}$ C are near each other, and charge Q_1 exerts a force F_1 on Q_2. How does F_1 change if the distance between Q_1 and Q_2 is increased by a factor of 4?

    A. Decreases by a factor of 4   **C.** Decreases by a factor of 16

    B. Increases by a factor of 16   **D.** Increases by a factor of 4   **E.** Remains the same

5. A proton is located at ($x = 1$ nm, $y = 0$ nm) and an electron is located at ($x = 0$ nm, $y = 4$ nm). Find the attractive Coulomb force between them. (Use Coulomb's constant $k = 9 \times 10^9$ N·m^2/C^2 and the charge of an electron $e = -1.6 \times 10^{-19}$ C)

    A. 5.3×10^8 N   **C.** 9.3×10^4 N

    B. 1.9×10^{-15} N   **D.** 2.6×10^{-18} N   **E.** 1.4×10^{-11} N

6. Which form of electromagnetic radiation has photons with the highest energy?

    A. Gamma rays   **C.** Microwaves

    B. Visible light   **D.** Ultraviolet radiation   **E.** Infrared radiation

7. A 54,000 kg asteroid carrying a negative charge of 15 μC is 180 m from another 51,000 kg asteroid carrying a negative charge of 11 μC. What is the net force the asteroids exert upon each other? (Use gravitational constant $G = 6.673 \times 10^{-11}$ N·m^2/kg^2 and Coulomb's constant $k = 9 \times 10^9$ N·m^2/C^2)

    A. 400,000 N   **B.** 5,700 N   **C.** -4.0×10^{-5} N   **D.** 4.0×10^{-5} N   **E.** 5.7×10^{-5} N

8. Two small beads are 30 cm apart with no other charges or fields present. Bead A has 20 µC of charge and bead B has 5 µC. Which of the following statements is true about the electric forces on these beads?

A. The force on A is 120 times the force on B
B. The force on A is exactly equal to the force on B
C. The force on B is 4 times the force on A
D. The force on A is 20 times the force on B
E. The force on B is 120 times the force on A

Questions **9-10** are based on the following:

Two parallel metal plates separated by 0.01 m are charged to create a uniform electric field of 3.5×10^4 N/C between them, which points down. A small, stationary 0.008 kg plastic ball m is located between the plates and has a small charge Q on it. The only forces acting on it are the force of gravity and of the electric field. (Use Coulomb's constant $k = 9 \times 10^9$ N·m^2/C^2, charge of an electron $= -1.6 \times 10^{-19}$ C, charge of a proton $= 1.6 \times 10^{-19}$ C, mass of a proton $= 1.67 \times 10^{-27}$ kg, mass of an electron $= 9.11 \times 10^{-31}$ kg and acceleration due to gravity $g = 9.8$ m/s^2)

9. What is the charge on the ball?

A. –250 C   B. 250 C   C. 3.8×10^{-6} C   D. -2.2×10^{-6} C   E. 2.5×10^{-3} C

10. How would the acceleration of an electron between the plates compare to the acceleration of a proton between the plates?

A. One thousand eight hundred thirty times as large, and in the opposite direction
B. The square root times as large, and in the opposite direction
C. Twice as large, and in the opposite direction
D. The same magnitude, but in the opposite direction
E. One hundred times as large, and in the opposite direction

11. A positive charge $Q = 2.3 \times 10^{-11}$ C is 10^{-2} m away from a negative charge of equal magnitude. Point P is located equidistant between them. What is the magnitude of the electric field at point P? (Use Coulomb's constant $k = 9 \times 10^9$ N·m^2/C^2)

A. 9.0×10^3 N/C   C. 3.0×10^4 N/C
B. 4.5×10^3 N/C   D. 1.7×10^4 N/C   E. 6.6×10^5 N/C

12. A point charge $Q = -10$ µC. What is the number of excess electrons on charge Q? (Use charge of an electron $e = -1.6 \times 10^{-19}$ C)

A. 4.5×10^{13} electrons   C. 9.0×10^{13} electrons
B. 1.6×10^{13} electrons   D. 8.5×10^{13} electrons   E. 6.3×10^{13} electrons

13. An electron and a proton are separated by a distance of 3 m. What happens to the magnitude of the force on the proton if the electron is moved 1.5 m closer to the proton?

A. It increases to twice its original value

B. It decreases to one-fourth its original value

C. It increases to four times its original value

D. It decreases to one-half its original value

E. It remains the same

14. How will the magnitude of the electrostatic force between two objects be affected, if the distance between them and both of their charges are doubled?

A. It will increase by a factor of 4

B. It will increase by a factor of 2

C. It will decrease by a factor of 2

D. It will increase by a factor of $\sqrt{2}$

E. It will be unchanged

15. Which statement is true for an H nucleus, which has a charge $+e$ that is situated to the left of a C nucleus, which has a charge $+6e$?

A. The electrical force experienced by the H nucleus is to the right, and the magnitude is equal to the force exerted on the C nucleus

B. The electrical force experienced by the H nucleus is to the right, and the magnitude is less than the force exerted on the C nucleus

C. The electrical force experienced by the H nucleus is to the left, and the magnitude is greater than the force exerted on the C nucleus

D. The electrical force experienced by the H nucleus is to the left, and the magnitude is equal to the force exerted on the C nucleus

E. The electrical force experienced by the H nucleus is to the right, and the magnitude is greater than the force exerted on the C nucleus

16. Two oppositely charged particles are slowly separated from each other. What happens to the force as the particles are slowly moved apart?

A. attractive and decreasing

B. repulsive and decreasing

C. attractive and increasing

D. repulsive and increasing

E. none of the above

17. An object with a 6 μC charge is accelerating at 0.006 m/s^2 due to an electric field. If the object has a mass of 2 μg, what is the magnitude of the electric field?

A. 0.002 N/C   B. –0.005 N/C   C. 2 N/C   D. –2 N/C   E. –0.07 N/C

18. If the number of turns on the secondary coil of a transformer are less than those on the primary, the result is a:

A. 240 V transformer

B. 110 V transformer

C. step-up transformer

D. step-down transformer

E. impedance transformer

19. Two charges $Q_1 = 3 \times 10^{-8}$ C and $Q_2 = 9 \times 10^{-8}$ C are near each other, and charge Q_1 exerts a force F_1 on Q_2. What is F_2, the force that charge Q_2 exerts on charge Q_1?

A. $F_1 / 3$ B. F_1 C. $3F_1$ D. $2F_1$ E. $F_1 / 2$

20. Two electrons are passing 30 mm apart. What is the electric repulsive force that they exert on each other? (Use Coulomb's constant $k = 9 \times 10^9$ N·m^2/C^2 and charge of an electron $= -1.6 \times 10^{-19}$ C)

    A. 1.3×10^{-25} N   **B.** 3.4×10^{-27} N   **C.** 1.3×10^{27} N   **D.** 3.4×10^{10} N   **E.** 2.56×10^{-25} N

21. A light bulb is connected in a circuit and has a wire leading to it in a loop. What happens when a strong magnet is quickly passed through the loop?

    A. The brightness of the light bulb dims or gets brighter due to an induced emf produced by the magnet
    B. The light bulb's brightness remains the same although current decreases
    C. The light bulb gets brighter because more energy is being added to the system by the magnet inside the coil
    D. The light bulb gets brighter because there is an induced emf that drives more current through the light bulb
    E. This does not affect the light bulb's brightness because the coil does not shift the magnitude of the current through the light bulb

22. Suppose a van de Graaff generator builds a negative static charge, and a grounded conductor is placed near enough to it so that a 8 μC of negative charge arcs to the conductor. What is the number of electrons that are transferred? (Use charge of an electron $e = -1.6 \times 10^{-19}$ C)

    A. 1.8×10^{14} electrons   **C.** 5×10^{13} electrons
    B. 48 electrons   **D.** 74 electrons   **E.** 5×10^{20} electrons

23. Which statement must be true if two objects are electrically attracted to each other?

    A. One of the objects could be electrically neutral
    B. One object must be negatively charged and the other must be positively charged
    C. At least one of the objects must be positively charged
    D. At least one of the objects must be negatively charged
    E. None of the above statements are true

24. A proton is traveling to the right and encounters a region S which contains an electric field or a magnetic field or both. The proton is observed to bend up the page. Which of the statements is true regarding region S?

        I. There is a magnetic field pointing into the page
        II. There is a magnetic field pointing out of the page
        III. There is an electric field pointing up the page
        IV. There is an electric field pointing down the page.

    A. I only   **B.** II only   **C.** I and III   **D.** II and IV   **E.** II and III

25. A loop of wire is rotated about a diameter (which is perpendicular to a given magnetic field). In one revolution, the induced current in the loop reverses direction how many times?

    A. 2   **B.** 1   **C.** 0   **D.** 4   **E.** 3

26. Two charges ($Q_1 = 2.3 \times 10^{-8}$ C and $Q_2 = 2.5 \times 10^{-9}$ C) are a distance 0.1 m apart. How much energy is required to bring them to a distance 0.01 m apart? (Use Coulomb's constant k = 9×10^9 N·m^2/C^2)

    A. 2.2×10^{-4} J   **C.** 1.7×10^{-5} J

    B. 8.9×10^{-5} J   **D.** 4.7×10^{-5} J   **E.** 6.2×10^{-5} J

27. A solid aluminum cube rests on a wooden table in a region where a uniform external electric field is directed straight upward. What can be concluded regarding the charge on the top surface of the cube?

    A. The top surface is neutral
    B. The top surface is charged negatively
    C. The top surface fluctuates between being charged neutral and positively
    D. The top surface's charge cannot be determined without further information
    E. The top surface is charged positively

28. A point charge of $+Q$ is placed at the center of an equilateral triangle, as shown. When a second charge of $+Q$ is placed at one of the triangle's vertices, an electrostatic force of 5 N acts on it. What is the magnitude of the force that acts on the center charge when a third charge of $+Q$ is placed at one of the other vertices?

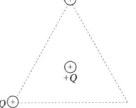

    A. 0 N   **B.** 4 N   **C.** 5 N   **D.** 8 N   **E.** 12 N

29. In the figure below, the charge in the middle is fixed and $Q = -7.5$ nC. For what fixed, positive charge q_1 will non-stationary, negative charge q_2 be in static equilibrium?

    A. 53 nC   **C.** 15 nC

    B. 7.5 nC   **D.** 30 nC   **E.** 12.8 nC

30. Which form of electromagnetic radiation has the highest frequency?

    A. Gamma radiation   **C.** Visible light

    B. Ultraviolet radiation   **D.** Radio waves   **E.** Infrared radiation

31. All of the following affect the electrostatic field strength at a point at a distance from a source charge, EXCEPT:

    A. the sign of the source charge
    B. the distance from the source charge
    C. the magnitude of the source charge
    D. the nature of the medium surrounding the source charge
    E. the presence of nearby conducting objects

32. A charged particle is observed traveling in a circular path in a uniform magnetic field. If the particle had been traveling twice as fast, the radius of the circular path would be:

A. three times the original radius
B. twice the original radius

C. one-half of the original radius
D. four times the original radius
E. one-third of the original radius

33. Two charges separated by 1 m exert a 1 N force on each other. If the magnitude of each charge is doubled, the force on each charge is:

A. 1 N   B. 2 N   C. 4 N   D. 6 N   E. 10 N

34. In a water solution of NaCl, the NaCl dissociates into ions surrounded by water molecules. Consider a water molecule near a Na^+ ion. What tends to be the orientation of the water molecule?

A. The hydrogen atoms are nearer the Na^+ ion because of their positive charge
B. The hydrogen atoms are nearer the Na^+ ion because of their negative charge
C. The oxygen atom is nearer the Na^+ ion because of the oxygen's positive charge
D. The oxygen atom is nearer the Na^+ ion because of the oxygen's negative charge
E. The hydrogen and oxygen atom center themselves on either side of the Na^+ ion because an atom itself has no charge

35. A metal sphere is insulated electrically and is given a charge. If 30 electrons are added to the sphere in giving a charge, how many Coulombs are added to the sphere? (Use Coulomb's constant $k = 9 \times 10^9$ N·m^2/C^2 and charge of an electron $e = -1.6 \times 10^{-19}$ C)

A. -2.4 C   B. -30 C   C. -4.8×10^{-18} C   D. -4.8×10^{-16} C   E. -13 C

36. What happens to the cyclotron frequency of a charged particle if its speed doubles?

A. It is ¼ as large
B. It is ½ as large

C. It doubles
D. It is $\sqrt{2}$ times as large   E. It remains the same

37. A positive test charge q is released near a positive fixed charge Q. As q moves away from Q, it experiences:

A. increasing acceleration
B. decreasing acceleration

C. constant velocity
D. decreasing velocity
E. constant momentum

38. If a value has SI units kg m^2/s^2/C, this value can be:

A. electric potential difference
B. resistance

C. electric field strength
D. Newton's forces
E. electric potential energy

39. Two uncharged metal spheres, A and B, are mounted on insulating support rods. A third metal sphere, C, carrying a positive charge, is then placed near B. A copper wire is momentarily connected between A and B, and then removed. Finally, sphere C is removed. In this final state:

    A. spheres A and B both carry equal positive charges
    B. sphere A carries a negative charge and B carries a positive charge
    C. sphere A carries a positive charge and B carries a negative charge
    D. spheres A and B both carry positive charges, but B's charge is greater
    E. sphere A remains uncharged and B carries a positive charge

40. In the figure, $Q = 5.1$ nC. What is the magnitude of the electrical force on the charge Q? (Use Coulomb's constant $k = 9 \times 10^9$ N·m²/C²)

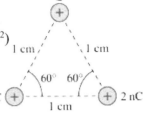

    A. 4.2×10^{-3} N
    B. 0.4×10^{-3} N
    C. 1.6×10^{-3} N
    D. 3.2×10^{-3} N
    E. 7.1×10^{-3} N

41. Two charges $Q_1 = 1.7 \times 10^{-10}$ C and $Q_2 = 6.8 \times 10^{-10}$ C are near each other. How would F change if the charges were both doubled, but the distance between them remained the same?

    A. F increases by a factor of 2
    B. F increases by a factor of 4
    C. F decreases by a factor of $\sqrt{2}$
    D. F decreases by a factor of 4
    E. F increases by a factor of $\sqrt{2}$

42. Two like charges of the same magnitude are 10 mm apart. If the force of repulsion they exert upon each other is 4 N, what is the magnitude of each charge? (Use Coulomb's constant $k = 9 \times 10^9$ N·m²/C²)

    A. 6×10^{-5} C   **B.** 6×10^5 C   **C.** 2×10^{-7} C   **D.** 1.5×10^{-7} C   **E.** 6×10^{-7} C

43. A circular loop of wire is rotated about an axis whose direction at constant angular speed can be varied. In a region where a uniform magnetic field points straight down, what orientation of the axis of the rotation guarantees that the emf will be zero (regardless of how the axis is aligned to the loop)?

    A. It must be vertical
    B. It must make an angle of 45° to the direction South
    C. It could have any horizontal orientation
    D. It must make an angle of 45° to the vertical
    E. It must make an angle of 90° to the direction South

44. Two identical small charged spheres are a certain distance apart, and each initially experiences an electrostatic force of magnitude F due to the other. With time, charge gradually diminishes on both spheres. What is the magnitude of the electrostatic force when each of the spheres has lost half its initial charge?

    A. $1/16$ F **B.** $1/8$ F **C.** $1/4$ F **D.** 2 F **E.** F

45. A proton, moving in a uniform magnetic field, moves in a circle perpendicular to the field lines and takes time T for each circle. If the proton's speed tripled, what would now be its time to go around each circle?

   A. T/3   **B.** T   **C.** 6T   **D.** 3T   **E.** T/6

46. As measurements of the electrostatic field strength are taken at points that progressively approach a negatively-charged particle, the field vectors will point:

   A. away from the particle and have constant magnitude
   B. away from the particle and have progressively decreasing magnitude
   C. towards the particle and have progressively increasing magnitude
   D. towards the particle and have progressively decreasing magnitude
   E. towards the particle and have constant magnitude

47. Every proton in the universe is surrounded by its own:

      I. electric field   II. gravitational field   III. magnetic field

   A. I only   **B.** II only   **C.** III only   **D.** I and III only   **E.** I, II and III

48. A charge $Q = 3.1 \times 10^{-5}$ C is fixed in space while another charge $q = -10^{-6}$ C is 6 m away. Charge q is slowly moved 4 m in a straight line directly toward the charge Q. How much work is required to move charge q? (Use Coulomb's constant $k = 9 \times 10^9$ N·m^2/C^2)

   A. –0.09 J   **B.** –0.03 J   **C.** 0.16 J   **D.** 0.08 J   **E.** 0.8 J

49. A point charge $Q = -600$ nC. What is the number of excess electrons in charge Q? (Use the charge of an electron $e = -1.6 \times 10^{-19}$ C)

   A. 5.6×10^{12} electrons   **C.** 2.8×10^{11} electrons
   B. 2.1×10^{10} electrons   **D.** 3.8×10^{12} electrons   **E.** 4.3×10^{8} electrons

50. In electricity, what quantity is analogous to acceleration of gravity, g (i.e. a force per unit mass)?

   A. Electric charge   **C.** Electric field
   B. Electric current   **D.** Electromagnetic force   **E.** Electric dipole

Electric Circuits

1. What is the new resistance of a wire if the length of a certain wire is doubled and its radius is also doubled?

A. It is $\sqrt{2}$ times as large   **C.** It stays the same

B. It is ½ as large   **D.** It is 2 times as large   **E.** It is ¼ as large

2. A 6 Ω resistor is connected across the terminals of a 12 V battery. If 0.6 A of current flows, what is the internal resistance of the battery?

   A. 2 Ω   **B.** 26 Ω   **C.** 20 Ω   **D.** 14 Ω   **E.** 3.6 Ω

3. Three 8 V batteries are connected in series in order to power light bulbs A and B. The resistance of light bulb A is 60 Ω and the resistance of light bulb B is 30 Ω. How does the current through light bulb A compare with the current through light bulb B?

   A. The current through light bulb A is less
   B. The current through light bulb A is greater
   C. The current through light bulb A is the same
   D. The current through light bulb A is exactly doubled that through light bulb B
   E. None are true

4. A sphere with radius 2 mm carries a 1 μC charge. What is the potential difference, $V_B - V_A$, between point B 3.5 m from the center of the sphere and point A 8 m from the center of the sphere? (Use Coulomb's constant $k = 9 \times 10^9$ N·m²/C²)

   A. –485 V   **B.** 1,140 V   **C.** –140 V   **D.** 1,446 V   **E.** 2,457 V

5. Which of the following affect(s) capacitance of capacitors?

     I. material between the conductors
     II. distance between the conductors
     III. geometry of the conductors

   A. I only   **B.** II only   **C.** III only   **D.** I and III only   **E.** I, II and III

6. A proton with an initial speed of 1.5×10^5 m/s falls through a potential difference of 100 volts, gaining speed. What is the speed reached? (Use the mass of a proton = 1.67×10^{-27} kg and the charge of a proton = 1.6×10^{-19} C)

   A. 2×10^5 m/s   **C.** 8.6×10^5 m/s

   B. 4×10^5 m/s   **D.** 7.6×10^5 m/s   **E.** 6.6×10^5 m/s

7. The current flowing through a circuit of constant resistance is doubled. What is the effect on the power dissipated by that circuit?

A. Decreases to one-half its original value
B. Decreases to one-fourth its original value
C. Quadruples its original value
D. Doubles its original value
E. Decreases to one-eighth its original value

8. A positively-charged particle is at rest in an unknown medium. What is the magnitude of the magnetic field generated by this particle?

A. Constant everywhere and dependent only on the mass of the medium
B. Less at points near to the particle compared to a distant point
C. Greater at points near to the particle compared to a distant point
D. Equal to zero
E. Constant everywhere and dependent only on the density of the medium

9. The heating element of a toaster is a long wire of some metal, often a metal alloy, which heats up when a 120 V potential difference is applied across it. Consider a 300 W toaster connected to a wall outlet. Which statement would result in an increase in the rate by which heat is produced?

A. Use a longer wire
B. Use a thicker wire
C. Use a thicker and longer wire
D. Use a thinner and longer wire
E. Use a thinner wire of the same length

10. A 4 μC point charge and an 8 μC point charge are initially infinitely far apart. How much work is required to bring the 4 μC point charge to ($x = 2$ mm, $y = 0$ mm), and the 8 μC point charge to ($x = -2$ mm, $y = 0$ mm)? (Use Coulomb's constant $k = 9 \times 10^9$ N·m²/C²)

A. 32.6 J   B. 9.8 J   C. 47 J   D. 81 J   E. 72 J

11. A 3 Ω resistor is connected in parallel with a 6 Ω resistor, both resistors are connected in series with a 4 Ω resistor, and all three resistors are connected to an 18 V battery as shown. If 3 Ω resistor burnt out and exhibits infinite resistance, which of the following is true?

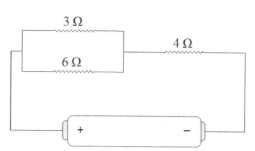

A. The power dissipated in the circuit increases
B. The current provided by the battery remains the same
C. The current in the 6 Ω resistor decreases
D. The current in the 4 Ω resistor decreases to zero
E. The current in the 6 Ω resistor increases

12. Which statement is accurate for when different resistors are connected in parallel across an ideal battery?

    A. Power dissipated in each is the same
    B. Their equivalent resistance is greater than the resistance of any one of the individual resistors
    C. Current flowing in each is the same
    D. Their equivalent resistance is equal to the average of the individual resistances
    E. Potential difference across each is the same

13. An electron was accelerated from rest through a potential difference of 990 V. What is its speed? (Use mass of an electron = 9.11×10^{-31} kg, mass of a proton = 1.67×10^{-27} kg and charge of a proton = 1.6×10^{-19} C)

    A. 0.8×10^7 m/s   **C.** 7.4×10^7 m/s
    B. 3.7×10^7 m/s   **D.** 1.9×10^7 m/s   **E.** 6.9×10^7 m/s

14. A circular conducting loop with a radius of 0.5 m and a small gap filled with a 12 Ω resistor is oriented in the *xy*-plane. If a magnetic field of 1 T, making an angle of 30° with the *z*-axis, increases to 12 T, in 5 s, what is the magnitude of the current flowing in the conductor?

    A. 0.33 A   **B.** 0.13 A   **C.** 0.88 A   **D.** 1.5 A   **E.** 4.5 A

15. Two parallel circular plates with radii 7 mm carrying equal-magnitude surface charge densities of ±3 µC/m² are separated by a distance of 1 mm. How much stored energy do the plates have? (Use dielectric constant $k = 1$ and electric permittivity $\varepsilon_0 = 8.854 \times 10^{-12}$ F/m)

    A. 226 nJ   **B.** 17 nJ   **C.** 127 nJ   **D.** 78 nJ   **E.** 33 nJ

16. A charged parallel-plate capacitor has an electric field E_0 between its plates. The bare nuclei of a stationary ^{1}H and ^{4}He are between the plates. Ignoring the force of gravity, how does the magnitude of the acceleration of the hydrogen nucleus a_H compare with the magnitude of the acceleration of the helium nucleus a_{He}? (Use mass of an electron = 9×10^{-31} kg, mass of a proton = 1.67×10^{-27} kg, mass of a neutron = 1.67×10^{-27} kg and charge of a proton = 1.6×10^{-19} C)

    A. $a_H = 2a_{He}$ **B.** $a_H = 4a_{He}$ **C.** $a_H = \frac{1}{4}a_{He}$ **D.** $a_H = a_{He}$ **E.** $a_H = \frac{1}{2}a_{He}$

17. Identical light bulbs are attached to identical batteries in three different ways (A, B, or C), as shown in the figure. What is the ranking (from lowest to highest) of the total power produced by the battery?

    A. C, B, A   **C.** A, C, B
    B. B, A, C   **D.** A, B, C
                     E. C, A, B

18. A parallel-plate capacitor consists of two parallel, square plates that have dimensions 1 cm by 1 cm. If the plates are separated by 1 mm, and the space between them is filled with Teflon, what is the capacitance? (Use dielectric constant k for Teflon = 2.1 and electric permittivity ε_0 = 8.854 × 10^{-12} F/m)

    A. 0.83 pF   **B.** 2.2 pF   **C.** 0.46 pF   **D.** 1.9 pF   **E.** 0.11 pF

19. The resistor R has a variable resistance. Which statement is true when R is decreased? (Neglect the very small internal resistance r of the battery)

    A. I_1 decreases, I_2 increases
    B. I_1 increases, I_2 remains the same
    C. I_1 remains the same, I_2 increases
    D. I_1 remains the same, I_2 decreases
    E. I_1 increases, I_2 increases

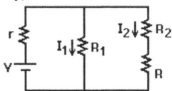

20. What physical quantity does the slope of the graph represent?

    A. 1 / Current
    B. Voltage
    C. Current
    D. Resistivity
    E. 1 / Voltage

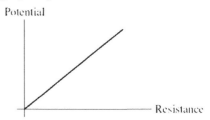

21. An alternating current is supplied to an electronic component with a rating that it be used only for voltages below 12 V. What is the highest V_{rms} that can be supplied to this component while staying below the voltage limit?

    A. 6 V   **B.** 12 V   **C.** 3√2 V   **D.** 12√2 V   **E.** 6√2 V

22. A generator produces alternating current electricity with a frequency of 40 cycles per second. What is the maximum potential difference created by the generator, if the rms voltage is 150 V?

    A. 54 V   **B.** 91 V   **C.** 212 V   **D.** 141 V   **E.** 223 V

23. Kirchhoff's junction rule is a statement of:

    A. Law of conservation of energy   **C.** Law of conservation of momentum
    B. Law of conservation of angular momentum   **D.** Law of conservation of charge
                                         E. Newton's Second Law

24. Four identical capacitors are connected in parallel to a battery. If a total charge of Q flows from the battery, how much charge does each capacitor carry?

    A. $Q/4$ **B.** Q **C.** $4Q$ **D.** $16Q$ **E.** $Q/16$

25. Which statement is correct for two conductors that are joined by a long copper wire?

    A. The electric field at the surface of each conductor is the same
    B. Each conductor must be at the same potential
    C. Each conductor must have the same resistivity
    D. A free charge must be present on either conductor
    E. The potential of the wire is the average of the potential of each conductor

26. Electromagnetic induction occurs in a coil when there is a change in the:

    A. coil's charge   **C.** magnetic field intensity in the coil
    B. current in the coil   **D.** electric field intensity in the coil
                                           E. electromagnetic polarity

27. The resistivity of gold is $2.22 \times 10^{-8}\ \Omega{\cdot}m$ at a temperature of 22 °C. A gold wire, 2 mm in diameter and 18 cm long, carries a current of 500 mA. What is the power dissipated in the wire?

    A. 0.17 mW   **B.** 0.54 mW   **C.** 0.77 mW   **D.** 0.32 mW   **E.** 0.44 mW

28. Electric current flows only from a point of:

    A. equal potential
    B. high pressure to a point of lower pressure
    C. low pressure to a point of higher pressure
    D. high potential to a point of lower potential
    E. low potential to a point of higher potential

29. Consider the group of charges in this figure. All three charges have $Q = 3.8$ nC. What is their electric potential energy? (Use Coulomb's constant $k = 9.0 \times 10^9\ N{\cdot}m^2/C^2$)

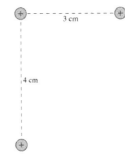

    A. 1.9×10^{-6} J   **C.** 8.8×10^{-6} J
    B. 7.4×10^{-5} J   **D.** 9.7×10^{-6} J
                                   E. 1×10^{-5} J

30. A positively-charged and negatively-charged particle are traveling on the same path perpendicular to a constant magnetic field. How do the forces experienced by the two particles differ, if the magnitudes of the charges are equal?

    A. Differ in direction, but not in magnitude
    B. Differ in magnitude, but not in direction
    C. No difference in magnitude or direction
    D. Differ in both magnitude and direction
    E. Cannot be predicted

31. An electron moves in a direction opposite to an electric field. The potential energy of the system:

    A. decreases, and the electron moves toward a region of lower potential
    B. increases, and the electron moves toward a region of higher potential
    C. decreases, and the electron moves toward a region of higher potential
    D. remains constant, and the electron moves toward a region of higher potential
    E. remains constant, and the electron moves toward a region of lower potential

32. What is the name of a device that transforms electrical energy into mechanical energy?

    A. Magnet   **C.** Turbine
    B. Transformer   **D.** Generator   **E.** Motor

33. A hydrogen atom consists of a proton and an electron. If the orbital radius of the electron increases, the absolute magnitude of the potential energy of the electron:

    A. remains the same   **C.** increases
    B. decreases   **D.** depends on the potential of the electron
                         E. is independent of the orbital radius

34. Copper wire A has a length L and a radius r. Copper wire B has a length $2L$ and a radius $2r$. Which of the following is true regarding the resistances across the ends of the wires?

    A. The resistance of wire A is one-half that of wire B
    B. The resistance of wire A is four times higher than that of wire B
    C. The resistance of wire A is twice as high as that of wire B
    D. The resistance of wire A is equal to that of wire B
    E. The resistance of wire A is one-fourth that of wire B

35. When a negative charge is free, it tries to move:

    A. toward infinity   **C.** from high potential to low potential
    B. away from infinity   **D.** from low potential to high potential
                          E. in the direction of the electric field

36. Four 6 V batteries (in a linear sequence of A → B → C → D) are connected in series in order to power lights A and B. The resistance of light A is 50 Ω and the resistance of light B is 25 Ω. What is the potential difference at a point between battery C and battery D? (Assume that the potential at the start of the sequence is zero)

    A. 4 volts   **B.** 12 volts   **C.** 18 volts   **D.** 26 volts   **E.** 30 volts

37. By what factor does the dielectric constant change when a material is introduced between the plates of a parallel-plate capacitor, if the capacitance increases by a factor of 4?

    A. ½   **B.** 4   **C.** 0.4   **D.** ¼   **E.** 2

38. Two isolated copper plates, each of area 0.4 m^2, carry opposite charges of magnitude 6.8 × 10^{-10} C. They are placed opposite each other in parallel alignment. What is the potential difference between the plates when their spacing is 4 cm? (Use the dielectric constant $k = 1$ in air and electric permittivity $\varepsilon_0 = 8.854 \times 10^{-12}$ F/m)

    A. 1.4 V   **B.** 4.1 V   **C.** 5.8 V   **D.** 3.2 V   **E.** 7.7 V

39. The force on an electron moving in a magnetic field is largest when its direction is:

    A. perpendicular to the magnetic field direction
    B. at any angle greater than 90° to the magnetic field direction
    C. at any angle less than 90° to the magnetic field direction
    D. exactly opposite to the magnetic field direction
    E. parallel to the magnetic field direction

40. In a parallel-plate capacitor, a positively-charged plate is on the left, and a negatively-charged plate is on the right. An electron is moving in between the plates to the right. Which statement is true?

    A. The PE of the electron decreases and it moves to a region of higher potential
    B. The PE of the electron decreases and it moves to a region of lower potential
    C. The PE of the electron increases and it moves to a region of higher potential
    D. The PE of the electron increases and it moves to a region of lower potential
    E. The PE of the electron remains constant and it moves to a region of higher potential

41. A proton with a speed of 1.7 × 10^5 m/s falls through a potential difference V and thereby increases its speed to 3.2 × 10^5 m/s. Through what potential difference did the proton fall? (Use the mass of a proton = 1.67 × 10^{-27} kg and the charge of a proton = 1.6 × 10^{-19} C)

    A. 880 V   **B.** 1,020 V   **C.** 384 V   **D.** 430 V   **E.** 130 V

42. Three capacitors are connected to a battery as shown. The capacitances are: $C_1 = 2C_2$ and $C_1 = 3C_3$. Which of the three capacitors stores the smallest amount of charge?

    A. C_1 **C.** C_2
    B. C_1 or C_3 **D.** C_3
    E. The amount of charge is the same in all three
        capacitors

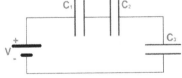

43. Two isolated copper plates, each of area 0.6 m^2, carry opposite charges of magnitude 7.08 × 10^{-10} C. They are placed opposite each other in parallel alignment, with a spacing of 2 mm. What will be the potential difference between the plates when their spacing is increased to 6 cm? (Use the dielectric constant $k = 1$ in air and electric permittivity $\varepsilon_0 = 8.854 \times 10^{-12}$ F/m)

    A. 8.0 V   **B.** 3.1 V   **C.** 4.3 V   **D.** 7.2 V   **E.** 0.9 V

44. A charged parallel-plate capacitor has an electric field of 140 N/C between its plates. If a stationary proton is placed between the plates, what is its speed after 0.18 milliseconds? (Use mass of a proton = 1.67×10^{-27} kg and charge of a proton = 1.6×10^{-19} C)

A. 3.7×10^{1} m/s   **C.** 3.2×10^{-6} m/s

B. 2.4×10^{6} m/s   **D.** 3.2×10^{-8} m/s   **E.** 4.8×10^{7} m/s

45. The metal detectors used to screen passengers at airports operate via:

A. Newton's Laws   **C.** Faraday's Law

B. Bragg's Law   **D.** Ohm's Law   **E.** Ampere's Law

46. A 7 μC negative charge is attracted to a large, well-anchored, positive charge. How much kinetic energy does the negatively-charged object gain if the potential difference through which it moves is 3.5 mV?

A. 0.86 J   **B.** 6.7 μJ   **C.** 36.7 μJ   **D.** 0.5 kJ   **E.** 24.5 nJ

47. A wire of resistivity ρ is replaced in a circuit by a wire of the same material but four times as long. If the total resistance remains the same, the diameter of the new wire must be:

A. one-fourth the original diameter
B. two times the original diameter
C. the same as the original diameter
D. one-half the original diameter
E. four times the original diameter

48. The addition of resistors in series to a resistor in an existing circuit, while voltage remains constant, would result in [ ] in the original resistor.

A. an increase in current   **C.** an increase in resistance

B. a decrease in resistance   **D.** a decrease in current   **E.** no change

49. In an experiment, a battery is connected to a variable resistor R, where resistance can be adjusted by turning a knob. The potential difference across the resistor and the current through it are recorded for different settings of the resistor knob. The battery is an ideal potential source in series with an internal resistor. The emf of the potential source is 9 V and the internal resistance is 0.1 Ω. What is the current if the variable resistor is set at 0.5 Ω?

A. 15 A   **B.** 0.9 A   **C.** 4.5 A   **D.** 45 A   **E.** 9 A

50. Two parallel plates that are initially uncharged are separated by 1.6 mm. What charge must be transferred from one plate to the other if 10 kJ of energy is to be stored in the plates? The area of each plate is 24 mm². (Use dielectric constant $k = 1$ in air and electric permittivity $\mathcal{E}_0 = 8.854 \times 10^{-12}$ F/m)

A. 78 μC   **B.** 15 mC   **C.** 52 μC   **D.** 29 μC   **E.** 66 mC **1211**

Light and Optics

1. What is the minimum thickness of a soap film that reflects a given wavelength of light?

   A. ¼ the wavelength
   B. ½ the wavelength
   C. One wavelength
   D. Two wavelengths
   E. There is no minimum thickness

2. If a distant galaxy is moving away from the Earth at 4,300 km/s, how do the detected frequency (f_{det}) and λ of the visible light detected on Earth compare to the f and λ of the light emitted by the galaxy?

   A. The f_{det} is lower and the λ is shifted towards the red end of the visible spectrum
   B. The f_{det} is lower and the λ is shifted towards the blue end of the visible spectrum
   C. The f_{det} is the same, but the λ is shifted towards the red end of the visible spectrum
   D. The f_{det} is the same, but the λ is shifted towards the blue end of the visible spectrum
   E. The f_{det} and the λ are the same as the sources

3. At what distance from a concave spherical mirror (with a focal length of 100 cm) must a woman stand in order to see an upright image of herself that is twice her actual height?

   A. 100 cm   B. 50 cm   C. 300 cm   D. 25 cm   E. 150 cm

4. If a person's eyeball is too long from front to back, what is the name of the condition that the person likely suffers?

   A. Hyperopia
   B. Astigmatism
   C. Presbyopia
   D. Myopia
   E. Diplopia

5. According to the relationship between frequency and energy of light ($E = hf$), which color of light has more energy?

   A. Red   B. Yellow   C. Green   D. Orange   E. Blue

6. A candle 18 cm tall sits 4 m away from a diverging lens with a focal length of 3 m. What is the size of the image?

   A. 6.3 cm   B. 7.7 cm   C. 2.9 cm   D. 13.5 cm   E. 18 cm

Questions **7-8** are based on the following:

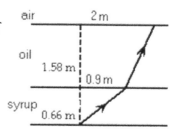

A tank holds a layer of oil 1.58 m thick that floats on a layer of syrup that is 0.66 m thick. Both liquids are clear and do not intermix. A ray, which originates at the bottom of the tank on a vertical axis (see figure), crosses the oil-syrup interface at a point 0.9 m to the right of the vertical axis. The ray continues and arrives at the oil-air interface, 2 m from the axis and at the critical angle. (Use the refractive index $n = 1$ for air)

7. The index of refraction of the oil is closest to:

   A. 1.39   **B.** 1.56   **C.** 1.75   **D.** 1.82   **E.** 1.94

8. What is the index of refraction of the syrup?

   A. 1.53   **B.** 1.46   **C.** 1.17   **D.** 1.24   **E.** 1.33

9. Which of the following cannot be explained with the wave theory of light?

   A. Photoelectric effect   **C.** Polarization
   B. Interference   **D.** Diffusion   **E.** All of the above

10. The use of wave fronts and rays to describe optical phenomena is known as:

   A. dispersive optics   **C.** wave optics
   B. reflector optics   **D.** geometrical optics   **E.** array optics

11. In the investigation of a new type of optical fiber (index of refraction $n = 1.26$), a laser beam is incident on the flat end of a straight fiber in air, as shown in the figure below. What is the maximum angle of incidence (θ_1) if the beam is not to escape from the fiber?

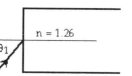

   A. 36°   **B.** 43°   **C.** 58°   **D.** 50°   **E.** 28°

12. An object is placed at a distance of 0.5 m from a converging lens with a power of 10 diopters. At what distance from the lens does the image appear?

   A. 0.13 m   **B.** 0.47 m   **C.** 0.7 m   **D.** 1.5 m   **E.** 1.8 m

13. A virtual image is:

      I. produced by light rays
      II. the brain's interpretations of light rays
      III. found only on a concave mirror

   A. I only   **B.** II only   **C.** III only   **D.** I and II only   **E.** I and III only

14. If Karen stands in front of a convex mirror, at the same distance from it as its radius of curvature:

    A. Karen does not see her image because it's focused at a different distance
    B. Karen sees her image and she appears the same size
    C. Karen does not see her image and she is not within its range
    D. Karen sees her image and she appears larger
    E. Karen sees her image and she appears smaller

15. An object is viewed at various distances using a mirror with a focal length of 10 m. If the object is 20 m away from the mirror, what best characterizes the image?

    A. Inverted and real
    B. Inverted and virtual
    C. Upright and real
    D. Upright and virtual
    E. Real, but it cannot be determined if it is inverted or upright

16. If an object is placed at a position beyond $2f$ of the focal point of a converging lens, the image is:

    A. real, upright and enlarged
    B. virtual, inverted and enlarged
    C. virtual, upright and reduced
    D. real, inverted and enlarged
    E. real, inverted and reduced

17. An amateur astronomer grinds a double-convex lens whose surfaces have radii of curvature of 40 cm and 60 cm. What is the focal length of this lens in air? (Use index of refraction for glass $n = 1.54$)

    A. 44 cm   **B.** 88 cm   **C.** 132 cm   **D.** 22 cm   **E.** 1.32 cm

18. If the index of refraction of diamond is 2.43, a given wavelength of light travels:

    A. 2.43 times faster in diamond than it does in air
    B. 2.43 times faster in a vacuum than it does in diamond
    C. 2.43 times faster in diamond than it does in a vacuum
    D. 2.43 times faster in vacuum than it does in air
    E. 2.43 times faster in air than it does in a vacuum

19. An object is placed 15 cm to the left of a double-convex lens of focal length 20 cm. Where is the image of this object located?

    A. 15 cm to the left of the lens
    B. 30 cm to the left of the lens
    C. 60 cm to the right of the lens
    D. 60 cm to the left of the lens
    E. 30 cm to the right of the lens

20. A sheet of red paper appears black when it is illuminated with:

    A. orange light
    B. cyan light
    C. red light
    D. yellow light
    E. violet light

21. Where is an object if the image produced by a lens appears very close to its focal point?

    A. near the center of curvature of the lens   **C.** near the lens
    B. far from the lens   **D.** near the focal point
                                                 E. requires more information

22. A light with the frequency 4.9×10^{14} Hz is produced by a source located 6 m from a converging lens with a focal length of 3 m. For a different frequency of light, the focal length of the lens is different than 3 m. This phenomenon is called:

    A. Diffusion   **C.** Interference
    B. Incidence   **D.** Refraction   **E.** Dispersion

23. If an image appears at the same distance from a mirror as the object, the size of the image is:

    A. exactly quadruple the size of the object   **C.** the same size as the object
    B. exactly ¼ the size of the object   **D.** exactly twice the size of the object
                                                 E. exactly ½ the size of the object

24. When viewed straight down (90° to the surface), an incident light ray moving from water to air is refracted:

    A. 37° away from the normal   **C.** 28° toward the normal
    B. 37° toward the normal   **D.** 28° away from the normal   **E.** 0°

25. Suppose that a beachgoer uses two lenses from a pair of disassembled polarized sunglasses and places one on top of the other. What would he observe if he rotates one lens 90° with respect to the normal position of the other lens and looks directly at the sun overhead?

    A. Light with an intensity reduced to about 50% of what it would be with one lens
    B. Light with an intensity that is the same of what it would be with one lens
    C. Complete darkness, since no light would be transmitted
    D. Light with an intensity reduced to about 25% of what it would be with one lens
    E. Light with an intensity increased to about 150% of what it would be with one lens

26. A glass plate with an index of refraction of 1.45 is immersed in a liquid. The liquid is an oil with an index of refraction of 1.35. The surface of the glass is inclined at an angle of 54° with the vertical. A horizontal ray in the glass is incident on the interface of glass and liquid. The incident horizontal ray refracts at the interface. The angle that the refracted ray in the oil makes with the horizontal is closest to:

    A. 8.3°   **B.** 14°   **C.** 6°   **D.** 12°   **E.** 17°

27. Two plane mirrors make an angle of 30°. A light ray enters the system and is reflected once off each mirror. Through what angle is the ray turned?

    A. 60°   **B.** 90°   **C.** 120°   **D.** 160°   **E.** 180°

28. An incident ray traveling in air makes an angle of 30° with the surface of a medium with an index $n = 1.73$. What is the angle that the refracted ray makes with the surface? (Use the index of refraction for air $n = 1$)

    A. 30°   **B.** $90 \sin^{-1}(0.5)$ **C.** 60°   **D.** $\sin^{-1}(0.5)$ **E.** 90°

29. A lens has a focal length of 2 m. What lens could you combine with it to get a combination with a focal length of 3 m?

    A. A lens of power 1/6 diopters   **C.** A lens of power –6 diopters
    B. A lens of power 6 diopters   **D.** A lens of power –1/6 diopters
                                               E. A lens of power 3 diopters

30. A 5-foot-tall woman stands next to a plane mirror on a wall. As she walks away from the mirror, her image:

    A. is always a real image, no matter how far she is from the mirror.
    B. changes from being upright to being inverted as she passes the focal point.
    C. has a height less than 5 feet.
    D. may or may not get smaller, depending on where she is positioned.
    E. remains 5 feet tall.

31. If a spherical concave mirror has a radius of curvature R, its focal length is:

    A. $2R$ **B.** R **C.** $R/2$ **D.** $R/4$ **E.** $4R$

32. Let n_1 be the index of refraction of the incident medium, and let n_2 be the index of refraction of the refracting medium. Which of the following must be true if the angle that the refracted ray makes with the boundary (not with the normal) is less than the angle that the incident ray makes with the boundary?

    A. $n_1 < n_2$ **B.** $n_1 > n_2$ **C.** $n_1 < 1$ **D.** $n_2 < 1$ **E.** $n_1 = n_2$

33. If a person's eyeball is too short from front to back, the person is likely to suffer from:

    A. nearsightedness   **C.** presbyopia
    B. farsightedness   **D.** astigmatism   **E.** diplopia

34. The shimmering that is observed over a hot surface is:

    A. changing refraction from the mixing of warm and cool air
    B. a mirage
    C. heat rays
    D. reflections from evaporating water vapor
    E. reflections from condensing water vapor

35. When two parallel white rays pass through the outer edges of a converging glass lens, chromatic aberrations cause colors to appear on the screen in what order, from the top down?

 A. blue, blue, red, red   **C.** blue, red, blue, red

 B. red, blue, blue, red   **D.** red, red, blue, blue   **E.** blue, red, red, blue

36. Two thin converging lenses are near each other, so that the lens on the left has a focal length of 2 m and the one on the right has a focal length of 4 m. What is the focal length of the combination?

 A. 1/4 m   **B.** 4/3 m   **C.** 3/4 m   **D.** 4 m   **E.** 8 m

37. A cylindrical tank is 50 ft deep, 37.5 ft in diameter, and filled to the top with water. A flashlight shines into the tank from above. What is the minimum angle θ that its beam can make with the water surface if the beam is to illuminate part of the bottom? (Use the index of refraction $n = 1.33$ for water)

 A. 25°   **B.** 31°   **C.** 37°   **D.** 53°   **E.** 18°

38. A convex lens has a focal length of f. If an object is placed at a distance of $2f$ from the lens on the principal axis, the image is located at a distance from the lens:

 A. between the lens and f **C.** between f and $2f$

 B. of f **D.** of $2f$ **E.** of infinity

39. An object is placed at a distance d in front of a plane mirror. The size of the image is:

 A. dependent on where the observer is positioned when looking at the image
 B. twice the size of the object
 C. half the size of the object
 D. dependent on the distance d
 E. the same as the object, independent of the position of the observer or distance d

40. If a single lens forms a virtual image of an object, then the:

  I. image must be upright
  II. lens must be a converging lens
  III. lens could be either diverging or converging

 A. I only   **B.** I and III only   **C.** III only   **D.** I and II only   **E.** II only

41. When neon light passes through a prism, what is observed?

 A. White light   **C.** The same neon light

 B. Bright spots or lines   **D.** Continuous spectrum   **E.** Both A and B

42. Which of the following cannot be explained with the particle theory of light?

　　I. Polarization　　　　II. Photoelectric effect　　　III. Quantization of energy

A. I only　　　**B.** II only　　　**C.** III only　　　**D.** I and II only　　　**E.** I and III only

43. The image formed by a single concave lens:

A. can be real or virtual, but is always real when the object is placed at the focal point
B. can be real or virtual, depending on the object's distance compared to the focal length
C. is always virtual
D. is always real
E. is always inverted

44. A lens forms a virtual image of an object. Which of the following must be true of the image?

A. It is inverted
B. It is upright
C. It is larger than the object and upright
D. It is smaller than the object and inverted
E. It is the same size as the object and upright

45. The radius of curvature of the curved side of a plano-convex lens made of glass is 33 cm. What is the focal length of the lens? (Use index of refraction for glass $n = 1.64$)

A. −28 cm　　　**B.** 28 cm　　　**C.** 38 cm　　　**D.** 52 cm　　　**E.** 16 cm

46. A 0.1 m tall candle is observed through a converging lens that is 3 m away and has a focal length of 6 m. The resulting image is:

A. 3 m from the lens on the opposite side of the object
B. 6 m from the lens on the opposite side of the object
C. 3 m from the lens on the same side as the object
D. 6 m from the lens on the same side as the object
E. 0.5 m from the lens on the opposite side of the object

47. Which statement about thin lenses is correct when considering only a single lens?

A. A diverging lens always produces a virtual erect image
B. A diverging lens always produces a real erect image
C. A diverging lens always produces a virtual inverted image
D. A diverging lens always produces a real inverted image
E. A converging lens always produces a real inverted image

48. A double-concave lens has equal radii of curvature of 15 cm. An object placed 14 cm from the lens forms a virtual image 5 cm from the lens. What is the index of refraction of the lens material?

A. 0.8　　　**B.** 1.4　　　**C.** 2　　　**D.** 2.6　　　**E.** 2.8

49. The magnification m for an object reflected from a mirror is the ratio of what characteristic of the image to the object?

    A. Center of curvature   **C.** Orientation

    B. Focal distances   **D.** Angular size   **E.** Distance

50. Suppose Mike places his face in front of a concave mirror. Which of the following statements is correct?

    A. Mike's image is diminished in size

    B. Mike's image is always inverted

    C. No matter where Mike places himself, a virtual image is formed

    D. If Mike positions himself between the center of curvature and the focal point of the mirror, he will not be able to see his image

    E. Mike's image is enlarged in size

Heat and Thermodynamics

1. Compared to the initial value, what is the resulting pressure for an ideal gas that is compressed isothermally to one-third of its initial volume?

    A. Equal   **C.** Larger, but less than three times larger
    B. Three times larger   **D.** More than three times larger
                                    E. Requires more information

2. A uniform hole in a brass plate has a diameter of 1.2 cm at 25 °C. What is the diameter of the hole when the plate is heated to 225 °C? (Use the coefficient of linear thermal expansion for brass = 19×10^{-6} K^{-1})

    A. 2.2 cm   **B.** 2.8 cm   **C.** 1.2 cm   **D.** 1.6 cm   **E.** 0.8 cm

3. A student heats 90 g of water using 50 W of power, with 100% efficiency. How long does it take to raise the temperature of the water from 10 °C to 30 °C? (Use specific heat of water c = 4.186 J/g·°C)

    A. 232 s   **B.** 81 s   **C.** 59 s   **D.** 151 s   **E.** 102 s

4. A runner generates 1,260 W of thermal energy. If her heat is to be dissipated only by evaporation, how much water does she shed in 15 minutes of running? (Use the latent heat of vaporization of water $L_v = 22.6 \times 10^5$ J/kg)

    A. 500 g   **B.** 35 g   **C.** 350 g   **D.** 50 g   **E.** 40 g

5. Phase changes occur as temperature:

    I. decreases   II. increases   III. remains the same
    A. I only   **B.** II only   **C.** III only   **D.** I and II only   **E.** I and III only

6. How much heat is needed to melt a 55 kg sample of ice that is at 0 °C? (Use latent heat of fusion for water L_f = 334 kJ/kg and latent heat of vaporization L_v = 2,257 kJ/kg)

    A. 0 kJ   **C.** 3×10^5 kJ
    B. 2.6×10^5 kJ   **D.** 4.6×10^6 kJ   **E.** 1.8×10^4 kJ

7. Metals are both good heat conductors and good electrical conductors because of the:

    A. relatively high densities of metals
    B. high elasticity of metals
    C. ductility of metals
    D. looseness of outer electrons in metal atoms
    E. crystal structure of metals

8. Solar houses are designed to retain the heat absorbed during the day so that the stored heat can be released during the night. A botanist produces steam at 100 °C during the day, and then allows the steam to cool to 0 °C and freeze during the night. How many kilograms of water are needed to store 200 kJ of energy for this process? (Use latent heat of vaporization of water $L_v = 22.6 \times 10^5$ J/kg, latent heat of fusion of water $L_f = 33.5 \times 10^4$ J/kg, and specific heat capacity of water $c = 4,186$ J/kg·K)

   A. 0.066 kg   **B.** 0.103 kg   **C.** 0.482 kg   **D.** 1.18 kg   **E.** 3.66 kg

9. A 0.3 kg ice cube at 0 °C has sufficient heat added to result in total melting, and the resulting water is heated to 60 °C. How much total heat is added? (Use latent heat of fusion for water $L_f = 334$ kJ/kg, latent heat of vaporization for water $L_v = 2,257$ kJ/kg and specific heat of water = 4.186 kJ/kg·K)

   A. 73 kJ   **B.** 48 kJ   **C.** 176 kJ   **D.** 144 kJ   **E.** 136 kJ

10. A glass beaker of unknown mass contains 65 ml of water. The system absorbs 1,800 cal of heat and the temperature rises 20 °C. What is the mass of the beaker? (Use specific heat of glass = 0.18 cal/g·°C and specific heat of water = 1 cal/g·°C)

   A. 342 g   **B.** 139 g   **C.** 546 g   **D.** 268 g   **E.** 782 g

11. An aluminum electric tea kettle with a mass of 500 g is heated with a 500 W heating coil. How many minutes are required to heat 1 kg of water from 18 °C to 98 °C in the tea kettle? (Use specific heat of aluminum = 900 J/kg·K and specific heat of water = 4,186 J/kg·K)

   A. 16 min   **B.** 12 min   **C.** 8 min   **D.** 4 min   **E.** 10 min

12. Heat is added at a constant rate to a pure substance in a closed container. The temperature of the substance as a function of time is shown in the graph. If L_f = latent heat of fusion and L_v = latent heat of vaporization, what is the value of the ratio L_v / L_f for this substance?

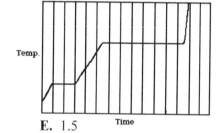

   A. 3.5   **B.** 7.2   **C.** 4.5   **D.** 5.0   **E.** 1.5

13. The moderate temperatures of islands throughout the world have much to do with water's:

   A. high evaporation rate   **C.** vast supply of thermal energy
   B. high specific heat capacity   **D.** poor conductivity
   E. absorption of solar energy

14. A 4.5 g lead BB moving at 46 m/s penetrates a wood block and comes to rest inside the block. If half of the kinetic energy is absorbed by the BB, what is the change in the temperature of the BB? (Use specific heat of lead = 128 J/kg·K)

   A. 2.8 K   **B.** 3.6 K   **C.** 1.6 K   **D.** 0.8 K   **E.** 4.1 K

15. Which of the following relationships is true for all types of Carnot heat engines?

    I. $\eta = 1 - T_C / T_H$
    II. $\eta = 1 - |Q_C / Q_H|$
    III. $T_C / T_H = Q_C / Q_H$

    A. I only   **B.** II only   **C.** III only   **D.** I, II and III   **E.** I and III only

16. A Carnot engine operating between a reservoir of liquid mercury at its melting point and a colder reservoir extracts 18 J of heat from the mercury and does 5 J of work during each cycle. What is the temperature of the colder reservoir? (Use melting temperature of mercury = 233 K)

    A. 168 K   **B.** 66 K   **C.** 57 K   **D.** 82 K   **E.** 94 K

17. A 920 g empty iron pan is put on a stove. How much heat in joules must the iron pan absorb to raise its temperature from 18 °C to 96 °C? (Use specific heat for iron = 113 cal/kg·°C and 1 cal = 4.186 J)

    A. 50,180 J   **B.** 81,010 J   **C.** 63,420 J   **D.** 33,940 J   **E.** 26,500 J

18. An 80-gram aluminum calorimeter contains 360 g of water at an equilibrium temperature of 20 °C. A 180 g piece of metal, initially at 305 °C, is added to the calorimeter. The final temperature at equilibrium is 35 °C. Assume there is no external heat exchange. What is the specific heat capacity of the metal? (Use specific heat capacity of aluminum = 910 J/kg·K and specific heat of water = 4,190 J/kg·K)

    A. 260 J/kg·K   **B.** 324 J/kg·K   **C.** 488 J/kg·K   **D.** 410 J/kg·K   **E.** 535 J/kg·K

19. Which of the following is an accurate statement about the work done for a cyclic process carried out in a gas? (Use P for pressure and V for volume on the graph)

    A. It is equal to the area under *ab* minus the area under *dc*
    B. It is equal to the area under the curve *adc*
    C. It is equal to the area under the curve *abc*
    D. It equals zero
    E. It is equal to the area enclosed by the cyclic process

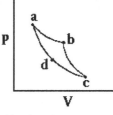

20. Substance A has a higher specific heat than substance B. With all other factors equal, which substance requires more energy to be heated to the same temperature?

    A. Substance A   **C.** Both require the same amount of heat
    B. Substance B   **D.** Depends on the density of each substance
                         E. Depends on the volume of each substance

21. A 6.5 g meteor hits the Earth at a speed of 300 m/s. If the meteor's kinetic energy is entirely converted to heat, by how much does its temperature rise? (Use specific heat of the meteor = 120 cal/kg·°C and conversion of 1 cal = 4.186 J)

    A. 134 °C   **B.** 68 °C   **C.** 120 °C   **D.** 90 °C   **E.** 44 °C

22. A substance has a melting point of 20 °C and a heat of fusion of 3.6×10^4 J/kg. The boiling point is 150 °C and the heat of vaporization is 7.2×10^4 J/kg at a pressure of one atmosphere. What is the quantity of heat released by 3.4 kg of the substance when it is cooled from 160 °C to 75 °C at a pressure of one atmosphere? (Use specific heat for the solid phase = 600 J/kg·K, specific heat for the liquid phase = 1,000 J/kg·K and specific heat for the gaseous phase = 400 J/kg·K)

    A. 448 kJ   **B.** 325 kJ   **C.** 249 kJ   **D.** 513 kJ   **E.** 671 kJ

23. A monatomic ideal gas (C_v = 3/2 R) undergoes an isothermal expansion at 300 K, as the volume increases from 0.05 m^3 to 0.2 m^3. The final pressure is 130 kPa. What is the heat transfer of the gas? (Use ideal gas constant R = 8.314 J/mol·K)

    A. −14 kJ   **B.** 36 kJ   **C.** 14 kJ   **D.** −21 kJ   **E.** 0 kJ

24. What is the maximum temperature rise expected for 1 kg of water falling from a waterfall with a vertical drop of 30 m? (Use acceleration due to gravity g = 9.8 m/s^2 and specific heat of water = 4,186 J/kg·K)

    A. 0.1 °C   **B.** 0.06 °C   **C.** 0.15 °C   **D.** 0.07 °C   **E.** 0.03 °C

25. When 0.75 kg of water at 0 °C freezes, what is the change in entropy of the water? (Use latent heat of fusion of water L_f = 33,400 J/kg)

    A. −92 J/K   **B.** −18 J/K   **C.** 44 J/K   **D.** 80 J/K   **E.** −60 J/K

26. When a bimetallic bar made of a copper and iron strip is heated, the copper part of the bar bends toward the iron strip. The reason for this is:

    A. copper expands more than iron   **C.** iron gets hotter before copper
    B. iron expands more than copper   **D.** copper gets hotter before iron
                                                   E. both copper and iron expand at the same rate

27. In a flask, 110 g of water is heated using 60 W of power, with perfect efficiency. How long does it take to raise the temperature of the water from 20 °C to 30 °C? (Use specific heat of water c = 4,186 J/kg·K)

    A. 132 s   **B.** 57 s   **C.** 9.6 s   **D.** 77 s   **E.** 41 s

28. A lamp radiates 80 J/s when the room is set on 25 °C but it radiates 95 J/s when the room temperature drops to 20 °C. What is the temperature of the lamp?

    A. 37 K   **B.** 48 °C   **C.** 101 °C   **D.** 84 °C   **E.** 73 K

29. A flask of liquid nitrogen is at a temperature of −243 °C. If the nitrogen is heated until the average energy of the particles is doubled, what is the new temperature?

    A. 356 °C   **B.** −356 °C   **C.** −134 °C   **D.** 134 °C   **E.** −213 °C

30. If a researcher is attempting to determine how much the temperature of a particular piece of material would rise when a known amount of heat is added to it, knowing which of the following quantities would be most helpful?

A. density   C. initial temperature

B. coefficient of linear expansion   D. specific heat   E. thermal conductivity

31. A substance has a density of 1,800 kg/m³ in the liquid state. At atmospheric pressure, the substance has a boiling point of 170 °C. The vapor has a density of 6 kg/m³ at the boiling point at atmospheric pressure. What is the change in the internal energy of 1 kg of the substance, as it vaporizes at atmospheric pressure? (Use heat of vaporization $L_v = 1.7 \times 10^5$ J/kg)

A. 180 kJ   B. 170 kJ   C. 6 kJ   D. 12 kJ   E. 200 kJ

32. If an aluminum rod that is at 5 °C is heated until it has twice the thermal energy, its temperature is:

A. 10 °C   B. 56 °C   C. 278 °C   D. 283 °C   E. 556 °C

33. A thermally isolated system is made up of a hot piece of aluminum and a cold piece of copper, with the aluminum and the copper in thermal contact. The specific heat capacity of aluminum is more than double that of copper. Which object experiences the greater temperature change during the time the system takes to reach thermal equilibrium?

A. Both experience the same magnitude of temperature change

B. The volume of each is required

C. The copper

D. The aluminum

E. The mass of each is required

34. In liquid water of a given temperature, the water molecules are moving randomly with different speeds. Electrostatic forces of cohesion tend to hold them together. However, occasionally one molecule gains enough energy through multiple collisions to pull away from the others and escape from the liquid. Which of the following is an illustration of this phenomenon?

A. When a large steel suspension bridge is built, gaps are left between the girders

B. When a body gets too warm, it produces sweat to cool itself down

C. Increasing the atmospheric pressure over a liquid causes the boiling temperature to decrease

D. If snow begins to fall when Mary is skiing, she feels colder than before it started to snow

E. A hot water bottle is more effective in keeping a person warm than would a rock of the same mass heated to the same temperature

35. A 2,200 kg sample of water at 0 °C is cooled to –30 °C, and freezes in the process. Approximately how much heat is liberated during this process? (Use heat of fusion for water $L_f = 334$ kJ/kg, heat of vaporization $L_v = 2,257$ kJ/kg and specific heat for ice = 2,050 J/kg·K)

A. 328,600 kJ   C. 637,200 kJ

B. 190,040 kJ   D. 870,100 kJ   E. 768,200 kJ

36. Object 1 has three times the specific heat capacity and four times the mass of Object 2. The same amount of heat is transferred to the two objects. If the temperature of Object 1 changes by an amount of ΔT, what is the change in temperature of Object 2?

    A. $(4/3)\Delta T$ **B.** $3\Delta T$ **C.** ΔT **D.** $(3/4)\Delta T$ **E.** $12\Delta T$

37. A sphere, 0.3 m in radius, has a surface emissivity of 0.55 and is at a temperature of 500 K. The sphere is surrounded by a concentric spherical shell whose inner surface has a radius of 0.8 m and emissivity of 1. The temperature of the shell is 400 K. What is the rate at which heat is radiated in the space between the sphere and the shell? (Use temperature of radiation T_H in K, temperature of surrounding T_C in K, Stefan Boltzmann constant $\sigma = 5.67 \times 10^{-8}$ W/m²K⁴)

    A. 1.3 kW   **B.** 4.3 kW   **C.** 3.6 kW   **D.** 7.8 kW   **E.** 9.2 kW

38. The graph shows a PV diagram for 5.1 g of oxygen gas in a sealed container. The temperature of T_1 is 20 °C. What are the values for temperatures of T_3 and T_4, respectively? (Use the gas constant R= 8.314 J/mol·K)

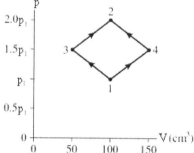

    A. −53 °C and 387 °C   **C.** 210 °C and 640 °C

    B. −14 °C and 34 °C   **D.** 12 °C and 58 °C

                                E. 29 °C and 171 °C

39. On a cold day, a piece of steel feels much colder to the touch than a piece of plastic. This is due to the difference in which one of the following physical properties of these materials?

    A. Emissivity   **C.** Density

    B. Thermal conductivity   **D.** Specific heat   **E.** Mass

40. What is the term for a process when a gas is allowed to expand as heat is added to it at constant pressure?

    A. Isochoric   **B.** Isobaric   **C.** Adiabatic   **D.** Isothermal   **E.** Isentropic

41. A Carnot engine is used as an air conditioner to cool a house in the summer. The air conditioner removes 20 kJ of heat per second from the house, and maintains the inside temperature at 293 K, while the outside temperature is 307 K. What is the power required for the air conditioner?

    A. 2.3 kW   **B.** 3.22 kW   **C.** 1.6 kW   **D.** 4.88 kW   **E.** 0.96 kW

42. Heat energy is measured in units of:

    I. Joules   II. calories   III. work

    A. I only   **B.** II only   **C.** I and II only   **D.** III only   **E.** I, II and III

43. If 800 kJ of heat is added to 800 g of water originally at 70 °C, how much water is left in the container? (Use latent heat of vaporization of water L_v= 22.6 × 10^5 J/kg and specific heat of water c = 4,186 J/kg·K)

    A. 321 g   **B.** 618 g   **C.** 433 g   **D.** 253 g   **E.** 490 g

44. How much heat must be removed from 435 g of water at 30 °C to change it into ice at –8 °C? (Use specific heat of ice = 2,090 J/kg·K, latent heat of fusion of water L_f= 33.5 × 10^4 J/kg and specific heat of water = 4,186 J/kg·K)

    A. 57 kJ   **B.** 420 kJ   **C.** 105 kJ   **D.** 145 kJ   **E.** 208 kJ

45. The figure shows 0.008 mol of gas that undergoes the process 1 → 2 → 3. What is the volume of V_3? (Use ideal gas constant R = 8.314 J/mol·K and 1 atm = 101,325 Pa)

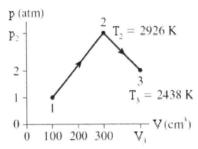

    A. 435 cm^3 **C.** 656 cm^3

    B. 568 cm^3 **D.** 800 cm^3 **E.** 940 cm^3

46. When a gas expands adiabatically:

    A. it does no work   **C.** the internal (thermal) energy of the gas decreases

    B. work is done on the gas   **D.** the internal (thermal) energy of the gas increases

    E. the temperature of the gas remains constant

47. Why is it that when a swimmer gets out of a swimming pool and stands in a breeze dripping wet, he feels much colder compared to when he dries off?

    A. This is a physiological effect resulting from the skin's sensory nerves

    B. The water on his skin is colder than the surrounding air

    C. The moisture on his skin has good thermal conductivity

    D. Water has a relatively small specific heat

    E. To evaporate a gram of water from his skin requires heat and most of this heat flows out of his body

48. A 200 L electric water heater uses 4 kW. Assuming no heat loss, how many hours would it take to heat the water in this tank from 28 °C to 80 °C? (Use specific heat of water = 4,186 J/kg·K, density of water = 1,000 kg/m^3 and the conversion of 1 L = 0.001 m^3)

    A. 12 h   **B.** 9 h   **C.** 1.5 h   **D.** 3 h   **E.** 6 h

49. An ideal gas is compressed via an isobaric process to one-third of its initial volume. Compared to the initial pressure, the resulting pressure is:

    A. more than three times greater   **C.** three times greater

    B. nine times greater   **D.** the same   **E.** requires more information

50. Which of the following would be the best radiator of thermal energy?

    A. A metallic surface   **C.** A white surface

    B. A black surface   **D.** A shiny surface   **E.** Styrofoam

Quantum Mechanics

1. The work function of a certain metal is 1.90 eV. What is the longest wavelength of light that can cause photoelectron emission from this metal?

    A. 64 nm   **B.** 98 nm   **C.** 247 nm   **D.** 449 nm   **E.** 653 nm

2. Which of the following statements is correct if the frequency of the light in a laser beam is doubled while the number of photons per second in the beam is fixed?

    I. The power in the beam does not change
    II. The intensity of the beam doubles
    III. The energy of individual photons does not change

    A. I only   **C.** III only
    B. II only   **D.** I and II only   **E.** I, II and III

3. Upon being struck by 240 nm photons, a material ejects electrons with a maximum kinetic energy of 2.58 eV. What is the work function of this material?

    A. 1.17 eV   **C.** 2.60 eV
    B. 2.04 eV   **D.** 3.26 eV   **E.** 4.34 eV

4. A high energy photon collides with matter and creates an electron-positron pair. What is the minimum frequency of the photon? (Use $m_{electron} = 9.11 \times 10^{-31}$ kg, $c = 3.00 \times 10^8$ m/s, and $h = 6.626 \times 10^{-34}$ J·s)

    A. greater than 1.24×10^{12} Hz   **C.** greater than 2.47×10^{20} Hz
    B. greater than 2.47×10^{16} Hz   **D.** greater than 2.47×10^{22} Hz
                                       E. greater than 1.24×10^{24} Hz

5. What is the longest wavelength of light that can cause photoelectron emission from a metal that has a work function of 2.20 eV?

    A. 216 nm   **C.** 484 nm
    B. 372 nm   **D.** 564 nm   **E.** 642 nm

6. In 1932, C. D. Anderson:

    A. set the limits on the probability of measurement accuracy
    B. predicted the positron from relativistic quantum mechanics
    C. discovered the positron using a cloud chamber
    D. was the first to produce diffraction patterns of electrons in crystals
    E. was the first to produce X-ray-like diffraction patterns of electrons passing through thin metal foil

7. What is the energy of an optical photon of frequency 6.43×10^{14} Hz (Use $h = 6.626 \times 10^{-34}$ J·s and 1 eV = 1.60×10^{-19} J)

    A. 1.04 eV   **B.** 1.86 eV   **C.** 2.66 eV   **D.** 3.43 eV   **E.** 5.37 eV

8. A photocathode has a work function of 2.4 eV. The photocathode is illuminated with monochromatic radiation whose photon energy is 3.4 eV. What is the maximum kinetic energy of the photoelectrons produced? (Use 1 eV = 1.60×10^{-19} J)

    A. 3.4×10^{-20} J   **C.** 4.6×10^{-19} J
    B. 1.6×10^{-19} J   **D.** 5.8×10^{-19} J   **E.** 7.2×10^{-18} J

9. A photocathode whose work function is 2.9 eV is illuminated with white light that has a continuous wavelength band from 400 nm to 700 nm. What is the range of the wavelength band in this white light illumination for which photoelectrons are NOT produced?

    A. 360 to 440 nm   **C.** 430 to 500 nm
    B. 400 to 480 nm   **D.** 430 to 700 nm   **E.** 460 to 760 nm

10. Photon A has twice the momentum of photon B as both travel in a vacuum. Which of the following statements about these photons is correct?

    A. Both photons have the same speed
    B. Both photons have the same wavelength
    C. Photon A is traveling twice as fast as photon B
    D. The energy of photon A is half as great as the energy of photon B
    E. The wavelength of photon B is half as great as the wavelength of photon A

11. What is the energy of the photon emitted when an electron drops from the n = 20 state to the n = 7 state in a hydrogen atom?

    A. 0.244 eV   **C.** 0.336 eV
    B. 0.288 eV   **D.** 0.404 eV   **E.** 0.492 eV

12. Protons are being accelerated in a particle accelerator. What is the de Broglie wavelength when the energy of the protons is doubled if the protons are non-relativistic (i.e. their kinetic energy is much less than mc^2)?

    A. increases by a factor of 2   **C.** decreases by a factor of 2
    B. increases by a factor of 3   **D.** decreases by a factor of $\sqrt{2}$
                                         E. increases by a factor of $\sqrt{2}$

13. A certain photon, after being scattered from a free electron that was at rest, moves at an angle of 120° with respect to the incident direction. If the wavelength of the incident photon is 0.591 nm, what is the wavelength of the scattered photon? (Use $m_{electron} = 9.11 \times 10^{-31}$ kg, $c = 3.00 \times 10^8$ m/s and $h = 6.626 \times 10^{-34}$ J·s)

    A. 0.0 nm   **B.** 0.180 nm   **C.** 0.252 nm   **D.** 0.366 nm   **E.** 0.595 nm

14. Increasing the *brightness* of a beam of light without changing its color, increases the:

    A. speed of the photons
    B. frequency of the light
    C. number of photons per second traveling in the beam
    D. energy of each photon
    E. wavelength of the photons

15. What is the frequency of the light emitted by atomic Hydrogen according to the Balmer formula with $m = 4$ and $n = 9$?

    A. 820 Hz   **B.** 1,640 Hz   **C.** 1,820 Hz   **D.** 2.24×10^{-6} m   **E.** 1.65×10^{14} Hz

16. One of the emission lines described by the original version of the Balmer formula has wavelength 377 nm. What is the value of n in the Balmer formula that gives this emission line?

    A. 5   **B.** 7   **C.** 9   **D.** 11   **E.** 13

17. What is the wavelength of the most intense light emitted by a giant star of surface temperature 5000 K? (Use the constant in Wien's law = 0.00290 m·K)

    A. 366 nm   **B.** 448 nm   **C.** 490 nm   **D.** 540 nm   **E.** 580 nm

18. In 1928, Paul Dirac:

    A. set the limits on the probability of measurement accuracy
    B. developed a wave equation for matter waves
    C. suggested the existence of matter waves
    D. discovered the positron using a cloud chamber
    E. predicted the positron from relativistic quantum mechanics

19. A photocathode has a work function of 2.4 eV. The photocathode is illuminated with monochromatic radiation whose photon energy is 3.4 eV. What is the maximum kinetic energy of the photoelectrons produced?

    A. 0.9×10^{-19} J   **C.** 2.8×10^{-19} J
    B. 1.6×10^{-19} J   **D.** 4.2×10^{-19} J   **E.** 5.8×10^{-19} J

20. In a Compton scattering experiment, which scattering angle produces the greatest change in wavelength?

    A. 0°   **B.** 45°   **C.** 90°   **D.** 180°   **E.** 270°

21. A photocathode has a work function of 2.4 eV. The photocathode is illuminated with monochromatic radiation whose photon energy is 3.5 eV. What is the wavelength of the illuminating radiation?

    A. 280 nm   **B.** 325 nm   **C.** 350 nm   **D.** 395 nm   **E.** 420 nm

22. If the wavelength of a photon is doubled, what happens to its energy?

  A. It is reduced to one-half of its original value
  B. It stays the same
  C. It is doubled
  D. It is increased to four times its original value
  E. It is reduced to one-fourth of its original value

23. A photocathode has a work function of 2.8 eV. The photocathode is illuminated with monochromatic radiation. What is the threshold frequency for the monochromatic radiation required to produce photoelectrons?

  A. 1.2×10^{14} Hz   **C.** 4.6×10^{14} Hz
  B. 2.8×10^{14} Hz   **D.** 6.8×10^{14} Hz   **E.** 8.4×10^{14} Hz

24. If the de Broglie wavelength of an electron is 380 nm, what is the speed of this electron? (Use $m_{electron} = 9.11 \times 10^{-31}$ kg and $h = 6.626 \times 10^{-34}$ J·s)

  A. 0.6 km/s   **C.** 3.4 km/s
  B. 1.9 km/s   **D.** 4.6 km/s   **E.** 5.8 km/s

25. What is the wavelength of the scattered photon if a photon of wavelength 1.50×10^{-10} m is scattered at an angle of 90° in the Compton effect?

  A. 1.29×10^{-10} m   **C.** 1.84×10^{-10} m
  B. 1.52×10^{-10} m   **D.** 2.42×10^{-10} m   **E.** 3.50×10^{-10} m

26. When the surface of a metal is exposed to blue light, electrons are emitted. Which of the following increases if the intensity of the blue light increases?

  I. the maximum kinetic energy of the ejected electrons
  II. the number of electrons ejected per second
  III. the time lag between the onset of the absorption of light and the ejection of electrons

  A. I only   **C.** III only
  B. II only   **D.** I and II only   **E.** I, II and III

27. A proton has a speed of 7.2×10^4 m/s. What is the energy of a photon that has the same wavelength as the de Broglie wavelength of this proton? (Use $m_{proton} = 1.67 \times 10^{-27}$ kg and $c = 3.00 \times 10^8$ m/s)

  A. 80 keV   **C.** 160 keV
  B. 120 keV   **D.** 230 keV   **E.** 360 keV

28. In the Compton effect, as the scattering angle increases monotonically from 0° to 180°, the frequency of the X-rays scattered at that angle:

  A. decreases by the $\sqrt{2}$ **C.** increases by the $\sqrt{2}$ **E.** remains the same
  B. decreases monotonically   **D.** increases monotonically

29. In the spectrum of Hydrogen the lines obtained by setting m = 1 in the Rydberg formula is referred to as the Lyman series. What is the wavelength of the spectral line of the 15th member of the Lyman series?

- **A.** 91.6 nm
- **B.** 126.2 nm
- **C.** 244.6 nm
- **D.** 368.2 nm
- **E.** 462.8 nm

30. If the frequency of the light in a laser beam is doubled while the number of photons per second in the beam is fixed, which of the following statements is correct?

    I. The energy of individual photons doubles
    II. The wavelength of the individual photons doubles
    III. The intensity of the beam doubles

- **A.** I only
- **B.** II only
- **C.** III only
- **D.** I and III only
- **E.** I, II and III

31. The spacing of the surface planes of a crystal is 159.0 pm. A beam directed normally at the surface of the crystal undergoes first order diffraction at an angle of 58° from the normal. What is the energy of the neutrons if the diffraction is done with a beam of monenergistic neutrons? (Use 1.67×10^{-27} kg for the mass of a neutron)

- **A.** 0.0155 eV
- **B.** 0.0106 eV
- **C.** 0.0909 eV
- **D.** 0.1450 eV
- **E.** 0.2401 eV

32. A photocathode whose work function is 2.5 eV is illuminated with white light that has a continuous wavelength band from 360 nm to 700 nm. What is the stopping potential for this white light illumination?

- **A.** 0.95 V
- **B.** 1.45 V
- **C.** 1.90 V
- **D.** 2.6 V
- **E.** 3.2 V

33. If the momentum of an electron is 1.95×10^{-27} kg·m/s, what is its de Broglie wavelength? (Use $h = 6.626 \times 10^{-34}$ J·s)

- **A.** 86.2 nm
- **B.** 130.6 nm
- **C.** 240.8 nm
- **D.** 340.0 nm
- **E.** 640.5 nm

34. A Hydrogen atom is excited to the n = 9 level. Its decay to the n = 6 level is detected in a photographic plate. What is the frequency of the light photographed?

- **A.** 3,810 Hz
- **B.** 7,240 Hz
- **C.** 5.08×10^{13} Hz
- **D.** 3.28×10^{-9} Hz
- **E.** 2.24×10^{6} Hz

35. How much energy is carried by a photon of light having frequency 110 GHz? (Use $h = 6.626 \times 10^{-34}$ J·s)

- **A.** 7.3×10^{-23} J
- **B.** 2.9×10^{-25} J
- **C.** 1.7×10^{-26} J
- **D.** 1.1×10^{-21} J
- **E.** 4.4×10^{-22} J

36. How many of the infinite number of Balmer spectrum lines are in the visible spectrum range?

A. 0   **B.** 2   **C.** 4   **D.** 6   **E.** infinite

37. Each photon in a beam of light has an energy of 4.20 eV. What is the wavelength of this light? ($c = 3.00 \times 10^8$ m/s, $h = 6.626 \times 10^{-34}$ J·s and 1 eV $= 1.60 \times 10^{-19}$ J)

A. 118.0 nm   **C.** 365.0 nm

B. 296.0 nm   **D.** 462.0 nm   **E.** 520.0 nm

38. Electrons are emitted from a surface when light of wavelength 500.0 nm is shone on the surface but electrons are not emitted for longer wavelengths of light. What is the work function of the surface?

A. 0.5 eV   **C.** 2.5 eV

B. 1.6 eV   **D.** 3.8 eV   **E.** 5.6 eV

39. In the Bohr theory, the orbital radius depends upon the principal quantum number in what way?

A. n   **B.** 1/n   **C.** n^2 **D.** n^3 **E.** $1/n^2$

40. The uncertainty in the position of a proton is 0.053 nm. What is the uncertainty in its speed? (Use 1.67×10^{-27} kg as the proton mass)

A. 0.6 m/s   **C.** 2.4 m/s

B. 1.2 m/s   **D.** 3.6 m/s   **E.** 8.2 m/s

41. What is the wavelength of the light emitted by atomic Hydrogen according to the Balmer formula with m = 9 and n = 11?

A. 8,500 nm   **C.** 22,300 nm

B. 14,700 nm   **D.** 31,900 nm   **E.** 39,400 nm

42. A certain particle's energy is known within 10^{-18} J. What is the minimum uncertainty in its arrival time at a detector?

A. 10^{-12} s   **C.** 10^{-14} s

B. 10^{-13} s   **D.** 10^{-15} s   **E.** 10^{-16} s

43. Upon being struck by 240.0 nm photons, a material ejects electrons with a maximum kinetic energy of 2.58 eV. What is the work function of this material?

A. 1.20 eV   **C.** 2.60 eV

B. 2.82 eV   **D.** 3.46 eV   **E.** 4.60 eV

Atomic and Nuclear Structure

1. Which statement(s) about alpha particles is/are FALSE?

    I. They are a harmless form of radiation
    II. They have low penetrating power
    III. They have high ionization power

  A. I only   **B.** II only   **C.** III only   **D.** I and II only   **E.** I and III only

2. What is the term for nuclear radiation that is identical to an electron?

  A. Positron
  B. Gamma ray
  C. Beta minus particle
  D. Alpha particle
  E. Beta plus particle

3. Protons are being accelerated in a particle accelerator. When the speed of the protons is doubled, by what factor does their de Broglie wavelength change? Note: consider this situation non-relativistic.

  A. Increases by $\sqrt{2}$
  B. Decreases by $\sqrt{2}$
  C. Increases by 2
  D. Increases by 4
  E. Decreases by 2

4. The Bohr model of the atom was able to explain the Balmer series because:

  A. electrons were allowed to exist only in specific orbits and nowhere else
  B. differences between the energy levels of the orbits matched the differences between the energy levels of the line spectra
  C. smaller orbits require electrons to have more negative energy to match the angular momentum
  D. differences between the energy levels of the orbits were exactly half the differences between the energy levels of the line spectra
  E. none of the above

5. What nucleus results when ^{55}Ni decays by positron emission?

  A. ^{55}Ca   **B.** ^{55}Ni   **C.** ^{55}Co   **D.** ^{55}Fe   **E.** None of the above

6. Which is the missing species in the nuclear equation: $^{100}_{44}\text{Ru} + ^{0}_{-1}\text{e}^- \rightarrow$ ___?

  A. $^{100}_{45}\text{Ru}$ **B.** $^{100}_{43}\text{Ru}$ **C.** $^{101}_{44}\text{Ru}$ **D.** $^{100}_{43}\text{Tc}$ **E.** $^{101}_{43}\text{Tc}$

7. The square of the wave function represents the:

  A. inertia of the particle
  B. probability density for finding the particle
  C. velocity of the particle
  D. momentum of the particle
  E. specific quadrants for the particle

8. An isolated ^{9}Be atom spontaneously decays into two alpha particles. What can be concluded about the mass of the ^{9}Be atom?

    A. The mass is less than twice the mass of the ^{4}He atom, but not equal to the mass of ^{4}He
    B. No conclusions can be made about the mass
    C. The mass is exactly twice the mass of the ^{4}He atom
    D. The mass is equal to the mass of the ^{4}He atom
    E. The mass is greater than twice the mass of the ^{4}He atom

9. Which of the following isotopes contains the most neutrons?

    A. $^{178}_{84}$Po   **B.** $^{178}_{87}$Fr   **C.** $^{181}_{86}$Rn   **D.** $^{170}_{83}$Bi   **E.** $^{177}_{86}$Rn

10. Which of the following correctly balances this nuclear fission reaction?

$$^1_0\text{n} + ^{235}_{92}\text{U} \rightarrow ^{131}_{53}\text{I} + \underline{\hspace{1cm}} + 3\,^1_0\text{n}$$

    A. $^{102}_{39}$X   **B.** $^{102}_{36}$Kr   **C.** $^{104}_{39}$Y   **D.** $^{105}_{36}$Kr   **E.** $^{131}_{54}$I

11. What is the frequency of the light emitted by atomic hydrogen according to Balmer's formula where n = 12? (Use Balmer series constant B = 3.6×10^{-7} m and speed of light $c = 3 \times 10^8$ m/s)

    A. 5.3×10^6 Hz   **C.** 5.9×10^{13} Hz
    B. 9.8 Hz   **D.** 1.2×10^{11} Hz   **E.** 8.1×10^{14} Hz

12. Gamma rays require the heaviest shielding of all the common types of nuclear radiation because gamma rays have the:

    A. heaviest particles   **C.** most intense color
    B. lowest energy   **D.** highest energy   **E.** lowest frequency

13. In making a transition from state n = 1 to state n = 2, the hydrogen atom must [ ] a photon of [ ]. (Use Planck's constant $h = 4.14 \times 10^{-15}$ eV·s, speed of light $c = 3 \times 10^8$ m/s and Rydberg constant R = 1.097×10^7 m^{-1})

    A. absorb … 10.2 Ev   **C.** emit … 8.6 eV
    B. absorb … 8.6 eV   **D.** emit … 10.2 eV   **E.** absorb … 4.3 eV

14. Rubidium $^{87}_{37}$Rb is a naturally-occurring nuclide which undergoes β^- decay. What is the resultant nuclide from this decay?

    A. $^{86}_{36}$Rb   **B.** $^{87}_{38}$Kr   **C.** $^{87}_{38}$Sr   **D.** $^{87}_{36}$Kr   **E.** $^{86}_{37}$Rb

15. Which of the following statements best describes the role of neutrons in the nucleus?

   A. The neutrons stabilize the nucleus by attracting protons
   B. The neutrons stabilize the nucleus by balancing charge
   C. The neutrons stabilize the nucleus by attracting other nucleons
   D. The neutrons stabilize the nucleus by repelling other nucleons
   E. The neutrons stabilize the nucleus by attracting electrons

16. A Geiger–Muller counter detects radioactivity by:

   A. ionizing argon gas in a chamber which produces an electrical signal
   B. analyzing the mass and velocity of each particle
   C. developing film which is exposed by radioactive particles
   D. slowing the neutrons using a moderator and then counting the secondary charges produced
   E. converting electrical charges from a chemical reaction into light

17. An electron in a hydrogen atom is in its n = 2 excited state. What is the wavelength of photon needed to ionize this electron? (Use Planck's constant $h = 4.135 \times 10^{-15}$ eV·s and speed of light $c = 3 \times 10^8$ m/s)

   A. 365 nm   **B.** 248 nm   **C.** 137 nm   **D.** 69 nm **E.** 476 nm

18. The Lyman series is formed by electron transitions in hydrogen that:

   A. begin on the n = 2 shell   **C.** begin on the n = 1 shell
   B. end on the n = 2 shell   **D.** end on the n = 1 shell
                              E. are between the n = 1 and n = 3 shells

19. Most of the volume of an atom is occupied by:

   A. neutrons   **B.** empty space   **C.** electrons   **D.** protons   **E.** interface with protons

20. Which of the following statements regarding a nucleon is true?

   I. Attraction between nucleons changes their mass
   II. Some of the mass of a nucleon can be converted into energy by breaking certain nuclei
   III. The mass of a nucleon is different outside the nucleus

   A. I only   **B.** II only   **C.** III only   **D.** I and II only   **E.** I, II and III

21. The isotope $^{36}_{17}$Cl most likely undergoes:

   I. α decay   II. β⁻ decay   III. β⁺ decay

   A. I only   **B.** II only   **C.** III only   **D.** I and II only   **E.** II and III only

22. What is the term given to the amount of a radioactive substance that undergoes 3.7×10^{10} disintegrations per second?

   A. Rem   **B.** Rad   **C.** Curie   **D.** Roentgen   **E.** Sievert

23. An isolated ^{235}U atom spontaneously undergoes fission into two approximately equal-sized fragments. What is missing from the product side of the reaction:

$$^{235}U \rightarrow {}^{141}Ba + {}^{92}Kr + \underline{\quad}?$$

A. A neutron   **C.** Two protons and two neutrons

B. Two neutrons   **D.** Two protons and a neutron   **E.** A proton and two neutrons

24. A common reaction in the Sun involves the encounter of two nuclei of light helium ($^{3}_{2}$He). If one ^{3}He nucleus encounters another, which products are possible?

A. $^{2}H + {}^{2}H + {}^{2}H$ **C.** $^{4}He + {}^{1}H + {}^{1}H$

B. $^{7}Li + {}^{1}H$ **D.** $^{4}He + {}^{2}H$ **E.** $^{4}He + {}^{1}H$

25. Which isotope has the maximum binding energy per nucleon and therefore is represented as the maximum in the binding energy per nucleon curve?

A. ^{56}Fe   **B.** ^{1}H   **C.** ^{251}Cf   **D.** ^{197}Au   **E.** ^{4}He

26. Which of the following nuclear equations correctly describes alpha emission?

A. $^{238}_{92}U \rightarrow {}^{242}_{94}Pu + {}^{4}_{2}He$ **C.** $^{238}_{92}U \rightarrow {}^{234}_{90}Th + {}^{4}_{2}He$

B. $^{238}_{92}U \rightarrow {}^{4}_{2}He$ **D.** $^{238}_{92}U \rightarrow {}^{235}_{90}Th + {}^{4}_{2}He$ **E.** None of the above

27. A hydrogen atom makes a downward transition from the n = 20 state to the n = 5 state. Find the wavelength of the emitted photon. (Use Planck's constant $h = 4.14 \times 10^{-15}$ eV·s, speed of light $c = 3 \times 10^8$ m/s and the Rydberg constant $R = 1.097 \times 10^7$ m^{-1})

A. 1.93 µm   **B.** 2.82 µm   **C.** 1.54 µm   **D.** 1.38 µm   **E.** 2.43 µm

28. A nuclear equation is balanced when the:

A. same elements are found on both sides of the equation

B. sums of the atomic numbers of the particles and atoms are the same on both sides of the equation

C. sum of the mass numbers of the particles and the sum of atoms are the same on both sides of the equation

D. sum of the mass numbers and the sum of the atomic numbers of the particles and atoms are the same on both sides of the equation

E. charges of the particles and atoms are the same on both sides of the equation

29. A blackbody is an ideal system that:

A. absorbs 50% of the light incident upon it, and emits 50% of the radiation it generates

B. absorbs 0% of the light incident upon it, and emits 100% of the radiation it generates

C. absorbs 100% of the light incident upon it, and emits 100% of the radiation it generates

D. emits 100% of the light it generates, and absorbs 50% of the radiation incident upon it

E. absorbs 50% of the light incident upon it, and emits 100% of the radiation it generates

30. Recent nuclear bomb tests have created an extra-high level of atmospheric ^{14}C. When future archaeologists date samples, without knowing of these nuclear tests, will the dates they calculate be correct?

    A. Correct, because biological materials do not gather ^{14}C from bomb tests
    B. Correct, since the ^{14}C decays within the atmosphere at the natural rate
    C. Incorrect, they would appear too old
    D. Incorrect, they would appear too young
    E. Incorrect, since there is more ^{14}C than there should be

31. When an isotope releases gamma radiation, the atomic number:

    A. and the mass number remain the same
    B. and the mass number decrease by one
    C. and the mass number increase by one
    D. remains the same and the mass number increases by one
    E. remains the same and the mass number decreases by one

32. If $^{14}Carbon$ is a beta emitter, what is the likely product of radioactive decay?

    A. $^{22}Silicon$ **C.** $^{14}Nitrogen$
    B. $^{13}Boron$ **D.** $^{12}Carbon$ **E.** None of the above

33. In a nuclear equation, the:

    I. sum of the mass numbers on both sides must be equal
    II. sum of the atomic numbers on both sides must be equal
    III. daughter nuclide appears on the right side of the arrow

    A. I only   **B.** II only   **C.** III only   **D.** I and III only   **E.** I, II and III

34. A metal surface is illuminated with blue light and electrons are ejected at a given rate, each with a certain amount of energy. If the intensity of the blue light is increased, electrons are ejected at:

    A. an increased rate with no change in energy per electron
    B. an increased rate with an increase in energy per electron
    C. the same rate, but with an increase in energy per electron
    D. the same rate, but with a decrease in energy per electron
    E. a reduced rate with no change in energy per electron

35. Hydrogen atoms can emit four spectral lines with visible colors from red to violet. These four visible lines emitted by hydrogen atoms are produced by electrons that:

    A. end in the ground state   **C.** end in the $n = 2$ level
    B. end in the $n = 3$ level   **D.** start in the ground state   **E.** start in the $n = 3$ level

36. The electron was discovered through experiments with:

    A. quarks   **B.** foil   **C.** light   **D.** electricity   **E.** magnets

Questions **37-39** are based on the following:

The image shows a beam of radiation passing between two electrically-charged plates.

I. a
II. b
III. c

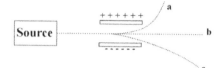

37. Which of the beams is due to an energetic light wave?

  A. I only   **B.** II only   **C.** III only   **D.** I and II only   **E.** None

38. Which of the beams is/are composed of particles?

  A. I only   **B.** II only   **C.** III only   **D.** I and III only   **E.** I, II and III

39. Which of the beams is due to a positively-charged helium nucleus?

  A. I only   **B.** II only   **C.** III only   **D.** I, II and III   **E.** None of the above

40. Lithium atoms are able to absorb photons transitioning from the ground state (at −5.37 eV) to an excited state with one electron removed from the atom, which corresponds to the zero energy state. What is the wavelength of light associated with this transition? (Use Planck's constant $h = 4.14 \times 10^{-15}$ eV·s and speed of light $c = 3 \times 10^{8}$ m/s)

  A. 6.6×10^{-6} m   **C.** 3.6×10^{6} m
  B. 2.3×10^{-7} m   **D.** 4.2×10^{5} m   **E.** 2.6×10^{-6} m

41. All of the elements with atomic numbers of 84 and higher are radioactive because:

  A. strong attractions between their nucleons make them unstable
  B. their atomic numbers are larger than their mass numbers
  C. strong repulsions between their electrons make them unstable
  D. strong repulsions between their protons make their nuclei unstable
  E. strong repulsions between their neutrons make their nuclei unstable

42. Which of the following statements about β particles is FALSE?

  A. They have a smaller mass than α particles
  B. They have high energy and a charge
  C. They are created when neutrons become protons and vise versa
  D. They can be positively or negatively charged
  E. They are a harmless form of radioactivity

43. According to the Pauli Exclusion Principle, how many electrons in an atom may have a particular set of quantum numbers?

    A. 1   **B.** 2   **C.** 3   **D.** 4   **E.** 5

44. Which statement regarding Planck's constant is true?

    A. It relates mass to the amount of energy that can be emitted
    B. It sets a lower limit to the amount of energy that can be absorbed or emitted
    C. It sets an upper limit to the amount of energy that can be absorbed
    D. It sets an upper limit to the amount of energy that can be absorbed or emitted
    E. It relates mass to the amount of energy that can be absorbed or emitted

45. The decay rate of a radioactive isotope will NOT be increased by increasing the:

    I. surface area   II. pressure   III. temperature

    A. I only   **B.** II only   **C.** III only   **D.** I and III only   **E.** I, II and III

46. Why are some smaller nuclei such as ^{14}Carbon often radioactive?

    I. The attractive force of the nucleons has a limited range
    II. The neutron to proton ratio is too large or too small
    III. Most smaller nuclei are not stable

    A. I only   **B.** II only   **C.** III only   **D.** II and III only   **E.** I and III only

47. Scandium ^{44}Sc decays by emitting a positron. What is the resultant nuclide which is produced by this decay?

    A. $^{43}_{21}$Sc   **B.** $^{45}_{21}$Sc   **C.** $^{44}_{20}$Ca   **D.** $^{43}_{20}$Ca   **E.** $^{45}_{22}$Ti

48. A scintillation counter detects radioactivity by:

    A. analyzing the mass and velocity of each electron
    B. ionizing argon gas in a chamber which produces an electrical signal
    C. emitting light from a NaI crystal when radioactivity passes through the crystal
    D. developing film which is exposed by radioactive particles
    E. slowing the neutrons using a moderator and then counting the secondary charges produced

49. Which of the following is indicated by each detection sound by a Geiger counter?

    A. One half-life   **C.** One neutron being emitted
    B. One nucleus decaying   **D.** One positron being emitted   **E.** None of the above

Special Relativity

1. Consider three galaxies, Alpha, Beta and Gamma. An astronomer in Beta sees each of the other two galaxies moving away from him in opposite directions at $0.70c$. At what speed would an observer in Alpha see the galaxy Gamma moving?

A. $0.94c$ **B.** $0.84c$ **C.** $1.2c$ **D.** $0.65c$ **E.** $0.98c$

2. A super high-speed train moves in a direction parallel to its length with a speed that approaches the speed of light. The height of the train, as measured by a stationary observer on the ground:

A. decreases slightly
B. increases slightly
C. approaches zero
D. approaches infinity
E. does not change due to the motion

3. A spaceship visits Alpha Centauri and returns to Earth. Alpha Centauri is 4.367 light-years from Earth. If the spaceship travels at one-half the speed of light for essentially all of its expedition, how long was the ship gone according to an observer on Earth?

A. 2.184 years
B. 2.090 years
C. 4.367 years
D. 17.468 years
E. 19.010 years

4. A muon at rest decays in 2.2 μs. Moving at 99% the speed of light, it would be seen to "live" for how long?

A. 0.31 μs
B. 0.218 μs
C. 2.178 μs
D. 4.356 μs
E. 16 μs

5. A spaceship approaching an asteroid at a speed of $0.6c$ launches a scout rocket with speed $0.4c$. At what speed is the scout rocket approaching the asteroid from the point of view of the asteroid?

A. $0.52c$ **B.** $1.15c$ **C.** $0.66c$ **D.** $0.81c$ **E.** $0.73c$

6. An astronaut is resting on a bed inclined at an angle above the floor of a spaceship, with his head elevated near the front of the capsule while his feet are lower and facing the rear of the capsule. From the point of view of an observer who sees the spaceship moving near the speed of light parallel to the floor, the angle the bed makes with the floor:

A. could be greater or smaller than the angle observed by the astronaut depending on whether the rocket is moving to the right or to the left
B. is smaller than the angle observed by the astronaut
C. is the same as the angle observed by the astronaut
D. is greater than the angle observed by the astronaut
E. cannot be determined from the information provided

7. As measured in Earth's rest frame, a spaceship traveling at $0.9640c$ takes 10.5 years to travel between two planets that are not moving relative to each other. How many years does the trip take as measured by someone on the spaceship?

    A. 2.79   **B.** 5.43   **C.** 8.42   **D.** 19.25   **E.** 28.65

8. A hydrogen atom and a neutron fuse to form deuterium. If the energy released is 3.6×10^{-13} J, what is the mass of the deuterium? (Use the H atom nucleus as a single proton.).

    A. 0.85×10^{-20} kg   **C.** 3.3×10^{-27} kg

    B. 1.6×10^{-27} kg   **D.** 4.1×10^{-27} kg   **E.** 5.3×10^{-27} kg

9. Steve is moving past Earth at $0.99c$ and notices his heart beating 88 times/minute. What does his doctor on Earth observe his heart rate to be?

    A. 8 beats/min   **C.** 22 beats/min

    B. 12 beats/min   **D.** 28 beats/min   **E.** 33 beats/min

10. Two spaceships are approaching one another, each at a speed of $0.31c$ relative to a stationary observer on Earth. What speed, in terms of the speed of light, does an observer on one spaceship record for the other approaching spaceship?

    A. $0.71c$ **B.** $0.38c$ **C.** $0.57c$ **D.** $0.64c$ **E.** $0.69c$

11. The special theory of relativity predicts that there is an upper limit to the speed of a particle. It thus follows that there is also an upper limit on which of the following property of a particle:

    A. the kinetic energy   **C.** the linear momentum

    B. the total energy   **D.** more than one of these is correct

                                              E. none of the above

12. Two fixed navigation beacons mark the approach lane to a star. The beacons are in line with the star and are 49 million meters apart. A spaceship approaches the star with a relative velocity of $0.50c$ and passes the beacons. The passage of the ship between the beacons is timed by an observer on the ship. What is the time interval of the passage?

    A. 240 ms   **B.** 280 ms   **C.** 360 ms   **D.** 140 ms   **E.** 90 ms

13. A pion is an unstable particle that has a mean lifetime of 2.55×10^{-8} s. This is the time interval between its creation in a nuclear process and its extinction into decay products, as measured in a frame of reference at rest with respect to the pion. How far does it travel in its lifetime, relative to Earth? (Use the value that an average pion travels at $0.230c$ relative to Earth).

    A. 1.81 m   **B.** 1.09 m   **C.** 2.46 m   **D.** 3.83 m   **E.** 4.56 m

14. Astronaut Yuri is space-travelling from planet Y to planet Z at a speed of $0.60c$. When he is precisely halfway between the planets, a distance of 1 light-hour from each as measured in the frame of the planets, nuclear devices are detonated. The explosions are simultaneous in the frame of the planets. What is the difference in time of arrival of the flashes from the explosions as observed by Yuri?

A. 45 min   **C.** 125 min

B. 90 min   **D.** 300 min   **E.** 385 min

15. From Earth, humans see the Enterprise approaching from the west at $0.800c$ and the Klingons approaching from the east at $0.900c$. What speed, in terms of the speed of light, does the crew of the Enterprise measure for the Klingon ship?

A. $0.721c$ **B.** $0.378c$ **C.** $0.547c$ **D.** $0.988c$ **E.** $0.659c$

16. Sofia is a passenger on a spaceship. After the speed of the spaceship has increased, she observes:

A. her watch moving slower

B. her watch moving faster

C. her watch got bigger

D. her watch got smaller

E. nothing unusual about the behavior of her watch

17. Two fixed navigation beacons mark the approach lane to a star. The beacons are in line with the star and are 40 million meters apart. A spaceship approaches the star with a relative velocity of $0.30c$ and passes the beacons. The passage of the ship between the beacons is timed by observers on the beacons. What is the time interval of the passage?

A. 610 ms   **B.** 560 ms   **C.** 444 ms   **D.** 240 ms   **E.** 180 ms

18. Calculate the kinetic energy of an electron moving at $0.737c$. (Use the rest energy of an electron = 511 keV)

A. 184 keV   **C.** 292 keV

B. 245 keV   **D.** 338 keV   **E.** 446 keV

19. In a common rest frame, event A happens on planet A and event B occurs on planet B 100 years later. If the space time interval between these two events is 90 light-years, how far apart are the 2 planets in their common rest frame?

A. 18 light-years   **C.** 32 light-years

B. 22 light-years   **D.** 44 light-years   **E.** 52 light-years

20. At what speed are lengths contracted to half and times dilated by a factor of 2?

A. $0.866c$ **B.** $0.986c$ **C.** $1.007c$ **D.** $1.134c$ **E.** $1.472c$

21. Suppose one twin takes a ride in a spaceship traveling at a very high speed to a distant star and then back again, while the other twin remains on Earth. Compared to the twin who remained on Earth, the twin who rode in the spaceship is:

    A. younger than the Earth-twin
    B. the same age as the Earth-twin
    C. older than the Earth-twin
    D. The ages cannot be determined from the information provided
    E. Both younger and older than the Earth-twin

22. Two satellites with equal rest masses of 100 kg are traveling toward each other in deep space. One is traveling at $0.650c$ and the other at $0.850c$. The satellites collide and somehow manage to stick together. What is the rest mass of the combined object after the collision?

    A. 100 kg   **B.** 208 kg   **C.** 246 kg   **D.** 366 kg   **E.** 312 kg

23. What is the momentum of a proton when it is moving with a speed of $0.60c$? (Use the mass of a proton $m_{proton} = 1.67 \times 10^{-27}$ kg)

    A. 1.4×10^{-19} kg·m/s   **C.** 5.3×10^{-19} kg·m/s
    B. 2.6×10^{-19} kg·m/s   **D.** 3.8×10^{-19} kg·m/s
                                               E. 8.8×10^{-19} kg·m/s

24. How many joules of energy are required to accelerate a 1.0 kg rock from rest to a speed of $0.866c$? (Use speed of light $c = 3.0 \times 10^8$ m/s)

    A. 2.6×10^{16} J   **C.** 6.8×10^{17} J
    B. 9.0×10^{16} J   **D.** 4.3×10^{16} J   **E.** 5.6×10^{16} J

25. A spaceship traveling at $0.50c$ away from Earth launches a secondary rocket in the forward direction at $0.50c$ relative to the spaceship. As measured from the frame of Earth, how fast is the secondary rocket moving away from Earth?

    A. $0.92c$ **B.** $0.56c$ **C.** $0.80c$ **D.** $0.72c$ **E.** c

26. Observer A sees a pendulum oscillating back and forth in a relativistic rocket and measures its period to be T_A. Observer B moves along with the rocket and measures the period of the pendulum to be T_B. What is true about these two time measurements?

    A. $T_A > T_B$
    B. $T_A = T_B$
    C. $T_A < T_B$
    D. T_A could be greater or smaller than T_A depending on the direction of the motion
    E. T_A is greater than or equal to T_B

27. A spaceship travels to Alpha Centauri. The nearby star Alpha Centauri is 4.367 light-years from Earth. If the spaceship travels at one-half the speed of light for essentially all of its expedition, how long was the ship gone according to an observer on the spaceship?

   A. 4.5 years   **C.** 8.7 years

   B. 7.6 years   **D.** 11.3 years   **E.** 12.4 years

28. A particle physicist observes cosmic rays creating a new particle high in the atmosphere, and the speed of this particle is measured at $0.997c$. It is unstable, and is observed to decay in an average 37.0 μs. If this particle were at rest in the laboratory, what would be its average lifetime?

   A. 8.4 μs   **B.** 7.3 μs   **C.** 16.4 μs   **D.** 2.9 μs   **E.** 4.8 μs

29. If, instead of the correct formula for kinetic energy, someone carelessly uses the classical expression for kinetic energy for a particle moving at half the speed of light, by what magnitude percent will their calculation be in error? (Use the speed of light $c = 3.0 \times 10^8$ m/s)

   A. 8%   **B.** 12%   **C.** 19%   **D.** 27%   **E.** 31%

30. In their common rest frame, two stars are 90.0 light-years apart. If they appear to be 68.7 light-years apart to a spaceship, how fast is the spaceship moving?

   A. $0.323c$ **C.** $0.246c$

   B. $0.646c$ **D.** $0.810c$ **E.** $1.40c$

31. Robert is riding in a spaceship that has no windows, radios, or other means for him to observe or measure what is outside. How can he determine if the ship is stopped or moving at constant velocity?

   A. He determines if the ship is moving by measuring the apparent velocity of light in the spaceship

   B. He can determine if the ship is moving by checking his precision time piece. If it's running slow, the ship is moving

   C. He can determine if the ship is moving by lying down and measuring his height. If he is shorter than usual, the ship is moving

   D. It is not possible for him to determine if the ship is stopped or moving at constant velocity

   E. He can determine if the ship is moving by lying down facing one direction and measuring his height and then turning to face a different direction and again measuring his height. If the two measurements are different, then he is moving

32. Two satellites with equal rest masses are traveling toward each other in deep space. One is traveling at $0.550c$ and the other at $0.750c$. What is the speed of the combined object after the collision if the satellites collide and stick together?

   A. $0.108c$ **B.** $0.124c$ **C.** $0.245c$ **D.** $0.175c$ **E.** $0.328c$

33. A spaceship approaches Earth with a speed 0.50c. A passenger in the spaceship measures his heartbeat as 70 beats per minute. What is his heartbeat rate according to an observer that is at rest relative to Earth?

A. 61 beats per minute

B. 55 beats per minute

C. 68 beats per minute

D. 76 beats per minute

E. 82 beats per minute

34. A particle in a 453-m long particle accelerator is moving at 0.875c. How long does the particle accelerator appear to the particle?

A. 148 m

B. 219 m

C. 264 m

D. 462 m

E. 517 m

35. Someone in Earth's rest frame says that a spaceship's trip between two planets took 10.0 years, while an astronaut on the space ship says that the trip took 5.78 years. What is the speed of the spaceship, assuming the planets are at essentially at rest?

A. 0.244c B. 0.515c C. 0.816c D. 1.17c E. 2.37c

36. A super-speed train moves in a direction parallel to its length with a speed that approaches the speed of light. The length of the train, as measured by a stationary observer on the ground:

A. approaches infinity

B. increases due to the motion

C. decreases due to the motion

D. is not affected by the motion

E. cannot be measured because the train is moving

37. A spaceship enters the solar system moving toward the sun at a constant speed relative to the sun. By its own clock, the time elapsed between the time it crosses the orbit of Jupiter and the time it crosses the orbit of Mars is 50.0 minutes. As measured in the coordinate system of the sun, how many minutes did it take for the spaceship to travel that distance? (Use the radius of the orbit of Jupiter = 778×10^9 m and the orbit of Mars = 228×10^9 m)

A. 28.4 minutes

B. 44.8 minutes

C. 58.6 minutes

D. 66.2 minutes

E. 88.8 minutes

38. Two fixed navigation beacons mark the approach lane to a star. The beacons are in line with the star and are 65×10^6 meters apart. A spaceship approaches the star with a relative velocity of 0.90c and passes the beacons. As the ship passes the first beacon the ship emits a short radar pulse toward the second beacon, and the radar echo is received at the ship. What is the time interval between the emission of the radar pulse and the reception of the radar echo as measured on the spaceship?

A. 210 ms   B. 420 ms   C. 130 ms   D. 100 ms   E. 60 ms

39. An electron that was initially at rest reaches a speed of $0.648c$. Through what potential difference would the electron need to be accelerated to reach this speed? (Use the rest energy of an electron = 511 keV)

    A. 120 keV   **B.** 160 keV   **C.** 190 keV   **D.** 230 keV   **E.** 280 keV

40. A certain unstable particle has a mean lifetime of 1.52×10^{-6} s. This is the time interval between its creation in a nuclear process and its extinction into decay products, as measured in a frame of reference at rest with respect to the particle. An average such particle is observed by a scientist on Earth to travel 342 m in its lifetime. What is the speed of the particle relative to Earth? (Use the speed of light $c = 3.00 \times 10^8$ m/s)

    A. $0.844c$ **B.** $0.486c$ **C.** $0.600c$ **D.** $0.754c$ **E.** $0.324c$

41. The relativistic kinetic energy formula is valid:

    I. for speeds near the speed of light
    II. for subatomic particles, such as electrons and protons
    III. at all speeds

    A. I only   **C.** III only
    B. II only   **D.** I and II only   **E.** I and III only

42. A spaceship with a constant velocity of $0.800c$ relative to Earth travels to the star that is 4.30 light-years from Earth. Measured by a passenger on the ship, what distance does the space ship travel?

    A. 1.32 light-years   **C.** 3.82 light-years
    B. 2.58 light-years   **D.** 4.60 light-years   **E.** 6.44 light-years

43. A spaceship is moving away from an asteroid with a speed of $0.80c$ relative to the asteroid. The spaceship then fires a missile with a speed of $0.50c$ relative to the spaceship. What is the speed of the missile measured by astronauts on the asteroid if the missile is fired away from the asteroid?

    A. $0.43c$ **B.** $0.93c$ **C.** $0.18c$ **D.** $0.37c$ **E.** $0.72c$

44. What is the total energy of an electron moving with a speed of $0.950c$? (Use the speed of light $c = 3.0 \times 10^8$ m/s and $m_{el} = 9.11 \times 10^{-31}$ kg)

    A. 2.6×10^{-13} J   **C.** 1.8×10^{-13} J
    B. 7.4×10^{-14} J   **D.** 3.6×10^{-14} J   **E.** 6.6×10^{-13} J

45. A spaceship carrying a light clock moves at a speed of $0.960c$ relative to an observer on Earth. If the clock on the ship advances by 1.00 s as measured by the space travelers aboard the ship, how long did that advance take as measured by the observer on Earth?

    A. 0.84 s   **B.** 1.9 s   **C.** 2.4 s   **D.** 3.6 s   **E.** 4.8 s

46. In an "atom smasher," two particles collide head on at relativistic speeds. The velocity of the first particle is $0.741c$ to the left, and the velocity of the second particle is $0.543c$ to the right (both of these speeds are measured in Earth's rest frame). How fast are the particles moving with respect to each other?

A. $0.916c$ C. $0.744c$

B. $1.164c$ D. $0.836c$ E. $0.448c$

47. A particle is moving at approximately $0.86c$. Expressed as a percentage error for the difference between the erroneous and correct expressions, relative to the correct one, by what percentage is the Newtonian expression for momentum in error?

A. 49%   C. 57%

B. 38%   D. 64%   E. 22%

48. A spaceship, traveling at $0.100c$ away from a stationary space platform, launches a secondary rocket towards the station, with a speed of $0.560c$ relative to the spaceship. What is the speed of the secondary rocket relative to the space platform?

A. $0.364c$ B. $0.487c$ C. $0.524c$ D. $0.588c$ E. $0.682c$

49. An electron slowing from $0.998c$ to $0.500c$ loses how much momentum?

A. 2.17 MeV/c   C. 5.28 MeV/c

B. 4.36 MeV/c   D. 7.77 MeV/c   E. 12.44 MeV/c

50. A star is moving toward Earth at $0.90c$. The star emits light, which moves away from the star at the speed of light. What do Earth-based astronomers measure for the speed of this light?

A. $0.88c$ B. $1.1c$ C. $1.8c$ D. c E. $0.90c$

Diagnostic Tests

Answer Keys & Explanations

Diagnostic test #1

1	A	Kinematics & dynamics	31	B	Kinematics & dynamics
2	E	Force, motion, gravitation	32	A	Work & energy
3	C	Heat & thermodynamics	33	B	Waves & periodic motion
4	B	Work & energy	34	D	Heat & thermodynamics
5	E	Waves & periodic motion	35	B	Light & geometrical optics
6	B	Sound	36	E	Electric circuits
7	A	Fluids & solids	37	C	Electrostatics & electromagnetism
8	A	Electrostatics & electromagnetism	38	A	Fluids & solids
9	D	Electric circuits	39	A	Heat & thermodynamics
10	E	Light & optics	40	E	Waves & periodic motion
11	B	Atomic & nuclear structure	41	D	Work & energy
12	B	Equilibrium & momentum	42	C	Equilibrium & momentum
13	E	Work & energy	43	C	Special relativity
14	A	Waves & periodic motion	44	A	Waves & periodic motion
15	A	Sound	45	D	Heat & thermodynamics
16	B	Rotational motion	46	C	Work & energy
17	C	Electrostatics & electromagnetism	47	B	Sound
18	A	Electric circuits	48	C	Electrostatics & electromagnetism
19	C	Light & geometrical optics	49	D	Fluids & solids
20	C	Sound	50	D	Kinematics & dynamics
21	B	Heat & thermodynamics	51	D	Equilibrium & momentum
22	E	Force, motion, gravitation	52	E	Light & optics
23	D	Sound	53	C	Sound
24	C	Waves & periodic motion	54	E	Electric circuits
25	B	Electrostatics & electromagnetism	55	E	Rotational motion
26	E	Electric circuits	56	E	Heat & thermodynamics
27	A	Light & geometrical optics	57	C	Kinematics & dynamics
28	C	Quantum mechanics	58	D	Force, motion, gravitation
29	B	Kinematics & dynamics	59	C	Electrostatics & electromagnetism
30	D	Force, motion, gravitation	60	B	Atomic & nuclear structure

61	**A**	Electrostatics & electromagnetism	**81**	**D**	Special relativity
62	**B**	Force, motion, gravitation	**82**	**C**	Atomic & nuclear structure
63	**E**	Heat & thermodynamics	**83**	**B**	Sound
64	**C**	Work & energy	**84**	**E**	Fluids & solids
65	**C**	Waves & periodic motion	**85**	**D**	Electrostatics & electromagnetism
66	**B**	Sound	**86**	**A**	Heat & thermodynamics
67	**C**	Fluids & solids	**87**	**A**	Light & optics
68	**D**	Electrostatics & electromagnetism	**88**	**B**	Atomic & nuclear structure
69	**C**	Electric circuits	**89**	**D**	Fluids & solids
70	**C**	Light & optics	**90**	**D**	Force, motion, gravitation
71	**C**	Atomic & nuclear structure	**91**	**B**	Equilibrium & momentum
72	**B**	Equilibrium & momentum	**92**	**B**	Work & energy
73	**C**	Work & energy	**93**	**A**	Waves & periodic motion
74	**A**	Waves & periodic motion	**94**	**D**	Heat & thermodynamics
75	**B**	Sound	**95**	**D**	Light & optics
76	**A**	Fluids & solids	**96**	**E**	Quantum mechanics
77	**E**	Electrostatics & electromagnetism	**97**	**B**	Heat & thermodynamics
78	**C**	Electric circuits	**98**	**B**	Fluids & solids
79	**C**	Light & optics	**99**	**C**	Sound
80	**A**	Atomic & nuclear structure	**100**	**A**	Waves & periodic motion

Diagnostic test #2

1	B	Work & energy
2	E	Equilibrium & momentum
3	D	Force, motion, gravitation
4	A	Kinematics & dynamics
5	B	Rotational motion
6	E	Work & energy
7	D	Sound
8	A	Electrostatics & electromagnetism
9	B	Work & energy
10	B	Kinematics & dynamics
11	E	Equilibrium & momentum
12	D	Waves & periodic motion
13	C	Fluids & solids
14	D	Electric circuits
15	D	Atomic & nuclear structure
16	E	Heat & thermodynamics
17	C	Kinematics & dynamics
18	A	Force, motion, gravitation
19	C	Equilibrium & momentum
20	B	Atomic & nuclear structure
21	D	Kinematics & dynamics
22	A	Force, motion, gravitation
23	D	Heat & thermodynamics
24	E	Work & energy
25	E	Waves & periodic motion
26	D	Sound
27	C	Fluids & solids
28	B	Electrostatics & electromagnetism
29	D	Special relativity
30	C	Light & optics
31	E	Atomic & nuclear structure
32	C	Equilibrium & momentum
33	C	Work & energy
34	B	Waves & periodic motion
35	C	Sound
36	B	Electrostatics & electromagnetism
37	E	Electrostatics & electromagnetism
38	B	Electric circuits
39	B	Light & optics
40	C	Atomic & nuclear structure
41	E	Heat & thermodynamics
42	C	Force, motion, gravitation
43	D	Sound
44	D	Fluids & solids
45	B	Electrostatics & electromagnetism
46	C	Electric circuits
47	E	Light & optics
48	B	Atomic & nuclear structure
49	E	Quantum mechanics
50	B	Force, motion, gravitation
51	E	Equilibrium & momentum
52	A	Work & energy
53	D	Waves & periodic motion
54	C	Heat & thermodynamics
55	D	Light & optics
56	A	Electric circuits
57	B	Electrostatics & electromagnetism
58	E	Sound
59	A	Waves & periodic motion
60	B	Waves & periodic motion

61	A	Work & energy	**81**	E	Kinematics & dynamics
62	C	Equilibrium & momentum	**82**	B	Force, motion, gravitation
63	D	Rotational motion	**83**	B	Heat & thermodynamics
64	A	Kinematics & dynamics	**84**	B	Work & energy
65	B	Light & optics	**85**	E	Waves & periodic motion
66	A	Work & energy	**86**	D	Sound
67	A	Light & optics	**87**	A	Fluids & solids
68	A	Electrostatics & electromagnetism	**88**	D	Electrostatics & electromagnetism
69	B	Special relativity	**89**	C	Electric circuits
70	A	Kinematics & dynamics	**90**	B	Light & optics
71	C	Equilibrium & momentum	**91**	C	Atomic & nuclear structure
72	C	Quantum mechanics	**92**	D	Equilibrium & momentum
73	E	Fluids & solids	**93**	A	Work & energy
74	A	Electric circuits	**94**	D	Waves & periodic motion
75	B	Atomic & nuclear structure	**95**	E	Sound
76	A	Heat & thermodynamics	**96**	C	Fluids & solids
77	B	Kinematics & dynamics	**97**	B	Electrostatics & electromagnetism
78	C	Force, motion, gravitation	**98**	A	Electric circuits
79	B	Equilibrium & momentum	**99**	A	Light & optics
80	E	Atomic & nuclear structure	**100**	C	Atomic & nuclear structure

Diagnostic test #3

1	D	Electric circuits	31	C	Equilibrium & momentum
2	C	Force, motion, gravitation	32	B	Waves & periodic motion
3	E	Sound	33	A	Fluids & solids
4	A	Fluids & solids	34	B	Electric circuits
5	D	Rotational motion	35	C	Atomic & nuclear structure
6	C	Electric circuits	36	D	Heat & thermodynamics
7	D	Light & optics	37	B	Kinematics & dynamics
8	D	Atomic & nuclear structure	38	D	Force, motion, gravitation
9	E	Kinematics & dynamics	39	B	Equilibrium & momentum
10	A	Force, motion, gravitation	40	E	Atomic & nuclear structure
11	B	Equilibrium & momentum	41	B	Quantum mechanics
12	E	Work & energy	42	A	Force, motion, gravitation
13	C	Waves & periodic motion	43	B	Heat & thermodynamics
14	C	Heat & thermodynamics	44	A	Work & energy
15	B	Light & optics	45	B	Waves & periodic motion
16	A	Atomic & nuclear structure	46	E	Sound
17	B	Electrostatics & electromagnetism	47	D	Fluids & solids
18	A	Fluids & solids	48	D	Electrostatics & electromagnetism
19	A	Sound	49	B	Electric circuits
20	D	Waves & periodic motion	50	B	Light & optics
21	C	Work & energy	51	D	Atomic & nuclear structure
22	C	Equilibrium & momentum	52	C	Equilibrium & momentum
23	D	Special relativity	53	E	Work & energy
24	E	Kinematics & dynamics	54	A	Waves & periodic motion
25	A	Heat & thermodynamics	55	E	Fluids & solids
26	D	Work & energy	56	E	Fluids & solids
27	D	Sound	57	A	Electric circuits
28	B	Electrostatics & electromagnetism	58	B	Electric circuits
29	B	Light & optics	59	C	Light & optics
30	D	Heat & thermodynamics	60	B	Rotational motion

61	D	Atomic & nuclear structure	**81**	A	Work & energy
62	C	Force, motion, gravitation	**82**	B	Equilibrium & momentum
63	B	Sound	**83**	C	Force, motion, gravitation
64	A	Fluids & solids	**84**	B	Kinematics & dynamics
65	D	Electrostatics & electromagnetism	**85**	C	Heat & thermodynamics
66	E	Electric circuits	**86**	A	Work & energy
67	B	Fluids & solids	**87**	E	Sound
68	D	Electrostatics & electromagnetism	**88**	A	Electrostatics & electromagnetism
69	B	Kinematics & dynamics	**89**	D	Light & optics
70	D	Force, motion, gravitation	**90**	C	Electric circuits
71	A	Equilibrium & momentum	**91**	C	Equilibrium & momentum
72	B	Work & energy	**92**	C	Waves & periodic motion
73	B	Waves & periodic motion	**93**	E	Fluids & solids
74	B	Special relativity	**94**	C	Electric circuits
75	A	Light & optics	**95**	C	Atomic & nuclear structure
76	B	Electric circuits	**96**	D	Heat & thermodynamics
77	D	Electrostatics & electromagnetism	**97**	B	Kinematics & dynamics
78	A	Fluids & solids	**98**	D	Quantum mechanics
79	C	Sound	**99**	E	Equilibrium & momentum
80	E	Waves & periodic motion	**100**	A	Atomic & nuclear structure

Diagnostic test #4

1	D	Kinematics & dynamics	31	B	Equilibrium & momentum
2	A	Force, motion, gravitation	32	A	Work & energy
3	A	Fluids & solids	33	D	Waves & periodic motion
4	C	Work & energy	34	B	Heat & thermodynamics
5	A	Waves & periodic motion	35	E	Light & optics
6	B	Sound	36	B	Electric circuits
7	C	Fluids & solids	37	B	Electric circuits
8	A	Electrostatics & electromagnetism	38	E	Fluids & solids
9	C	Electric circuits	39	C	Sound
10	E	Light & optics	40	D	Waves & periodic motion
11	B	Atomic & nuclear structure	41	E	Work & energy
12	C	Equilibrium & momentum	42	A	Equilibrium & momentum
13	B	Work & energy	43	C	Force, motion, gravitation
14	D	Waves & periodic motion	44	E	Kinematics & dynamics
15	B	Sound	45	A	Heat & thermodynamics
16	D	Fluids & solids	46	C	Work & energy
17	D	Electrostatics & electromagnetism	47	A	Quantum mechanics
18	A	Electric circuits	48	D	Electrostatics & electromagnetism
19	C	Light & optics	49	B	Light & optics
20	D	Rotational motion	50	C	Electrostatics & electromagnetism
21	B	Heat & thermodynamics	51	C	Equilibrium & momentum
22	E	Force, motion, gravitation	52	E	Waves & periodic motion
23	B	Sound	53	D	Fluids & solids
24	C	Fluids & solids	54	A	Electric circuits
25	A	Electrostatics & electromagnetism	55	B	Atomic & nuclear structure
26	C	Electric circuits	56	D	Heat & thermodynamics
27	D	Light & optics	57	E	Kinematics & dynamics
28	C	Atomic & nuclear structure	58	B	Force, motion, gravitation
29	C	Heat & thermodynamics	59	D	Equilibrium & momentum
30	B	Special relativity	60	E	Atomic & nuclear structure

61	A	Kinematics & dynamics	**81**	E	Heat & thermodynamics
62	D	Force, motion, gravitation	**82**	C	Force, motion, gravitation
63	C	Heat & thermodynamics	**83**	A	Sound
64	B	Work & energy	**84**	B	Fluids & solids
65	A	Waves & periodic motion	**85**	B	Electrostatics & electromagnetism
66	A	Sound	**86**	E	Special relativity
67	A	Fluids & solids	**87**	B	Light & optics
68	D	Electrostatics & electromagnetism	**88**	C	Atomic & nuclear structure
69	C	Electric circuits	**89**	B	Kinematics & dynamics
70	B	Light & optics	**90**	E	Force, motion, gravitation
71	A	Atomic & nuclear structure	**91**	D	Equilibrium & momentum
72	E	Equilibrium & momentum	**92**	A	Work & energy
73	D	Work & energy	**93**	C	Waves & periodic motion
74	E	Rotational motion	**94**	D	Heat & thermodynamics
75	D	Sound	**95**	E	Light & optics
76	E	Fluids & solids	**96**	E	Electric circuits
77	A	Electrostatics & electromagnetism	**97**	B	Force, motion, gravitaion
78	A	Electric circuits	**98**	D	Quantum mechanics
79	C	Light & optics	**99**	D	Sound
80	D	Atomic & nuclear structure	**100**	B	Waves & periodic motion

Diagnostic test #5

1	D	Work & energy	31	C	Atomic & nuclear structure
2	D	Equilibrium & momentum	32	B	Equilibrium & momentum
3	A	Rotational motion	33	E	Work & energy
4	E	Kinematics & dynamics	34	B	Waves & periodic motion
5	D	Heat & thermodynamics	35	C	Sound
6	A	Work & energy	36	E	Fluids & solids
7	D	Sound	37	B	Electrostatics & electromagnetism
8	E	Electrostatics & electromagnetism	38	C	Electric circuits
9	C	Light & optics	39	D	Light & optics
10	B	Kinematics & dynamics	40	E	Atomic & nuclear structure
11	C	Equilibrium & momentum	41	A	Heat & thermodynamics
12	E	Waves & periodic motion	42	B	Force, motion, gravitation
13	A	Fluids & solids	43	B	Sound
14	B	Kinematics & dynamics	44	B	Fluids & solids
15	C	Atomic & nuclear structure	45	A	Electrostatics & electromagnetism
16	E	Heat & thermodynamics	46	C	Electric circuits
17	C	Special relativity	47	C	Light & optics
18	B	Quantum mechanics	48	E	Atomic & nuclear structure
19	A	Equilibrium & momentum	49	A	Kinematics & dynamics
20	C	Atomic & nuclear structure	50	D	Force, motion, gravitation
21	D	Kinematics & dynamics	51	B	Equilibrium & momentum
22	E	Force, motion, gravitation	52	C	Work & energy
23	C	Heat & thermodynamics	53	E	Waves & periodic motion
24	B	Work & energy	54	D	Heat & thermodynamics
25	D	Waves & periodic motion	55	D	Light & optics
26	B	Sound	56	E	Electric circuits
27	C	Fluids & solids	57	A	Electrostatics & electromagnetism
28	A	Electrostatics & electromagnetism	58	B	Fluids & solids
29	C	Electric circuits	59	D	Sound
30	A	Light & optics	60	C	Waves & periodic motion

61	D	Work & energy	**81**	B	Kinematics & dynamics
62	C	Equilibrium & momentum	**82**	C	Force, motion, gravitation
63	A	Force, motion, gravitation	**83**	E	Heat & thermodynamics
64	B	Kinematics & dynamics	**84**	A	Work & energy
65	A	Heat & thermodynamics	**85**	B	Waves & periodic motion
66	C	Kinematics & dynamics	**86**	C	Sound
67	B	Rotational motion	**87**	A	Waves & periodic motion
68	C	Electrostatics & electromagnetism	**88**	A	Special relativity
69	D	Light & optics	**89**	E	Electric circuits
70	C	Heat & thermodynamics	**90**	D	Light & optics
71	D	Equilibrium & momentum	**91**	B	Atomic & nuclear structure
72	B	Waves & periodic motion	**92**	D	Equilibrium & momentum
73	A	Fluids & solids	**93**	C	Work & energy
74	D	Electric circuits	**94**	A	Waves & periodic motion
75	E	Atomic & nuclear structure	**95**	C	Sound
76	B	Heat & thermodynamics	**96**	E	Fluids & solids
77	E	Kinematics & dynamics	**97**	C	Electrostatics & electromagnetism
78	E	Force, motion, gravitation	**98**	B	Electric circuits
79	D	Equilibrium & momentum	**99**	B	Quantum mechanics
80	E	Atomic & nuclear structure	**100**	A	Atomic & nuclear structure

Diagnostic test #6

1	D	Heat & thermodynamics	31	A	Equilibrium & momentum
2	A	Force, motion, gravitation	32	B	Waves & periodic motion
3	B	Sound	33	E	Fluids & solids
4	A	Fluids & solids	34	D	Electric circuits
5	E	Electrostatics & electromagnetism	35	C	Atomic & nuclear structure
6	B	Electric circuits	36	D	Heat & thermodynamics
7	C	Light & optics	37	C	Kinematics & dynamics
8	D	Atomic & nuclear structure	38	C	Special relativity
9	B	Rotational motion	39	B	Equilibrium & momentum
10	B	Special relativity	40	C	Atomic & nuclear structure
11	B	Equilibrium & momentum	41	D	Kinematics & dynamics
12	C	Work & energy	42	C	Force, motion, gravitation
13	E	Waves & periodic motion	43	D	Heat & thermodynamics
14	A	Heat & thermodynamics	44	A	Work & energy
15	A	Light & optics	45	C	Waves & periodic motion
16	B	Electric circuits	46	B	Sound
17	D	Electrostatics & electromagnetism	47	A	Fluids & solids
18	E	Fluids & solids	48	C	Electrostatics & electromagnetism
19	C	Sound	49	E	Electric circuits
20	E	Waves & periodic motion	50	C	Light & optics
21	D	Work & energy	51	E	Atomic & nuclear structure
22	C	Equilibrium & momentum	52	D	Equilibrium & momentum
23	B	Quantum mechanics	53	B	Work & energy
24	A	Kinematics & dynamics	54	A	Waves & periodic motion
25	C	Heat & thermodynamics	55	B	Sound
26	E	Work & energy	56	D	Fluids & solids
27	B	Sound	57	A	Electrostatics & electromagnetism
28	C	Rotational motion	58	C	Electric circuits
29	D	Light & optics	59	E	Light & optics
30	E	Kinematics & dynamics	60	A	Atomic & nuclear structure

61	A	Heat & thermodynamics	**81**	A	Work & energy
62	E	Force, motion, gravitation	**82**	E	Equilibrium & momentum
63	C	Sound	**83**	E	Force, motion, gravitation
64	A	Fluids & solids	**84**	D	Kinematics & dynamics
65	B	Electrostatics & electromagnetism	**85**	C	Heat & thermodynamics
66	D	Electric circuits	**86**	E	Work & energy
67	B	Light & optics	**87**	D	Sound
68	C	Atomic & nuclear structure	**88**	D	Electrostatics & electromagnetism
69	B	Kinematics & dynamics	**89**	A	Light & optics
70	E	Force, motion, gravitation	**90**	D	Kinematics & dynamics
71	D	Equilibrium & momentum	**91**	D	Quantum mechanics
72	B	Work & energy	**92**	B	Waves & periodic motion
73	A	Waves & periodic motion	**93**	D	Fluids & solids
74	E	Heat & thermodynamics	**94**	E	Electric circuits
75	C	Light & optics	**95**	B	Atomic & nuclear structure
76	C	Electric circuits	**96**	C	Heat & thermodynamics
77	A	Electrostatics & electromagnetism	**97**	A	Kinematics & dynamics
78	C	Fluids & solids	**98**	E	Force, motion, gravitation
79	E	Sound	**99**	A	Equilibrium & momentum
80	C	Waves & periodic motion	**100**	B	Atomic & nuclear structure

Diagnostic Test #1 – Explanations

1. A is correct.

An object's resistance to change in its state of motion is characterized by its inertia.

Inertia is not a physical property but is directly related to an object's mass. Thus, mass determines resistance to change in motion.

2. E is correct. The three forces are in equilibrium, so the net force $F_{net} = 0$

$$F_{net} = F_1 + F_2 + F_3$$

$$0 = F_1 + F_2 + F_3$$

Since the forces F_1 and F_2 are mirror images of each other along the *x*-axis, their net force in the *y* direction is zero. Therefore, F_3 is also zero in the *y* direction.

The net force along the *x* direction must add to zero, so set the sum of the *x* components to zero.

The angles for F_1 and F_2 are equal and measured with respect to the *x*-axis, so θ_1 and θ_2 are both 20°.

Since F_3 has no *y* component, $\theta_3 = 0°$. Note that force components to the left are set negative in this answer and components to the right are set positive.

$$0 = F_{1x} + F_{2x} + F_{3x}$$

$$0 = F_1 \cos \theta_1 + F_2 \cos \theta_2 + F_3 \cos \theta_3$$

$$0 = (-4.6 \text{ N} \cos 20°) + (-4.6 \text{ N} \cos 20°) + (F_3 \cos 0°)$$

Since $\cos 0° = 1$:

$$0 = (-4.3 \text{ N}) + (-4.3 \text{ N}) + F_3$$

$$-F_3 = -8.6 \text{ N}$$

$$F_3 = 8.6 \text{ N, to the right}$$

3. C is correct. Heat transfer between two materials occurs until both materials reach the same temperature, so the amount of heat lost by the hotter material is gained by the colder material.

4. B is correct.

$$W = Fd$$

$$W = (20 \text{ N}) \cdot (3.5 \text{ m})$$

$$W = 70 \text{ J}$$

5. E is correct.

Constructive interference occurs when two or more waves of equal frequency and phase produce a single amplitude wave that is the sum of amplitudes of the individual waves.

If there is any phase difference the interference will not be the sum total of the amplitude of each individual wave.

If the phase difference is 180° there will be total destructive interference.

6. B is correct. The expression for the Doppler shift is:

$$f = f_s[(c + v_o) / (c + v_s)]$$

where f is the frequency heard by the observer, f_s is the frequency of the source, c is the speed of sound, v_o is the velocity of the observer, v_s is the velocity of the source

The velocity of the source v_s is positive when the source is moving away from the observer and negative when it is moving toward the observer

Since the train is traveling away, once it passes the velocity of the source (i.e. train) is positive.

Kevin is standing still, so the velocity of the observer is zero.

$$f = f_s[(c + v_o) / (c + v_s)]$$

$$f = (420 \text{ Hz}) \cdot [(350 \text{ m/s} + 0 \text{ m/s}) / (350 \text{ m/s} + 50 \text{ m/s})]$$

$$f = (420 \text{ Hz}) \cdot [(350 \text{ m/s}) / (400 \text{ m/s})]$$

$$f = (147{,}000 \text{ Hz} \cdot \text{m/s}) / (400 \text{ m/s})$$

$$f = 368 \text{ Hz}$$

7. A is correct.

$$F_B = V\rho g$$

where F_B = buoyant force upward, V = volume of fluid that the object displaces, ρ = density of the fluid, g = acceleration due to gravity

The lead weight starts in the air above the water so at its origin it is experiencing zero buoyant force from the water.

As the weight breaks the surface of the water and sinks, the buoyant force increases until the weight is fully submerged, after which the force remains constant since the density of water is uniform.

8. A is correct.

A moving charge experiences a magnetic force from a magnetic field, but the force is perpendicular to the velocity (as well as the magnetic field), so the speed does not change.

$$F_B = qvB \sin \theta$$

F_B is perpendicular to both v and B

9. D is correct. If one mass is halved, then the gravitational attraction between them is halved.

For equilibrium, the electrostatic repulsion must also be halved.

$$F_e = F_g$$

$$F_e = kQ_1Q_2 / r^2$$

$$F_g = Gm_1m_2 / r^2$$

$$kQ_1Q_2 / r^2 = Gm_1m_2 / r^2$$

$$kQ_1Q_2 = Gm_1m_2, k \text{ and } G \text{ are constants and cannot be manipulated.}$$

If the mass of object 1 is halved, while equilibrium is maintained:

$G(m_1 / 2)m_2 = (Gm_1m_2) / 2$

If the electrostatic force is halved, the charge of one of the objects must be halved:

$(kQ_1Q_2) / 2 = kQ_1(Q_2 / 2)$

10. E is correct.

Calculate the focal length:

$1 / f = 1 / d_i + 1 / d_o$

where f is focal length d_o is distance to the object and d_i is distance to the image

$1 / f = 1 / 2 \text{ m} + 1 / 4 \text{ m}$

$1 / f = 2 / 4 \text{ m} + 1 / 4 \text{ m}$

$1 / f = 3 / 4 \text{ m}$

$f = 4 / 3 \text{ m}$

11. B is correct.

$$_Z^A n + e^- \rightarrow \, _{Z-1}^A (n-1) + v_e$$

A proton captures an electron and transforms it into a neutron. Therefore, the atomic number Z decreases by 1 because the nucleus contains one less proton. The $(n-1)$ signifies the new element name (since the atomic number changed), and v_e is the release of an electron neutrino.

12. B is correct. To balance the torques due to the weight, the fulcrum must be placed 4 times farther from the son than from the man, because the father weighs 4 times more.

Since the total length of the seesaw is 10 m, the fulcrum must be placed 8 m from the son and 2 m from the father who is on the heavier end.

$x + 4x = 10 \text{ m}$

$5x = 10 \text{ m}$

$x = 2 \text{ m}$

Another method to solve the problem:

<table>
<tr><td>200 N</td><td></td><td>800 N</td></tr>
<tr><td>10 − x</td><td>Δ</td><td>x</td></tr>
</table>

$(200 \text{ N}) \cdot (10 - x) = (800 \text{ N})x$

$x = 2 \text{ m}$

13. E is correct.

The energy before release and at the top of each bounce equals gravitational PE:

$PE = mgh$

Gravitational potential energy is proportional to height, and mass and g stay constant.

Multiply by 0.8 (80%) to determine the height after a bounce if 20% of the energy is lost.

$h_{\text{initial}} = 250$ cm

250 cm × (0.8 × 0.8 × 0.8), equals h after 3 bounces

$h_3 = (250 \text{ cm}) \cdot (0.8)^3$

$h_3 = 128$ cm

14. A is correct.

$T = 1 / f$

$T = 1 / (10 \text{ Hz})$

$T = 0.1$ s

15. A is correct.

$f = v / \lambda$

$f = (1{,}600 \text{ m/s}) / (2.5 \text{ m})$

$f = 640$ Hz

16. B is correct.

Consider this formula for rotational kinematics:

$\omega_f = \omega_i + \alpha \Delta t$

Solve for Δt:

$\Delta t = (\omega_f - \omega_i) / \alpha$

$\Delta t = (33.3 \text{ rad/s} - 15.0 \text{ rad/s}) / 3.45 \text{ rad/s}^2$

$\Delta t = 5.30$ s

17. C is correct.

18. A is correct.

Find Capacitive Reactance:

$X_c = 1 / 2\pi Cf$

$X_c = 1 / (2\pi) \cdot (26 \times 10^{-6} \text{ F}) \cdot (60 \text{ Hz})$

$X_c = 102 \ \Omega$

Find rms current:

$I = V_{rms} / X_c$

$I = 120 \text{ V} / 102 \ \Omega$

$I = 1.2$ A

19. C is correct.

Snell's Law:

$$n_g / n_w = (\sin \phi) / (\sin \theta)$$

Find the index of refraction for glass:

$$n_g / 1.33 = (\sin 61°) / (\sin 48°)$$

$$n_g / 1.33 = (0.875) / (0.743)$$

$$n_g / 1.33 = 1.18$$

$$n_g = (1.18) \cdot (1.33)$$

$$n_g = 1.57$$

Solve for the new angle of refraction after the angle of incidence has changed:

$$1.57 / 1.33 = (\sin \phi) / (\sin 25°)$$

$$1.18 = (\sin \phi) / (0.423)$$

$$(1.18) \cdot (0.423) = \sin \phi$$

$$\sin \phi = 0.5$$

$$\phi = 30°$$

20. C is correct.

$$f = nv / 2L$$

n = 1 for the frequency of the fundamental

$$f = v / 2L$$

$$f = (340 \text{ m/s}) / 2(0.1 \text{ m})$$

$$f = 1,700 \text{ Hz}$$

21. B is correct.

Enthalpy of fusion.

As a solid undergoes a phase change, the temperature will always stay constant until the phase change is complete. To calculate the amount of heat absorbed to completely melt the solid, multiply the heat of fusion by the mass undergoing the phase change.

Heat needed to melt a solid:

$$q = m\Delta H_f$$

22. E is correct.

$$a = g \sin \theta$$

An object's acceleration down a frictionless ramp (with an incline angle) is constant.

23. D is correct.

Sound cannot travel through a vacuum because there is no medium to propagate the wave.

In air, sound waves travel through gas, in the ocean they travel through liquid, and in the Earth they travel through solids. These are all mediums in which sound waves can propagate.

However, vacuums are devoid of matter; there is no medium, and the wave cannot pass.

24. C is correct.

The *lowest* harmonic (i.e. fundamental) frequency (f_1) corresponds to the *longest* harmonic (i.e. fundamental) wavelength (λ_1).

$$f_1 = v / \lambda_1$$
$$f_1 = (8 \text{ m/s}) / 4 \text{ m}$$
$$f_1 = 2 \text{ Hz}$$

25. B is correct.

By Newton's Third Law, F_1 and F_2 form an *action–reaction* pair.

The ratio of their magnitudes equals 1.

26. E is correct.

$$P = IV$$
$$P = (2 \text{ A}){\cdot}(120 \text{ V})$$
$$P = 240 \text{ W}$$

An ampere (A) is a rate of electric charge flowing in a circuit in coulombs per second (C/s), where 1 A = 1 C/s. The volt (V) measures the difference in electric potential between two points, where 1 V is defined as the electric potential difference when 1 ampere consumes 1 watt (W) of power.

Power is a measure of energy per unit time:

$$1 \text{ W} = 1 \text{ A}{\cdot}\text{V}$$
$$1 \text{ W} = 1 \text{ J} / \text{s}$$
$$1 \text{ W} = 1 \text{ N}{\cdot}\text{m/s}$$
$$1 \text{ W} = 1 \text{ kg}{\cdot}\text{m}^2/\text{s}^3$$

27. A is correct.

When an atom absorbs energy their valence electrons move to higher "orbits". As the electrons fall back to their original (ground state), they emit the absorbed energy as light.

28. C is correct.

The de Broglie wavelength of a matter wave is:

$\lambda = h / p$

$\lambda = h / (mv)$

$\lambda = (6.626 \times 10^{-34} \text{ J·s}) / [(1.30 \text{ kg})·(28.10 \text{ m/s})]$

$\lambda = (6.626 \times 10^{-34} \text{ J·s}) / [(1.30 \text{ kg})·(28.10 \text{ m/s})]$

$\lambda = 1.81 \times 10^{-35} \text{ m}$

29. B is correct.

$d = \frac{1}{2}gt^2$

$t^2 = 2d / g$

$t^2 = 2(42 \text{ m}) / 10 \text{ m/s}^2$

$t^2 = 8.4 \text{ s}^2$

$t \approx 2.9 \text{ s}$

30. D is correct.

$F = ma$

$W = mg$

$m = W / g$

$F = (W / g)a$

$a = F / m$

The $F_{\text{friction}} = 8.8$ N, and the mass is known from the box's weight.

$8.8 \text{ N} = (40 \text{ N} / 10 \text{ m/s}^2)a$

$a = (8.8 \text{ N}) / (4 \text{ N/m/s}^2)$

$a = 2.2 \text{ m/s}^2$

Since the box moves at constant velocity when force F is applied, F = force due to kinetic friction.

Once the force F is removed, the net force that causes its deceleration is the frictional force.

31. B is correct.

A longer barrel gives the propellant a longer time to impart a force upon a bullet and thus a higher velocity. This is characterized by impulse.

$J = F\Delta t$

32. A is correct.

$KE_{\text{final}} = 0$ since $v_f = 0$

The length of the skid marks are irrelevant.

$$\Delta Energy = KE_{final} - KE_{initial}$$

$$\Delta E = \frac{1}{2}mv_f^2 - \frac{1}{2}mv_i^2$$

$$\Delta E = 0 \text{ J} - \frac{1}{2}(1{,}000 \text{ kg}){\cdot}(30 \text{ m/s})^2$$

$$\Delta E = -4.5 \times 10^5 \text{ J}$$

33. B is correct.

The position of an object in simple harmonic motion (SHM) is represented as a function of time using sine or cosine:

$$x = A \sin (\omega t - \theta)$$

where x = position, A = amplitude (i.e. max displacement of object from equilibrium position), ω = angular velocity in radians/sec (or degrees/sec), t = time elapsed, θ = phase

Here, $\theta = 0$ since the graph matches the phase of the standard sine graph, so there is no need for a phase correction. $A = 1$ is used for simplicity.

$$x = \sin (\omega t)$$

The object's velocity in SHM is represented by the derivative of the position function:

$$v = \omega \cos (\omega t)$$

The object's acceleration in SHM is represented by the derivative of the velocity function:

$$a = -\omega^2 \sin (\omega t)$$

Therefore, the acceleration of objects in SHM is represented as the opposite value of position, multiplied by the square of angular velocity.

ω is constant, so the graphs keep the same wavelengths.

34. D is correct.

$$KE_{avg} = (3/2)kT$$

$$KE_{avg} = (3/2){\cdot}(1.38 \times 10^{-23} \text{ J/K}){\cdot}(740 \text{ K})$$

$$KE_{avg} = 1.5 \times 10^{-20} \text{ J}$$

35. B is correct.

The power of the combination is:

$$P = P_1 + P_2$$

Since power is the reciprocal of the focal length (in meters),

$$f_1 = 10 \text{ cm} = 1 / 10 \text{ m}$$

$$P_1 = 1 / f_1$$

$$P_1 = 1 / (1 / 10 \text{ m})$$

$$P_1 = 10 \text{ D}$$

$f_2 = 20$ cm $= 1 / 5$ m

$P_2 = 1 / f_2$

$P_2 = 1 / (1 / 5$ m$)$

$P_2 = 5$ D

$P = P_1 + P_2$

$P = 10$ D $+ 5$ D $= 15$ D

36. E is correct.

$C = 1 / (2\pi Rf)$

$C = 1 / (2\pi \times 4{,}000\ \Omega \times 600$ Hz$)$

$C = 6.6 \times 10^{-8}$ F

Because the answers are in the micro-Faradays, divide by 10^{-6} to find proper units (μFaradays)

$C = 6.6 \times 10^{-8}$ F $/ (10^{-6})$

$C = 0.066$ μF

37. C is correct.

If the voltage drop across the 3 Ω resistor is 2 V, the current through the 3 Ω resistor is:

$I = V / R$

$I = 2$ V $/ 3\ \Omega$

$I = 2/3$ amp

Since the 1.5 Ω resistor is connected in parallel with the 3 Ω resistor, voltage drop = 2 V (parallel resistors always share the same voltage drop).

The current through the 1.5 Ω resistor is:

$I = 2$ V $/ 1.5\ \Omega$

$I = 4/3$ amps

Then, sum the currents:

$I_{total} = 2/3$ amp $+ 4/3$ amps

$I_{total} = 2$ amps

38. A is correct.

mass = density $\times$ volume

$m = \rho V$

$m = (1 \times 10^{18}$ kg/m$^3)\cdot(1.76 \times 10^{-6}$ m$)^3$

$m = 5.45$ kg ≈ 5.5 kg

39. A is correct. An isothermal process does more work than an adiabatic process and thus there is more area under the curve of the isothermal process than the adiabatic.

40. E is correct.

$\lambda = vt$

$\lambda = (4.6 \text{ m/s}) \cdot (10 \text{ s}) = 46 \text{ m}$

41. D is correct.

$W = Fd \cos \theta$

$W = (20 \text{ N}) \cdot (2 \text{ m})$

$W = 40 \text{ J}$

42. C is correct. Total momentum of the system is always conserved. Before the ball was thrown the momentum was zero because all mass on the canoe was stationary.

After the ball is thrown and caught on the canoe the momentum must still be equal to zero so the canoe must remain stationary.

$p = mv$

43. C is correct.

In Joseph's frame the two events are separated by $\Delta x = 0$ and $\Delta t = (61 - 21)$ years and in the Earth's frame $\Delta x' = 50$ light-years. The Lorentz transformation is:

$\Delta x' = \gamma (\Delta x + v \Delta t)$ where $\gamma = 1/\sqrt{(1 - \beta^2)}$ $\beta = v/c$

50 light-years $= [1/\sqrt{(1 - \beta^2)}] \cdot (0 + \beta \cdot 40 \text{ light-years})$

Squaring both sides:

$2500 = 1600 \cdot \beta^2 / (1 - \beta^2)$

Solving for β^2:

$\beta^2 = (25/16) / (1 + 25/16) = 0.610$

and:

$v = 0.781c$

44. A is correct.

$f = 1 / T$

Period $= (60 \text{ s}) / (10 \text{ oscillations})$

$T = 6 \text{ s}$

$f = 1 / 6 \text{ s}$

$f = 0.17 \text{ Hz}$

45. D is correct. For materials with a positive coefficient of thermal expansion, a hole drilled in the material expands as temperature increases. Regardless of the surrounding metal's expansion, the hole's diameter always increases with higher temperature.

46. C is correct.

The kinetic energy of a falling object is directly proportional to height from which it falls. This is because mass and gravity are constants so only the height varies the kinetic energy of a dropped object.

$KE = PE$

$\frac{1}{2}mv^2 = mgh$

47. B is correct.

If the two sound sources are in phase then there is no destructive interference.

The point can be related to the wavelength of the sound wave.

$0.5 \text{ m} = x\lambda$

$0.5 \text{ m} = x(1 \text{ m})$

$x = \frac{1}{2}$

The microphone is located one-half wavelength from the speaker. The speaker is a source of the sound pressure wave, so is an antinode. One-half wavelength from an antinode is also an antinode.

48. C is correct. An object becomes electrostatically charged when a charge imbalance exists.

Charge can only be transferred by electrons because protons are not mobile, thus electron transfer creates electrostatic charge.

49. D is correct. Volume strain:

$\Delta V / V$

$B = -\Delta P / (\Delta V / V)$

$\Delta P = -B(\Delta V / V)$

$\Delta P = (-6.3 \times 10^9 \text{ Pa}) \cdot (-3 \times 10^{-4})$

$\Delta P = 19 \times 10^5 \text{ Pa}$

$\Delta P = (19 \times 10^5 \text{ Pa} / 1) \cdot (1 \text{ atm} / 10^5 \text{ Pa})$

$\Delta P = 19 \text{ atm}$

The negative sign indicates that the final volume is lower than the initial volume; since the volume has decreased, the pressure increased.

50. D is correct.

Velocity is in the direction of the current:

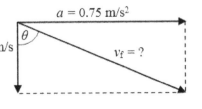

$v_c = at$

$v_c = (0.75 \text{ m/s}^2) \cdot (33.5 \text{ s})$

$v_c = 25 \text{ m/s}$

Final velocity:

$$v_f^2 = v^2 + v_c^2$$

$$v_f^2 = (3.35 \text{ m/s})^2 + (25 \text{ m/s})^2$$

$$v_f^2 = 636.2 \text{ m}^2/\text{s}^2$$

$$v_f = 25 \text{ m/s}$$

The angle of motion with respect to the initial velocity:

$$\theta = \tan^{-1}(v_c / v)$$

$$\theta = \tan^{-1}[(25 \text{ m/s}) / (3.35 \text{ m/s})]$$

$$\theta = \tan^{-1} 7.5$$

$$\theta = 82.4°$$

51. D is correct.

Divide the problem into three parts: initial acceleration, constant velocity, final deceleration stage.

1) Initial acceleration: determine α, then solve for the displacement during the acceleration. The initial velocity is zero.

Convert the displacement in radians to revolutions.

$$\alpha = (\omega_f - \omega_i) / t$$

$$\alpha = (58 \text{ radians/s} - 0) / 10 \text{ s}$$

$$\alpha = 5.8 \text{ radians/s}^2$$

$$\theta = \tfrac{1}{2}\alpha t^2$$

$$\theta = \tfrac{1}{2}(5.8 \text{ radians/s}^2) \cdot (10 \text{ s})^2$$

$$\theta = 290 \text{ radians}$$

$$Rev = \theta / 2\pi$$

$$Rev = 290 \text{ radians} / 2\pi$$

$$Rev = 46 \text{ revolutions}$$

2) Constant velocity: solve θ using constant angular velocity.

Convert radians to revolutions.

$$\theta = \omega t$$

$$\theta = (58 \text{ radians/s}) \cdot (30 \text{ s})$$

$$\theta = 1{,}740 \text{ radians}$$

$$Rev = \theta / 2\pi$$

$$Rev = 1{,}740 \text{ radians} / 2\pi$$

$$Rev = 277 \text{ revolutions}$$

3) Final deceleration: determine t for the period of deceleration using the final velocity as zero.

Solve for the displacement during this constant deceleration and convert to revolutions.

$\alpha = (\omega_f - \omega_i) / t$

$t = (\omega_f - \omega_i) / \alpha$

$t = (0 - 58 \text{ radians/s}) / (-1.4 \text{ radians/s}^2)$

$t = 41 \text{ s}$

$\theta = \omega_i t + \frac{1}{2} \alpha t^2$

$\theta = [(58 \text{ radians/s}) \cdot (41 \text{ s})] + [\frac{1}{2}(-1.4 \text{ radians/s}^2) \cdot (41 \text{ s})^2]$

$\theta = 1{,}201 \text{ radians}$

$Rev = 1{,}201 \text{ radians} / 2\pi$

$Rev = 191 \text{ revolutions}$

Add the revolutions:

$Rev_{total} = 46 \text{ rev} + 277 \text{ rev} + 191 \text{ rev}$

$Rev_{total} = 514 \approx 510 \text{ revolutions}$

52. E is correct. Snell's Law:

$n_1 \sin \theta_1 = n_2 \sin \theta_2$

$n_1 = n_2 (\sin \theta_2 / \sin \theta_1)$

$n_1 = (1.33) \cdot [\sin (72°) / \sin (48°)]$

$n_1 = 1.7$

$(1.7) \sin (37°) = (1.33) \sin \theta_2$

$\sin \theta_2 = 0.769$

$\theta_2 = 50°$

53. C is correct. Label the tuning forks I, II, III, and IV.

Beats: I & II, I & III, I & IV, II & III, II & IV and III & IV

From six pairs, there is the possibility of six different beat frequencies. This is a combination problem since order does not matter.

The formula for combinations is:

$C(n, k) = n! / (n - k)! k!$

where n is the given sample size and k is the number of tuning forks per pair.

When solving combination problems, the best way to choose n and k is to ask: "how do I find all the ways to pick n and k?"

$C(4,2) = 4! / (4 - 2)! 2!$

$C(4,2) = 4! / 2! 2!$

$C(4,2) = 6$

54. E is correct.

Capacitance:

$C = Q / V$

$Q = CV$

$V = IR$

$Q = C \times (IR)$

$Q = (12 \times 10^{-6}\,\text{F}) \cdot (33 \times 10^{-6}\,\text{A}) \cdot (8.5 \times 10^{6}\,\Omega)$

$Q = 0.0034\,\text{C}$

Divide by 10^{-6} to determine micro-coulombs:

$Q = (0.0034\,\text{C}) / 10^{-6}$

$Q = 3,400\,\mu\text{C}$

55. E is correct.

Use conservation of energy. Note that in the initial state, the ball is at rest, so the initial kinetic energy is zero. Take the zero of gravitational potential energy to be the height of the ball at its final position. The final kinetic energy has a translational part and a rotational part:

$E_f = E_i$

$KE_f = PE_i$

$KE_{\text{translation}} + KE_{\text{rotation}} = PE_i$

$\frac{1}{2}mv^2 + \frac{1}{2}I\omega^2 = mgh$

The ball is rolling without slipping, so the relationship between translational velocity and rotational velocity is $v = r\omega$. Then, the above becomes:

$\frac{1}{2}mr^2\omega^2 + \frac{1}{2}(2/5)mr^2\omega^2 = mgh$

$(7/10)mr^2\omega^2 = mgh$

Solving for the angular speed:

$\omega = \sqrt{(10gh / 7r^2)}$

$\omega = \sqrt{\{[10 \cdot (9.8\,\text{m/s}^2) \cdot (5.3\,\text{m})] / [7 \cdot (1.7\,\text{m})^2]\}}$

$\omega = 5.1\,\text{rad/s}$

56. E is correct.

57. C is correct.

$$y = v_i t + \tfrac{1}{2}at^2$$

$$50 \text{ m} = 0 + \tfrac{1}{2}(10 \text{ m/s}^2)t^2$$

$$50 \text{ m} = \tfrac{1}{2}(10 \text{ m/s}^2)t^2$$

$$t^2 = 50 \text{ m} / 5 \text{ m/s}^2$$

$$t^2 = 10 \text{ s}^2$$

$$t = 3.2 \text{ s}$$

Solve for speed:

$$v_f = v_i + at$$

$$v_f = 0 + (10 \text{ m/s}^2){\cdot}(3.2 \text{ s})$$

$$v_f = 32 \text{ m/s}$$

58. D is correct. Newton's Second Law for each block:

$$ma = F_{net} \text{ acting on the object.}$$

The tension and acceleration on each block are equal in magnitude, but act in different directions.

The only nonzero net forces will be in the horizontal direction for the 15 kg block and in the vertical direction for the 60 kg block.

For the 15 kg block:

$$ma = \text{tension acting to the right}$$

$$(15 \text{ kg})a = F_T$$

For the 60 kg block:

$$ma = (\text{weight acting downward}) - (\text{tension acting upward})$$

$$(60 \text{ kg})a = (60 \text{ kg}){\cdot}(10 \text{ m/s}^2) - F_T$$

Substitute F_T from the first equation into the second:

$$(60 \text{ kg})a = (60 \text{ kg}){\cdot}(10 \text{ m/s}^2) - (15 \text{ kg})a$$

$$(60 \text{ kg})a + (15 \text{ kg})a = (60 \text{ kg}){\cdot}(10 \text{ m/s}^2)$$

$$(75 \text{ kg})a = (60 \text{ kg}){\cdot}(10 \text{ m/s}^2)$$

$$a = [(60 \text{ kg}){\cdot}(10 \text{ m/s}^2)] / (75 \text{ kg})$$

$$a = 8 \text{ m/s}^2$$

59. C is correct. charge = (# electrons)·(electron charge)

$$Q = n(e^-)$$

$$n = Q / e^-$$

$$n = (-9 \times 10^{-6} \text{ C}) / (-1.6 \times 10^{-19} \text{ C})$$

$$n = 5.6 \times 10^{13} \text{ electrons}$$

60. B is correct.

$_0^0 \gamma$ is a gamma particle, so the atomic mass and atomic number do not change.

Alpha decay: during alpha decay, the parent nuclide sheds two protons and two neutrons which is identical to the nucleus of ^{4}He.

$$_Z^A X \rightarrow {}_{Z-2}^{A-4} Y + {}_2^4 \alpha$$

Beta Decay (minus): during beta minus decay, the parent nuclide sheds an electron and electron antineutrino. However, in the process a neutron converts to a proton so the mass number remains the same but the atomic number increases by 1.

$$_Z^A X \rightarrow {}_{Z+1}^A Y + {}_{-1}^0 e^- + {}_0^0 v_e$$

Beta Decay (plus): during beta plus decay, the parent nuclide sheds a positron and neutrino. However, in the process a proton converts to a neutron so the mass number remains the same but the atomic number decreases by 1.

$$_Z^A X \rightarrow {}_{Z-1}^A Y + {}_{+1}^0 e^+ + {}_0^0 v_e$$

61. A is correct.

Coulomb's Law:

$$F = kQ_1Q_2 / r^2$$

When charges are doubled:

$$F_2 = k(2Q_1)(2Q_2) / r^2$$
$$F_2 = 4kQ_1Q_2 / r^2$$
$$F_2 = 4F$$

F increases by a factor of 4 (quadruples).

62. B is correct.

The angle the board makes before the pot slides is dependent upon the static friction coefficient as static friction influences the force of friction before the pot slides. Kinetic friction only occurs after movement of the pot.

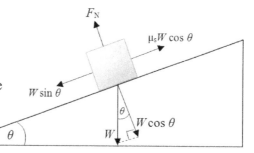

63. E is correct.

$$Q = mc\Delta T, \text{ where } \Delta T \text{ is constant}$$

If $m = 4$ times increase and $c = 3$ times increase

$$Q = (4)\cdot(3)\Delta T$$
$$Q = (12)\Delta T$$
$$Q_1 / 12 = \Delta T$$

64. C is correct.

Ignoring air resistance, energy is conserved. The loss in PE = the gain in KE.

$KE = \frac{1}{2}mv^2$

$KE = \frac{1}{2}(20 \text{ kg}) \cdot (30 \text{ m/s})^2$

$KE = 9,000 \text{ J}$

This equals the amount of PE that is lost (i.e. converted into KE).

65. C is correct.

velocity = frequency × wavelength

$v = f\lambda$

$\lambda = v / f$

$f = 1 / T$

$\lambda = v \times T$

$\lambda = 360 \text{ m/s} \times 4.2 \text{ s}$

$\lambda \approx 1,512 \text{ m}$

66. B is correct.

$PE = \frac{1}{2}kx^2$

$PE = \frac{1}{2}k(2x)^2$

$PE = 4(\frac{1}{2}kx^2)$

67. C is correct.

Young's Modulus is expressed as:

$E = \sigma \text{ (stress)} / \varepsilon \text{ (strain)}$

$E = (F / A) / (\Delta L / L)$

$E = (FL) / (\Delta LA)$

Solve for E:

$E = (8.8 \text{ kg}) \cdot (9.8 \text{ m/s}^2) \cdot (4.4 \text{ m}) / (0.0033 \text{ m}) \cdot (\pi / 4) \cdot (0.0016 \text{ m})^2$

$E = 5.7 \times 10^{10} \text{ N/m}^2$

68. D is correct.

From Coulomb's Law, the electrostatic force is *inversely proportional* to the square of the distance between the charges.

$F = kq_1q_2 / r^2$

If the distance increases by a factor of 2, then the force decreases by a factor of $2^2 = 4$.

69. C is correct.

$P = IV$

$I = P / V$

$I = (1 \times 10^{-3} \text{ W}) / (9 \text{ V})$

$P = 0.00011 \text{ A} = 0.11 \text{ mA}$

70. C is correct.

The plane mirror is double the distance from an object, so $\frac{1}{2}h$ is required for the minimum length.

Law of reflection:

$\theta_1 = \theta_2$

$h = 2x$

$x = \frac{1}{2}h$

71. C is correct.

Fission occurs when an atom with a larger atomic number is struck by a free neutron and splits.

For example:

$$^{235}_{92}\text{U} + ^{1}_{0}\text{n} \rightarrow ^{92}_{36}\text{Kr} + ^{141}_{56}\text{Ba} + 3 ^{1}_{0}\text{n}$$

72. B is correct.

Momentum is conserved

$m_1v_1 + m_2v_2 = m_3v_3$

momentum before = momentum after

$p_i = p_f$

$p_{total} = m_1v_1 + m_2v_2$

$p_{total} = (1 \text{ kg}) \cdot (1 \text{ m/s}) + (6 \text{ kg}) \cdot (0 \text{ m/s})$

$p_{total} = 1 \text{ kg} \cdot \text{m/s}$

73. C is correct.

The work done by the force can be related to kinetic energy.

6 kg mass:

$KE = W$

$\frac{1}{2}(6 \text{ kg}) \cdot (2 \text{ m/s})^2 = Fd_1$

$d_1 = 12 / F$

3 kg mass:

$$KE = W$$

$$½(3 \text{ kg}) \cdot (4 \text{ m/s})^2 = Fd_2$$

$$d_2 = 24 / F$$

$$d_2 = 2(12 / F)$$

Therefore:

$$2d_1 = d_2$$

74. A is correct.

Separation between maxima in a double slit interference pattern is given by:

$$\Delta y = \lambda D / d$$

where y = maximum separation, λ = wavelength, D = distance from slit to diffraction pattern and d = slit separation.

Red light has the highest value wavelength and has the largest maximum separation.

75. B is correct.

The λ of a stretched string of length L that is fixed at both ends is:

$$\lambda = 2L / \text{n}$$

where n = 1 for the fundamental frequency.

Therefore, if the fundamental frequency (f_1) is 860 Hz, then:

$$\lambda = 2(0.25 \text{ m})$$

$$\lambda = 0.5 \text{ m}$$

$$v = f\lambda$$

$$v = (860 \text{ Hz}) \cdot (0.5 \text{ m})$$

$$v = 430 \text{ m/s}$$

76. A is correct. Volume flow rate (Q) is how much water is flowing per second.

Find the cross-sectional area of the pipe and multiply the area with the velocity of the water.

$$Q = A_{\text{pipe}} v$$

$$Q = \pi (0.03 \text{ m})^2 \times (4 \text{ m/s})$$

$$Q = 0.0113 \text{ m}^3/\text{s}$$

$$Q = 1.1 \times 10^{-2} \text{ m}^3/\text{s}$$

77. E is correct.

78. C is correct. When two conductors are joined by a copper wire they must have the same potential because the wire allows for charge to flow. Any potential difference is neutralized by charge flow.

79. C is correct.

$d = 130$ m

$f = 3.6$ MHz

$\theta = ?$

velocity = frequency × wavelength

$\lambda = c / f$

$\lambda = (3 \times 10^8 \text{ m/s}) / (3.6 \times 10^6 \text{ Hz})$

$\lambda = 83.3$ m

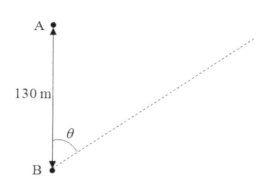

The condition for constructive interference is:

$m\lambda = d \cos \theta$

or

$\cos \theta = m\lambda / d$

The value of cosine gets closer to 1.0 as the angle gets *smaller*. Thus, to find the smallest angle, find the largest possible value of $\cos \theta$, as long as the value does not exceed 1.0.

With $m = 1$:

$\theta = \cos^{-1} (83.3 \text{ m} / 130 \text{ m})$

$\theta = \cos^{-1}(0.641)$

$\theta = 50°$

With $m = 2$:

$\theta = \cos^{-1} (2 \times 83.3 \text{ m} / 130 \text{ m})$

$\theta = \cos^{-1}(1.281)$, which has no solution.

Therefore, the smallest angle for which constructive interference occurs is 50°.

80. A is correct. The magnetic quantum number is an interval from $-\ell$ to $+\ell$ (includes zero and an allowable value). The total amount of magnetic quantum numbers possible is:

$2(\ell) + 1$

For example:

$\ell = 2$

$m_\ell = -2, -1, 0, 1, 2$

$m_{\ell \text{ total possible}} = 2(2) + 1 = 5$

In the range from $-\ell$ to $+\ell$, there are 5 possible magnetic quantum numbers.

Verification through the equation:

$m_{\ell \text{ tot possible}} = 2(\ell) + 1$

81. D is correct.

In the frame of the earth:

$$d = vt$$

$$t = d / v$$

$$t = (4.367 \text{ years} \cdot c) / [0.8c]$$

$$t = 5.49 \text{ years}$$

82. C is correct.

Within the nucleus, the Coulomb repulsion is overcome by the strong nuclear forces. The strong nuclear force counteracts the repulsion and binds the nucleus together.

83. B is correct.

Sound intensity is defined as power per unit area and is usually expressed as W/m^2.

Thus, sound intensity is directly proportional to power.

84. E is correct.

$$\text{Output pressure } (P_2) = \text{input pressure } (P_1)$$

$$P_2 = P_1$$

$$(F_2 / A_2) = (F_1 / A_1)$$

$$F_1 = (A_1 / A_2)F_2$$

$$F_1 = [\pi(3 \text{ cm})^2 / \pi(12.5 \text{ cm})^2] \cdot (12,000 \text{ N})$$

$$F_1 = (9 \text{ cm} / 156.25 \text{ cm}) \cdot (12,000 \text{ N})$$

$$F_1 = 691 \text{ N}$$

85. D is correct.

$$E = F / q$$

$$F = Eq_{proton}$$

$$F = (4 \times 10^4 \text{ N/C}) \cdot (1.6 \times 10^{-19} \text{ C})$$

$$F = 6.4 \times 10^{-15} \text{ N}$$

86. A is correct.

$$Q = mc\Delta T$$

$$c = Q / m\Delta T$$

$$c = (200 \text{ kcal}) / [(3 \text{ kg}) \cdot (90 \text{ °C})]$$

$$c = 0.74 \text{ kcal/kg} \cdot \text{°C}$$

87. A is correct.

Optical density is related to the index of refraction of a material and describes how electromagnetic waves travel in a medium.

The optical density of a material is not related to its mass (physical) density.

88. B is correct.

Beta radiation is more powerful than alpha radiation, but less powerful than gamma rays. Beta radiation can penetrate skin, paper or even a light layer of clothing.

89. D is correct. Increasing the viscosity will decrease the Reynold's number, decreasing the likelihood of turbulence occurring. Increasing the flow rate or increasing the radius of the pipe increases the likelihood of turbulence. Reynold's number does not include a term for temperature (i.e., it has no bearing on the value of Reynold's number).

90. D is correct.

$$T = W \pm ma$$

$$F = W \pm ma$$

Positive (add) if body is moving upward and negative (subtract) if moving downward.

$$T = mg + ma$$

$$T = m(g + a)$$

$$T = (900 \text{ kg}) \cdot (9.8 \text{ m/s}^2 + 0.6 \text{ m/s}^2)$$

$$T = 9{,}360 \text{ N}$$

91. B is correct. Check if KE is conserved:

$$KE_{before} = KE_{after} \text{ if collision is elastic}$$

Before:

$$(\tfrac{1}{2}) \cdot (4 \text{ kg}) \cdot (1.8 \text{ m/s})^2 + (\tfrac{1}{2}) \cdot (6 \text{ kg}) \cdot (0.2 \text{ m/s})^2 = KE_{before}$$

$$KE_{before} = 6.6 \text{ J}$$

After:

$$(\tfrac{1}{2}) \cdot (4 \text{ kg}) \cdot (0.6 \text{ m/s})^2 + (\tfrac{1}{2}) \cdot (6 \text{ kg}) \cdot (1.4 \text{ m/s})^2 = KE_{after}$$

$$KE_{after} = 6.6 \text{ J}$$

Therefore:

$$KE_{before} = KE_{after}$$

The collision was completely elastic because kinetic energy was conserved.

92. B is correct. Assuming that the swing was at rest at the beginning and end of Steve's pull:

$$W = mgh$$

Referring to the figure:

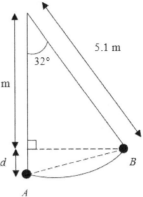

$h = L(1 - \cos\theta)$, where L is the length of the chain.

Hence:

$$W = mgL(1 - \cos\theta)$$

Therefore:

$m = W / [gL(1 - \cos\theta)]$
$m = (174 \text{ J}) / [(9.8 \text{ m/s}^2) \cdot (5.1 \text{ m}) \cdot (1 - \cos(32°)]$
$m = (174 \text{ J}) / [(9.8 \text{ m/s}^2) \cdot (5.1 \text{ m}) \cdot (1 - 0.834)]$
$m = 21.0 \text{ kg}$

93. A is correct. It takes 2 s for the object to travel from one end of its displacement to the other (½ a cycle).

The time for a complete cycle is 2 s + 2 s = 4 s.

$f = 1 / T$
$f = 1 / (4 \text{ s})$
$f = 0.25 \text{ s}^{-1} = 0.25 \text{ Hz}$

94. D is correct.

2 (10 cm aluminum rods) + 5 (8 cm steel rods) = 20 cm + 40 cm = 60 cm

$\Delta L = L\alpha\Delta T$, where α is the coefficient of linear expansion

$\Delta L_{alum} = (20 \text{ cm})(2.4 \times 10^{-5} \text{ K}^{-1})(80 \text{ °C} - 5 \text{ °C})$

$\Delta L_{alum} = 3.6 \times 10^{-2} \text{ cm} = 0.36 \text{ mm}$

$\Delta L_{steel} = (40 \text{ cm})(1.2 \times 10^{-5} \text{ K}^{-1})(80 \text{ °C} - 5 \text{ °C})$

$\Delta L_{steel} = 3.6 \times 10^{-2} \text{ cm} = 0.36 \text{ mm}$

The change in length of the composite rod is the sum of these: 0.72 mm

95. D is correct.

Diverging mirrors (i.e. convex mirrors) are curved outward toward the light source and therefore have a focal point *behind* the mirror, so the focal length f is a negative value.

Using the equation for focal length:

$1 / f = 1 / d_o + 1 / d_i$

where d_o is the distance to the light source and d_i is the distance to the image.

$-1 / 6 \text{ m} = 1 / 12 \text{ m} + 1 / d_i$

$1 / d_i = -1 / 4 \text{ m}$

$d_i = -4 \text{ m}$

96. E is correct.

By doubling the frequency of the light, the energy of each photon doubles, but not the number of photons (hence B is wrong). Although doubling the energy of each photon would cause more electrons to be ejected, it does not, necessarily, double that number, since the number is not linearly proportional to the incident energy (hence A is not always true). The kinetic energy of the ejected electrons would more than double since the initial kinetic energy is less than the energy of the incident photons - it was reduced by the work function of the surface (hence C is wrong). The kinetic energy would increase by at least 2 but not necessarily by 4 (hence D is wrong).

97. B is correct. Efficiency of a heat engine:

$n = Q_H - Q_C / Q_H$

$n = (8,500 \text{ J} - 4,500 \text{ J}) / (8,500 \text{ J})$

$n = 0.47$

$n = 47\%$

98. B is correct. Buoyancy force:

$F_B = \rho g h \text{A}$

$F_B = \rho g \text{V}$

Because the cube is lowered at a constant rate the volume of the cube underwater increases linearly and thus the F_B increases linearly.

After the cube is submerged, F_B stays constant because the volume of displaced water is constant.

Thus a linearly increasing line then steady flat slope of zero describes the buoyant force vs. time graph.

99. C is correct. The source is stationary and the detector is traveling towards the source at $v_d = 50$ m/s. Since they are moving toward each other, the velocity of the detector is positive and the detected frequency will be higher than the emitted frequency.

For the frequency perceived when the source of noises is approaching; the Doppler calculation takes the form:

$f_{observed} = f_{source} (v + v_{observer}) / (v - v_{source})$

$f_{observed} = (420 \text{ Hz}) \times [(350 \text{ m/s} + 50 \text{ m/s}) / (350 \text{ m/s} - 0 \text{ m/s})]$

$f_{observed} = 420 \text{ Hz} \times 1.14$

$f_{observed} = 480 \text{ Hz}$

100. A is correct. Beats are observed when two sound waves of different frequency approach and the alternating constructive/destructive causes the sound to be soft and loud.

$f_{beat} = |f_1 - f_2|$

Diagnostic Test #2 – Explanations

1. B is correct.

The extension x beyond the resting length is given by:

$x = F_{spring} / k$

spring force $\leftarrow$ M $\rightarrow$ centripetal force

$F_{spring} = F_{centripetal}$

$x = (12 \text{ N}) / (40 \text{ N/m})$

$x = 0.3 \text{ m}$

Since the radius of the circle of revolution is 2 m and the spring is pulling, the resting length of the spring is (2 m – 0.3 m) = 1.7 m.

2. E is correct.

The acceleration of a point on a rotating circle is the centripetal acceleration:

$a_c = v^2 / r$

where $r = 7.2 \text{ cm} = 0.072 \text{ m}$

Convert rpm to rps:

$(2,640 \text{ rotation/min}) \cdot (1 \text{ min} / 60 \text{ s}) = 44 \text{ rps}$

The speed of a point on the edge of the motor is:

$v = C / T$,

where C is the circumference and T is the period of revolution.

Calculate the circumference:

$C = 2\pi r$

$C = 2\pi(0.072 \text{ m}) = 0.45 \text{ m}$

Calculate the speed:

$v = (0.45 \text{ m}) / (1 \text{ s} / 44 \text{ rps})$

$v = 19.81 \text{ m/s}$

$a = v^2 / r$

$a = (19.81 \text{ m/s})^2 / (0.072 \text{ m})$

$a = 5,451 \text{ m/s}^2$

3. D is correct.

$$x = x_0 + v_0 t + \tfrac{1}{2}at^2,$$

where $t = 0.51$ s

$$x = 0 + 0 + \tfrac{1}{2}at^2$$

$$x = \tfrac{1}{2}at^2$$

$$2x / t^2 = a$$

$$2(1 \text{ m}) / (0.51 \text{ s})^2 = a$$

$$a = 2 \text{ m} / 0.26 \text{ s}^2$$

$$a = 7.7 \text{ m/s}^2$$

$$(m_1 + m_2)a = m_1 g - m_2 g$$

$$m_1 a + m_2 a = m_1 g - m_2 g$$

$$m_2(a + g) = m_1(g - a)$$

$$m_2 = [m_1(g - a)] / (a + g)$$

$$m_2 = [(100 \text{ kg}){\cdot}(9.8 \text{ m/s}^2 - 7.7 \text{ m/s}^2)] / (7.7 \text{ m/s}^2 + 9.8 \text{ m/s}^2)$$

$$m_2 = [(100 \text{ kg}){\cdot}(2.1 \text{ m/s}^2)] / (17.5 \text{ m/s}^2)$$

$$m_2 = 12 \text{ kg}$$

4. A is correct.

In projectile motion, the projectile is always experiencing a net force downward due to gravity, which is why the acceleration is negative. Since deceleration upward is equivalent to acceleration downward, the rock is always accelerating downward.

5. B is correct. We have three rotating bodies. The total angular momentum is the sum of their angular momenta.

$$L_{\text{total}} = L_1 + L_2 + L_3$$

The angular momentum of a rotating object is:

$$L = I\omega$$

The flywheels are identical, so they each have the same rotational inertia I, so:

$$L = I(\omega_1 + \omega_2 + \omega_3)$$

The moment of inertia of the flywheels is:

$$I = \tfrac{1}{2}mr^2$$

$$I = 0.5(65.0 \text{ kg})(1.47 \text{ m})^2$$

$$I = 70.23 \text{ kg m}^2$$

Thus:

$$L = (70.23 \text{ kg m}^2){\cdot}(3.83 \text{ rad/s} + 3.83 \text{ rad/s} - 3.42 \text{ rad/s})$$

$$L = 298 \text{ kg m}^2/\text{s}$$

6. E is correct. The object has constant velocity upward and the force necessary to propel the object is also constant and upward.

> Power = Watts / time
>
> W = *Fd*
>
> *P = Fd / t*
>
> *d / t = v*
>
> *P = Fv*
>
> *P* = (50 N)·(10 m/s)
>
> *P* = 500 W

7. D is correct.

For a pipe closed at one end, the harmonic frequencies are odd multiples of the fundamental frequency, so n = 1, 3, 5….

The harmonic frequency has a wavelength λ_n = 4*L* / n

The wavelength of the fundamental frequency is:

> λ_1 = 4*L* / 1
>
> λ_1 = 4*L*

Since the wavelength is four times greater than the length of the pipe, the pipe accommodates ¼λ, and therefore it has a displacement node at the closed end and an antinode at the open end.

8. A is correct. Charged objects always interact with other charged objects.

If electric charge is conserved, by definition charge cannot be created or destroyed.

Electrons and protons are the fundamental particles that carry charge.

Therefore the charge of any object is a whole-number multiple of an electron ($Q = ne^-$).

The electric charge of an object can be infinitely large, so there are infinite whole-number multiples of an electron's charge.

Because charge is a whole-number multiple of an electron's charge, it cannot have a value that is not a whole-number multiple, and therefore it occurs in restricted quantities.

9. B is correct.

Hooke's Law:

F = –kx, so force and distance stretched are inversely proportional.

The negative sign indicates that the force is in a direction opposite to the direction of the displacement.

10. B is correct.

Area under a curve is the same as taking the integral of velocity with respect to time.

The integral of velocity with respect to time gives displacement.

11. E is correct.

Momentum is conserved in the collision, so it neither increases nor decreases.

Kinetic energy is also conserved in the collision since the collision is elastic; the pucks are made of rubber and, due to the frictionless surface, bounce off each other without losing any speed.

If these pucks have identical masses and travel towards each other with identical speeds, each puck will have a final velocity that is equal in magnitude but opposite in direction to its initial velocity.

12. D is correct.

$$c = \lambda f$$

$$\lambda = c / f$$

$$\lambda = (3 \times 10^8 \text{ m/s}) / (2.4 \times 10^{20} \text{ Hz})$$

$$\lambda = 1.25 \times 10^{-12} \text{ m}$$

$$r = 5 \times 10^{-13} \text{ cm} = 5 \times 10^{-15} \text{ m}$$

$$\lambda / r = (1.25 \times 10^{-12} \text{ m}) / (5 \times 10^{-15} \text{ m})$$

$$\lambda / r = 250$$

13. C is correct.

The pressure in the hose depends on the height of the water above it and the pressure in the atmosphere. So the pressure in the hose is given by:

$$P = \rho g h + P_{atm}$$

where h = height of water

The 12 m water tank is 25 m above the ground, so $h = 37$ m

So the water pressure in the hose is:

$$P = (1{,}000 \text{ kg/m}^3){\cdot}(9.8 \text{ m/s}^2){\cdot}(37 \text{ m}) + 101{,}325 \text{ N/m}^2$$

$$P = 362{,}600 \text{ N/m}^2 + 101{,}325 \text{ N/m}^2$$

$$P = 4.6 \times 10^5 \text{ N/m}^2$$

14. D is correct.

Series: $R_{tot} = R_1 + R_2 + R_3$

Parallel: $1 / R_{tot} = 1 / R_1 + 1 / R_2 + 1 / R_3$

15. D is correct. In the photoelectric effect, photons from a light source are absorbed by electrons on a metal surface and cause them to be ejected. The energy of the ejected electrons is only dependent upon photon frequency and is found by:

$$KE = hf - \phi$$

where h = Planck's constant, f = frequency and ϕ = stopping potential

Increasing the intensity of the light only increases the number of photons incident upon the metal and thus the number of ejected electrons but their KE does not change.

16. E is correct. The Carnot cycle is an idealized thermodynamic cycle consisting of two isothermal processes and two adiabatic processes. It is the most efficient heat engine operating between two temperatures.

17. C is correct.

$$\Delta d = v\Delta t$$

$$\Delta d = (-3 \text{ m/s}) \cdot (4 \text{ s})$$

$$\Delta d = -12 \text{ m}$$

$$d - d_0 = -12 \text{ m}$$

$$d - 4 \text{ m} = -12 \text{ m}$$

$$d = -8 \text{ m}$$

18. A is correct. Horizontal velocity has no effect on the pebble's downward trajectory, so it is effectively in free fall like the second pebble.

19. C is correct.

Efficiency is defined as $KE_{final}/KE_{initial}$.

Kinetic energy:

$$KE = \tfrac{1}{2}mv^2$$

$$KE = p^2/2m$$

Note that momentum is always conserved in a collision:

$$p_{initial} = p_{final} = p$$

Therefore:

$$\text{Efficiency} = KE_{final}/KE_{initial}$$

$$\text{Efficiency} = (p^2/2m_2) / (p^2/2m_1)$$

$$\text{Efficiency} = m_1 / m_2$$

$$\text{Efficiency} = (2.0 \text{ kg}) / (2.5 \text{ kg})$$

$$\text{Efficiency} = 0.8 \times 100\% = 80\%$$

20. B is correct.

The nucleus of an atom consists of protons and neutrons held together by the strong nuclear force. This force counteracts the electrostatic force of repulsion between the protons in the nucleus.

The gravitational and weak nuclear forces are negligible when discussing the nucleus and the force acting within it.

21. D is correct.

There is no acceleration in the horizontal direction, so velocity is constant.

$v_{0x} = v_x$

$d = v_x \times t$

$d = (30 \text{ m/s}) \cdot (75 \text{ s})$

$d = 2{,}250 \text{ m}$

22. A is correct. The friction described in the scenario is between the tires and the road, because the problem asks for the force of friction *on the car*. Note that the car is skidding, meaning that the wheels are locked and are being dragged along the road; therefore, there is relative motion between the tires and the road. This is the condition for *kinetic friction*.

Static friction applies when there is no relative motion between the tires and the road at the point of contact, such as when the wheels are rotating normally.

$F_{\text{friction}} = \mu_k N$

Because the angle is described as *slight*, the incline can be ignored.

23. D is correct.

The rate of heat transfer:

$Q / t = k A \Delta T / d$

where k is the thermal conductivity of the wall material, A is the surface area of the wall, d is the wall's thickness and ΔT is the temperature difference on either side.

Therefore, if thickness d is doubled, the rate is halved.

24. E is correct. Energy can exist as PE, KE, heat, waves, etc.

Energy in any of its forms can be defined as the ability to do work, and the various mathematical expressions for energy specify the amount of work that can be done. The conversion between energy and work goes both ways: work can generate any form of energy.

25. E is correct. The displacement of the tines of a tuning fork from their resting positions is a measure of the amplitude of the resulting sound wave.

26. D is correct.

$I \text{ (dB)} = 10 \log_{10}(I / I_o)$

27. C is correct.

Hydrostatic equilibrium:

$$P_{bottom} = P_{atm} + \rho g(h_3 - h_1)$$

Absolute pressure:

$$P = P_{atm} + \rho g(h_3 - h_1)$$

Gauge pressure:

$$P = \rho g(h_3 - h_1)$$

28. B is correct.

Voltage results in a current but not vice versa.

Voltage is a potential difference across a circuit but does not flow through it.

29. D is correct.

In the stationary observer's time frame the time between clock ticks ($\Delta t'$) will appear to be twice that as measured in the clock's frame (Δt). The Lorentz transformation for the time interval from the clock's frame (in which $\Delta x = 0$) to the observer's frame is:

$$\Delta t' = \gamma \, (\Delta t - v \, \Delta x \, / \, c^2) \quad \text{where } \gamma = 1 \, / \, \sqrt{(1 - \beta^2)} \qquad \beta = v \, / \, c$$

$$\Delta t' = \gamma \, \Delta x$$

We want:

$$\Delta t' \, / \, \Delta t = 2.0$$

Therefore:

$$\gamma = 2.0$$

Solving for β:

$$\beta = 0.866c$$

30. C is correct.

Ultraviolet radiation has the highest frequency among the choices.

Energy is related to frequency by:

$$E = hf$$

Thus ultraviolet light has the most energy per photon because it has the highest frequency which is directly proportional to energy.

31. E is correct.

This is an example of a β^- decay.

A neutron converts to a proton and an electron (e^-) along with an electron neutrino (v_e).

32. C is correct.

Moment of inertia I is defined as the ratio of the angular momentum L of a system to its angular velocity ω around a principal axis.

Moment of inertia:

$I = L \, / \, \omega$

Angular acceleration around a fixed axis:

$\tau = \alpha I$

Mass moment of inertia of a thin disk:

$I = \tfrac{1}{2}mr^2$

$\tau = \alpha(\tfrac{1}{2}mr^2)$

$m = (2\tau) \, / \, \alpha r^2$

$m = [(2)\cdot(14 \text{ N·m})] \, / \, [(5.3 \text{ rad/s}^2)\cdot(0.6 \text{ m})^2]$

$m = 14.7 \text{ kg}$

33. C is correct.

$v = v_0 + at$

$29 \text{ m/s} = 0 + (10 \text{ m/s}^2)t$

$v = at$

$t = v \, / \, a$

$t = (29 \text{ m/s}) \, / \, (10 \text{ m/s}^2)$

$t = 2.9 \text{ s}$

$y = \tfrac{1}{2}at^2$

$y = \tfrac{1}{2}(10 \text{ m/s}^2)\cdot(2.9 \text{ s})^2 + 1 \text{ m}$

$y = \tfrac{1}{2}(10 \text{ m/s}^2)\cdot(8.41 \text{ s}^2) + 1 \text{ m}$

$y = 42 \text{ m} + 1 \text{ m}$

$y = 43 \text{ m}$

34. B is correct. Resonant frequency of a spring mass system:

$\omega = \sqrt{(k \, / \, m)}$

Increasing the spring constant k results in a higher resonant frequency.

35. C is correct.

Sound velocity in an ideal gas:

$v_{sound} = \sqrt{(yRT \, / \, M)}$

where y = adiabatic constant, R = gas constant, T = temperature and M = molecular mass of gas.

Increasing the temperature increases the velocity of sound in air.

36. B is correct. The work is path-independent.

$W = q\Delta V$

$W = q(V_D - V_A)$

$W = (10^{-14}\ C)\cdot(750\ V - 750\ V)$

$W = 0\ J$

The force does positive work during the first part of the motion and negative work in the final part. The total work is zero.

37. E is correct. The Earth's magnetic field is thought to be created by circulating electric currents in the Earth's mantle (liquid portion). These charges move slowly due to the convection currents in the mantle and create the magnetic field through the large number of charges present.

38. B is correct. Polarity switches twice per wavelength.

There are 60 λ per second.

$2 \times f = \#$ polarity switches

$2 \times 60 = 120$ times/s

39. B is correct. A blue object illuminated with yellow light appears black because it absorbs the yellow light and reflects none.

40. C is correct.

$$^A_Z X \rightarrow\ ^{A-4}_{Z-2} Y + ^4_2 \alpha$$

Alpha decay: the parent nuclide ejects two protons and two neutrons as $^4_2 He$ (essentially a helium nucleus). The daughter nucleus has an atomic number of two less than the parent nucleus and an atomic weight of four less than the parent nucleus.

41. E is correct. From the Second Law of Thermodynamics: it is not possible to extract heat from a hot reservoir and convert it all into useful work.

The maximum efficiency is that of a Carnot cycle given as:

$\eta = (Q_H - Q_C) / Q_H$

42. C is correct. Centripetal acceleration:

$F_c = (m)\cdot(v^2 / r)$

$F_c = (1{,}200\ kg)\cdot[(3.5\ m/s)^2 / 4\ m]$

$F_c = (1{,}200\ kg)\cdot[(12.25\ m^2/s^2) / 4\ m]$

$F_c = 3{,}675\ N$

43. D is correct.

Frequency, length, and velocity are related by:

$f = v / 2L$

$v = f \times 2L$

$v = (440 \text{ Hz}) \cdot (2 \times 0.14 \text{ m})$

$v = 123.2 \text{ m/s} \approx 123 \text{ m/s}$

$L = v / 2f$

$L = (123 \text{ m/s}) / (2) \cdot (520 \text{ Hz})$

$L = 0.118 \text{ m}$

$\Delta L = 0.14 \text{ m} - 0.118 \text{ m}$

$\Delta L = 0.022 \text{ m} = 2.2 \text{ cm}$

44. D is correct.

gauge pressure $= \rho g h$

gauge pressure $= (1{,}000 \text{ kg/m}^3) \cdot (10 \text{ m/s}^2) \cdot (110 \text{ m})$

gauge pressure $= 1.1 \times 10^6 \text{ Pa}$

45. B is correct.

Magnetic moment of a circular loop:

$\mu = \text{IA}$

$\text{A} = (\pi r^2)$

$\mu = \text{I}(\pi r^2)$

If r is doubled:

$\mu = \text{I}\pi(2r)^2$

$\mu = \text{I}\pi(4r^2)$

The magnetic moment increases by a factor of 4.

46. C is correct. First, find the total resistance of each set of resistors in parallel.

Resistors in parallel:

$1 / R_{\text{total}} = 1 / R_1 + 1 / R_2 \ldots + 1 / R_n$

$1 / R_{\text{total}} = 1 / 600 \ \Omega + 1 / 600 \ \Omega$

$R_{\text{total}} = 300 \ \Omega$

The two sets of parallel resistors are in series. Resistors in series:

$R_{\text{total}} = R_1 + R_2 \ldots + R_n$

$R_{\text{total}} = 300 \ \Omega + 300 \ \Omega$

$R_{\text{total}} = 600 \ \Omega$

47. E is correct.

48. B is correct.

De Broglie equation:

$\lambda = h / mv$

If velocity increases then λ decreases because they are inversely proportional.

49. E is correct.

The Balmer formula for Hydrogen is:

$1 / \lambda = (1 / 91.2 \text{ nm})(1 / m^2 - 1 / n^2)$

From the n = 3 level, the transition to the n = 2 level has the lowest energy and therefore the longest wavelength. The Balmer formula for n = 3, m = 2 is:

$1 / \lambda = (1 / 91.2 \text{ nm})(1 / 2^2 - 1 / 3^2)$

$1 / \lambda = (1 / 91.2 \text{ nm})(5 / 36)$

$\lambda = 656 \text{ nm}$

50. B is correct.

Newton's Third Law: when two objects interact, the force exerted on one object is equal in strength and opposite in direction to the force exerted on the other object.

51. E is correct.

$F = ma$

$m = F / a$

$m_1 = (69 \text{ N}) / (9.8 \text{ m/s}^2)$

$m_1 = 7.04 \text{ kg}$

$m_2 = (94 \text{ N}) / (9.8 \text{ m/s}^2)$

$m_2 = 9.59 \text{ kg}$

$m_1 r_1 = m_2 r_2$

$m_1 / m_2 = r_2 / r_1$

$m_1 / m_2 = (7.04 \text{ kg}) / (9.59 \text{ kg})$

$m_1 / m_2 = 0.734$

$r_2 / r_1 = 0.734$

$r_2 + r_1 = 10 \text{ m}$

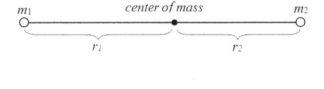

Two equations, two unknowns:

Eq$_1$: $r_2 + r_1 = 10 \text{ m}$

Eq$_2$: $r_2 - (0.734) \cdot (r_1) = 0$

Multiply Eq_2 by -1 and add to Eq_1:

$(1.734)r_1 = 10$ m

$r_1 = 5.8$ m

Alternatively:

For the object to be in equilibrium, the torques due to the two forces must sum to zero:

$\tau L + \tau R = 0$

Taking a counterclockwise torque to be positive:

$F_L x_L - F_R x_R = 0$

Let L be the length of the object, 10 m. Then:

$x_R = (L - x_L)$

and:

$F_L x_L - F_R (L - x_L) = 0$

Solve for x_L:

$x_L = LF_R / (F_L + F_R)$

$x_L = (10$ m$) \cdot (94$ N$) / (69$ N $+ 94$ N$)$

$x_L = 5.77$ m ≈ 5.8 m

52. A is correct.

The potential energy of a system can be zero because potential energy is defined against an arbitrary reference point. In a gravitational potential problem, if the reference point is ground level and the object is below ground level, it will have a negative potential energy relative to the reference point.

53. D is correct.

$\lambda = 2$ m and $T = 1$ s

$f = 1 / T$

$f = 1 / 1$ s

$f = 1$ Hz

$v = f\lambda$

$v = (1$ Hz$) \cdot (2$ m$)$

$v = 2$ m/s

54. C is correct.

$\Delta E = E_2 - E_1$

$\Delta E = 110$ J $- 40$ J

$\Delta E = 70$ J

55. D is correct. A plane mirror has a magnification of m = 1.

$m = -d_i / d_o$

$m = h_i / h_o$

$1 = -d_i / d_o$

$1 = h_i / h_o$

$-d_i = d_o$

$h_i = h_o$

The negative image distance indicates that the image is virtual and the positive image height indicates that the image is erect.

56. A is correct. The voltage through the 8 Ω resistor is:

$V = IR$

$V = (8\ \Omega)\cdot(0.8\ A)$

$V = 6.4\ V$

Since the 8 Ω resistor is in parallel with the 16 Ω resistor, the voltage across the 16 Ω resistor is also 6.4 V, and the current through it is:

$I = V / R$

$I = (6.4\ V) / (16\ \Omega)$

$I = 0.4\ A$

The total current in the upper branch is the sum of these:

$I_{upper} = 0.4\ A + 0.8\ A$

$I_{upper} = 1.2\ A$

The voltage across 20 Ω resistor:

$V = IR$

$V = (1.2\ A)\cdot(20\ \Omega)$

$V = 24\ V$

The total voltage across the upper branch is:

$V_{upper} = 6.4\ V + 24\ V$

$V_{upper} = 30.4\ V$

This is also the power supply voltage, and the voltage across the lower branch. The 2 Ω and 4 Ω resistors are in parallel, so it's also the voltage across the 2 Ω resistor.

Therefore, the current in the 2 Ω resistor is:

$I = V / R$

$I = (30.4\ V) / (2\ \Omega)$

$I = 15.2\ A$

57. B is correct. Force exerted on a particle of charge q:

$F = qE$

The acceleration of the proton is to the right so the force is also to the right. Therefore, the electric field must be to the right.

58. E is correct. Since a beat of frequency 4 Hz is produced, the violin string must be vibrating at either:

(340 Hz − 4 Hz) = 336 Hz

or

(340 Hz + 4 Hz) = 344 Hz

Since the string is too taut, the perceived f is too high.

Therefore, the string vibrates at 344 Hz.

Period is the reciprocal of frequency.

$T = 1 / f$

$T = 1 / 344$ sec

59. A is correct. Simple harmonic motion is described by Hooke's Law:

$F = -kx$

Combining it with Newton's Second law ($F = ma$), find:

$a = -(k/m)x$

Acceleration is proportional to displacement.

60. B is correct. Period of a pendulum:

$T = 2\pi\sqrt{(L / g)}$

The period does not depend on mass, so changes to M do not affect the period.

61. A is correct. Work equation:

$W = Fd$

$W = (70 \text{ N})\cdot(45 \text{ m})$

$W = 3,150 \text{ J}$

Power equation:

$P = W / t$

$P = (3,150 \text{ J}) / (60 \times 30 \text{ s})$

$P = (3,150 \text{ J}) / (180 \text{ s})$

$P = 18 \text{ W}$

62. C is correct. To balance the seesaw, the total torque about the center must be zero.

Let the subscripts S, M and J represent Shawn, Mark and John, respectively. Then:

$\tau_S + \tau_M + \tau_J = 0$

Take the positive sense of torque to be counter-clockwise. Then:

$F_S x_S - F_M x_M - F_J x_J = 0$

$(m_S g)\, x_S - (m_M g)\, x_M - (m_J g)\, x_J = 0$

$m_S x_S - m_M x_M - m_J x_J = 0$

Now, solve for John's position, x_J:

$x_J = (m_S x_S - m_M x_M) / m_J$

$x_J = [(105\ \text{kg}){\cdot}(5.5\ \text{m}) - (20\ \text{kg})(10\ \text{m})] / (20\ \text{kg})$

$x_J = [(105\ \text{kg}){\cdot}(5.5\ \text{m}) - (20\ \text{kg})(10\ \text{m})] / (20\ \text{kg})$

$x_J = (377.5\ \text{kg}{\cdot}\text{m}) / (20\ \text{kg})$

$x_J = 18.9\ \text{m} \approx 19\ \text{m}$

63. D is correct. It seems that there is not enough information because neither the masses nor the radii of the sphere and cylinder are known. However, various parameters often cancel out.

Try to find the acceleration of the two objects. The object with the larger acceleration will reach the bottom first.

An object rolling down an incline experiences three forces, and hence three torques. The forces are the force of gravity acting on the center of mass of the object, the normal force between the incline and the object, and the force of friction between the incline and the object.

If the origin is taken to be the center of the object, the force of gravity provides zero torque. This can be seen by noting that the distance between the origin and the point of application of the force is zero. $\tau_{gravity} = F_{gravity} r = mg(0) = 0$. Similarly, the normal force contributes zero torque because the direction of the force is directly through the origin (pivot point). $\tau_{normal} = F_{normal}\, r \sin\theta = F_{normal}(R)(\sin 180°) = F_{normal}(R)(0) = 0$.

Use a coordinate system in which the x-axis is parallel to the incline and the y-axis is perpendicular. The object is rolling in the positive x-direction.

The dynamical equation for linear motion along the x-direction is:

$F_{net} = ma$

$(mg \sin\theta - f) = ma$

Note that the normal force is only in the y-direction, and thus does not directly contribute to the acceleration in the x-direction. The dynamical equation for rotational motion is:

$\tau_{net} = I\alpha$

$fR = I\alpha$

(Note that the frictional force is perpendicular to the r vector, and $\sin 90° = 1$)

where R is the radius of the object, f is the force of friction, and I is the moment of inertia.

A relation is needed to couple these two dynamical equations. This is the equation of constraint imposed by the restriction that the object rolls without slipping:

$\alpha = a / R$

To find the linear acceleration, use the equation of constraint to eliminate α from the rotational equation by replacing it with a / R:

$fR = I(a / R)$

The force of friction is of no interest, so rearrange this last expression:

$f = Ia / R^2$

Substitute this into the linear dynamic equation from above in place of f:

$mg \sin \theta - (Ia / R^2) = ma$

Solving this for a:

$a = mg \sin \theta / [(m + (I / R^2)]$

$a = g\sin \theta / [1 + (I / mR^2)]$

For a sphere, $I = (2/5)mR^2$, so:

$a_{sphere} = g \sin \theta / (1 + 2/5)$

$a_{sphere} = (5/7)g \sin \theta$

For the cylinder, $I = \frac{1}{2}mR^2$, so:

$a_{cylinder} = g \sin \theta / (1 + \frac{1}{2})$

$a_{cylinder} = (2/3)g \sin \theta$

Since 5/7 > 2/3, the acceleration of the sphere is greater than the acceleration of the cylinder, so the sphere will reach the bottom first. Interestingly, neither the mass nor the size of the sphere or cylinder enters into the result. Indeed, both the mass and radius cancel out. Since neither the masses nor the radii were given in the statement of the problem, it would not be possible to solve this problem by brute force numerical calculation.

64. A is correct.

$v_y = 3.13 \sin 30°$

$v_y = 1.6$ m/s

$v_f = v_o + at$

$0 = (1.6$ m/s$) + (-9.8$ m/s$^2)t$

$(9.8$ m/s$^2)t = (1.6$ m/s$)$

$t = (1.6$ m/s$) / (9.8$ m/s$^2)$

$t = 0.16$ s

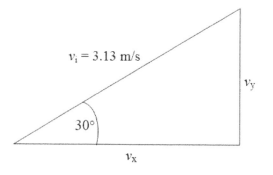

65. B is correct.

For a concave mirror with the object located at a distance equal to the focal length:

$d_o = f$

An object located at the focal point of a concave mirror will form no image.

66. A is correct. Before it is released, the hammer has zero velocity and a gravitational PE of *mgh*. This PE is converted completely into KE when it reaches the ground.

PE (top) = KE (bottom)

$mgh_0 = \frac{1}{2}m(v_0^2)$, cancel *m* from both sides of the expression

$v_0 = \sqrt{(2gh_0)}$

If h_0 increases by a factor of 2, substitute $2h_0$ for h_0

$v = \sqrt{[2g(2h_0)]}$

$v = \sqrt{2} \times \sqrt{2gh_0}$

$v = \sqrt{2} \times (v_0)$

The new velocity is $\sqrt{2}$ times faster.

67. A is correct. There is a common notion that a light's color is dependent on its wavelength (ranging from 700 nm at the red end of the spectrum to 400 nm at the violet end for visible light). However, this is true *only* when the light is traveling through one medium (e.g., air). When the light enters another medium (e.g., water), the wavelength changes, even though the color remain the same. If the color was always dependent on wavelength, it would change when the light enters a medium with a different refraction index.

The color of light is *always* dependent on frequency – the number of cycles per second (i.e., the number of waves of the light per second passing a given plane in space per second).

To illustrate this concept, visualize a ball floating in a swimming pool. If one were to dive into the pool and view the ball while under water, all the colors of the ball will appear the same as they did when they were observed in the air. When light goes from one medium to another, both the speed of the light and the wavelength of the light change. However, the frequency of the series of light waves does not.

68. A is correct. An electric current measures the amount of charge passing a point in the circuit per unit of time. In a flow of water, the analogous parameter is the volume (i.e. amount) of water passing a point per unit of time (i.e. volume flow rate).

By analogy, the current is the same for resistors in series, and the volume flow rate is constant (absent any branching) along a flow, which is not true of flow velocity.

69. B is correct.

Because of time dilation, clocks that are moving with respect to Earth run more slowly than clocks that are at rest on Earth. So during the length of the mission, fewer days will have passed for the astronaut than for observers on Earth.

70. A is correct. For constant acceleration, the velocity increases with time. If velocity increases with time, the position vs. time line of the graph is curved over each time interval.

71. C is correct. Use conservation of momentum for momenta in the x coordinate to solve for the x component of the second ball's final velocity.

Use m as the mass for the first ball and $1.4m$ as mass of the second ball.

$p_{before} = p_{after}$

$m(4 \text{ m/s}) \cos 60° = 1.4mv_x$

$v_x = (4 \text{ m/s}) \cdot (\cos 60°) / 1.4$

$v_x = (4 \text{ m/s}) \cdot (0.5) / 1.4$

$v_x = 1.4 \text{ m/s}$

72. C is correct. Photons are light and the speed of light is invariant, therefore I is wrong. The energy of the photons in a beam of light determines the color of the light. If the color is unchanged, then the average energy of the photons is unchanged, making II wrong. Changing the brightness of a beam of light increases the number of photons in the beam of light.

73. E is correct.

The flow rate must be equal in both parts of the pipe:

$A_1v_1 = A_2v_2$

$(\pi / 4)D_1^2v_1 = (\pi / 4)D_2^2v_2$, cancel $(\pi / 4)$ from both sides of the expression

$D_1^2v_1 = D_2^2v_2$

$v_2 = (D_1^2v_1) / D_2^2$

$v_2 = [(0.2 \text{ m})^2 / (0.004 \text{ m})^2] \cdot (0.03 \text{ m/s})$

$v_2 = (2,500) \cdot (0.03 \text{ m/s})$

$v_2 = 75 \text{ m/s}$

74. A is correct. The magnetic force on a charged particle can change the velocity and direction of the particle but cannot change its speed.

Kinetic energy is calculated using the square of speed:

$KE = \frac{1}{2}mv^2$

Thus if speed does not change the energy of the charge does not change.

75. B is correct. Beta (β^-) decay: the parent nuclide ejects an electron and electron antineutrino. However, in the process a neutron converts to a proton so the mass number remains the same but the atomic number increases by 1.

$$^A_Z X \rightarrow\ ^A_{Z+1} Y +\ ^0_{-1}e^- +\ ^0_0 v_e$$

76. A is correct.

$$Q = c_p m \Delta T$$

$$c_{p1} m_w \Delta T = c_{p2} m \Delta T$$

$$c_{p2} = (c_{p1} m_w \Delta T_w) / (m_2 \Delta T_2)$$

$$c_{p2} = (1 \text{ kcal/kg·°C})·(0.2 \text{ kg})·(40 \text{ °C}) / (0.06 \text{ kg})·(60 \text{ °C})$$

$$c_{p2} = 2.2 \text{ kcal/kg·°C}$$

77. B is correct. First, determine how long it takes the ball to drop 50 m:

$$PE = KE$$

$mgh = \tfrac{1}{2}mv_{yf}^2$, cancel m from both sides of the expression

$$gh = \tfrac{1}{2}v_{yf}^2$$

$$v_{yf}^2 = 2gh$$

$$v_{yf}^2 = (2)·(10 \text{ m/s}^2)·(50 \text{ m})$$

$$v_{yf}^2 = 1{,}000 \text{ m}^2/\text{s}^2$$

$$v_{yf} \approx 32 \text{ m/s}$$

$$t = (v_{yf} - v_{yi}) / a$$

$$t = (32 \text{ m/s} - 0) / (10 \text{ m/s}^2)$$

$$t = 3.2 \text{ s}$$

Calculate the distance traveled horizontally in 3.2 s:

$$d_x = v_x \times t$$

$$d_x = (5 \text{ m/s})·(3.2 \text{ s})$$

$$d_x = 16 \text{ m}$$

78. C is correct.

$$F_{tot} = F_{gravity} + F_{friction}$$

$ma_{tot} = mg \sin \theta + \mu_k mg \cos \theta$, cancel m from both sides

$$a_{tot} = g(\sin \theta + \mu_k \cos \theta)$$

$$a_{tot} = -9.8 \text{ m/s}^2(\sin 30° + 0.3 \cos 30°)$$

$$a_{tot} = -7.44 \text{ m/s}^2$$

Find time taken to reach 0 m/s:

$$v_f = v_0 + at$$

$$0 \text{ m/s} = 14 \text{ m/s} + (-7.44 \text{ m/s}^2)t$$

$$t = 1.88 \text{ s}$$

$$x = x_0 + v_0 t + \tfrac{1}{2}at^2$$

$$x = 0 \text{ m} + (14 \text{ m/s})·(1.88 \text{ s}) + \tfrac{1}{2}(-7.44 \text{ m/s}^2)·(1.88 \text{ s})^2$$

$$x = 13.2 \text{ m}$$

Find vertical component of x:

$$y = x \sin \theta$$

$$y = (13.2 \text{ m}) \sin 30°$$

$$y = 6.6 \text{ m}$$

79. B is correct.

The forces on the block (with bullet) are gravity and the tension of the string. The tension is perpendicular to the direction of travel, so the tension does no work. This problem is solved using conservation of energy, assuming a full transfer of KE into gravitational PE.

KE (block with bullet at bottom) = PE (block with bullet at top)

$\frac{1}{2}mv^2 = mgh$, cancel m from both sides of the expression

$$\frac{1}{2}v^2 = gh$$

$$\frac{1}{2}(2 \text{ m/s})^2 = (9.8 \text{ m/s}^2)h$$

$$\frac{1}{2}(4 \text{ m}^2/\text{s}^2) = (9.8 \text{ m/s}^2)h$$

$$(2 \text{ m}^2/\text{s}^2) = (9.8 \text{ m/s}^2)h$$

$$h = (2 \text{ m}^2/\text{s}^2) / (9.8 \text{ m/s}^2)$$

$$h = 0.20 \text{ m} = 20 \text{ cm}$$

80. E is correct.

Photon energy:

$$E = hf$$

$$f = c / \lambda$$

$$f = (3 \times 10^8 \text{ m/s}) / (6.5 \times 10^{-6} \text{ μm})$$

$$f = 4.6 \times 10^{13} \text{ Hz}$$

$$E = (4.136 \times 10^{-15} \text{ eV·s}) \cdot (4.6 \times 10^{13} \text{ Hz})$$

$$E = 0.19 \text{ eV}$$

81. E is correct.

$$v_f^2 = v_0^2 + 2ad$$

where $v_0 = 0$

$$v_f^2 = 0 + 2ad$$

$$v_f^2 = 2ad$$

Since a is constant, d is proportional to v_f^2

If v_f increases by a factor of 4, then d increases by a factor of $4^2 = 16$.

82. B is correct. The period of a satellite is found through Kepler's Third Law:

$$T = 2\pi\sqrt{(r^3 / GM)}$$

where T = period, r = distance from Earth's center, G = gravitational constant and M = mass of Earth

The period does not depend on the mass of the satellite so the period remains the same.

83. B is correct.

Heat conduction follows the equation:

$$\Delta Q / \Delta t = kA\Delta T / d$$

Assuming all other values are constant the equation can be written as:

$$\Delta Q / \Delta t = (1 / d)x$$

where x is a constant

The rate of heat loss is inversely proportional to the thickness, so by increasing d, the slope of the curve is negative.

84. B is correct. The arrows experience the same stopping force when they impart the hay bales.

The kinetic energy can be related to the work done by the force:

Arrow 1: $KE_1 = W$

                    $KE_1 = Fd_1$

                    $d_1 = KE_1 / F$

Arrow 2: $KE_2 = 2KE_1$

                    $2KE_1 = W$

                    $2KE_1 = Fd_2$

                    $d_2 = 2KE_1 / F$

                    $d_2 = 2d_1$

85. E is correct.

The period of a pendulum:

$$T = 2\pi\sqrt{(L / g)}$$

where L is the length of the pendulum and g is acceleration due to gravity.

Use $g / 6$ for g.

$$T = 2\pi\sqrt{(L / (g / 6))}$$

$$T = 2\pi\sqrt{(6L / g)}$$

$$T = 2\pi\sqrt{(L / g)} \times \sqrt{6}$$

New period = $T\sqrt{6}$

86. D is correct.

Decibels use a logarithmic scale.

$$\text{Intensity (dB)} = 10\log_{10}[I / I_0]$$

Where I_0 is the intensity at the threshold of hearing (10^{-12} W/m^2)

$$I = 10\log_{10}[10^{-7}\text{ W/m}^2 / 10^{-12}\text{ W/m}^2]$$

$$I = 10\log_{10}[10^5]$$

$$I = 50\text{ dB}$$

87. A is correct.

The buoyant force is given by:

$$F_B = \rho V g$$

ρ = density of fluid, V = volume of fluid displaced, g = acceleration due to gravity

To calculate how much the brick *appears* to weigh, subtract the buoyant force from the force due to gravity, where *m* is the *actual* mass of the brick:

$$F_{\text{apparent}} = F_{\text{gravity}} - F_{\text{buoyant}}$$

$$F_{\text{apparent}} = mg - \rho V g$$

The *actual* mass of the brick can be calculated as density × volume

$$V_{\text{brick}} = (2\text{ in} \times 4\text{ in} \times 6\text{ in})$$

$$V_{\text{brick}} = 48\text{ in}^3$$

$$V_{\text{brick}} = (48\text{ in}^3)\cdot(16.4\text{ cm}^3/1\text{ in}^3)$$

$$V_{\text{brick}} = 787\text{ cm}^3$$

$$\text{mass} = \text{density} \times \text{volume}$$

$$m = (11.4\text{ g/cm}^3)\cdot(787\text{ cm}^3)$$

$$m = 8{,}972\text{ g}$$

To get the apparent *mass*, divide the apparent force by *g*:

$$m_{\text{apparent}} = F_{\text{apparent}} / g$$

$$m_{\text{apparent}} = (m_{\text{brick}}g - \rho V g) / g$$

$$m_{\text{apparent}} = m_{\text{brick}} - \rho V$$

$$m_{\text{apparent}} = 8{,}972\text{ g} - [(0.92\text{ g/cm}^3)\cdot(787\text{ cm}^3)]$$

$$m_{\text{apparent}} = (8{,}972\text{ g} - 724\text{ g})$$

$$m_{\text{apparent}} = 8.2\text{ kg}$$

88. D is correct.

Acceleration is always positive and away from charge Q.

Therefore, velocity increases (no opposing force of friction).

The energy of the system starts as electrical PE.

$$PE_{elec} = (kQq) / r$$

where r is the initial distance between the point charges.

Electrical PE is the energy required to bring a system together from the charges starting at infinity.

After charge Q has moved very far away, the energy of the system is only KE = $\frac{1}{2}mv^2$

v has a limit because KE cannot exceed kQq / r

89. C is correct.

Resistance in series experience equal current because there is only one path for the current to travel.

90. B is correct. For the critical angle, the refracted angle is 90°

$$n_{water} \sin \theta_{crit} = n_{air} \sin 90°$$

$$\sin \theta_{crit} = (n_{air} / n_{water}) \sin 90°$$

$$\theta_{crit} = \sin^{-1} [(1 / 1.33)\cdot(1)]$$

$$\theta_{crit} = \sin^{-1} (3/4)$$

91. C is correct. Energy needed to change hydrogen from one state to another:

$E = -13.6 \text{ eV}[(1 / n_1^2) - (1 / n_2^2)]$

To ionize hydrogen, the electron must be removed to the n = ∞ state.

Energy needed to change from ground state:

$$E = -13.6[(1 / 1) - (1 / \infty)]$$

$$E = -13.6 \text{ eV}$$

Energy is expressed as a negative number to indicate that this much energy is needed to be input to the atom.

92. D is correct. Find the perimeter (i.e. circumference) of the carousel: distance traveled in one revolution.

$$Perimeter = \pi \times d$$

$$Perimeter = \pi \times 18 \text{ m}$$

$$Perimeter = 56.5 \text{ m}$$

Convert to rev/min, to rev/s

$$v = (5 \text{ rev/min})\cdot(1 \text{ min/60 s})$$

$$v = 0.083 \text{ rev/s}$$

Convert rev/s to m/s:

where 1 rev = 56.5 m

$v = (0.083 \text{ rev/s}) \cdot (56.5 \text{ m/1 rev})$

$v = 4.7$ m/s

93. A is correct.

Power = work / time

Power = (force × distance) / time

Newton's First Law: no force is required to keep the object moving with constant velocity.

The projectile maintains horizontal v since no forces are acting on the horizontal axis.

The vertical forces must also be balanced since it maintains its elevation (only moving horizontally).

Since there is no net force, no work is done, and therefore no power is required.

94. D is correct. Solve for spring constant k:

$PE = \frac{1}{2}kx^2$

$k = 2(PE) / x^2$

where x is the amplitude (maximum distance traveled from rest).

$k = 2(10 \text{ J}) / (0.2 \text{ m})^2$

$k = 500$ N/m

Solve for the period:

$T = 2\pi[\sqrt{(m / k)}]$

$T = 2\pi[\sqrt{(0.4 \text{ kg} / 500 \text{ N/m})}]$

$T = 0.18$ s

Convert the period to frequency:

$f = 1 / T$

$f = 1 / (0.18 \text{ s})$

$f = 5.6$ Hz

95. E is correct.

Electromagnetic waves propagate at the speed of light oscillations of electric and magnetic fields that propagate at the speed of light.

The oscillations of the two fields form a transverse wave perpendicular to each other and perpendicular to the direction of energy and wave propagation.

96. C is correct.

Under one meter of water the gauge pressure is:

$P = \rho g h$

Jack's lungs are open to atmospheric pressure due to the snorkel so he only needs to overcome the gauge pressure.

The force needed is:

$P = F / A$

$F = PA$

$F = (\rho g h)A$

The area is the area of his chest as this is what the pressure acts against.

$F = (\text{gauge pressure})\cdot(\text{chest area})$

97. B is correct.

Before the switch is closed, there is no current and no magnetic field in either solenoid. After the switch is closed, current in the first solenoid begins to flow from positive to negative, and a magnetic field is created pointing to the right (according to the solenoid right-hand rule).

According to Lenz's Law, an EMF is induced in the second solenoid to oppose the change in magnetic flux. Since the field from the first solenoid points to the right, the induced current in the second solenoid must induce a current pointing to the left to oppose it.

By the right-hand solenoid rule, the current in the galvanometer must flow from right to left to create a temporary magnetic field in the direction opposite to the original field.

98. A is correct.

Resistance in a wire:

$R = (\rho L) / A$

where ρ = resistivity, L = length of wire and A = cross-sectional area of wire

Cross-sectional area of a wire:

$A = \pi r^2$

$A = \pi D^2 / 4$

If D is doubled:

$A = \pi(2D)^2 / 4$

$A = \pi(4D^2) / 4$

The area is increased by a factor of 4.

The new resistance if D is doubled and L is doubled:

$R = (\rho \times 2L) / (4A)$

$R = \frac{1}{2}(\rho L / A)$

99. A is correct.

Magnification is defined as:

$$m = -d_i / d_o$$

For a mirror:

$$1 / f = 1 / d_i + 1 / d_o$$

Multiplying both sides by d_o gives:

$$d_o / f = d_o / d_i + 1$$

$$d_o / f = -(1 / m) + 1$$

Or:

$$1 / m = 1 - d_o / f$$

$$m = 1 / (1 - d_o / f)$$

$$m = 1 / (1 - 5 \text{ m} / 10 \text{ m})$$

$$m = +2$$

The magnification is positive, so the image is upright, and twice as large.

100. C is correct.

Diagnostic Test #3 – Explanations

1. D is correct.

The magnitude of the acceleration is given by:

$F = ma$

$a = F / m$

$F = qE_0$

$a = qE_0 / m$

$| a_p / a_e | = | (q_p E_0 / m_p) / (q_e E_0 / m_e) |$

$a_p / a_e = (m_e / m_p)$

$a_p = (m_e / m_p)a_e$

$a_p = (9 \times 10^{-31} \text{ kg} / 1.67 \times 10^{-27} \text{ kg})a_e$

$a_p \approx (1 / 1{,}850)a_e$

The electric field is constant.

The charges of the proton and the electron are equal in magnitude and are opposite in sign.

1.67×10^{-27} kg divided by 9×10^{-31} kg $\approx 1{,}850$.

The proton is about 1,850 times more massive, so its acceleration is 1,850 times smaller.

2. C is correct.

By Newton's second law, the acceleration is:

$a = F_{net} / m$

There are two forces on the object: gravity (F_g), pointing down the slope, and friction (F_f), opposing the motion, pointing up the slope.

Therefore:

$F_{net} = F_g - F_f,$

where the positive direction points down the slope, in the direction of motion.

From the diagram, the force due to gravity is:

$F_g = mg \sin \theta$

The force of friction is:

$F_f = \mu_k F_{normal}$

$F_f = \mu_k mg \cos\theta$

Therefore:

$a = (mg \sin \theta - \mu_k mg \cos \theta) / m$

Cancel m from both sides of the expression:

$a = g (\sin \theta - \mu_k \cos \theta)$

$a = (9.8 \text{ m/s}^2) \cdot (\sin 40° - 0.19 \times \cos 40°)$

$a = (9.8 \text{ m/s}^2) \cdot (0.49)$

$a = 4.9 \text{ m/s}^2$

3. E is correct.

The difference in intensity between a shout and a whisper is given by:

90 dB – 20 dB = 70 dB

A change of 10 decibels corresponds to a factor change of 10 in the intensity I in W/m^2.

An increase of 70 dB corresponds to an intensity increase of seven factors of 10, which equals a 10^7 or a ten million-fold increase in the intensity of the sound.

4. A is correct.

$F_B = mg$

$F_B = \rho V g$

$\rho V g = mg$, cancel g from both sides of the expression

$m = \rho V$

$m = (\pi r^2 h) \cdot (1 \text{ g/cm}^3)$

$m = \pi (1 \text{ cm})^2 \cdot (14 \text{ cm}) \cdot (1 \text{ g/cm}^3)$

$m = 14\pi \text{ g}$

$m = 44 \text{ g}$

5. D is correct.

813.0 rpm · (1 min / 60 s) · (2π rad/rev) = 85.14 rad/s

6. C is correct.

$V = IR$

Resistivity is the measure of resistance along the length of a given material:

$R = \rho L / A$

where ρ is resistivity

$\rho = RA / L$

$\rho = (\Omega) \cdot (\text{m}^2) / (\text{m})$

$\rho = \Omega \cdot \text{m}$

7. D is correct.

The magnification:

$$m = -d_i / d_o$$

$$m = -3\ m\ /\ 6\ m$$

$$m = -\tfrac{1}{2},\ \text{where the negative sign indicates that the image is inverted}$$

8. D is correct.

Uranium decays because the electromagnetic repulsion of the protons overcomes the strong nuclear force due to its limited range and the massive size of the uranium nucleus.

9. E is correct.

To achieve a due north bearing, the east-west velocity must be made to be zero.

Find the horizontal component of the NE drift:

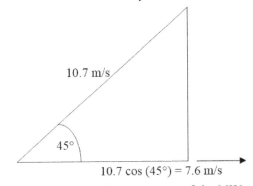

10.7 cos (45°) = 7.6 m/s

Find the horizontal component of the NW acceleration:

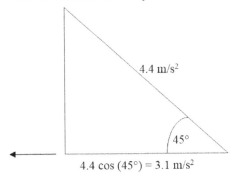

4.4 cos (45°) = 3.1 m/s²

The drift is fully corrected when there is zero east-west veloctity.

$$v_f = v_i + a_x t$$

$$0 = (7.6\ \text{m/s}) + (3.1\ \text{m/s}^2)(t)$$

$$t = (7.6\ \text{m/s}) / (3.1\ \text{m/s}^2)$$

$$t = 2.4\ \text{s}$$

10. A is correct.

For constant acceleration, average speed is:

$$v_{avg} = (v_{final} + v_{initial}) / 2$$

In this case:

$$v_{initial} = 0 \text{ m/s}$$

So:

$$v_{avg} = v_{final} / 2$$

With that:

$$d = v_{avg} t$$

$$d = v_{avg} t / 2$$

$$d = (20 \text{ m/s})(10 \text{ s}) / 2$$

$$d = 100 \text{ m}$$

11. B is correct.

The relationship between final speed and initial height can be found using conservation of energy:

$$PE_{initial} = KE_{final}$$

$$mgh = \tfrac{1}{2}mv^2$$

Therefore:

$$v^2 = gh$$

To double v, h increases by a factor of 4.

12. E is correct.

There are two forces on the ball: tension and the force of gravity. When the ball is at the bottom of its circular path, tension points up and the force of gravity points down.

The tension at the bottom is related to the net force on the ball and the force of gravity:

$$F_{net} = T - F_{gravity}$$

$$F_{net} = T - mg$$

or

$$T = F_{net} + mg$$

The ball will be executing circular motion, but its speed will be changing. Consider the speed to be approximately constant if observed for short intervals of time, so the motion is uniform circular motion during a short interval.

For any object executing uniform circular motion the net force is the centripetal force:

$$F_{net} = F_{centripetal}$$

$$F_{net} = mv^2/r$$

Putting this into the previous equation:

$T = mv^2/r + mg$

The velocity at the bottom can be related to the initial height using conservation of energy:

$KE_{final} = PE_{initial}$

$\frac{1}{2}\,mv^2 = mgh$

The height change is equal to twice the radius:

$\frac{1}{2}\,mv^2 = mg(2r)$

Therefore:

$mv^2 = 4mgr$

Putting this into the equation for the tension:

$T = (4mgr)/r + mg$

$T = 5mg$

$T = 5(4\ \text{kg}){\cdot}(9.8\ \text{m/s}^2)$

$T = 196.0\ \text{N}$

13. C is correct.

$T = 12\ \text{s}$

$f = 1\ /\ T$

$f = (1\ /\ 12\ \text{s})$

$f = 0.083\ \text{Hz}$

$\lambda = v\ /\ f$

$\lambda = (4.5\ \text{m/s}\ /\ 0.083\ \text{Hz})$

$\lambda = 54\ \text{m}$

14. C is correct. Although an iceberg has a much lower temperature than hot coffee it contains far more thermal energy due to its much greater mass.

For example, assume coffee at 90 °C goes to 80 °C:

$Q = mc\Delta T$

$Q = (1\ \text{kg}){\cdot}(4.2\ \text{kJ/kg{\cdot}K}){\cdot}(90\ °C - 80\ °C)$

where specific heat for water = 4.2 kJ/kg·K

$Q = 42$ kJ were released during temperature change

If a 10,000 kg iceberg (very small iceberg) were to go from 0 °C to –10 °C:

$Q = mc\Delta T$

$Q = (10{,}000\ \text{kg}){\cdot}(2.05\ \text{kJ/kg{\cdot}K}){\cdot}(0\ °C - (-10\ °C))$

where specific heat for ice = 2.05 kJ/kg·K

$Q = 205,000$ kJ were released during temperature change

Therefore, even a small iceberg at a much lower temperature contains more thermal energy due to its far greater mass.

15. B is correct.

The equation for focal length is:

$1/f = 1/d_o + 1/d_i$

where d_o is object distance and d_i is image distance

$1/f = 1/d_o + 1/d_i$

$1/f = 1/24$ cm $+ 1/3$ cm

$1/f = 1/24$ cm $+ 8/24$ cm

$1/f = 0.375$ cm

$f = 2.7$ cm

16. A is correct.

When an electron is emitted the parent nucleus is undergoing β^- decay:

$$_Z^A X \rightarrow {}_{Z+1}^A Y + {}_{-1}^0 e^- + {}_0^0 v_e$$

The parent nuclide ejects an electron and electron antineutrino. However, in the process a neutron converts to a proton so the mass number remains the same but the atomic number increases by 1.

The daughter nuclei should have the same mass number but an atomic number one higher than the parent nuclei. This causes the daughter nuclei to be a different element, in this example an atomic number of 91 is Pa.

17. B is correct. The equation for the magnetic field of an infinitely long straight wire is given as:

$B = \mu I / 2\pi r$

Where μ = permittivity of free space, I = current and r is radial distance from the wire

When r doubles, B decreases by a factor of ½.

18. A is correct.

Flow velocity:

$v = f / A$

where flow rate $f = 0.04$ m³/s

$v = f / (\pi r^2)$

$v = (0.04 \text{ m}^3/\text{s}) / [\pi(0.06 \text{ m})^2]$

$v = 3.5$ m/s

19. A is correct.

Intensity related to decibels may be expressed as:

$I \text{ (dB)} = 10\log_{10}(I / I_0)$

If intensity is increased by 100:

$I \text{ (dB)} = 10\log_{10}(100 / 1)$

$I \text{ (dB)} = 20$

20. D is correct.

Velocity in a wire:

$v = \sqrt{[T / (m / L)]}$

$T = v^2(m / L)$

$\text{volume} = A_{\text{cross-section}} \times \text{length}$

$V = (\pi D^2 / 4) \cdot (L)$

$m = V\rho$

$m = (\rho) \cdot (\pi D^2 / 4) \cdot (L)$

Rewrite tension formula with mass:

$T = v^2[(\rho) \cdot (\pi D^2 / 4) (L) / (L)]$

$T = v^2(\rho \times \pi D^2 / 4)$

$T = (42 \text{ m/s})^2 \times (\pi / 4) \cdot (2{,}600 \text{ kg/m}^3) \cdot (0.0044 \text{ m})^2$

$T = (1{,}764 \text{ m}^2/\text{s}^2) \cdot (\pi / 4) \cdot (2{,}600 \text{ kg/m}^3) \cdot (0.00001936 \text{ m}^2)$

$T = 69.74 \approx 70 \text{ N}$

21. C is correct.

Force along the incline:

$F = mg \sin \theta$

$F = (5 \text{ kg}) \cdot (9.8 \text{ m/s}^2) \sin 30°$

$F = (5 \text{ kg}) \cdot (9.8 \text{ m/s}^2) \cdot (0.5)$

$F = 24.5 \text{ N}$

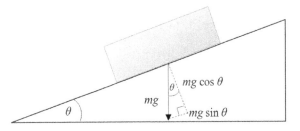

Solving for work:

$\text{Work} = \text{force} \times \text{distance}$

$W = (24.5 \text{ N}) \cdot (10 \text{ m})$

$W = 245 \text{ J}$

22. C is correct.

Momentum is:

$p = mv$

$v = 400 \text{ m} / 50 \text{ s}$

$v = 8 \text{ m/s}$

$p = (65 \text{ kg}) \cdot (8 \text{ m/s})$

$p = 520 \text{ kg} \cdot \text{m/s}$

23. D is correct. The speed of light has the same value for any observer regardless of the state of motion of the source or the observer. This is a fundamental principle of special relativity.

24. E is correct.

$\Delta v = at$

$a = \Delta v / t$

$a = (v_f - v_i) / t$

$(v_f - v_i) = at$

$v_f = at + v_i$

$v_f = (2 \text{ m/s}^2) \cdot (6 \text{ s}) + (5 \text{ m/s})$

$v_f = 17 \text{ m/s}$

25. A is correct.

Stay in SI units for consistency. Express the specific heat in SI units:

$c = 108 \text{ cal/kg/}^\circ\text{C}$

$c = 108 \text{ cal/kg/}^\circ\text{C} (4.186 \text{ J/cal})$

$c = 450.09 \text{ J/kg/}^\circ\text{C}$

Calculate ΔT:

$\Delta T = Q/(mc) = (1/2 \; mv^2) / (mc) = v^2/(4c)$

$\Delta T = (1{,}250 \text{ m/s})^2 / [4 (450.09 \text{ J/kg/}^\circ\text{C})]$

$\Delta T = 1728 \; ^\circ\text{C}$

Note that the temperature increase is independent of the mass of the meteorite.

26. D is correct.

Relate KE to PE:

$KE_B = PE_B$

$\tfrac{1}{2}mv_B^2 = mgh_B$, cancel m from both sides of the expression

$$\tfrac{1}{2}v_B{}^2 = gh_B$$

$$h_B = v_B{}^2 / 2g$$

If $v_M = 2v_B$

$$h_M = (2v_B)^2 / 2g$$

$$h_M = 4v_B{}^2 / 2g$$

$$h_M = 4h_B$$

Mary's ball travels four times as high as Brittany's ball.

27. D is correct.

For tubes open at both ends:

$$\lambda = 2L / n$$

where n = 1 is the fundamental

$$\lambda = 2 \,(0.2 \text{ m}) / 1$$

$$\lambda = 0.4 \text{ m}$$

28. B is correct. According to the Lorentz force law for a charged particle in a magnetic field, the magnetic force on a particle acts in a direction given by the right-hand rule.

For particles with velocity perpendicular to the field (as in this case), the magnitude of the force is:

$$F_B = qvB$$

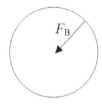

The centripetal force F_C on the proton is the magnetic force F_B:

$$F_B = F_C$$

$$qvB = (mv^2) / r$$

Therefore:

$$r = (mv) / (qB)$$

The values for m, q and B are fixed. If the speed is increased by a factor of three, so is the radius.

Thus, the time needed to complete one circular path is:

$t = 2\pi(3r) / 3v$

$t = 2\pi r / v$, unchanged from the original time.

29. B is correct.

$1 / f = 1 / d_i + 1 / d_o$

$1 / 2 \text{ m} = 1 / d_i + 1 / 6 \text{ m}$

$1 / 3 \text{ m} = 1 / d_i$

$d_i = 3 \text{ m}$

$m = -d_i / d_o$

$m = h_i / h_o$

$-3 \text{ m} / 6 \text{ m} = h_i / h_o$

$-\frac{1}{2} = h_i / h_o$

For a converging lens, a positive image distance indicates a real image.

The image is inverted because $h_i / h_o = -\frac{1}{2}$ and h_o cannot be negative so h_i must be negative.

A negative image height indicates an inverted image.

30. D is correct.

Break into three parts: heating the ice, melting the ice, heating the water.

Heating ice:

$\Delta Q_1 = mc\Delta T$

$\Delta Q_1 = (10 \text{ kg}) \cdot (0.5 \text{ kcal/kg} \cdot °C) \cdot [0 °C - (-8 °C)]$

$\Delta Q_1 = 40 \text{ kcal}$

Melting ice:

$\Delta Q_2 = mL_f$

$\Delta Q_2 = (10 \text{ kg}) \cdot (80 \text{ kcal/kg})$

$\Delta Q_2 = 800 \text{ kcal}$

Heating water:

$\Delta Q_3 = mc\Delta T$

$\Delta Q_3 = (10 \text{ kg}) \cdot (1 \text{ kcal/kg} \cdot °C) \cdot (14 °C - 0 °C)$

$\Delta Q_3 = 140 \text{ kcal}$

Combine:

$\Delta Q_{total} = (40 \text{ kcal} + 800 \text{ kcal} + 140 \text{ kcal})$

$\Delta Q_{total} = 980 \text{ kcal}$

31. C is correct. Conservation of energy states that momentum before and after the collision is consistent.

$$p_i = p_f$$

$$p = mv$$

$$m_1 v_1 = m_2 v_2$$

$$m_1 \Delta v_1 = m_2 \Delta v_2$$

$$(6 \text{ kg}) \cdot (v_f - v_i)_1 = (8 \text{ kg}) \cdot (v_f - v_i)_2$$

$(v_f - v_i)_1$ must be larger

32. B is correct.

The period of a pendulum is:

$$T = 2\pi \sqrt{(L / g)}$$

If the elevator is accelerating upwards then the constant acceleration adds to apparent acceleration due to gravity and the period decreases.

$$g < g + a$$

The period decreases as the gravitational acceleration increases.

33. A is correct.

The 400 m distance between the aircraft (i.e. source) and the observer remains constant.

Since there is no relative motion between the source and the detector, f_d equals f_s.

34. B is correct.

The magnetic force on an object changes the direction of the charge and thus the velocity. However the speed does not change. Kinetic energy is calculated using speed thus if the magnetic force does not change the speed it does not change its kinetic energy.

35. C is correct. Heavy nuclides with atomic numbers greater than 83 almost always undergo alpha decay to reduce the number of neutrons and protons in the nucleus.

36. D is correct.

A larger coefficient of thermal expansion causes a greater size increase compared to materials with smaller coefficients of thermal expansion. If the pin were removed easily while hot it did not expand as much as material X and must have a smaller coefficient.

37. B is correct.

According to Newton's First Law: every object remains at rest or in motion in a straight line unless acted upon by an unbalanced force. Thus if the object's motion changes an unbalanced force is being applied.

38. D is correct.

Objects in orbit around Earth still experience the force of gravity. The reason the astronauts feel weightless in space is because they are in free fall and cannot feel the force of gravity.

39. B is correct.

Find the amount of time it takes the ball to fall 1 m from the apex:

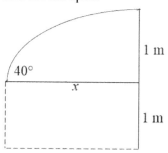

$$\Delta x = v_0 t + \tfrac{1}{2}at^2$$

$$1\ m = (0\ m/s)t + \tfrac{1}{2}(9.8\ m/s^2)t^2$$

$$1\ m = \tfrac{1}{2}(9.8\ m/s^2)t^2$$

$$1\ m = 4.9\ m/s^2\, t^2$$

$$t = \sqrt{(1\ m\ /\ 4.9\ m/s^2)}$$

$$t = 0.452\ s$$

Find initial upward velocity of the ball:

$$v^2 = v_0^2 + 2a\Delta x$$

$$0\ m/s = v_0^2 + 2(-9.8\ m/s^2)\cdot(1\ m)$$

$$0\ m/s = v_0^2 + (-19.6\ m^2/s^2)$$

$$19.6\ m^2/s^2 = v_0^2$$

$$v_0 = \sqrt{(19.6\ m^2/s^2)}$$

$$v_0 = 4.427\ m/s$$

Calculate the horizontal velocity:

$$\tan(40°) = (4.427\ m/s)\ /\ v_h$$

$$0.839 = (4.427\ m/s)\ /\ v_h$$

$$v_h = (4.427\ m/s)\ /\ 0.839$$

$$v_h = 5.277\ m/s$$

Calculate the distance from fence using elapsed time and horizontal velocity:

$$d = v_h t$$

$$d = 5.277\ m/s \times 0.452\ s$$

$$d = 2.39\ m \approx 2.4\ m$$

40. E is correct. During beta minus decay, the parent nuclide ejects an electron and electron antineutrino. However, in the process a neutron converts to a proton so the mass number remains the same but the atomic number increases by 1.

$$^{A}_{Z}X \rightarrow\ ^{A}_{Z+1}Y + ^{0}_{-1}e^- + ^{0}_{0}\nu_e$$

41. B is correct. Using the Compton Equation:

$$\Delta \lambda = \lambda_{Compton} (1 - \cos \theta), \text{ where } \lambda_{Compton} = 2.43 \times 10^{-12} \text{ m}$$

At $\theta = 180°$, it is required that $\Delta \lambda = \lambda$.

Thus:

$$\lambda = 2\lambda_{Compton}$$
$$\lambda = 4.86 \times 10^{-12} \text{ m}$$

42. A is correct. An object in motion with constant nonzero velocity experiences no acceleration and thus cannot have any net force upon it.

If v = constant, then:

$$a = 0$$
$$F = ma$$
$$F = m(0 \text{ m/s}^2)$$
$$F = 0 \text{ N}$$

43. B is correct.

Heat conduction equation:

$$Q \, / \, t = (kA\Delta T) \, / \, d$$

where k is the thermal conductivity of the wall material, A is the surface area of the wall, d is the wall's thickness and ΔT is the temperature difference on either side.

Assume heat flow is lengthwise so barrier distance:

$$d = 2d_0$$

The important value here is A ($A = \pi r^2$), which is surface area of object with respect to direction of heat flow and d, which is barrier thickness.

The surface area with respect to heat flow:

$$A_0 = (\pi \, / \, 4)D_0^2$$
$$A = (\pi \, / \, 4) \cdot (2D_0)^2$$
$$A = 4(\pi \, / \, 4) \, D_0^2$$
$$A = 4A_0$$

Substitute values into original equation:

$$Q \, / \, t = (k\Delta T) \cdot (4A_0 \, / \, 2d_0)$$
$$Q \, / \, t = 2(kA_0\Delta T \, / \, d_0)$$
$$Q \, / \, t = 2(Q_0 \, / \, t)$$
$$Q \, / \, t = 2(30 \text{ W})$$
$$Q \, / \, t = 60 \text{ W}$$

44. A is correct.

The spring already has the 0.9 kg mass attached to it so its original equilibrium length is the length needed to counteract the force of gravity.
If the spring is stretched further then the net force only includes the component from the spring force:

$F_{spring} = k\Delta x$

$F_{spring} = (3 \text{ N/m}) \cdot (0.18 \text{ m})$

$F_{spring} = 0.54 \text{ N}$

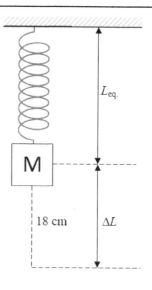

45. B is correct.

Convert weight to mass:

$F = ma$

$m = F / a$

$m = 30 \text{ N} / (9.8 \text{ m/s}^2)$

$m = 3.061 \text{ kg}$

Frequency of a spring system:

$\omega = \sqrt{(k / m)}$

$\omega = \sqrt{(40.0 \text{ N/m} / 3.061 \text{ kg})}$

$\omega = 3.615 \text{ rad/s}$

$f = \omega / 2\pi$

$f = (3.615 \text{ rad/s}) / 2\pi$

$f = 0.58 \text{ Hz}$

46. E is correct.

$f_{beat} = |f_2 - f_1|$

$f_{beat} = |786.3 \text{ Hz} - 785.8 \text{ Hz}|$

$f_{beat} = 0.5 \text{ Hz}$

47. D is correct.

The weight of the piston surface area is a ratio:

$F_1 / A_1 = F_2 / A_2$

$F_2 = F_1 \times A_2 / A_1$

$F_2 = (600 \text{ N}) \cdot (50 \text{ cm}^2) / 5 \text{ cm}^2$

$F_2 = 6,000 \text{ N}$

48. D is correct.

Equation for potential energy:

$$\Delta PE = q\Delta V$$

Note: q is negative because electrons are negatively charged

$$\Delta PE = (-1.6 \times 10^{-19} \text{ C}) \cdot (-500 \text{ V} - 500 \text{ V})$$

$$\Delta PE = (-1.6 \times 10^{-19} \text{ C}) \cdot (-1,000 \text{ V})$$

$$\Delta PE = 1.6 \times 10^{-16} \text{ J}$$

Moving this electron increases its PE energy.

49. B is correct.

$$P = VI$$

$$V = IR, \text{ substituting into the equation}$$

$$P = (IR) \times I$$

$$P = I^2 \times R$$

If P is on y-axis and R is on x-axis,

$$\text{slope} = P / R$$

$$\text{slope} = I^2$$

50. B is correct.

The resolution is the smallest distance between two objects where they are still capable of being distinguished as separate objects.

Therefore, the light with shorter wavelength gives a smaller distance between peaks and therefore a higher resolution.

51. D is correct.

The photoelectric effect is the phenomenon where light incident upon a metallic surface causes electrons to be emitted.

The photoelectric effect is described by the equation:

$$KE_{max} = hf - \phi$$

where h = Planck's constant, f = frequency and ϕ = work function.

If light of a threshold frequency such that $hf > \phi$ shines upon a metallic surface, the electrons will be ejected with KE. Increasing frequency increases the KE.

Note: hf is the energy carried by one incident photon. Since the incident intensity remains constant, but the energy per photon has increased, the rate of incident photons must decrease, resulting in a decrease in the rate of ejection events.

52. C is correct.

First calculate the stone's speed at impact:

$$v^2 = v_0{}^2 + 2ad$$

where $v_0 = 0$ and $a = g$

$$v^2 = 2ad$$

$$v^2 = 2(10 \text{ m/s}^2){\cdot}(5 \text{ m})$$

$$v^2 = 100 \text{ m}^2/\text{s}^2$$

$$v = 10 \text{ m/s}$$

Use the speed of impact to calculate momentum p:

$$p = mv$$

$$p = (3 \text{ kg}){\cdot}(10 \text{ m/s})$$

$$p = 30 \text{ kg}{\cdot}\text{m/s}$$

Another method to solve this problem:

$$PE = KE$$

$mgh = \frac{1}{2}mv^2$, cancel m from both sides of the expression

$$gh = \frac{1}{2}v^2$$

$$2(gh) = v^2$$

$$v^2 = 2(10 \text{ m/s}^2 \times 5 \text{ m})$$

$$v^2 = 100 \text{ m}^2/\text{s}^2$$

$$v = 10 \text{ m/s}$$

$$p = mv$$

$$p = (3 \text{ kg}){\cdot}(10 \text{ m/s})$$

$$p = 30 \text{ kg}{\cdot}\text{m/s}$$

53. E is correct.

Find kinetic energy and set equal to the work done by friction:

$$KE = W_\text{f}$$

$$\tfrac{1}{2}mv^2 = F_\text{f} \times d$$

$$\tfrac{1}{2}m \,/\, F_\text{f} = d \,/\, v^2$$

Because the mass is constant, $d \,/\, v^2$ = constant regardless of velocity.

Solve for the new skid distance:

$$d_1 \,/\, v_1{}^2 = d_2 \,/\, v_2{}^2$$

$$d_2 = (d_1){\cdot}(v_2{}^2) \,/\, (v_1{}^2)$$

$$d_2 = (30 \text{ m}){\cdot}(150 \text{ km/h})^2 \,/\, (45 \text{ km/h})^2$$

$$d_2 = 333 \text{ m}$$

54. A is correct. The time it takes to complete one cycle is the period T.

$$T = 1 / f$$

Period is measured in seconds.

$$\text{Frequency} = s^{-1} \text{ or } Hz$$

55. E is correct.

Volume strain = Δ Volume / Volume

$$\Delta\text{Volume} = \text{Volume strain} \times \text{Volume}$$

$$\Delta V = (-3 \times 10^{-4})\cdot(12\ L)$$

$$\Delta V = -3.6 \times 10^{-3}\ L$$

$$\Delta V = -3.6\ mL$$

The value of ΔV is negative, meaning the final volume is smaller than the initial volume, confirming that it is a reduction.

56. E is correct.

First, find the total mass of the mixture once the ethanol has been added to the chloroform:

$$\text{Total Mass} = x + 5 \text{ grams}$$

where x is the mass of the ethanol added.

Then, find the volume of the resulting mixture. Volume is found using the specific gravity formula:

$$\text{Volume (mL)} = \text{Mass (g)} / SG$$

Therefore:

$$V_e = x / 0.8$$

$$V_c = 5\ g / 1.5$$

$$\text{Total Volume} = V_e + V_c$$

$$\text{Total Volume} = (x / 0.8) + (5\ g / 1.5)$$

$$\text{Total Volume} = 1.25x + 3.33\ mL$$

Find the mass of added ethanol using the given specific gravity of the mixture:

$$SG_{\text{mixture}} = \text{Total Mass} / \text{Total Volume}$$

$$1.2 = (x + 5\ g) / (1.25x + 3.33\ mL)$$

$$(1.2)\cdot(1.25x + 3.33\ mL) = (x + 5\ g)$$

$$1.5x + 3.96\ g = x + 5\ g$$

$$0.5x = 1.04\ g$$

$$x = 2.08\ g \approx 2\ g$$

57. A is correct.

Batteries in series add voltage:

$$V_{eq} = 4(8\ V)$$

$$V_{eq} = 32\ V$$

Resistors in series add resistance:

$$R_{eq} = 45\ \Omega + 25\ \Omega$$

$$R_{eq} = 70\ \Omega$$

Ohm's law:

$$V = IR$$

$$I = V\ /\ R$$

Current through series circuit is constant:

$$I = 32\ V\ /\ 70\ \Omega$$

$$I = 0.46\ A$$

The point at which the current is measured does not matter because the circuit is connected in series.

58. B is correct.

The equivalent resistance of resistors in parallel:

$$R_{eq} = 1\ /\ (1\ /\ R_1 + 1\ /\ R_2 + 1\ /\ R_3\ ...)$$

The equivalent resistance is always smaller than the smallest resistance:

For example:

$R_1 = 20\ \Omega,\ R_2 = 30\ \Omega,\ R_3 = 30\ \Omega$

$$R_{eq} = 1\ /\ (1\ /\ 20\ \Omega + 1\ /\ 30\ \Omega + 1\ /\ 30\ \Omega\ ...)$$

$$R_{eq} = 8.75\ \Omega$$

$$R_{eq} < R_1$$

59. C is correct.

First, assume that the distance of the Moon from the lens is ∞.

$$d_o = \infty$$

Next, assume d_i is the distance from the lens where the image forms.

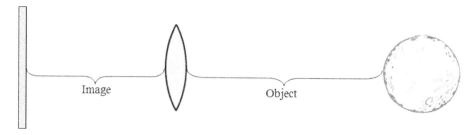

By the thin lens equation:

$$1 / d_i + 1 / d_o = 1 / f$$

$$1 / d_i + 1 / \infty = 1 / f$$

$$1 / d_i + 0 = 1 / f$$

$$1 / d_i = 1 / f$$

$$d_i = f$$

60. B is correct.

The angular speed changes according to the kinematic relation:

$$\Delta\omega = \alpha\Delta t$$

$$\Delta t = \Delta\omega / \alpha$$

$$\Delta t = (0 \text{ rad/s} - 96.0 \text{ rad/s}) / (-1.5 \text{ rad/s}^2)$$

The angular acceleration is negative because the wheel is slowing down and the initial ω is in the positive direction.

$$\Delta t = 64.0 \text{ s}$$

61. D is correct. If ^{23}Na absorbs a proton and releases a neutron then the atomic number increases by one and the mass number remains constant.

Thus ^{23}Mg has the same mass number but has an atomic number one higher than ^{23}Na.

62. C is correct. The coefficient of static friction (object at rest) is larger than the coefficient of kinetic friction (object in motion). It is proportional to the force needed to take a stationary object out of static equilibrium and accelerate it. The coefficient of kinetic friction is proportional to the force needed to maintain dynamic equilibrium in an object moving at constant speed.

Therefore, the force required to take a stationary object out of static equilibrium and accelerate it is greater than the force required to keep a moving object in dynamic equilibrium. It is more difficult to set an object in motion than it is to keep it in motion.

63. B is correct.

The two ends count as nodes. From a standing wave with four nodes, there are three antinodes.

Therefore, there are three half-wavelengths.

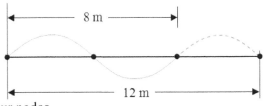

Each dot on the curve represents one of the four nodes.

One complete wave (the solid line) includes three nodes.

$$1 \text{ wave} = (2/3) \text{ entire string}$$

$$1 \text{ wave} = (2/3)\cdot(12 \text{ m}) = 8 \text{ m}$$

64. A is correct.

The reading on the meter is the net force between the necklace weight and buoyant force.

$$F_{total} = F_O - F_B$$

$$F_{total} = mg - \rho V g$$

$$F_{total} = g(m - \rho V)$$

$$F_{total} = (9.8 \text{ m/s}^2) \cdot [(0.06 \text{ kg}) - (1 \text{ g/cm}^3) \cdot (5.7 \text{ cm}^3) \cdot (1 \text{ kg/1,000 g})]$$

$$F_{total} = 0.53 \text{ N}$$

65. D is correct.

The centripetal force F_C on a charged particle in a magnetic field is the magnetic Lorentz force:

$$F_M = qvB$$

Therefore:

$$F_C = F_M$$

$$mv^2 / r = qvB$$

or

$$r = mv / qB$$

Increasing the speed by a factor of two increases the radius by a factor of two.

66. E is correct.

The equation for force in a magnetic field (B):

$$F = qv \times B$$

The direction of B is given by the right-hand rule.

If the thumb is oriented upward as shown for F, the magnetic field B points into the page.

67. B is correct.

$$PV = nRT$$

$$T_0 = PV / nR$$

$$T_1 = (2P) \cdot (2V) / (nR)$$

$$T_1 = 4(PV / nR)$$

68. D is correct. Electric field lines go from positive charge to negative charge. The electron will go against the field lines due to attraction to the positive charge emitting the field lines.

They do not follow path X because momentum in the horizontal direction must be conserved.

69. B is correct. The maximum and minimum of position vs. time is always equal to zero velocity.

70. D is correct.

$$F_f = \mu_k F_N$$

$$F_f = \mu_k mg \cos\theta$$

Find the length of travel:

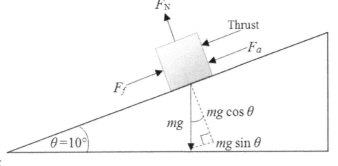

$$L = 50 \text{ m} / \sin 10°$$

$$L = 50 \text{ m} / 0.174$$

$$L = 288 \text{ m}$$

Find acceleration to reach 40 m/s:

$$v_f^2 = v_i^2 + 2ad$$

$$(40 \text{ m/s})^2 = 0 + 2a(288 \text{ m})$$

$$1,600 \text{ m}^2/\text{s}^2 = a(576 \text{ m})$$

$$a = (1,600 \text{ m}^2/\text{s}^2) / (576 \text{ m})$$

$$a = 2.8 \text{ m/s}^2$$

Find normal (F_N) and gravitational (F_G) forces:

$$F_N = mg \cos\theta$$

$$F_N = (50 \text{ kg}) \cdot (9.8 \text{ m/s}^2) \cos 10°$$

$$F_N = (50 \text{ kg}) \cdot (9.8 \text{ m/s}^2) \cdot (0.985)$$

$$F_N = 483 \text{ N}$$

$$F_G = mg \sin\theta$$

$$F_G = (50 \text{ kg}) \cdot (9.8 \text{ m/s}^2) \sin 10°$$

$$F_G = (50 \text{ kg}) \cdot (9.8 \text{ m/s}^2) \cdot (0.174)$$

$$F_G = 85 \text{ N}$$

$$F_{total} = (260 \text{ N} + 85 \text{ N})$$

$$F_{total} = 345 \text{ N, total force experienced by the skier}$$

The skier experiences acceleration down the slope that was reduced by friction.

The coefficient of kinetic friction can be calculated by:

$$F_{total} - F_{friction} = F_{experienced}$$

$$F_{total} - \mu F_N = F_{experienced}$$

$$345 \text{ N} - \mu_k 483 \text{ N} = (2.8 \text{ m/s}^2 \times 50 \text{ kg})$$

$$345 \text{ N} - \mu_k 483 \text{ N} = 140 \text{ N}$$

$$345 \text{ N} - 140 \text{ N} = \mu_k 483 \text{ N}$$

$$205 \text{ N} = \mu_k 483 \text{ N}$$

$$205 \text{ N} / 483 \text{ N} = \mu_k$$

$$\mu_k = 0.42$$

71. A is correct.

Conservation of momentum:

$$m_1v_1 = m_2v_2$$

m_1 = putty

m_2 = putty + bowling ball

$m_2 = (1 \text{ kg} + 7 \text{ kg})$

$m_2 = 8 \text{ kg}$

$v_2 = (m_1v_1) / m_2$

$v_2 = (1 \text{ kg})·(1 \text{ m/s}) / 8 \text{ kg}$

$v_2 = 1/8 \text{ m/s}$

72. B is correct.

Upward force due to the spring (Hooke's law):

$$F = k\Delta x$$

where k is the spring constant and Δx is the distance the spring is stretched

The downward force due to gravity:

$$F = mg$$

System is in equilibrium so set the expressions equal to each other:

$k\Delta x = mg$

$\Delta x = mg / k$

$\Delta x = (4 \text{ kg})·(10 \text{ m/s}^2) / (10 \text{ N/m})$

$\Delta x = 4 \text{ m}$

73. B is correct.

The overtone or harmonic can be found by the following:

harmonic	overtone
n^{th} harmonic	$(n^{th} - 1)$ overtone

Thus the third harmonic has the 2nd $(3 - 1)$ overtone

74. B is correct.

Proper time is the elapsed time between two events in the frame in which the events happen at the same location. The two events here are the spaceship passing Earth and the spaceship passing Mars. In the frame of the spaceship, both events occur in the same place: at the spaceship.

75. A is correct.

$m = -d_i / d_o$

$m = -(-6 \text{ m}) / (2 \text{ m})$

$m = 3$

Positive magnification means an upright image.

76. B is correct.

Calculate impedance for each circuit element.

Resistor:

$Z_r = 30 \ \Omega$

Inductor:

$Z_i = j2\pi fL$

where j is an imaginary number used in calculating complex impedance.

$Z_i = j2\pi(50 \text{ Hz}) \cdot (0.4 \text{ H})$

$Z_i = j125.6 \ \Omega$

Capacitor:

$Z_c = -j / (2\pi fC)$

$Z_c = -j / [2\pi(50 \text{ Hz}) \cdot (50 \times 10^{-6} \text{ F})]$

$Z_c = -j63.7 \ \Omega$

Adding in series:

$Z_{total} = 30 \ \Omega + j(125.6 \ \Omega - 63.7 \ \Omega)$

To find magnitude, use Pythagorean Theorem:

$|Z| = \sqrt{[(30 \ \Omega)^2 + (61.9 \ \Omega)^2]}$

$|Z| = 68.79 \ \Omega$

$V = IR$

Using impedance (Z) as resistance:

$V = (1.8 \text{ A}) \cdot (68.79 \ \Omega)$

$V = 124 \text{ V}$

77. D is correct.

Coulomb's Law, which describes repulsive force between two particles, is given as:

$F = kq_1q_2 / r^2$

The expression does not include mass, so the repulsive force remains the same when m changes.

Note: gravitational (attractive) forces do rely on the masses of the objects.

78. A is correct.

The gauge pressure is referenced at ambient air pressure thus:

$$P = \rho g h$$
$$P = (1{,}000 \text{ kg/m}^3){\cdot}(9.8 \text{ m/s}^2){\cdot}(6 \text{ m} + 22 \text{ m})$$
$$P = 2.7 \times 10^5 \text{ N/m}^2$$

79. C is correct.

$$f_{\text{beat}} = |f_2 - f_1|$$
$$\pm f_{\text{beat}} = f_2 - f_1$$
$$f_2 = \pm f_{\text{beat}} + f_1$$
$$f_2 = \pm 5 \text{ Hz} + 822 \text{ Hz}$$
$$f_2 = 817 \text{ Hz, } 827 \text{ Hz}$$

Only 827 Hz is an answer choice.

80. E is correct.

A phase change occurs when waves reflect from the surface of a medium with a higher refractive index than the medium they are traveling in. Glass has a higher refractive index than air and therefore, when the light ray moves from glass to air, no change occurs.

81. A is correct.

Convert PE (before release) into KE (as it is about to strike the ground):

$$mgh = \text{KE}$$

KE is proportional to *h*.

82. B is correct.

Determine distance in one revolution (the perimeter or circumference):

$$P = \pi d$$
$$P = \pi(18 \text{ m})$$
$$P = 56.55 \text{ m}$$

Convert rev/min to rev/s:

$$v = (5.3 \text{ rev/min}){\cdot}(1 \text{ min}/60 \text{ s})$$
$$v = 0.0883 \text{ rev/s}$$

Convert rev/s to m/s, where 1 rev = 56.55 m

$$v = (0.0883 \text{ rev/s}){\cdot}(56.55 \text{ m}/1 \text{ rev})$$
$$v = 5 \text{ m/s}$$

83. C is correct.

$$F_{net} = ma$$

The only acceleration is centripetal:

$$a_{cent} = v^2 / r$$

$$a_{cent} = (4 \text{ m/s})^2 / 16 \text{ m}$$

$$a_{cent} = (16 \text{ m}^2/\text{s}^2) / 16 \text{ m}$$

$$a_{cent} = 1 \text{ m/s}^2$$

$$F_{net} = ma$$

$$F_{net} = (40 \text{ kg}) \cdot (1 \text{ m/s}^2)$$

$$F_{net} = 40 \text{ kg} \cdot \text{m/s}^2 = 40 \text{ N}$$

84. B is correct. When an object is accelerating its velocity must change in either speed or direction. The speed or direction do not always change but velocity does.

85. C is correct. Solve for heat required:

$$Q = cm\Delta T$$

$$Q = (113 \text{ cal/kg} \cdot °\text{C}) \cdot (1.14 \text{ kg}) \cdot (90 \text{ °C} - 18 \text{ °C})$$

$$Q = 9,275 \text{ cal}$$

Convert to Joules:

$$Q = (9,275 \text{ cal} / 1) \cdot (4.186 \text{ J} / \text{cal})$$

$$Q = 38,825 \text{ J}$$

86. A is correct.

Include the term for work done by air resistance in the conservation of energy equation.

$$KE_i + PE_i + W_{air\ resis} = KE_f + PE_f$$

$$0 + mgh + (-F_{air} \times d) = \tfrac{1}{2}mv_f^2 + 0$$

$$mgh + (-mad) = \tfrac{1}{2}mv_f^2$$

$$(1.2 \text{ kg}) \cdot (10 \text{ m/s}^2) \cdot (6 \text{ m}) + (-3.4 \text{ kg} \cdot \text{m/s}^2) \cdot (6 \text{ m}) = \tfrac{1}{2}(1.2 \text{ kg})v_f^2$$

$$v_f^2 = 86 \text{ m}^2/\text{s}^2$$

$$v_f = 9.2 \text{ m/s}$$

87. E is correct.

Sound intensity is expressed as power / area:

Units of intensity: $W/m^2 = J/s/m^2 = J/m^2/s$

which is the unit of energy per unit area per unit time.

88. A is correct. Unit of watt = work / time

Multiply by time, time cancels and work is left.

Alternatively, 1 kilowatt-hour:

1 watt = 1 J/s

1 watt·second = 1 J

$(1\ hr/60\ s)\cdot(60\ min/1\ hr)\cdot(60\ s/1min) = 60^2\ s$

$1 \times 10^3\ Watt \times (1\ hour)\cdot(60^2\ s/1\ hour) = 36 \times 10^5\ J$

Work = force × distance

Joule is a unit of work.

89. D is correct.

Critical angle = $\sin^{-1} (n_2 / n_1)$

Critical angle = $\sin^{-1} (1.3 / 1.6)$

Critical angle = $\sin^{-1} (0.81)$

Critical angle = 54°

90. C is correct. $PE_e = PE_1 + PE_2 + PE_3$

$PE_e = (kQ_1Q_2) / r_1 + (kQ_2Q_3) / r_2 + (kQ_1Q_3) / r_3$

The distance between the bottom charge and the right charge can be found using the Pythagorean Theorem.

$d^2 = (0.06\ m)^2 + (0.04\ m)^2$

$d^2 = 0.0036\ m^2 + 0.0016\ m^2$

$d^2 = 0.0052\ m^2$

$d = 0.072\ m$

$Q_1 = Q_2 = Q_3$, so:

$PE_e = kQ^2[(1 / 0.06\ m) + (1 / 0.04\ m) + (1 / 0.072\ m)]$

$PE_e = (9 \times 10^9\ Nm^2/C^2)\cdot(6.2 \times 10^{-9}\ C)^2\cdot[(1 / 0.06\ m) + (1 / 0.04\ m) + (1 / 0.072\ m)]$

$PE_e = (9 \times 10^9\ Nm^2/C^2)\cdot(6.2 \times 10^{-9}\ C)^2 \times (16.7\ m^{-1} + 25\ m^{-1} + 13.9\ m^{-1})$

$PE_e = 1.9 \times 10^{-5}\ J$

91. C is correct. If the cylinder's center of mass does not move it must be stationary and the forces must balance:

$F = mg \sin \theta$

Force produced by torque is:

$\tau = I\alpha$

where I is mass moment of inertia and α is angular acceleration.

The moment of inertia for a solid cylinder is:

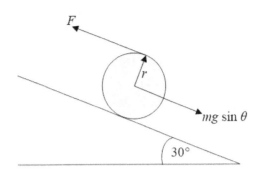

$I = \frac{1}{2}mr^2$

$\tau = I\alpha$

$\tau = Fr$

$I\alpha = Fr$

$(\frac{1}{2}mr^2)\alpha = (mg \sin \theta)r$

$\alpha = (2g \sin \theta) / r$

$\alpha = (2) \cdot (10 \text{ m/s}^2) \sin 30° / (0.8 \text{ m})$

$\alpha = (2) \cdot (10 \text{ m/s}^2) \cdot (0.5) / (0.8 \text{ m})$

$\alpha = 12.5 \text{ rad/s}^2$

92. C is correct. Frequency = # cycles / time

$f = 2 \text{ cycles} / 1 \text{ s}$

$f = 2 \text{ s}^{-1}$

$v = \lambda f$

where λ is wavelength

$v = (12 \text{ m}) \cdot (2 \text{ s}^{-1})$

$v = 24 \text{ m/s}$

93. E is correct. Atmospheric pressure is not taken into account because it acts at the surface of the water and all around Mike's finger so it cancels.

$P_{water} = \rho gh$

$P_{water} = (10^3 \text{ kg/m}^3) \cdot (10 \text{ m/s}^2) \cdot (1 \text{ m})$

$P_{water} = 10^4 \text{ N/m}^2$

Area of hole:

$A = (0.01 \text{ m}) \cdot (0.01 \text{ m})$

$A = 10^{-4} \text{ m}^2$

$F = PA$

$F = (10^4 \text{ N/m}^2) \cdot (10^{-4} \text{ m}^2)$

$F = 1 \text{ N}$

94. C is correct. $P = IV$

Voltage is considered potential in a DC circuit.

Slope = Voltage / Power

Slope = V / IV

Slope = 1 / I

Slope = 1 / current

95. C is correct. Energy needed to change hydrogen from one state to another:

$E = -13.6 \text{ eV}[(1 / n_1^2) - (1 / n_2^2)]$

To ionize hydrogen, the electron must be removed to the $n = \infty$ state.

Energy needed to change from ground state:

$E = -13.6[(1 / 1) - (1 / \infty)]$

$E = -13.6 \text{ eV}$

Energy is expressed as a negative number to indicate that this much energy is needed to be input to the atom.

96. D is correct. Heat required to melt a solid:

$Q = mL_f$

$Q = (70 \text{ kg}) \cdot (334 \times 10^3 \text{ J/kg})$

$Q = 2.3 \times 10^4 \text{ kJ}$

97. B is correct. Distance traveled is represented by the area under the velocity vs. time curve.

At the point where each of those curves intersect on this plot, there is more area under the curve of the truck velocity than there is under the curve of the car velocity.

98. D is correct. The energy of the photons in the beam depends linearly on the frequency of the beam. Since the frequency of beam B is twice the frequency of beam A, the photons in beam B have twice the energy as the photons in beam A. The intensity depends on the energy of the photons and the number of photons per second carried by the beam. Nothing is known about the intensity or the number of photons per second.

99. E is correct.

$\tau = 120 \text{ N·m}$

$\tau = I\alpha$

Mass moment of inertia: mass moment of inertia of disk about z-axis

$I = \frac{1}{2}mr^2$

$\tau = [\frac{1}{2}mr^2]\alpha$

$120 \text{ N} = \frac{1}{2}(12 \text{ kg}) \cdot (4 \text{ m})^2 \, \alpha$

$\alpha = (120 \text{ N}) / [\frac{1}{2}(12 \text{ kg}) \cdot (4 \text{ m})^2]$

$\alpha = 1.25 \text{ rad/s}^2$

$\omega = \alpha t$

$7.35 \text{ rad/s} = (1.25 \text{ rad/s}^2)t$

$t = (7.35 \text{ rad/s}) / (1.25 \text{ rad/s}^2)$

$t = 5.9 \text{ s}$

100. A is correct. Beam A is due to high energy electrons because it deflects towards the positive plate indicating attraction.

Diagnostic Test #4 – Explanations

1. D is correct.

When an object is thrown into the air, the acceleration vector is always equal to gravity (for objects in free fall). The velocity vector changes direction when the object starts to come down.

2. A is correct.

As shown in the diagram, *mg* (i.e. the force of the mass due to gravity) is broken down into two components.

The *mg* sin θ component is parallel to the slope of the road.

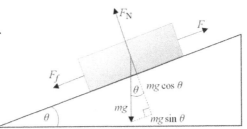

3. A is correct.

Archimedes' principle: the buoyant force acting on an object of volume V that is completely submerged in a liquid of a specific density has a magnitude that is expressed as:

$$F_B = \rho(V_{displaced})g$$

A change in the density of the liquid and thus, the volume affects the buoyant force.

$$density = mass / volume$$

F_B does not include the density of the object.

Differences in the density of a liquid that results from depth can be ignored.

4. C is correct.

$$P = W / t$$

$$W = Fd$$

$$P = (Fd) / t$$

$$F = mg$$

$$P = (mgd \sin \theta) / t$$

$$P = [(54 \text{ kg})\cdot(9.8 \text{ m/s}^2)\cdot(10 \text{ m}) \sin 30°] / (4 \text{ s})$$

$$P = [(54 \text{ kg})\cdot(9.8 \text{ m/s}^2)\cdot(10 \text{ m})\cdot(0.5)] / (4 \text{ s})$$

$$P = 2,646 \text{ J} / (4 \text{ s})$$

$$P = 661 \text{ J/s}$$

$$P = 661 \text{ W}$$

Convert watts into horsepower:

$$1 \text{ hp} = 745 \text{ W}$$

$$P = (661 \text{ W})\cdot(1 \text{ hp} / 745 \text{ W})$$

$$P = 0.89 \text{ hp}$$

5. A is correct. The amplitude of a wave is a measure of the energy of the wave. Thus if energy is dissipated the amplitude is reduced.

6. B is correct.

To determine the frequency of the fundamental:

$f_n = nf_1$

where f_1 = fundamental

$f_1 = f_3 / 3$

$f_1 = 783 \text{ Hz} / 3$

$f_1 = 261 \text{ Hz}$

7. C is correct.

To calculate the buoyant force due to the water:

$F_B = 7.86 \text{ N} - 6.92 \text{ N}$

$F_B = 0.94 \text{ N}$

Volume of displaced water is equal to volume of object:

$F_B = \rho g V$

$V = F_B / \rho g$

$V = 0.94 \text{ N} / (1{,}000 \text{ kg/m}^3) \cdot (9.8 \text{ m/s}^2)$

$V = 9.6 \times 10^{-5} \text{ m}^3$

Mass of the object:

$m = W / g$

$m = 7.86 \text{ N} / 9.8 \text{ m/s}^2$

$m = 0.8 \text{ kg}$

$\rho = \text{mass} / \text{volume}$

$\rho = 0.8 \text{ kg} / 9.6 \times 10^{-5} \text{ m}^3$

$\rho = 8{,}333 \text{ kg/m}^3$

8. A is correct. Height determines the energy per mass required to position the water at a particular point.

This is analogous to electric potential, as a measure of energy per charge required to position the charge at a particular point.

9. C is correct. As the copper sheet is quickly passed through the magnetic field eddy currents form.

According to Lenz's Law the eddy currents rotate in such a way to produce magnetic fields that oppose the changing magnetic flux. This opposing magnetic force acts to impede the motion of the copper sheet.

10. E is correct.

$n_1 \sin \theta_1 = n_2 \sin \theta_2$

$1.33 \sin 42° = 1 \sin \theta_2$

$1.33 \times (0.67) = 1 \sin \theta_2$

$\sin \theta_2 = 0.89$

$\theta_2 = \sin^{-1} (0.89)$

$\theta_2 = 63°$

11. B is correct.

Half-life is the time it takes for ½ of the quantity to decay.

    1st half-life: 3,200 µg / 2 = 1,600 µg

    2nd half-life: 1,600 µg / 2 = 800 µg

If two periods took 24.6 years, then one cycle takes 12.3 years.

Mathematically solving for half-life:

$A_{final} = A_{initial} \times (½)^{t/h}$

where t = time and h = half-life

$800 \text{ µg} = (3,200 \text{ µg}) \cdot (½)^{24.6 \text{ yr}/h}$

$(800 \text{ µg}) / (3,200 \text{ µg}) = (½)^{24.6 \text{ yr}/h}$

$0.25 = (½)^{24.6 \text{ yr}/h}$

$\ln (0.25) = (24.6 \text{ yr} / h) \ln (½)$

$h = 12.3 \text{ yr}$

12. C is correct.

If the object's velocity is constant, then the net force is zero.

In the y direction:

$0 = F_N + F_g$

In the x direction:

$0 = F_{friction} + F$

$F_N + F_g = F_{friction} + F$

$-F = F_{friction}$

Since kinetic friction is exerting a force opposing the object's motion, there must be an equal and opposing force propelling it forward for net force to be zero.

13. B is correct.

According to the principle of conservation of mechanical energy: total mechanical energy in a system remains constant as long as the only forces acting are conservative forces.

14. D is correct.

This is a thin film interference problem. When light strikes the surface of the oil some will be transmitted and some light will be reflected off the surface. This process is repeated when the light reaches the oil-water interface.

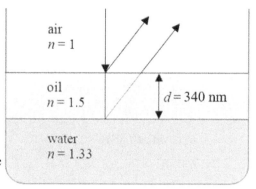

However, the light reflected from the oil-water interface may combine with the light originally reflected off the oil from before in either constructive or destructive interference.

The light which is strongly reflected is formed through constructive interference, the rays that destructively interfere with the originally reflected light cannot be seen.

Use the thin film constructive interference equation:

$$2n_{oil}d = (m + \tfrac{1}{2})\lambda \qquad (m = 0, 1, 2...)$$

where m is the order of the reflected light.

$$\lambda = (2n_{oil}d) / (m + \tfrac{1}{2})$$

Solve for range: 400 nm $\leq \lambda \leq$ 800 nm

Use m = 0

$$\lambda_0 = (2) \cdot (1.5) \cdot (340 \times 10^{-9} \text{ m}) / (0 + \tfrac{1}{2}),$$

$$\lambda_0 = 1{,}020 \times 10^{-9} \text{ m} = 1{,}020 \text{ nm}$$

λ_0 is out of range

Use m = 1

$$\lambda_1 = (2) \cdot (1.5) \cdot (340 \times 10^{-9} \text{ m}) / (1 + \tfrac{1}{2})$$

$$\lambda_1 = 680 \times 10^{-9} \text{ m} = 680 \text{ nm}$$

λ_1 is in range

Use m = 2

$$\lambda_2 = (2) \cdot (1.5) \cdot (340 \times 10^{-9} \text{ m}) / (2 + \tfrac{1}{2})$$

$$\lambda_2 = 408 \times 10^{-9} \text{ m} = 408 \text{ nm}$$

λ_2 is in range

If m is a value greater than 2, it produces wavelength outside the 400 nm to 800 nm range.

Thus the two most strongly reflected wavelengths are:

$$\lambda_1 = 680 \text{ nm}$$

$$\lambda_2 = 408 \text{ nm}$$

15. B is correct.

The harmonic wavelength λ_n occurs when:

$\lambda_n = (2L) / n$

where L is the length of the string and n is the harmonic (n = 1, 2, 3...).

The fourth harmonic wavelength occurs at n = 4.

$\lambda_4 = (2L) / 4$

$\lambda_4 = (2 \times 1 \text{ m}) / 4$

$\lambda_4 = 0.5 \text{ m}$

16. D is correct.

The elastic modulus is calculated as stress divided by strain.

$E = \sigma / \varepsilon$

Stress is measured in N/m^2, strain is unitless and work is measured in Joules so the other choices are incorrect based upon the units being dissimilar.

17. D is correct.

Electric field at a distance:

$E = kQ / d^2$

Solve for $Q_1 = 18 \text{ µC}$, where d is half the distance:

$E_1 = (9 \times 10^9 \text{ N·m}^2\text{·C}^{-2})\cdot(18 \times 10^{-6} \text{ C}) / (0.075 \text{ m})^2$

$E_1 = 28.8 \times 10^6 \text{ N/C}$

Solve for Q_2:

$E_2 = (9 \times 10^9 \text{ N·m}^2\text{·C}^{-2})\cdot(-6 \times 10^{-6} \text{ C}) / (0.075 \text{ m})^2$

$E_2 = -9.6 \times 10^6 \text{ N/C}$

Note that the negative sign indicates that the electric field goes into the charge, because the charge is negative.

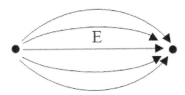

Because the electric fields generated by both charges point in the same direction, sum E_1 and E_2 to find the strength halfway between the charges:

$E_{total} = E_1 + E_2$

$E_{total} = (28.8 \times 10^6 \text{ N/C}) + (9.6 \times 10^6 \text{ N/C})$

$E_{total} = 38.4 \times 10^6 \text{ N/C}$ towards the negative charge.

18. A is correct.

$P = I^2R$

$P = (4I)^2R$

$P = (16)I^2R$

Power increased by a factor of 16

19. C is correct.

$1/f = 1/d_o + 1/d_i$

$1/d_i = 1/f - 1/d_o$

Since $d_o > f$,

$1/f - 1/d_o$ is always positive, so the image is real.

$m = -d_i/d_o$

Since i is positive, m = –(+i / o) is negative, so the image is inverted.

If the resulting magnification is positive, the image is upright.

If the magnification is negative, the image is inverted (upside down).

20. D is correct.

Apply the law of conservation of energy. There is no potential energy in this situation – all of the energy is kinetic (rotational kinetic energy in the initial state, translational kinetic energy in the final state).

$E_f = E_i$

$K_f = K_i$

$\frac{1}{2}m_{car}v^2 = \frac{1}{2}I\omega^2$

The moment of inertia of a disk is:

$\frac{1}{2}mR^2$,

where m is the mass of the disk, and R is its radius.

Then:

$\frac{1}{2}m_{car}v^2 = \frac{1}{2}(\frac{1}{2}m_{wheel}R^2)\omega^2$

Solving for velocity:

$v = R\omega\sqrt{(m_{wheel}/2m_{car})}$

The angular speed in rev/s must be converted to rad/s:

200.0 rev/s·(2π rad/rev) = 1,256.6 rad/s

Finally:

$v = (0.50\text{ m})\cdot(1{,}256.6\text{ rad/s})\cdot\sqrt{[370.0\text{ kg}/(2\cdot1{,}500.0\text{ kg})]}$

$v = 221$ m/s

21. B is correct.

Solve for heat required:

$Q = cm\Delta T$

$Q = (92 \text{ cal/kg·°C})·(0.5 \text{ kg})·(70 \text{ °C} - 20 \text{ °C})$

$Q = 2,300 \text{ cal}$

Convert to Joules:

$Q = (2,300 \text{ cal} / 1 \text{ J})·(4.186 \text{ J/cal})$

$Q = 9,628 \text{ J}$

22. E is correct.

The force of gravity depends only on the *m* and the distance between their centers.

$F_{grav} = GM_1M_2 / d^2$

If one *m* decreases by a factor of 2, then F_{grav} decreases by a factor of 2.

23. B is correct. The Doppler effect for a receeding source:

$f_{observed} = [v_{sound} / (v_{sound} + v_{source})]f_{source}$

Thus a receding source has a lower pitch (higher frequency) and decreases further as he falls due to the increase in the source velocity.

24. C is correct. As the block just enters the water the total pressure will be the sum of atmospheric pressure and the pressure produced by submersion.

$P_{total} = P_{atmosphere} + \rho gh$

When the block just enters the water:

$P_{total} = P_{atmosphere} + 0$

Graph C depicts the scenario as the block will experience an initial pressure of $P_{atmosphere}$ and this will linearly increase (from ρgh) as the block is lowered further into the water.

25. A is correct.

$F = qE$

where *q* is the charge and *E* is the electric field

They both act in the same direction because they have a positive charge and are moving opposite the negative charge generated by the plates.

Since *E* is constant, and *q* is twice as large for the α particle (He has two protons and two neutrons), the charge is multiplied by +2.

$F \propto q$

F is twice as large.

26. C is correct.

   Resistance = resistivity × (length / area)

   $A = \pi r^2$

   $R = (1.68 \times 10^{-8} \ \Omega \cdot m) \cdot [(57 \ m) / \pi (5.7 \times 10^{-3} \ m)^2]$

   $R = 9.4 \times 10^{-3} \ \Omega$

   $V = IR$

   $I = V / R$

   $I = 70 \ V / 9.4 \times 10^{-3} \ \Omega$

   $I = 7{,}447 \ A$

27. D is correct.

Virtual images can be seen (image in a plane mirror) but cannot be projected onto a screen.

28. C is correct.

Beta Decay (plus): the parent nuclide ejects a positron and neutrino. However, in the process a proton converts to a neutron so the mass number remains the same but the atomic number decreases by 1.

$$^{A}_{Z}X \rightarrow\ ^{A}_{Z-1}Y +\ ^{0}_{+1}e^{+} +\ ^{0}_{0}v$$

29. C is correct.

Isothermal means that temperature is constant.

Therefore if there is no temperature change, U (internal energy) experiences no change.

   $\Delta U = 0$

30. B is correct.

The speed of an object as measured in the rest frame of a second object is the same as the speed of the second as measured in the rest frame of the first. Note that the question did not ask for the speed of Beta. An observer on Alpha will observe that speed to be $0.94c$ (ignoring the effects of the curvature of the universe).

31. B is correct.

In projectile motion, the acceleration due to gravity always acts in the vertical component. Thus acceleration due to gravity remains a nonzero constant.

32. A is correct.

Power = current × voltage

$P = I\Delta V$

$P = (5 \text{ A}) \cdot (25 \text{ V})$

$P = 125 \text{ W}$

Energy = power × time

Energy = $(125 \text{ W}) \cdot (60 \text{ s})$

Energy = 7,500 J

At 30% efficiency, the energy converted into PE:

7,500 J × 30% = 2,250 J

Set PE equal to *mgh*:

$2,250 \text{ J} = mgh$

$2,250 \text{ J} = (50 \text{ kg}) \cdot (10 \text{ m/s}^2)h$

$2,250 \text{ J} = (500 \text{ kg m/s}^2)h$

$2,250 \text{ J} = (500 \text{ J/m})h$

$h = 2,250 \text{ J} / (500 \text{ J/m})$

$h = 4.5 \text{ m}$

33. D is correct.

Gravitational PE is converted into KE as the pendulum swings back from its maximum height.

To calculate the pendulum's speed as it passes through its lowest point:

$mgh = \frac{1}{2}mv^2$, cancel *m* from both sides of the expression

$gh_0 = \frac{1}{2}v_0^2$

$v_0 = \sqrt{(2gh_0)}$

If h_0 is doubled the velocity is:

$v = \sqrt{[2g(2h_0)]}$

$v = \sqrt{(2gh_0)} \times \sqrt{2}$

$v = v_0\sqrt{2}$

The velocity increases by a factor of $\sqrt{2}$.

34. B is correct.

$\Delta L / L = \alpha \Delta T$

where α is coefficient of linear expansion

$\Delta L = \alpha \Delta T L$

Using $3L$ for L:

$$\Delta L = \alpha \Delta T (3L)$$

$$\Delta L = 3(\alpha \Delta T L)$$

ΔL is 3 times larger

35. E is correct.

$$n_1 \sin \theta_1 = n_2 \sin \theta_2$$

When the critical angle is reached:

$$\theta_2 = 90°$$

$$\sin \theta_C = (n_2 / n_1)$$

For this statement to be valid:

$$n_1 > n_2$$

36. B is correct.

37. B is correct.

In a circuit with capacitors connected in parallel, the charge in each branch of the circuit is not constant (like the current in different branches is different).

The equivalent capacitance of the two capacitors in series, C_2 and C_3, is lower than the capacitance of each capacitor ($1 / C_{eq} = 1 / C_2 + 1 / C_3$).

The charge across these capacitors is lower than across C_1 due to the relation $V = Q / C$ and the fact that voltage across C_1 and the voltage across the branch containing C_2 and C_3 is the same.

For a capacitor:

$$U = (1/2) C V^2$$

Note: U is the symbol for potential energy.

Since C is the same for each capacitor, but V is higher in C_1 than in C_2 or C_3, the PE is higher.

38. E is correct.

$$F_B = \rho g V$$

Buoyant force is directly proportional to volume.

Volume of a sphere is given as:

$$V = 4 / 3 \pi r^3$$

If radius doubles:

$$V = 4 / 3 \pi (2r)^3$$

$$V = (8) \cdot (4 / 3 \pi r^3)$$

Therefore, when r doubles, F_B increase by a factor of 8 times.

39. C is correct.

Speed of sound in a gas:

$$V_{sound} = \sqrt{[(\gamma RT) / M]}$$

where γ = adiabatic constant, R = gas constant, T = temperature and M = molar mass of a gas

$$V_{sound\ H} = \sqrt{[(\gamma RT) / M]}$$

If M is doubled, the speed of sound in He compared to in H is:

$$V_{sound\ He} = \sqrt{[(\gamma RT) / 2M]}$$

$$V_{sound\ He} = (1 / \sqrt{2}) \cdot \sqrt{[(\gamma RT) / M]}$$

$$V_{sound\ He} = (0.707) \cdot \sqrt{[(\gamma RT) / M]}$$

Comparing the two with respect to He:

$$V_{sound\ He} = (0.707) \cdot (V_{sound\ H})$$

$$(1 / 0.707) V_{sound\ He} = V_{sound\ H}$$

$$V_{sound\ H} = 1.41\ V_{sound\ He}$$

40. D is correct. The amplitude of a wave is a measure of the energy of the wave. If energy increases, the amplitude increases.

41. E is correct.

I: PE = work

II: PE = $(mg)h$

III: PE = (weight)h

All the statements are measurements of potential energy of the box.

42. A is correct.

Conservation of momentum:

$$m v_{im} + M v_{iM} = m v_{fm} + M v_{fM}$$

$$v_{fM} = [m(v_{im} - v_{fm}) + M v_{im}] / M$$

$$v_{fM} = [(3.3\ kg) \cdot (8.5\ m/s - (-3\ m/s)) + (6.5\ kg) \cdot (0\ m/s)] / 6.5\ kg$$

$$v_{fM} = (3.3\ kg) \cdot (11.5\ m/s) / 6.5\ kg$$

$$v_{fM} = 5.8\ m/s$$

43. C is correct.

$$(m_1 + m_2)a = m_1 g$$

$$(70\ kg + 10\ kg)a = (70\ kg) \cdot (10\ m/s^2)$$

$$a = 8.8\ m/s^2$$

351

Or another method to solve this problem:

Sum of forces for each system equals zero:

(A) $0 = T + ma$

       $T = -(10 \text{ kg})a$

(B) $0 = T - ma - mg$

       $0 = T - (70 \text{ kg})a - (70 \text{ kg})\cdot(10 \text{ m/s}^2)$

       $0 = T - (70 \text{ kg})a - 700 \text{ N}$

Substituting (A) into (B):

       $0 = [(-10 \text{ kg})a] - (70 \text{ kg})a - 700 \text{ N}$

       $0 = (-80 \text{ kg})a - 700 \text{ N}$

       $700 \text{ N} / 80 \text{ kg} = a$

       $a = 8.8 \text{ m/s}^2$

44. E is correct.

       $v_f = v_i + at$

       $a = (v_f - v_i) / t$

       $a = (16 \text{ m/s} - 4 \text{ m/s}) / 2 \text{ s}$

       $a = 6 \text{ m/s}^2$

       $d = d_i + v_i t + \frac{1}{2}(6 \text{ m/s}^2)\cdot(2 \text{ s})^2$

       $d = 0 + (4 \text{ m/s})\cdot(2 \text{ s}) + \frac{1}{2}(6 \text{ m/s}^2)\cdot(2 \text{ s})^2$

       $d = (8 \text{ m}) + \frac{1}{2}(6 \text{ m/s}^2)\cdot(4 \text{ s}^2)$

       $d = 20 \text{ m}$

45. A is correct.

       $Q = m_s c_p \Delta T$

       $Q = (70 \text{ g})\cdot(0.11 \text{ cal/g}\cdot°\text{C})\cdot(450 °\text{C} - 100 °\text{C})$

       $Q = 2{,}695 \text{ cal}$

       $Q = m_w c_p \Delta T$

       $m_w = Q / c_p \Delta T$

       $m_w = 2{,}695 \text{ cal} / [(1 \text{ cal/g}\cdot°\text{C})\cdot(100 °\text{C} - 25 °\text{C})]$

       $m_w = 36 \text{ g}$

46. C is correct.

$$PE_{spring} = KE_{mass}$$

$$\tfrac{1}{2}kx^2 = \tfrac{1}{2}mv^2$$

$$x = \sqrt{[(m / k) / v^2]}$$

$$m / k = 0.031 \text{ kg·m/N}$$

$$x = \sqrt{[(0.031 \text{ kg·m/N})·(30 \text{ m/s})^2]}$$

$$x = 5.3 \text{ m}$$

47. A is correct.

The Balmer formula for Hydrogen is:

$$1 / \lambda = (1 / 91.2 \text{ nm})·(1 / m^2 - 1 / n^2)$$

From the n = 3 level, the transition to the n = 1 level has the greatest energy and therefore the shortest wavelength. The Balmer formula for n = 3, m = 1 is:

$$1 / \lambda = (1 / 91.2 \text{ nm})·(1 / 1^2 - 1 / 3^2)$$

$$1 / \lambda = (1 / 91.2 \text{ nm})·(8 / 9)$$

$$\lambda = 102.6 \text{ nm}$$

48. D is correct.

According to Coulomb's Law, like charges repel with equal and opposite force:

$$F_1 = F_2 = kq_1q_2 / r^2$$

49. B is correct.

$$1 / f = 1 / d_i + 1 / d_o$$

$$1 / 10 \text{ m} = 1 / d_i + 1 / 20 \text{ m}$$

$$1 / 10 \text{ m} - 1 / 20 \text{ m} = 1 / d_i$$

$$1 / 20 \text{ m} = 1 / d_i$$

$$d_i = 20 \text{ m, positive so it must be in front of the mirror}$$

The image is 20 m in front of the mirror – same position as the object (i.e. in front), only inverted.

50. C is correct.

$$E = kQ / r^2$$

$$E_2 = k(2Q) / r^2$$

$$E_2 = 2E$$

51. C is correct.

Note that the collision of the bullet and the block is inelastic because the bullet and block stuck together after the collision so the momentum is conserved but kinetic energy is not.

First find the velocity of the bullet-block system through conservation of energy when it compressed the spring. Then the velocity of the bullet can be found using conservation of momentum in the bullet-block collision.

To determine the final velocity of the system, use *conservation of energy*:

$\text{KE}_{system} = \text{PE}_{system}$

$\frac{1}{2}m_{system}v_{system}^2 = \frac{1}{2}kx^2$

$m_{system}v_{system}^2 = kx^2$

$v_{system}^2 = kx^2 / m_{system}$

$v_{system} = \sqrt{(kx^2 / m_{system})}$

$v_{system} = \sqrt{[(2{,}400 \text{ N/m}) \cdot (0.034 \text{ m})^2 / (4 \text{ kg} + 0.009 \text{ kg})]}$

$v_{system} = 0.832 \text{ m/s}$

To determine the initial velocity of the bullet, use *conservation of momentum*:

$p = mv$

$m_{bullet}v_{bullet} = m_{final:\ block+bullet}v_{final:\ block+bullet}$

$v_{bullet} = m_{final:\ block+bullet}v_{final:\ block+bullet} / m_{bullet}$

$v_{bullet} = (4.009 \text{ kg} \times 0.832 \text{ m/s}) / (0.009 \text{ kg})$

$v_{bullet} \approx 370 \text{ m/s}$

52. E is correct.

$T = 2\pi\sqrt{(L / g)}$

When L is tripled:

$T_2 = 2\pi\sqrt{(3L / g)}$

$T_2 = 2\pi\sqrt{3}\sqrt{(L / g)}$

$T_2 / T_1 = [2\pi\sqrt{3}\sqrt{(L / g)}] / [2\pi\sqrt{(L / g)}]$

$T_2 / T_1 = \sqrt{3}$

53. D is correct.

Static fluid pressure only depends on fluid density, height and acceleration

$P = \rho gh$

$P = (1{,}000 \text{ kg/m}^3) \cdot (9.8 \text{ m/s}^2) \cdot (15 \text{ m} + 30 \text{ m})$

$P = 4.4 \times 10^5 \text{ N/m}^2$

54. A is correct.

The resistance of a wire is given by:

$$R = \rho L / A$$

where ρ = resistivity, L = length and A = cross-sectional area

Resistance of thin wire:

$$R_0 = \rho L / A_0$$

Resistance of thicker wire:

$$A = 2A_0$$

$$R = \rho L / 2A_0$$

$$R = \tfrac{1}{2} R_0$$

The thicker wire has ½ the resistance of the thinner wire.

55. B is correct.

The orbital angular momentum is given by:

$$L = \sqrt{[\ell(\ell + 1)]}\, h$$

Allowable angular momentum quantum numbers: $\ell = 0, 1, 2\ldots n - 1$

56. D is correct.

$$Q = mc_p \Delta T$$

$$c_p = Q / m\Delta T$$

$$c_p = (14\ \text{J}) / (0.185\ \text{kg}) \cdot (10\ ^\circ\text{C})$$

$$c_p = 7.6\ \text{J/kg} \cdot \text{C}$$

$$1\ ^\circ\text{C} = 1\ \text{K}$$

$$c_p = 7.6\ \text{J/kg} \cdot \text{K}$$

57. E is correct.

$$v_f = v_0 + at$$

The only force causing acceleration acting on the ball after it has been thrown is gravity. Thus acceleration due to gravity is $-10\ \text{m/s}^2$ because it acts opposite the upward direction.

The acceleration due to gravity points downwards, giving a negative value.

58. B is correct.

$$a = \Delta v / \Delta t$$

$$a = (0.9\ \text{m/s}) / (8\ \text{s})$$

$$a = 0.1125\ \text{m/s}^2$$

$$F = ma$$

Total mass:

$$m = F_{net} / a$$

$$m = 900 \text{ N} / 0.1125 \text{ m/s}^2$$

$$m = 8{,}000 \text{ kg}$$

The mass of the rocket:

$$m_{rocket} = m - m_{spacecraft}$$

$$m_{rocket} = (8{,}000 \text{ kg} - 3{,}500 \text{ kg})$$

$$m_{rocket} = 4{,}500 \text{ kg}$$

59. D is correct.

An impulse is a change in momentum.

If the ball's initial direction is in the positive direction, then after the bounce it is negative.

$$\Delta p = p_2 - p_1$$

$$\Delta p = mv_i - mv_f$$

$$\Delta p = [(0.3 \text{ kg}){\cdot}(7 \text{ m/s})] - [(0.3 \text{ kg}){\cdot}(-5 \text{ m/s})]$$

$$\Delta p = (2.1 \text{ kg·m/s}) - (-1.5 \text{ kg·m/s})$$

$$\Delta p = 3.6 \text{ kg·m/s}$$

60. E is correct.

The Bohr model of the atom has two major failures:

1. It could not explain why some spectral emission lines were brighter than others.

2. It defines a radius and momentum for the electron which violates the Heisenberg uncertainty principle.

61. A is correct.

Involves proportions: what change in h (distance) is required for t to double?

$$t = (v_f - v_i) / a$$

$$t = v_f / g$$

If t is doubled, then v_f is also doubled:

$$2t = 2(v_f / g)$$

$$2t = (2v_f) / g$$

The height h is related to the velocity v_f through the equation for conservation of energy:

$$mgh = \tfrac{1}{2}mv_f^2$$

Cancel m from both sides and rearrange for h:

$$h = v_f^2 / 2g$$

Since v_f was doubled when t was doubled, the new height is:

$$h = (2v_f)^2 / 2g$$

$$h = (4)v_f^2 / 2g$$

If t is doubled, h increases by a factor of $2^2 = 4$.

62. D is correct. Take the system to comprise both the lower block and Rope 2. There are two forces on this system: the tension due to Rope 1 (pointing up) and gravity (pointing down).

The net force is:

$$F_{net} = T - m_{system}\, g$$

The mass of the system is the sum of the mass of the lower block and Rope 2:

$$m_{system} = m_{block} + m_{Rope2}$$

By Newton's second law:

$$F_{net} = m_{system}\, a$$

Combine these:

$$T - (m_{block} + m_{Rope2})g = (m_{block} + m_{Rope2})a$$

Or:

$$T = (m_{block} + m_{Rope2}) \cdot (g + a)$$

$$T = (1.0 \text{ kg} + 0.35 \text{ kg}) \cdot (9.8 \text{ m/s}^2 + 5.5 \text{ m/s}^2)$$

$$T = (1.35 \text{ kg}) \cdot (15.3 \text{ m/s}^2)$$

$$T = 20.7 \text{ N} \approx 21 \text{ N}$$

63. C is correct.

$$Q = 9 \text{ kJ}$$

$$W = -5 \text{ kJ}$$

By the first law of thermodynamics:

$$\Delta U = Q + W$$

$$\Delta U = 9 \text{ kJ} - 5 \text{ kJ}$$

$$\Delta U = 4 \text{ kJ}$$

64. B is correct. The force of gravity and the normal force on the table sum to zero.

The spring provides the centripetal force:

$$F_{spring} = mv^2 / r$$

$$20 \text{ N} = (5 \text{ kg})v^2 / (4 \text{ m})$$

$$80 \text{ N} \cdot \text{m} = (5 \text{ kg})v^2$$

$$v^2 = 16 \text{ m}^2/\text{s}^2$$

$$v = 4 \text{ m/s}$$

One revolution is equivalent to the circumference:

$$C = 2\pi r$$

$$C = 2\pi(4 \text{ m})$$

$$C = 25.1 \text{ m}$$

$$t = C / v$$

$$t = (25.1 \text{ m}) / (4 \text{ m/s})$$

$$t = 6.3 \text{ s}$$

65. A is correct. Waves transport energy from one region to another but do not transport matter.

66. A is correct.

An organ pipe produces sounds of wavelength:

$$\lambda_n = (2L / n)$$

where n is harmonic number: n = 1, 2, 3…

The lowest tone is the fundamental where n = 1.

$$\lambda_1 = (2L / 1)$$

$$\lambda_1 = 2L$$

The next lowest tone is the second harmonic where n = 2.

$$\lambda_2 = (2L / 2)$$

$$\lambda_2 = L$$

The next lowest tone is the third harmonic where n = 3.

$$\lambda_3 = (2L / 3)$$

$$\lambda_3 = 2L/3$$

67. A is correct.

Young's Modulus (E) is given as:

$$E = FL / A\Delta L$$

where $F = mg$

$$E = mgL / A\Delta L$$

Rearranging for m:

$$m = EA\Delta L / gL_i$$

$$A = \pi r^2$$

$$m = E\pi r^2 \Delta L / gL_i$$

$$m = [(2 \times 10^{11} \text{ N/m}^2)\cdot\pi(0.9 \times 10^{-3} \text{ m})^2\cdot(1.8 \times 10^{-3} \text{ m})] / (9.8 \text{ m/s}^2)\cdot(4.2 \text{ m})$$

$$m = 916.8 \text{ kg}\cdot\text{m}^2 / 41.2 \text{ m}^2/\text{s}^2$$

$$m = 22 \text{ kg}$$

68. D is correct.

Parallel to the field direction.

Faraday's Law (induced emf in a coil with changing magnetic flux):

$$V_{generated} = -N\Delta(BA) / \Delta t$$

where N = number of turns, B = magnetic field, A = area of coil and t = time

Positioning the loop such that the area vector is parallel to the magnetic field maximizes the flux through the loop (BA) and maximizes $V_{generated}$.

69. C is correct. The nuclei have the same charge because each has one proton.

Therefore, the forces are the same.

70. B is correct.

A diverging thin lens always produces images that are virtual, erect and reduced in size.

A converging thin lens produces images that are real or virtual, erect or inverted and reduced or magnified.

71. A is correct. Beta Decay (plus): the parent nuclide ejects a positron and neutrino. However, in the process a proton converts to a neutron so the mass number remains the same but the atomic number decreases by 1.

$$_Z^A X \rightarrow \, _{Z-1}^{A} Y + \, _{+1}^{0} e^+ + \, _0^0 v_e$$

72. E is correct.

Conservation of momentum for inelastic collision:

$$m_A v_A = (m_A + m_B)v$$

$$v = m_A v_A / (m_A + m_B)$$

Calculate velocity:

$$v = (2 \text{ kg}){\cdot}(2 \text{ m/s}) / (2 \text{ kg} + 5 \text{ kg})$$

$$v = 0.6 \text{ m/s}$$

73. D is correct.

Potential energy is equal to the work performed:

$$PE = W$$

$$PE = mgh$$

$$mgh = W$$

$$m = W / gh$$

$$m = 400 \text{ J} / (9.8 \text{ m/s}^2){\cdot}(4 \text{ m})$$

$$m = 10.2 \text{ kg}$$

74. E is correct. Since the motor spins at constant speed, there is no tangential component for the linear acceleration. The linear acceleration is just the centripetal acceleration:

$a = r\omega^2$

Angular speed is in rpm, but needs to be in rad/s:

2695.0 rpm·(1 min/60 s)·(2π rad/rev) = 282.22 rad/s

$a = (0.07165 \text{ m})·(282.22 \text{ rad/s})^2$

$a = 5{,}707 \text{ m/s}^2$

75. D is correct.

The diagram represents the Doppler effect for a source with velocity with respect to the observer (positioned to the right).

The siren on truck changes pitch because as the source approaches, the pitch is higher.

As the source is receding, the pitch is lower.

76. E is correct.

$P = F / A$

$F = PA$

$F = (3 \text{ atm})·(1.01 \times 10^5 \text{ Pa/1 atm})·(0.2 \text{ m})^2$

$F = 12{,}120 \text{ N} = 1.2 \times 10^4 \text{ N}$

77. A is correct.

Force from a magnetic field on a charged particle equals the electric field force on the charged particle.

For an electromagnetic wave:

$B = E / c$

$B = (1{,}200 \text{ V/m}) / (3 \times 10^8 \text{ m/s})$

$B = 4 \times 10^{-6} \text{ T}$

78. A is correct.

$V_{rms} = V_{max} / \sqrt{2}$

$V_{rms} = 200 \text{ V} / 1.41$

$V_{rms} = 142 \text{ V}$

79. C is correct.

In the situation of a diverging lens, the image is always located on the same side as the object.

The equation is:

$1 / f = 1 / d_i + 1 / d_o$

For a diverging lens, the focal length is negative by convention.

$$-1 / 3 \text{ m} = 1 / d_i + 1 / 4 \text{ m}$$

$$1 / d_i = -1 / 3 \text{ m} - 1 / 4 \text{ m}$$

$$1 / d_i = -4 / 12 \text{ m} - 3 / 12 \text{ m}$$

$$1 / d_i = -7 / 12 \text{ m}$$

$$d_i = -12 / 7 \text{ m}$$

For a diverging lens, the image distance is always negative.

For a concave or diverging lens the focal length is negative because the focus used in the ray diagram is located on the left side (*x*- and *y*-axis coordinate system) of the lens.

The image distance will be negative because it is also formed on the left-hand side.

80. D is correct.

The transition from level 3 to 2 produces a wavelength λ so that wavelength has energy of:

$$E_{3,2} = hf$$

$$f = c / \lambda$$

$$E_{3,2} = h(c / \lambda)$$

$$E_{3,2} = (1 / \lambda) \cdot (hc)$$

Then the energy from 2 to 1 is:

$$E_{2,1} = 2E_{3,2}$$

Then the energy from 3 to 1 is:

$$E_{3,1} = 3E_{3,2}$$

Because the energy and wavelength are inversely related, the transition from 2 to 1 must have ½ λ and the transition from 3 to 1 must have 1/3 λ.

81. E is correct.

$$PE = mgh$$

Energy used in one repetition:

$$PE = (2) \cdot (3 \text{ kg}) \cdot (9.8 \text{ m/s}^2) \cdot (0.5 \text{ m})$$

$$PE = 29.4 \text{ J}$$

Convert 19kcal to joules:

$$PE = (19 \text{ kcal} / 1) \cdot (1{,}000 \text{ cal} / \text{kcal}) \cdot (4.186 \text{ J} / \text{cal})$$

$$PE = 79{,}534 \text{ J}$$

Divide by 29.4 J to find the # of repetitions

$$\# = (79{,}534 \text{ J}) / (29.4 \text{ J})$$

$$\# = 2{,}705 \text{ repetitions}$$

82. C is correct.

Find force due to gravity on 18 kg block:

$F_{g1} = mg \sin \theta$

$F_{g1} = (18 \text{ kg}) \cdot (9.8 \text{ m/s}^2) \sin 20°$

$F_{g1} = 60.3 \text{ N}$

Find force due to gravity on 21 kg block:

$F_{g2} = m_2 g$

$F_{g2} = (21 \text{ kg}) \cdot (9.8 \text{ m/s}^2)$

$F_{g2} = 205.8 \text{ N}$

Sum forces (note opposite signs so the F_{g1} values is subtracted):

$F_{\text{tot}} = F_{g2} - F_{g1}$

$F_{\text{tot}} = (205.8 \text{ N} - 60.3 \text{ N})$

$F_{\text{tot}} = 145.5 \text{ N}$

Find the acceleration of system:

$F = m_{\text{tot}}a$

$a = F / m_{\text{tot}}$

$a = 145.5 \text{ N} / (18 \text{ kg} + 21 \text{ kg})$

$a = 3.7 \text{ m/s}^2$

83. A is correct.

The time it takes for the point on the string to move from $+x$ to $-x$ is half a period, or $T / 2$.

$\lambda = vT$,

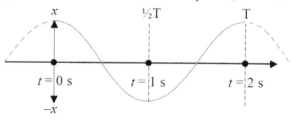

where v is the velocity of the wave

$T = \lambda / v$

$T = (8 \text{ m}) / (4 \text{ m/s})$

$T = 2 \text{ s}$

In general, calculating the frequency of a repeating event is accomplished by counting the number of times that event occurs within a specific time period, then dividing the count by the time period.

$t = \frac{1}{2}T$

$t = 1 \text{ s}$

84. B is correct.

The equation of continuity:

$f = Av$ remains constant.

$A_2V_2 = A_1V_1$

$V_2 = A_1V_1 / A_2$

$V_2 = \pi(16 \text{ cm})^2 \cdot (V_1) / \pi(4 \text{ cm})^2$

$V_2 = 16V_1$

If the radius decreases by a factor of 4 then the velocity increases by a factor of 16.

85. B is correct.

Coulomb's Law equation:

$F = kQ_1Q_2 / d$

Because of the multiplication of Q_1 and Q_2 by Coulomb's Law, each ball will experience the same force regardless of the magnitude of its own charge.

$F_1 = k(2Q_1)Q_2 / d$

$F_2 = k(2Q_1)Q_2 / d$

$F_1 = F_2$

86. E is correct.

The principle of relativity requires that the laws of physics be the same in all inertial reference frames. There can be no difference in any observation between one taken in a frame at rest and one taken in a uniformly moving frame.

87. B is correct.

Linear magnification of lens:

$m = -d_i / d_o$

The negative in the image distance is because all real images are inverted.

If the image distance value is negative, the image is virtual, m is positive and the image is erect:

m	Image	Inverted / Erect
+	virtual	erect
–	real	inverted

88. C is correct. All the masses of the elements are determined relative to 12C (Carbon-12), which is defined as an exact number 12 amu. Elements exist as a variety of isotopes and two major isotopes of carbon are 12C and 13C. Each carbon atom has the same number of protons and electrons – 6. 12C has 6 neutrons, 13C has 7 neutrons.

89. B is correct. Kinetic energy is equal to potential energy at top of flight.

PE = KE

$mgh = \frac{1}{2}mv^2$, cancel m from the expression

$gh = \frac{1}{2}v^2$

$h = \frac{1}{2}v^2 / g$

$h = v^2 / 2g$

Thus, height does not depend on mass.

Objects thrown at the same velocity travel to equal heights, regardless of mass.

90. E is correct. According to Newton's First Law: "An object at rest, or in uniform motion, will remain that way unless acted upon by an outside force."

Because there are no outside forces acting on the puck, no force is required to keep the puck in uniform motion.

91. D is correct.

Final velocity of an object with respect to time:

$v_f = v_i + at$

Solve for acceleration:

$0 = 16 \text{ m/s} + a(0.091 \text{ s})$

$a = -175.8 \text{ m/s}^2$

The acceleration is negative because it acts opposite the velocity vector. Calculate force using the magnitude of acceleration:

$F = ma$

$F = (0.24 \text{ kg}) \cdot (175.8 \text{ m/s}^2)$

$F = 42 \text{ N}$

92. A is correct.

$d_{tot} = d_1 + d_2 + d_3$

$d_{tot} = (5 \text{ km} + 7.3 \text{ km} + 3.4 \text{ km})$

$d_{tot} = 15.7 \text{ km}$

$d_{tot} = 15.7 \times 10^3 \text{ m}$

Force to work relationship:

W = Fd

$F = W / d$

$F = (2.6 \times 10^6 \text{ J}) / (15.7 \times 10^3 \text{ m})$

$F = 1.7 \times 10^2 \text{ N}$

93. C is correct.

A redshift is created when a light source moves away from the observer and thereby its wavelength is perceived to be longer due to the Doppler effect.

A blueshift occurs when the light source moves towards the observer and the perceived wavelength is shorter.

94. D is correct.

Stefan-Boltzmann Law:

$$P = A\varepsilon\sigma T^4$$

Temperature is doubled:

$$P = A\varepsilon\sigma(2T)^4$$

$$P = A\varepsilon\sigma(16)T^4$$

The power increases by a factor of 16.

$$P_2 = P(16)$$

$$P_2 = (15\ W)\cdot(16)$$

$$P_2 = 240\ W$$

95. E is correct.

Angular magnification equation:

$$M_\alpha = NP\ /\ f$$

where NP = near point

$$M_\alpha = (250\ mm\ /\ 50\ mm)$$

$$M_\alpha = 5$$

96. E is correct.

Faraday's Law states that a voltage will be induced in a coil exposed to a magnetic field:

$$V = -N\Delta(BA)\ /\ \Delta t$$

All three choices are correct because options I and III would increase the rate of change of the magnetic field (B) and thereby increase the voltage. Option II is correct because it would increase the number of turns (N) and therefore increase the induced voltage.

97. B is correct.

Use a rotated coordinate system in which the normal force points along the positive *y*-axis and "up the incline" is in the negative *x*-direction. In this coordinate system, there is no motion or acceleration in the *y*-direction; this means the normal force F_N must be equal to $mg \cos \theta$, so the *y*-forces balance.

Next, consider forces and components of forces in the *x*-direction. There is the frictional force to the right ("down the incline," since friction opposes the motion and is stopping the car) and there is a component of the gravitational force to the right *mg* sin *θ*.

$$F_{net} = F_{net,x} = F_{friction} + F_{gravity,x}$$

$$F_{friction} = \mu_k F_N = \mu_k (mg \cos \theta)$$

$$F_{net,x} = \mu_k (mg \cos \theta) + mg \sin \theta$$

$$F_{net,x} = mg (\mu_k \cos \theta + \sin \theta),$$

where downhill is positive.

Note: use μ_k because the tires locked up, meaning the tires are sliding over the road surface. If the tires were gripping the surface (a condition called "smooth rolling"), the static friction would be used because in that case the tires are *not* sliding against the surface in that case.

98. D is correct.

The uncertainty principle states that the uncertainty in position and momentum must be at least:

$$\Delta x \Delta p \approx h / 2\pi$$

$$\Delta p \approx h / (2\pi \Delta x)$$

If:

$$\Delta x = 5.0 \times 10^{-15} \text{ m}$$

Then:

$$\Delta p \approx 6.626 \times 10^{-34} \text{ J·s} / (2\pi \cdot 5.0 \times 10^{-15} \text{ m})$$

$$\Delta p \approx 2.11 \times 10^{-20} \text{ kg·m/s}$$

The uncertainty in the (non-relativistic) kinetic energy of the proton is then:

$$\Delta KE \approx (\Delta p)^2 / (2m)$$

$$\Delta KE \approx [h / (2\pi \Delta x)]^2 / (2m)$$

$$\Delta KE \approx [(6.626 \times 10^{-34} \text{ J·s}) / (2\pi \cdot 5.0 \times 10^{-15} \text{ m})]^2 / (2 \cdot 1.67 \times 10^{-27} \text{ kg})$$

$$\Delta KE \approx (1.33 \times 10^{-13} \text{ J})$$

Converting to MeV:

$$\Delta KE \approx (1.33 \times 10^{-13} \text{ J}) / (1.6 \times 10^{-13} \text{ J/MeV})$$

$$\Delta KE \approx (0.83 \text{ MeV})$$

99. D is correct.

Standing wave: relationship of wavelength to length and harmonic number.

$$\lambda = 2L / n$$

$$\lambda = 2(0.2 \text{ m}) / 5$$

$$\lambda = 0.08 \text{ m}$$

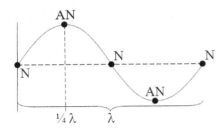

In a wave, the length between a node and antinode is ¼λ:

$d = \frac{1}{4}\lambda$

$d = \frac{1}{4}(0.08 \text{ m})$

$d = 0.02 \text{ m} = 20 \text{ mm}$

100. B is correct.

Notice that every time the position graph reads a maximum it must be changing direction. Therefore velocity must be zero at these points.

Graphs B and C have zero velocity at the maximum of the position graph. Graph B is the correct answer because graph C displays a negative velocity while the position graph is increasing which is not possible. Graph B is correct because it has positive velocity as the position increases and negative velocity as the position decreases.

Diagnostic Test #5 – Explanations

1. D is correct.

Potential energy:

$$PE = mgh$$

$$PE = (2 \text{ kg}) \cdot (9.8 \text{ m/s}^2) \cdot (4 \text{ m})$$

$$PE \approx 80 \text{ J}$$

2. D is correct. At point D the diver has maximum velocity because all the PE from point B is converted into KE at point D.

If velocity is maximized then momentum is maximized:

$$p = mv$$

3. A is correct.

The kinetic energy stored in a rotating object is:

$$K = \tfrac{1}{2} I\omega^2$$

With this, the angular speed as a function of energy is:

$$\omega^2 = 2K / I$$

The moment of inertia of a disk is:

$$I = \tfrac{1}{2}mr^2$$

Giving:

$$\omega^2 = 4K / mr^2$$

$$\omega = \sqrt{(4K / mr^2)}$$

$$\omega = \sqrt{[4 \cdot (3.2 \times 10^7 \text{ J})] / [(400.0 \text{ kg}) \cdot (0.60 \text{ m})^2]}$$

$$\omega = 943 \text{ rad/s}$$

4. E is correct. Constant velocity means balanced forces are acting on the box. Therefore the horizontal forces must be equal.

5. D is correct. Isometric refers to constant volume. Since the container does not expand when heat energy is added, it undergoes an isometric process.

6. A is correct.

A watt is a J/s

$$J = N \cdot m$$

$$N = \text{kg} \cdot \text{m/s}^2$$

$$J = (\text{kg} \cdot \text{m/s}^2)\text{m}$$

$$W = J/s$$

$$W = N \cdot m/s$$

$$W = kg \cdot m^2/s^3$$

7. D is correct.

Sound speed and frequency are related:

$$f = v / \lambda$$

where λ is twice the length of the organ pipe.

If sound speed is 3% slower, then v decreases by a factor of 0.97, and f decreases by a factor of 0.97 because f is directly proportional to v.

Thus f decreases by 3%.

8. E is correct. Particle 1 is negative because it is deflected in the magnetic field but goes in the opposite direction of the right-hand rule.

Particle 2 is neutral because it is unaffected by the magnetic field.

Particle 3 is positive because is deflected in the presence of the magnetic field and obeys the right-hand rule.

9. C is correct. Among the choices listed, radio waves have the lowest frequency.

$$f_{radio} < f_{microwave} < f_{infrared} < f_{X\text{-ray}} < f_{\gamma \text{ rays}}$$

10. B is correct. If both marbles are thrown with speed v_0 then both marbles have equal KE_0.

When they reach the ground their final KE is:

$$KE_0 + PE_0 = KE_{final}$$

Because the height of the cliff is the same, the PE_0 of both marbles is equal.

Thus both marbles have equal KE_{final} and equal speed at the bottom.

11. C is correct.

Moment of inertia solid cylinder:

$$I_1 = \tfrac{1}{2}mr^2$$

Moment of inertia thin loop:

$$I_2 = mr^2$$

If both have the same mass and radius, then:

$$I_1 = \tfrac{1}{2}I_2$$

The thin loop has a greater moment of inertia.

12. E is correct.

Calculate cable tension:

$$T = mg$$

$$T = (2{,}500 \text{ kg}) \cdot (9.8 \text{ m/s}^2)$$

$$T = 24{,}500 \text{ N}$$

Calculate wave velocity:

$$v = \sqrt{[T / (m / L)]}$$

$$v = \sqrt{(24{,}500 \text{ N} / 0.65 \text{ kg/m})}$$

$$v = 194 \text{ m/s}$$

13. A is correct.

Volumetric flow rate:

$$V_f = Av$$

$$A = \pi d^2 / 4$$

So, for the original pipe:

$$V_f = (\pi d^2 / 4) \cdot v$$

If diameter is doubled:

$$V_f = [\pi (2d)^2 / 4] \, v$$

$$V_f = (\pi / 4) \cdot (4d^2) \, v$$

$$V_f = 4 \, [(\pi d^2 / 4) \, v]$$

where the term in square brackets is identical to the original flow rate. Thus, the flow rate increases by a factor of 4.

14. B is correct.

15. C is correct. Because protons are positively charged they repel each other in the nucleus due to the forces from electrostatic repulsion. The strong nuclear force keeps the protons together because it overcomes the electrostatic repulsion and thus binds the nucleus together.

16. E is correct.

$$10 \text{ °C} = 10 \text{ K}$$

$$Q = mc\Delta T$$

$$Q = (0.3 \text{ kg}) \cdot (128 \text{ J/kg} \cdot \text{K}) \cdot (10 \text{ K})$$

$$Q = 384 \text{ J}$$

17. C is correct.

The relativistic expression for momentum is $p = \gamma m v = \gamma m \beta c$, where as usual $\beta = v / c$ and $\gamma = 1 / \sqrt{(1 - \beta^2)}$.

The two particles are to have the same momentum:

$\gamma_1 m_1 \beta_1 c = \gamma_2 m_2 \beta_2 c$

$(m_1 \beta_1) / \sqrt{(1 - \beta_1^2)} = (m_2 \beta_2) / \sqrt{(1 - \beta_2^2)}$

$\beta_1^2 / (1 - \beta_1^2) = (m_2 / m_1)^2 \cdot [\beta_2^2 / (1 - \beta_2^2)]$

For clarity, the right-hand side is set equal to a temporary variable x.

$x = (m_2 / m_1)^2 \cdot [\beta_2^2 / (1 - \beta_2^2)]$

$x = [(1.30 \text{ kg}) / (0.723 \text{ kg})]^2 \cdot [0.515^2 / (1 - 0.515)^2]$

$x = 1.1670$

Furthermore:

$\beta_1^2 / (1 - \beta_1^2) = x$

Solving this for β_1:

$\beta_1 = \sqrt{[x / (1 + x)]}$

$\beta_1 = \sqrt{(1.1670 / 2.1670)}$

$\beta_1 = 0.734$

$v_1 = 0.734c$

18. B is correct. The electron absorbs the full energy of the photon, losing 2.4 eV as it escapes from the photocathode and an additional 1.1 eV of kinetic energy after it escapes from the photocathode. This allows it to be stopped only with a potential exceeding 1.1 volts. It therefore absorbs 2.4 eV + 1.1 eV = 3.5 eV from the incident photon. A photon with energy 3.5 eV has a wavelength given by:

$h v = h c / \lambda = E$

$\lambda = h c / E = (6.626 \times 10^{-34} \text{ J·s}) \cdot (3.00 \times 10^8 \text{ m/s}) / (3.5 \text{ eV} \cdot 1.60 \times 10^{-19} \text{ J /eV})$

$\lambda = 355 \text{ nm}$

19. A is correct. The collision is inelastic because the bullet and block stick together after impact so kinetic energy is not conserved in the collision. Use energy conservation after the collision to find the velocity of the bullet and block system.

$KE = PE$

$\frac{1}{2}(m_{bullet} + m_{block})v_{system}^2 = (m_{bullet} + m_{block})gh$

$v_{system} = \sqrt{(2gh)}$

$v_{system} = \sqrt{[2(9.8 \text{ m/s}^2) \cdot (0.4 \text{ m})]}$

$v_{system} = 2.8 \text{ m/s}$

Conservation of momentum to find the velocity of the bullet:

$$(m_{bullet})·(v_{bullet}) = (m_{bullet} + m_{block})v_{system}$$

$$v_{bullet} = (0.01 \text{ kg} + 1.5 \text{ kg})·(2.8 \text{ m/s}) / (0.01 \text{ kg})$$

$$v_{bullet} = 423 \text{ m/s}$$

20. C is correct. Heavy nuclei tend to have more neutrons than protons because neutrons contribute to the nuclear strong force but do not contribute to the electrostatic repulsion (i.e. protons) because of their neutral charge. Thus, an excess of neutrons help keep the nuclei together without adding repulsion forces within the nuclei.

21. D is correct.

$$v_f = v_0 + at$$

$$5 \text{ m/s} = (0 \text{ m/s}) + a(1 \text{ s})$$

$$a = 5 \text{ m/s}^2$$

$$x = x_0 + v_0 t + \tfrac{1}{2}at^2$$

$$x = (0 \text{ m}) + (0 \text{ m/s})·(3 \text{ s}) + \tfrac{1}{2}(5 \text{ m/s}^2)·(3 \text{ s})^2$$

$$x = 22.5 \text{ m}$$

22. E is correct. The component of the block's weight (w) that is perpendicular to the inclined plane equals the normal force (N) on the block.

N is given by the expression $w \cos θ$, where $θ$ is the angle of incline.

As the angle increases toward 90°, $\cos θ$ decreases.

Therefore, N also decreases.

23. C is correct.

Linear expansion:

$$ΔL = L_i α ΔT$$

Total linear expansion of two rods:

$$ΔL_{total} = ΔL_A + ΔL_S$$

$$ΔL_{total} = L_{iA} α_A ΔT + L_{iS} α_S ΔT$$

$$ΔL_{total} = ΔT(L_{iA} α_A + L_{iS} α_S)$$

$$ΔL_{total} = (90 \text{ °C} - 15 \text{ °C})·[(0.1 \text{ m})·(2.4 × 10^{-5} \text{ K}^{-1}) + (0.8 \text{ m})·(1.2 × 10^{-5} \text{ K}^{-1})]$$

$$ΔL_{total} = 9 × 10^{-4} \text{ m}$$

Convert to mm:

$$ΔL_{total} = (9 × 10^{-4} \text{ m/1})·(1{,}000 \text{ mm/1 m})$$

$$ΔL_{total} = 0.9 \text{ mm}$$

24. B is correct.

The object's KE and momentum become zero after impact.

The total energy of the system (including heat, sound, etc.) remains constant.

25. D is correct. Frequency is the number of cycles per second.

f = cycles / sec

$2f$ = 2 cycles / sec

By doubling the frequency, the number of cycles per second is doubled.

The speed increases by a factor of two to accomplish this in the same amount of time.

26. B is correct. For a pipe that has one end closed and one end open, the diagram for the 3rd overtone looks as following:

Note that the closed end of the pipe must have an antinode and the open end will have a node. Because the open end can't have an antinode, the even-numbered harmonics can't occur in a pipe like this. That means that the 3rd overtone corresponds to the *seventh* harmonic in this case. The fundamental frequency for this pipe is 1/7 the frequency of the 3rd overtone. Looking at the diagram, the number of antinodes (points on the waveform that have zero displacement) can be counted – there are four of them.

27. C is correct.

Both the solid circle and wire circle have the same diameters but the wire has two surface areas exposed to the water (i.e. inner and outer circumference) where the difference in circumference length is assumed to be negligible. The solid circle only has the outer edge exposed to the water's surface (i.e. circumference).

$L_{wire} = 2(2\pi r)$ = the relevant length for the wire circle

$2\pi r$ = the relevant length for the solid circle

Solid circle on water: Wire on water:

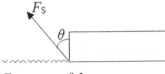   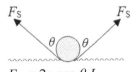

$F_{s1} = y \cos \theta\, L$ $F_{s2} = 2y \cos \theta\, L$

$F_{s2} = 2F_{s1}$

Balance weight vs. surface tension where F_s point up and F_w points down.

For solid circle:

$F_{w1} = F_{s1}$

For wire circle:

$$F_{w2} = F_{s2}$$

$$F_{w2} = 2F_{s1}$$

$$F_{w2} = 2F_{w1}$$

The wire circle can have double the mass without sinking.

28. A is correct.

The volt is expressed in Joules per Coulomb:

$$1\ V = 1\ J\ /\ 1\ C$$

Thus 120 V is 120 J per Coulomb of charge.

29. C is correct.

Current:

$$6\ mA = 0.006\ A$$

$$0.006\ A = 0.006\ Coulombs/sec$$

During 1 minute (60 sec), calculate the charge that has flowed:

$$0.006\ C/s \times 60\ s = 0.36\ C$$

Each electron carries: $1.602 \times 10^{-19}\ C$

Calculate the # of electrons:

$$(0.36\ C)\cdot(1\ electron\ /\ 1.602 \times 10^{-19}\ C) = 2.25 \times 10^{18}\ electrons$$

30. A is correct.
A convex mirror always produces an image that is upright, virtual and smaller regardless of object location.

31. C is correct.

32. B is correct.
Assume that the system is the massless spring and the two masses.

Although KE is not conserved, the sum of KE and spring PE is conserved because KE is converted into PE.

Momentum is conserved only if the system is isolated. The fixed wall provides an external force on the back of the spring, therefore the system is not isolated and momentum is not conserved. This results in the changing speed of the massive objects.

33. E is correct.

The potential energy of the pebble at the top of its flight is equal to its kinetic energy right as it is being thrown.

$$KE = PE$$

$\frac{1}{2}mv_0^2 = mgh_0$, cancel m from both sides of the expression

$v_0 = \sqrt{(2gh_0)}$

When the height doubles:

$v = \sqrt{(2g2h_0)}$

$v = \sqrt{2}\,\sqrt{2gh_0}$

$v = \sqrt{2} \times v_0$

34. B is correct.

Period of a simple pendulum only depends on the length:

$T = 2\pi\sqrt{(L\,/\,g)}$

Double the length:

$T = 2\pi\sqrt{(2L\,/\,g)}$

When the length is doubled, the period increases by a factor of $\sqrt{2}$.

35. C is correct.

Open pipes can produce even and odd # harmonics.

Closed pipes only produce odd # harmonics.

36. E is correct.

Bernoulli's Equation:

$P_1 + \frac{1}{2}\rho v_1^2 + \rho gh_1 = P_2 + \frac{1}{2}\rho v_2^2 + \rho gh_2$

When simplifying Bernoulli's Equation, both the top opening and the bottom opening experience atmospheric pressure so P_1 and P_2 cancel.

Likewise, $v_1 << v_2$ so it can be assumed to be negligible and go to zero.

Finally, $h_2 = 0$ because it is at the bottom of the tank and is the reference for all further heights in the problem

This results in the simplified expression:

$\rho gh_1 = \frac{1}{2}\rho v_2^2$, cancel ρ from both sides of the expression

$gh_1 = \frac{1}{2}v_2^2$

$v_2 = \sqrt{(2gh_1)}$

$v_2 = \sqrt{[(2)\cdot(9.8 \text{ m/s}^2)\cdot(0.5 \text{ m})]}$

$v_2 = 3.1 \text{ m/s}$

37. B is correct.

Electric field strength of parallel-plate capacitors:

Energy = voltage / distance

$E = V / d$

If V remains constant and d increases, E decreases

38. C is correct.

The force on a charged particle due to an electric field:

$F = qE_0$

The charge on the deuteron (1 proton and 1 neutron) has a charge equal and opposite to that of an electron.

The forces on the two particles have the same magnitude but opposite directions.

39. D is correct. When wave enters a different medium, both its speed and wavelength change.

An electromagnetic wave always transports its energy in a vacuum at a speed of approximately 3.00×10^8 m/s (a speed of light or c).

The frequency remains constant and is related to wavelength by:

$\lambda = c / f$

$\lambda = (3 \times 10^8 \text{ m/s}) / (1.8 \times 10^{14} \text{ Hz})$

$\lambda = 1.667 \times 10^{-6} \text{ m} = 1{,}667 \text{ nm}$

40. E is correct.

Wavelength relates to photon energy:

$E = hc / \lambda$

$E = [(6.626 \times 10^{-34} \text{ J·s}) \cdot (3 \times 10^8 \text{ m/s})] / (580 \times 10^{-9} \text{ m})$

$E = 3.4 \times 10^{-19} \text{ J}$

41. A is correct. Graham's Law: $\text{rate}_1 / \text{rate}_2 = \sqrt{(m_2 / m_1)}$

42. B is correct.

W = mg

On a slope, the force on an object due to the acceleration of gravity:

$F = mg \sin \theta$

$F = \text{W} \sin \theta$

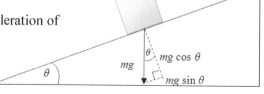

43. B is correct.

Velocity of sound in ideal gas:

$v_0 = \sqrt{(YRT / M)}$

where Y = adiabatic constant, R = gas constant, T = temperature and M = molecular mass.

if T is doubled:

$v_1 = \sqrt{(YR2T / M)}$

$v_1 = \sqrt{2}\, v_0$

The velocity increases by $\sqrt{2}$

44. B is correct.

The flow rate must be constant along the flow because water is incompressible.

Volumetric Flow Rate is:

$\upsilon = Av$

Volumetric Flow Rate at different points in a pipe with different areas:

$A_1v_1 = A_2v_2$

Thus the Volumetric Flow Rate at one point must match that of the other.

$A_2v_2 = 0.09 \text{ m}^3/\text{s}$

45. A is correct.

According to the right hand rule for a negative charge, the magnetic field causes the electron to curve by path X.

If the charge were positive the charge would curve by path Z.

46. C is correct.

For the magnetic field around a current-carrying wire, the magnetic field strength is:

$B = (\mu_0 I) / (2\pi r)$

where B is the magnetic field strength, μ_0 is the magnetic constant, I is the current in the wire and r is the distance of the particle from the wire.

According to the equation for magnetic field strength, there are two ways to increase B:

1) increase the current I through the wire, or

2) decrease the distance r from the wire

Changing the particle's charge does not affect the field, nor does changing the particle's speed. The field becomes weaker as the particle moves away from the wire (r increases).

47. C is correct.

Relationship between lens power and focal length:

$P = 1 / f$, with f expressed in meters

$f = 1 / P$

$f = 1/4$ m

The lens is a converging lens because the focal length of ¼ m is more than 0.

48. E is correct. An alpha particle is more massive than a beta particle and thus has more inertia.

An alpha particle deflects less in a magnetic field because its extra inertia requires more forced to change it from its path.

49. A is correct.

The marble and sponge balls should fall at the same rate. Air resistance prevents this from happening because it causes more friction that increases the time for the sponge ball to reach the ground.

50. D is correct.

Newton's Third Law of Motion: the gravitational pull of the Earth on the Moon is equal to the gravitational pull of the Moon on the Earth.

51. B is correct.

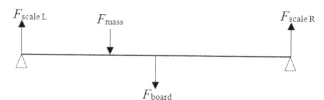

where $F_{scale\,L}$ and $F_{scale\,R}$ are forces from the scales.

$F_{mass} = (4 \text{ kg}) \cdot (9.8 \text{ m/s}^2)$

$F_{mass} = 39.2$ N

$F_{board} = (16 \text{ kg}) \cdot (9.8 \text{ m/s}^2)$

$F_{board} = 156.8$ N

F_{board} acts at $L / 2$ because the board is uniform.

Movement of a force (torque) is:

$\tau = L \times F$

The board is in equilibrium, so sum of torques = 0. Taking torque about left side of the board:

$\Sigma \tau = 0$

$0 = (0) \cdot (F_{scale\,L}) + (L / 3) \cdot (-F_{mass}) + (L / 2) \cdot (-F_{board}) + (L) \cdot (F_{scale\,R})$

Note: F_{mass} and F_{board} are negative because they turn the board clockwise, which is designated negative.

$$0 = (L / 3) \cdot (-39.2 \text{ N}) + (L / 2) \cdot (-156.8 \text{ N}) + (L) \cdot (F_{scale R})$$

Divide by L:

$$0 = (-39.2 \text{ N}) / 3 + (-156.8 \text{ N}) / 2 + (F_{scale R})$$

$$0 = -13.1 \text{ N} - 78.4 \text{ N} + F_{scale R}$$

$$F_{scale R} = (13.1 \text{ N} + 78.4 \text{ N})$$

$$F_{scale R} = 91.5 \text{ N}$$

52. C is correct. The KE of the car must be completely dissipated by work due to friction.

Additionally, the friction is static friction and has a constant normal force involved, so the frictional force is constant in both scenarios. So:

$$\tfrac{1}{2}mv^2 = F_f \times d$$

where d is the distance of the skid

$$\tfrac{1}{2}mv_0^2 = F_f \times d_0$$

When the velocity is doubled,

$$d = \tfrac{1}{2}m(2v_0)^2 / F_f$$

$$d = \tfrac{1}{2}mv_0^2 \, (4) / F_f$$

$$d = 4d_0$$

If the velocity is doubled, the car will skid 4 times further.

53. E is correct.

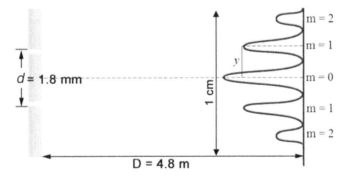

Double slit interference equation:

$$y = (m\lambda \text{D}) / d$$

$$\lambda = (yd) / (m\text{D})$$

Because 5 bright spots are visible in 1 cm, the first order fringe m = 1 will be separated by a distance y from the central fringe m = 0.

$$y = (1 \text{ cm}) / (5)$$
$$y = 0.2 \text{ cm}$$
$$\lambda = (yd) / (mD)$$

Solve:

$$\lambda = (0.002 \text{ m}) \cdot (0.0018 \text{ m}) / (1) \cdot (4.8 \text{ m})$$
$$\lambda = 7.5 \times 10^{-7} \text{ m} = 750 \text{ nm}$$

54. D is correct.

Heat required to melt a solid:

$$Q_1 = mL_f$$
$$Q_1 = (0.4 \text{ kg}) \cdot (334 \times 10^3 \text{ J/kg})$$
$$Q_1 = 133.6 \text{ kJ}$$

Heat required to raise temperature of water from 0 °C to 60 °C:

$$Q_2 = mc\Delta T$$
$$Q_2 = (0.4 \text{ kg}) \cdot (4.186 \times 10^3 \text{ J/Kg} \cdot °C) \cdot (60 °C)$$
$$Q_2 = 100.5 \text{ kJ}$$

Total heat added:

$$Q_1 + Q_2 = Q_{total}$$
$$Q_{total} = (133.6 \text{ kJ} + 100.5 \text{ kJ})$$
$$Q_{total} = 234.1 \text{ kJ}$$

55. D is correct. Lens equation:

$$1 / f = 1 / d_i + 1 / d_o$$
$$1 / 20 \text{ cm} = 1 / d_i + 1 / 10 \text{ cm}$$
$$-1 / 20 \text{ cm} = 1 / d_i$$
$$d_i = -20 \text{ cm}$$

The negative sign indicates the image should be on the object side of the mirror.

By the sign convention for mirrors, a negative value places the image behind the mirror.

56. E is correct.

57. A is correct.

$$W = Q\Delta V \text{ (for work or energy with charges)}$$

The charge transferred is:

$$Q = 10^{-10} \text{ C}$$

A positive charge moving from 8,000 V to –8,000 V is a negative sign.

$$W = (10^{-10} \text{ C}) \cdot (-8,000 \text{ V} - 8,000 \text{ V})$$

$$W = (10^{-10} \text{ C}) \cdot (-1.6 \times 10^4 \text{ V})$$

$$W = -1.6 \times 10^{-6} \text{ J}$$

58. B is correct.

Archimedes Principle:

$$\rho_{object} / \rho_{fluid} = W_{object} / W_{fluid}$$

$$\rho_{object} / \rho_{fluid} = (11.3 \text{ g/cm}^3) / (13.6 \text{ g/cm}^3)$$

$$\rho_{object} / \rho_{fluid} = 0.83$$

83% of the lead ball is below the surface by weight. The ball has 17% above the surface because the density is assumed to be consistent throughout the sphere.

The weight is directly correlated to volume.

59. D is correct.

For an approaching sound source, the Doppler equation becomes:

$$f_{observed} = [v / (v - v_{source})] \cdot (f_{source})$$

$$f_{observed} = [350 \text{ m/s} / (350 \text{ m/s} - 50 \text{ m/s})] \cdot (420 \text{ Hz})$$

$$f_{observed} = (1.17) \cdot (420 \text{ Hz})$$

$$f_{observed} = 490 \text{ Hz}$$

60. C is correct.

The period T of a pendulum is:

$$T = 2\pi\sqrt{(L / g)}$$

where L is the length of the pendulum and g is the acceleration due to gravity.

Since the gravity on the Moon is 1/6 of that on Earth, the period of the pendulum on the Moon is:

$$T_M = 2\pi\sqrt{(L / (1/6)g)}$$

$$T_M = 2\pi\sqrt{(6L / g)}$$

$$T_M = (\sqrt{6}) \cdot 2\pi \cdot \sqrt{(L / g)}$$

Since $T = 2\pi\sqrt{(L / g)}$, the period of the pendulum on the Moon can be rewritten as:

$$T_M = (\sqrt{6})T$$

$$T_M = (\sqrt{6}) \cdot (3 \text{ s})$$

$$T_M = 7.3 \text{ s}$$

61. D is correct.

The gravitational force and the spring force add to zero; they are equal in magnitude (Newton's Second Law of Motion).

The magnitude of the force is:

$F_{grav} = mg$

$F_{grav} = (1.2 \text{ kg}) \cdot (10 \text{ m/s}^2)$

$F_{grav} = 12 \text{ N}$

Use the spring equation:

$F_{spring} = kx$

$x = F_{spring} / k$

$x = (12 \text{ N}) / (3 \text{ N/m})$

$x = 4 \text{ m}$

Add the amount that the spring stretches to the resting length of 0.25 m.

Total length = (0.25 m + 4 m) = 4.25 m

62. C is correct.

The horizontal component of velocity is:

$v_x = v \cos \theta$

$v_x = (20 \text{ m/s}) \cos 25°$

$v_x = 18.1 \text{ m/s}$

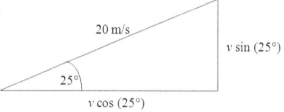

63. A is correct.

Force due to friction is expressed as:

$F_f = \mu F_N$

where μ = coefficient of friction and F_N = the normal force on the block.

$F_N = W \cos \theta$

As θ decreases, $\cos \theta$ becomes larger.

F_N increases, and substituting F_N back into the equation for frictional force, the value of F_f increases.

Weight is the force of the mass due to gravity, which are both constants.

Therefore, weight remains constant.

64. B is correct.

If the velocity of an object is constant then the instantaneous velocity at any arbitrary time equals the average velocity. However, if the velocity is increasing or decreasing at a constant rate then the instantaneous velocity at an arbitrary time will not equal the average velocity.

65. A is correct.

Stefan-Boltzmann Law:

$$P = \varepsilon A \sigma T^4$$

$$P = (1) \cdot (1.25 \text{ m}^2) \cdot (5.67 \times 10^{-8} \text{ W/m}^2\text{K}^4) \cdot (100 + 273 \text{ K})^4$$

$$P = 1{,}371.9 \text{ W} \approx 1.4 \text{ kW}$$

66. C is correct.

$$t = d_x / v_x$$

$$t = (1{,}000 \text{ m}) / (50 \text{ m/s})$$

$$t = 20 \text{ s}$$

Check that the projectile is still moving upwards during the duration of the allotted time:

$$v_{fy} = v_{iy} + at$$

$$v_{fy} = 240 \text{ m/s} + (-9.8 \text{ m/s}^2)t$$

$$v_{fy} = 240 \text{ m/s} + (-9.8 \text{ m/s}^2) \cdot (20 \text{ s})$$

$$v_{fy} = 240 \text{ m/s} + (-196 \text{ m/s})$$

$$v_{fy} = 44 \text{ m/s, positive value so projectile is still moving upwards}$$

$$d_y = v_{iy}t + \tfrac{1}{2}at^2$$

$$d_y = (240 \text{ m/s}) \cdot (20 \text{ s}) + \tfrac{1}{2}(-9.8 \text{ m/s}^2) \cdot (20 \text{ s})^2$$

$$d_y = (4{,}800 \text{ m}) + \tfrac{1}{2}(-9.8 \text{ m/s}^2) \cdot (400 \text{ s}^2)$$

$$d_y = (4{,}800 \text{ m}) - (1{,}960 \text{ m})$$

$$d_y = 2{,}840 \text{ m}$$

67. B is correct. An object having moment of inertia I rotating with an angular speed of ω has angular momentum:

$$L = I\omega$$

The moment of inertia of a solid right circular cylinder about the axis indicated is $\tfrac{1}{2}mR^2$:

$$L = (\tfrac{1}{2}mR^2)\omega$$

$$L = 0.5(15.0 \text{ kg}) \cdot (1.4 \text{ m})^2 \cdot (2.7 \text{ rad/s})$$

$$L = 39.69 \text{ kg m}^2/\text{s}$$

$$L = 40 \text{ kg m}^2/\text{s}$$

68. C is correct.

$$F = kq_1q_2 / r^2$$

If both the charge and the separation distance are doubled:

$$F = k(2q_1) \cdot (2q_2) / (2r)^2$$

$$F = 4kq_1q_2 / 4r^2$$

$$F = kq_1q_2 / r^2 \quad \text{(same as the first expression)}$$

69. D is correct. For a diverging lens, regardless of the object position, the image is:

- virtual
- upright
- reduced

70. C is correct. Work during an isothermal process:

$$W = nRT \times \ln(V_f / V_i)$$

$$W = (4 \text{ mol}) \cdot (8.134 \text{ J/mol·K}) \cdot (650 \text{ K}) \times \ln(0.33 \text{ m}^3 / 0.025 \text{ m}^3)$$

$$W = 56 \text{ kJ}$$

71. D is correct.

$$p = mv$$

Sum momentum:

$$p_{tot} = m_1v_1 + m_2v_2 + m_3v_3$$

Objects moving left have negative velocity.

$$p_{tot} = 7 \text{ kg} \times 6 \text{ m/s} + 12 \text{ kg} \times (-3 \text{ m/s}) + 4 \text{ kg} \times 2 \text{ m/s}$$

$$p_{tot} = 42 \text{ kg·m/s} + (-36 \text{ kg·m/s}) + 8 \text{ kg·m/s}$$

$$p_{tot} = 14 \text{ kg·m/s}$$

72. B is correct. Sound velocity in an ideal gas:

$$v_{sound} = \sqrt{(yRT / M)}$$

where y = adiabatic constant, R = gas constant, T = temperature and M = molecular mass of gas.

Increasing the temperature increases the velocity of sound in air.

73. A is correct.

The Bernoulli Equation originated as a conservation of energy relationship for flowing fluids:

$$P_1 + \tfrac{1}{2}\rho v_1^2 + \rho gh_1 = P_2 + \tfrac{1}{2}\rho v_2^2 + \rho gh_2$$

where P_1 = pressure energy, $\tfrac{1}{2}\rho v_1^2$ = kinetic energy (volumetric) and ρgh_1 = potential energy (volumetric)

Thus, the Bernoulli Equation is a statement of the conservation of pressure energy, kinetic energy and potential energy of a flowing fluid.

74. D is correct.

Resistance in a wire:

$R = (\rho L) / A$

where ρ = resistivity, L = length of wire and A = cross-sectional area of wire

If the first wire has resistance R_1:

$R_1 = \rho L_1 / A_1$

The second wire has:

$L_2 = 2L_1$

$A_2 = 2A_1$

$R_2 = \rho 2L_1 / 2A_1$

$R_2 = \rho L_1 / A_1$

$R_2 = R_1$

The resistances are equal.

75. E is correct.

Positron: $^{0}_{1}\beta^{+}$

The atomic mass remains the same but the atomic number decreases.

76. B is correct.

77. E is correct.

$a = (v_2 - v_1) / \Delta t$

$a = [12 \text{ m/s} - (-6 \text{ m/s})] / 10 \text{ s}$

$a = 1.8 \text{ m/s}^2$

78. E is correct.

Force of gravity on a mass:

$F = mg$

Force of gravity on the 1 kg book:

$F_{\text{book}} = (1 \text{ kg})\cdot(9.8 \text{ m/s}^2)$

$F_{\text{book}} = 9.8 \text{ N}$

Force of gravity on the 10 kg brick:

$F_{\text{brick}} = (10 \text{ kg})\cdot(9.8 \text{ m/s}^2)$

$F_{\text{brick}} = 98 \text{ N}$

The force on the brick is 10 times that on the book.

79. D is correct.

Find acceleration:

$$v_f = v_0 + at$$

$$106 \text{ m/s} = (0 \text{ m/s}) + a(0.85 \times 10^{-3} \text{ s})$$

$$106 \text{ m/s} = a(0.85 \times 10^{-3} \text{ s})$$

$$a = (106 \text{ m/s}) / (0.85 \times 10^{-3} \text{ s})$$

$$a = 1.25 \times 10^5 \text{ m/s}^2$$

Find average force:

$$F = ma$$

$$F = (0.6 \text{ kg}) \cdot (1.25 \times 10^5 \text{ m/s}^2)$$

$$F = 7{,}500 \text{ N}$$

80. E is correct.

During beta minus decay, the parent nuclide ejects an electron and electron antineutrino. However, in the process a neutron converts to a proton so the mass number remains the same but the atomic number increases by 1.

$$^A_Z X \rightarrow {^A_{Z+1}} Y + {^0_{-1}} e^- + {^0_0} v_e$$

81. B is correct.

The equation for displacement given an initial velocity and constant acceleration is:

$$d = v_i t + \tfrac{1}{2} a t^2$$

$$a = (v_f - v_i) / t$$

$$a = (1.8 \text{ m/s} - 0.4 \text{ m/s}) / 4 \text{ s}$$

$$a = 0.35 \text{ m/s}^2$$

Substituting $a = 0.35 \text{ m/s}^2$ into the equation for displacement,

$$d = v_i t + \tfrac{1}{2} a t^2$$

$$d = (0.4 \text{ m/s}) \cdot (4 \text{ s}) + \tfrac{1}{2}(0.35 \text{ m/s}^2) \cdot (4 \text{ s})^2$$

$$d = 4.4 \text{ m}$$

82. C is correct.

The object experiencing the force increases in speed due to the acceleration from the force:

$$F = ma$$

However, because the force is decreasing the rate of increase of its speed will decrease.

83. E is correct.

$Q = mc\Delta T$

$c = Q / m\Delta T$

$c = (150 \text{ kcal}) / [(3 \text{ kg}) \cdot (200 \text{ °C})]$

$c = 0.25 \text{ kcal/kg·°C}$

84. A is correct.

$W = F \times d \cos \theta$

$F = W / d$

$F = 40 \text{ J} / 4 \text{ m}$

$F = 10 \text{ N}$

85. B is correct. Equation for the period T of a simple pendulum:

$T = 2\pi\sqrt{(L / g)}$

Rearranging the equation for *g*:

$g = (2\pi / T)^2 L$

$g = (4\pi^2)L / T^2$

$g = 4\pi^2(0.58 \text{ m}) / (2.5 \text{ s})^2$

$g = 3.7 \text{ m/s}^2$

86. C is correct.

Electromagnetic waves are created by accelerating electric charges (change in velocity or speed).

87. A is correct.

Speed of the wave = wavelength × frequency

$v = \lambda f$

$v = (0.5 \text{ m}) \cdot (800 \text{ Hz})$

$v = 400 \text{ m/s}$

Distance = velocity × time, the distance covered in one second is:

$d = vt$

$d = (400 \text{ m/s}) \cdot (1 \text{ s})$

$d = 400 \text{ m}$

88. A is correct. In Elena's inertial frames of reference, one before the spaceship increased its speed and one after, the spaceship is at rest. Therefore, the measurements of length must give the same result. Otherwise, the laws of physics would be different in these two inertial frames of reference. During the acceleration of the spaceship, there are some unusual effects caused by the acceleration. Those effects are the subject of General Relativity.

89. E is correct. Connecting two identical batteries in parallel yields the same voltage but twice the total available charge.

90. D is correct. The power of the combination of the lenses is the sum of the powers.

$$5\,D + 3\,D = 8\,D$$

91. B is correct. A nucleon is a proton or neutron.

An alpha particle consists of two neutrons and two protons.

A hydrogen atom only has one proton, so it is not possible for it to emit an alpha particle.

92. D is correct.

$$m_1 v_1 = m_2 v_2$$

$$(1{,}450\ \text{kg})v_1 = (90\ \text{kg}){\cdot}(30\ \text{m/s})$$

$$v_1 = (90\ \text{kg}){\cdot}(30\ \text{m/s}) / (1{,}450\ \text{kg})$$

$$v_1 = 1.9\ \text{m/s}$$

93. C is correct.

$$\text{work} = \text{force} \times \text{distance}$$

$$W = Fd$$

Machines reduce the amount of force required, but the distance through which the force acts increases. They do not reduce the amount of work required.

If 900 J of energy are expended to lift the block to a certain height, then, even if a perfectly efficient pulley were used, the engineer expends a total of 900 J of work to lift the block to the same height using the pulley.

94. A is correct.

$$\text{amplitude} = \tfrac{1}{2}(\text{total displacement})$$

$$\text{amplitude} = \tfrac{1}{2}(0.4\ \text{m})$$

$$\text{amplitude} = 0.2\ \text{m}$$

The amplitude is the displacement from the position of equilibrium. The amplitude is 0.2 m because the mass travels 0.2 m to the left of equilibrium and 0.2 m to the right of equilibrium in one oscillation.

95. C is correct. One wave is completed at the 3rd node.

From the figure, the given wave has 1.5 λ:

$L = 1.5\ \lambda$

$\lambda = 2/3\ L$

$\lambda = (2/3) \cdot (\text{total length})$

$\lambda = (2/3) \cdot (0.6\ m)$

$\lambda = 0.4\ m$

$v = f \lambda$

$1\ Hz = 1\ s^{-1}$

$v = (900\ s^{-1}) \cdot (0.4\ m)$

$v = 360\ m/s$

96. E is correct.

density = mass / volume

$\rho = m\ /\ V$

$\rho = kg/m^3$

97. C is correct.

The charge q is equally attracted to both Qs because q is equidistant from each.

$q_{net} = 0$

$F_{1 \to 2} = kq_1 q_2\ /\ r^2$

$F_{2 \to 1} = -kq_1 q_2\ /\ r^2$

One force is attractive to the first Q, but the other force is attractive to the second Q and therefore points in the opposite direction. The sign of the second force is reversed.

$F_{net} = 0$

98. B is correct. A simple LC circuit with 0 resistance acts as an oscillator with charge flowing back and forth across the capacitor and inductor.

99. B is correct. The Compton effect is a measure of the reduction in wavelength of an x-ray beam as it scatters off a sample. The reduction in wavelength can be explained if the incident x-ray beam is considered as being made up of individual particles each with momentum and energy, and that those particles are scattered by electrons in the sample. Hence, the Compton effect demonstrates the particle nature of electromagnetic radiation. While the energy content and momenta of the individual x-rays are included in the scattering calculation, they are not directly demonstrated in the Compton effect.

100. A is correct.

Diagnostic Test #6 – Explanations

1. D is correct.

Because the path *ca* is adiabatic, no heat is added or lost by the system during this process.

Adiabatic process:

$Q = 0$ kJ

2. A is correct.

$\Sigma F_x = 0$

$0 = F_{Ax} + F_{Bx} + F_{Cx} + F_x$

$0 = (30$ N$)\cdot(\sin 35°) - (40$ N$)\cdot(\cos 25°) + (50$ N$)\cdot(\cos 40°) + F_x$

$0 = (30$ N$)\cdot(0.57) - (40$ N$)\cdot(0.91) + (50$ N$)\cdot(0.77) + F_x$

$0 = (17$ N $- 36$ N $+ 39$ N$) + F_x$

$F_x = -20$ N

3. B is correct.

The 4th harmonic has four nodes (i.e. three nodes more than the fundamental) and the ends are antinodes.

The harmonic to wavelength relationship for an organ pipe is calculated by:

$\lambda_n = 2L / n$

where *L* is the length of the pipe and n is the harmonic number (1, 2, 3,…)

For n = 4:

$\lambda_4 = (2)\cdot(0.2$ m$) / 4$

$\lambda_4 = 0.1$ m

4. A is correct.

Volumetric flow rate = velocity × area

$V = vA$

Water is incompressible, so volumetric flow rate is constant.

$(vA)_{in} = (vA)_{out}$

$(0.02$ m/s$)(\pi/4)(0.15$ m$)^2 = v_{out}(\pi/4)(0.003$ m$)^2$

$v_{out} = [(0.02$ m/s$)(0.15$ m$)^2] / (0.003$ m$)^2$

$v_{out} = 50$ m/s

5. E is correct.

Both microwaves and blue light are electromagnetic radiation.

The difference between them is with respect to their frequency, wavelength and corresponding energy.

$$c = \lambda f$$

$$E = hf$$

6. B is correct.

The internal resistance is added to the external resistance of the circuit.

If the external resistance is large, then current is small and the internal resistance can be ignored.

7. C is correct.

A plane mirror does not magnify the image and always produces an erect, virtual image.

$$m = 1$$

$$1 = d_i / d_o$$

$$1 = h_i / h_o$$

8. D is correct.

An alpha particle is essentially a helium nucleus and consists of two protons and two neutrons.

Alpha decay: during alpha decay, the parent nuclide sheds two protons and two neutrons.

$$^A_Z X \rightarrow ^{A-4}_{Z-2} Y + ^4_2 \alpha$$

9. B is correct.

The angular speed changes according to the kinematic relation:

$$\Delta \omega = \alpha \Delta t$$

$$\Delta t = \Delta \omega / \alpha$$

The torque is given and the moment of inertia of a right circular cylinder is $\frac{1}{2}mR^2$. Find the angular acceleration from the dynamic relation:

$$\tau = I\alpha$$

$$\alpha = \tau / I = \tau / (\frac{1}{2}mR^2) = 2\tau / mR^2$$

Combining the two results:

$$\Delta t = mR^2 \Delta \omega / 2\tau$$

$$\Delta t = (10.0 \text{ kg}) \cdot (3.00 \text{ m})^2 \cdot (8.13 \text{ rad/s}) / [2(110.0 \text{ N m})]$$

$$\Delta t = 3.33 \text{ s}$$

10. B is correct.

The speed of the missile as measured in the frame of the asteroid is the relativistic addition of the speed of the spaceship as measured from the asteroid, plus the speed of the missile as measured from the spaceship. The two velocities are in opposite direction. The formula for the relativistic addition of two speeds in opposite directions is:

$$\beta = (\beta_1 - \beta_2) / (1 - \beta_1\beta_2)$$

$$\beta = (0.8 - 0.5) / [1 - (0.8)(0.5)]$$

$$\beta = 0.50$$

$$v = 0.50c$$

11. B is correct.

Impulse:

$$J = F\Delta t$$

Increase in Δt = decrease in F

Decreased force means that it is less likely to break.

Impulse and change in momentum are directly related.

$$F\Delta t = m\Delta v$$

Because the wine glass always goes from terminal velocity to zero in both cases, and the mass is constant, the impulse is constant and equal in both cases.

Thus the only way to decrease force is to increase Δt which is the stopping time.

12. C is correct.

$$W = Fd \cos \theta$$

θ is perpendicular to direction of velocity

$$\cos 90° = 0$$

$Fd \cos \theta = 0$ J, no work is done against the force of gravity.

Since the velocity is constant, there is no net horizontal force, so no net work is done by horizontal forces.

13. E is correct.

velocity = wavelength × frequency

$$v = \lambda f$$

For velocity to remain constant, as frequency decreases, wavelength must increase.

14. A is correct.

$\Delta L \, / \, L_i = \alpha_L \Delta T$

$\alpha_L = \Delta L \, / \, L_i \Delta T$

$\alpha_L = (2.0005 \text{ m} - 2.0000 \text{ m}) \, / \, (2.0000 \text{ m}) \cdot (40 \,°C - 20 \,°C)$

$\alpha_L = 0.0005 \text{ m} \, / \, 40 \text{ m} \cdot °C$

$\alpha_L = 1.25 \times 10^{-5} \text{ K}^{-1}$

15. A is correct.

$1 \, / \, f = 1 \, / \, d_i + 1 \, / \, d_o$

$1 \, / \, 12 \text{ m} = 1 \, / \, d_i + 1 \, / \, 6 \text{ m}$

$1 \, / \, 12 \text{ m} - 2 \, / \, 12 \text{ m} = 1 \, / \, d_i$

$-1 \, / \, 12 \text{ m} = 1 \, / \, d_i$

$d_i = -12 \text{ m}$

A negative sign indicates that the image is behind the mirror.

16. B is correct. The total resistance for a circuit with parallel resistors decreases as more resistors are added. A decrease in the total resistance increases the total current in the circuit.

17. D is correct.

$E = kQ \, / \, r^2$

E is directly proportional to Q and inversely proportional to r^2:

$2Q = 2E$

The only solution that doubles the magnitude of E is to double Q.

18. E is correct.

If an object's entire volume is suspended in a liquid, the object's density is equal to that of the liquid.

If 20% of the floating buoy is above the surface of the liquid, 80% of its volume is suspended in the liquid.

Since 80% of the buoy's volume is in the liquid, it is only 80% as dense as the liquid.

19. C is correct.

The wave of fundamental frequency for an open pipe is shown in the figure.

Therefore:

$\lambda = 2L$

The two endpoints are antinodes and the midpoint is a node.

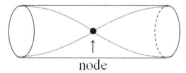

node

20. E is correct.

Wave interference occurs for all types of waves, both mechanical and electromagnetic.

21. D is correct.

$$F = -kx$$
$$-k = F / x$$
$$-k = 30 \text{ N} / -0.75 \text{ m}$$
$$k = 40 \text{ N/m}$$

22. C is correct.

Since the two objects come to rest immediately, they must have equal but opposite momenta before the collision:

$$p_A = p_B$$
$$p = mv$$
$$m_A v_A = m_B v_B$$
$$v_A / v_B = m_B / m_A$$

v_A is 5 times greater than v_B

$$v_A / v_B = 5$$
$$5 = m_B / m_A, \text{ take the reciprocal of each side}$$
$$m_A / m_B = 1 / 5$$

The ratio of the mass of A to the mass of B is 1: 5

23. B is correct.

The de Broglie wavelength of a matter wave is:

$$\lambda = h / p$$
$$\lambda = h / (m\gamma v)$$

(Since $v / c < 0.1$, this will equal about 1.005 and can be ignored)

$$\lambda = (6.626 \times 10^{-34} \text{ J·s}) / [(9.11 \times 10^{-31} \text{ kg})·(2.5 \times 10^7 \text{ m/s})]$$
$$\lambda = 29 \times 10^{-12} \text{ m}$$
$$\lambda = 29 \text{ pm}$$

24. A is correct.

$$v_{\text{Parallel}} = v \sin \theta$$

The component of velocity in the direction of the slope is:

$$v_P = v \sin \theta, \text{ where } \theta = 20°$$

The velocity parallel to the slope:

$v_P = v \sin \theta$

$v_P = v \sin 20°$

$v_P = (16 \text{ m/s}) \cdot (0.34)$

$v_P = 5.47 \approx 5.5 \text{ m/s}$

25. C is correct. In isothermal compression all heat is released to the surroundings and is equal to the work needed to compress the gas.

$Q_{released} = W$

$W = nRT \ln (V_2 / V_1)$

26. E is correct. All three answer choices are correct because they all describe PE:

$PE = mgh$

PE equals the work done by the pile driver:

$PE = W$

$PE = Fd$

$PE / d = F$

The force is directly proportional to PE so all three choices are correct because they relate to the PE of the pile driver.

27. B is correct. An organ pipe is either open at both ends or closed at one end.

Open pipe:

$f_n = nv / 2L$

where n = 1, 2, 3…

Closed pipe:

$f_n = nv / 4L$

where n = 1, 3, 5…

Observing the equation for frequencies produced by an open or closed pipe, there are an infinite number of frequencies possible depending on the value of n.

28. C is correct. The gravitational force is the only influence making the satellite move in a circular path, so the centripetal acceleration in orbit is the gravitational acceleration at that orbital radius.

$v^2 / r = g'$

$v = \sqrt{(g'r)}$

$v = \sqrt{[(2.3 \text{ m/s}^2) \cdot (34{,}000 \text{ m})]}$

$v = 280 \text{ m/s}$

29. D is correct.

A diopter is a unit of measurement of the optical power of a lens or curved mirror.

The power equals the reciprocal of the focal length (i.e. $1/f$). Therefore, the diopter is a unit of reciprocal length.

For example, a 3 diopter lens brings parallel rays of light to focus at 1/3 m.

$$1/d_o + 1/d_i = 1/f$$

Setting object at infinity (∞):

$$1/\infty + 1/d_i = 1/f$$

$$0 + 1/d_i = 1/f$$

$$1/d_i = 1/f$$

Power of the lens:

$$P = 1/f$$

$$3 = 1/d_i$$

$$d_i = 1/3 \text{ m} = 0.33 \text{ m}$$

30. E is correct.

Accelerating uniformly for 8 s:

$$\Delta v = a\Delta t$$

$$v_2 - v_1 = a\Delta t$$

$$v_2 = v_1 + a\Delta t$$

$$v_2 = 0 \text{ m/s} + (2.5 \text{ m/s}^2)\cdot(8 \text{ s})$$

$$v_2 = 20 \text{ m/s}$$

31. A is correct.

Set North as the positive direction.

Conservation of momentum:

$$(m_1 + m_2)v = m_1v_1 + m_2v_2$$

$$(m_1 + m_2)v = (2{,}500 \text{ kg})\cdot(7 \text{ m/s}) + (2{,}000 \text{ kg})\cdot(-14 \text{ m/s})$$

$$(m_1 + m_2)v = 17{,}500 \text{ kg·m/s} + (-28{,}000 \text{ kg·m/s})$$

$$(m_1 + m_2)v = -10{,}500 \text{ kg·m/s}$$

$$-10{,}500 \text{ kg·m/s} = (4{,}500 \text{ kg})v$$

Velocity immediately after the inelastic collision:

$$v = (-10{,}500 \text{ kg·m/s}) / (4{,}500 \text{ kg})$$

$$v = -2.3 \text{ m/s, the minus sign indicates } v \text{ points South.}$$

32. B is correct.

$$T = 2\pi\sqrt{(L / g)}$$

If the clock is too slow, that means the period (T) is too large.

Decrease T by raising the weight which effectively decreases *L*.

33. E is correct. When the air above the paper is blown the air moves faster, and the decrease in pressure causes the air below the paper to attempt to fill that void, pushing the paper upward in the process.

34. D is correct.

voltage = current × resistance

$V = IR$

$4 \text{ V} = I(20 \text{ }\Omega)$

$I = 4 \text{ V} / 20 \text{ }\Omega$

$I = 0.2 \text{ A}$

35. C is correct. Becquerel (Bq) is the SI unit of radioactivity. One Bq is defined as the activity of a quantity of radioactive material in which one nucleus decays per second (s^{-1}).

36. D is correct. As the temperature rises both the mercury and glass will expand by:

$$\Delta V = \alpha V_i \Delta T$$

Thus in order to reach 450 ml the expansion of both the glass and the mercury must be taken into account:

$V_G + \Delta V_G = V_M + \Delta V_M$

$450 \text{ ml} + \Delta V_G = 442 \text{ ml} + \Delta V_M$

$8 \text{ ml} = \Delta V_M - \Delta V_G$

$8 \text{ ml} = \alpha_M V_{iM} \Delta T - \alpha_G V_{iG} \Delta T$

$8 \text{ ml} = \Delta T(\alpha_M V_{iM} - \alpha V_{iG})$

$8 \text{ ml} = \Delta T[(18 \times 10^{-5} \text{ K}^{-1}){\cdot}(442 \text{ ml}) - (2 \times 10^{-5} \text{ K}^{-1}){\cdot}(450 \text{ ml})]$

$8 \text{ ml} = \Delta T(0.0706 \text{ K}^{-1}\text{ ml})$

$\Delta T = 113.4 \text{ }^{\circ}\text{C}$

$T_f = T_i + \Delta T$

$T_f = 22 \text{ }^{\circ}\text{C} + 113.4 \text{ }^{\circ}\text{C}$

$T_f = 135 \text{ }^{\circ}\text{C}$

37. C is correct.

A constant positive acceleration increases the velocity linearly upwards over time. The graph with a positive slope represents a constant positive acceleration on the velocity vs. time graph.

38. C is correct.

This is one of the two postulates of special relativity. The other is that the speed of light is the same in all frames moving with constant velocity with respect to an inertial frame.

39. B is correct.

Torque can be written as:

$\tau = I\alpha$

where τ = torque, I = moment of inertia and α = angular acceleration

Thus if torque is constant then the angular acceleration must be constant as well because the moment of inertia does not change

40. C is correct.

Dosimeter badges are used to monitor cumulative radiation dose from gamma radiation. Typically, they do not measure beta or alpha radiation as they cannot penetrate the badges due to their lower energies.

41. D is correct.

Let $y = 0$ be the ground, which is also the final position of the package.

Then:

$y_f = y_i + v_i \Delta t - \frac{1}{2}g(\Delta t)^2$

$0 = d + v_i \Delta t - \frac{1}{2}g(\Delta t)^2$

$d = v_i \Delta t + \frac{1}{2}g \Delta t^2$

$d = (-15 \text{ m/s}) \cdot (16 \text{ s}) + \frac{1}{2}(10 \text{ m/s}^2) \cdot (16 \text{ s})^2$

$d = (-240 \text{ m} + 1,280 \text{ m})$

$d = 1,040 \text{ m}$

42. C is correct.

$F = ma$

$m = F / a$

$m = 3,000 \text{ N} / (2 \text{ m/s}^2)$

$m = 1,500 \text{ kg}$

43. D is correct.

If metal A has a larger coefficient of thermal expansion it will elongate more than metal B when the strip is heated. Because the two strips are bound together, the bimetallic strip will curve downward when heated as the configuration gives strip A more room for expansion.

44. A is correct.

$$F = -kx$$

The negative sign is only by convention. It indicates that the spring resting force is opposite the stretch direction.

$$x = F / k$$

$$x = mg / k$$

$$x = [(30 \text{ kg}) \cdot (10 \text{ m/s}^2)] / 4{,}600 \text{ N/m}$$

$$x = 0.0652 \text{ m}$$

$$PE = \tfrac{1}{2}kx^2$$

$$PE = \tfrac{1}{2}(4{,}600 \text{ N/m}) \cdot (0.0652 \text{ m})^2$$

$$PE = 9.8 \text{ J}$$

An increase in PE due to the addition of the weight.

45. C is correct.

Frequency = # of cycles / time

$$f = 2 \text{ cycles} / 1 \text{ s}$$

$$f = 2 \text{ s}^{-1}$$

$$v = \lambda f$$

$$v = (6 \text{ m}) \cdot (2 \text{ s}^{-1})$$

$$v = 12 \text{ m/s}$$

46. B is correct. The decibel rating for sound is based on a logarithmic scale.

Sound intensity equation:

$$I \text{ (dB)} = 10 \log_{10}(I / I_0)$$

where $I_0 = 10^{-12}$ W/m^2 and is the threshold of human hearing.

Example:

sound intensity decreases from 10 W/m^2 to 1 W/m^2

$$I_1 \text{ (dB)} = 10 \log_{10}(10 \text{ W/m}^2 / 10^{-12} \text{ W/m}^2)$$

$$I_1 = 130 \text{ dB}$$

$$I_2 \text{ (dB)} = 10 \log_{10}(1 \text{ W/m}^2 / 10^{-12} \text{ W/m}^2)$$

$$I_1 = 120 \text{ dB}$$

$$I_1 - I_2 = 130 \text{ dB} - 120 \text{ dB}$$

$$I_1 - I_2 = 10 \text{ dB}$$

Thus the sound intensity decreases by 10 dB if the intensity decreases by a factor of 10.

47. A is correct.

Buoyancy force:

$F_B = \rho g V$, where V is the volume of water displaced.

When the two blocks are stacked on each other:

$F_B = \rho g V_0 = F_1 + F_2$

When the two blocks are both in the water:

$F_{B1} = \rho g V_1 = F_1$

$F_{B2} = \rho g V_2 = F_2$

Total volume displaced in both cases:

$V_0 = (1/\rho g) \cdot (F_1 + F_2)$

$V_1 + V_2 = (1/\rho g) \cdot (F_1 + F_2)$

$V_0 = V_1 + V_2$

Same displacement of water in both cases so the water level does not change.

48. C is correct.

To find # excess electrons, divide Q_1 by the charge of a single electron:

excess electrons = Q_1 / e

excess electrons = $(-1 \times 10^{-6}\,C) / (-1.60 \times 10^{-19}\,C)$

excess electrons = 6.3×10^{12}

49. E is correct.

Capacitance only depends on the geometry (i.e. surface area) of a conductor and the permittivity of the dielectric used.

50. C is correct.

A flat plane mirror has no curvature so the radius is considered to be infinite.

51. E is correct.

$m = m_0 y$

where m_0 = rest mass, y = Lorentz factor and m = relativistic mass

$m = m_0 / \sqrt{(1 - v^2 / c^2)}$

$m = (1.675 \times 10^{-24}\,g) / \sqrt{[1 - (54,300 \times 10^3\,m/s)^2 \cdot (3.8 \times 10^8\,m/s)^2]}$

$m = 1.7 \times 10^{-24}\,g$

52. D is correct.

The moment of inertia:

I = mass × the square of the distance from the rotational axis

$I = mr^2$

Since $r_1 = r_2$,

I_1 / I_2 is simply the ratio of the masses.

Therefore, moment of inertia I is directly proportional to the mass m.

Doubling the mass doubles the moment of inertia, giving a ratio of 2 : 1 comparing the more massive to the less massive sphere.

53. B is correct.

power = work / time

$P = W / t$

$P = (1{,}000 \text{ J}) / (40 \text{ s})$

$P = 25 \text{ W}$

54. A is correct.

A spring mass oscillator has a frequency:

$\omega = \sqrt{(k / m_0)}$

$f = \omega / 2\pi$

$f = \sqrt{(k / m_0)} / 2\pi$

Period:

$T = 1 / f$

$T_0 = 2\pi / \sqrt{(k / m_0)}$

If mass is doubled:

$T = 2\pi / \sqrt{(k / 2\, m_0)}$

$T = 2\pi / \sqrt{(k / m_0)} \times \sqrt{2}$

$T = \sqrt{2}\, T_0$

The period increases by a factor of $\sqrt{2}$.

55. B is correct.

For a pipe or tube that is closed at one end and open at the other end:

harmonic wavelengths λ_n have values of n which are only odd (n = 1, 3, 5, …).

After the fundamental wavelength (n = 1), the next consecutive harmonic wavelength is the third harmonic (n = 3).

The harmonic wavelength can be determined from the equation:

$\lambda = 4L / n$

$\lambda = 4(1.5 \text{ m}) / 3$

$\lambda = 2 \text{ m}$

56. D is correct.

$\rho = m / V$

$V = (4/3)\pi r^3$

$\rho = m / (4/3)\pi r^3$

$\rho = (115 \text{ kg}) / (4/3)\pi \times (0.6 \text{ m})^3$

$\rho = 127 \text{ kg/m}^3$

57. A is correct. When a potential difference exists across a wire (for example connecting a battery to both ends of the wire) electrons flow in order to move from high potential to low potential.

In the case of a battery the electrons flow along the wire towards the positive terminal to lower their potential.

58. C is correct. $1 \text{ A} = 1 \text{ C/s}$

59. E is correct. For a concave spherical mirror:

$r = 2f$

If the object is located at the radius of curvature:

$r = d_o$

$d_o = 2f$

Use the mirror equation:

$1 / f = 1 / d_o + 1 / d_i$

$1 / f = 1 / 2f + 1 / d_i$

$1 / 2f = 1 / d_i$

$d_i = 2f = d_o$, the image and object are located at the same point.

Use the magnification equation:

$m = -d_i / d_o$

$m = h_i / h_o$

$-(2f) / 2f = h_i / h_o$

$-1 = h_i / h_o$

$-h_i = h_o$

If the object is located at the radius of curvature then the image distance is equal to the object distance and the image is inverted because the height is the negative of the object height.

60. A is correct.

61. A is correct.

An isobaric process is a process in which the pressure remains constant throughout.

From the diagram, the volume changes but the pressure is constant, consistent with an isobaric process.

62. E is correct. $F = ma$, on Earth

$20 \text{ N} = m(4 \text{ m/s}^2)$

$m = 20 \text{ N} / (4 \text{ m/s}^2)$

$m = 5 \text{ kg}$

$W = ma$, on Moon

$W = (5 \text{ kg}) \cdot (1.62 \text{ m/s}^2)$

$W = 8.1 \text{ N}$

63. C is correct. Frequency is the amount of cycles that a wave makes in a certain amount of time.

$f = \#$ cycles / time

The figure shows the wave making 2 cycles in 4 seconds.

$f = 2$ cycles / 4 s

$f = 0.5 \text{ s}^{-1} = 0.5 \text{ Hz}$

64. A is correct.

$\frac{1}{2}\rho v^2 = \rho gh$, cancel ρ from both sides of the expression

$\frac{1}{2}v^2 = gh$

$v^2 = 2gh$

$v^2 = 2(9.8 \text{ m/s}^2) \cdot (0.8 \text{ m})$

$v^2 = 15.68 \text{ m}^2/\text{s}^2$

$v = 3.95 \text{ m/s} \approx 4 \text{ m/s}$

65. B is correct. Faraday's Law:

$V = N\Delta BA / \Delta t$

where N = number of turns, B = magnetic field, A = area of coil and t = time

The magnetic flux is the product of the magnetic field strength and area of the coil exposed to the field:

magnetic flux = BA

If the magnetic flux and the number of turns are doubled then the numerator increases by a factor of four and the induced emf increases by a factor of four.

66. D is correct.

$$P = I^2R$$
$$I^2 = P / R$$
$$I^2 = 16 \text{ W} / 18 \text{ } \Omega$$
$$I^2 = 0.89 \text{ A}^2$$
$$I = 0.94 \text{ A}$$

67. B is correct.

$$c = \lambda f$$
$$f = c / \lambda$$

Wavelength and frequency are inversely proportional.

68. C is correct. Ionizing power and penetrating power are inversely related.

Alpha particles have the lowest penetrating power but have the highest ionizing power. This is due to their high mass and charge.

69. B is correct.

Given the angular velocity, the linear velocity at a given radius is calculated by:

$$v = \omega r$$

where v is the linear velocity and ω is the angular velocity

Convert from revolutions/minute to radians/second to arrive at an answer in m/s. Since 1 revolution = 2π radians and 1 min = 60 sec, angular velocity in radians/s is given by:

$$\omega = (8.3 \text{ rev/min}) \cdot (2\pi \text{ rad/rev}) \cdot (1 \text{ min/60 s})$$
$$\omega = 0.87 \text{ rad/s}$$

Calculate linear velocity. The problem gives the diameter, but the formula requires radius:

$$v = (0.87 \text{ rad/s}) \cdot (9 \text{ m})$$
$$v = 7.8 \text{ m/s}$$

70. E is correct.

71. D is correct. In an elastic collision, KE and momentum are conserved:

KE before collision = KE after collision

Block$_1$ + Block$_2$ = Block$_1$ + Block$_2$

$$\tfrac{1}{2}m_1v_1^2 + \tfrac{1}{2}m_2v_2^2 = \tfrac{1}{2}m_1u_1^2 + \tfrac{1}{2}m_2u_2^2$$

Initially $v_2 = 0$

$$\tfrac{1}{2}m_1v_1^2 = \tfrac{1}{2}m_1u_1^2 + \tfrac{1}{2}m_2u_2^2$$

Solve for u_2:

$$[m_1(v_1{}^2 - u_1{}^2) / m_2]^{1/2} = u_2$$

Momentum:

$$m_1 v_1 = m_1 u_1 + m_2 u_2$$

Solve for u_2:

$$m_1(v_1 - u_1) / m_2 = u_2$$

Set equal and isolate m_2:

$$[m_1(v_1{}^2 - u_1{}^2) / m_2]^{1/2} = m_1(v_1 - u_1) / m_2$$

$$m_2 = m_1(v_1 - u_1)^2 / (v_1{}^2 - u_1{}^2)$$

Solve for the m_2:

$$m_2 = [(2.8 \text{ kg}) \cdot (8.5 \text{ m/s} - (-1.1 \text{ m/s}))^2] / [(8.5 \text{ m/s})^2 - (-1.1 \text{ m/s})^2]$$

$$m_2 = [(2.8 \text{ kg}) \cdot (92 \text{ m}^2/\text{s}^2)] / (71 \text{ m}^2/\text{s}^2)$$

$$m_2 = 3.6 \text{ kg}$$

72. B is correct.

Work is defined as:

$$W = Fd,$$

where d is the displacement in the direction of the force; in this case it is –h, where the minus sign indicates that the direction of the displacement is down.

The force is the force of gravity:

$$F = -mg,$$

where again the minus sign indicates that the force is directed downward.

Therefore:

$$W = Fd$$

$$W = (-mg) \cdot (-h)$$

$$W = mgh$$

73. A is correct.

Frequency = 1 / period

$$f = 1 / T$$

$$f = 1.6 \text{ kHz}$$

$$v = \lambda f$$

$$v = (0.25 \text{ m}) \cdot (1.6 \text{ kHz})$$

$$v = (0.25 \text{ m}) \cdot (1{,}600 \text{ s}^{-1})$$

$$v = 400 \text{ m/s}$$

74. E is correct.

60 mL = 60 g water

$Q = (mc\Delta T)_{beaker} + (mc\Delta T)_{water}$

Change in temperature is the same.

$Q = \Delta T[(m_{beaker})\cdot(c_{beaker}) + (m_{water})\cdot(c_{water})]$

$2{,}200 \text{ cal} = (25 \ ^{\circ}C)\cdot[(m_{beaker})(0.18 \text{ cal/g}\cdot^{\circ}C) + (60 \text{ g})\cdot(1 \text{ cal/g}\cdot^{\circ}C)]$

$2{,}200 \text{ cal} / 25 \ ^{\circ}C = (m_{beaker})\cdot(0.18 \text{ cal/g}\cdot^{\circ}C) + 60 \text{ cal/}^{\circ}C$

$88 \text{ cal/}^{\circ}C = (m_{beaker})\cdot(0.18 \text{ cal/g}\cdot^{\circ}C) + 60 \text{ cal/}^{\circ}C$

$m_{beaker} = (88 \text{ cal/}^{\circ}C - 60 \text{ cal/}^{\circ}C) / (0.18 \text{ cal/g}\cdot^{\circ}C)$

$m_{beaker} = (28 \text{ cal/}^{\circ}C) / (0.18 \text{ cal/g}\cdot^{\circ}C)$

$m_{beaker} = 156 \text{ g}$

75. C is correct. Spherical miror equation:

$f = -r / 2$

The negative is only included to imply convergence of the lens.

$f = r / 2$

$r = 2f$

$r = (2)\cdot(20 \text{ cm})$

$r = 40 \text{ cm}$

76. C is correct.

Find R_{eq} for entire circuit:

R₁: ⎯⎯W⎯⎯⎯W⎯⎯   in series:
$\quad$ 2 Ω $\quad$ 1 Ω

$\quad R_1 = 2 \ \Omega + 1 \ \Omega$

$\quad R_1 = 3 \ \Omega$

R₂: ⎯⎯W⎯⎯⎯W⎯⎯   in series:
$\quad$ 5Ω $\quad$ 1 Ω

$\quad R_2 = 5 \ \Omega + 1 \ \Omega$

$\quad R_2 = 6 \ \Omega$

R_1 and R_2 are in parallel:

$1 / R_3 = 1 / R_1 + 1 / R_2$

$1 / R_3 = 1 / 3 \ \Omega + 1 / 6 \ \Omega$

$1 / R_3 = 2 / 6 \ \Omega + 1 / 6 \ \Omega$

$1 / R_3 = 1 / 2 \ \Omega$

$R_3 = 2 \ \Omega$

R_3 is in series with the 4 Ω resistor:

$R_{\text{total}} = 2 \, \Omega + 4 \, \Omega$

$R_{\text{total}} = 6 \, \Omega$

Calculate the current around the entire circuit:

$V = IR$

$12 \, \text{V} = I(6 \, \Omega)$

$I = 2 \, \text{A}$

Calculate voltage drop across parallel section using R_3 as equivalent resistor:

$V = IR$

$V = (2 \, \text{A}) \cdot (2 \, \Omega)$

$V = 4 \, \text{V}$

*Note: voltage drop is equal across parallel branches.

Calculate current running through the branch the 2 Ω is on:

$V = IR$

$4 \, \text{V} = I(3 \, \Omega)$

$I = 1.33 \, \text{A}$

Calculate power dissipated by the 2 Ω resistor:

$P = I^2 R$

$P = (1.33 \, \text{A})^2 (2 \, \Omega)$

$P = 3.5 \, \text{W}$

77. A is correct. $F = qv \times B$

The charge density ρ and the charge q are properties of the particle and do not change. Because of the cross product, the force is always perpendicular to the velocity, and thus perpendicular to the displacement of the charge over any infinitesimal interval of time.

Since the force is always perpendicular to the displacement, no work is done, so the kinetic energy will not change.

Since the force is always perpendicular to the velocity, the force is centripetal and the motion is uniform circular motion, so the magnitude of the acceleration does not change.

The force does change the direction of the velocity, and thus the vector velocity itself.

78. C is correct. gauge pressure $= P_{\text{absolute}} - P_{\text{atm}}$

$\rho g h = P_{\text{absolute}} - P_{\text{atm}}$

gauge pressure $= \rho g h$

gauge pressure $= (10^3 \, \text{kg/m}^3) \cdot (9.8 \, \text{m/s}^2) \cdot (10 \, \text{m})$

gauge pressure $= 9.8 \times 10^4 \, \text{Pa}$

79. E is correct. The distance between any two adjacent nodes is $= \frac{1}{2}\lambda$.

$$\frac{1}{2}\lambda = 75 \text{ cm}$$

$$\lambda = 150 \text{ cm}$$

80. C is correct. $v = \lambda f$

$$\lambda = v / f$$

$$\text{Hz} = \text{s}^{-1}$$

$$\lambda = (4{,}900 \text{ m/s}) / (640 \text{ s}^{-1})$$

$$\lambda = 7.7 \text{ m}$$

81. A is correct. There is no force acting in the direction of motion (constant velocity), so there is no work done.

$$\text{W} = Fd \cos \theta$$

Assuming there is no friction, Stacey performed no work because the mass experienced no acceleration due to its constant velocity.

$$F = ma$$

$$F = (15 \text{ kg}) \cdot (0 \text{ m/s}^2)$$

$$F = 0 \text{ N}$$

$$\text{W} = (0 \text{ N}) \cdot (100 \text{ m})$$

$$\text{W} = 0 \text{ J}$$

82. E is correct. The force delivered by the block to her hand and her hand to the block are equal by Newton's Third Law. The time of impact is the same for the block and the hand.

Impulse is calculated by:

$$J = F\Delta t$$

Thus if the force and time are equal for the block and for the hand then they experience the same impulse.

83. E is correct. The textbooks are following a straight path. By turning the car's steering wheel, Karen pulls her car door into the path of the textbooks, giving the illusion that the textbooks have a force acting on them.

84. D is correct.

$$d = (v_f^2 - v_i^2) / 2a$$

$$d = [(21 \text{ m/s})^2 - (5 \text{ m/s})^2] / 2(4 \text{ m/s}^2)$$

$$d = [(441 \text{ m}^2/\text{s}^2) - (25 \text{ m}^2/\text{s}^2)] / (8 \text{ m/s}^2)$$

$$d = (416 \text{ m}^2/\text{s}^2) / (8 \text{ m/s}^2)$$

$$d = 52 \text{ m}$$

85. C is correct.

$$\Delta L / L_0 = \alpha \Delta T$$

$$\Delta T = \Delta L / \alpha L_0$$

$$\Delta T = 3 \times 10^{-3}\,\text{m} / (30 \times 10^{-6}\,\text{K}^{-1}) \cdot (10\,\text{m})$$

$$\Delta T = 10\,\text{K}$$

86. E is correct.

$$F = ma$$

$$a = F / m$$

$$a = 10\,\text{N} / 2\,\text{kg}$$

$$a = 5\,\text{m/s}^2$$

$$v_f = v_i + at$$

$$v_f = 0\,\text{m/s} + (5\,\text{m/s}) \cdot (15\,\text{s})$$

$$v_f = 75\,\text{m/s}$$

$$KE = \tfrac{1}{2}mv^2$$

$$KE = \tfrac{1}{2}(2\,\text{kg}) \cdot (75\,\text{m/s})^2$$

$$KE = 5{,}625\,\text{J}$$

87. D is correct. The beat frequency is twice per second, or 2 Hz.

$$f_{beat} = |f_1 - f_2|$$

$$2\,\text{Hz} = |680\,\text{Hz} - f_2|$$

$$f_2 = 678\,\text{Hz or }682\,\text{Hz}$$

88. D is correct.

$$F = ma$$

$$a = F / m$$

The force is an inverse-square with respect to distance.

$$F = (kqQ) / r^2$$

F decreases as q moves away from Q, and F decreases asymptotically (never reaching zero).

The charges move away from each other because both are positive.

89. A is correct.

For a diverging lens, regardless of the object position, the image is:

- virtual
- upright
- reduced

90. D is correct.

91. D is correct.

The energy uncertainty is given by the uncertainty principle:

$\Delta E \Delta t \geq h / 2\pi$

$\Delta E \geq (6.626 \times 10^{-34} \text{ J·s} / 2\pi) / (30 \times 10^{-12} \text{ s})$

$\Delta E \geq (3.5 \times 10^{-24} \text{ J})$

Converting to eV (1.6×10^{-19} J /eV):

$\Delta E \geq 2.2 \times 10^{-5}$ eV

92. B is correct.

Ignoring the dissipative forces due to friction, the total mechanical energy of a pendulum is conserved. Gravitational PE is constantly being converted into KE, and vice versa.

The total mechanical energy (i.e. KE + PE) remains constant.

93. D is correct.

Volumetric flow rate is constant:

$v_1 A_1 = v_2 A_2$

$v_1 / v_2 = A_2 / A_1$

$v_1 / v_2 = (\pi / 4 \ D_2^2) / (\pi / 4 \ D_1^2)$

$v_1 / v_2 = (8 \text{ cm})^2 / (3 \text{ cm})^2$

$v_1 / v_2 = 7$

$v_1 = 7v_2$

If the diameter increases, then the speed decreases by a factor of 7.

94. E is correct.

Changing the current in a nearby wire changes the magnetic field around it and induces a voltage in the wire close to it by Faraday's Law.

Moving a magnet close to the wire or moving the wire close to a magnetic field changes the magnetic field around the wire and induces a voltage by Faraday's Law.

95. B is correct.

96. C is correct.

Isothermal process change in entropy:

$$\Delta s = Q \,/\, T$$

An isothermal process has work equal to the heat added.

$$Q = W$$

$$\Delta s = W \,/\, T$$

$$W = T\Delta s$$

$$W = (273 \text{ K}) \cdot (2.6 \text{ J/K})$$

$$W = 710 \text{ J}$$

$$W = 7.1 \times 10^2 \text{ J}$$

97. A is correct.

The rock starts at the velocity Jack throws it, which is downward and therefore negative.

The velocity continues to increase negatively due to acceleration from gravity which is constant. Thus the velocity is linear with a downward slope.

$$v_f = v_i + at$$

$$y = mx + b$$

98. E is correct. By the definition of impulse:

$$F\Delta t = m\Delta v$$

Therefore:

$$F = m\Delta v / \Delta t$$

The problem is asking to find the force on the block. Proceed by focusing on the block, first finding Δv, and then using the relation above to find the force.

To determine Δv, calculate velocity after the collision using conservation of momentum:

$$m_i v_i = (m_i + m_f)v_f$$

$$v_f = m_i v_i / (m_i + m_f)$$

$$v_f = (0.1 \text{ kg}) \cdot (50 \text{ m/s}) / (0.1 \text{ kg} + 0.9 \text{ kg})$$

$$v_f = (5 \text{ kg·m/s}) / 1 \text{ kg}$$

$$v_f = 5 \text{ m/s}$$

$$F\Delta t = m(v_f - v_i)$$

$$F = m(v_f - v_i) / \Delta t$$

$$F = (0.9 \text{ kg})(5 \text{ m/s} - 0 \text{ m/s}) / 0.01 \text{ s}$$

$$F = (4.5 \text{ kg m/s}) / (0.01 \text{ s})$$

$$F = 450 \text{ N}$$

99. A is correct.

Use conservation of momentum:

$$m_A v_{Ai} + m_B v_{Bi} = m_A v_{Af} + m_B v_{Bf}$$

$$(2 \text{ kg}) \cdot (0.6 \text{ m/s}) + 0 = 0 + (2.5 \text{ kg}) v_{Bf}$$

$$v_{Bf} = (1.2 \text{ kg} \cdot \text{m/s}) / (2.5 \text{ kg})$$

$$v_{Bf} = 0.48 \text{ m/s}$$

100. B is correct.

Radioactivity is the process by which a nucleus of an unstable atom loses energy by emitting ionizing radiation (e.g. α particles, β particles and γ rays).

The rad is a unit of absorbed radiation dose.

Roentgen (rem) is a related unit to the rad. It is used to quantify the number of rad deposited into a target after radiation exposure.

Becquerel (Bq) is the SI unit of radioactivity. One Bq is defined as the activity of a quantity of radioactive material in which one nucleus decays per second (s^{-1}).

Curie (Ci) is a non-SI unit of radioactivity. 1 Ci = 3.7×10^{10} decays per second.

Sievert (Sv) is the SI unit for a dosage of ionizing radiation and measures the health effect of low levels of ionizing radiation on the human body.

Topical
Practice Questions

Answer Keys &
Explanations

Kinematics & Dynamics

1: D	11: C	21: E	31: B	41: C
2: B	12: B	22: A	32: C	42: A
3: B	13: A	23: B	33: B	43: E
4: A	14: D	24: D	34: E	44: B
5: C	15: B	25: B	35: C	45: A
6: E	16: D	26: E	36: E	46: C
7: D	17: E	27: C	37: D	47: E
8: B	18: B	28: D	38: D	48: C
9: A	19: D	29: D	39: E	49: D
10: E	20: C	30: D	40: E	50: E

Force, Motion, Gravitation

1: B	11: A	21: B	31: C	41: A
2: E	12: E	22: A	32: E	42: C
3: A	13: B	23: C	33: D	43: B
4: C	14: D	24: E	34: A	44: C
5: E	15: E	25: D	35: E	45: A
6: D	16: A	26: B	36: A	46: D
7: A	17: C	27: E	37: D	47: E
8: E	18: C	28: D	38: B	48: E
9: A	19: E	29: A	39: B	49: B
10: C	20: B	30: D	40: C	50: A

Equilibrium & Momentum

1: A	11: E	21: D	31: C	41: B
3: D	12: C	22: B	32: E	42: A
3: E	13: D	23: A	33: C	43: C
4: C	14: B	24: E	34: B	44: B
5: E	15: E	25: D	35: E	45: D
6: E	16: D	26: A	36: C	46: C
7: D	17: B	27: E	37: B	47: B
8: A	18: E	28: C	38: C	48: A
9: B	19: B	29: D	39: E	49: D
10: C	20: C	30: B	40: A	50: C

Rotational Motion

1: D	11: A	21: B	31: D	41: C
2: B	12: E	22: D	32: D	42: D
3: A	13: C	23: B	33: B	43: C
4: D	14: B	24: A	34: C	44: C
5: C	15: C	25: A	35: D	45: B
6: C	16: D	26: A	36: B	46: C
7: E	17: E	27: A	37: C	
8: A	18: A	28: C	38: B	
9: C	19: D	29: C	39: B	
10: B	20: D	30: C	40: D	

Work & Energy

1: D	11: D	21: B	31: B	41: A
2: B	12: B	22: D	32: C	42: A
3: A	13: A	23: B	33: D	43: C
4: B	14: C	24: C	34: E	44: E
5: D	15: B	25: E	35: B	45: D
6: A	16: A	26: A	36: B	46: E
7: D	17: E	27: D	37: D	47: A
8: C	18: A	28: E	38: D	48: A
9: A	19: D	29: B	39: E	49: E
10: B	20: A	30: C	40: B	50: B

Waves & Periodic Motion

1: B	11: D	21: B	31: B	41: A
2: D	12: A	22: E	32: D	42: C
3: D	13: B	23: B	33: E	43: B
4: D	14: C	24: A	34: D	44: E
5: A	15: E	25: E	35: C	45: A
6: E	16: B	26: A	36: E	46: B
7: B	17: C	27: D	37: B	47: A
8: D	18: E	28: B	38: C	48: C
9: E	19: A	29: E	39: D	49: D
10: E	20: D	30: A	40: D	50: A

Sound

1: B	11: B	21: E	31: C	41: A
2: C	12: A	22: D	32: D	42: C
3: B	13: E	23: B	33: A	43: D
4: C	14: C	24: B	34: E	44: A
5: C	15: D	25: E	35: A	45: B
6: E	16: E	26: D	36: E	46: C
7: D	17: C	27: B	37: B	47: C
8: A	18: B	28: A	38: D	48: A
9: C	19: A	29: E	39: E	49: C
10: D	20: B	30: A	40: C	50: E

Fluids & Solids

1: C	11: A	21: E	31: C	41: A
2: D	12: A	22: C	32: A	42: D
3: A	13: A	23: D	33: B	43: B
4: A	14: E	24: E	34: D	44: E
5: E	15: C	25: D	35: C	45: A
6: C	16: B	26: B	36: D	46: C
7: B	17: C	27: E	37: B	47: A
8: E	18: B	28: D	38: D	48: C
9: A	19: C	29: B	39: B	49: E
10: C	20: D	30: B	40: E	50: D

Electrostatics & Electromagnetism

1: C	11: D	21: A	31: A	41: B
2: D	12: E	22: C	32: B	42: C
3: A	13: C	23: A	33: C	43: A
4: C	14: E	24: C	34: D	44: C
5: E	15: D	25: A	35: C	45: B
6: A	16: A	26: D	36: E	46: C
7: D	17: A	27: E	37: B	47: E
8: B	18: D	28: C	38: A	48: A
9: D	19: B	29: D	39: C	49: D
10: A	20: E	30: A	40: C	50: C

Electric Circuits

1: B	11: E	21: E	31: C	41: C
2: D	12: E	22: C	32: E	42: E
3: C	13: D	23: D	33: B	43: A
4: D	14: B	24: A	34: C	44: B
5: E	15: D	25: B	35: D	45: C
6: A	16: A	26: C	36: C	46: E
7: C	17: B	27: D	37: B	47: B
8: D	18: D	28: D	38: E	48: D
9: B	19: C	29: E	39: A	49: A
10: E	20: C	30: A	40: D	50: C

Light & Optics

1: A	11: D	21: B	31: C	41: B
2: A	12: A	22: E	32: B	42: A
3: B	13: D	23: C	33: B	43: C
4: D	14: E	24: E	34: A	44: B
5: E	15: A	25: C	35: E	45: D
6: B	16: E	26: C	36: B	46: D
7: C	17: A	27: A	37: C	47: A
8: D	18: B	28: A	38: D	48: C
9: A	19: D	29: D	39: E	49: E
10: D	20: B	30: E	40: B	50: D

Heat & Thermodynamics

1: B	11: B	21: D	31: B	41: E
2: C	12: A	22: D	32: D	42: C
3: D	13: B	23: B	33: E	43: E
4: A	14: E	24: D	34: B	44: E
5: C	15: D	25: A	35: D	45: D
6: E	16: A	26: A	36: E	46: C
7: D	17: D	27: D	37: A	47: E
8: A	18: C	28: B	38: A	48: D
9: C	19: E	29: E	39: B	49: D
10: B	20: A	30: D	40: B	50: B

Quantum Mechanics

1: E	11: A	21: C	31: B	41: C
2: B	12: D	22: A	32: A	42: E
3: C	13: E	23: D	33: D	43: C
4: C	14: C	24: B	34: C	
5: D	15: E	25: B	35: A	
6: C	16: D	26: B	36: C	
7: C	17: E	27: D	37: B	
8: B	18: E	28: B	38: C	
9: D	19: B	29: A	39: C	
10: A	20: D	30: D	40: B	

Atomic & Nuclear Structure

1: A	11: E	21: B	31: A	41: D
2: C	12: D	22: C	32: C	42: E
3: E	13: A	23: B	33: E	43: A
4: B	14: C	24: C	34: A	44: B
5: C	15: C	25: A	35: C	45: E
6: D	16: A	26: C	36: D	46: B
7: B	17: A	27: E	37: B	47: C
8: E	18: D	28: D	38: E	48: C
9: C	19: B	29: C	39: C	49: B
10: A	20: E	30: D	40: B	

Special Relativity

1: A	11: E	21: A	31: D	41: C
2: E	12: B	22: E	32: D	42: B
3: D	13: A	23: D	33: A	43: B
4: E	14: B	24: B	34: B	44: A
5: D	15: D	25: C	35: C	45: D
6: D	16: E	26: A	36: C	46: A
7: A	17: C	27: B	37: C	47: A
8: C	18: B	28: D	38: D	48: B
9: B	19: D	29: C	39: B	49: D
10: C	20: A	30: B	40: C	50: D

Kinematics and Dynamics – Explanations

1. D is correct.

$$t = (v_f - v_i) / a$$

$$t = (60 \text{ mi/h} - 0 \text{ mi/h}) / (13.1 \text{ mi/h·s})$$

$$t = 4.6 \text{ s}$$

Acceleration is in mi/h·s, so miles and hours cancel and the answer is in units of seconds.

2. B is correct.

At the top of the parabolic trajectory, the vertical velocity $v_{yf} = 0$

The initial upward velocity is the vertical component of the initial velocity:

$$v_{yi} = v \sin \theta$$

$$v_{yi} = (20 \text{ m/s}) \sin 30°$$

$$v_{yi} = (20 \text{ m/s}) \cdot (0.5)$$

$$v_{yi} = 10 \text{ m/s}$$

$$t = (v_{yf} - v_{yi}) / a$$

$$t = (0 - 10 \text{ m/s}) / (-10 \text{ m/s}^2)$$

$$t = (-10 \text{ m/s}) / (-10 \text{ m/s}^2)$$

$$t = 1 \text{ s}$$

3. B is correct.

$$\Delta d = 31.5 \text{ km} = 31,500 \text{ m}$$

$$1.25 \text{ hr} \times 60 \text{ min/hr} = 75 \text{ min}$$

$$\Delta t = 75 \text{ min} \times 60 \text{ s/min} = 4,500 \text{ s}$$

$$v_{avg} = \Delta d / \Delta t$$

$$v_{avg} = 31,500 \text{ m} / 4,500 \text{ s}$$

$$v_{avg} = 7 \text{ m/s}$$

4. A is correct. Instantaneous speed is the scalar magnitude of velocity. It can only be positive or zero (because magnitudes cannot be negative).

5. C is correct.

$$d = (v_f^2 - v_i^2) / 2a$$

$$d = [(21 \text{ m/s})^2 - (5 \text{ m/s})^2] / [2(3 \text{ m/s}^2)]$$

$$d = (441 \text{ m}^2/\text{s}^2 - 25 \text{ m}^2/\text{s}^2) / 6 \text{ m/s}^2$$

$$d = (416 \text{ m}^2/\text{s}^2) / 6 \text{ m/s}^2$$

$$d = 69 \text{ m}$$

6. E is correct.

$$a = (v_f - v_i) / t$$

$$a = [0 - (-30 \text{ m/s})] / 0.15 \text{ s}$$

$$a = (30 \text{ m/s}) / 0.15 \text{ s}$$

$$a = 200 \text{ m/s}^2$$

To represent the acceleration in terms of g, divide a by 9.8 m/s²:

$$\# \text{ of } g = (200 \text{ m/s}^2) / 9.8 \text{ m/s}^2$$

$$\# \text{ of } g = 20 \text{ } g$$

The initial velocity (v_i) is negative due to the acceleration of the car being a positive value. Since the car is decelerating, its acceleration is opposite of its initial velocity.

7. D is correct.

When a bullet is fired it is in projectile motion. The only force in projectile motion (if air resistance is ignored) is the force of gravity.

8. B is correct.

When a car is slowing down, it is decelerating, which is equivalent to acceleration in the opposite direction.

9. A is correct .

Uniform acceleration:

$$a = \text{change in velocity} / \text{change in time}$$

$$a = \Delta v / \Delta t$$

$$\Delta v = a\Delta t$$

$$\Delta v = (20 \text{ m/s}^2) \cdot (1 \text{ s})$$

$$\Delta v = 20 \text{ m/s}$$

10. E is correct.

$$d = v_0 t + \tfrac{1}{2}gt^2$$

Set g as negative because it is in the opposite direction as +800 m/s:

$$d = (800 \text{ m/s}) \cdot (200 \text{ s}) + \tfrac{1}{2}(-10 \text{ m/s}^2) \cdot (200 \text{ s})^2$$

$$d = (160,000 \text{ m}) - (200,000 \text{ m})$$

$$d = -40,000 \text{ m}$$

The projectile traveled –40,000 m from the top of the cliff to the sea at point P, which means the cliff is 40,000 m from the base to the top.

11. C is correct. $t = d / v$

$t = (540 \text{ mi}) / (65 \text{ mi/h})$

$t = 8.3 \text{ h}$

The time she can stop is the difference between her total allowed time and the time t that it takes to make the trip:

$t_{\text{stop}} = 9.8 \text{ h} - 8.3 \text{ h}$

$t_{\text{stop}} = 1.5 \text{ h}$

12. B is correct. Average velocity is the change in position with respect to time:

$v = \Delta x / \Delta t$

After one lap, the racecar's final position is the same as its initial position.

Thus $x = 0$, which implies the average velocity of 0 m/s.

13. A is correct. $d = v_i\Delta t + \frac{1}{2}a\Delta t^2$

$d = (0.2 \text{ m/s}) \cdot (5 \text{ s}) + \frac{1}{2}(-0.05 \text{ m/s}^2) \cdot (5 \text{ s})^2$

$d = 1 \text{ m} + \frac{1}{2}(-0.05 \text{ m/s}^2) \cdot (25 \text{ s}^2)$

$d = 1 \text{ m} + (-0.625 \text{ m})$

$d = 0.375 \text{ m} \approx 0.38 \text{ m}$

Decelerating is set to negative.

The net displacement is the difference between the final and initial positions after 5 s.

14. D is correct.

The solution is measured in feet, so first convert the car velocity into feet per second:

$v = (49 \text{ mi/h}) \cdot (5280 \text{ ft/mi}) \cdot (1 \text{ h}/3600 \text{ s})$

$v = 72 \text{ ft/s}$

The sober driver's distance:

$d = vt$

$d_{\text{sober}} = (72 \text{ ft/s}) \cdot (0.33 \text{ s})$

$d_{\text{sober}} = 24 \text{ ft}$

The intoxicated driver's distance:

$d = vt$

$d_{\text{drunk}} = (72 \text{ ft/s}) \cdot (1 \text{ s})$

$d_{\text{drunk}} = 72 \text{ ft}$

The differences between the distances:

$\Delta d = 72 \text{ ft} - 24 \text{ ft}$

$\Delta d = 48 \text{ ft}$

15. B is correct.

Convert the final speed from km/h to m/s:

v_f = (210 km/h) × [(1,000 m/1 km)] × [(1 h/3,600 s)]

v_f = 58.33 m/s

Calculate the acceleration necessary to reach this speed:

$a = (v_f^2 - v_i^2) / 2d$

a = [(58.33 m/s)² – (0 m/s)²] / 2(1,800 m)

a = (3,402.39 m²/s²) / (3,600 m)

a = 0.95 m/s²

16. D is correct.

The distance the rocket travels during its acceleration upward is calculated by:

$d_1 = \frac{1}{2}at^2$

$d_1 = \frac{1}{2}$(22 m/s²)·(4 s)²

d_1 = 176 m

The distance from when the motor shuts off to when the rocket reaches maximum height can be calculated using the conservation of energy:

$mgd_2 = \frac{1}{2}mv^2$, cancel m from both sides of the expression

$gd_2 = \frac{1}{2}v^2$

where $v = at$

$gd_2 = \frac{1}{2}(at)^2$

$d_2 = \frac{1}{2}(at)^2 / g$

$d_2 = \frac{1}{2}$[(22 m/s²)·(4 s)]² / (10 m/s²)

Magnitudes are not vectors but scalars, so no direction is needed

d_2 = 387 m

For the maximum elevation, add the two distances:

$h = d_1 + d_2$

h = 176 m + 387 m

h = 563 m

17. E is correct.

Calculate the vertical component of the initial velocity:

$v_{up} = v(\sin \theta)$

v_{up} = (2.74 m/s) sin 60°

v_{up} = 2.37 m/s

Then solve for the upward displacement given the initial upward velocity:

$$d = (v_f^2 - v_i^2) / 2a$$

$$d = [(0 \text{ m/s})^2 - (2.37 \text{ m/s})^2] / 2(-9.8 \text{ m/s}^2)$$

$$d = (-5.62 \text{ m}^2/\text{s}^2) / (-19.6 \text{ m/s}^2)$$

$$d = 0.29 \text{ m}$$

18. B is correct. Acceleration due to gravity is constant and independent of mass.

19. D is correct. As an object falls its acceleration is constant due to gravity. However, the magnitude of the velocity increases due to the acceleration of gravity and the displacement increases because the object is going further away from its starting point.

20. C is correct. The man is moving at constant velocity (no acceleration), so it's known immediately that the net force is zero. The only objects interacting with the man directly are Earth and the floor of the elevator. The cable is not touching the man; it pulls the elevator car up and the floor of the elevator is what pushes on the man.

21. E is correct.

Horizontal velocity (v_x):

$$v_x = d_x / t$$

$$v_x = (44 \text{ m}) / (2.9 \text{ s})$$

$$v_x = 15.2 \text{ m/s}$$

The x component of a vector is calculated by:

$$v_x = v \cos \theta$$

Rearrange the equation to determine the initial velocity of the ball:

$$v = v_x / \cos \theta$$

$$v = (15.2 \text{ m/s}) / (\cos 45°)$$

$$v = (15.2 \text{ m/s}) / 0.7$$

$$v = 21.4 \text{ m/s}$$

22. A is correct. Conservation of energy:

$$mgh = \tfrac{1}{2}mv_f^2, \text{ cancel } m \text{ from both sides of the expression}$$

$$gh = \tfrac{1}{2}v_f^2$$

$$(10 \text{ m/s}^2)h = \tfrac{1}{2}(14 \text{ m/s})^2$$

$$(10 \text{ m/s}^2)h = \tfrac{1}{2}(196 \text{ m}^2/\text{s}^2)$$

$$h = (98 \text{ m}^2/\text{s}^2) / (10 \text{ m/s}^2)$$

$$h = 9.8 \text{ m} \approx 10 \text{ m}$$

23. B is correct.

$$d = v_i t + \tfrac{1}{2}at^2$$
$$d = (20 \text{ m/s}){\cdot}(7 \text{ s}) + \tfrac{1}{2}(1.4 \text{ m/s}^2){\cdot}(7 \text{ s})^2$$
$$d = (140 \text{ m}) + \tfrac{1}{2}(1.4 \text{ m/s}^2){\cdot}(49 \text{ s}^2)$$
$$d = 174.3 \text{ m} \approx 174 \text{ m}$$

24. D is correct.

Force is not a scalar because it has a magnitude and direction.

25. B is correct.

$$d = \tfrac{1}{2}at^2$$
$$d_A = \tfrac{1}{2}at^2$$
$$d_B = \tfrac{1}{2}a(2t)^2$$
$$d_B = \tfrac{1}{2}a(4t^2)$$
$$d_B = 4 \times \tfrac{1}{2}at^2$$
$$d_B = 4d_A$$

26. E is correct.

$$d = v_{\text{average}} \times \Delta t$$
$$d = \tfrac{1}{2}(v_i + v_f)\Delta t$$
$$d = \tfrac{1}{2}(5 \text{ m/s} + 30 \text{ m/s}){\cdot}(10 \text{ s})$$
$$d = 175 \text{ m}$$

27. C is correct.

$$a = (v_i^2 + v_f^2) / 2d$$
$$a = [(0 \text{ m/s})^2 + (42 \text{ m/s})^2] / [2(5{,}600 \text{ m})]$$
$$a = (1{,}764 \text{ m}^2/\text{s}^2) / 11{,}200 \text{ m}$$
$$a = 0.16 \text{ m/s}^2$$

28. D is correct.

The gravitational force between two objects in space, each having masses of m_1 and m_2, is:

$$F_G = Gm_1m_2 / r^2$$

where G is the gravitational constant and r is the distance between the two objects.

Doubling the distance between the two objects:

$$F_{G2} = Gm_1m_2 / (2r)^2$$

$$F_{G2} = Gm_1m_2 / (4r^2)$$

$$F_{G2} = \tfrac{1}{4}Gm_1m_2 / r^2$$

$$F_{G2} = \tfrac{1}{4}Gm_1m_2 / r^2$$

$$F_{G2} = \tfrac{1}{4}F_G$$

Therefore, when the distance between the objects is doubled, the force (F_G) is one fourth as much.

29. D is correct.

I: If the velocity is constant, the instantaneous velocity is always equal to the average velocity.

II and III: If the velocity is increasing, the average value of velocity over an interval must lie between the initial velocity and the final velocity. In going from its initial value to its final value, the instantaneous velocity must cross the average value at one point, regardless of whether or not the velocity is changing at a constant rate, or changing irregularly.

30. D is correct.

Before determining the average speed and velocity of the trip, first calculate the total time of the trip:

$$t_{total} = (d_{North} / v_{North}) + (d_{South} / v_{South})$$

$$t_{total} = (95 \text{ km} / 70 \text{ km/h}) + (21.9 \text{ km} / 80 \text{ km/h})$$

$$t_{total} = 1.36 \text{ h} + 0.27 \text{ h}$$

$$t_{total} = 1.63 \text{ h}$$

Calculate the average speed of the trip:

$$speed_{avg} = (d_{North} + d_{South}) / t_{total}$$

$$speed_{avg} = (95 \text{ km} + 21.9 \text{ km}) / 1.63 \text{ h}$$

$$speed_{avg} = (116.9 \text{ km}) / 1.63 \text{ h}$$

$$speed_{avg} = 72 \text{ km/h}$$

Calculate the average velocity of the trip, remembering that velocity is directional so set South as the negative direction:

$$v_{avg} = (d_{North} - d_{South}) / t_{total}$$

$$v_{avg} = (95 \text{ km} - 21.9 \text{ km}) / 1.63 \text{ h}$$

$$v_{avg} = (73.1 \text{ km}) / 1.63 \text{ h}$$

$$v_{avg} = 45 \text{ km/h}$$

The difference between the average speed and average velocity is:

$$speed_{avg} - v_{avg} = 72 \text{ km/h} - 45 \text{ km/h}$$

$$speed_{avg} - v_{avg} = 27 \text{ km/h}$$

31. B is correct. velocity = distance / time

$v = d / t$

d is constant, while t decreases by a factor of 3

32. C is correct. The equation for distance, given a constant acceleration and both the initial and final velocity, is:

$d = (v_i^2 + v_f^2) / 2a$

Since the car is coming to rest, $v_f = 0$

$d = v_i^2 / 2a$

If the initial velocity is doubled while acceleration and final velocity remain unchanged, the new distance traveled is:

$d_2 = (2v_i)^2 / 2a$

$d_2 = 4(v_i^2 / 2a)$

$d_2 = 4d_1$

Another method to solve this problem:

$d_1 = (29 \text{ mi/h})^2 / 2a$

$d_2 = (59 \text{ mi/h})^2 / 2a$

$d_2 / d_1 = [(59 \text{ mi/h})^2 / 2a] / [(29 \text{ mi/h })^2 / 2a]$

$d_2 / d_1 = (59 \text{ mi/h})^2 / (29 \text{ mi/h})^2$

$d_2 / d_1 = (3,481 \text{ mi/h}) / (841 \text{ mi/h})$

$d_2 / d_1 = 4$

33. B is correct.

$d = v_0t + \frac{1}{2}at^2$, where $v_0 = 0$

$d = \frac{1}{2}at^2$

$t^2 = d / \frac{1}{2}a$

$t = \sqrt{(2d / a)}$

$t = \sqrt{[2 (10 \text{ m}) / 9.8 \text{ m/s}^2]}$

$t = \sqrt{(2.04 \text{ s}^2)}$

$t = 1.4 \text{ s}$

34. E is correct.

$\Delta v = a\Delta t$

$(v_f - v_i) = a\Delta t$, where $v_f = 0$ m/s (when the car stops)

$a = -0.1 \text{ m/s}^2$ (negative because deceleration), $\Delta t = 5$ s

$$v_i = v_f - a\Delta t$$

$$v_i = [(0 \text{ m/s}) - (-0.1 \text{ m/s}^2)] \cdot (5 \text{ s})$$

$$v_i = (0.1 \text{ m/s}^2) \cdot (5 \text{ s}) = 0.5 \text{ m/s}$$

35. C is correct.

If acceleration is constant then the velocity vs. time graph is linear and the average velocity is the average of the final and initial velocity.

$$v_{average} = v_f - v_i / \Delta t$$

If acceleration is not constant then the velocity vs. time graph is nonlinear.

$$v_{average} \neq v_f - v_i / \Delta t$$

36. E is correct.

Find velocity of thrown rock:

$$v_{f1}^2 - v_i^2 = 2ad$$

$$v_{f1}^2 = v_i^2 + 2ad$$

$$v_{f1}^2 = (10 \text{ m/s})^2 + [2(9.8 \text{ m/s}^2) \cdot (300 \text{ m})]$$

$$v_{f1}^2 = 100 \text{ m}^2/\text{s}^2 + 5{,}880 \text{ m}^2/\text{s}^2$$

$$v_{f1}^2 = 5{,}980 \text{ m}^2/\text{s}^2$$

$$v_{f1} = 77.33 \text{ m/s}$$

$$t_1 = (v_f - v_i) / a$$

$$t_1 = (77.33 \text{ m/s} - 10 \text{ m/s}) / 9.8 \text{ m/s}^2$$

$$t_1 = (67.33 \text{ m/s}) / (9.8 \text{ m/s}^2)$$

$$t_1 = 6.87 \text{ s}$$

Find velocity of dropped rock:

$$v_{f2} = \sqrt{2ad}$$

$$v_{f2} = \sqrt{[(2) \cdot (9.8 \text{ m/s}^2) \cdot (300 \text{ m})]}$$

$$v_{f2} = 76.7 \text{ m/s}$$

$$t_2 = (76.7 \text{ m/s}) / (9.8 \text{ m/s}^2)$$

$$t_2 = 7.82 \text{ s}$$

$$\Delta t = (7.82 \text{ s} - 6.87 \text{ s})$$

$$\Delta t = 0.95 \text{ s}$$

37. D is correct.

$$F = ma$$

Force and acceleration are directly proportional so doubling force doubles acceleration.

38. D is correct.

Approach the problem by finding the distance traveled in each of the three segments.

$$d_1 = \tfrac{1}{2}a_1\Delta t_1$$

$$d_1 = (0.5)\cdot(2 \text{ m/s}^2)\cdot(10 \text{ s}) = 100 \text{ s}$$

The second segment:

$$d_2 = v_2\Delta t_2$$

where $\Delta t_2 = 10$ s, the duration of interval 2 and v_2 is the speed during interval 2, which is the speed at the end of interval 1.

$$v_2 = v_{1f} = a_1\Delta t_1$$

$$v_2 = (2 \text{ m/s})\cdot(10 \text{ s}) = 20 \text{ m/s}$$

So:

$$d_2 = (20 \text{ m/s})\cdot(10 \text{ s}) = 200\text{m}$$

Next, the third segment:

$$d_3 = (v^2_{3f} - v^2_{3i}) \,/\, 2a_3$$

$$d_3 = [(0 \text{ m/s})^2 - (20 \text{ m/s})^2] \,/\, 2(-2 \text{ m/s}^2)$$

$$d_3 = 100 \text{ m}$$

The total distance traveled is the sum of d_1, d_2 and d_3:

$$d = 100 \text{ m} + 200 \text{ m} + 100 \text{ m}$$

$$d = 400 \text{ m}$$

39. E is correct.

The acceleration is negative because it acts to slow the car down against the $+y$ direction.

It is unclear if the acceleration decreases in magnitude from the data provided.

40. E is correct.

Total distance is represented by the area under the velocity-time curve with respect to the x-axis.

This graph can be broken up into sections; calculate the area under the curve.

$$d_{total} = d_A + d_B + d_C + d_D$$

$$d_A = \tfrac{1}{2}(4 \text{ m/s})\cdot(2 \text{ s}) = 4 \text{ m}$$

$$d_B = \tfrac{1}{2}(4 \text{ m/s} + 2 \text{ m/s})\cdot(2 \text{ s}) = 6 \text{ m}$$

$$d_C = (2 \text{ m/s})\cdot(4 \text{ s}) = 8 \text{ m}$$

Since the total distance traveled needs to be calculated, the area under the curve when the velocity is negative is calculated as a positive value. Distance is a scalar quantity and therefore has no direction.

$d_D = \frac{1}{2}(2 \text{ m/s}) \cdot (1 \text{ s}) + \frac{1}{2}(2 \text{ m/s}) \cdot (1 \text{ s}) = 2 \text{ m}$

$d_{total} = 4 \text{ m} + 6 \text{ m} + 8 \text{ m} + 2 \text{ m}$

$d_{total} = 20 \text{ m}$

If the question was asking to find the displacement, the area under the curve would be calculated as negative and the answer would be 18 m.

41. C is correct. The two bullets have different velocities when hitting the water, but they both only experience the force due to gravity. Thus the acceleration due to gravity is the same for each bullet.

42. A is correct.

$v_f = v_i + at$

$v_f = 0 + (2.5 \text{ m/s}^2) \cdot (9 \text{ s})$

$v_f = 22.5 \text{ m/s}$

43. E is correct.

The equation for impulse is used for contact between two objects over a specified time period:

$F\Delta t = m\Delta v$

$ma\Delta t = m(v_f - v_i)$, cancel m from both sides of the expression

$a\Delta t = (v_f - v_i)$

$a = (v_f - v_i) / \Delta t$

$a = (-2v - v) / (0.45 \text{ s})$

$a = (-3v) / (0.45 \text{ s})$

$a = (-6.7 \text{ s}^{-1})v$

Ratio $a : v = -6.7 \text{ s}^{-1} : 1$

44. B is correct.

The time for the round trip is 4 s.

The weight reaches the top of its path in ½ time:

$\frac{1}{2}(4 \text{ s}) = 2 \text{ s}$, where $v = 0$

$a = \Delta v / t$ for the first half of the trip

$a = (v_f - v_i) / t$

$a = (0 - 3.2 \text{ m/s}) / 2 \text{ s}$

$a = -1.6 \text{ m/s}^2$

$|a| = 1.6 \text{ m/s}^2$

Acceleration is a vector and the negative direction only indicates direction.

45. A is correct.

$$\Delta v = a\Delta t$$

$$\Delta v = (0.3 \text{ m/s}^2) \cdot (3 \text{ s})$$

$$\Delta v = 0.9 \text{ m/s}$$

46. C is correct.

Since the car is initially traveling North, let North be the positive direction and South be the negative direction:

$$a = (v_f - v_i) / t$$

$$a = (14.1 \text{ m/s} - 17.7 \text{ m/s}) / 12 \text{ s}$$

$$a = (-3.6 \text{ m/s}) / 12 \text{ s}$$

$$a = -0.3 \text{ m/s}^2$$

$$a = 0.3 \text{ m/s}^2 \text{ South}$$

47. E is correct.

$$d = d_0 + (v_i^2 + v_f^2) / 2a$$

$$d = 64 \text{ m} + (0 \text{ m/s} + 60 \text{ m/s})^2 / 2(9.8 \text{ m/s}^2)$$

$$d = 64 \text{ m} + (3{,}600 \text{ m}^2/\text{s}^2) / (19.6 \text{ m/s}^2)$$

$$d = 64 \text{ m} + 184 \text{ m}$$

$$d = 248 \text{ m}$$

48. C is correct.

$$a = (v_f^2 + v_i^2) / 2d$$

$$a = [(60 \text{ m/s})^2 + (0 \text{ m/s})^2] / [2(64 \text{ m})]$$

$$a = (3{,}600 \text{ m}^2/\text{s}^2) / 128 \text{ m}$$

$$a = 28 \text{ m/s}^2$$

49. D is correct.

Expression for the time interval during constant acceleration upward:

$$d = \tfrac{1}{2}at^2$$

Solving for acceleration:

$$a = (v_f^2 + v_i^2) / 2d$$

$$a = [(60 \text{ m/s})^2 + (0 \text{ m/s})^2] / [2(64 \text{ m})]$$

$$a = (3{,}600 \text{ m}^2/\text{s}^2) / (128 \text{ m})$$

$$a = 28.1 \text{ m/s}^2$$

Solving for time:

$$t^2 = 2d/a$$

$$t^2 = 2(64 \text{ m}) / 28.1 \text{ m/s}^2$$

$$t^2 = 4.5 \text{ s}^2$$

$$t = 2.1 \text{ s}$$

50. E is correct.

$$d = (v_i^2 + v_f^2) / 2a, \text{ where } v_i = 0$$

$$d = v_f^2 / 2a$$

For half the final velocity:

$$d_2 = (v_f / 2)^2 / 2a$$

$$d_2 = \tfrac{1}{4}v_f^2 / 2a$$

$$d_2 = \tfrac{1}{4}d$$

Force, Motion, Gravitation – Explanations

1. B is correct. The tension of the string keeps the weight traveling in a circular path, otherwise it would move linearly on a tangent path to the circle. Without the string, there are no horizontal forces on the weight and no horizontal acceleration. The horizontal motion of the weight is in a straight line at constant speed.

2. E is correct.

The vertical force on the garment bag from the left side of the clothesline is:

$$T_{y,left} = T \cos \theta$$

Similarly, for the right side:

$$T_{y,right} = T \cos \theta$$

where $T = 10$ N (tension) and $\theta = 60°$.

Since the garment bag is at rest, its acceleration is zero. Therefore, according to Newton's second law:

$$T_{y,left} + T_{y,right} - mg = 0 = 2T (\cos \theta) - mg$$

Or: $\quad 2T (\cos \theta) = mg$

$$m = 2T (\cos \theta) / g$$

$$m = 2(10 \text{ N}) \cdot (\cos 60°) / (10.0 \text{ m/s}^2)$$

$$m = 2(10 \text{ N}) \cdot (0.5) / (10.0 \text{ m/s}^2)$$

$$m = 1 \text{ kg}$$

3. A is correct. An object's inertia is its resistance to change in motion. The milk carton has enough inertia to overcome the force of static friction.

4. C is correct.

$$(F_{net})_y = (F_N)_y - (F_g)_y$$

The car is not moving up or down, so $a_y = 0$:

$$(F_{net})_y = 0$$

$$0 = (F_N)_y - (F_g)_y$$

$$F_N = (F_g)_y$$

$$F_N = F_g \cos \theta$$

$$F_N = mg \cos \theta$$

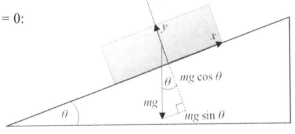

The normal force is a force that is perpendicular to the plane of contact (the slope).

5. E is correct.

If θ is the angle with respect to a horizontal line, then:

$\theta = \frac{1}{2}(40°)$

$\theta = 20°$

Therefore, in order for the third force to cause equilibrium, the sum of all three forces' components must equal zero. Since F_1 and F_2 mirror each other in the y direction:

$F_{1y} + F_{2y} = 0$

Therefore, in order for F_3 to balance the forces in the y direction, its y component must also equal zero:

$F_{1y} + F_{2y} + F_{3y} = 0$

$0 + F_{3y} = 0$

$F_{3y} = 0$

Since the y component of F_3 is zero, the angle that F_3 makes with the horizontal is zero:

$\theta_3 = 0°$

The x component of F_3:

$F_{1x} + F_{2x} + F_{3x} = 0$

$F_1 \cos \theta + F_2 \cos \theta + F_3 \cos \theta = 0$

$F_3 = -(F_2 \cos \theta_2 + F_3 \cos \theta_3)$

$F_3 = -[(2.3 \text{ N}) \cos 20° + (2.3 \text{ N}) \cos 20°]$

$F_3 = -4.3 \text{ N}$

$F_3 = 4.3 \text{ N to the right}$

6. D is correct.

The mass on the table causes a tension force in the string that acts against the force of gravity.

7. A is correct.

Although the net force acting on the object is decreasing with time and the magnitude of the object's acceleration is decreasing there exists a positive acceleration. Therefore, the object's speed continues to increase.

8. E is correct. An object moving at constant velocity experiences zero net force.

9. A is correct. The sine of an angle is equal to the opposite side over the hypotenuse:

$\sin \theta = \text{opposite} / \text{hypotenuse}$

$\sin \theta = h / L$

$h = L \sin \theta$

10. C is correct.

A car accelerating horizontally does not rely on the force of gravity to move it. Since mass does not depend on gravity, a car on Earth and a car on the Moon that experience the same horizontal acceleration also experience the same force.

11. A is correct.

$$a = (v_f - v_i) / t$$
$$a = (3.5 \text{ m/s} - 1.5 \text{ m/s}) / (3 \text{ s})$$
$$a = (2 \text{ m/s}) / (3 \text{ s})$$
$$a = 0.67 \text{ m/s}^2$$

12. E is correct.

An object with uniform circular motion (i.e. constant angular velocity) only experiences centripetal acceleration directed toward the center of the circle.

13. B is correct.

$F = ma$, so zero force means zero acceleration in any direction.

14. D is correct.

Each scale weighs the fish at 17 kg, so the sum of the two scales is:

$$17 \text{ kg} + 17 \text{ kg} = 34 \text{ kg}$$

15. E is correct.

The only force acting on a projectile in motion is the force due to gravity. Since that force always acts downward, there is always only a downward acceleration.

16. A is correct.

$$F_{net} = ma$$

If an object moves with constant v, its $a = 0$, so:

$$F_{net} = 0$$

Since gravity pulls down on the can with a force of mg:

$$F_g = mg$$
$$F_g = (10 \text{ kg}) \cdot (10 \text{ m/s}^2)$$
$$F_g = 100 \text{ N}$$

The rope pulls *up* on the can with the same magnitude of force, so the tension is 100 N, for a net force = 0.

17. C is correct.

Find equal and opposite forces:

$$F_{Rx} = -F_1$$

$$F_{Rx} = -(-6.6 \text{ N})$$

$$F_{Rx} = 6.6 \text{ N}$$

$$F_{Ry} = -F_2$$

$$F_{Ry} = -2.2 \text{ N}$$

Pythagorean Theorem ($a^2 + b^2 = c^2$) to calculate the magnitude of the resultant force:

The magnitude of F_R:

$$F_R{}^2 = F_{Rx}{}^2 + F_{Ry}{}^2$$

$$F_R{}^2 = (6.6 \text{ N})^2 + (-2.2 \text{ N})^2$$

$$F_R{}^2 = 43.6 \text{ N}^2 + 4.8 \text{ N}^2$$

$$F_R{}^2 = 48.4 \text{ N}^2$$

$$F_R = 7 \text{ N}$$

The direction of F_R:

$$\theta = \tan^{-1}(-2.2 \text{ N} / 6.6 \text{ N})$$

$$\theta = \tan^{-1}(-1 / 3)$$

$$\theta = 342°$$

The direction of F_R with respect to F_1:

$$\theta = 342° - 180°$$

$$\theta = 162° \text{ counterclockwise of } F_1$$

18. C is correct.

$$a_{cent} = v^2 / r$$

$$a_{cent} = (4 \text{ m/s})^2 / (4 \text{ m})$$

$$a_{cent} = (16 \text{ m}^2/\text{s}^2) / (4 \text{ m})$$

$$a_{cent} = 4 \text{ m/s}^2$$

19. E is correct.

Solve for m_1:

$$F_{net} = 0$$

$$m_2 g = F_T$$

$$m_1 g \sin\theta + F_f = F_T$$

$$m_1 g \sin\theta + \mu_s m_1 g \cos\theta = m_2 g$$

cancel g from both sides

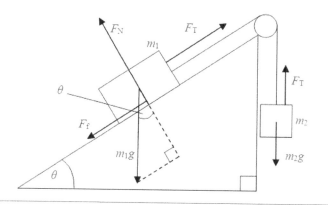

$$m_1(\sin\theta + \mu_s \cos\theta) = m_2$$

$$m_1 = m_2 / (\sin\theta + \mu_s \cos\theta)$$

$$m_1 = 2 \text{ kg} / [\sin 20° + (0.55) \cos 20°]$$

$$m_1 = 2 \text{ kg} / 0.86$$

$$m_1 = 2.3 \text{ kg}$$

Kinetic friction is only used when the mass is in motion.

20. B is correct. Since the masses are identical, the force of gravity on each is the same. The force of gravity on one of the masses produces the tension force in the string, which in turn pulls on the other mass. Since this tension force is equal to the force of gravity, there is no net force and the objects remain at rest.

21. B is correct.

Newton's Third Law states that for every action there is an equal and opposite reaction.

22. A is correct.

Newton's Third Law states that for every action there is an equal and opposite reaction.

23. C is correct. If w denotes the magnitude of the box's weight, then the component of this force that is parallel to the inclined plane is $w \sin\theta$, where θ is the incline angle.

If θ is less than 90°, then $\sin\theta$ is less than 1.

The component of w parallel to the inclined plane is less than w.

24. E is correct. The package experiences projectile motion upon leaving the truck, so it experiences no horizontal forces and its initial velocity of 30 m/s remains unchanged.

25. D is correct.

$$f = \text{revolutions / unit of time}$$

The time (period) for one complete revolution is:

$$T = 1 / f$$

Each revolution represents a length of $2\pi r$.

Velocity is the distance traveled in one revolution over duration of one revolution (circumference over period):

$$v = 2\pi r / t$$

$$v = 2\pi r f$$

If f doubles, then v doubles.

26. B is correct.

$$F_g = Gm_{Earth}m_{moon} / d^2$$

d is the distance between the Earth and the Moon.

If d decreases by a factor of 4, F_g increases by a factor of $4^2 = 16$

27. E is correct.

Newton's First Law states that every object will remain at rest or in uniform motion unless acted upon by an outside force.

In this case, Steve and the bus are in uniform constant motion until the bus stops due to sudden deceleration (the ground exerts no frictional force on Steve). There is no force acting upon Steve. However, his inertia carries him forward because he is still in uniform motion while the bus comes to a stop.

28. D is correct.

The ball is in a state of rest, so $F_{net} = 0$

$$F_{down} = F_{up}$$

$$F_{external} + F_w = F_{buoyant}$$

$$F_{external} = F_{buoyant} - F_w$$

$$F_{external} = 8.4 \text{ N} - 4.4 \text{ N}$$

$$F_{external} = 4 \text{ N, in the same direction as the weight}$$

29. A is correct.

The luggage and the train move at the same speed, so when the luggage moves forward with respect to the train, it means the train has slowed down while the luggage is continuing to move at the train's original speed.

30. D is correct.

The mass does not change by changing the object's location.

Since the object is outside of Earth's atmosphere, the object's weight is represented by the equation:

$$F_g = GmM_{Earth} / R^2$$

If the altitude is $2R_{Earth}$, then the distance from the center of the Earth is $3R_{Earth}$.

The gravitational acceleration decreases by a factor of $3^2 = 9$ ($g = GmM / R^2$).

Weight decreases by a factor of 9.

$$\text{New weight} = 360 \text{ N} / 9 = 40 \text{ N}$$

31. C is correct. The velocity of the rock just after its release is the same as the truck's. Once in free fall, there are no horizontal forces on the rock. The rock's velocity remains unchanged and is equal to that of the truck.

32. E is correct. The acceleration of Jason due to thrust is $F_{net} = ma_1$:

$$ma_1 = F_{ski} - \mu_k mg$$

$$a_1 = (F_{ski} - \mu_k mg) / m$$

$$a_1 = [200 \text{ N} - (0.1) \cdot (75 \text{ kg}) \cdot (9.8 \text{ m/s}^2)] / 75 \text{ kg}$$

$$a_1 = (126.5 \text{ N}) / 75 \text{ kg}$$

$$a_1 = 1.69 \text{ m/s}^2$$

The distance traveled during the acceleration stage is:

$$d_1 = \frac{1}{2}a_1 t^2$$

$$d_1 = \frac{1}{2}(1.69 \text{ m/s}^2) \cdot (67 \text{ s})^2$$

$$d_1 = 3{,}793 \text{ m}$$

The distance traveled after the skis run out of fuel is:

$$d_2 = (v_f^2 - v_i^2) / 2a_2$$

a_2 is Jason's acceleration after the fuel runs out:

$$F_{net} = ma_2$$

$ma_2 = -\mu_k mg$, cancel m from both sides of the expression

$$a_2 = -\mu_k g$$

$$a_2 = -(0.1) \cdot (9.8 \text{ m/s}^2)$$

$$a_2 = -0.98 \text{ m/s}^2$$

The acceleration is negative since the frictional force opposes the direction of motion.

v_i is the velocity at the moment when the fuel runs out:

$$v_i = a_1 t$$

$$v_i = (1.69 \text{ m/s}^2) \cdot (67 \text{ s})$$

$$v_i = 113.2 \text{ m/s}$$

Substitute a_2 and v_i into the equation for d_2:

$$d_2 = [(0 \text{ m/s})^2 - (113.2 \text{ m/s})^2] / 2(-0.98 \text{ m/s}^2)$$

$$d_2 = (-12{,}814.2 \text{ m}^2/\text{s}^2) / -1.96 \text{ m/s}^2$$

$$d_2 = 6{,}538 \text{ m}$$

The total distance Jason traveled is:

$$d_{total} = d_1 + d_2$$

$$d_{total} = 3{,}793 \text{ m} + 6{,}538 \text{ m}$$

$$d_{total} = 10{,}331 \text{ m}$$

33. D is correct. Using the force analysis:

$$F_{net} = F_g + F_{fk}$$

$$F_g = mg \sin \theta$$

$$F_g = (0.2 \text{ kg}) \cdot (-9.8 \text{ m/s}^2) \sin 30°$$

$$F_g = (0.2 \text{ kg}) \cdot (-9.8 \text{ m/s}^2) \cdot (1/2)$$

$$F_g = -1 \text{ N}$$

$$F_{fk} = \mu_k F_N$$

$$F_{fk} = \mu_k mg \cos \theta$$

$$F_{fk} = (0.3) \cdot (0.2 \text{ kg}) \cdot (-9.8 \text{ m/s}^2) \cos 30°$$

$$F_{fk} = (0.3) \cdot (0.2 \text{ kg}) \cdot (-9.8 \text{ m/s}^2) \cdot (0.866)$$

$$F_{fk} = -0.5 \text{ N}$$

$$F_{net} = -1 \text{ N} + (-0.5 \text{ N})$$

$$F_{net} = -1.5 \text{ N}$$

$$a = F_{net} / m$$

$$a = -1.5 \text{ N} / 0.2 \text{ kg}$$

$$a = -7.5 \text{ m/s}^2$$

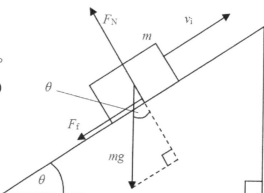

The distance it travels until it reaches a velocity of 0 at its maximum height:

$$d = (v_f^2 - v_i^2) / 2a$$

$$d = [(0 \text{ m/s})^2 - (63 \text{ m/s})^2] / 2(-7.5 \text{ m/s}^2)$$

$$d = (-4,000 \text{ m}^2/\text{s}^2) / (-15 \text{ m/s}^2)$$

$$d = 267 \text{ m}$$

The vertical height is:

$$h = d \sin \theta$$

$$h = (267 \text{ m}) \sin 30°$$

$$h = (267 \text{ m}) \cdot (0.5)$$

$$h = 130 \text{ m}$$

Using energy to solve the problem:

$$KE = PE + W_f$$

$$\tfrac{1}{2}mv^2 = mgd \sin \theta + \mu_k mgd \cos \theta, \text{ cancel } m \text{ from the expression}$$

$$\tfrac{1}{2}v^2 = gd \sin \theta + \mu_k gd \cos \theta$$

$$\tfrac{1}{2}v^2 = d(g \sin \theta + \mu_k g \cos \theta)$$

$$d = v^2 / [2g(\sin \theta + \mu_k \cos \theta)]$$

$$d = (63 \text{ m/s})^2 / [(2) \cdot (9.8 \text{ m/s}^2) \cdot (\sin 30° + 0.3 \times \cos 30°)]$$

$$d = 267 \text{ m}$$

$$h = d \sin \theta$$

$$h = (267 \text{ m}) \sin 30° = 130 \text{ m}$$

34. A is correct.

$F = ma$

$a = F / m$

$a_1 = F / 4 \text{ kg}$

$a_2 = F / 10 \text{ kg}$

$4a_1 = 10a_2$

$a_1 = 2.5a_2$

35. E is correct. The acceleration of the 2 kg block is the acceleration of the system because the blocks are linked together. Balance forces and solve for acceleration:

$F_{net} = m_3g - m_2g\mu_k - m_1g$

$(m_3 + m_2 + m_1)a = m_3g - m_2g\mu_k - m_1g$

$a = (m_3 - m_2\mu_k - m_1)g / (m_3 + m_2 + m_1)$

$a = [3 \text{ kg} - (2 \text{ kg}){\cdot}(0.25) - 1 \text{ kg}]{\cdot}(9.8 \text{ m/s}^2) / (3 \text{ kg} + 2 \text{ kg} + 1 \text{ kg})$

$a = 2.5 \text{ m/s}^2$

36. A is correct. Newton's Third Law describes that any time one object pushes on another, the second object pushes right back with the same force. Mathematically, it can be expressed as:

$F_{AonB} = -F_{BonA}$

In the described scenario, the force that the truck exerts on the car is in the opposite direction to the force that the car exerts on the truck (since they push on each other) and, crucially, the *magnitudes* of the two forces are the same.

This may seem counterintuitive, since it is known that the car will get far more damaged than the truck. To understand this apparent contradiction, remember Newton's Second Law which states that the car will *accelerate* at a much higher rate (since it is less massive than the truck). It is this extreme acceleration that causes the car to be completely destroyed.

Therefore, to understand this situation fully, two Newton's laws must be applied: The Third Law, which states that each vehicle experiences a force of the same magnitude, and The Second Law, which describes why the car *responds* to that force more violently due to its smaller mass.

37. D is correct.

$m = F / a_{Earth}$

$m = 20 \text{ N} / 3 \text{ m/s}^2$

$m = 6.67 \text{ kg}$

$F_{Moon} = mg_{Moon}$

$F_{Moon} = (6.67 \text{ kg}){\cdot}(1.62 \text{ m/s}^2)$

$F_{Moon} = 11 \text{ N}$

38. B is correct.

Pythagorean Theorem ($a^2 + b^2 = c^2$) to calculate the net force:

$$F_1^2 + F_2^2 = F_{net}^2$$

$$(500\ N)^2 + (1{,}200\ N)^2 = F_{net}^2$$

$$250{,}000\ N^2 + 1{,}440{,}000\ N^2 = F_{net}^2$$

$$F_{net}^2 = 1{,}690{,}000\ N^2$$

$$F_{net} = 1{,}300\ N$$

Newton's Second Law:

$$F = ma$$

$$a = F_{net} / m$$

$$a = 1{,}300\ N / 500\ kg$$

$$a = 2.6\ m/s^2$$

39. B is correct.

Need an expression which connects time and mass.

Given information for F, v_1, and d:

$$a = F / m$$

$$d = v_1 t + \tfrac{1}{2} a t^2$$

Combine the expressions and set $v_i = 0$ m/s because initial velocity is zero:

$$d = \tfrac{1}{2} a t^2$$

$$a = F / m$$

$$d = \tfrac{1}{2} (F / m) t^2$$

$$t^2 = 2dm / F$$

$$t = \sqrt{(2dm / F)}$$

If m increases by a factor of 4, t increases by a factor of $\sqrt{4} = 2$

40. C is correct.

$$a = (v_f^2 - v_i^2) / 2d$$

$$a = [(0\ m/s)^2 - (27\ m/s)^2] / 2(578\ m)$$

$$a = (-729\ m^2/s^2) / 1{,}056\ m$$

$$a = -0.63\ m/s^2$$

$$F = ma$$

$$F = (1{,}100\ kg) \cdot (-0.63\ m/s^2)$$

$$F = -690\ N$$

The car is decelerating, so the acceleration (and therefore the force) is negative.

41. A is correct. Constant speed upward means no net force.

Tension = weight (equals Mg)

42. C is correct.

    Weight = mg

    75 N = mg

    m = 75 N / 9.8 m/s^2

    m = 7.65 kg

    $F_{net} = F_{right} - F_{left}$

    F_{net} = 50 N – 30 N

    F_{net} = 20 N

    $F_{net} = ma$

    $a = F_{net} / m$

    a = 20 N / 7.65 kg

    a = 2.6 m/s^2

43. B is correct. The string was traveling at the same velocity as the plane with respect to the ground outside. When the plane began accelerating backward (decelerating), the string continued to move forward at its original velocity and appeared to go towards the front of the plane.

Since the string is attached to the ceiling at one end, only the bottom of the string moved.

44. C is correct. If the object slides down the ramp with a constant speed, velocity is constant.

Acceleration and the net force = 0

    $F_{net} = F_{grav\ down\ ramp} - F_{friction}$

    $F_{net} = mg \sin \theta - \mu_k mg \cos \theta$

    $F_{net} = 0$

    $mg \sin \theta - \mu_k mg \cos \theta = 0$

    $mg \sin \theta = \mu_k mg \cos \theta$

    $\mu_k = \sin \theta / \cos \theta$

45. A is correct. The net force on an object in free fall is equal to its weight.

46. D is correct. The scale measures the force of interaction between the person and the floor, the normal force. The question asks to find the normal force.

Use Newton's Second Law:

    $F = ma$,

where the net force is the result of the force of gravity and the normal force.

$$F_{net} = F_{normal} - F_{gravity} = N - W$$

Here, W is the normal weight of the object, $W = mg$. Therefore, Newton's Law becomes:

$$N - W = ma = (W / g) a$$

Solve for the reading of the scale, N, noting that the acceleration is negative:

$$N = W (1 + a / g)$$

$$N = (600 \text{ N}) \cdot (1 + -6 \text{ m/s}^2 / 9.8 \text{ m/s}^2)$$

$$N = (600 \text{ N}) \cdot (0.388)$$

$$N = 233 \text{ N}$$

47. E is correct. Since the object does not move, it is in a state of equilibrium, so there are forces acting on it that equal and oppose the force F that Yania applies to the object.

48. E is correct. Newton's Third Law describes that any time one object pushes on another, the second object pushes right back with the same force. Mathematically, it can be expressed as:

$$F_{AonB} = -F_{BonA}$$

In this situation, this means if one pushes on an object with force F, the object must push back on them equally strongly (magnitude is F) and in the opposite direction (hence the negative sign); therefore, the force vector of the object is just $-F$.

49. B is correct.

Arrow in flight:

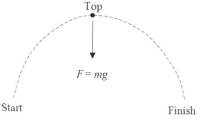

The weight of the arrow is:

$$W = mg$$

At the top of its flight and throughout its flight, the acceleration of gravity acts on the arrow:

$$F = ma$$

$$F = mg$$

$$F = W$$

50. A is correct. $m_{Bob} = 4m_{Sarah}$

Conservation of momentum, since the system (Bob and Sarah combined) initially had total momentum of 0, in the final state Sarah's momentum and Bob's momentum must add to 0 (i.e., they will be the same magnitude, but opposite directions):

$$m_{Bob}v_{Bob} = m_{Sarah}v_{Sarah}$$

$$4m_{Sarah} \, v_{Bob} = m_{Sarah}v_{Sarah}$$

$$4v_{Bob} = v_{Sarah}$$

Equilibrium and Momentum – Explanations

1. A is correct.

The rate of change of angular momentum of a system is equal to the net external torque:

$$\tau_{net} = \Delta L \,/\, \Delta t$$

If the angular momentum is constant, then the net external torque must be zero.

2. D is correct.

If the velocity is 7 m/s down the mountain, the horizontal component v_x is:

$$v_x = v \cos \theta$$

$$1.8 \text{ m/s} = (7 \text{ m/s}) \cos \theta$$

$$\cos \theta = 0.26$$

$$\theta \approx 75°$$

3. E is correct.

The hill exerts a normal force on the sled. However, this force is *perpendicular* to the surface of the hill. There is no parallel force that the hill exerts because it is frictionless.

4. C is correct.

Assuming that the water flow is tangent to the wheel, it is perpendicular to the radius vector at the point of contact.

The torque around the center of the wheel is:

$$\tau = rF$$

$$\tau = (10 \text{ m}){\cdot}(300 \text{ N})$$

$$\tau = 3,000 \text{ N·m}$$

5. E is correct.

$$1 \text{ revolution} = 360°, \; 1 \text{ min} = 60 \text{ s}$$

$$33 \text{ rpm} = 33 \text{ revs/min}$$

$$(33 \text{ revs/min}){\cdot}(360°/\text{rev}) = 11,880°/\text{min}$$

$$(11,880°/\text{min}){\cdot}(1 \text{ min}/60 \text{ s}) = 198°/\text{s}$$

Degrees per second is a *rate*:

$$\text{rate} \times \text{time} = \text{total degrees}$$

$$(198°/\text{s}){\cdot}(0.32 \text{ s}) \approx 63°$$

6. E is correct.

Conservation of momentum:

$$mv_i = mv_f + Mv$$

Conservation of energy:

$$\tfrac{1}{2}mv_i^2 = \tfrac{1}{2}mv_f^2 + \tfrac{1}{2}Mv^2$$

Rearranging this, the energy equation becomes:

$$m(v_i^2 - v_f^2) = Mv^2$$

Both M and v are unknown. As the question asks to find M, solving the momentum equation for v^2 eliminates v from this system of equations.

$$v^2 = (m\,/\,M)^2\,(v_i - v_f)^2$$

Putting this into the energy equation:

$$m(v_i^2 - v_f^2) = Mv^2 = M(m\,/\,M)^2\,(v_i - v_f)^2$$

$$(v_i^2 - v_f^2) = (m\,/\,M)\cdot(v_i - v_f)^2$$

Divide both sides by $(v_i - v_f)$:

$$(v_i + v_f) = (m\,/\,M)\cdot(v_i - v_f)$$

Solve for M:

$$M = m(v_i - v_f)\,/\,(v_i + v_f)$$

$$M = (2.2\ \text{kg})\cdot[(9.2\ \text{m/s}) - (-2.5\ \text{m/s})]\,/\,[(9.2\ \text{m/s}) + (-2.5\ \text{m/s})]$$

$$M = (2.2\ \text{kg})\cdot(11.7\ \text{m/s})\,/\,(6.7\ \text{m/s})$$

$$M = 3.8\ \text{kg}$$

7. D is correct.

The total momentum before the collision is:

$$p_{total} = m_I v_I + m_{II} v_{II} + m_{III} v_{III}$$

$$p_{before} = (1\ \text{kg})\cdot(0.5\ \text{m/s}) + (1.5\ \text{kg})\cdot(-0.3\ \text{m/s}) + (3.5\ \text{kg})\cdot(-0.5\ \text{m/s})$$

$$p_{before} = (0.5\ \text{kg·m/s}) + (-0.45\ \text{kg·m/s}) + (-1.75\ \text{kg·m/s})$$

$$p_{before} = -1.7\ \text{kg·m/s}$$

8. A is correct. The collision of I and II does not affect the momentum of the system:

$$p_{before} = p_{after}$$

$$p_{I\ \&\ II} = (1\ \text{kg})\cdot(0.5\ \text{m/s}) + (1.5\ \text{kg})\cdot(-0.3\ \text{m/s})$$

$$p_{I\ \&\ II} = (0.5\ \text{kg·m/s}) - (0.45\ \text{kg·m/s})$$

$$p_{I\ \&\ II} = 0.05\ \text{kg·m/s}$$

$$p_{III} = (3.5\ \text{kg})\cdot(-0.5\ \text{m/s})$$

$$p_{III} = -1.75\ \text{kg·m/s}$$

$$p_{net} = p_{I\ and\ II} + p_{III}$$

$$p_{net} = (0.05\ kg{\cdot}m/s) + (-1.75\ kg{\cdot}m/s)$$

$$p_{net} = -1.7\ kg{\cdot}m/s$$

Momentum is conserved at all times.

9. B is correct.

Set the initial momentum equal to the final momentum after all the collisions have occurred.

$$p_{before} = p_{after}$$

$$p_{before} = (m_I + m_{II} + m_{III})v_f$$

$$-1.7\ kg{\cdot}m/s = (1\ kg + 1.5\ kg + 3.5\ kg)v_f$$

$$v_f = (-1.7\ kg{\cdot}m/s)\ /\ (6\ kg)$$

$$v_f = -0.28\ m/s$$

10. C is correct.

Momentum is conserved in this system. The momentum of each car is given by mv, and the sum of the momenta before the collision must equal the sum of the momenta after the collision:

$$p_{before} = p_{after}$$

Solve for the velocity of the first car after the collision. Each car is traveling in the same direction before and after the collision, so each velocity value has the same sign.

$$m_1v_{i1} + m_2v_{i2} = m_1v_{f1} + m_2v_{f2}$$

$$(480\ kg){\cdot}(14.4\ m/s) + (570\ kg){\cdot}(13.3\ m/s) = (480\ kg){\cdot}(v_{f2}) + (570\ kg){\cdot}(17.9\ m/s)$$

$$(480\ kg){\cdot}(v_{f2}) = (480\ kg){\cdot}(14.4\ m/s) + (570\ kg){\cdot}(13.3\ m/s) - (570\ kg){\cdot}(17.9\ m/s)$$

$$v_{f2} = [(480\ kg){\cdot}(14.4\ m/s) + (570\ kg){\cdot}(13.3\ m/s) - (570\ kg){\cdot}(17.9\ m/s)]\ /\ (480\ kg)$$

$$v_{f2} = 8.9\ m/s \approx 9\ m/s$$

11. E is correct.

Impulse is a force acting over a period of time:

$$J = F\Delta t$$

An impulse changes a system's momentum, so:

$$F\Delta t = \Delta p_{system}$$

The moving block with the lodged bullet comes to a stop when it compresses the spring, losing all momentum.

The initial velocity of the block and bullet separately can be determined by conservation of energy. The two values of interest are the KE of the block and bullet and the PE of the spring.

$$(KE + PE)_{before} = (KE + PE)_{after}$$

$$\tfrac{1}{2}mv^2 + 0 = 0 + \tfrac{1}{2}kx^2$$

x = distance of compression of the spring

k = spring constant

½(4 kg + 0.008 kg)v^2 = ½(1,400 N/m)·(0.089 m)^2

v^2 = (1,400 N/m)·(0.089 m)^2 / (4.008 kg)

v^2 = 2.76 m^2/s^2

v = 1.66 m/s

Thus, the block with the lodged bullet hits the spring with an initial velocity of 1.66 m/s.

Since there is no friction, the block is sent in the opposite direction with the same speed of 1.66 m/s when the spring decompresses. Calculate the momentum, with initial momentum toward the spring and final momentum away from the spring.

$\Delta p = p_{final} - p_{initial}$

Δp = (4.008 kg)·(−1.66 m/s) − (4.008 kg)·(1.66 m/s)

Δp = (−6.65 kg·m/s) − (6.65 kg·m/s)

$\Delta p \approx -13$ kg·m/s

$\Delta p \approx -13$ N·s

Since $F\Delta t = \Delta p$, the impulse is also −13 kg·m/s = −13 N·s

The negative sign signifies the coordinate system chosen in this calculation: toward the spring is the positive direction, and away from the spring is the negative direction.

12. C is correct. For a rotating body, kinetic energy is:

$K = ½ I \omega^2$

Angular momentum is:

$L = I \omega$

Therefore:

$I = L / \omega$

Replacing this for I in the expression for kinetic energy:

$K = L^2 / 2I$

Taking the ice to be frictionless, there is no external torque on the skater. Thus, angular momentum is conserved and does not change as she brings in her arms. The moment of inertia of a body of a given mass is smaller if its mass is more concentrated toward the rotation axis (e.g., when she draws her arms in close). Therefore, the moment of inertia of the skater decreases. Consequently, the skater's kinetic energy increases.

13. D is correct.

The centripetal force is the net force required to maintain an object in uniform circular motion.

$F_{centripetal} = mv^2/r$

where r is the radius of the circular path

Since m is constant and r remains unchanged, the centripetal force is proportional to v^2.

$2^2 = 4$

Thus, if v is doubled, then $F_{\text{centripetal}}$ is quadrupled.

14. B is correct. $1\ \text{J} = \text{kg·m}^2/\text{s}^2$

$p = mv = \text{kg·m/s}$

$\text{J·s/m} = (\text{kg·m}^2/\text{s}^2)\cdot(\text{s/m})$

$\text{J·s/m} = \text{kg·m/s}$

$\text{kg·m/s} = p$

$\text{J·s/m} = p$

15. E is correct. Impulse is a change in momentum.

$J = \Delta p$

$J = m\Delta v$

Impulse is also the product of average force and time.

$J = F\Delta t$

$F\Delta t = m\Delta v$

$ma\Delta t = m\Delta v$, cancel m from both sides of the expression

$a\Delta t = \Delta v$

Because acceleration g is constant impulse depends only upon time and velocity.

The speed of the apple affects the impulse as this is included in the Δv term.

Bouncing results in a change in direction. This means a greater change in velocity (the Δv term), so the impulse is greater.

The time of impulse changes the impulse as it is included in the Δt term.

16. D is correct.

$F\Delta t = m\Delta v$

$F = m\Delta v\ /\ \Delta t$

Choosing toward the wall as the positive direction, the initial velocity is 25 m/s and the final velocity is –25 m/s:

$F = m(v_{\text{f}} - v_{\text{i}})\ /\ \Delta t$

$F = (0.8\ \text{kg})\cdot(-25\ \text{m/s} - 25\ \text{m/s})\ /\ (0.05\ \text{s})$

$F = -800\ \text{N}$

Thus, the wall exerts an average force of 800 N on the ball in the negative direction. From Newton's Third Law, the ball exerts a force of 800 N on the wall in the opposite direction.

17. B is correct.

$$p = mv$$

Sum momentum:

$$p_{total} = m_1v_1 + m_2v_2 + m_3v_3$$

All objects moving to the left have negative velocity.

$$p_{total} = (7 \text{ kg}) \cdot (6 \text{ m/s}) + (12 \text{ kg}) \cdot (3 \text{ m/s}) + (4 \text{ kg}) \cdot (-2 \text{ m/s})$$

$$p_{total} = (42 \text{ kg·m/s}) + (36 \text{ kg·m/s}) + (-8 \text{ kg·m/s})$$

$$p_{total} = 70 \text{ kg·m/s}$$

18. E is correct.

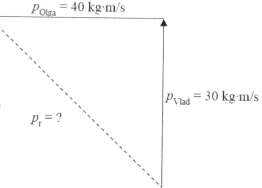

Use conservation of momentum to determine the momentum after the collision. Since they stick together, treat it as a perfectly inelastic collision.

Before the collision, Vladimir's momentum is: (60 kg)·(0.5 m/s) = 30 kg·m/s pointing North

Before the collision, Olga's momentum is:

(40 kg)·(1 m/s) = 40 kg·m/s pointing West

Write two expressions: one for conservation of momentum on the y-axis (North-South) and one for conservation of momentum on the x-axis (East-West). They do not interact since they are perpendicular to each other. Since Olga and Vladimir stick together, the final mass is the sum of their masses.

Simply use the Pythagorean Theorem:

$$a^2 + b^2 = c^2$$

$$(30 \text{ kg·m/s})^2 + (40 \text{ kg·m/s})^2 = p^2$$

$$900 \text{ (kg·m/s)}^2 + 1{,}600 \text{ (kg·m/s)}^2 = p^2$$

$$2{,}500 \text{(kg·m/s)}^2 = p^2$$

$$p = 50 \text{ kg·m/s}$$

Use this to solve for velocity:

$$p = mv$$

$$50 \text{ kg·m/s} = (100 \text{ kg})v$$

$$v = 50 \text{ kg·m/s} / 100 \text{ kg}$$

$$v = 0.5 \text{ m/s}$$

Also, this problem can be solved algebraically:

$$p_{before} = p_{after}$$

$$p = mv$$

On the y coordinate:

$$(60 \text{ kg}) \cdot (0.5 \text{ m/s}) = (60 \text{ kg} + 40 \text{ kg})v_y$$

$$v_y = (30 \text{ kg·m/s}) / (100 \text{ kg})$$

$$v_y = 0.3 \text{ m/s}$$

On the x coordinate:

$$(40 \text{ kg}) \cdot (1 \text{ m/s}) = (60 \text{ kg} + 40 \text{ kg})v_x$$

$$v_x = (40 \text{ kg·m/s}) / (100 \text{ kg})$$

$$v_x = 0.4 \text{ m/s}$$

Combine these final velocity components using the Pythagorean Theorem since they are perpendicular.

$$v^2 = v_x^2 + v_y^2$$

$$v^2 = (0.4 \text{ m/s})^2 + (0.3 \text{ m/s})^2$$

$$v = 0.5 \text{ m/s}$$

19. B is correct.

Use conservation of momentum to determine the momentum after the collision. Since they stick together, treat it as a perfectly inelastic collision.

Before collision, Vladimir's momentum is $(60 \text{ kg}) \cdot (0.5 \text{ m/s}) = 30 \text{ kg·m/s}$ pointing North

Before collision, Olga's momentum is $(40 \text{ kg}) \cdot (1 \text{ m/s}) = 40 \text{ kg·m/s}$ pointing West

Write two expressions: one for conservation of momentum on the y coordinate (North-South) and one for conservation of momentum on the x coordinate (East-West). They do not interact since they are perpendicular to each other. Since they stick together, the final mass is the sum of their masses.

Simply use the Pythagorean Theorem:

$$a^2 + b^2 = c^2$$

$$(30 \text{ kg·m/s})^2 + (40 \text{ kg·m/s})^2 = p^2$$

$$900 (\text{kg·m/s})^2 + 1{,}600 (\text{kg·m/s})^2 = p^2$$

$$2{,}500 (\text{kg·m/s})^2 = p^2$$

$$p = 50 \text{ kg·m/s}$$

This problem can also be solved algebraically:

$$p_{before} = p_{after}$$

$$p = mv$$

On the y coordinate:

$$(60 \text{ kg}) \cdot (0.5 \text{ m/s}) = (60 \text{ kg} + 40 \text{ kg})v_y$$

$$v_y = (30 \text{ kg·m/s}) / (100 \text{ kg})$$

$$v_y = 0.3 \text{ m/s}$$

On the x coordinate:

$$(40 \text{ kg}) \cdot (1 \text{ m/s}) = (60 \text{ kg} + 40 \text{ kg}) v_x$$

$$v_x = (40 \text{ kg·m/s}) / (100 \text{ kg})$$

$$v_x = 0.4 \text{ m/s}$$

Combine these final velocity components using the Pythagorean Theorem since they are perpendicular:

$$v^2 = v_x{}^2 + v_y{}^2$$

$$v^2 = (0.4 \text{ m/s})^2 + (0.3 \text{ m/s})^2$$

$$v = 0.5 \text{ m/s}$$

Use the final weight and final velocity to find the final momentum directly after the collision:

$$p = mv$$

$$p = (60 \text{ kg} + 40 \text{ kg}) \cdot (0.5 \text{ m/s})$$

$$p = 50 \text{ kg·m/s}$$

20. C is correct.

$$p_0 = mv$$

If m and v are doubled:

$$p = (2m) \cdot (2v)$$

$$p = 4mv$$

$$p = 4p_0$$

The momentum increases by a factor of 4.

21. D is correct. Balance forces on box Q to solve for tension on box P cable:

$$m_Q a = F - T_P$$

$$T_P = F - m_Q a$$

$$0 < T_P < F$$

Thus the tension on the cable connected to box P is less than F because it is equal to the difference of F and $m_Q a$ but is not equal because the boxes are accelerating.

22. B is correct.

At all points on a rotating body the angular velocity is equal. The speed at different points along a rotating body is directly proportional to the radius.

$$v = \omega r$$

where v = speed, ω = angular velocity and r = radius

Thus Melissa and her friend have different speeds due to their different radial locations.

23. A is correct.

Impulse is directly proportional to force and change in time:

$$J = F\Delta t$$

Increasing the change in time lowers the impact force, while decreasing the change in time increases the force.

24. E is correct.

Angular momentum is always conserved unless a system experiences a net torque greater than zero. This is the rotational equivalent of Newton's First Law of motion.

25. D is correct.

$$F\Delta t = m\Delta v$$

$$F = (m\Delta v) / (\Delta t)$$

$$F = (6.8 \text{ kg})\cdot(-3.2 \text{ m/s} - 5.4 \text{ m/s}) / (2 \text{ s})$$

$$F = (-58.48 \text{ kg}\cdot\text{m/s}) / (2 \text{ s})$$

$$F = -29.2 \text{ N}$$

$$| F | = 29.2 \text{ N}$$

26. A is correct.

Before collision, the total momentum of the system = 0 kg·m/s.

Momentum is conserved in the explosion.

The momentum of the moving rifle and bullet are in opposite directions:

Therefore, $p = 0$

The total momentum after the explosion = 0 kg·m/s

27. E is correct. $p = mv$

Conservation of momentum:

$$p_{initial} = p_{final}$$

$$0 \text{ kg}\cdot\text{m/s} = (0.01 \text{ kg})\cdot(300 \text{ m/s}) + (4 \text{ kg})v_{recoil}$$

$$0 \text{ kg}\cdot\text{m/s} = 3 \text{ kg}\cdot\text{m/s} + (4 \text{ kg})v_{recoil}$$

$$-3 \text{ kg}\cdot\text{m/s} = (4 \text{ kg})v_{recoil}$$

$$(-3 \text{ kg}\cdot\text{m/s}) / (4 \text{ kg}) = v_{recoil}$$

$$v_{recoil} = -0.75 \text{ m/s}$$

Velocity is negative since the gun recoils in the opposite direction of the bullet.

28. C is correct. Since the initial velocity only has a horizontal component, the y component of the initial velocity $= 0$.

Use 24 m to calculate the time the ball is in the air:

$$d_y = \frac{1}{2}at^2$$

$$t^2 = 2d_y / a$$

$$t^2 = 2(24 \text{ m}) / (9.8 \text{ m/s}^2)$$

$$t^2 = 4.89 \text{ s}^2$$

$$t = 2.21 \text{ s}$$

Use the time in the air and the horizontal distance to calculate the horizontal speed of the ball:

$$v_x = d_x / t$$

$$v_x = (18 \text{ m}) / (2.21 \text{ s})$$

$$v_x = 8.1 \text{ m/s}$$

29. D is correct.

The percentage of energy lost is:

$$p = [(E_{\text{initial}} - E_{\text{final}}) / E_{\text{initial}}] \times 100\%$$

The initial energy is the kinetic energy of the 3.3 kg object:

$$E_{in} = \frac{1}{2} m_1 v_1^2$$

The final kinetic energy is found from the speed and mass of the two objects stuck together:

$$E_f = \frac{1}{2} (m_1 + m_2)v_2^2$$

We can express v_2 in terms of v_1 through conservation of momentum:

$$m_1 v_1 = (m_1 + m_2)v_2$$

or:

$$v_2 = v_1[m_1 / (m_1 + m_2)]$$

Therefore:

$$E_f = \frac{1}{2} (m_1 + m_2)v_2^2$$

$$E_f = \frac{1}{2} (m_1 + m_2)v_1^2[m_1 / m_1 + m_2)]^2$$

$$E_f = \frac{1}{2} m_1 v_1^2[m_2 / (m_1 + m_2)]$$

$$E_i - E_f = \frac{1}{2} m_1 v_1^2[1 - m_1 / (m_1 + m_2)]$$

$$E_i - E_f = \frac{1}{2} m_1 v_1^2[m_2 / (m_1 + m_2)]$$

Finally resulting in:

$$p = [m_2 / (m_1 + m_2)] \times 100\%$$

$$p = [3.6 \text{ kg} / (3.3 \text{ kg} + 3.6 \text{ kg})] \times 100\%$$

$$p = 52\%$$

30. B is correct.

Impulse:

$$J = F\Delta t$$

$$J = \Delta p$$

where p is momentum

31. C is correct.

Conservation of energy:

$$KE_i + PE_i = KE_f + PE_f$$

$$KE_i + PE_i = KE_f + 0$$

$$KE_f = \tfrac{1}{2}mv_i^2 + mgh_i$$

$$KE_f = \tfrac{1}{2}(4 \text{ kg}){\cdot}(20 \text{ m/s})^2 + (4 \text{ kg}){\cdot}(10 \text{ m/s}^2){\cdot}(10 \text{ m})$$

$$KE_f = 800 \text{ J} + 400 \text{ J}$$

$$KE_f = 1{,}200 \text{ J}$$

32. E is correct.

The force needed to stop a car can be related to KE and work:

$$KE = W$$

$$\tfrac{1}{2}mv^2 = Fd$$

$$F = \tfrac{1}{2}mv^2 \,/\, d$$

Momentum is included in the KE term.

$$p = mv$$

$$F = \tfrac{1}{2}(mv)v \,/\, d$$

$$F = \tfrac{1}{2}(p)v \,/\, d$$

If there is less stopping distance the force increases as they are inversely proportional.

If the momentum or mass increase the force increases as they are directly proportional.

33. C is correct.

Impulse:

$$J = F\Delta t$$

Based on Newton's Third Law, the force experienced by these two objects is equal and opposite.

Therefore, the magnitudes of impulse are the same.

34. B is correct.

Balance the counterclockwise (CCW) torque with the clockwise (CW) torque. Let the axis of rotation be at the point where the rope attaches to the bar. This placement causes the torque from the rope to be zero since the lever arm is zero.

$$\Sigma \tau : \tau_1 - \tau_2 = 0$$

$$\tau_1 = \tau_2$$

The CCW torque due to the weight of the 6 kg mass:

$$\tau = r_1 F_1$$

$$r_1 F_1 = (x) \cdot (6 \text{ kg}) \cdot (9.8 \text{ m/s}^2)$$

The CW torque due to the weight of the 30 kg mass:

$$r_2 F_2 = (5 \text{ m} - x) \cdot (30 \text{ kg}) \cdot (9.8 \text{ m/s}^2)$$

Set the two expressions equal to each other

$$(9.8 \text{ m/s}^2) \cdot (x) \cdot (6 \text{ kg}) = (5 \text{ m} - x) \cdot (30 \text{ kg}) \cdot (9.8 \text{ m/s}^2)$$

Cancel g and kg from each side of the equation:

$$6x = 30(5 \text{ m} - x)$$

$$6x = 150 \text{ m} - 30x$$

$$36x = 150 \text{ m}$$

$$x = 4.2 \text{ m}$$

35. E is correct.

If the block is at rest then the force of static friction is equal to the force of gravity at angle θ.

$$F_f = mg \sin \theta$$

36. C is correct.

$F_{net} = 0$ is necessary to maintain constant velocity.

If 45 N must be exerted on the block to maintain constant velocity, the force due to kinetic friction against the block equals 45 N.

For a horizontal surface and no other vertical forces acting, the normal force on the block equals its weight.

$$N = mg$$

$$F_{friction} = \mu_k N$$

$$F_{friction} = \mu_k mg$$

$$\mu_k = (F_{friction}) / mg$$

$$\mu_k = (45 \text{ N}) / [(30 \text{ kg}) \cdot (10 \text{ m/s}^2)]$$

$$\mu_k = 0.15$$

37. B is correct.

Newton's Second Law:

$$F = ma$$

The impulse-momentum relationship can be derived by multiplying Δt on both sides:

$$F\Delta t = ma\Delta t$$

$$F\Delta t = m\Delta v$$

$$J = m\Delta v$$

Thus, the impulse is equal to the change in momentum.

38. C is correct.

Force X acts perpendicular to the short arm of the rectangle, this is the lever arm.

$$\tau = rF$$

$$\tau = (0.5 \text{ m}) \cdot (15 \text{ N})$$

$$\tau = 7.5 \text{ N·m}$$

Since the torque causes the plate to rotate clockwise its sign is negative.

$$\tau = -7.5 \text{ N·m}$$

39. E is correct.

$$\tau = rF$$

Force Z acts directly at the pivot so the lever arm equals zero.

$$\tau = (0 \text{ m}) \cdot (30 \text{ N})$$

$$\tau = 0 \text{ N·m}$$

40. A is correct.

$$\tau = rF$$

Force Y acts perpendicular to the long arm of the rectangle, this is the lever arm.

$$\tau = (0.6 \text{ m}) \cdot (25 \text{ N})$$

$$\tau = 15 \text{ N·m}$$

The torque is clockwise, so its sign is negative.

$$\tau = -15 \text{ N·m}$$

41. B is correct.

The tension in the string provides the centripetal force.

$T = mv^2 / r$

$m = 50 \text{ g} = 0.05 \text{ kg}$

$T = [(0.05 \text{ kg}) \cdot (20 \text{ m/s})^2] / (2 \text{ m})$

$T = [(0.05 \text{ kg}) \cdot (400 \text{ m}^2/\text{s}^2)] / (2 \text{ m})$

$T = (20 \text{ kg} \cdot \text{m}^2/\text{s}^2) / (2 \text{ m})$

$T = 10 \text{ N}$

42. A is correct. Newton's Third Law states that each force is paired with an equal and opposite reaction force. Therefore, the small car and the truck each receive the same force.

43. C is correct. Choose the axis of rotation at the point where the bar attaches to the wall. Since the lever arm of the force that the wall exerts is zero, the torque at that point is zero and can be ignored.

The two other torques present arise from the weight of the bar exerting force downward and the cable exerting force upward. The weight of the bar acts at the center of mass, so its lever arm is 1 m. The lever arm for the cable is 2 m, since it acts the full 2 m away from the wall at the end of the bar.

Torque is the product of the length of the lever arm and the component of force perpendicular to the arm. The torque applied by the wire is:

$F_T l \sin \theta$

The sum of torques = 0, since the bar is in rotational equilibrium.

Let the torque of the cable be positive and the torque of the weight be negative.

$(F_T \sin 30°) \cdot (2 \text{ m}) - (10 \text{ kg}) \cdot (10 \text{ m/s}^2) \cdot (1 \text{ m}) = 0$

$F_T = [(10 \text{ kg}) \cdot (10 \text{ m/s}^2) \cdot (1 \text{ m})] / [(2 \text{ m}) \cdot (\sin 30°)]$

$F_T = [(10 \text{ kg}) \cdot (10 \text{ m/s}^2) \cdot (1 \text{ m})] / [(2 \text{ m}) \cdot (0.5)]$

$F_T = 100 \text{ N}$

44. B is correct.

Momentum is defined as:

$p = mv$

$m_A = 2m_B$

$p_A = 2m_B v$

$p_B = m_B v$

$p_A = 2p_B$

If both objects reach the ground at the same time they have equal velocities.

However, because A is twice the mass, it has twice the momentum as object B.

45. D is correct.

Use conservation of momentum to make equations for momenta along the *x*-axis and the *y*-axis. Since the mass ratio is 1 : 4, one car has a mass of *m* and the other has a mass of 4*m*. The entangled cars after the collision have a combined mass of 5*m*.

Let the car of mass *m* be traveling in the positive *x* direction and the car of mass 4*m* be traveling in the positive *y* direction. The choice of directions here is arbitrary, but the angle of impact is important.

$p_{\text{initial}} = p_{\text{final}}$ for both the *x*- and *y*-axes

$p = mv$

For the *x*-axis:

$m_i v_i = m_f v_{fx}$

$m(12\ \text{m/s}) = 5mv_x$, cancel *m*

$12\ \text{m/s} = 5v_x$

$v_x = 2.4\ \text{m/s}$

For the *y*-axis:

$m_i v_i = m_f v_{fy}$

$4m(12\ \text{m/s}) = 5mv_y$, cancel *m*

$4(12\ \text{m/s}) = 5v_y$

$v_y = 9.6\ \text{m/s}$

The question asks for the magnitude of the final velocity, so combine the *x* and *y* components of the final velocity using the Pythagorean Theorem.

$v^2 = (2.4\ \text{m/s})^2 + (9.6\ \text{m/s})^2$

$v^2 = 5.76\ \text{m}^2/\text{s}^2 + 92.16\ \text{m}^2/\text{s}^2$

$v = 9.9\ \text{m/s}$

46. C is correct. Use conservation of momentum on the horizontal plane. Before the throw, the total momentum of the skater-ball system is zero. Thus, after the throw, the total horizontal momentum must sum to zero: the horizontal component of the ball's momentum equals the momentum of the skater moving the opposite way.

Use m_s for the skater's mass and $m_s/3$ for the ball's mass.

$p = mv$

$p_{\text{skater}} = p_{\text{ball}}$

$m_s v_s = m_b v_b$

$m_s(2.9\ \text{m/s}) = (1/3)m_s v \cos 5°$, cancel *m*

$v = (2.9\ \text{m/s}) \cdot (3) / (\cos 5°)$

$v = (2.9\ \text{m/s}) \cdot (3) / (0.996)$

$v = 8.73\ \text{m/s}$

47. B is correct.

weight = mass × gravity

$W = mg$

$m = W / g$

$m = (98 \text{ N}) / (9.8 \text{ m/s}^2)$

$m = 10 \text{ kg}$

Newton's Second Law:

$F = ma$

$F = (10 \text{ kg}){\cdot}(10 \text{ m/s}^2)$

$F = 100 \text{ N}$

48. A is correct.

KE is constant because speed is constant.

PE increases because the cart is at a greater height at point B.

The cart as a system is not isolated since the winch does work on it and so its energy is not conserved.

Conservation of energy: PE increase of the cart = work done by the winch

49. D is correct.

The vertical component of the initial velocity:

$v_{iy} = (140 \text{ m/s}) \sin 35°$

$v_{iy} = (140 \text{ m/s}){\cdot}(0.57)$

$v_{iy} = 79.8 \text{ m/s}$

The initial velocity upward, time elapsed, and acceleration due to gravity is known.

Determine the final velocity after 4 s.

$v_y = v_{iy} + at$

$v_y = 79.8 \text{ m/s} + (-9.8 \text{ m/s}^2){\cdot}(4 \text{ s})$

$v_y = 41 \text{ m/s}$

50. C is correct.

impulse = force × time

$J = F\Delta t$

Rotational Motion – Explanations

1. D is correct. An object rolling down an incline experiences three forces, and hence three torques. The forces are the force of gravity acting on the center of mass of the object, the normal force between the incline and the object, and the force of friction between the incline and the object.

If the origin is taken to be the center of the object, the force of gravity provides zero torque. This can be seen by noting that the distance between the origin and the point of application of the force is zero. $\tau_{gravity} = F_{gravity}r = mg(0) = 0$. Similarly, the normal force contributes zero torque because the direction of the force is directly through the origin (pivot point). $\tau_{normal} = F_{normal} r \sin \theta = F_{normal}(R)(\sin 180°) = F_{normal}(R)(0) = 0$.

Use a coordinate system in which the *x*-axis is parallel to the incline and the *y*-axis is perpendicular. The object is rolling in the positive *x*-direction. The dynamical equation for linear motion along the *x*-direction is:

$F_{net} = ma$

$(mg \sin \theta - f) = ma$

Note that the normal force is only in the *y*-direction, and thus does not directly contribute to the acceleration in the *x*-direction. The dynamical equation for rotational motion is:

$\tau_{net} = I\alpha$

$fR = I\alpha$ (Note that the frictional force is perpendicular to the *r* vector, and $\sin 90° = 1$)

where *R* is the radius of the object, *f* is the force of friction, and *I* is the moment of inertia.

A relation coupling these two dynamical equations is needed. This is the equation of constraint imposed by the restriction that the object rolls without slipping:

$\alpha = a / R$

To find the linear acceleration, use the equation of constraint to eliminate α from the rotational equation by replacing it with *a / R*:

$fR = I(a / R)$

The force of friction is of no interest, so rearrange this last expression:

$f = Ia / R^2$

Substitute this into the linear dynamic equation from above in place of *f*:

$(mg \sin \theta - Ia / R^2) = ma$

Solving this for *a*:

$a = mg \sin \theta / [m + (I / R^2)]$

$a = g \sin \theta / [1 + (I / mR^2)$

The moment of inertia of any circular object can be written as NmR^2, where *N* is some real number that is different for different shapes. For example, for a sphere $I = (2/5)mR^2$, so for a sphere $N = 2/5$. So for any rolling object, the linear acceleration is:

$a = g \sin \theta / (1 + N)$, which depends on neither the radius nor the mass of the object.

Only the shape of the object is important.

2. B is correct.

Use conservation of energy. The initial and final states are the sphere at the top and bottom of the ramp, respectively. Take the zero of gravitational potential energy to be the configuration in which the sphere is at the bottom. The potential energy at the bottom is zero. The sphere starts from rest, so the kinetic energy at the top is zero. With that:

$$mgh = K_{\text{linear}} + K_{\text{rotation}}$$

$$mgh = \tfrac{1}{2}mv^2 + \tfrac{1}{2}I\omega^2$$

For a sphere, $I = (2/5)mr^2$. Because the sphere rolls without slipping, $v = r\omega$. Substituting these into the conservation of energy equation:

$$mgh = \tfrac{1}{2}mr^2\omega^2 + \tfrac{1}{2}(2/5)mr^2\omega^2$$

$$mgh = \tfrac{1}{2}mr^2\omega^2 + (2/10)mr^2\omega^2$$

$$mgh = (7/10)mr^2\omega^2$$

Isolating ω:

$$\omega = \sqrt{(10gh / 7r^2)}$$

$$\omega = \sqrt{[10 \cdot (9.8 \text{ m/s}^2) \cdot (5.3 \text{ m})] / [7 \cdot (1.7 \text{ m})^2]}$$

$$\omega = 5.1 \text{ rad/s}$$

3. A is correct.

There is no torque on the ball during the fall; therefore, its rotational speed does not change during the fall. Therefore, the rotational kinetic energy just before the ball hits the floor is the same as it was when it was rolling on the horizontal surface.

The rotational kinetic energy when it was rolling on the surface can be calculated directly. Recall that the moment of inertia of a solid sphere is $I = 2/5mR^2$.

$$K_{\text{rot}} = \tfrac{1}{2}I\omega^2$$

$$K_{\text{rot}} = \tfrac{1}{2}(2/5)mR^2\omega^2$$

Since the ball is rolling without slipping, $\omega = v / R$:

$$K_{\text{rot}} = \tfrac{1}{2}(2/5)mR^2(v / R)^2$$

$$K_{\text{rot}} = (2/10)mv^2$$

$$K_{\text{rot}} = (2/10)mv^2$$

$$K_{\text{rot}} = (2/10) \cdot (0.125 \text{ kg}) \cdot (4.5 \text{ m/s})^2$$

$$K_{\text{rot}} = 0.51 \text{ J}$$

4. D is correct.

The angular momentum of an object in circular motion is:

$$L = I\omega$$

where I is the moment of inertia with respect to the center of motion and ω is the angular speed.

The moment of inertia of a point mass is:

$$I = mr^2$$

The angular momentum is then:

$$L = mr^2\omega$$

Angular speed is in rev/s. Express in rad/s:

$$1.2 \text{ rev/s}\cdot(2\pi \text{ rad/rev}) = 7.540 \text{ rad/s}$$

Finally:

$$L = (0.38 \text{ kg})\cdot(1.3 \text{ m})^2\cdot(7.540 \text{ rad/s})$$

$$L = 4.8 \text{ kg m}^2/\text{s}$$

5. C is correct.

Conservation of angular momentum requires:

$$L_f = L_i$$

$$I_f\omega_f = I_i\omega_i$$

The final angular speed is:

$$\omega_f = \omega_i \, (I_i \, / \, I_f)$$

$$\omega_f = (3.0 \text{ rev/s})\cdot(5.0 \text{ kg}\cdot\text{m}^2) \, / \, (2.0 \text{ kg m}^2)$$

$$\omega_f = 7.5 \text{ rev/s}$$

6. C is correct. An external torque changes the angular velocity of a system ($\alpha = \sum\tau \, / \, I$), and hence its angular momentum. To maintain a constant angular momentum, the sum of external torques must be zero.

7. E is correct.

For a rotating circular object:

$$\omega = v \, / \, r$$

$$\omega = v \, / \, (d \, / \, 2)$$

$$\omega = (4.0 \text{ m/s}) \, / \, [(0.60 \text{ m}) \, / \, 2]$$

$$\omega = 13.3 \text{ rad/s}$$

8. A is correct.

$$K = \tfrac{1}{2}I\omega^2$$

The moment of inertia of a rod with respect to its "short axis" is $I = (1/12)ml^2$

$$K = (1/24)ml^2\omega^2$$

$$K = (1/24)\cdot(0.4500 \text{ kg})\cdot(1.20 \text{ m})^2\cdot(3.60 \text{ rad/s})^2$$

$$K = 0.350 \text{ J}$$

9. C is correct. The moment of inertia can be found from the dynamic relation:

$$\tau = I\alpha$$

$$I = \tau / \alpha$$

where τ is the torque applied to the pulley, and α is the pulley's angular acceleration.

The torque is defined as $FR \sin \theta$. In this case, the force F is the tension force from the rope, R is the radius of the wheel, and $\theta = 90°$. Thus, the torque is just the product of the tension of the rope and the radius of the pulley:

$$\tau = TR$$

The angular acceleration is related to the acceleration of a point on the circumference of the pulley:

$$\alpha = a / R$$

where a is the linear acceleration at the circumference, and R is the pulley's radius. Combining these two results, the moment of inertia is:

$$I = TR^2 / a$$

If the rope does not slip on the pulley, then the rope, and hence the hanging mass, also has acceleration a. To continue, find the acceleration and the tension.

The tension is found by applying Newton's Second Law to the hanging mass. There are two forces on the hanging mass, the force of gravity pointing down, and the tension of the rope pointing up. From Newton's Second Law (with down as the positive direction):

$$(mg - T) = ma$$

$$T = m(g - a)$$

With that, the moment of inertia becomes:

$$I = mR^2[(g - a) / a]$$

The acceleration can be found from the kinematic information given about the movement of the hanging mass. The relation needed is:

$$\Delta y = \tfrac{1}{2}a(\Delta t)^2 + v_0(\Delta t)$$

$$a = 2\Delta y / (\Delta t)^2 = 2\cdot(10 \text{ m}) / (2 \text{ s})^2 = 5.000 \text{ m/s}^2$$

Calculate the moment of inertia:

$$I = (14 \text{ kg})\cdot(2.0 \text{ m})^2\cdot[(9.8 \text{ m/s}^2 - 5.000 \text{ m/s}^2) / (5.000 \text{ m/s}^2)]$$

$$I = 53.76 \text{ kg}\cdot\text{m}^2$$

$$I = 53.8 \text{ kg}\cdot\text{m}^2$$

10. B is correct.

The final speed of the string can be found if the acceleration is known:

$$v_f^2 = v_i^2 + 2ad = 0 + 2ad$$

$$v_f = \sqrt{(2ad)}$$

where d is the distance over which the acceleration occurs.

The acceleration of the string is related to the acceleration of the pulley:

$$a = r\alpha$$

The angular acceleration follows from the dynamical equation for rotational motion:

$$\tau = I\alpha$$

The torque is the force applied times the radius of the pulley:

$$Fr = I\alpha$$

Combining these equations gives:

$$a = r^2 F / I$$

The final velocity of the string is:

$$v_f = \sqrt{(2r^2 Fd / I)}$$

$$v_f = \sqrt{[2 \cdot (0.125 \text{ m})^2 \cdot (5.00 \text{ N}) \cdot (1.25 \text{ m}) / (0.0352 \text{ kg} \cdot \text{m}^2)]}$$

$$v_f = 2.36 \text{ m/s}$$

11. A is correct.

The angle of every point remains fixed relative to all other points. The tangential acceleration increases as one moves away from the center ($a_t = \alpha r$). The radial (or centripetal) acceleration also depends on the distance r from the center ($a_c = \omega^2 r$). The only choice that does not depend on r (i.e., is the same for all the points in the object) is I.

12. E is correct.

Linear velocity is related to angular velocity by $v = r\omega$.

13. C is correct.

For a rotating object:

$$K = \tfrac{1}{2} I \omega^2$$

The moment of inertia of a cylinder is:

$$I = \tfrac{1}{2} m r^2$$

Combining these:

$$K = \tfrac{1}{4} m r^2 \omega^2$$

Solving for the angular speed:

$$\omega = \sqrt{(4K / m r^2)}$$

$$\omega = \sqrt{\{4 \cdot (3.2 \times 10^7 \text{ J}) / [(400.0 \text{ kg})(0.60 \text{ m})^2]\}}$$

$$\omega = 940 \text{ rad/s}$$

14. B is correct.

For a rotating object subject to a constant torque which has undergone a total angular displacement of $\Delta\theta$, the work done on the wheel is:

$$W = \tau\Delta\theta$$

Since work is the change in energy of the wheel from external forces, and since the wheel started with $E = 0$ ("from rest"), the final kinetic energy can be written as:

$$K = \tau\Delta\theta$$

By rotational kinematics:

$$\Delta\theta = \tfrac{1}{2}\alpha t^2$$

The equation of rotational dynamics is:

$$\tau = I\alpha, \text{ or } \alpha = \tau / I$$

So:

$$\Delta\theta = t^2\tau / 2I$$

and

$$K = t^2\tau^2 / 2I$$

(Note that this expression can be developed by finding the final angular velocity and using the definition of rotational kinetic energy.)

$$K = [(8.0 \text{ s})^2 \cdot (3.0 \text{ N} \cdot \text{m})^2] / [2 \cdot (5.0 \text{ kg} \cdot \text{m}^2)]$$

$$K = 58 \text{ J}$$

15. C is correct.

Tangential speed depends on the distance of the point from the fixed axis, so points at different radii have different tangential speeds. Angular speed and acceleration of a rigid object does not depend on radius, and is the same for all points (since each point on the object must rotate through the same angle in the same time interval, or else it would not be rigid).

16. D is correct.

The angular momentum of a rotating object is:

$$L = I\omega$$

For a cylinder, $I = \tfrac{1}{2}mr^2$, giving:

$$L = \tfrac{1}{2}mr^2\omega$$

$$L = (0.5) \cdot (15.0 \text{ kg}) \cdot (1.4 \text{ m})^2 \cdot (2.4 \text{ rad/s})$$

$$L = 35 \text{ kg m}^2/\text{s}$$

17. E is correct.

The speed of an accelerating object is related to the distance covered by the kinematic relation:

$$v_f^2 - v_i^2 = 2ad$$

In this case, the initial speed is zero, so:

$$v_f = \sqrt{(2ad)}$$

Thus, find the linear acceleration of the disk.

An object rolling down an incline experiences three forces, and hence three torques. The forces are the force of gravity acting on the center of mass of the object, the normal force between the incline and the object, and the force of friction between the incline and the object.

If the origin is taken to be the center of the object, the force of gravity provides zero torque. This can be seen by noting that the distance between the origin and the point of application of the force is zero. $\tau_{gravity} = F_{gravity}r = mg(0) = 0$. Similarly, the normal force contributes zero torque because the direction of the force is directly through the origin (pivot point). $\tau_{normal} = F_{normal}\, r \sin\theta = F_{normal}(R)(\sin 180°) = F_{normal}(R)(0) = 0$.

Use a coordinate system in which the *x*-axis is parallel to the incline and the *y*-axis is perpendicular. The object is rolling in the positive *x*-direction. The dynamical equation for linear motion along the *x*-direction is:

$$F_{net} = ma$$

$$(mg \sin\theta - f) = ma$$

Note that the normal force is only in the *y*-direction, and thus does not directly contribute to the acceleration in the *x*-direction. The dynamical equation for rotational motion is:

$$\tau_{net} = I\alpha$$

$$fR = I\alpha \quad \text{(Note that the frictional force is perpendicular to the } r \text{ vector, and } \sin 90° = 1)$$

where R is the radius of the object, f is the force of friction, and I is the moment of inertia.

A relation coupling these two dynamical equations is needed. This is the equation of constraint imposed by the restriction that the object rolls without slipping:

$$\alpha = a \,/\, R$$

To find the linear acceleration, use the equation of constraint to eliminate α from the rotational equation by replacing it with $a \,/\, R$:

$$fR = I(a \,/\, R)$$

The force of friction is of no interest, so rearrange this last expression:

$$f = Ia \,/\, R^2$$

Substitute this into the linear dynamic equation from above in place of f:

$$(mg \sin\theta - Ia \,/\, R^2) = ma$$

Solving this for a:

$$a = mg \sin\theta \,/\, [m + (I \,/\, R^2)]$$

$$a = g \sin\theta \,/\, [1 + (I \,/\, mR^2)]$$

For a disk, $I = \frac{1}{2}mR^2$, so:

$$a = g \sin \theta / (1 + \frac{1}{2}) = (2/3)g \sin \theta$$

Using this in the kinematic equation above:

$$v_f = \sqrt{(4gd \sin \theta / 3)}$$

$$v_f = \sqrt{[(4/3) \cdot (9.8 \text{ m/s}^2) \cdot (3.0 \text{ m}) \cdot \sin (25°)]}$$

$$v_f = \sqrt{[(4/3) \cdot (9.8 \text{ m/s}^2) \cdot (3.0 \text{ m}) \cdot (0.4226)]}$$

$$v_f = 4.1 \text{ m/s}$$

18. A is correct.

The center of the tire is moving at velocity v, but the bottom of the tire is in contact with the ground without slipping, so the speed at the bottom of the tire is 0 m/s. Thus, with respect to the ground, the tire is *instantaneously* rotating about the point of contact with the ground, and all points in the tire have the same instantaneous angular speed. The top of the tire is twice the distance from the ground as the center. For the center of the tire:

$$v = r\omega$$

At the top:

$$v_{top} = (2r)\omega = 2(r\omega) = 2v$$

19. D is correct.

The string does not slip. This means that the speed of the string is the same as the speed of a point on the circumference of the pulley. The angular speed of the pulley (radius R) and the speed of a point on its circumference are related be:

$$\omega = v / R$$

$$\omega = (5.0 \text{ m/s}) / (0.050 \text{ m})$$

$$\omega = 100 \text{ rad/s}$$

20. D is correct.

One way of expressing the magnitude of angular momentum is:

$$L = rp \sin \theta$$

where r is the magnitude of the object's absolute position vector, p is the magnitude of the object's linear momentum and θ is the angle between the position vector and the momentum vector.

The magnitude of the position vector is:

$$r = \sqrt{(r_x^2 + r_y^2)}$$

$$r = \sqrt{[(2.00 \text{ m})^2 + (3.10 \text{ m})^2]}$$

$$r = 3.689 \text{ m}$$

Its angle with respect to the positive x axis is:

$\theta_r = \operatorname{atan}(r_y / r_x)$

$\theta_r = \operatorname{atan}(3.10 / 2.00)$

$\theta_r = 57.17°$

The magnitude of the momentum vector is:

$p = mv$

$p = (1.4 \text{ kg})(4.62 \text{ m/s})$

$p = 6.468 \text{ kg·m/s}$

The angle of the momentum vector is given in the problem:

$\theta_p = 45°$

Thus, the angle between the two vectors is:

$\theta = \theta_r - \theta_p$

$\theta = 57.17° - 45°$

$\theta = 12.17°$

The angular momentum is then:

$L = (3.689 \text{ m})·(6.468 \text{ kg m/s})·\sin(12.17°)$

$L = 5.0 \text{ kg·m}^2\text{/s}$

21. B is correct. Average angular acceleration is defined by:

$\alpha_{avg} = \Delta\omega / \Delta t$

$\alpha_{avg} = |(6.3 \text{ rad/s} - 10.0 \text{ rad/s}) / (5.0 \text{ s})|$

$\alpha_{avg} = 0.74 \text{ rad/s}$

22. D is correct.

The kinematic equation for angular velocity is:

$\omega_f = \omega_i + \alpha\Delta t$

Note that the sign of angular velocity is opposite from the sign of angular acceleration. That means that the wheel is slowing down. In order for the final kinetic energy to be larger than the initial kinetic energy, the wheel must slow and continue beyond zero speed so that it gains speed in the opposite direction. That is, the final angular velocity must be negative.

The kinetic energy of a rotating wheel is:

$K = \frac{1}{2}I\omega^2$

The kinetic energy scales as the square of the angular speed. To double the kinetic energy, the angular speed must increase by a factor of $\sqrt{2}$. That is:

$\omega_f = -\omega_i\sqrt{2}$

Putting the result in the kinematic equation:

$$-\omega_i\sqrt{2} = \omega_i + \alpha\Delta t$$

Solving for Δt:

$$\Delta t = -(1 + \sqrt{2})\omega_i / \alpha)$$

$$\Delta t = -(1 + \sqrt{2})\cdot(26.0 \text{ rad/s}) / (-0.43 \text{ rad/s}^2)$$

$$\Delta t = 146 \text{ s}$$

23. B is correct.

Apply conservation of energy. Take the zero of gravitational potential energy to be the configuration when the disk is at the bottom of the ramp. Conservation of energy demands:

$$E_{\text{top}} = E_{\text{bottom}}$$

At the top of the ramp, the disk is at rest, so the kinetic energy is zero. The total energy at the top is:

$$E_{\text{top}} = K_{\text{top}} + U_{\text{top}}$$

$$E_{\text{top}} = 0 + mgh$$

At the bottom of the ramp, the gravitational potential energy is zero, and the kinetic energy is the sum of the linear and rotational kinetic energies:

$$E_{\text{bottom}} = K_{\text{bottom}} + U_{\text{bottom}}$$

$$E_{\text{bottom}} = K_{\text{linear}} + K_{\text{rotational}} + 0$$

$$E_{\text{bottom}} = \tfrac{1}{2}\,mv^2 + \tfrac{1}{2}\,I\omega^2$$

Final linear velocity is not given, but rather the final angular velocity is given. Eliminate the linear velocity in favor of the angular velocity by applying the constraint that applies to a circular object rolling without slipping.

$$v = \omega r$$

$$E_{\text{bottom}} = \tfrac{1}{2}m\omega^2 r^2 + \tfrac{1}{2}I\omega^2$$

The moment of inertia of a disk is:

$$I = \tfrac{1}{2}mr^2$$

Thus:

$$E_{\text{bottom}} = \tfrac{1}{2}m\omega^2 r^2 + \tfrac{1}{2}(\tfrac{1}{2}\,mr^2)\omega^2$$

$$E_{\text{bottom}} = \tfrac{1}{2}m\omega^2 r^2 + \tfrac{1}{4}mr^2\omega^2$$

$$E_{\text{bottom}} = \tfrac{3}{4}m\omega^2 r^2$$

Combining results into the expression for conservation of energy:

$$mgh = \tfrac{3}{4}m\omega^2 r^2$$

or

$$h = 3\omega^2 r^2 / 4g$$

Note that the mass has canceled, a common occurrence in mechanics problems. The chance of error is reduced by proceeding algebraically (rather than plugging in numbers in the beginning), by which mass can be cancelled out.

Finally, note that diameter is given, not the radius. $r = d / 2 = 1.6$ m

$$h = [3(4.27 \text{ rad/s})^2 \cdot (1.60 \text{ m})^2] / [4(9.8 \text{ m/s}^2)]$$

$$h = 3.57 \text{ m}$$

24. A is correct. The direction of angular velocity is taken by convention to be given by applying the right hand rule to the rotation. In the case of a wheel of a forward-moving bicycle, that direction is to the left of the rider.

25. A is correct. Angular acceleration can be found if linear acceleration is calculated from:

$$\alpha = a / R$$

The linear acceleration follows from the kinematic relationship:

$$v_f^2 - v_i^2 = 2ad$$

In this case, v_f is zero.

$$-v_i^2 = 2ad$$

Only the absolute value of the acceleration is needed, so drop the minus sign and solve for a:

$$a = v_i^2 / 2d$$

The angular acceleration is:

$$\alpha = v_i^2 / 2dR$$

$$\alpha = (8.4 \text{ m/s})^2 / [2(115.0 \text{ m})(0.34 \text{ m})]$$

$$\alpha = 0.90 \text{ rad/s}^2$$

26. A is correct.

For a rotating object:

$$K = \tfrac{1}{2}I\omega^2$$

The moment of inertia of a cylinder is:

$$I = \tfrac{1}{2}mr^2$$

Combining these:

$$K = \tfrac{1}{4}mr^2\omega^2$$

The angular speed is given in rpm, but needs to be in rad/s:

$$33.4 \text{ rpm} \cdot (1 \text{ min} / 60 \text{ s}) \cdot (2\pi \text{ rad/rev}) = 3.498 \text{ rad/s}$$

Thus:

$$K = (0.25) \cdot (3.0 \text{ kg}) \cdot (0.10 \text{ m})^2 \cdot (3.489 \text{ rad/s})^2$$

$$K = 0.091 \text{ J}$$

27. A is correct.

The angular momentum of a spinning object can be written as:

$L = I\omega$

The moment of inertia of a long thin uniform object of length *l* about an axis through the center perpendicular to the long axis is:

$I = (1/12)ml^2$

Giving:

$L = (1/12)ml^2\omega$

$L = (1/12)\cdot(0.1350 \text{ kg})\cdot(1.000 \text{ m})^2\cdot(3.5 \text{ rad/s})$

$L = 0.0394 \text{ kg·m}^2/\text{s}$

28. C is correct.

The period of a rotating object can be expressed as:

$T = 2\pi / \omega$

ω can be extracted from the definition of centripetal force:

$F = mv^2 / r$

Combining this with the relationship $v = \omega r$ gives:

$F = mr\omega^2$

Thus:

$\omega = \sqrt{(F / mr)}$

Then:

$T = 2\pi\sqrt{(mr / F)}$

$T = 2\pi\sqrt{[(23.0 \text{ kg})(1.3 \text{ m}) / (51.0 \text{ N})]}$

$T = 4.8 \text{ s}$

29. C is correct.

Angular acceleration is:

$\alpha = \Delta\omega / \Delta t$

$\alpha = (38.0 \text{ rad/s} - 0.00 \text{ rad/s}) / (10.0 \text{ s})$

$\alpha = 3.80 \text{ rad/s}$

The other information given in the question is not needed.

30. C is correct.

The magnitude of torque can be expressed as:

$$\tau = rF \sin \theta$$

where r is the distance from the origin (taken here to be the location of the pivot point) to the point of application of the force F, and θ is the angle between the position vector of the point of application and the force vector.

$$\tau = (0.63 \text{ m}) \cdot (17.0 \text{ N}) \cdot \sin (45°)$$

$$\tau = 7.6 \text{ N m}$$

31. D is correct.

Use conservation of energy. Take the zero of potential energy to be the configuration in which the sphere is at the bottom. The potential energy at the bottom is zero. The disk starts from rest, so the kinetic energy at the top is zero. With that:

$$mgh = K_{\text{linear}} + K_{\text{rotation}}$$

$$mgh = \tfrac{1}{2}mv^2 + \tfrac{1}{2}I\omega^2$$

For a disk, $I = \tfrac{1}{2}mr^2$. Because the disk rolls without slipping, $v = r\omega$. Substituting these into the conservation of energy equation:

$$mgh = \tfrac{1}{2}m(r^2\omega^2) + \tfrac{1}{2}(\tfrac{1}{2}mr^2)\omega^2$$

$$mgh = \tfrac{1}{2}mr^2\omega^2 + \tfrac{1}{4}mr^2\omega^2$$

$$mgh = \tfrac{3}{4}mr^2\omega^2$$

Isolating h:

$$h = 3r^2\omega^2 / 4g$$

$$h = [3\cdot(1.60 \text{ m})^2\cdot(4.27 \text{ rad/s})^2] / [4\cdot(9.8 \text{ m/s}^2)]$$

$$h = 3.57 \text{ m}$$

32. D is correct.

The moment of inertia is proportional to the square of the distance of an object from the center of rotation. As Paul moves toward the center, the moment of inertia decreases. Angular momentum, $L = I\omega$ is conserved. As I decreases, ω, the angular speed, increases to compensate.

33. B is correct.

Converting units:

$$210.0 \text{ rpm} \cdot (1 \text{ min} / 60 \text{ s}) \cdot (2\pi \text{ rad/revolution}) = 22.0 \text{ rad/s}$$

34. C is correct. Use the conservation of energy:

$$E_f = E_i$$

$$KE_f + PE_f = KE_i + PE_i$$

Take the zero of potential energy at the initial height, so that PE_i is zero. The kinetic energy of a rolling object is the sum of the kinetic energy of translation plus the kinetic energy of rotation:

$$KE = \tfrac{1}{2}mv^2 + \tfrac{1}{2}I\omega^2$$

If the object rolls without slipping, as is the case here, then $v = r\omega$, where R is the radius of the sphere. The moment of inertia of a sphere is $I = (2/5)m\omega^2$. With these we can write the kinetic energy of a sphere that rolls without slipping:

$$KE = \tfrac{1}{2}mv^2 + \tfrac{1}{2}(2/5)mr^2(v/r)^2$$

$$KE = \tfrac{1}{2}mv^2 + (1/5)mv^2$$

$$KE = (7/10)mv^2$$

Conservation of energy becomes:

$$(7/10)mv_f^2 + mgh = (7/10)mv_i^2$$

Canceling the mass and solving for the final speed:

$$v_f = \sqrt{[v_i^2 - (10/7)gh]}$$

The height, h, is related to the distance travelled and the angle of incline:

$$h = d \sin \theta$$

So:

$$v_f = \sqrt{[v_i^2 - (10/7)gd \sin \theta]}$$

$$v_f = \sqrt{[(5.5 \text{ m/s})^2 - (10/7) \cdot (9.8 \text{ m/s}^2) \cdot (3.0 \text{ m}) \cdot \sin (25°)]}$$

$$v_f = \sqrt{[(5.5 \text{ m/s})^2 - (10/7) \cdot (9.8 \text{ m/s}^2) \cdot (3.0 \text{ m}) \cdot (0.4226)]}$$

$$v_f = 3.5 \text{ m/s}$$

35. D is correct. The dynamical relation for rotational motion is:

$$\tau = I\alpha$$

$$I = \tau / \alpha$$

where τ is the torque applied to the wheel, and α is the wheel's angular acceleration.

The torque is the product of the force and the radius of the pulley: $\tau = FR$ (note that $\sin \theta = 1$, since $\theta = 90°$ [the problem mentions the force is applied tangentially]).

So:

$$I = \tau / \alpha$$

$$I = FR / \alpha$$

$$I = (16.88 \text{ N}) \cdot (0.340 \text{ m}) / (1.20 \text{ rad/s}^2)$$

$$I = 4.78 \text{ kg·m}^2$$

36. B is correct.

The energy required to bring a rotating object to rest is:

$$E = \tfrac{1}{2}I\omega_0^2$$

The moment of inertia of a cylinder is:

$$I = \tfrac{1}{2}mr^2$$

So the energy needed to stop the object is:

$$E = \tfrac{1}{4}mr^2\omega_0^2$$

Solving for the mass:

$$m = 4E / r^2\omega_0^2$$

We are given the angular speed in rpm, but should be in rad/s:

500.0 rpm·(1 min / 60 sec)·(2π rad / 1 rev) = 52.36 rad/s

The mass of the object is:

$$m = 4(3900 \text{ J}) / (1.2 \text{ m})^2 \cdot (52.36 \text{ rad/s})^2$$

$$m = 4.0 \text{ kg}$$

37. C is correct.

The torque at P_2 due to the weight of the billboard is:

$$\tau = r_{perp}F = r_{perp}mg$$

where r_{perp} is the perpendicular distance between P_2 and the line of application of the force.

Here, the weight of the billboard acts as if all of the mass is concentrated at the center of mass, which is the center of the billboard. Thus, the line of application of the force of gravity is P_1P_3, the vertical line that passes through P_1 and P_3.

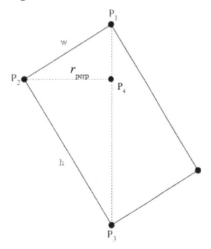

The length r_{perp} is the length of the horizontal line segment between P_2 and the line of application of the force (P_1P_3). This line segment is perpendicular to P_1P_3 and intersects P_1P_3 at point P_4.

To find r_{perp} note that the triangle $P_1P_2P_3$ is similar to the triangle formed by $P_1P_4P_2$. The ratios of the lengths of corresponding sides of similar triangles are equal. Apply this by forming the ratio of the length of the long side to the length of the hypotenuse of these two triangles:

$$h / \sqrt{(h^2 + w^2)} = r_{perp} / w$$

$$r_{perp} = hw / \sqrt{(h^2 + w^2)}$$

Giving an expression for torque:

$$\tau = mg[hw / \sqrt{(h^2 + w^2)}]$$

$$\tau = (5.0 \text{ kg}) \cdot (9.8 \text{ m/s}^2) \cdot (0.20 \text{ m}) \cdot (0.11 \text{ m}) / \sqrt{[(0.20 \text{ m})^2 + (0.11 \text{ m})^2]}$$

$$\tau = 4.7 \text{ N m}$$

38. B is correct.

An object rolling down an incline experiences three forces, and hence three torques. The forces are the force of gravity acting on the center of mass of the object, the normal force between the incline and the object, and the force of friction between the incline and the object.

If the origin is taken to be the center of the object, the force of gravity provides zero torque. This can be seen by noting that the distance between the origin and the point of application of the force is zero. $\tau_{gravity} = F_{gravity}r = mg(0) = 0$. Similarly, the normal force contributes zero torque because the direction of the force is directly through the origin (pivot point). $\tau_{normal} = F_{normal} r \sin \theta = F_{normal}(R)(\sin 180°) = F_{normal}(R)(0) = 0$.

Use a coordinate system in which the x-axis is parallel to the incline and the y-axis is perpendicular. The object is rolling in the positive x-direction. The dynamical equation for linear motion along the x-direction is:

$$F_{net} = ma$$

$$(mg \sin \theta - f) = ma$$

Note that the normal force is only in the y-direction, and thus does not directly contribute to the acceleration in the x-direction. The dynamical equation for rotational motion is:

$$\tau_{net} = I\alpha$$

$$fR = I\alpha \quad \text{(Note that the frictional force is perpendicular to the } r \text{ vector, and } \sin 90° = 1\text{)}$$

where R is the radius of the object, f is the force of friction, and I is the moment of inertia.

A relation coupling these two dynamical equations is necessary. This is the equation of constraint imposed by the restriction that the object rolls without slipping.

$$\alpha = a / R$$

To find the linear acceleration, use the equation of constraint to eliminate α from the rotational equation by replacing it with a / R:

$$fR = I(a / R)$$

The force of friction is of no interest, so rearrange this last expression:

$$f = Ia / R^2$$

Substitute this into the linear dynamic equation from above in place of f:

$$(mg \sin \theta - Ia / R^2) = ma$$

Solving this for *a*:

$$a = mg \sin \theta \, / \, [m + (I \, / \, R^2)]$$

$$a = g \sin \theta \, / \, [1 + (I \, / \, mR^2)]$$

For a sphere, $I = (2/5)mR^2$, so:

$$a_{sphere} = g \sin \theta \, / \, [1 + (2/5)]$$

$$a_{sphere} = (5/7)g \sin \theta$$

$$a_{sphere} = (0.714)g \sin \theta$$

For the disk, $I = \frac{1}{2} mR^2$, so:

$$a_{disk} = g \sin \theta \, / \, (1 + \frac{1}{2})$$

$$a_{disk} = (2/3)g \sin \theta$$

$$a_{disk} = (0.667)g \sin \theta$$

For the hoop, $I = mR^2$, so:

$$a_{hoop} = g \sin \theta \, / \, (1 + 1)$$

$$a_{hoop} = (1/2)g \sin \theta$$

$$a_{hoop} = (0.500)g \sin \theta$$

The object with the largest acceleration will reach the bottom first. The order is sphere, disk, hoop.

39. B is correct. The kinetic energy of a rotation object is:

$$K = \frac{1}{2}I\omega^2$$

The moment of inertia is given in SI units, but the angular speed is in rpm, which is not an SI unit. Convert:

$$96.0 \text{ rpm} \cdot (1 \text{ m}/ \, 60 \text{ s}) \cdot (2\pi \text{ rad/rev}) = 10.05 \text{ rad/s}$$

$$K = (0.5) \cdot (6.0 \times 10^{-3} \text{ kg·m}^2) \cdot (10.05 \text{ rad/s})^2$$

$$K = 0.30 \text{ J}$$

40. D is correct. If a wheel of radius *r* rolls without slipping on the pavement, the relationship between angular speed ω and translational speed is:

$$v = r\omega$$

$$\omega = v \, / \, r$$

$$\omega = (6.00 \text{ m/s}) \, / \, (0.120 \text{ m})$$

$$\omega = 50.00 \text{ rad/s}$$

Converting this to rpm:

$$\omega = (50.00 \text{ rad/s}) \cdot (1 \text{ rev} \, / \, 2\pi \text{ rad}) \cdot (60 \text{ s} \, / \, 1 \text{ min})$$

$$\omega = 477.5 \text{ rpm}$$

$$\omega = 478 \text{ rpm}$$

41. C is correct. Her moment of inertia does not remain constant because the radial position of her hands is changing. Angular momentum does remain constant because there is no torque on her, assuming the ice is frictionless.

Her kinetic energy changes. To see this, notice that her hands initially execute uniform circular motion, and hence there is no tangential force. As long as this condition is maintained, her kinetic energy will be constant. However, *as she pulls her hands in* they are no longer in uniform circular motion. During this time, there will be a tangential component of force, and work will be done. Another way to think about it is to recognize that, because *L* is conserved,

$$L_0 = L_f$$

$$I_0\omega_0 = I_f\omega_f$$

I will decrease by some amount, and *ω* will multiply by that same amount, e.g., *I* halves and *ω* doubles. When examining $KE = \frac{1}{2}I\omega^2$, *I* has gone down by half but *ω* has doubled. Since *KE* depends on *ω* squared, the change to *ω* has a greater impact on *KE*. *KE* will go up.

42. D is correct. There are two perpendicular components to Tanya's acceleration. Centripetal acceleration:

$$a_c = r\omega^2$$

and tangential acceleration:

$$a_t = r\alpha$$

Since these two acceleration components are perpendicular to each other, find the magnitude of the total linear acceleration:

$$a = \sqrt{(a_c^2 + a_t^2)}$$

$$a = \sqrt{[(r\omega^2)^2 + (r\alpha)^2]}$$

$$a = r\sqrt{(\omega^4 + \alpha^2)}$$

$$a = (4.65 \text{ m})\cdot\sqrt{[(1.25 \text{ rad/s})^4 + (0.745 \text{ rad/s}^2)^2]}$$

$$a = 8.05 \text{ m/s}^2$$

43. C is correct. For a rotating object:

$$\Delta\theta = \omega\Delta t$$

The angular speed is given in rpm, but needs to be in deg/s:

$$33.0 \text{ rpm}\cdot(1 \text{ min} / 60 \text{ s})\cdot(360 \text{ deg} / \text{rev}) = 198.0 \text{ deg/s}$$

$$\Delta\theta = (198.0 \text{ deg/s})\cdot(0.32 \text{ s})$$

$$\Delta\theta = 63°$$

44. C is correct.

The question asks to find the *magnitude* of the force of the floor on the bottom of the ladder. There are two forces acting on the bottom of the ladder: the normal force of the floor, *N*, which acts in the vertical direction, and the force of friction, *f*, which acts horizontally.

These two forces are directed in mutually perpendicular directions, so the magnitude of the net force of the floor on the bottom of the ladder is:

$$F_{net,\,bottom} = \sqrt{(N^2 + f^2)}$$

The values of N and f can be found by applying the laws of rotational and linear static equilibrium. Assume the ladder is static (not moving), but this is not a valid assumption until it is known whether or not the force of friction exceeds the limit imposed by static friction. This will be verified at the end. If the ladder is in equilibrium, the sum of the forces in both the x- and y-directions is zero and the sum of the torques is zero:

$$\sum F_x = 0; \ \sum F_y = 0; \ \sum \tau = 0$$

The force equations are straightforward to fill in:

$$\sum F_x = F_w - f = 0$$

$$\sum F_y = N - Mg - mg = 0$$

where F_w is the normal force from the wall on the top of the ladder, M is the mass of the hanging block, and m is the mass of the ladder. Note that since in the problem statement the wall is "smooth," there is no frictional force from the wall on the ladder. The $\sum F_y$ equation has only one unknown quantity and can be solved for N:

$$N = (M + m)g = (80\text{kg} + 50\text{kg})(9.8\text{m/s}^2) = 1274 \text{ N}$$

For the torque equation, choose the origin to be the point where the top of the ladder touches the wall. With that choice the torque due to the normal force of the wall is zero, and the torque due to the hanging block is also zero (since these forces are exerted right at the origin). There are three non-zero torques. One is the torque due to gravity on the ladder. This acts as if all of the mass of the ladder is concentrated on the center of mass. The next torque is due to the normal force of the floor on the bottom of the ladder, and the third is the force of friction acting on the bottom of the ladder. Using the general formula for torque $\tau = Fr \sin \phi$, where F is the force, r is the distance from the origin to the point where the force is being applied, and ϕ is the angle between the force vector and the r vector (which points from the origin to the point where the force is being applied):

$$\sum \tau = 0 + 0 - mg(L\,/\,2) \sin \beta - fL \sin \alpha + NL \sin \beta = 0$$

where m is the mass of the ladder and α and β are the angles in the figure shown. Take counterclockwise torques to be positive and clockwise torques to be negative. Use trigonometry to find α and β:

$$\alpha = \sin^{-1}(h\,/\,L) = \sin^{-1}(3.7\,/\,5) = 47.73°$$

$$\beta = 90° - \alpha = 42.27°$$

There is only one unknown quantity in the torque equation, so, dividing by L and rearranging, solve for f:

$$f \sin \alpha = N \sin \beta - \tfrac{1}{2}mg \sin \beta$$

$$f = [(N - \tfrac{1}{2}mg) \cdot \sin \beta]\,/\,\sin \alpha$$

$$f = [1274 \text{ N} - \tfrac{1}{2}(50 \text{ kg}) \cdot (9.8 \text{ m/s}^2) \cdot (\sin 42.27°)]\,/\,[\sin 47.73°]$$

$$f = 935.3 \text{ N}$$

Calculate the magnitude of the force on the bottom of the latter due to the floor:

$$F_{net,\ bottom} = \sqrt{(N^2 + f^2)}$$

$$F_{net,\ bottom} = \sqrt{[(1274\ N)^2 + (935.3\ N)^2]}$$

$$F_{net,\ bottom} = 1580\ N$$

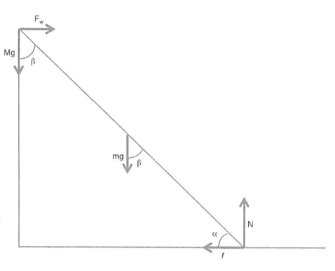

Finally, check to see if the force of friction is lower than the limit imposed by static friction.

$$f_{max} = \mu_s N = (0.750)\cdot(1274\ N) = 955\ N.$$

The calculated value for the force of static friction is 935.3 N, lower than the limit imposed by static friction, so the assumption that the system is in static equilibrium is valid. If this number had been lower than the value of f, the static frictional force would *not* be able to hold the ladder stationary.

45. B is correct.

The maximum displacement occurs when the acceleration stops the forward motion and the wheel reverses direction. Since $\theta_0 = 0$, $\Delta\theta = \theta - 0 = \theta$. The kinematic relation is:

$$\omega_f^2 - \omega_i^2 = 2\alpha\theta$$

The final angular speed is zero at the instant that the wheel changes direction.

$$-\omega_i^2 = 2\alpha\theta$$

Thus, the angular displacement at that instant is:

$$\theta = -(\omega_i^2 / 2\alpha)$$

$$\theta = -(29.0\ rad/s)^2 / [2\cdot(-0.52\ rad/s^2)]$$

$$\theta = 809\ rad$$

46. C is correct.

The simplest way to determine the direction of the angular momentum for a rotating object is to use the *right-hand rule*. Take the fingers of your right hand and curl them in the direction that the object is rotating, and stick your thumb out perpendicular to your fingers (as in a "thumbs-up" or "thumbs down" signal). The direction your thumb points is the direction of the angular momentum – in this case, down.

For a mathematical approach, use the definition $L = r \times p$ applied to a point on the outer edge of the object. Taking a point on the disk along the positive x-axis, the position vector r is in the positive x-direction and the momentum vector p is in the positive z-direction. The cross-product of these two vectors points down in the negative y-direction.

Work and Energy – Explanations

1. D is correct.

The final velocity in projectile motion is related to the maximum height of the projectile through conservation of energy:

$$KE = PE$$

$$\tfrac{1}{2}mv^2 = mgh$$

When the stone thrown straight up passes its starting point on its way back down, its downward speed is equal to its initial upward velocity (2D motion). The stone thrown straight downward contains the same magnitude of initial velocity as the stone thrown upward, and thus both the stone thrown upward and the stone thrown downward have the same final speed.

A stone thrown horizontally (or for example, a stone thrown at 45°) does not achieve the same height h as a stone thrown straight up, so it has smaller final vertical velocity.

2. B is correct.

$$\text{Work} = \text{force} \times \text{displacement} \times \cos \theta$$

$$W = Fd \cos \theta, \text{ where } \theta \text{ is the angle between the vectors } F \text{ and } d$$

$$W = (5 \text{ N}) \cdot (10 \text{ m}) \cos 45°$$

$$W = (50 \text{ J}) \cdot (0.7)$$

$$W = 35 \text{ J}$$

3. A is correct.

$$KE = \tfrac{1}{2}mv^2$$

KE is influenced by mass and velocity. However, since velocity is squared, its influence on KE is greater than the influence of mass.

4. B is correct.

$$\text{Work} = \text{force} \times \text{displacement} \times \cos \theta$$

$$W = Fd \cos \theta$$

$$\cos 90° = 0$$

$$W = 0$$

Since the force of gravity acts perpendicular to the distance traveled by the ball, the force due to gravity does no work in moving the ball.

5. D is correct.

$h_0 = 3.5$ m

$PE_0 = mgh$

$PE_1 = mgh(0.69) \rightarrow$ after first bounce

$PE_2 = mgh(0.69)^2 \rightarrow$ after second bounce

$PE_3 = mgh(0.69)^3 \rightarrow$ after third bounce

Because mass and gravity are constant, the final height is:

final height $= h(0.69)^3$

final height $= (4$ m$)\cdot(0.69)^3$

final height $= 1.31$ m

final height $= 131$ cm

6. A is correct.

$W = Fd \cos \theta$

$\cos \theta = 1$

$F = W / d$

$F = (360$ J$) / (8$ m$)$

$F = 45$ N

$F = ma$

$m = F / a$

$m = (45$ N$) / (10$ m/s$^2)$

$m = 4.5$ kg

7. D is correct.

On a displacement (x) vs. force (F) graph, the displacement is the y-axis and the force is the x-axis.

The slope is x / F, (in units of m/N) which is the reciprocal of the spring constant k, which is measured in N/m.

8. C is correct.

Work done by a spring equation:

$W = \frac{1}{2}kx^2$

$W = \frac{1}{2}(22$ N/m$)\cdot(3$ m$)^2$

$W = 99$ J

9. A is correct.

The force of gravity always points down. When the ball is moving upwards, the direction of its displacement is opposite of that of the force of gravity, and therefore the work done by gravity is negative.

On the way down, the direction of displacement is the same as that of the force of gravity, and therefore the work done by gravity is positive.

10. B is correct.

Work done by gravity is an object's change in gravitational PE.

$$W = -PE$$

$$A_1 = 400 \text{ J}$$

By the work-energy theorem,

$$W = KE$$

$$B_1 = 400 \text{ J}$$

11. D is correct.

Work is calculated as the product of force and displacement parallel to the direction of the applied force:

$$W = Fd \cos \theta$$

where some component of d is in the direction of the force.

12. B is correct.

Work only depends on force and distance:

$$W = Fd \cos \theta$$

Power = W / t is the amount of work done in a unit of time.

13. A is correct.

The area under the curve on a graph is the product of the values of $y \times x$.

Here, the y value is force and the x value is distance:

$$Fd = W$$

14. C is correct.

The initial kinetic energy of the helicopter is entirely converted to the potential energy of the landing gear and heat. By conversation of energy:

$$\Delta KE = \Delta PE + Q$$

Let the equilibrium length of the landing gear's spring be L_0 and the compressed length be L.

The change in potential energy of the landing gear is:

$$\Delta PE = \frac{1}{2}k(\Delta x)^2$$

$$\Delta PE = \frac{1}{2}k(L_0 - L)^2$$

$$\Delta PE = \frac{1}{2}k(L_0 - (0.23)L_0)^2$$

$$\Delta PE = \frac{1}{2}k(0.77)^2 L_0{}^2$$

The energy lost to heat is 23% of the initial kinetic energy. The final kinetic energy is zero, therefore:

$$Q = (0.23)\ \Delta KE$$

$$Q = (0.23)\ \frac{1}{2}mv^2$$

Conservation of energy becomes:

$$\frac{1}{2}mv^2 = (0.23)^2 L_0{}^2 + (0.23)\frac{1}{2}mv^2$$

Solving for $k\,/\,m$:

$$k\,/\,m = [(0.77)\ v^2]\,/\,[(0.23)^2 L_0{}^2]$$

$$k\,/\,m = 819\ \text{s}^{-2}$$

$$k\,/\,m = 0.8\ \text{kN m}^{-1}\ \text{kg}^{-1}$$

15. B is correct.

Although the book is stationary with respect to the plank, the plank is applying a force to the book causing it to accelerate in the direction of the force. Since the displacement of the point of application of the force is in the same direction as the force, the work done is positive. Choices D and E are not correct because work is a scalar and has no direction.

16. A is correct.

Find the final speed using conservation of energy.

Let the energy added as work be represented by W. Then, conservation of energy requires:

$$E_f = E_i + W$$

$$\frac{1}{2}mv^2{}_f = \frac{1}{2}mv^2{}_i + W$$

Solving for v_f:

$$v_f = \sqrt{v^2{}_i + (2W)\,/\,m}$$

$$v_f = \sqrt{[(10\ \text{m/s})^2 + (2)\cdot(4.5 \times 10^5\ \text{J})\,/\,(1150\ \text{kg})]}$$

$$v_f = 29.7\ \text{m/s} \approx 30\ \text{m/s}$$

17. E is correct. Conservation of energy between kinetic energy and potential energy:

KE = PE

KE = $\frac{1}{2}mv^2$ and PE = mgh

Set the equations equal to each other:

$\frac{1}{2}mv^2 = mgh$, cancel m from both sides

$\frac{1}{2}v^2 = gh$

h is only dependent on the initial v, which is equal between both objects, so the two objects rise to the same height.

18. A is correct.

Work = Power × time

$P_1 = W / t$

$P_2 = (3\ W) / (1/3\ t)$

$P_2 = 3(3/1) \cdot (W / t)$

$P_2 = 9(W / t)$

$P_2 = 9(P_1)$

19. D is correct.

Conservation of energy:

KE = PE

KE = mgh

W = mg

KE = Wh

KE = (450 N)·(9 m)

KE = 4,050 J

20. A is correct.

$F_1 = -kx_1$

Solve for the spring constant k:

$k = F / x_1$

$k = (160\ \text{N}) / (0.23\ \text{m})$

$k = 696\ \text{N/m}$

$F_2 = -kx_2$

$F_2 = (696\ \text{N/m}) \cdot (0.34\ \text{m})$

$F_2 = 237\ \text{N}$

21. B is correct. There is a frictional force since the net force = 0

The mule pulls in the same direction as the direction of travel so $\cos \theta = 1$

$$W = Fd \cos \theta$$

$$d = v\Delta t$$

$$W = Fv\Delta t$$

22. D is correct.

$$W = Fd \cos \theta$$

$$F_T = W / (d \times \cos \theta)$$

$$F_T = (540 \text{ J}) / (18 \text{ m} \times \cos 32°)$$

$$F_T = (540 \text{ J}) / (18 \text{ m} \times 0.848)$$

$$F_T = 35 \text{ N}$$

23. B is correct. The spring force balances the gravitational force on the mass. Therefore:

$$F_g = -kx$$

$$mg = -kx$$

By adding an extra 120 grams, the mass is doubled:

$$(2m)g = -kx$$

Since the weight mg and the spring constant k are constant, only x changes.

Thus, after the addition of 120 g, x doubles:

$$PE_1 = \tfrac{1}{2}kx^2$$

$$PE_2 = \tfrac{1}{2}k(2x)^2$$

$$PE_2 = \tfrac{1}{2}k(4x^2)$$

$$PE_2 = 4(\tfrac{1}{2}kx^2)$$

The potential energy increases by a factor of 4.

24. C is correct. In each case the car's energy is reduced to zero by the work done by the frictional force, or in other words:

$$KE + (-W) = 0$$

$$KE = W$$

Each car starts with kinetic energy $KE = (1/2)mv^2$. The initial speed is the same for each car, so due to the differences in mass, the Ferrari has the most KE. Thus, to reduce the Ferrari's energy to zero requires the most work.

25. E is correct. The hammer does work on the nail as it drives it into the wood. The amount of work done is proportional to the amount of kinetic energy lost by the hammer:

$$\Delta KE = \Delta W$$

26. A is correct. The only force doing work is the road's friction, so the work done by the road's friction is the total work. This work equals the change in KE.

$W = \Delta KE$

$W = KE_f - KE_i$

$W = \frac{1}{2}mv_2^2 - \frac{1}{2}mv_1^2$

$W = 0 - [\frac{1}{2}(1{,}500 \text{ kg})\cdot(25 \text{ m/s})^2]$

$W = -4.7 \times 10^5 \text{ J}$

27. D is correct.

$KE = \frac{1}{2}mv^2$

$KE_{car} = \frac{1}{2}(1{,}000 \text{ kg})\cdot(4.72 \text{ m/s})^2$

$KE_{car} = 11{,}139 \text{ J}$

Calculate the KE of the 2,000 kg truck with 20 times the KE:

$KE_{truck} = KE_{car} \times 20$

$KE_{truck} = (11{,}139 \text{ J}) \times 20$

$KE_{truck} = 222.7 \text{ kJ}$

Calculate the speed of the 2,000 kg truck:

$KE = \frac{1}{2}mv^2$

$v^2 = 2KE / m$

$v^2 = 2(222.7 \text{ kJ}) / (2{,}000 \text{ kg})$

$v_{truck} = \sqrt{[2(222.7 \text{ kJ}) / (2{,}000 \text{ kg})]}$

$v_{truck} = 14.9 \text{ m/s}$

28. E is correct. Gravity and the normal force are balanced, vertical forces.

Since the car is slowing (i.e. accelerating backwards) there is a net force backwards, due to friction (i.e. braking).

Newton's First Law of Motion states that in the absence of any forces, the car would keep moving forward.

29. B is correct. Energy is always conserved so the work needed to lift the piano is 0.15 m is equal to the work needed to pull the rope 1 m:

$W_1 = W_2$

$F_1 d_1 = F_2 d_2$

$F_1 d_1 / d_2 = F_2$

$F_2 = (6{,}000 \text{ N})\cdot(0.15 \text{ m}) / 1 \text{ m}$

$F_2 = 900 \text{ N}$

30. C is correct. The area under the curve on a graph is the product of the values of $y \times x$.

Here, the y value is force and the x value is distance:

$$Fd = W$$

31. B is correct. The vast majority of the Earth's energy comes from the sun, which produces radiation that penetrates the Earth's atmosphere. Likewise, radiation is emitted from the Earth's atmosphere.

32. C is correct.

$$W = Fd$$

$$W = \Delta KE$$

$$F \times d = \tfrac{1}{2}mv^2$$

If v is doubled:

$$F \times d_2 = \tfrac{1}{2}m(2v)^2$$

$$F \times d_2 = \tfrac{1}{2}m(4v^2)$$

$$F \times d_2 = 4(\tfrac{1}{2}mv^2)$$

For equations to remain equal to each other, d_2 must be 4 times d.

33. D is correct.

$$\text{Work} = \text{Power} \times \text{time}$$

$$P = W / t$$

$$W = Fd$$

$$P = (Fd) / t$$

$$P = [(2{,}000 \text{ N}) \cdot (320 \text{ m})] / (60 \text{ s})$$

$$P = 10{,}667 \text{ W} = 10.7 \text{ kW}$$

34. E is correct.

Solution using the principle of conservation of energy.

Assuming the system to consist of the barbell alone, the force of gravity and the force of the hands raising the barbell are both external forces. Since the system contains only a single object, potential energy is not defined.

The net power expended is:

$$P_{net} = W_{ext} / \Delta t$$

Conservation of energy requires:

$$W_{ext} = \Delta KE$$

$$W_{ext} = \tfrac{1}{2}m(v_f^2 - v_i^2)$$

For constant acceleration situations:

$$(v_f + v_i) / 2 = v_{average} = \Delta y / \Delta t$$

$$(v_f + 0.0 \text{ m/s}) / 2 = 3.0 \text{ m} / 3.0 \text{ s}$$

$$v_f = 2.0 \text{ m/s}$$

Therefore:

$$W_{ext} = \tfrac{1}{2}(25 \text{ kg}) \cdot (2.0 \text{ m/s})^2$$

$$W_{ext} = 50.0 \text{ J}$$

The net power expended is:

$$P_{net} = 50.0 \text{ J} / 3.0 \text{ s} = 17 \text{ W}$$

$$P_{net} = 17 \text{ W}$$

Solution using work.

The power expended in raising the barbell is:

$$P_{net} = W_{net} / \Delta t$$

The net work is defined as:

$$W_{net} = F_{net}\Delta y$$

By Newton's Second law:

$$F_{net} = ma$$

Find the acceleration:

$$\Delta y = \tfrac{1}{2}a\Delta t^2$$

$$a = (2) \cdot (3.0 \text{ m}) / (3.0 \text{ s})^2$$

$$a = 0.67 \text{ m/s}^2$$

The net force on the barbell is:

$$F_{net} = (25 \text{ kg}) \cdot (0.67 \text{ m/s}^2)$$

$$F_{net} = (50 / 3) \text{ N}$$

The net work is:

$$W_{net} = F_{net}\Delta y$$

$$W_{net} = [(50 / 3) \text{ N}] \cdot (3.0 \text{ m})$$

$$W_{net} = 50.0 \text{ J}$$

The net power expended:

$$P_{net} = 50.0 \text{ J} / 3.0 \text{ s}$$

$$P_{net} = 17 \text{ W}$$

35. B is correct.

The bag was never lifted off the ground and moved horizontally at constant velocity.

$F = 0$

$W = Fd$

$W = 0$ J

Because there is no acceleration, the force is zero and thus the work is zero.

36. B is correct.

Using energy conservation to solve the problem:

$W = |\Delta KE|$

$Fd = |\frac{1}{2}m(v_f^2 - v_0^2)|$

$d = |m(v_f^2 - v_0^2)/2F|$

$d = |(1{,}000 \text{ kg})\cdot[(22 \text{ m/s})^2 - (30 \text{ m/s})^2]/(2)\cdot(9{,}600 \text{ N})|$

$d = |(1{,}000 \text{ kg})\cdot(484 \text{ m}^2/\text{s}^2 - 900 \text{ m}^2/\text{s}^2)/19{,}200 \text{ N}|$

$d = 22$ m

Kinematic approach:

$F = ma$

$a = F/m$

$a = (9{,}600 \text{ N})/(1{,}000 \text{ kg})$

$a = 9.6 \text{ m/s}^2$

$v_f^2 = v_0^2 + 2a\Delta d$

$(v_f^2 - v_0^2)/2a = \Delta d$

Note that acceleration is negative due to it acting opposite the velocity.

$\Delta d = [(22 \text{ m/s})^2 - (30 \text{ m/s})^2]/2(-9.6 \text{ m/s}^2)$

$\Delta d = (484 \text{ m}^2/\text{s}^2 - 900 \text{ m}^2/\text{s}^2)/(-19.2 \text{ m/s}^2)$

$\Delta d = (-416 \text{ m}^2/\text{s}^2)/(-19.2 \text{ m/s}^2)$

$\Delta d = 21.7 \text{ m} \approx 22 \text{ m}$

37. D is correct.

$v = (70 \text{ km/h})\cdot(1{,}000 \text{ m/km})\cdot(1 \text{ h/60 min})\cdot(1 \text{ min/60 s})$

$v = 19.4$ m/s

Force acting against the car:

$F = mg \sin\theta$

$F = (1{,}320 \text{ kg})\cdot(9.8 \text{ m/s}^2)\sin 5°$ ($\sin 5° = 0.0872$, round it to 0.09)

$F = (1{,}320 \text{ kg})\cdot(9.8 \text{ m/s}^2)\cdot(0.09)$

$F = 1{,}164$ N

$N = \text{kg}\cdot\text{m/s}^2$

Rate of energy is power:

Watts = $kg \cdot m^2/s^3$

Multiply velocity by the downward force:

$P = Fv$

$P = (1{,}164 \text{ N}) \cdot (19.4 \text{ m/s})$

$P = 22.6 \text{ kW}$

38. D is correct. All of the original potential energy (with respect to the bottom of the cliff) is converted into kinetic energy.

$mgh = \frac{1}{2} m v_f^2$

Therefore:

$v_f = \sqrt{2gh}$

$v_f = \sqrt{(2) \cdot (10 \text{ m/s}^2) \cdot (58 \text{ m})}$

$v_f = 34 \text{ m/s}$

Kinematic approach:

$v_f^2 = v_0^2 + 2a\Delta x$

$v_f^2 = 0 + 2a\Delta x$

$v_f = \sqrt{2a\Delta x}$

$v_f = \sqrt{[2(10 \text{ m/s}^2) \cdot (58 \text{ m})]}$

$v_f = \sqrt{(1{,}160 \text{ m}^2/s^2)}$

$v_f = 34 \text{ m/s}$

39. E is correct.

$PE = mgh$

If height and gravity are constant then potential energy is directly proportional to mass.

As such, if the second stone has four times the mass of the first, then it must have four times the potential energy of the first stone.

$m_2 = 4m_1$

$PE_2 = 4PE_1$

Therefore, the second stone has four times the potential energy.

40. B is correct.

$W = Fd$

$W = mgh$, work done by gravity

$W = (1.3 \text{ kg}) \cdot (10 \text{ m/s}^2) \cdot (6 \text{ m}) = 78 \text{ J}$

41. A is correct.

Potential energy is the energy associated with the relative positions of pairs of objects, regardless of their state of motion. Kinetic energy is the energy associated with the motion of single particles, regardless of their location.

42. A is correct.

$F_{spring} = F_{centripetal}$

$F_{spring} = kx$

$kx = 15$ N

$x = (15$ N$) / (65$ N/m$)$

$x = 0.23$ m

$PE_{spring} = \frac{1}{2}kx^2$

$PE_{spring} = \frac{1}{2}(65$ N/m$)\cdot(0.23$ m$)^2$

$PE_{spring} = 1.7$ J

43. C is correct.

total time $= (3.5$ h/day$)\cdot(7$ days$)\cdot(5$ weeks$)$

total time $= 122.5$ h

cost $= (8.16$ cents/kW·h$)\cdot(122.5$ h$)\cdot(0.12$ kW$)$

cost $= 120$ cents $= \$1.20$

44. E is correct.

$x = 5.1$ m $\times (\cos 32°)$

$x = 4.33$ m

$h = 5.1$ m $- 4.33$ m

$h = 0.775$ m

$W = Fd$

$W = mg \times h$

$m = W / gh$

$m = (120$ J$) / (9.8$ m/s$^2)\cdot(0.775$ m$)$

$m = 15.8$ kg

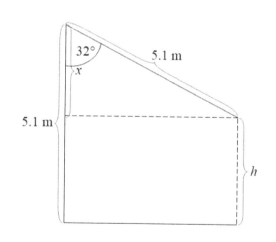

45. D is correct. Potential energy of spring:

$PE_i + W = PE_f$

$\frac{1}{2}\,k\,x_i^2 + 111$J $= \frac{1}{2}\,k\,x_f^2$

111J $= \frac{1}{2}\,k\,(x_f^2 - x_i^2)$

$111J = \frac{1}{2} k [(2.9m)^2 - (1.4m)^2]$

$111J = \frac{1}{2} k [(8.41m^2) - (1.96m^2)]$

$111J = \frac{1}{2} k (6.45m^2)$

$k = 2(111\ J)\ /\ (6.45\ m^2)$

$k = 34\ N/m$

Unit check:

$J = kg \cdot m^2/s^2$

$J/m^2 = (kg \cdot m^2/s^2) \cdot (1/m^2)$

$J/m^2 = (kg/s^2)$

$N/m = (kg \cdot m/s^2) \cdot (1/m)$

$N/m = (kg/s^2)$

46. E is correct.

Potential energy, kinetic energy and work are all measured in joules:

$J = kg \cdot m^2/s^2$

$KE = \frac{1}{2}mv^2 = kg(m/s)^2 = J$

$PE = mgh$

$PE = kg(m/s^2) \cdot (m) = J$

$W = Fd = J$

47. A is correct.

Potential energy of spring:

$PE = \frac{1}{2}kx^2$

Kinetic energy of mass:

$KE = \frac{1}{2}mv^2$

Set equal to each other and rearrange:

$\frac{1}{2}kx^2 = \frac{1}{2}mv^2$, cancel $\frac{1}{2}$ from both sides of the expression

$kx^2 = mv^2$

$x^2 = (mv^2)\ /\ k$

$x^2 = (m\ /\ k)v^2$

Since $m\ /\ k$ is provided:

$x^2 = (0.038\ kg \cdot m/N) \cdot (18\ m/s)^2$

$x^2 = 12.3\ m^2$

$x = \sqrt{12.3}\ m$

$x = 3.5\ m$

48. A is correct.

$$m_t = 2m_c$$

$$v_t = 2v_c$$

KE of the truck:

$$KE_t = \frac{1}{2}m_t v_t^2$$

Replace mass and velocity of the truck with the equivalent mass and velocity of the car:

$$KE_t = \frac{1}{2}(2m_c)\cdot(2v_c)^2$$

$$KE_t = \frac{1}{2}(2m_c)\cdot(4v_c^2)$$

$$KE_t = \frac{1}{2}(8m_c v_c^2)$$

The truck has 8 times the kinetic energy of the car.

49. E is correct.

When a car stops the KE is equal to the work done by the force of friction from the brakes.
Through friction the KE is transformed into heat.

50. B is correct.

When the block comes to rest at the end of the spring, the upward force of the spring balances the downward force of gravity.

$$F = kx$$

$$mg = kx$$

$$x = mg\,/\,k$$

$$x = (30 \text{ kg})\cdot(10 \text{ m/s}^2)\,/\,900 \text{ N/m}$$

$$x = 0.33 \text{ m}$$

Waves and Periodic Motion – Explanations

1. B is correct.

Frequency is the measure of the amount of cycles per second a wave experiences, which is independent of the wave's amplitude.

2. D is correct.

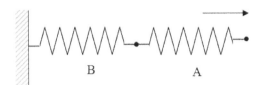

Hooke's Law:

$$F = kx$$

It is known that the force on each spring must be equal if they are in static equilibrium, therefore:

$$F_A = F_B$$

Therefore, the expression can be written as:

$$k_A L_A = k_B L_B$$

Solve for the spring constant of spring B:

$$k_B = (k_A L_A) / L_B$$

3. D is correct.

In a longitudinal wave, particles of a material are displaced parallel to the direction of the wave.

4. D is correct.

When it rains the brightly colored oil slicks on the road are due to thin film interference effects. This is when light reflects from the upper and lower boundaries of the oil layer and form a new wave due to interference effects. These new waves are perceived as different colors.

5. A is correct.

$$E_{stored} = PE = \tfrac{1}{2}kA^2$$

Stored energy is potential energy.

In simple harmonic motion (e.g., a spring), the potential energy is just:

$$PE = \tfrac{1}{2}kx^2 \text{ or } \tfrac{1}{2}kA^2,$$

where k is a constant and A (or x) is the distance from equilibrium

A is the amplitude of a wave in simple harmonic motion (SHM).

6. E is correct.

The spring will oscillate around its new equilibrium position (which is 3 cm below the equilibrium position with no mass hanging) with period $T = 2\pi\sqrt{m/k}$ since it's a mass-spring system undergoing simple harmonic motion.

To find k, consider how much the spring stretched when the mass was hung from it. Since the spring found a new equilibrium point 3 cm below its natural length, the upwards force from the spring (F_s) must balance the downwards gravitational force (F_g) at that displacement:

$$|F_s| = |F_g|$$

$$kd = mg$$

$$k\,(0.03\text{ m}) = (11\text{ kg})\cdot(9.8\text{ m/s}^2)$$

$$k = 3593\text{ N/m}$$

Now, solve for T:

$$T = 2\pi\sqrt{m/k}$$

$$T = 2\pi\sqrt{11\text{ kg}/3593\text{ N/m}}$$

$$T = 0.35\text{ s}$$

The frequency is the reciprocal of the period:

$$f = 1/T$$

$$f = 1/(0.35\text{ s})$$

$$f = 2.9\text{ Hz}$$

7. B is correct. When displacement is greatest, the force on the object is greatest. When force is maximized, then acceleration is maximum.

8. D is correct. The period of a pendulum:

$$T = 2\pi\sqrt{(L/g)}$$

The period only depends on the pendulum's length and gravity.

In an elevator, the apparent force of gravity only changes if the elevator is accelerating in either direction.

9. E is correct.

$$T = 2\pi[\sqrt{(L/g)}]$$

No effect on the period because T is independent of mass.

10. E is correct.

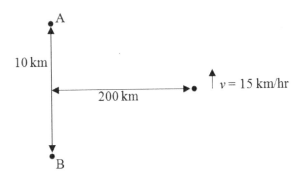

Convert v to m/s:

$$v = (15 \text{ km/1 h}) \cdot (1 \text{ h/60 min}) \cdot (1 \text{ min/60 s}) \cdot (10^3 \text{ m/1 km})$$

$$v = 4.2 \text{ m/s}$$

Convert frequency to λ:

$$\lambda = c / f$$

$$\lambda = (3 \times 10^8 \text{ m/s}) / (4.7 \times 10^6 \text{ Hz})$$

$$\lambda = 63.8 \text{ m}$$

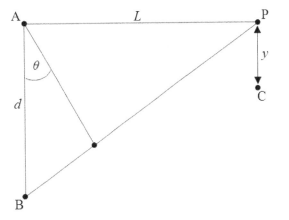

According to Young's Equation:

$$\lambda = yd / mL, \text{ where m = 0, 1, 2, 3, 4...}$$

Solve for y by rearranging to isolate y:

$$y = \lambda Lm / d$$

y = distance travelled by the ship:

$$y = vt$$

Since the first signal came at the point of maximum intensity, m = 0 at that time, at the next maximum m = 1.

Therefore:

$$t = L\lambda / vd$$

$$t = (200{,}000 \text{ m}) \cdot (63.8 \text{ m}) / (4.2 \text{ m/s}) \cdot (10{,}000 \text{ m})$$

$$t = 304 \text{ s}$$

Convert time from seconds to minutes:

$$t = (304 \text{ s}) \cdot (1 \text{ min/60 s})$$

$$t = 5.06 \text{ min} \approx 5.1 \text{ min}$$

For all m values greater than 1, the calculated times are beyond the answer choices so 5.1 min is the correct answer.

11. D is correct.

The tension in the rope is given by the equation:

$T = (mv^2) / L$

where v is the velocity of the wave and L is the length of the rope.

Substituting:

$v = L / t$

$T = [m(L / t)^2] / L$

$T = mL / t^2$

$t^2 = mL / T$

$t = \sqrt{(mL / T)}$

$t = \sqrt{[(2.31 \text{ kg}) \cdot (10.4 \text{ m}) / 74.4 \text{ N}]}$

$t = \sqrt{(0.323 \text{ s}^2)} = 0.57 \text{ s}$

12. A is correct.

$\omega_A = 2\omega_B$

$\omega_B = \sqrt{g / l_B}$

Therefore:

$l_B = g / \omega^2_B$

Similarly for A:

$l_A = g / \omega^2_A$

$l_A = g / (2\omega_B)^2$

$l_A = \frac{1}{4}g / \omega^2_B$

$l_A = \frac{1}{4}l_B$

13. B is correct. $F = -kx$

Since the motion is simple harmonic, the restoring force is proportional to displacement.

Therefore, if the displacement is 5 times greater, then so is the restoring force.

14. C is correct.

Period = (60 s) / (10 oscillations)

T = 6 s

The period is the time for one oscillation.

If 10 oscillations take 60 s, then one oscillation takes 6 s.

15. E is correct. Conservation of Energy:

total ME = ΔKE + ΔPE = constant

$\frac{1}{2}mv^2 + \frac{1}{2}kx^2$ = constant

16. B is correct. A displacement from the position of maximum elongation to the position of maximum compression represents *half* a cycle. If it takes 1 s, then the time required for a complete cycle is 2 s.

$f = 1 / T$

$f = 1 / 2$ s

$f = 0.5$ Hz

17. C is correct.

Sound waves are longitudinal waves.

18. E is correct.

speed = wavelength $\times$ frequency

speed = wavelength / period

$v = \lambda / T$

$\lambda = vT$

$\lambda = (362 \text{ m/s})\cdot(0.004 \text{ s})$

$\lambda = 1.5$ m

19. A is correct.

$a = -A\omega^2 \cos (\omega t)$

where A is the amplitude, or displacement from resting position.

20. D is correct.

The acceleration of a simple harmonic oscillation is:

$a = -A\omega^2 \cos (\omega t)$

Its maximum occurs when cos (ωt) is equal to 1

$a_{max} = -\omega^2 x$

If ω is doubled:

$a = -(2\omega)^2 x$

$a = -4\omega^2 x$

The maximum value of acceleration changes by a factor of 4.

21. B is correct. Resonant frequency of a spring and mass system in any orientation:

$\omega = \sqrt{(k \, / \, m)}$

$f = \omega \, / \, 2\pi$

$T = 1 \, / \, f$

$T = 2\pi\sqrt{(m \, / \, k)}$

Period of a spring does not depend on gravity.

The period remains constant because only mass and the spring constant affect the period.

22. E is correct.

$v = \lambda f$

$\lambda = v \, / \, f$

An increase in v and a decrease in f must increase λ.

23. B is correct.

Frequency is the measure of oscillations or vibrations per second.

frequency = 60 vibrations in 1 s

frequency = 60 Hz

speed = 30 m / 1 s

speed = 30 m/s

24. A is correct.

$T = (mv^2) \, / \, L$

$m = TL \, / \, v^2$

$m = (60 \text{ N}) \cdot (16 \text{ m}) \, / \, (40 \text{ m/s})^2$

$m = (960 \text{ N·m}) \, / \, (1{,}600 \text{ m}^2/\text{s}^2)$

$m = 0.6 \text{ kg}$

25. E is correct.

Amplitude is independent of frequency.

26. A is correct.

$f = (1/2\pi)\sqrt{(k/m)}$

An increase in m causes a decrease in f.

27. D is correct.

Transverse waves are characterized by their crests and valleys, which are caused by the particles of the wave traveling "up and down" with respect to the lateral movement of the wave.

The particles in longitudinal waves travel parallel to the direction of the wave.

28. B is correct.

The velocity vs. time graph shows that at $t = 0$, the velocity of the particle is positive, and the speed is increasing. When speed increases, velocity and acceleration point in the same direction. Therefore, the acceleration is non-zero and positive. Only graph B displays a positive acceleration at $t = 0$.

29. E is correct.

The speed of a wave is determined by the characteristics of the medium (and the type of wave). Speed is independent of amplitude.

30. A is correct. Period of a pendulum:

$$T_P = 2\pi\sqrt{(L / g)}$$

Period of a spring:

$$T_S = 2\pi\sqrt{(m / k)}$$

The period of a spring does not depend on gravity and is unaffected.

31. B is correct.

$$f = v / \lambda$$

$$\lambda = v / f$$

$$\lambda = (340 \text{ m/s}) / (2{,}100 \text{ Hz})$$

$$\lambda = 0.16 \text{ m}$$

32. D is correct.

$$\text{Period (T)} = 2\pi\sqrt{(L / g)}$$

The period is independent of the mass.

33. E is correct.

$$v = \omega x$$

$$\omega = v / x$$

$$\omega = (15 \text{ m/s}) / (2.5 \text{ m})$$

$$\omega = 6.0 \text{ rad/s}$$

34. D is correct. Unpolarized light on a polarizer reduces the intensity by ½.

$$I = (½)I_0$$

After that, the light is further reduced in intensity by the second filter.

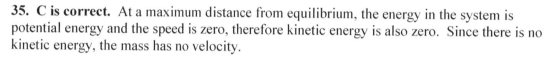

Law of Malus:

$$I = I_0 \cos^2 \theta$$

$$(0.14\ I_0) = (0.5\ I_0) \cos^2 \theta$$

$$0.28 = \cos^2 \theta$$

$$\cos^{-1} \sqrt{(0.28)} = \theta$$

$$\theta = 58°$$

35. C is correct. At a maximum distance from equilibrium, the energy in the system is potential energy and the speed is zero, therefore kinetic energy is also zero. Since there is no kinetic energy, the mass has no velocity.

36. E is correct. At the top of its arc, the pendulum comes to rest momentarily; the KE and the velocity equal zero.

Since its height above the bottom of its arc is at a maximum at this point, its (angular) displacement from the vertical equilibrium position is at a maximum also.

The pendulum constantly experiences the forces of gravity and tension, and is therefore continuously accelerating.

37. B is correct. In a transverse wave the vibrations of particles are perpendicular to the direction of travel of the wave. Transverse waves have crests and troughs that move along the wave.

In a longitudinal wave the vibrations of particles are parallel to the direction of travel of the wave. Longitudinal waves have compressions and rarefactions that move along the wave.

38. C is correct.

$$v = \sqrt{(T / \mu)},$$

where μ is the linear density of the wire.

$$T = v^2\mu$$

$$\mu = \rho A,$$

where A is the cross-sectional area of the wire and equals πr^2.

$$\mu = (2{,}700 \text{ kg/m}^3)\pi(4.6 \times 10^{-3} \text{ m})^2$$

$$\mu = 0.18 \text{ kg/m}$$

$$T = (36 \text{ m/s})^2 \cdot (0.18 \text{ kg/m})$$

$$T = 233 \text{ N}$$

39. D is correct. Refraction is the change in direction of a wave, caused by the change in the wave's speed. Examples of waves include sound waves and light waves. Refraction is seen most often when a wave passes from one medium to a different medium (e.g. from air to water and vice versa).

40. D is correct. The Doppler effect is the observed change in frequency when a sound source is in motion relative to an observer (away or towards). If the sound source moves with the observer then there is no relative motion between the two and the Doppler effect does not occur.

41. A is correct.

Pitch is how the brain perceives frequency. Pitch becomes higher as frequency increases.

42. C is correct.

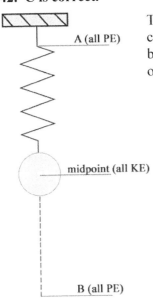

A (all PE)

midpoint (all KE)

B (all PE)

The KE is maximum when the spring is neither stretched nor compressed. If the object is bobbing, KE is maximum at the midpoint between fully stretched and fully compressed because this is where all of the spring's energy is KE rather than a mix of KE and PE.

43. B is correct.

Torque = $rF \sin \theta$

$F = ma$, substitute mg for F

$\tau = rmg \sin \theta$

$\tau = (1 \text{ m}) \cdot (0.5 \text{ kg}) \cdot (10 \text{ m/s}^2) \sin 60°$

$\tau = (5 \text{ kg} \cdot \text{m}^2/\text{s}^2) \times 0.87$

$\tau = 4.4 \text{ N} \cdot \text{m}$

44. E is correct. The Doppler effect can be observed to occur in all types of waves.

45. A is correct.

$v = \sqrt{(T / \mu)}$ where μ is the linear density of the wire.

$F_T = ma$

$F_T = (2{,}500 \text{ kg}){\cdot}(10 \text{ m/s}^2)$

$F_T = 25{,}000 \text{ N}$

$v = \sqrt{(25{,}000 \text{ N} / 0.65 \text{ kg/m})}$

$v = 196 \text{ m/s}$

The weight of the wire can be assumed to be negligible compared to the cement block.

46. B is correct.

$f = \tfrac{1}{2}\pi[\sqrt{(g / L)}]$, frequency is independent of mass

47. A is correct.

$T = 2\pi\sqrt{(L / g)}]$

$T = 2\pi\sqrt{(3.3 \text{ m} / 10 \text{ m/s}^2)}$

$T = 3.6 \text{ s}$

48. C is correct.

$f = (1/2\pi)\sqrt{(k / m)}$

If k increases by a factor of 2, then f increases by a factor of $\sqrt{2}$ (or 1.41).

Increasing by a factor of 1.41 or 41%

49. D is correct. In simple harmonic motion, the acceleration is greatest at the ends of motions (points A and D) where velocity is zero.

Velocity is greatest at the nadir where acceleration is equal to zero (point C).

50. A is correct.

At the lowest point, the KE is at a maximum and the PE is at a minimum.

The loss of gravitational PE equals the gain in KE:

$mgh = \tfrac{1}{2}mv^2$, cancel m from both sides of the expression

$gh = \tfrac{1}{2}v^2$

$(10 \text{ m/s}^2){\cdot}(10 \text{ m}) = \tfrac{1}{2}v^2$

$(100 \text{ m}^2/\text{s}^2) = \tfrac{1}{2}v^2$

$200 \text{ m}^2/\text{s}^2 = v^2$

$v = 14 \text{ m/s}$

Sound – Explanations

1. B is correct. Intensity is inversely proportional to distance (in W/m², not dB).

$$I_2 / I_1 = (d_1 / d_2)^2$$

$$I_2 / I_1 = (3 \text{ m} / 30 \text{ m})^2$$

$$100 \, I_2 = I_1$$

The intensity is 100 times greater at 3 m away than 30 m away.

Intensity to decibel relationship:

$$I \text{ (dB)} = 10 \log_{10} (I / I_0)$$

The intensity to dB relationship is logarithmic. Thus if I_1 is 100 times the original intensity then it is two times the dB intensity because:

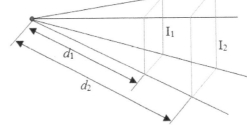

$$\log_{10} (100) = 2$$

Thus the decibel level at 3 m away is:

$$I \text{ (dB)} = (2) \cdot (20 \text{ dB})$$

$$I = 40 \text{ dB}$$

2. C is correct. If beats are heard every 500 ms (i.e. ½ s), or 2 beats per second.

Since f_{beat} = 2 Hz, the frequencies of the two tuning forks differ by 2 Hz.

One tuning fork has an f of 490 Hz:

f is (490 Hz – 2 Hz) = 488 Hz

or

f is (490 Hz + 2 Hz) = 492 Hz

3. B is correct. Resonance occurs when a vibrating system is driven at its resonance frequency, resulting in a relative maximum of the vibrational energy of the system. When the force associated with the vibration exceeds the strength of the material, the glass shatters.

4. C is correct. The third harmonic is shown in the figure below:

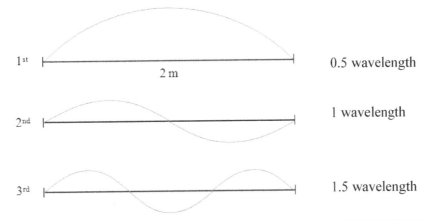

There are $(3/2)\lambda$ in the 2 m wave in the third harmonic

$L = (n / 2)\lambda$ (for n harmonic)

$L = (3 / 2)\lambda$ (for 3rd harmonic)

$L(2 / 3) = \lambda$

$\lambda = (2\ m) \cdot (2 / 3)$

$\lambda = 4/3\ m$

5. C is correct.

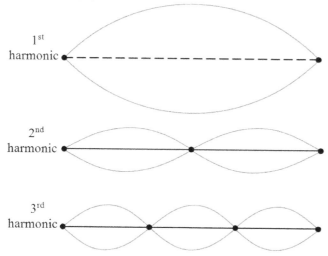

From the diagram, the wave is a 3rd harmonic standing wave.

Find wavelength:

$\lambda_1 = 2L$

$\lambda_n = 2L / n$

where n = 1, 2, 3, 4…

$\lambda_n = (2 \times 0.6\ m) / 3$

$\lambda_n = 0.4\ m$

Find speed:

$\lambda = v / f$

$v = \lambda f$

$v = (0.4\ m) \cdot (670\ Hz)$

6. E is correct.

Snell's law:

$n_1 \sin \theta_1 = n_2 \sin \theta_2$

Solve for θ_2:

$$(n_1 / n_2) \sin \theta_1 = \sin \theta_2$$

$$\sin \theta_1 = (n_1 / n_2) \sin \theta_2$$

$$\theta_2 = \sin^{-1}[(n_1 / n_2) \sin \theta_1]$$

Substituting the given values:

$$\theta_2 = \sin^{-1}[(1 / 1.5) \sin 60°]$$

$$\theta_2 = \sin^{-1}(0.67 \sin 60°)$$

7. D is correct.

For a standing wave, the length and wavelength are related:

$$L = (n / 2)\lambda \text{ (for n harmonic)}$$

From the diagram, the wave is the 6th harmonic:

$$L = (6 / 2)\lambda$$

$$\lambda = (2 \text{ m}) \cdot (2 / 6)$$

$$\lambda = 0.667 \text{ m}$$

$$f = v / \lambda$$

$$f = (92 \text{ m/s}) / (0.667 \text{ m})$$

$$f = 138 \text{ Hz}$$

8. A is correct.

$$v = d / t$$

$$v = (0.6 \text{ m}) / (0.00014 \text{ s})$$

$$v = 4,286 \text{ m/s}$$

$$\lambda = v / f$$

$$\lambda = (4,286 \text{ m/s}) / (1.5 \times 10^6 \text{ Hz})$$

$$\lambda = 0.0029 \text{ m} = 2.9 \text{ mm}$$

9. C is correct. The wave velocity is increased by a factor of 1.3.

$$v^2 = T / \rho_L$$

$$T = v^2 \times \rho_L$$

Increasing v by a factor of 1.3:

$$T = (1.3v)^2 \rho_L$$

$$T = 1.69v^2 \rho_L$$

T increases by 69%

10. D is correct.

$$\rho_L = \rho A$$

$$\rho_L = \rho(\pi r^2)$$

Thus if the diameter decreases by a factor of 2, then the radius decreases by a factor of 2, and the area decreases by a factor of 4. The linear mass density decreases by a factor of 4.

11. B is correct.

The v and period (T) of wire C are equal to wire A so the ρ_L must be equal as well.

$$\rho_{LA} = \rho_{LC}$$

$$\rho_A A_A = \rho_C A_C$$

$$A_C = (\rho_A A_A) / \rho_C$$

$$(\pi / 4)\cdot(d_C)^2 = (7 \text{ g/cm}^3)(\pi / 4)\cdot(0.6 \text{ mm})^2 / (3 \text{ g/cm}^3)$$

$$(d_C)^2 = (7 \text{ g/cm}^3)\cdot(0.6 \text{ mm})^2 / (3 \text{ g/cm}^3)$$

$$d_C^2 = 0.84 \text{ mm}^2$$

$$d_C = \sqrt{(0.84 \text{ mm}^2)} = 0.92 \text{ mm}$$

12. A is correct.

$$A = \pi r^2$$

If d increases by a factor of 4, r increases by a factor of 4. A increases by a factor of 16.

13. E is correct.

Since the bird is moving toward the observer, the $f_{observed}$ must be higher than f_{source}.

Doppler shift for an approaching sound source:

$$f_{observed} = (v_{sound} / v_{sound} - v_{source})f_{source}$$

$$f_{observed} = [340 \text{ m/s} / (340 \text{ m/s} - 10 \text{ m/s})]f_{source}$$

$$f_{observed} = (340 \text{ m/s} / 330 \text{ m/s})\cdot(60 \text{ kHz})$$

$$f_{observed} = (1.03)\cdot(60 \text{ kHz})$$

$$f_{observed} = 62 \text{ kHz}$$

14. C is correct.

When an approaching sound source is heard, the observed frequency is higher than the frequency from the source due to the Doppler effect.

15. D is correct.

Sound requires a medium of solid, liquid or gas substances to be propagated through. A vacuum is none of these.

16. E is correct.

According to the Doppler effect, frequency increases as the sound source moves towards the observer. Higher frequency is perceived as higher pitch.

Conversely, as the sound source moves away from the observer, the perceived pitch decreases.

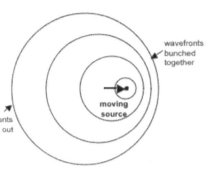

17. C is correct.

If waves are out of phase, the combination has its minimum amplitude of (0.6 – 0.4) Pa = 0.2 Pa.

If waves are in phase, the combination has its maximum amplitude of (0.6 + 0.4) Pa = 1.0 Pa.

When the phase difference has a value between in phase and out of phase, the amplitude will be between 0.2 Pa and 1.0 Pa.

18. B is correct.

$$I = P / A$$

$$I = P / \pi d^2$$

Intensity at 2d:

$$I_2 = P / \pi (2d)^2$$

$$I_2 = P / 4\pi d^2$$

$$I_2 = \tfrac{1}{4} P / \pi d^2$$

The new intensity is ¼ the original.

19. A is correct.

speed of sound = √[resistance to compression / density]

$$v_{sound} = \sqrt{(E / \rho)}$$

Low resistance to compression and high density result in low velocity because this minimizes the term under the radical and thus minimizes velocity.

20. B is correct. A pipe open at each end has no constraint on displacement at the ends. Furthermore, the pressure at the ends must equal the ambient pressure. Thus, the pressure is maximum at the ends: an antinode.

21. E is correct.

For a pipe open at both ends, the resonance frequency:

$$f_n = n f_1$$

where n = 1, 2, 3, 4…

Therefore only a multiple of 200 Hz can be a resonant frequency.

22. D is correct.

Unlike light, sound waves require a medium to travel through and its speed is dependent upon the medium.

Sound is fastest in solids, then liquids and slowest in air.

$$v_{solid} > v_{liquid} > v_{air}$$

23. B is correct.

Magnetic fields are induced by currents or moving charges.

24. B is correct.

$$I = \text{Power / area}$$

The intensity I is proportional to the power, so an increase by a factor of 10 in power leads to an increase by a factor of 10 in intensity.

$$I\,(dB) = 10\log_{10}(I / I_0)$$

dB is related to the logarithm of intensity.

If the original intensity was 20 dB then:

$$20\,dB = 10\log_{10}(I_1 / I_0)$$

$$2 = \log_{10}(I_1 / I_0)$$

$$100 = I_1 / I_0$$

The new intensity is a factor of 10 higher than before:

$$I_2 = 10\,I_1$$

$$1{,}000 = I_2 / I_0$$

$$I\,(dB) = 10\log_{10}(1{,}000)$$

$$I\,(dB) = 30\,dB$$

25. E is correct.

Sound intensity radiating spherically:

$$I = P / 4\pi r^2$$

If r is doubled:

$$I = P / 4\pi(2r)^2$$

$$I = \tfrac{1}{4}P / 4\pi r^2$$

The intensity is reduced by a factor of $\tfrac{1}{4}$.

26. D is correct.

As the sound propagates through a medium it spreads out in an approximately spherical pattern. Thus the power is radiated along the surface of the sphere and the intensity can be given by:

$$I = P / (4\pi r^2) \leftarrow \text{for surface area of a sphere}$$

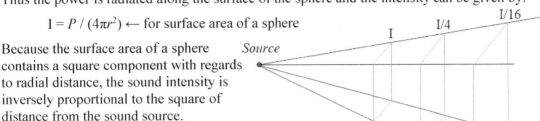

Because the surface area of a sphere contains a square component with regards to radial distance, the sound intensity is inversely proportional to the square of distance from the sound source.

27. B is correct.

The closed end is a node and the open end is an antinode.

$$\lambda = (4 / n)L$$

where n = 1, 3, 5 …

For the fundamental n = 1:

$$\lambda = (4 / 1) \cdot (1.5 \text{ m})$$

$$\lambda = 6 \text{ m}$$

The 1.5 m tube (open at one end) is a quarter of a full wave, so the wavelength is 6 m.

28. A is correct.

The 1.5 m is ¼ a full wave, so the wavelength is 6 m, for the fundamental.

$$f = v / \lambda$$

$$f = (960 \text{ m/s}) / 6 \text{ m}$$

$$f = 160 \text{ Hz}$$

29. E is correct.

For a closed-ended pipe the wavelength to the harmonic relationship is:

$$\lambda = (4 / n)L$$

where n = 1, 3, 5…

For the 5th harmonic n = 5

$$\lambda = (4 / 5) \cdot (1.5 \text{ m})$$

$$\lambda_n = 1.2 \text{ m}$$

Closed end tube				
Harmonic # (n)	# of waves in tube	# of nodes	# of antinodes	Wavelength to length
1	1/4	1	1	$\lambda = 4 L$
3	3/4	2	2	$\lambda = 4/3 L$
5	5/4	3	3	$\lambda = 4/5 L$
7	7/4	4	4	$\lambda = 4/7 L$

30. A is correct. $f = v / \lambda$

$$f = (340 \text{ m/s}) / (6 \text{ m})$$

$$f = 57 \text{ Hz}$$

31. C is correct.

Wavelength to harmonic number relationship in a standing wave on a string:

$$\lambda = (2L / n)$$

where n = 1, 2, 3, 4, 5 …

For the 3rd harmonic:

$$\lambda = (2)\cdot(0.34 \text{ m}) / 3$$

$$\lambda = 0.23 \text{ m}$$

32. D is correct.

Beat frequency equation:

$$f_{beat} = |f_2 - f_1|$$

If one of the tones increases in frequency, then the beat frequency increases or decreases, but this cannot be determined unless the two tones are known.

33. A is correct.

For a closed-ended pipe, the wavelength to harmonic relationship is:

$$\lambda = (4 / n)L$$

where n = 1, 3, 5, 7…

The lowest three tones are n = 1, 3, 5

$$\lambda = (4 / 1)L; \lambda = (4 / 3)L; \lambda = (4 / 5)L$$

34. E is correct.

The sound was barely perceptible, the intensity at Mary's ear is $I_0 = 9.8 \times 10^{-12}$ W/m^2.

Since the mosquito is 1 m away, imagine a sphere 1 m in radius around the mosquito.

If 9.8×10^{-12} W emanates from each area 1 m^2, then the surface area is $4\pi(1 \text{ m})^2$.

This is the power produced by one mosquito:

$$P = 4\pi r^2 I_0$$

$$P = 4\pi(1 \text{ m})^2 \times (9.8 \times 10^{-12} \text{ W/m}^2)$$

$$P = 1.2 \times 10^{-10} \text{ W}$$

energy = power × time

$$E = Pt$$

Energy produced in 200 s:

$$Pt = (1.2 \times 10^{-10} \text{ W})\cdot(200 \text{ s})$$

$$E = 2.5 \times 10^{-8} \text{ J}$$

35. A is correct.

    $v = c / n$

    where c is the speed of light in a vacuum

    $v = \Delta x / \Delta t$

    $\Delta x / \Delta t = c / n$

    $\Delta t = n \Delta x / c$

    $\Delta t = (1.33) \cdot (10^3 \text{ m}) / (3 \times 10^8 \text{ m/s})$

    $\Delta t = 4.4 \times 10^{-6} \text{ s}$

36. E is correct.

When waves interfere constructively (i.e. in phase), the sound level is amplified. When they interfere destructively (i.e. out of phase), they cancel and no sound is heard. Acoustic engineers work to ensure that there are no "dead spots" and the sound waves add.

An engineer should minimize destructive interference which can distort sound.

37. B is correct.

Velocity of a wave on a string in tension can be calculated by:

    $v = \sqrt{(TL / m)}$

Graph B gives a curve of a square root relationship which is how velocity and tension are related.

    $y = x^{1/2}$

38. D is correct.

From the diagram, the wave is a 6th harmonic standing wave.

Find wavelength:

    $\lambda = (2L / n)$

    $\lambda = (2) \cdot (4 \text{ m}) / (6)$ 1st

    $\lambda = 1.3 \text{ m}$

Find frequency: 2nd

    $f = v / \lambda$

    $f = (20 \text{ m/s}) / (1.3 \text{ m})$

    $f = 15.4 \text{ Hz}$ 3rd

39. E is correct.

Sound wave velocity is independent of frequency and does not change.

40. C is correct. First, find the frequency of the string, then the length of the pipe excited to the second overtone using that frequency.

The speed of sound in the string is:

$v_{string} = \sqrt{T/\mu}$

where T is the tension in the string, and μ is linear mass density.

$v_{string} = \sqrt{[(75\ N) / (0.00040\ kg)]}$

$v_{string} = 433.01\ m/s$

The wavelength of a string of length L_{string} vibrating in harmonic n_{string} is:

$\lambda_{string} = 2L_{string} / n_{string}$

Therefore, the vibration frequency of the string is:

$f = v_{string} / \lambda_{string}$

$f = [(n_{string})(v_{string})] / 2L_{string}$

$f = [(6)(433.01\ m/s)] / (2 \times 0.50\ m)$

$f = (2{,}598.06\ m/s) / 1\ m$

$f = 2{,}598.1\ Hz$

Now, consider the open pipe. The relationship between length, wavelength and harmonic number for an open pipe is the same as that for a string. Therefore:

$L_{pipe} = n_{pipe} (\lambda_{pipe} / 2)$

However, since $\lambda_{pipe} = v_{air} / f$:

$L_{pipe} = n_{pipe} (v_{air} / 2f)$

Noting that the second overtone is the third harmonic ($n_{pipe} = 3$):

$L_{pipe} = (3 \times 345\ m/s) / (2 \times 2{,}598.1\ Hz)$

$L_{pipe} = 0.20\ m$

Note that it is not necessary to calculate the frequency; its value cancels out.

There is less chance for error if the two steps that use frequency are skipped.

In $L_{pipe} = n_{pipe} (v_{air} / 2f)$ substitute $f = [(n_{string})(v_{string})] / 2L_{string}$, which gives:

$L_{pipe} = L_{string} (v_{air} / v_{string}) \cdot (n_{pipe} / n_{string})$

It yields the same answer but with fewer calculations.

41. A is correct.

$v = \sqrt{(T / \mu)}$

$\mu = m / L$

$v = \sqrt{(TL / m)}$

$v_2 = \sqrt{(T(2L) / m)}$

$v_2 = \sqrt{2} \sqrt{(TL / m)}$

$v_2 = v\sqrt{2}$

42. C is correct.

For a standing wave, the resonance frequency:

$f_n = nf_1$

where n is the harmonic number, n = 1, 2, 3, 4 …

Therefore, only a multiple of 500 Hz can be a resonant frequency.

43. D is correct.

The angle of incidence always equals the angle of reflection.

A light beam entering a medium with a greater refractive index than the incident medium refracts *toward* the normal. Thus, the angle of refraction is less than the angles of incidence and reflection.

Snell's law:

$n_1 \sin \theta_1 = n_2 \sin \theta_2$

where $n_1 < n_2$

For Snell's law to be true, then:

$\theta_1 > \theta_2$

44. A is correct.

Speed of sound in gas:

$v_{sound} = \sqrt{(yRT / M)}$

where y = adiabatic constant, R = gas constant, T = temperature and M = molecular mass

The speed of sound in a gas is only dependent upon temperature and not frequency or wavelength.

45. B is correct.

Waves only transport energy and not matter.

46. C is correct.

An overtone is any frequency higher than the fundamental.

In a stopped pipe (i.e. open at one end and closed at the other):

Harmonic #	Tone
1	fundamental tone
3	1st overtone
5	2nd overtone
7	3rd overtone

The first overtone is the 3rd harmonic.

Find wavelength:

$\lambda_n = (4L / n)$, for stopped pipe

where n = 1, 3, 5, 7...

$\lambda_3 = [(4) \cdot (3 \text{ m}) / 3]$

$\lambda_3 = 4 \text{ m}$

Find frequency:

$f = v / \lambda$

$f = (340 \text{ m/s}) / (4 \text{ m})$

$f = 85 \text{ Hz}$

Find velocity of a standing wave on the violin:

$f = v / 2L$

$v = (2L) \cdot (f)$

$v = (2) \cdot (0.36 \text{ m}) \cdot (85 \text{ Hz})$

$v = 61 \text{ m/s}$

Convert linear density to kg/m:

$\mu = (3.8 \text{ g/cm}) \cdot (1 \text{ kg} / 10^3 \text{ g}) \cdot (100 \text{ cm} / 1 \text{ m})$

$\mu = 0.38 \text{ kg/m}$

Find tension:

$v = \sqrt{(T / \mu)}$

$T = v^2 \mu$

$T = (61 \text{ m/s})^2 \times (0.38 \text{ kg/m})$

$T = 1{,}414 \text{ N}$

47. C is correct.

$v = \lambda f$

$f = v / \lambda$

Distance from sound source is not part of the equation for frequency.

48. A is correct. Velocity of a wave in a rope:

$v = \sqrt{[T / (m / L)]}$

$t = d / v$

$d = L$

$t = d / \sqrt{[T / (m / L)]}$

$t = (8 \text{ m}) / [40 \text{ N} / (2.5 \text{ kg} / 8 \text{ m})]^{1/2}$

$t = 0.71 \text{ s}$

49. C is correct. Intensity to decibel relationship:

$$I \, (dB) = 10 \log_{10} (I_1 / I_0)$$

where I_0 = threshold of hearing

$$dB = 10\log_{10}[(10^{-5} \text{ W/m}^2) / (10^{-12} \text{ W/m}^2)]$$

$$I = 70 \text{ decibels}$$

50. E is correct. The diagram represents the described scenario.

The wave is in the second harmonic with a wavelength of:

$$\lambda = (2 / n)L$$

$$\lambda = (2 / 2)\cdot(1 \text{ m})$$

$$\lambda = 1 \text{ m}$$

$$f = v / \lambda$$

$$f = (3.8 \times 10^4 \text{ m/s}) / (1 \text{ m})$$

$$f = 3.8 \times 10^4 \text{ Hz}$$

The lowest frequency corresponds to the lowest possible harmonic number.

For this problem, n = 2.

Fluids and Solids – Explanations

1. C is correct.

Refer to the unknown liquid as "A" and the oil as "O".

$\rho_A h_A g = \rho_O h_O g$, cancel g from both sides of the expression

$\rho_A h_A = \rho_O h_O$

$h_A = 5$ cm

$h_O = 20$ cm

$h_A = \frac{1}{4} h_O$

$\rho_A(\frac{1}{4})h_O = \rho_O h_O$

$\rho_A = 4\rho_O$

$\rho_A = 4(850$ kg/m$^3)$

$\rho_A = 3{,}400$ kg/m^3

2. D is correct.

$P = \rho_{oil} \times V_{oil} \times g / (A_{tube})$

$P = [\rho_O \pi (r_{tube})^2 \times hg] / \pi(r_{tube})^2$

cancel $\pi(r_{tube})^2$ from both the numerator and the denominator.

$P = \rho_O g h$

$P = (850$ kg/m$^3) \cdot (9.8$ m/s$^2) \cdot (0.2$ m$)$

$P = 1{,}666$ Pa

3. A is correct.

$m_{oil} = \rho_{oil} V_{oil}$

$V = \pi r^2 h$

$m_{oil} = \rho_{oil} \pi r^2 h$

$m_{oil} = \pi(850$ kg/m$^3) \cdot (0.02$ m$)^2 \times (0.2$ m$)$

$m_{oil} = 0.21$ kg $= 210$ g

4. A is correct.
Gauge pressure is the pressure experienced by an object referenced at atmospheric pressure. When the block is lowered its gauge pressure increases according to:

$P_G = \rho g h$

Thus at $t = 0$, the block just enters the water and $h = 0$ so $P_G = 0$. As time passes, the height of the block below the water increases linearly so P_G increases linearly as well.

5. E is correct.

Using Bernoulli's principle and assuming the opening of the tank is so large that the initial velocity is essentially zero:

$\rho gh = \frac{1}{2}\rho v^2$, cancel ρ from both sides of the expression

$gh = \frac{1}{2}v^2$

$v^2 = 2gh$

$v^2 = 2 \cdot (9.8 \text{ m/s}^2) \cdot (0.8 \text{ m})$

$v^2 = 15.68 \text{ m}^2/\text{s}^2$

$v = 3.96 \text{ m/s} \approx 4 \text{ m/s}$

Note: the diameter is not used to solve the problem.

6. C is correct.

The ideal gas law is:

$PV = nRT$

Keeping nRT constant:

If $P_{final} = \frac{1}{2}P_{initial}$

$V_{final} = \frac{1}{2}V_{initial}$

However, in an isothermal process there is no change in internal energy.

Therefore, because energy must be conserved:

$\Delta U = 0$

7. B is correct.

Hooke's Law for a spring:

$F = kx$

Solve for k:

$k = F / x$

$k = (9.5 \text{ kg}) \cdot (9.8 \text{ m/s}^2) / (0.004 \text{ m})$

$k = 23{,}275 \text{ N/m} = 2.3 \times 10^4 \text{ N/m}$

8. E is correct.

The object sinks when the buoyant force is less than the weight of the object.

Since the buoyant force is equal to the weight of the displaced fluid, an object sinks precisely when the weight of the fluid it displaces is less than the weight of the object itself.

9. A is correct.

$P = \rho g h$

$P = (10^3 \text{ kg/m}^3) \cdot (9.8 \text{ m/s}^2) \cdot (100 \text{ m})$

$P = 9.8 \times 10^5 \text{ N/m}^2$

10. C is correct.

Absolute pressure = gauge pressure + atmospheric pressure

$P_{abs} = P_G + P_{atm}$

$P_{abs} = \rho g h + P_{atm}$

Atmospheric pressure is added to the total pressure at the bottom of a volume of liquid.

Therefore, if the atmospheric pressure increases, absolute pressure increases by the same amount.

11. A is correct. Surface tension increases as temperature decreases. Generally, the cohesive forces maintaining surface tension decrease as molecular thermal activity increases.

12. A is correct. The stretch of a wire is caused by a force per unit area.

If force is constant, an increase in weight increases the area, related to d^2.

$E = \sigma / \varepsilon$

where E = Young's modulus, σ = stress (F / A) and ε = strain ($\Delta L / L$)

$E = (F / A) / (\Delta L / L)$

$E = FL / A\Delta L$

Relate force and area:

$F = (E) \cdot (\Delta L) \cdot (A) / (L)$

$F = (E) \cdot (\Delta L) \cdot (\pi / 4 \times d^2) / (L)$

The force is directly proportional to the ΔL and is directly proportional to d^2.

13. A is correct. The buoyant force upward must balance the weight downward.

Buoyant force = weight of the volume of water displaced

$F_B = W_{object}$

$\rho V g = W_{object}$

$W_{object} = 60 \text{ N}$

$W_{object} = (\rho_{water}) \cdot (V_{water}) \cdot (g)$

$60 \text{ N} = (1{,}000 \text{ kg/m}^3) \cdot (V_{water}) \cdot (10 \text{ m/s}^2)$

$V_{water} = 60 \text{ N} / (1{,}000 \text{ kg/m}^3) \cdot (10 \text{ m/s}^2)$

$V_{water} = 0.006 \text{ m}^3$

14. E is correct.

Volume flow rate:

$$Q = v\text{A}$$

$$Q = (2.5 \text{ m/s})\pi r^2$$

$$Q = (2.5 \text{ m/s}) \cdot (0.015 \text{ m})^2 \pi$$

$$Q = 1.8 \times 10^{-3} \text{ m}^3/\text{s}$$

15. C is correct. Force equation for the cork that is not accelerating:

$$F_\text{B} - mg = 0$$

Let *m* be the mass and V be the volume of the cork.

Replace:

$$m = \rho \text{V}$$

$$F_\text{B} = (\rho_\text{water}) \cdot (\text{V}_\text{disp}) \cdot (g)$$

$$(\rho_\text{water}) \cdot (\text{V}_\text{disp}) \cdot (g) = (\rho_\text{cork}) \cdot (\text{V}) \cdot (g)$$

$$\text{V}_\text{disp} = \tfrac{3}{4}\text{V}$$

$$\rho_\text{water} (\tfrac{3}{4}\text{V}g) = (\rho_\text{cork}) \cdot (\text{V}) \cdot (g), \text{ cancel } g \text{ and V from both sides of the expression}$$

$$\tfrac{3}{4}\rho_\text{water} = \rho_\text{cork}$$

$$\rho_\text{cork} / \rho_\text{water} = \tfrac{3}{4} = 0.75$$

16. B is correct.

By Poiseuille's Law, the volumetric flow rate of a fluid is given by:

$$V = \Delta \text{PA}r^2 / 8\eta L$$

Volumetric flow rate is the volume of fluid that passes a point per unit time:

$$V = \text{A}v$$

where *v* is the speed of the fluid.

Therefore:

$$\text{A}v = \Delta \text{PA}r^2 / 8\eta L$$

$$v = \Delta \text{P}r^2 / 8\eta L$$

$$v = (225 \times 10^3 \text{ Pa}) \cdot (0.0032 \text{ m})^2 / [8 \, (0.3 \text{ Ns/m}^2) \cdot (1 \text{ m})]$$

$$v = 0.96 \text{ m/s}$$

17. C is correct.

For monatomic gases:

$$U = 3/2 k_\text{B}T$$

where U is average KE per molecule and k_B is the Boltzmann constant

18. B is correct. The object weighs 150 N less while immersed because the buoyant force is supporting 150 N of the total weight of the object.

Since the object is totally submerged, the volume of water displaced equals the volume of the object.

$$F_B = 150 \text{ N}$$

$$F_B = \rho_{water} \times V_{water} \times g$$

$$V = F_B / \rho g$$

$$V = (150 \text{ N}) / (1{,}000 \text{ kg/m}^3){\cdot}(10 \text{ m/s}^2)$$

$$V = 0.015 \text{ m}^3$$

19. C is correct.

$$F_B / \rho_w = (m_c g) / \rho_c$$

$$F_B = (\rho_w m_c g) / \rho_c$$

$$F_B = [(1 \text{ g/cm}^3){\cdot}(0.03 \text{ kg}){\cdot}(9.8 \text{ m/s}^2)] / (8.9 \text{ g/cm}^3)$$

$$F_B = 0.033 \text{ N}$$

$$m_{total} = m_w + (F_B / g)$$

$$m_{total} = (0.14 \text{ kg}) + [(0.033 \text{ N}) / (9.8 \text{ m/s}^2)]$$

$$m_{total} = 0.143 \text{ kg} = 143 \text{ g}$$

20. D is correct.

$$v_1 A_1 = v_2 A_2$$

$$v_2 = v_1 A_1 / A_2$$

$$v_2 = [v_1(\pi/4)d_1^2] / (\pi/4)d_2^2$$

cancel ($\pi/4$) from both the numerator and denominator

$$v_2 = v_1(d_1^2 / d_2^2)$$

$$v_2 = (1 \text{ m/s}){\cdot}[(6 \text{ cm})^2 / (3 \text{ cm})^2]$$

$$v_2 = 4 \text{ m/s}$$

21. E is correct.

Static fluid pressure:

$$P = \rho g h$$

Pressure is only dependent on gravity (g), the height (h) of the fluid above the object and density (ρ) of the fluid. It does depend on the depth of the object but does not depend on surface area of the object.

Both objects are submerged to the same depth, so the fluid pressure is equal. Note that the buoyant force on the blocks is NOT equal, but pressure (force / area) is equal.

22. C is correct.

Surface tension force acts as the product of surface tension and total length of contact.

$F = AL$

For a piece of thread the length of contact is l as shown:

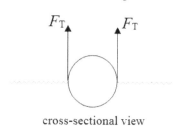

cross-sectional view

$F = 2L$ because the force acts on both sides of the thread.

Thus, for a thread rectangle, the total contact length is the total length times two.

$L = 2(l + w + l + w)$

$F_{max} = 2A(l + w + l + w)$

$F_{max} = 2A(2l + 2w)$

$F_{max} = 4A(l + w)$

23. D is correct.

Gauge pressure is the measure of pressure with respect to the atmospheric pressure.

So if the pressure inside the tire is equal to the air pressure outside, the gauge reads zero.

24. E is correct. Pressure is measured in force per unit area, which is the force divided by the area.

25. D is correct. The sheer stress is the force per unit area and has units of N/m^2.

26. B is correct. Because the area of the reservoir is assumed to be essentially infinite, the velocity of the flow at the top of the tank is assumed to be zero.

Using Bernoulli's equation, find the speed through the 3 cm pipe:

$(\frac{1}{2}\rho v^2 + \rho gh)_{out} = (\frac{1}{2}\rho v^2 + \rho gh)_{in}$

$\frac{1}{2}\rho v^2 = \rho gh$, cancel ρ from both sides of the expression

$\frac{1}{2}v^2 = gh$

$v^2 = 2gh$

$v = \sqrt{(2gh)}$

$v = \sqrt{[2(9.8 \text{ m/s}^2) \cdot (4 \text{ m})]}$

$v_{3cm} = 8.9 \text{ m/s}$

To find the speed through the 5 cm pipe use the continuity equation:

$A_{3cm}v_{3cm} = A_{5cm}v_{5cm}$

$(\pi / 4) \cdot (3 \text{ cm})^2 \cdot (8.9 \text{ m/s}) = (\pi / 4) \cdot (5 \text{ cm})^2 \cdot (v_{5cm})$

$v_{5cm} = 3.2 \text{ m/s}$

27. E is correct.

The ideal gas law is:

$PV = n\text{RT}$

where n, R and T are constants.

P is pressure, V is volume, n is the number of particles, R is the ideal gas law constant and T is temperature.

If $P \rightarrow 3P$, then $V \rightarrow (1/3)V$ to maintain constant temperature.

28. D is correct.

$F = \text{PA} + F_{cover}$

$P = \rho g h$

$F = \rho g h \text{A} + F_{cover}$

$F = [(1,000 \text{ kg/m}^3) \cdot (10 \text{ m/s}^2) \cdot (1 \text{ m}) \cdot (1 \text{ m}^2)] + 1,500 \text{ N}$

$F = 11,500 \text{ N}$

29. B is correct.

The buoyant force on a totally submerged object is independent of its depth below the surface (since any increase in the water's density is ignored).

The buoyant force on the ball at a depth of 4 m is 20 N, the same as the buoyant force at 1 m.

When it sits at the bottom of the pool, the two upward forces (i.e. the buoyant force F_B and the normal force F_N), must balance the downward force of gravity.

$F_B + F_N = F_g$

$(20 \text{ N}) + F_N = 80 \text{ N}$

$F_N = 80 \text{ N} - 20 \text{ N}$

$F_N = 60 \text{ N}$

30. B is correct.

$V_{\text{Fluid Displaced}} = \frac{1}{2} V_{block}$

Buoyant force:

$F_B = \rho g V$

$\rho_F g V_F = \rho_B g V_B$, cancel g from both sides of the expression

$$\rho_F V_F = \rho_B V_B$$

$$\rho_F(\tfrac{1}{2}V_B) = \rho_B V_B, \text{ cancel } V_B \text{ from both sides of the expression}$$

$$\tfrac{1}{2}\rho_F = \rho_B$$

$$\rho_F = (1.6)\rho_{\text{water}}$$

$$\rho_B = (1.6)\cdot(10^3 \text{ kg/m}^3)\cdot(\tfrac{1}{2})$$

$$\rho_B = 800 \text{ kg/m}^3$$

31. C is correct.

Terminal velocity:

$$v_t = \sqrt{(2mg / c\rho A)}$$

where c is the coefficient of air drag, ρ is the density of air and A is projected area (πr^2).

If the masses of the three balls are equal, then the velocity of each ball is:

$r = \text{R}$:

$$A = \pi r^2$$

$$v_1 = \sqrt{(2mg / c\rho A)}$$

$r = 2\text{R}$:

$$A_1 = \pi(2r)^2$$

$$A_1 = 4\pi r^2$$

$$A_1 = 4A$$

$$v_2 = \sqrt{(2mg / c\rho 4A)}$$

$$v_2 = (\tfrac{1}{2})\sqrt{(2mg / c\rho A)}$$

$$v_2 = (\tfrac{1}{2})v_1$$

$r = 3\text{R}$:

$$A_2 = \pi(3r)^2$$

$$A_2 = 9\pi r^2$$

$$A_2 = 9A$$

$$v_3 = \sqrt{(2mg / c\rho 9A)}$$

$$v_3 = (1/3)\sqrt{(2mg / c\rho A)}$$

$$v_3 = (1/3)v_1$$

As the ball becomes larger, its terminal velocity decreases, and therefore time until impact increases.

$$\text{velocity} = \text{distance} / \text{time}$$

32. A is correct. The pressure due to the density of a fluid surrounding an object submerged at depth *d* below the surface is given by:

$$P = \rho g d$$

Since the distance that the objects are below the surface is not specified, the only conclusion that can be drawn is that object B experiences less fluid pressure than object A. This difference is because object B is higher off the floor of the container and thus its depth is less than object A.

33. B is correct.

$$A_1 v_1 = A_2 v_2$$

$$A = \pi r^2$$

$$A_2 = \pi (2r)^2$$

$$A_2 = 4\pi r^2$$

$$A_2 = 4A_1$$

If r is doubled, then area is increased by 4 times

$$A_1 (14 \text{ m/s}) = (4A_1)v_2$$

$$v_2 = (A_1 \times 14 \text{ m/s}) / (4 \times A_1)$$

$$v_2 = (14 \text{ m/s}) / (4)$$

$$v_2 = 3.5 \text{ m/s}$$

Use Bernoulli's equation to find resulting pressure:

$$P_1 + \tfrac{1}{2}\rho v_1^2 = P_2 + \tfrac{1}{2}\rho v_2^2$$

$$(3.5 \times 10^4 \text{ Pa}) + \tfrac{1}{2}(1{,}000 \text{ kg/m}^3)\cdot(14 \text{ m/s})^2 = P_2 + \tfrac{1}{2}(1{,}000 \text{ kg/m}^3)\cdot(3.5 \text{ m/s})^2$$

$$P_2 = (13.3 \times 10^4 \text{ Pa}) - (6.1 \times 10^3 \text{ Pa})$$

$$P_2 = 12.7 \times 10^4 \text{ Pa}$$

34. D is correct. The pressure due to the atmosphere is equal to its weight per unit area. At an altitude of 2 km, there is less atmosphere pushing down than at the Earth's surface.

Therefore, atmospheric pressure decreases with increasing altitude.

35. C is correct. The buoyant force:

$$F_B = \rho_{air} V_{disp} g, \text{ and } V_{disp} \text{ is the volume of the man } m / \rho_{man}$$

$$F_B = (\rho_{air} / \rho_{man})mg$$

$$F_B = [(1.2 \times 10^{-3} \text{ g/cm}^3) / (1 \text{ g/cm}^3)]\cdot(80 \text{ kg})\cdot(9.8 \text{ m/s}^2)$$

$$F_B = 0.94 \text{ N}$$

36. D is correct.

Graham's law states that the rate at which a gas diffuses is inversely proportional to the square root of the density of the gas.

37. B is correct.

If the metal rod is thought of as a spring, then Hooke's law applies:

$$F = -kx$$

The force is proportional to the distance that the spring is stretched.

The proportional limit is reached when the deformation of the "spring" fails to obey Hooke's Law, but the "spring" can return to its original state (i.e., the deformation is not permanent).

The elastic limit is the point when the deformation becomes permanent.

The breaking point equals the fracture point and is when the rod snaps in two.

The elastic modulus is stress (σ) / strain (slope of the elastic region)

38. D is correct.

$$A = \pi r^2$$

$$A_T v_T = A_P v_P$$

$$v_T = v_P A_P / A_T$$

The ratio of the square of the diameter is equal to the ratio of area:

$$v_T = v_P (d_1 / d_2)^2$$

$$v_T = (0.03 \text{ m/s}) \cdot [(0.12 \text{ m}) / (0.002 \text{ m})]^2$$

$$v_T = 108 \text{ m/s}$$

39. B is correct.

Specific gravity:

$$\rho_{object} / \rho_{water}$$

Archimedes' principle:

$$F = \rho g V$$

$$\rho_{water} = F / g(0.9V)$$

$$\rho_{object} = F / gV$$

$$\rho_{object} / \rho_{water} = (F / gV) / [F / g(0.9V)]$$

$$\rho_{object} / \rho_{water} = 0.9$$

V_{water} is 0.9V because only 90% of the object is in the water, so 90% of the object's volume equals water displaced.

40. E is correct.

The factors considered are length, density, radius, pressure difference and viscosity.

The continuity equation does not apply here because it can only relate velocity and radius to the flow rate.

Bernoulli's equation does not apply because it only relates density and velocity.

The Hagen-Poiseuille equation is needed because it includes all the terms expect for density and therefore is the most applicable to this question.

Volumetric flow rate (Q) is:

$$Q = \Delta P \pi r^4 / 8\eta L$$

The radius is raised to the fourth power.

A 15% change to r results in the greatest change.

41. A is correct.

A force meter provides a force, and the reading indicates what the force is.

Since the hammer is not accelerating, the force equation is:

$$F_{meter} + F_B - m_h g = 0$$

$$m_h g = (0.68 \text{ kg}) \cdot (10 \text{ m/s}^2)$$

$$m_h g = 6.8 \text{ N}$$

The displaced volume is the volume of the hammer:

$$V_{disp} = m_h / \rho_{steel}$$

$$V_{disp} = (680 \text{ g}) / (7.9 \text{ g/cm}^3)$$

$$V_{disp} = 86 \text{ cm}^3$$

$$F_B = \rho_{water} \times V_{disp} \times g$$

$$F_B = (1 \times 10^{-3} \text{ kg/cm}^3) \cdot (86 \text{ cm}^3) \cdot (10 \text{ m/s}^2)$$

$$F_B = 0.86 \text{ N}$$

$$F_{meter} = m_h g - F_B$$

$$F_{meter} = 6.8 \text{ N} - 0.86 \text{ N}$$

$$F_{meter} = 5.9 \text{ N}$$

42. D is correct.

Poiseuille's law:

$$Q = \pi \Delta P r^4 / 8\eta L$$

$$D_B = 2D_A$$

$$r_B = 2r_A$$

$$Q_A = \pi \Delta P r_A{}^4 / 8\eta L$$

$$Q_B = \pi \Delta P (2r_A)^4 / 8\eta L$$

$$Q_B = 16(\pi \Delta P r_A{}^4 / 8\eta L)$$

$$Q_B = 16Q_A$$

43. B is correct.

The normal force exerted by the sea floor is the net force between the weight of the submarine and the buoyant force:

$$F_N = F_{net}$$

$$F_{net} = mg - F_B$$

$$F_{net} = mg - \rho g V$$

$$F_{net} = mg - W_{water}$$

$$F_N = mg - W_{water}$$

44. E is correct.

$$P = \rho g h$$

Because the bottom of the brick is at a lower depth than the rest of the brick, it will experience the highest pressure.

45. A is correct.

Mass flow rate:

$$\dot{m} = \text{cross-sectional area} \times \text{density} \times \text{velocity}$$

$$\dot{m} = A_C \rho v$$

$$\dot{m} = (7 \text{ m}) \cdot (14 \text{ m}) \cdot (10^3 \text{ kg/m}^3) \cdot (3 \text{ m/s})$$

$$\dot{m} = 2.9 \times 10^5 \text{ kg/s}$$

46. C is correct. Since the object is motionless:

$$a = 0$$

$$F_{net} = 0$$

The magnitude of the buoyant force upward = weight downward:

$$F = W$$

$$F = mg$$

$$F = (3 \text{ kg}) \cdot (10 \text{ m/s}^2)$$

$$F = 30 \text{ N}$$

47. A is correct.

$$P = P_{atm} + \rho g h$$

$$P = (1.01 \times 10^5 \text{ Pa}) + (10^3 \text{ kg/m}^3) \cdot (10 \text{ m/s}^2) \cdot (6 \text{ m})$$

$$P = (1.01 \times 10^5 \text{ Pa}) + (0.6 \times 10^5 \text{ Pa})$$

$$P = 1.6 \times 10^5 \text{ Pa}$$

48. C is correct.

Assuming there is a vacuum on the inside of the sphere, and using Archimedes' principle:

$$(\rho g V)_{\text{sphere}} = (\rho g V)_{\text{disp-water}}$$

$$(\rho V)_{\text{sphere}} = (\rho V)_{\text{disp-water}}$$

$$V_{\text{sphere}} = 4/3\pi r^3$$

Define r_o as outer radius and r_i as inner radius:

$$\rho_{\text{steel}}(4/3\pi)\cdot(r_o^3 - r_i^3) = \rho_{\text{water}}(4/3\pi r_o^3)$$

$$\rho_{\text{steel}}(r_o^3 - r_i^3) = \rho_{\text{water}}r_o^3$$

$$r_i^3 = [(-\rho_{\text{water}}r_o^3) / (\rho_{\text{steel}})] + r_o^3$$

$$r_i^3 = -[(10^3 \text{ kg/m}^3)\cdot(1.5 \text{ m})^3 / (7{,}870 \text{ kg/m}^3)] + (1.5 \text{ m})^3$$

$$r_i^3 = 2.95 \text{ m}^3$$

$$r_i = 1.43 \text{ m}$$

$$\text{Thickness} = r_o - r_i$$

$$\text{Thickness} = 1.5 \text{ m} - 1.43 \text{ m}$$

$$\text{Thickness} = 0.07 \text{ m} = 7 \text{ cm}$$

49. E is correct.

The bulk modulus is defined as how much a material is compressed under a given external pressure:

$$B = \Delta P / (\Delta V / V)$$

Most solids and liquids compress slightly under external pressure. However, gases have the highest change in volume and thus the lowest value of B.

50. D is correct.

Young's Modulus is expressed as:

$$E = \sigma \text{ (stress)} / \varepsilon \text{ (strain)}$$

$$E = (F / A) / (\Delta L / L)$$

$$E = (FL) / (\Delta LA)$$

Solve for ΔL:

$$\Delta L = FL / EA$$

$$\Delta L = [(8 \text{ kg})\cdot(9.8 \text{ m/s}^2)\cdot(2.7 \text{ m})] / [(20 \times 10^{10} \text{ N/m}^2)(\pi / 4)\cdot(8 \times 10^{-4} \text{ m})^2]$$

$$\Delta L = 0.0021 \text{ m} = 2.1 \text{ mm}$$

Electrostatics and Electromagnetism – Explanations

1. C is correct. Since charge is quantized, the charge Q must be a whole number (n) times the charge on a single electron:

Charge = # electrons × electron charge

$Q = n(e^-)$

$n = Q / e^-$

$n = (-1 \text{ C}) / (-1.6 \times 10^{-19} \text{ C})$

$n = 6.25 \times 10^{18} \approx 6.3 \times 10^{18}$ electrons

2. D is correct.

In Gaus's Law, the area is a vector perpendicular to the plane. Only the component of the electric field strength parallel is used.

Gaus's Law:

$\Phi = EA \cos \theta$

where Φ is electric flux (scalar), E is electric field strength and A is area vector.

Solve:

$\Phi = EA \cos (\pi / 6)$

$A = \pi r^2 = \pi D^2 / 4$

$\Phi = (740 \text{ N/C}) \cdot (\pi / 4) \cdot (1 \text{ m})^2 \cos (\pi / 6)$

$\Phi = 160\pi \text{ N·m}^2/\text{C}$

For calculation, use radians mode, not degree mode.

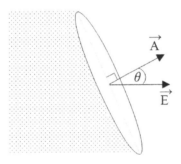

3. A is correct.

The magnitude of the negative charge's electric field:

$| E_2 | = kQ_2 / d_2{}^2$

$| E_2 | = (9 \times 10^9 \text{ N·m}^2/\text{C}^2) \cdot [(-1.3 \times 10^{-9} \text{ C}) / (+10^{-3} \text{ m})^2]$

$| E_2 | = 1.17 \times 10^7 \text{ N/C}$ to the left

The magnitude of the positive charge's electric field:

$| E_1 | = kQ_1 / d_1{}^2$

$| E_1 | = (9 \times 10^9 \text{ N·m}^2/\text{C}^2) \cdot [(1.3 \times 10^{-9} \text{ C}) / (2 \times 10^{-3} \text{ m})^2]$

$| E_1 | = 2.9 \times 10^6 \text{ N/C}$ to the right

$\Delta E = E_2 - E_1$

$\Delta E = (1.17 \times 10^7 \text{ N/C}) - (2.9 \times 10^6 \text{ N/C})$

$\Delta E = 8.8 \times 10^6 \text{ N/C}$, to the left

---

4. C is correct. Coulomb's law:

$$F_1 = kQ_1Q_2 / r^2$$

If r is increased by a factor of 4:

$$F_e = kQ_1Q_2 / (4r)^2$$

$$F_e = kQ_1Q_2 / (16r^2)$$

$$F_e = (1/16)kQ_1Q_2 / r^2$$

$$F_e = (1/16)F_1$$

As the distance increases by a factor of 4, the force decreases by a factor of $4^2 = 16$.

5. E is correct. Calculate the distance between the two charges using the Pythagorean Theorem:

$$r^2 = (1 \text{ nm})^2 + (4 \text{ nm})^2$$

$$r^2 = 17 \text{ nm}^2$$

$$r = 4.1 \text{ nm}$$

$$F = kQ_1Q_2 / r^2$$

$$F = [(9 \times 10^9 \text{ N·m}^2/\text{C}^2)·(1.6 \times 10^{-19} \text{ C})·(1.6 \times 10^{-19} \text{ C})] / (4.1 \times 10^{-9} \text{ m})^2$$

$$F = 1.4 \times 10^{-11} \text{ N}$$

6. A is correct.

7. D is correct. Use a coordinate system in which a repulsive force is in the positive direction and an attractive force is in the negative direction.

Gravitational Force: F_g

$$F_g = -Gm_1m_2 / r^2$$

$$F_g = -[(6.673 \times 10^{-11} \text{ N·m}^2/\text{kg}^2)·(54,000 \text{ kg})·(51,000 \text{ kg})] / (180 \text{ m})^2$$

$$F_g = -0.18 \text{ N·m}^2 / (32,400 \text{ m}^2)$$

$$F_g = -5.7 \times 10^{-6} \text{ N}$$

Electrostatic Force: F_e

$$F_e = kQ_1Q_2 / r^2$$

$$F_e = [(9 \times 10^9 \text{ N·m}^2/\text{C}^2)·(-15 \times 10^{-6} \text{ C})·(-11 \times 10^{-6} \text{ C})] / (180 \text{ m})^2$$

$$F_e = (1.49 \text{ N·m}^2) / (32,400 \text{ m}^2)$$

$$F_e = 4.6 \times 10^{-5} \text{ N}$$

Net Force:

$$F_{net} = F_g + F_e$$

$$F_{net} = (-5.7 \times 10^{-6} \text{ N}) + (4.6 \times 10^{-5} \text{ N})$$

$$F_{net} = 4 \times 10^{-5} \text{ N}$$

F_{net} is positive, which means there is a net repulsive force on the asteroids. In other words, the repulsive electrostatic force between them is stronger than the attractive gravitational force.

8. B is correct. Newton's Third Law states for every force there is an equal and opposite reaction force. This also applies to electrostatic forces.

Electrostatic Force:

$$F_1 = kQ_1Q_2 \,/\, r^2$$
$$F_2 = kQ_1Q_2 \,/\, r^2$$
$$F_1 = F_2$$

9. D is correct.

Forces balance to yield:

$$F_{electric} = F_{gravitation}$$
$$F_{electric} = mg$$

The values for an electric field are provided.

$$F_{electric} = QE$$
$$F_{electric} - F_{gravitation} = 0$$
$$QE - mg = 0, \text{ where } Q \text{ is the charge on the ball}$$
$$QE = mg$$
$$Q = mg \,/\, E$$
$$Q = (0.008 \text{ kg}) \cdot (9.8 \text{ m/s}^2) \,/\, (3.5 \times 10^4 \text{ N/C})$$
$$Q = -2.2 \times 10^{-6} \text{ C}$$

If the electric field points down, then a positive charge experiences a downward force. The charge must be negative, so the electric force balances gravity.

10. A is correct.

$$a = qE \,/\, m$$

The electron moves against the electric field, in the upward direction, so its acceleration:

$$a_e = qE \,/\, m_e$$

The proton moves with the electric field, which is down, so:

$$a_p = qE \,/\, m_p$$

However, the masses considered are small to where the gravity component is negligible.

$$m_p \,/\, m_e = (1.67 \times 10^{-27} \text{ kg}) \,/\, (9.11 \times 10^{-31} \text{ kg})$$
$$m_p \,/\, m_e = 1{,}830$$

The mass of an electron is about 1,830 times smaller than the mass of a proton.

$$(1{,}830)m_e = m_p$$
$$a_p = qE \,/\, (1{,}830)m_e$$
$$a_p = a_e \,/\, (1{,}830)$$
$$a_e = 1{,}830 a_p$$

11. D is correct.

Calculate the strength of the field at point P due to only one charge:

$$E = kQ / r^2$$

$$E_1 = (9 \times 10^9 \text{ N·m}^2/\text{C}^2) \cdot [(2.3 \times 10^{-11} \text{ C}) / (5 \times 10^{-3} \text{ m})^2]$$

$$E_1 = 8.3 \times 10^3 \text{ N/C}$$

Both electric field vectors point toward the negative charge, so the magnitude of each field at point P is doubled:

$$E_T = 2E_1$$

$$E_T = 2(8.3 \times 10^3 \text{ N/C})$$

$$E_T = 1.7 \times 10^4 \text{ N/C}$$

12. E is correct.

$$\text{charge} = \text{\# electrons} \times \text{electron charge}$$

$$Q = ne^-$$

$$n = Q / e^-$$

$$n = (-10 \times 10^{-6} \text{ C}) / (-1.6 \times 10^{-19} \text{ C})$$

$$n = 6.3 \times 10^{13} \text{ electrons}$$

13. C is correct.

Coulomb's law:

$$F_e = kQ_1Q_2 / r^2$$

If the separation is halved then r decreases by ½:

$$F_2 = kq_1q_2 / (\tfrac{1}{2}r)^2$$

$$F_2 = 4(kq_1q_2 / r^2)$$

$$F_2 = 4F_e$$

14. E is correct.

Coulomb's law:

$$F = kQ_1Q_2 / r^2$$

Doubling both the charges and distance:

$$F = [k(2Q_1) \cdot (2Q_2)] / (2r)^2$$

$$F = [4k(Q_1) \cdot (Q_2)] / (4r^2)$$

$$F = (4/4)[kQ_1Q_2 / (r^2)]$$

$$F = kQ_1Q_2 / r^2, \text{ remains the same}$$

15. D is correct.

Like charges repel each other.

From Newton's Third Law, the magnitude of the force experienced by each charge is equal.

16. A is correct.

Coulomb's law:

$$F = kQ_1Q_2 / r^2$$

The Coulomb force between opposite charges is attractive.

Since the strength of force is inversely proportional to the square of the separation distance (r^2), the force decreases as the charges are pulled apart.

17. A is correct.

Convert all units to their correct form:

$$F = ma$$

$$F = (2 \times 10^{-6} \text{ kg}) \cdot (0.006 \text{ m/s}^2)$$

$$F = 1.2 \times 10^{-8} \text{ N}$$

Substituting into the equation for electric field:

$$E = F / q$$

$$E = (1.2 \times 10^{-8} \text{ N}) / (6 \times 10^{-6} \text{ C})$$

$$E = 0.002 \text{ N/C}$$

Note: 1 N = 1 kg·m/s^2, not 1 g·m/s^2

18. D is correct.

Voltage is related to the number of coils in a wire. More coils yields a higher voltage.

Turns ratio:

$$V_s / V_p = n_s / n_p$$

In this case:

$$n_s < n_p$$

Therefore,

$$V_s < V_p$$

Because the secondary voltage (V_s) is lower than the primary voltage (V_p) the transformer is a step-down transformer.

19. B is correct.

Coulomb's Law:

$$F_1 = kQ_1Q_2 / r^2$$

$$F_2 = kQ_1Q_2 / r^2$$

$$F_1 = F_2$$

Newton's Third Law: the force exerted by one charge on the other has the same magnitude as the force the other exerts on the first.

20. E is correct.

$$F_e = kQ_1Q_2 / r^2$$

$$F_e = (9 \times 10^9 \text{ N·m}^2/\text{C}^2)·(-1.6 \times 10^{-19} \text{ C})·(-1.6 \times 10^{-19} \text{ C}) / (0.03 \text{ m})^2$$

$$F_e = 2.56 \times 10^{-25} \text{ N}$$

21. A is correct.

According to Lenz's Law, inserting a magnet into the coil causes the magnetic flux through the coil to change. This produces an emf in the coil which drives a current through the coil:

Lenz's Law:

$$\text{emf} = -N\Delta BA / \Delta t$$

The brightness of the bulb changes with a change in the current but it cannot be known if the bulb gets brighter or dimmer without knowing the orientation of the coil with respect to the incoming magnetic pole of the magnet.

22. C is correct.

Charge = # electrons × electron charge

$$Q = ne^-$$

$$n = Q / e^-$$

$$n = (8 \times 10^{-6} \text{ C}) / (1.6 \times 10^{-19} \text{ C})$$

$$n = 5 \times 10^{13} \text{ electrons}$$

23. A is correct.

An object with a charge can attract another object of opposite charge or a neutral charge.

Like charges cannot attract, but the type of charge does not matter otherwise.

24. C is correct. There is a force on the proton up the page. The electric field points in the direction of the force on positive particles, therefore it is pointed upwards.

The direction of the magnetic field is determined by the right hand rule.

$F = qvB$, where q is charge, v is velocity and B is magnetic field

When F is oriented upwards, curling your fingers from the direction of velocity gives B into the page.

25. A is correct. Initially, the current will flow clockwise but after 180° of rotation the current will reverse itself. After 360° of rotation the current will reverse itself again. Thus there are 2 current reverses in 1 revolution.

26. D is correct.

$W = Q\Delta V$

$V = kQ / r$

Consider the charge Q_1 to be fixed and move charge Q_2 from initial distance r_i to final distance r_f.

$W = Q_2(V_f - V_i)$

$W = Q_2[(kQ_1 / r_f) - (kQ_1 / r_i)]$

$W = kQ_1Q_2(1 / r_f - 1 / r_i)$

$W = (9 \times 10^9 \text{ N·m}^2/\text{C})·(2.3 \times 10^{-8} \text{ C})·(2.5 \times 10^{-9} \text{ C})·[(1 / 0.01 \text{ m}) - (1 / 0.1 \text{ m})]$

$W = 4.7 \times 10^{-5} \text{ J}$

27. E is correct. The electric field is oriented in a way that a positively-charged particle would be forced to move to the top because negatively-charged particles move to the bottom of the cube to be closer to the source of the electric field.

Therefore, all the positively charged particles are forced upward and the negatively-charged ones downward, leaving the top surface positively charged.

28. C is correct.

The magnitude of the force between the center charge and each charge at a vertex is 5 N. The net force of these two forces is directed toward the third vertex.

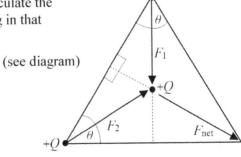

To determine the magnitude of the net force, calculate the magnitude of the component of each force acting in that direction:

$F_{net} = F_1 \sin (\tfrac{1}{2} \theta) + F_2 \sin (\tfrac{1}{2} \theta)$ (see diagram)

Since it is an equilateral triangle $\theta = 60°$,

$F_{net} = (5 \text{ N} \sin 30°) + (5 \text{ N} \sin 30°)$

$F_{net} = (5 \text{ N})·(\tfrac{1}{2}) + (5 \text{ N})·(\tfrac{1}{2})$

$F_{net} = 5 \text{ N}$

29. D is correct.

Equilibrium:

$$F = kq_1q_2 / r_1^2$$

$$F_{\text{attractive on } q2} = F_{\text{repulsive on } q2}$$

$$kq_1q_2 / r_1^2 = kq_2Q / r_2^2$$

$$q_1 = Qr_1^2 / r_2^2$$

$$q_1 = (7.5 \times 10^{-9} \text{ C}) \cdot (0.2 \text{ m})^2 / (0.1 \text{ m})^2$$

$$q_1 = 30 \times 10^{-9} \text{ C}$$

30. A is correct.

Gamma rays have the highest frequency on the electromagnetic spectrum, with frequencies greater than 3×10^{19} Hz.

31. A is correct.

The strength of the electrostatic field due to a single point charge is given by:

$E = kQ / r^2$, assumes that the source charge is in vacuum

E depends on both the magnitude of the source charge Q and the distance r from Q.

The sign of the source charge affects only the direction of the electrostatic field vectors.

The sign of the source charge does not affect the strength of the field.

32. B is correct.

$$F = qvB$$

$$F = mv^2 / r$$

$mv^2 / r = qvB$, cancel v from both sides of the expression

$$mv / r = qB$$

$$r = (mv) / (qB)$$

If the velocity doubles, the radius also doubles.

33. C is correct.

Coulomb's law:

$$F_e = kQ_1Q_2 / r^2$$

$$1 \text{ N} = kQ_1Q_2 / r^2$$

Doubling charges and keeping distance constant:

$$k(2Q_1) \cdot (2Q_2) / r^2 = 4kQ_1Q_2 / r^2$$

$$4kQ_1Q_2 / r^2 = 4F_e$$

$$4F_e = 4(1 \text{ N}) = 4 \text{ N}$$

34. D is correct. The Na^+ ion is positively charged and attracts the oxygen atom. Oxygen is slightly negative because it is more electronegative than the hydrogen atoms to which it is bonded.

35. C is correct.

Charge = # of electrons × electron charge

$$Q = ne^-$$
$$Q = (30) \cdot (-1.6 \times 10^{-19} \text{ C})$$
$$Q = -4.8 \times 10^{-18} \text{ C}$$

36. E is correct.

Cyclotron frequency is given as:

$$f = qB / 2\pi m$$

This expression does not take speed into consideration.

37. B is correct.

The repulsive force between two particles is:

$$F = kQ_1Q_2 / r^2$$

As r increases, F decreases

Using $F = ma$, a also decreases

38. A is correct. The given unit can be written $[\text{kg·m}^2/\text{s}^2] / \text{C} = \text{J} / \text{C}$, which is the definition of the Volt, the unit of electric potential difference.

39. C is correct.

When the positively charged sphere C is near sphere B it polarizes the sphere causing its negative charge to migrate towards C and a positive charge to build on the other side of sphere B.

The wire between sphere A and sphere B allows negative charge to flow to B and create a net positive charge on sphere A. Once the wire is removed and sphere C is removed, sphere A will have a net positive charge and B has a net negative charge.

40. C is correct.

$$F_e = kQ_1Q_2 / r^2$$
$$F_e = [(9 \times 10^9 \text{ N·m}^2/\text{C}^2) \cdot (5.1 \times 10^{-9} \text{ C})(2 \times 10^{-9} \text{ C})] / (0.1 \text{ m})^2$$
$$F_e = 9.18 \times 10^{-4} \text{ N}$$

$F_e \sin(60°)$ represents the force from one of the positive 2 nC charges.

Double to find the total force:

$$F_{total} = 2F_e \sin (60°)$$

$$F_{total} = 2(9.18 \times 10^{-4} \text{ N}) \sin (60°)$$

$$F_{total} = 1.6 \times 10^{-3} \text{ N}$$

The sine of the angle is used since only the vertical forces are added because the horizontal forces are equal and opposite and therefore they cancel.

41. B is correct.

Coulomb's Law:

$$F = kQ_1Q_2 / r^2$$

If both charges are doubled,

$$F = k(2Q_1) \cdot (2Q_2) / r^2$$

$$F = 4kQ_1Q_2 / r^2$$

F increases by a factor of 4.

42. C is correct.

Coulomb's law:

$$F = kQ_1Q_2 / r^2$$

$$Q_1 = Q_2$$

Therefore:

$$Q_1Q_2 = Q^2$$

$$F = kQ^2 / r^2$$

Rearranging:

$$Q^2 = Fr^2 / k$$

$$Q = \sqrt{(Fr^2 / k)}$$

$$Q = \sqrt{[(4 \text{ N}) \cdot (0.01 \text{ m})^2 / (9 \times 10^9 \text{ N} \cdot \text{m}^2/\text{C}^2)]}$$

$$Q = 2 \times 10^{-7} \text{ C}$$

43. A is correct.

Faraday's law states that electromotive force (emf) is equal to the rate of change of magnetic flux. Magnetic flux is the product of magnetic field and projected area:

$$\Phi = BA_\perp,$$

where $A_\perp$ is the area of the loop projected on a plane perpendicular to the magnetic field.

In this problem, B is vertical (and constant), so the projection plane is horizontal. Therefore, find the orientation of the axis of rotation that guarantees that as the loop rotates, the projection of its area on a horizontal plane does not change with time.

Notice that if the orientation of the axis is at an arbitrary angle to the field, the emf can be made to be zero by aligning the axis of rotation with the axis of the loop (i.e., perpendicular to the loop). With this orientation, the projection of the area never changes, which is not true of other alignments to the loop. Although the emf can be made to be zero, it is not *guaranteed* to be zero.

The only orientation of the axis that *guarantees* that the projected area is constant is the vertical orientation. One way to see this is to notice that because of the high symmetry of the vertical-axis orientation, rotating the loop about a vertical axis is equivalent to changing the perspective of the viewer from one angle to another. The answer cannot depend on the perspective of the viewer. Therefore, the projected area cannot change as the loop is rotated about the vertical axis; the emf is guaranteed to be zero.

44. C is correct. Coulomb's law:

$$F = kQ_1Q_2 / r^2$$

When each particle has lost ½ its charge:

$$F_2 = k(\tfrac{1}{2}Q_1)\cdot(\tfrac{1}{2}Q_2) / r^2$$

$$F_2 = (\tfrac{1}{4})kQ_1Q_2 / r^2$$

$$F_2 = (\tfrac{1}{4})F$$

F decreases by a factor of ¼

45. B is correct. The time taken for one revolution around the circular path is $T = 2\pi R/v$, where R is the radius of the circle and v is the speed of the proton. If the speed is increased, the radius also increases. The relationship between speed and radius follows from the fact that the centripetal force here is provided by the magnetic interaction:

$$mv^2/ R = qvB$$

Thus:

$$R = mv / qB.$$

If the speed is tripled, the radius triples, all other thigs being equal. The final period for a revolution is:

$$T_f = 2\pi R_f / v_f = 2\pi(3R) / 3v = 2\pi R / v = T$$

46. C is correct.

An electrostatic field shows the path that would be taken by a positively-charged particle.

As this positive particle moves closer to the negatively-charged one, the force between them increases.

Coulomb's law:

$$F = kQ_1Q_2 / r^2$$

By convention, electric field vectors always point towards negative source charges.

Since electrical field strength is inversely proportional to the square of the distance from the source charge, the magnitude of the electric field progressively increases as an object moves towards the source charge.

47. E is correct.

Protons are charges so they have an electric field.

Protons have mass so they have a gravitational field.

Protons have an intrinsic magnetic moment, so they have a magnetic field.

48. A is correct.

$W = Q\Delta V$

$V = kq / r$

$W = (kQq) \cdot (1 / r_2 - 1 / r_1)$

$W = (kQq) \cdot (1 / 2\text{ m} - 1 / 6\text{ m})$

$W = (kQq) \cdot (1 / 3\text{ m})$

$W = (9 \times 10^9\text{ N·m}^2/\text{C}^2) \cdot (3.1 \times 10^{-5}\text{ C}) \cdot (-10^{-6}\text{ C}) / (1 / 3\text{ m})$

$W = -0.093\text{ J} \approx -0.09\text{ J}$

The negative sign indicates that the electric field does the work on charge q.

49. D is correct.

charge = # electrons × electron charge

$Q = ne^-$

$n = Q / e^-$

$n = (-600 \times 10^{-9}\text{ C}) / (-1.6 \times 10^{-19}\text{ C})$

$n = 3.8 \times 10^{12}$ electrons

50. C is correct.

The analog to N/kg would be N/C, the unit for electric field.

Electric Circuits – Explanations

1. B is correct.

$R = \rho L / A$, where ρ is the resistivity of the wire material.

If the length L is doubled, the resistance R is doubled.

If the radius r is doubled, the area $A = \pi r^2$ is quadrupled and the resistance R is decreased by ¼.

If these two changes are combined:

$$R_{new} = \rho(2L) / \pi(2r)^2$$
$$R_{new} = (2/4)\cdot(\rho L / \pi r^2)$$
$$R_{new} = (2/4)R = \tfrac{1}{2}R$$

2. D is correct.

Internal resistance of battery is in series with resistors in circuit:

$$R_{eq} = R_1 + R_{battery}$$

where R_{eq} is equivalent resistance and R_1 is resistor connected to battery

$$V = IR_{eq}$$
$$V = I(R_1 + R_{battery})$$
$$R_{battery} = V / I - R_1$$
$$R_{battery} = (12\text{ V} / 0.6\text{ A}) - 6\ \Omega$$
$$R_{battery} = 14\ \Omega$$

3. C is correct.

An ohm Ω is defined as the resistance between two points of a conductor when a constant potential difference of 1 V, applied to these points, produces in the conductor a current of 1 A.

A series circuit experiences the same current through all resistors regardless of their resistance.

However, the voltage across each resistor can be different.

Since the light bulbs are in series, the current through them is the same.

4. D is correct.

$$V = kQ / r$$
$$V_B = kQ / r_B$$
$$V_B = (9 \times 10^9\,\text{N·m}^2/\text{C}^2)\cdot(1 \times 10^{-6}\,\text{C}) / 3.5\text{ m}$$
$$V_B = 2{,}571\text{ V}$$
$$V_A = kQ / r_A$$
$$V_A = (9 \times 10^9\,\text{N·m}^2/\text{C}^2)\cdot(1 \times 10^{-6}\,\text{C}) / 8\text{ m}$$
$$V_A = 1{,}125\text{ V}$$

Potential difference:

$$\Delta V = V_B - V_A$$
$$\Delta V = 2{,}571\ V - 1{,}125\ V$$
$$\Delta V = 1{,}446\ V$$

5. E is correct.

The capacitance of a parallel place capacitor demonstrates the influence of material, separation distance and geometry in determining the overall capacitance.

$$C = k\mathcal{E}_0 A / d$$

where k = dielectric constant or permittivity of material between the plates, A = surface area of the conductor and d = distance of plate separation

6. A is correct.

$$E = qV$$
$$E = \tfrac{1}{2}m(\Delta v)^2$$
$$qV = \tfrac{1}{2}m(v_f^2 - v_i^2)$$
$$v_f^2 = (2qV / m) + v_i^2$$
$$v_f^2 = [2(1.6 \times 10^{-19}\,C) \cdot (100\ V) / (1.67 \times 10^{-27}\ kg)] + (1.5 \times 10^5\ m/s)^2$$
$$v_f^2 = (1.9 \times 10^{10}\ m^2/s^2) + (2.3 \times 10^{10}\ m^2/s^2)$$
$$v_f^2 = 4.2 \times 10^{10}\ m^2/s^2$$
$$v_f = 2.04 \times 10^5\ m/s \approx 2 \times 10^5\ m/s$$

7. C is correct.

Power = current^2 × resistance

$$P = I^2 R$$

Double current:

$$P_2 = (2I)^2 R$$
$$P_2 = 4(I^2 R)$$
$$P_2 = 4P$$

Power is quadrupled.

8. D is correct.

A magnetic field is created only by electric charges in motion.

A stationary charged particle does not generate a magnetic field.

9. B is correct.

Combining the power equation with Ohm's law:

$P = (\Delta V)^2 / R$, where $\Delta V = 120$ V is a constant

To increase power, decrease the resistance.

A longer wire increases resistance, while a thicker wire decreases it:

$A = \pi r^2$

$R = \rho L / A$

Larger radius of the cross-sectional area means A is larger (denominator) which lowers *R*.

10. E is correct.

$W = k q_1 q_2 / r$

$r = \Delta x$

$r = 2$ mm $- (- 2$ mm$)$

$r = 4$ mm

$W = [(9 \times 10^9 \text{ N·m}^2/\text{C}^2)\cdot(4 \times 10^{-6} \text{ C})\cdot(8 \times 10^{-6} \text{ C})] / (4 \times 10^{-3} \text{ m})$

$W = (0.288 \text{ N·m}^2) / (4 \times 10^{-3} \text{ m})$

$W = 72$ J

11. E is correct.

The equivalent resistance of the 3 Ω and 6 Ω resistors is:

$1 / R_{eq} = 1 / (3 \text{ Ω}) + 1 / (6 \text{ Ω})$

$R_{eq} = 2$ Ω

The voltage across the equivalent resistor (i.e., the 6 Ω resistor) is given by the voltage divider relationship:

$V_6 = 18 \text{ V } (2 \text{ Ω}) / (2 \text{ Ω} + 4 \text{ Ω}) = 6$ V

The current through the 6 Ω resistor is:

$I_6 = V_6 / 6 \text{ Ω} = 1$ A

After the 3 Ω resistor burns out, the voltage across the 6 Ω resistor is again found using the voltage divider relationship:

$V_6' = 18 \text{ V } (6 \text{ Ω}) / (6 \text{ Ω} + 4 \text{ Ω}) = 10.8$ V

Now the current through the 6 Ω resistor is:

$I_6' = V_6' / 6 \text{ Ω} = 1.8$ A

The current has increased.

12. E is correct.

A parallel circuit experiences the same potential difference across each resistor.

However, the current through each resistor can be different.

13. D is correct.

$$E = q\text{V}$$

$$E = \tfrac{1}{2}mv^2$$

$$q\text{V} = \tfrac{1}{2}mv^2$$

$$v^2 = 2q\text{V} / m$$

$$v^2 = [2(1.6 \times 10^{-19}\,\text{C}){\cdot}(990\,\text{V})] / (9.11 \times 10^{-31}\,\text{kg})$$

$$v^2 = 3.5 \times 10^{14}\,\text{m}^2/\text{s}^2$$

$$v = 1.9 \times 10^7\,\text{m/s}$$

14. B is correct.

Calculate magnetic field perpendicular to loop:

$$\text{B}_{\text{Perp2}} = (12\,\text{T})\cos 30°$$

$$\text{B}_{\text{Perp2}} = 10.4\,\text{T}$$

$$\text{B}_{\text{Perp1}} = (1\,\text{T})\cos 30°$$

$$\text{B}_{\text{Perp1}} = 0.87\,\text{T}$$

Use Faraday's Law to calculate generated voltage:

$$\text{V} = N\Delta B A / \Delta t$$

$$\text{V} = N\Delta B(\pi r^2) / \Delta t$$

$$\text{V} = [(1){\cdot}(10.4\,\text{T} - 0.87\,\text{T}){\cdot}(\pi(0.5\,\text{m})^2)] / (5\,\text{s} - 0\,\text{s})$$

$$\text{V} = [(1){\cdot}(10.4\,\text{T} - 0.87\,\text{T}){\cdot}(0.785\,\text{m}^2)] / (5\,\text{s})$$

$$\text{V} = 1.5\,\text{V}$$

Use Ohm's Law to calculate current:

$$\text{V} = IR$$

$$I = \text{V} / R$$

$$I = (1.5\,\text{V}) / (12\,\Omega)$$

$$I = 0.13\,\text{A}$$

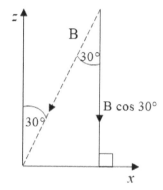

15. D is correct.

Find area:

$$A = \pi r^2$$

$$A = \pi(7 \times 10^{-3}\,\text{m})^2$$

$$A = 1.54 \times 10^{-4}\,\text{m}^2$$

Find capacitance:

$$C = A\varepsilon_{o}k / d$$

$$C = [(1.54 \times 10^{-4}\,\text{m}^2){\cdot}(8.854 \times 10^{-12}\,\text{F/m}){\cdot}(1)] / (1 \times 10^{-3}\,\text{m})$$

$$C = 1.36 \times 10^{-12}\,\text{F}$$

Find charge:

$$\sigma = 3 \times 10^{-6} \text{ C/m}^2$$

$$\sigma = Q / A$$

$$Q = \sigma A$$

$$Q = (3 \times 10^{-6} \text{ C/m}^2){\cdot}(1.54 \times 10^{-4} \text{ m}^2)$$

$$Q = 4.6 \times 10^{-10} \text{ C}$$

Find potential energy:

$$U = \tfrac{1}{2}Q^2 / C$$

$$U = \tfrac{1}{2}(4.6 \times 10^{-10} \text{ C})^2 / (1.36 \times 10^{-12} \text{ F})$$

$$U = 78 \times 10^{-9} \text{ J}$$

16. A is correct.

The magnitude of the acceleration is given by:

$$F = ma$$

$$a = F / m$$

$$F = qE_0$$

$$a = qE_0 / m$$

Bare nuclei = no electrons

^{1}H has 1 proton and ^{4}He has 2 protons and 2 neutrons

Thus ^{1}H has ½ the charge and ¼ the mass of ^{4}He.

$$a_H = q_H E_0 / m_H$$

$$a_{He} = q_{He} E_0 / m_{He}$$

$$a_H = (\tfrac{1}{2}q_{He})E_0 / (\tfrac{1}{4}m_{He})$$

$$a_H = 2(q_{He} E_0 / m_{He})$$

$$a_H = 2a_{He}$$

17. B is correct. The current will change as the choice of lamp arrangement changes.

Since $P = V^2/R$, power increases as resistance decreases.

To rank the power in increasing order, the equivalent resistance must be ranked in decreasing order.

For arrangement B, the resistors are in series, so:

$$R_{eq} = R + R = 2R$$

For arrangement C, the resistors are in parallel, so:

$$1/R_{eq} = 1/R + 1/R$$

$$R_{eq} = R/2$$

The ranking of resistance in decreasing order is B to A to C, which is therefore the ranking of power in increasing order.

18. D is correct.

$$C = k\varepsilon_0 A / d$$

where k = dielectric constant or permittivity of material between the plates, A = area and d = distance of plate separation

$$C = (2.1) \cdot (8.854 \times 10^{-12} \text{ F/m}) \cdot (0.01 \text{ m} \times 0.01 \text{ m}) / (0.001 \text{ m})$$

$$C = (1.9 \times 10^{-15} \text{ F/m}) / (0.001 \text{ m})$$

$$C = 1.9 \times 10^{-12} \text{ F} = 1.9 \text{ pF}$$

19. C is correct. Resistor R_1 is connected directly across the battery. Thus, the voltage across R_1 is V, and is held constant at that value regardless of whatever happens in the circuit. Similarly, the voltage across the series combination of R and R_2 is also held constant at V.

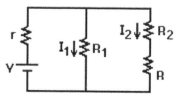

Since the voltage across R_1 will always be V, the current I_1 through R_1 will be unchanged as R changes (since R_1 didn't change, so $I_1 = V / R_1$ remains the same).

Since the voltage across the combination of R and R_2 will always be V, when R is decreased the effective resistance of the series combination $R + R_2$ will decrease, and the current I_2 through R_2 will increase.

20. C is correct.

$$V = IR$$

$$I = V / R$$

Ohm's law states that the current between two points is directly proportional to the potential difference between the points.

21. E is correct. Root mean square voltage equation:

$$V_{rms} = V_{max} / \sqrt{2}$$

$$V_{rms} = 12 / \sqrt{2}$$

$$V_{rms} = (12 / \sqrt{2}) \cdot (\sqrt{2} / \sqrt{2})$$

$$V_{rms} = (12\sqrt{2}) / 2$$

$$V_{rms} = 6\sqrt{2} \text{ V}$$

22. C is correct. By definition:

$$V_{rms} = V_{max} / \sqrt{2}$$

Therefore:

$$V_{max} = V_{rms}\sqrt{2}$$

$$V_{max} = (150 \text{ V})\sqrt{2}$$

$$V_{max} = 212 \text{ V}$$

23. D is correct.

Kirchhoff's junction rule states that the sum of all currents coming into a junction is the sum of all currents leaving a junction. This is a statement of conservation of charge because it defines that no charge is created nor destroyed in the circuit.

24. A is correct.

The capacitance of capacitors connected in parallel is the sum of the individual capacitances:

$$C_{eq} = C_1 + C_2 + C_3 + C_4 = 4C$$

The relationship between the total charge delivered by the battery and the voltage of the battery is:

$$V = Q / C_{eq} = Q / 4C$$

The charge on one capacitor is:

$$Q_1 = CV$$

$$Q_1 = C (Q / 4C)$$

$$Q_1 = Q / 4$$

25. B is correct.

If two conductors are connected by copper wire, each conductor will be at the same potential because current can flow through the wire and equalize the difference in potential.

26. C is correct.

Electromagnetic induction is the production of an electromotive force across a conductor.

When a changing magnetic field is brought near a coil, a voltage is generated in the coil thus inducing a current.

The voltage generated can be calculated by Faraday's Law:

$$\text{emf} = -N\Delta\phi / \Delta t$$

where N = number of turns and $\Delta\phi$ = change in magnetic flux

27. D is correct.

Calculate resistance:

$$R = \rho L / A$$

$$A = \pi r^2 = (\pi / 4)d^2$$

$$R = [(2.22 \times 10^{-8}\ \Omega\cdot m)\cdot(0.18\ m)] / (\pi / 4)\cdot(0.002\ m)^2$$

$$R = 1.3 \times 10^{-3}\ \Omega$$

$$P = I^2 R$$

$$P = (0.5\ A)^2 \times (1.3 \times 10^{-3}\ \Omega)$$

$$P = 0.32\ mW$$

28. D is correct. By convention, the direction of electric current is the direction that a positive charge migrates.

Therefore, current flows from a point of high potential to a point of lower potential.

29. E is correct. $PE_e = PE_1 + PE_2 + PE_3$

$PE_e = (kQ_1Q_2) / r_1 + (kQ_2Q_3) / r_2 + (kQ_1Q_3) / r_3$

$PE_e = kQ^2 [(1 / r_1) + (1 / r_2) + (1 / r_3)]$

$r_1 = 4$ cm and $r_2 = 3$ cm are known, use Pythagorean Theorem to find r_3:

$r_3^2 = r_1^2 + r_2^2$

$r_3^2 = (4 \text{ cm})^2 + (3 \text{ cm})^2$

$r_3^2 = 16 \text{ cm}^2 + 9 \text{ cm}^2$

$r_3^2 = 25 \text{ cm}^2$

$r_3 = 5$ cm

$PE_e = (9.0 \times 10^9 \text{ N·m}^2/\text{C}^2)·(3.8 \times 10^{-9} \text{ C})^2 \times [(1 / 0.04 \text{ m}) + (1 / 0.03 \text{ m}) + (1 / 0.05 \text{ m})]$

$PE_e = (1.2 \times 10^{-7} \text{ N·m}^2)·(25 \text{ m}^{-1} + 33 \text{ m}^{-1} + 20 \text{ m}^{-1})$

$PE_e = (1.2 \times 10^{-7} \text{ N·m}^2)·(78 \text{ m}^{-1})$

$PE_e = 1.0 \times 10^{-5}$ J

30. A is correct. The magnetic force acting on a charge q moving at velocity v in a magnetic field B is given by:

$F = qv \times B$

If q, v, and the angle between v and B are the same for both charges, then the magnitude of the force F is the same on both charges.

However, if the charges carry opposite signs, each experiences oppositely-directed forces.

31. C is correct. By convention, the direction of electric current is the direction that a positive charge migrates.

Electrons flow from regions of low potential to regions of high potential.

Electric Potential Energy:

$U = (kQq) / r$

Electric Potential:

$V = (kQ) / r$

Because the charge of an electron (q) is negative, as the electron moves opposite to the electric field, it must be getting closer to the positive charge Q. As this occurs, an increasingly negative potential energy U is produced; thus, potential energy is decreasing.

Conversely, as the electron approaches Q, the electric potential V increases with less distance. This is because the product is positive and reducing r increases V.

32. E is correct.

Magnets provide magnetic forces.

Generators convert mechanical energy into electrical energy, turbines extract energy from fluids (e.g. air and water), and transformers transfer energy between circuits.

33. B is correct. The potential energy of a system containing two point charges is:

$U = k q_1 q_2 / r$

In this problem, one of the charges is positive and the other is negative. To account for this, write:

$q_1 = +| q_1|$ and $q_2 = -| q_2|$

The potential energy can be written as:

$U = -k |q_1| |q_2| / r$

And the absolute value of the potential energy is:

$|U| = k |q_1| |q_2| / r$

All quantities are positive. The absolute value of the potential energy is inversely proportional to the orbital radius; therefore, the absolute value of the potential energy decreases as the orbital radius increases.

34. C is correct.

$R = (\rho L) / (\pi r^2)$

$R_A = (\rho L) / (\pi r^2)$

$R_B = [\rho(2L)] / [\pi(2r)^2]$

$R_B = (2/4)\cdot[(\rho L) / (\pi r^2)]$

$R_B = \frac{1}{2}[(\rho L) / (\pi r^2)]$

$R_B = \frac{1}{2}R_A$

35. D is correct.

By convention, current flows from high to low potential, but it represents the flow of positive charges.

Electron flow is in the opposite direction, from low potential to high potential.

36. C is correct.

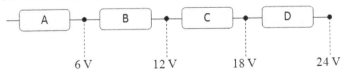

6 V   12 V   18 V   24 V

Batteries in series add voltage like resistors in series add resistance.

The resistances of the lights they power are not needed to solve the problem.

37. B is correct. $C = (k\mathcal{E}_0 A) / d$

$k = (Cd) / A\mathcal{E}_0$

If capacitance increases by a factor of 4:

$k_2 = (4C)d / A\mathcal{E}_0$

$k_2 = 4(Cd / A\mathcal{E}_0)$

$k_2 = 4k$

38. E is correct. $C = (k\mathcal{E}_0 A) / d$

$C = [(1)\cdot(8.854 \times 10^{-12}\ \text{F/m})\cdot(0.4\ \text{m}^2)] / (0.04\ \text{m})$

$C = 8.854 \times 10^{-11}\ \text{F}$

$V = Q / C$

$V = (6.8 \times 10^{-10}\ \text{C}) / (8.854 \times 10^{-11}\ \text{F})$

$V = 7.7\ \text{V}$

39. A is correct. Since force is the cross-product of velocity and magnetic field strength:

$F = qv \times B$

The force is at a maximum when v and B are perpendicular:

$F = qvB \sin 90°$

$\sin 90° = 1$

$F = qvB$

40. D is correct. Potential Energy:

$U = kQq / r$

Electric Potential:

$V = kQ / r$

Electric potential decreases when moving away from positive charges toward negative charges. Therefore, as the electron moves from left to right, the potential decreases.

Since the force on the electron points to the left, while its displacement is opposite of that (i.e., to the right), the work done by the field is negative. The change of potential energy is equal to the negative of the work done by the field, thus the potential energy increases.

41. C is correct.

$\Delta V = \Delta E / q$

$\Delta V = (1 / q)\cdot(\tfrac{1}{2}mv_f^2 - \tfrac{1}{2}mv_i^2)$

$\Delta V = (m / 2q)\cdot(v_f^2 - v_i^2)$

$\Delta V = [(1.67 \times 10^{-27}\ \text{kg}) / (2)\cdot(1.6 \times 10^{-19}\ \text{C})] \times [(3.2 \times 10^5\ \text{m/s})^2 - (1.7 \times 10^5\ \text{m/s})^2]$

$\Delta V = 684\ \text{V}$

42. E is correct.

$$Q = VC$$

Even though the capacitors have different capacitances, the voltage across each capacitor is inversely proportional to the capacitance of that capacitor.

Like current, charge is conserved across capacitors in series.

43. A is correct. Calculate capacitance:

$$C = k\mathcal{E}_\text{o}A / d$$

$$C = [(1){\cdot}(8.854 \times 10^{-12} \text{ F/m}){\cdot}(0.6 \text{ m}^2)] / (0.06 \text{ m})$$

$$C = 8.854 \times 10^{-11} \text{ F}$$

Find potential difference:

$$C = Q / V$$

$$V = Q / C$$

$$V = (7.08 \times 10^{-10} \text{ C}) / (8.854 \times 10^{-11} \text{ F})$$

$$V = 8 \text{ V}$$

44. B is correct. The force on the proton is given by:

$$F = qE$$

$$a = F / m, \ v_1 = 0 \text{ m/s}$$

The final velocity is given by:

$$v_2 = v_1 + a\Delta t$$

$$v_2 = (qE / m)\Delta t$$

$$v_2 = (1.6 \times 10^{-19} \text{ C}){\cdot}(140 \text{ N/C}){\cdot}(1.8 \times 10^{-4} \text{ s}) / (1.67 \times 10^{-27} \text{ kg})$$

$$v_2 = 2.4 \times 10^{6} \text{ m/s}$$

45. C is correct. Faraday's Law: a changing magnetic environment causes a voltage to be induced in a conductor. Metal detectors send quick magnetic pulses that cause a voltage (by Faraday's Law) and subsequent current to be induced in the conductor.

By Lenz's Law, an opposing magnetic field will then arise to counter the changing magnetic field. The detector picks up the magnetic field and notifies the operator.

Thus, metal detectors use Faraday's Law and Lenz's Law to detect metal objects.

46. E is correct.

$$E = qV$$

$$E = (7 \times 10^{-6} \text{ C}){\cdot}(3.5 \times 10^{-3} \text{ V})$$

$$E = 24.5 \times 10^{-9} \text{ J}$$

$$E = 24.5 \text{ nJ}$$

47. B is correct.

$R_1 = \rho L_1 / A_1$

$R_2 = \rho(4L_1) / A_2$

$R_1 = R_2$

$\rho L_1 / A_1 = \rho(4L_1) / A_2$

$A_2 = 4A_1$

$(\pi / 4)d_2^2 = (\pi / 4)\cdot(4)d_1^2$

$d_2^2 = 4d_1^2$

$d_2 = 2d_1$

48. D is correct.

The total resistance of a network of series resistors increases as more resistors are added.

$V = IR$

An increase in the total resistance results in a decrease in the total current through the network.

49. A is correct.

This is a circuit with two resistors in series.

Combine the two resistors into one resistor:

$R_T = R + R_{int}$

$R_T = 0.5\ \Omega + 0.1\ \Omega$

$R_T = 0.6\ \Omega$

Ohm's law:

$V = IR$

$I = V / R$

$I = 9\ V / 0.6\ \Omega$

$I = 15\ A$

50. C is correct.

Energy stored in capacitor:

$U = \frac{1}{2}(Q^2 / C)$

Capacitance:

$C = k\varepsilon_0 A / d$

$U = \frac{1}{2}(Q^2 d) / (k\varepsilon_0 A)$

$Q = \sqrt{[(2U \times k\varepsilon_0 A) / d]}$

$Q = \sqrt{\{[(2)\cdot(10 \times 10^3\ J)\cdot(1)\cdot(8.854 \times 10^{-12}\ F/m)\cdot(2.4 \times 10^{-5}\ m^2)] / 0.0016\ m\}}$

$Q = 52\ \mu C$

Light and Optics – Explanations

1. A is correct.

Soap film that reflects a given wavelength of light exhibits constructive interference.

The expression for constructive interference of a thin film:

$2t = (m + \frac{1}{2})\lambda$

where t = thickness, m = 0, 1, 2, 3… and λ = wavelength

To find the minimum thickness set m = 0:

$2t = (0 + \frac{1}{2})\lambda = \frac{1}{2}\lambda$

$t = \frac{1}{4}\lambda$

2. A is correct. The Doppler effect is qualitatively similar for both light and sound waves.

If the source and the observer move towards each other, the f_{det} is higher than the f_{source}.

If the source and the observer move away from each other, the f_{det} is lower than the f_{source}.

Since the galaxy is moving away from the Earth, the f_{det} is lower.

The speed of light through space is constant ($c = \lambda f$).

A lower f_{det} means a longer λ_{det}, so the λ_{det} is longer than the λ_{source}.

The λ has been shifted towards the red end of the visible spectrum because red light is the visible light with the longest λ.

3. B is correct.

If image is twice her height and upright, then:

$2h_o = h_i$

$m = h_i / h_o$

$m = -d_i / d_o$

$m = 2h_o / h_o$

$m = 2$

$2 = -d_i / d_o$

$-2d_o = d_i$

Use lens equation to solve:

$1 / f = 1 / d_o + 1 / d_i$

$1 / 100 \text{ cm} = 1 / d_o + (-1 / 2 d_o)$

$1 / 100 \text{ cm} = 1 / 2 d_o$

$2d_o = 100 \text{ cm}$

$d_o = 50 \text{ cm}$

4. D is correct.

If a person's eye is too long, the light entering the eye is focused in front of the retina causing myopia. This condition is also referred to as nearsightedness.

Hyperopia is also referred to as farsightedness.

5. E is correct.

Visible light:

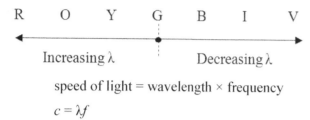

speed of light = wavelength × frequency

$c = \lambda f$

Wavelength to frequency:

$f = c / \lambda$

Frequency and wavelength are inversely proportional:

As λ increases, f decreases.

As λ decreases, f increases.

Thus, because $E = hf$:

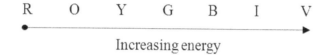

6. B is correct.

The lens equation:

$1 / f = 1 / d_o + 1 / d_i$

$1 / d_i = 1 / f - 1 / d_o$

$1 / d_i = -1 / 3 \text{ m} - 1 / 4 \text{ m}$

$1 / d_i = (-3 \text{ m} - 4 \text{ m}) / 12 \text{ m}$

$1 / d_i = -7 \text{ m} / 12 \text{ m}$

$d_i = -12 / 7 \text{ m}$

Magnification:

$m = -d_i / d_o$

$m = -(-12 / 7 \text{ m}) / 4 \text{ m}$

$m = 3 / 7$

Height of the candle image:

$h_i = m h_o$

$h_i = (3/7) \cdot (18 \text{ cm})$

$h_i = 54 / 7 \text{ cm}$

$h_i = 7.7 \text{ cm}$

7. C is correct.

$\theta_{syrup} = \tan^{-1} (0.9 \text{ m} / 0.66 \text{ m})$

$\theta_s = \tan^{-1} (1.36)$

$\theta_s = 53.7°$

$\theta_{oil} = \tan^{-1} [(2 \text{ m} - 0.9 \text{ m}) / 1.58 \text{ m}]$

$\theta_o = \tan^{-1} (0.7)$

$\theta_o = 34.8°$

$n_o \sin \theta_o = n_{air} \sin \theta_{air}$

$n_o \sin 34.8° = (1) \sin 90°$

$n_o = 1 / (\sin 34.8°)$

$n_o = 1.75$

8. D is correct.

$\theta_{syrup} = \tan^{-1} (0.9 \text{ m} / 0.66 \text{ m})$

$\theta_s = \tan^{-1} (1.36)$

$\theta_s = 53.7°$

$\theta_{oil} = \tan^{-1} [(2 \text{ m} - 0.9 \text{ m}) / 1.58 \text{ m}]$

$\theta_o = \tan^{-1} (0.7)$

$\theta_o = 34.8°$

$n_o \sin \theta_o = n_{air} \sin \theta_{air}$

$n_o \sin 34.8° = (1) \sin 90°$

$n_o = 1 / (\sin 34.8°)$

$n_o = 1.75$

$n_s \sin \theta_s = n_o \sin \theta_o$

$n_s = n_o \sin \theta_o / \sin \theta_s$

$n_s = (1.75) \cdot (\sin 34.8°) / (\sin 53.7°)$

$n_s = 1.24$

9. A is correct.

10. D is correct.

Geometrical optics, or ray optics, describes light propagation in terms of rays and fronts to approximate the path along which light propagates in certain circumstances.

11. D is correct.

First find the critical angle:

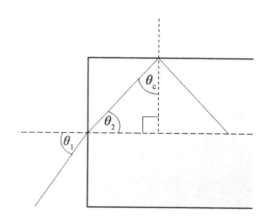

$$n_{fiber} \sin \theta_c = n_{air} \sin \theta_{air}$$

$$(1.26) \sin \theta_c = (1) \sin 90°$$

$$\sin \theta_c = 1 / 1.26$$

$$\theta_c = \sin^{-1} (1 / 1.26)$$

$$\theta_c = 52.5°$$

Find θ_2:

$$\theta_2 + \theta_c + 90° = 180°$$

$$(\theta_2 + 52.5° + 90°) = 180°$$

$$\theta_2 = 37.5°$$

Find θ_1:

$$n_{air} \sin \theta_1 = n_{fiber} \sin \theta_2$$

$$(1) \sin \theta_1 = (1.26) \sin 37.5°$$

$$\sin \theta_1 = 0.77$$

$$\theta_1 = \sin^{-1} (0.77)$$

$$\theta_1 = 50°$$

12. A is correct.

If the power of the lens is 10 diopters,

$$1 / f = 10 \text{ D}$$

where f is the focal length in m

Lens equation:

$$1 / f = 1 / d_o + 1 / d_i$$

$$10 \text{ m}^{-1} = 1 / 0.5 \text{ m} + 1 / d_i$$

$$1 / d_i = 10 \text{ m}^{-1} - 1 / 0.5 \text{ m}$$

$$1 / d_i = 8 \text{ m}^{-1}$$

$$d_i = 1 / 8 \text{ m}$$

$$d_i = 0.13 \text{ m}$$

13. D is correct. Most objects observed by humans are virtual images, or objects which reflect incoming light to project an image.

14. E is correct.

An image from a convex mirror will always have the following characteristics, regardless of object distance:

- located behind convex mirror
- virtual
- upright
- reduced in size from object (image < object)

15. A is correct.

The mirror has a positive focal length which indicates that the mirror is concave.

The object is at a distance greater than the focal length, therefore it is inverted.

Use lens equation to solve image distance:

$$1 / f = 1 / d_o + 1 / d_i$$

$$1 / 10 \text{ m} = 1 / 20 \text{ m} + 1 / d_i$$

$$d_i = 20 \text{ cm}$$

The image distance is positive so the image is real.

Use the magnification equation to determine if it is upright or inverted.

$$m = -d_i / d_o$$

$$m = h_i / h_o$$

$$-(20 \text{ m} / 20 \text{ m}) = h_i / h_o$$

$$-1 = h_i / h_o$$

The object height h_o is always positive so the image height h_i must be negative to satisfy the equation.

A negative image height indicates an inverted image.

16. E is correct.

For a converging lens, if an object is placed beyond $2f$ from the lens, the image is real, inverted and reduced.

Use the lens equation to determine if the image is real (or vitual):

Assume $f = 1$ m and $d_o = 3f$ (because $d_o > 2f$)

$$1 / f = 1 / d_o + 1/ d_i$$

$$1 / f = 1 / 3f + 1/ d_i$$

$$d_i = 1.5$$

A positive d_i indicates a real image.

Use the magnification equation to determine if the image is inverted and reduced.

$m = -d_i / d_o$

$m = -(1.5 \text{ m} / 3 \text{ m})$

$m = -\tfrac{1}{2}$

$|m| = \tfrac{1}{2}$

$|m| < 1$

A negative magnification factor with an absolute value less than 1 a reduced and inverted image.

17. A is correct.

Double convex lens:

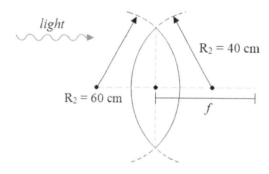

$R_2 = 40$ cm

$R_2 = 60$ cm

f

Lens maker formula:

$1 / f = (n - 1) \cdot (1 / R_1 - 1 / R_2)$

$1 / f = (1.54 - 1) \cdot (1 / 40 \text{ cm} - (1 / -60 \text{ cm}))$

$1 / f = -0.0225 \text{ cm}^{-1}$

$f = 44 \text{ cm}$

If light passes through the center of the radii of curvature (as it does to R_2) before the curve itself in the lens then that R is negative by convention.

18. B is correct.

A medium's index of refraction is the ratio of the speed of refracted light in a vacuum to its speed in the reference medium.

$n = c / v$

$n = 2.43$

$2.43 = c / v_{diamond}$

$c = 2.43(v_{diamond})$

19. D is correct.

$$1/f = 1/d_o + 1/d_i$$

$$1/20 \text{ cm} = 1/15 \text{ cm} + 1/d_i$$

$$3/60 \text{ cm} - 4/60 \text{ cm} = 1/d_i$$

$$-1/60 \text{ cm} = 1/d_i$$

$$d_i = -60 \text{ cm}$$

The negative sign indicates that the image is projected back the way it came.

20. B is correct.

Red paper absorbs all colors but reflects only red light giving it the appearance of being red. Cyan is the complementary color to red, so when the cyan light shines upon the red paper, no light is reflected and the paper appears black.

21. B is correct.

$$1/f = 1/d_o + 1/d_i$$

If $d_i = f$,

$$1/d_o = 0$$

Thus, d_o must be large.

22. E is correct.

Since the index of refraction depends on the frequency, and the focal length depends on the refraction of the beam in the lens, dispersion causes the focal length to depend on frequency.

23. C is correct.

Use the equation for magnification:

$$m = -d_i/d_o$$

$$d_i = d_o$$

$$m = 1$$

Thus, there is no magnification, so the image is the same size as the object.

24. E is correct.

25. C is correct.

26. C is correct.

First, find the angle that the ray makes with the normal of the glass:

$$180° = x + 90° + 54°$$

$$x = 36°$$

Find θ_1:

$$\theta_1 = 90° - 36°$$

$$\theta_1 = 54°$$

Referring to the diagram, $\theta_1 = 54°$

Snell's Law:

$$n_1 \sin \theta_1 = n_2 \sin \theta_2$$

$$\sin^{-1} [(n_1 / n_2) \sin \theta_1] = \theta_2$$

$$\theta_2 = \sin^{-1}[(1.45 / 1.35) \sin 54°]$$

$$\theta_2 = 60°$$

Solve for the angle with the horizontal:

$$\theta_H = 60° - 54°$$

$$\theta_H = 6°$$

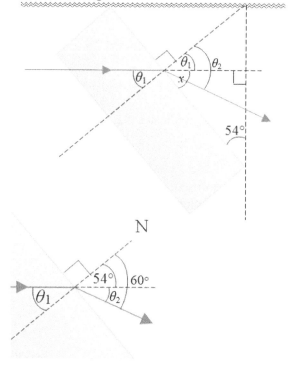

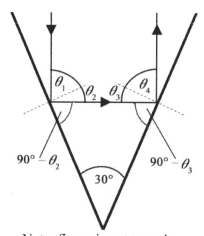

27. A is correct.

The angle at which the ray is turned is the sum of the angles if reflected off each mirror once:

$$\theta_{\text{turned}} = \theta_1 + \theta_2 + \theta_3 + \theta_4$$

By law of reflection:

$$\theta_1 = \theta_2$$

$$\theta_3 = \theta_4$$

Note the triangle formed (sum of interior angles is 180°):

$$30° + (90° - \theta_2) + (90° - \theta_3) = 180°$$

$$\theta_2 + \theta_3 = 30°$$

Given:

$$\theta_2 + \theta_3 = \theta_1 + \theta_4$$

Thus:

$$\theta_{\text{turned}} = 30° + 30°$$

$$\theta_{\text{turned}} = 60°$$

Note: figure is not to scale

In general: for two plane mirrors that meet at an angle of $\theta \leq 90°$ the ray that is deflected off both mirrors is deflected through an angle of 2θ.

28. A is correct.

$$n_1 \sin \theta_1 = n_1 \sin \theta_2$$

$$(1) \sin (90° - 30°) = (1.73) \sin \theta_2$$

$$\sin (60°) = 1.73 \sin \theta_2$$

$$\sin \theta_2 = \sin (60°) / 1.73$$

$$\sin \theta_2 = 0.5$$

$$\theta_2 = \sin^{-1} (0.5)$$

$$\theta_2 = 30°$$

29. D is correct.

The first lens has a power:

$$P_1 = 1 / f$$

$$P_1 = \tfrac{1}{2} \, D$$

For a combination of total power:

$$P_{tot} = 1 / f_{tot}$$

$$P_{tot} = 1/3 \, D$$

Thus,

$$P_2 = P_{tot} - P_1$$

$$P_2 = 1/3 \, D - 1/2 \, D$$

$$P_2 = -1/6 \, D$$

30. E is correct.

Plane mirrors do not distort the size or the shape of an object since light is reflected at the same angle it was received by the mirror.

Magnification equation:

$$m = h_i / h_o$$

For a plane mirror m = 1:

$$1 = h_i / h_o$$

$$h_i = h_o$$

Therefore, image size is the same as object size, and the image is virtual since it is located behind the mirror.

31. C is correct.

A spherical concave mirror has a focal length of:

$$f = R / 2$$

32. B is correct.

Refracted rays bend further from the normal than the original incident angle when the refracting medium is optically less dense than the incident medium. Therefore, $n_1 > n_2$.

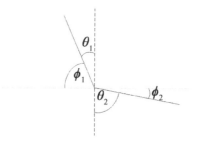

The index of refraction for a medium can never be less than 1.

33. B is correct. If a person's eye is too short, then the light entering the eye is focused behind the retina causing farsightedness (hyperopia).

34. A is correct. Hot air is less dense than cold air. Light traveling through both types of air experiences refractions, which appear as shimmering or "wavy" air.

35. E is correct.

Chromatic aberration occurs when a lens focuses different wavelengths of color at different positions in the focal plane.

It always occurs in the following pattern for converging lens:

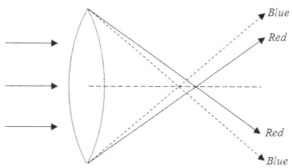

36. B is correct.

$$1 / f_{total} = 1 / f_1 + 1 / f_2$$
$$1 / f_{total} = 1 / 2 \text{ m} + 1 / 4 \text{ m}$$
$$1 / f_{total} = 3 / 4 \text{ m}$$
$$f_{total} = 4 / 3 \text{ m}$$

37. C is correct. The angle in the water respective to the normal:

$$\theta = \tan^{-1} (37.5 \text{ ft} / 50 \text{ ft})$$
$$\theta = \tan^{-1} (0.75)$$
$$\theta = 36.9°$$
$$n_{air} \sin (90 - \theta) = n_{water} \sin \theta$$
$$(1) \sin (90 - \theta) = (1.33) \sin 36.9°$$
$$\sin (90 - \theta) = 0.8$$
$$(90 - \theta) = \sin^{-1} (0.8)$$
$$(90 - \theta) = 52.9$$
$$\theta = 37.1° \approx 37°$$

38. D is correct.

$$1/f = 1/d_o + 1/d_i$$
$$1/f = 1/2f + 1/d_i$$
$$1/f - 1/2f = 1/d_i$$
$$1/2f = 1/d_i$$
$$d_i = 2f$$

39. E is correct. Objects directly in front of plane mirrors are reflected in their likeness, since plane mirrors are not curved and therefore reflect light perpendicularly to their surface.

40. B is correct. A virtual image is always upright and can be formed by both a diverging lens and converging lens.

Diverging lens → reduced and virtual image

Converging lens → enlarged and virtual image

41. B is correct. Neon light is the light emitted from neon atoms as their energized electrons cascade back down to ground level. When this occurs, energy is released in the form of light at very specific wavelengths known as the emission spectrum.

When this light is passed through a prism, a series of bright discontinuous spots or lines will be seen due to the specific wavelengths of emission spectrum of neon.

42. A is correct.

Both the photoelectric effect and quantization of energy rely upon the particle/wave nature of light to be explained. Polarization, however, is only a property of waves and cannot be explained through particle theory.

43. C is correct. A concave lens always forms an image that is virtual, upright and reduced in size.

44. B is correct. Virtual images are always upright.

There is no correlation between the size and nature – virtual or real – of an image.

Images may be larger, smaller, or the same size as the object.

45. D is correct. Lens maker formula:

$$1/f = (n - 1) \cdot (1/R_1 - 1/R_2)$$

For a flat surface:

$$R_2 = \infty$$
$$1/f = (1.64 - 1) \cdot [(1/33\ cm) - (1/\infty)]$$
$$1/f = (0.64) \cdot (1/33\ cm)$$
$$f = 51.6\ cm \approx 52\ cm$$

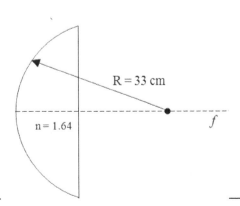

46. D is correct.

$1 / f = 1 / d_o + 1 / d_i$

$1 / 6 \text{ m} = 1 / 3 \text{ m} + 1 / d_i$

$1 / d_i = 1 / 6 \text{ m} - 1 / 3 \text{ m}$

$1 / d_i = -1 / 6 \text{ m}$

$d_i = -6 \text{ m}$

where the negative sign indicates the image is on the same side as the object.

The image is upright and virtual, since the rays must be extended to intersect.

47. A is correct. A diverging lens (concave) always produces an image that is virtual, upright and reduced in size.

48. C is correct. Thin lens formula:

$1 / f = 1 / d_o + 1 / d_i$

d_i is negative because the image is virtual

$1 / f = 1 / 14 \text{ cm} + 1 / -5 \text{ cm}$

$f = -7.8 \text{ cm}$

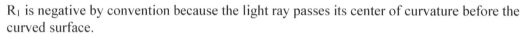

The focus is negative because the lens is diverging.

Lens maker formula:

$1 / f = (n - 1) \cdot (1 / R_1 - 1 / R_2)$

R_1 is negative by convention because the light ray passes its center of curvature before the curved surface.

$1 / (-7.8 \text{ cm}) = (n - 1) \cdot (1 / -15 \text{ cm} - 1 / 15 \text{ cm})$

$(1 / -7.8 \text{ cm}) \cdot (15 \text{ cm} / -2) + 1 = n$

$n = 2$

49. E is correct.

The magnification equation relates the image and object distance:

$m = -d_i / d_o$

or

The magnification equation relates the image and object height:

$m = h_i / h_o$

50. D is correct. (see image)

For a concave mirror, if an object is located between the focal point and center of curvature the image is formed beyond the center of curvature.

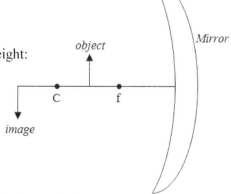

In this problem, Mike does not see his image because he is in front of where it forms.

Heat and Thermodynamics – Explanations

1. B is correct. Ideal gas law:

$$PV = nRT$$

$$P_0 = nRT / V_0$$

If isothermal expansion, then n, R and T are constant

$$P = nRT / (1/3 \, V_0)$$

$$P = 3(nRT / V_0)$$

$$P = 3P_0$$

2. C is correct. Area expansion equation:

$$\Delta A = A_0(2\alpha\Delta T)$$

$$\Delta A = (\pi / 4)\cdot(1.2 \text{ cm})^2\cdot(2)\cdot(19 \times 10^{-6} \text{ K}^{-1})\cdot(200 \text{ °C})$$

$$\Delta A = 8.6 \times 10^{-3} \text{ cm}^2$$

$$\Delta A = A_f - A_0$$

$$8.6 \times 10^{-3} \text{ cm}^2 = (\pi / 4)\cdot[d_f^2 - (1.2 \text{ cm})^2]$$

$$d_f = 1.2 \text{ cm}$$

3. D is correct.

$$1 \text{ Watt} = 1 \text{ J/s}$$

$$\text{Power} \times \text{Time} = Q$$

$$Q = mc\Delta T$$

$$P \times t = mc\Delta T$$

$$t = (mc\Delta T) / P$$

$$t = (90 \text{ g})\cdot(4.186 \text{ J/g·°C})\cdot(30 \text{ °C} - 10 \text{ °C}) / (50 \text{ W})$$

$$t = 151 \text{ s}$$

4. A is correct.

Convert 15 minutes to seconds:

$$t = (15 \text{ min}/1)\cdot(60 \text{ s}/1 \text{ min})$$

$$t = 900 \text{ s}$$

Find total energy generated:

$$Q = P \times t$$

$$Q = (1{,}260 \text{ J/s})\cdot(900 \text{ s})$$

$$Q = 1{,}134 \text{ kJ}$$

Find mass of water needed to carry away energy:

$$Q = mL_v$$

$$m = Q \,/\, L_v$$

$$m = (1{,}134 \text{ kJ}) \,/\, (22.6 \times 10^2 \text{ kJ/kg})$$

$$m = 0.5 \text{ kg}$$

$$m = 500 \text{ g}$$

5. C is correct. Phase changes occur at constant temperature. Once the phase change is complete the temperature of the substance then either increases or decreases.

For example, water remains at 0 °C until it has completely changed phase to ice before the temperature decreases further.

6. E is correct.

The amount of energy needed to melt a sample of mass m is:

$$Q = m \, L_f$$

Where L_f is the latent heat of fusion.

$$Q = (55 \text{ kg}) \cdot (334 \text{ kJ/kg})$$

$$Q = 1.8 \times 10^4 \text{ kJ}$$

7. D is correct.

Metals are good heat and electrical conductors because of their bonding structure. In metallic bonding, the outer electrons are held loosely and can travel freely. Electricity and heat require high electron mobility. Thus, the looseness of the outer electrons in the materials allows them to be excellent conductors.

8. A is correct. Find heat of phase change from steam to liquid:

$$Q_1 = mL_v$$

Find heat of phase change from liquid to solid:

$$Q_2 = mL_f$$

Find heat of temperature from 100 °C to 0 °C:

$$Q_3 = mc\Delta T$$

Total heat:

$$Q_{net} = Q_1 + Q_2 + Q_3$$

$$Q_{net} = mL_v + mL_f + mc\Delta T$$

To find mass:

$$Q_{net} = m(L_v + c\Delta T + L_f)$$

$$m = Q_{net} \,/\, (L_v + c\Delta T + L_f)$$

Solve:

$$Q_{net} = 200 \text{ kJ}$$

$$Q_{net} = 2 \times 10^5 \text{ J}$$

$$m = (2 \times 10^5 \text{ J}) / [(22.6 \times 10^5 \text{ J/kg}) + (4,186 \text{ J/kg·K})·(100 \text{ °C} - 0 \text{ °C}) + (33.5 \times 10^4 \text{ J/kg})]$$

$$m = 0.066 \text{ kg}$$

9. C is correct.

Heat to melt ice cube:

$$Q_1 = mL_f$$

Heat to raise the temperature:

$$Q_2 = mc\Delta T$$

Total heat:

$$Q_{total} = Q_1 + Q_2$$

$$Q_{total} = mL_f + mc\Delta T$$

$$Q_{total} = (0.3 \text{ kg})·(334 \text{ kJ/kg}) + (0.3 \text{ kg})·(4.186 \text{ kJ/kg·K})·(60 \text{ °C} - 0 \text{ °C})$$

$$Q_{total} = 176 \text{ kJ}$$

10. B is correct.

$$Q = (mc\Delta T)_{water} + (mc\Delta T)_{beaker}$$

Change in temperature is the same for both:

$$Q = \Delta T[(mc)_{water} + (mc)_{beaker}]$$

$$1,800 \text{ cal} = (20 \text{ °C})·[(65 \text{ g})·(1 \text{ cal/g·°C}) + (m_{beaker})·(0.18 \text{ cal/g·°C})]$$

$$90 \text{ cal/°C} = 65 \text{ cal/°C} + (m_{beaker})·(0.18 \text{ cal/g·°C})$$

$$25 \text{ cal/°C} / (0.18 \text{ cal/g·°C}) = (m_{beaker})$$

$$m_{beaker} = 139 \text{ g}$$

11. B is correct. Heat needed to raise temperature of aluminum:

$$Q_A = m_A c_A \Delta T$$

Heat needed to raise temperature of water:

$$Q_W = m_W c_W \Delta T$$

Total heat to raise temperature of system:

$$Q_{net} = Q_A + Q_W$$

$$Q_{net} = m_A c_A \Delta T + m_W c_W \Delta T$$

$$Q_{net} = \Delta T(m_A c_A + m_W c_W)$$

$$Q_{net} = (98 \text{ °C} - 18 \text{ °C})·[(0.5 \text{ kg})·(900 \text{ J/kg·K}) + (1 \text{ kg})·(4,186 \text{ J/kg·K})]$$

$$Q_{net} = 370,880 \text{ J}$$

Time to produce Q_{net} with 500 W:

$$Q_{net} = (500\ W)t$$

$$t = Q_{net} / (500\ W)$$

$$t = (370,880\ J) / 500\ W$$

$$t = 741.8\ s$$

Convert to minutes:

$$t = (741.8\ s/1)\cdot(1\ min/60\ s)$$

$$t = 12.4\ min \approx 12\ min$$

12. A is correct.

When a substance goes through a phase change, the temperature doesn't change.

It can be assumed that the lower plateau is L_f and the upper plateau is L_v.

Count the columns: $L_f = 2$, $L_v = 7$

$$L_v / L_f = 7 / 2$$

$$L_v / L_f = 3.5$$

13. B is correct.

Specific heat is the amount of heat (i.e. energy) needed to raise the temperature of the unit mass of a substance by a given amount (usually one degree).

14. E is correct.

Find ½ of KE of the BB:

$$KE = \tfrac{1}{2}mv^2$$

$$\tfrac{1}{2}KE = \tfrac{1}{2}(\tfrac{1}{2}mv^2)$$

$$\tfrac{1}{2}KE_{BB} = \tfrac{1}{2}(\tfrac{1}{2})\cdot(0.0045\ kg)\cdot(46\ m/s)^2$$

$$\tfrac{1}{2}KE_{BB} = 2.38\ J$$

The $\tfrac{1}{2}KE_{BB}$ is equal to energy taken to change temperature:

$$Q = \tfrac{1}{2}KE_{BB}$$
$$Q = mc\Delta T$$

$$mc\Delta T = \tfrac{1}{2}KE_{BB}$$

$$\Delta T = \tfrac{1}{2}KE_{BB} / mc$$

Calculate to find ΔT:

$$\Delta T = (2.38\ J) / (0.0045\ kg)\cdot(128\ J/kg\cdot K)$$

$$\Delta T = 4.1\ K$$

15. D is correct.

Carnot efficiency engines can be written as:

$$\eta = 1 - T_C / T_H$$

$$\eta = 1 - |\, Q_C / Q_H\,|$$

Thus:

$$Q_C / Q_H = T_C / T_H$$

16. A is correct.

Carnot efficiency:

$$\eta = \text{work done} / \text{total energy}$$

$$\eta = W / Q_H$$

$$\eta = 5 \text{ J} / 18 \text{ J}$$

$$\eta = 0.28$$

The engine's efficiency:

$$\eta = (T_H - T_C) / T_H$$

$$0.28 = (233 \text{ K} - T_C) / 233 \text{ K}$$

$$(0.28){\cdot}(233 \text{ K}) = (233 \text{ K} - T_C)$$

$$65.2 \text{ K} = 233 \text{ K} - T_C$$

$$T_C = 168 \text{ K}$$

17. D is correct. Heat needed to change temperature of a mass:

$$Q = mc\Delta T$$

Calculate to find Q:

$$Q = (0.92 \text{ kg}){\cdot}(113 \text{ cal/kg}{\cdot}°C){\cdot}(96 \text{ °C} - 18 \text{ °C})$$

$$Q = 8,108.9 \text{ cal}$$

Convert to joules:

$$Q = (8,108.9 \text{ cal}){\cdot}(4.186 \text{ J/cal})$$

$$Q = 33,940 \text{ J}$$

18. C is correct.

$$Q = mc\Delta T$$

Find heat added to aluminum calorimeter:

$$Q_A = (0.08 \text{ kg}){\cdot}(910 \text{ J/kg}{\cdot}K){\cdot}(35 \text{ °C} - 20 \text{ °C})$$

$$Q_A = 1,092 \text{ J}$$

Find heat added to water:

$$Q_W = (0.36 \text{ kg}) \cdot (4{,}190 \text{ J/kg} \cdot \text{K}) \cdot (35 \text{ °C} - 20 \text{ °C})$$

$$Q_W = 22{,}626 \text{ J}$$

Find total heat added to the system:

$$Q_{total} = Q_A + Q_W$$

$$Q_{total} = 1{,}092 \text{ J} + 22{,}626 \text{ J}$$

$$Q_{total} = 23{,}718 \text{ J}$$

Find specific heat of the metal:

$$Q = mc\Delta T$$

$$c = Q \, / \, m\Delta T$$

$$c = (23{,}718 \text{ J}) \, / \, [(0.18 \text{ kg}) \cdot (305 \text{ °C} - 35 \text{ °C})]$$

$$c = 488 \text{ J/kg} \cdot \text{K}$$

19. E is correct.

20. A is correct.

Specific heat of A is larger than B:

$$c_A > c_B$$

Energy to raise the temperature:

$$Q = mc\Delta T$$

If m and ΔT are equal for A and B:

$$Q_A = m_A c_A \Delta T_A$$

$$Q_B = m_B c_B \Delta T_B$$

$$Q_A > Q_B$$

This is valid because all other factors are equal and the magnitude of Q only depends on c.

21. D is correct.

Find kinetic energy of meteor:

$$KE = \tfrac{1}{2}mv^2$$

$$KE = \tfrac{1}{2}(0.0065 \text{ kg}) \cdot (300 \text{ m/s})^2$$

$$KE = 292.5 \text{ J}$$

Find temperature rise:

$$Q = KE$$

$$Q = mc\Delta T$$

$$mc\Delta T = KE$$

$$\Delta T = KE \, / \, mc$$

Convert KE to calories:

$$KE = (292.5 \text{ J/1}) \cdot (1 \text{ cal/4.186 J})$$

$$KE = 69.9 \text{ cal}$$

Calculate ΔT:

$$\Delta T = (69.9 \text{ cal}) / [(0.0065 \text{ kg}) \cdot (120 \text{ cal/kg} \cdot {}^\circ\text{C})]$$

$$\Delta T = 89.6 \ {}^\circ\text{C} \approx 90 \ {}^\circ\text{C}$$

22. D is correct.

$$Q = mc\Delta T$$

Find heat released for temperature drop from 160 °C to 150 °C:

$$Q_1 = (3.4 \text{ kg}) \cdot (400 \text{ J/kg} \cdot \text{K}) \cdot (160 \ {}^\circ\text{C} - 150 \ {}^\circ\text{C})$$

$$Q_1 = 13{,}600 \text{ J}$$

Find heat released due to condensation:

$$Q_2 = mL_v$$

$$Q_2 = (3.4 \text{ kg}) \cdot (7.2 \times 10^4 \text{ J/kg})$$

$$Q_2 = 244{,}800 \text{ J}$$

Find heat released for temperature drop from 150 °C to 75 °C:

$$Q_3 = mc\Delta T$$

$$Q_3 = (3.4 \text{ kg}) \cdot (1{,}000 \text{ J/kg} \cdot \text{K}) \cdot (150 \ {}^\circ\text{C} - 75 \ {}^\circ\text{C})$$

$$Q_3 = 255{,}000 \text{ J}$$

Sum the heats:

$$Q_{net} = Q_1 + Q_2 + Q_3$$

$$Q_{net} = (13{,}600 \text{ J} + 244{,}800 \text{ J} + 255{,}000 \text{ J})$$

$$Q_{net} = 513{,}400 \text{ J} = 513 \text{ kJ}$$

23. B is correct.

For an isothermal process:

$$\Delta U = 0$$

$$\Delta U = Q - W$$

$$Q = W$$

Work to expand an ideal gas in an isothermal process:

$$W = nRT \ln(V_f / V_i)$$

From the ideal gas law, $nRT = P_fV_f$, giving:

$W = P_fV_f \ln(V_f / V_i)$

$W = (130 \text{ kPa}) \cdot (0.2 \text{ m}^3) \ln[(0.2 \text{ m}^3) / (0.05 \text{ m}^3)]$

$W = 36 \text{ kJ}$

$Q = W$

$Q = 36 \text{ kJ}$

Since the process is isothermal, there is no change in the internal energy. Since the surroundings are doing negative work on the system:

$\Delta E = 0 = Q + W = Q - 36 \text{ kJ}$

Therefore:

$Q = 36 \text{ kJ}.$

24. D is correct. Find the potential energy of 1 kg of water:

$PE = mgh$

$PE = (1 \text{ kg}) \cdot (9.8 \text{ m/s}^2) \cdot (30 \text{ m})$

$PE = 294 \text{ J}$

Assume all potential energy is converted to heat for maximum temperature increase:

$PE = Q$

$Q = mc\Delta T$

$mc\Delta T = PE$

$\Delta T = PE / mc$

$\Delta T = (294 \text{ J}) / [(1 \text{ kg}) \cdot (4,186 \text{ J/kg/K})]$

$\Delta T = 0.07 \text{ °C}$

For temperature differences it is not necessary to convert to Kelvin because a temperature change in Kelvin is equal to a temperature change in Celsius.

25. A is correct. Find heat from phase change:

$Q = mL_f$

$Q = (0.75 \text{ kg}) \cdot (33,400 \text{ J/kg})$

$Q = 25,050 \text{ J}$

Because the water is freezing, Q should be negative due to heat being released.

$Q = -25,050 \text{ J}$

Find change in entropy:

$\Delta S = Q / T$

$\Delta S = -25,050 \text{ J} / (0 \text{ °C} + 273 \text{ K})$

$\Delta S = -92 \text{ J} / \text{K}$

A negative change in entropy indicates that the disorder of the isolated system has decreased. When water freezes the entropy is negative because water is more disordered than ice. Thus, disorder has decreased.

26. A is correct. Copper has a larger coefficient of linear expansion than iron, so it expands more than iron during a given temperature change. The bimetallic bar bends due to the difference in expansion between the copper and iron.

27. D is correct.

Calculate heat needed to raise temperature:

$Q = mc\Delta T$

$Q = (0.110 \text{ kg}) \cdot (4,186 \text{ J/kg·K}) \cdot (30 \text{ °C} - 20 \text{ °C})$

$Q = 4,605 \text{ J}$

Calculate time needed to raise temperature with 60 W power source:

$Q = P \times t$

$Q = (60 \text{ W})t$

$t = Q / (60 \text{ W})$

$t = (4,605 \text{ J}) / (60 \text{ W})$

$t = 77 \text{ s}$

28. B is correct.

Heat Radiation:

$Q / t = Ae\sigma(T_H^4 - T_C^4)$

Set constants $Ae\sigma = n$:

$Q / t = n(T_H^4 - T_C^4)$

$80 \text{ J/s} = n[T_H^4 - (25 \text{ °C} + 273 \text{ K})^4]$

$0 \text{ J/s} = n[T_H^4 - (298 \text{ K})^4] - 80 \text{ J/s}$

$95 \text{ J/s} = n[T_H^4 - (20 \text{ °C} + 273 \text{ K})^4]$

$0 \text{ J/s} = n[T_H^4 - (293 \text{ K})^4] - 95 \text{ J/s}$

Set equal and solve for n:

$n[T_H^4 - (298 \text{ K})^4] - 80 \text{ J/s} = n[(T_H^4 - (293 \text{ K})^4] - 95 \text{ J/s}$

$15 \text{ J/s} = n[T_H^4 - (293 \text{ K})^4] - n[T_H^4 - (298 \text{ K})^4]$

$15 \text{ J/s} = n[T_H^4 - (293 \text{ K})^4 - T_H^4 + (298 \text{ K})^4]$

$15 \text{ J/s} = n[(298 \text{ K})^4 - (293 \text{ K})^4]$

$15 \text{ J/s} = n(51.6 \times 10^7 \text{ K}^4)$

$n = 2.9 \times 10^{-8} \text{ W/K}^4$

Solve for T_H:

$$0 = (2.9 \times 10^{-8} \text{ W/K}^4)\cdot[T_H{}^4 - (293 \text{ K})^4] - 95 \text{ J/s}$$

$$T_H{}^4 = 1.06 \times 10^{10} \text{ K}^4$$

$$T_H = 321 \text{ K}$$

$$T_H = 48 \text{ °C}$$

29. E is correct.

Convert to Kelvin:

$$T = -243 \text{ °C} + 273$$

$$T = 30 \text{ K}$$

Double temperature:

$$T_2 = (30 \text{ K})\cdot(2)$$

$$T_2 = 60 \text{ K}$$

Convert back to Celsius:

$$T_2 = 60 \text{ K} - 273$$

$$T_2 = -213 \text{ °C}$$

30. D is correct.

31. B is correct.

Convert units:

$$1.7 \times 10^5 \text{ J/kg} = 170 \text{ kJ/kg}$$

Change in internal energy = heat added (Q)

$$Q = mL_v$$

$$Q = (1 \text{ kg})\cdot(170 \text{ kJ/kg})$$

$$Q = 170 \text{ kJ}$$

32. D is correct.

$$Q = mc\Delta T$$

If m and c are constant, the relationship is directly proportional.

To double Q, T must be doubled:

$$5 \text{ C} + 273 = 278 \text{ K}$$

$$278 \text{ K} \times 2 = 556 \text{ K}$$

$$556 \text{ K} - 273 = 283 \text{ C}$$

33. E is correct.

34. B is correct.

Body heat gives energy to the water molecules in the sweat. This energy is transferred via collisions until some molecules have enough energy to break the hydrogen bonds and escape the liquid (evaporation). However, if a body stayed dry, the heat would not be given to the water and the person would stay hot because the heat is not lost due to the evaporation of the water.

35. D is correct.

Calculate heat released when 0 °C water converts to 0 °C ice:

$$Q_1 = mL_f$$

$$Q_1 = (2{,}200 \text{ kg}) \cdot (334 \times 10^3 \text{ J/kg})$$

$$Q_1 = 734{,}800 \text{ kJ}$$

Calculate heat released for temperature drop ΔT

$$Q_2 = mc\Delta T$$

$$Q_2 = (2{,}200 \text{ kg}) \cdot (2{,}050 \text{ J/kg K}) \cdot [(0 \text{ °C} - (-30 \text{ °C})]$$

$\Delta K = \Delta °C$, so units cancel:

$$Q_2 = 135{,}300 \text{ kJ}$$

Add heat released to get Q_{net}:

$$Q_{net} = Q_1 + Q_2$$

$$Q_{net} = (734{,}800 \text{ kJ}) + (135{,}300 \text{ kJ})$$

$$Q_{net} = 870{,}100 \text{ kJ}$$

36. E is correct.

Object 1 has three times the specific heat capacity and four times the mass of Object 2:

$$c_1 = 3c_2; \; m_1 = 4m_2$$

A single-phase substance obeys the specific heat equation:

$$Q = mc\Delta T$$

In this case, the same amount of heat is added to each substance, therefore:

$$Q_1 = Q_2$$

$$m_1 c_1 \Delta T_1 = m_2 c_2 \Delta T_2$$

$$(4m_2)(3c_2)\Delta T_1 = m_2 \, c_2 \Delta T_2$$

$$12 m_2 c_2 \Delta T_1 = m_2 c_2 \Delta T_2$$

$$12 \, \Delta T_1 = \Delta T_2$$

37. A is correct. Stefan Boltzmann law for objects radiating energy to cooler surroundings:

$$Q / t = Ae\sigma(T_H^4 - T_C^4)$$

Surface area of a sphere:

$$A = 4\pi r^2$$

Surface area of hot inner sphere:

$$A = 4\pi(0.3 \text{ m})^2$$

$$A = 1.13 \text{ m}^2$$

Power radiated by hot inner sphere:

$$P = (1.13 \text{ m}^2){\cdot}(0.55){\cdot}(5.67 \times 10^{-8} \text{ W/m}^2\text{K}^4){\cdot}(500^4 \text{ K} - 400^4 \text{ K})$$

$$P = 1.3 \text{ kW outwards}$$

The direction is out because radiation always radiates from hot to cold.

38. A is correct.

From the ideal gas law:

$$p_3 V_3 = nRT_3$$

$$T_3 = p_3 V_3 / nR$$

$$T_3 = 1.5 p_1 V_3 / nR$$

$$T_3 = 1.5 V_3(p_1 / nR)$$

Also from the ideal gas law:

$$(p_1 / nR) = T_1 / V_1$$

$$(p_1 / nR) = (293.2 \text{ K}) / (100 \text{ cm}^3)$$

$$(p_1 / nR) = 2.932 \text{ K/cm}^3$$

Calculate T_3:

$$T_3 = 1.5 V_3 (2.932 \text{ K/cm}^3)$$

$$T_3 = 1.5 (50 \text{ cm}^3){\cdot}(2.932 \text{ K/cm}^3)$$

$$T_3 = 219.9 \text{ K}$$

$$T_3 = -53.3 \text{ °C} \approx -53 \text{ °C}$$

Calculate T_4:

$$T_4 = 1.5 V_4 (2.932 \text{ K/cm}^3)$$

$$T_4 = 1.5 (150 \text{ cm}^3){\cdot}(2.932 \text{ K/cm}^3)$$

$$T_4 = 659.6 \text{ K}$$

$$T_4 = 386.5 \text{ °C} \approx 387 \text{ °C}$$

39. B is correct. Steel is a very conductive material that is able to transfer thermal energy very well. The steel feels colder than the plastic because its higher thermal conductivity allows it to remove more heat and thus makes touching it feel colder.

40. B is correct. An isobaric process involves constant pressure.

An isochoric (also isometric) process involves a closed system at constant volume.

An adiabatic process occurs without transfer of heat or matter between a system and its surroundings.

An isothermal process involves the change of a system in which the temperature remains constant.

An isentropic process is an idealized thermodynamic process that is adiabatic of a frictionless system where work is transferred such that there is no transfer of heat or matter.

41. E is correct. Carnot coefficient of performance of a refrigeration cycle:

$C_P = T_C / (T_H - T_C)$

$C_P = Q_C / W$

$Q_C / W = T_C / (T_H - T_C)$

$W = (Q_C / T_C) \cdot (T_H - T_C)$

$W = (20 \times 10^3 \text{ J} / 293 \text{ K}) \cdot (307 \text{ K} - 293 \text{ K})$

$W = 955.6 \text{ J} = 0.956 \text{ kJ}$

Power = Work / time

$P = W / t$

$P = 0.956 \text{ kJ} / 1 \text{ s}$

$P = 0.956 \text{ kW} \approx 0.96 \text{ kW}$

42. C is correct.

43. E is correct. Find heat needed to raise temperature to boiling point:

$Q = mc\Delta T$

$Q = (0.8 \text{ kg}) \cdot (4,186 \text{ J/kg·K}) \cdot (100 \text{ °C} - 70 \text{ °C})$

$Q = 100,464 \text{ J}$

Subtract from 800 kJ:

$Q_{remaining} = (800 \times 10^3 \text{ J}) - 100,464 \text{ J}$

$Q_{remaining} = 699,536 \text{ J}$

Use $Q_{remaining}$ to find mass of water that has evaporated:

$Q_R = mL_v$

$m = Q_R / L_v$

$m = (699,536 \text{ J}) / (22.6 \times 10^5 \text{ J/kg})$

$m = 0.310 \text{ kg}$

Subtract from original mass to find mass remaining:

$m_R = 0.800 \text{ kg} - 0.310 \text{ kg}$

$m_R = 0.490 \text{ kg} = 490 \text{ g}$

44. E is correct. Find heat liberated from 30 °C to 0 °C:

$Q_1 = mc\Delta T$

$Q_1 = (0.435 \text{ kg}) \cdot (4{,}186 \text{ J/kg·K}) \cdot (30 \text{ °C} - 0 \text{ °C})$

$Q_1 = 54{,}600 \text{ J} = 54.6 \text{ kJ}$

Find heat liberated by phase change:

$Q_2 = mL_f$

$Q_2 = (0.435 \text{ kg}) \cdot (33.5 \times 10^4 \text{ J/kg})$

$Q_2 = 145{,}700 \text{ J} = 145.7 \text{ kJ}$

Find heat liberated by 0 °C to –8 °C:

$Q_3 = mc\Delta T$

$Q_3 = (0.435 \text{ kg}) \cdot (2{,}090 \text{ J/kg·K}) \cdot [(0 \text{ °C} - (-8 \text{ °C})]$

$Q_3 = 7{,}300 \text{ J} = 7.3 \text{ kJ}$

Find total Q heat liberated:

$Q_{net} = Q_1 + Q_2 + Q_3$

$Q_{net} = (54.6 \text{ kJ} + 145.7 \text{ kJ} + 7.3 \text{ kJ})$

$Q_{net} = 208 \text{ kJ}$

45. D is correct.

Convert P_3 to Pascals:

$P_3 = (2 \text{ atm} / 1) \cdot (101{,}325 \text{ Pa} / 1 \text{ atm})$

$P_3 = 202{,}650 \text{ Pa}$

Use the ideal gas law to find V_3:

$PV = nRT$

$V = (nRT) / P$

$V_3 = [(0.008 \text{ mol}) \cdot (8.314 \text{ J/mol·K}) \cdot (2{,}438 \text{ K})] / (202{,}650 \text{ Pa})$

$V_3 = 8 \times 10^{-4} \text{ m}^3$

Convert to cm³:

$V_3 = (8 \times 10^{-4} \text{ m}^3 / 1) \cdot (100^3 \text{ cm}^3 / 1 \text{ m}^3)$

$V_3 = 800 \text{ cm}^3$

46. C is correct. An adiabatic process involves no heat added or removed from the system.

From the First law of Thermodynamics:

$\Delta U = Q + W$

If $Q = 0$, then:

$\Delta U = W$

Because work is being done to expand the gas it is considered negative and then the change in internal energy is negative (decreases).

$$-\Delta U = -W$$

47. E is correct. Standing in a breeze while wet feels colder than when dry because of the evaporation of water off the skin. Water requires heat to evaporate so this is taken from the body making a person feel colder than if they were dry and the evaporation did not occur.

48. D is correct. Find mass of water:

$$V = (200 \text{ L}) \cdot (0.001 \text{ m}^3/\text{L})$$

$$V = 0.2 \text{ m}^3$$

density = mass / volume

$$m = V\rho$$

$$m = (0.2 \text{ m}^3) \cdot (1,000 \text{ kg/m}^3)$$

$$m = 200 \text{ kg}$$

Find heat added to raise temperature:

$$Q = mc\Delta T$$

$$Q = (200 \text{ kg}) \cdot (4,186 \text{ J/kg} \cdot \text{K}) \cdot (80 \text{ °C} - 28 \text{ °C})$$

$$Q = 43534.4 \text{ kJ}$$

Find time needed to raise temperature:

$$4 \text{ kW} = Q / t$$

$$t = Q / (4 \text{ kW})$$

$$t = 43,534.4 \text{ kJ} / 4 \text{ kW}$$

$$t = 10,884 \text{ s}$$

Convert to hours:

$$t = (10,884 \text{ s}) / (60 \text{ s}) / (60 \text{ min})$$

$$t = 3 \text{ hours}$$

49. D is correct. An isobaric process is a constant pressure process, so the resulting pressure is always the same.

50. B is correct. This question is asking which type of surface has higher emissivity than others and therefore can radiate more energy over a set time period. Blackbody is an idealized radiator and has the highest emissivity. As such, a surface most similar to a blackbody (the black surface) is the best radiator of thermal energy.

A black surface is considered to be an ideal blackbody and therefore has an emissivity of 1 (perfect emissivity). The black surface will be the best radiator as compared to other surface which cannot be considered as blackbodies and have emissivity of <1.

Quantum Mechanics – Explanations

1. E is correct.

The energy of each incident photon is transferred to an electron, which must then overcome the material's work function to be ejected. Therefore:

hc / λ = Work function

$\lambda = (6.626 \times 10^{-34} \text{ J·s} \cdot 3.00 \times 10^{8} \text{ m/s}) / (1.90 \text{ eV} \cdot 1.60 \times 10^{-19} \text{ J/eV})$

$\lambda = 6.53 \times 10^{-7} \text{ m}$

$\lambda = 653 \text{ nm}$

2. B is correct.

The power varies with the number of photons per second and the energy of the photons; therefore, I is incorrect. The energy of the photons varies with the frequency of the light; therefore, III is incorrect. The intensity of a laser beam depends on the number of photons and the energy of each photon. The energy of the photons varies linearly with the frequency. If the frequency doubles, the energy doubles. Since the number of photons is unchanged, the intensity doubles.

3. C is correct.

The energy of each incident photon is transferred to an electron, which must then overcome the material's work function to be ejected. Therefore, the maximum kinetic energy remaining in any electron is:

E = Energy in 240 nm photon − work function

$2.5 \text{ eV} = hc / \lambda -$ work function

Work function = $(6.626 \times 10^{-34} \text{ J·s} \cdot 3.00 \times 10^{8} \text{ m/s}) / (240 \times 10^{-9} \text{ m}) - 2.58 \text{ eV}$

Work function = $(8.28 \times 10^{-19} \text{ J}) / (1.60 \times 10^{-19} \text{ J/eV}) - 2.58 \text{ eV}$

Work function = 2.6 eV

4. C is correct.

The minimum energy of the electron-positron pair is its rest mass (E = $2m_{electron} c^2$). The photon that creates the pair must have more than the minimum energy. The energy of the photon (hv) must therefore be:

$hv > 2m_{electron} c^2$

$v > 2m_{electron} c^2 / h$

$v > 2 \cdot (9.11 \times 10^{-31} \text{ kg}) \cdot (3.00 \times 10^{8} \text{ m/s})^2 / (6.626 \times 10^{-34} \text{ J·s})$

$v > 2.47 \times 10^{20} \text{ Hz}$

5. D is correct.

The energy of each incident photon is transferred to an electron, which must then overcome the material's work function to be ejected. Therefore:

$hc / \lambda >$ Work function

$\lambda < (6.626 \times 10^{-34}$ J·s · 3.00×10^8 m/s$) / (2.20$ eV · 1.60×10^{-19} J/eV$)$

$\lambda < 564$ nm

6. C is correct. Anderson used a cloud chamber to observe the effects of cosmic rays. A cloud chamber is a device filled with saturated water or alcohol vapor and held in a magnetic field. As the cosmic rays interact with the molecules in the vapor, they form high energy charged particles. These high energy charged particles then move out from their point of creation in curved paths because of the magnetic field. Their path is visualized as they condense droplets from the saturated vapor. Anderson observed an event in which a pair of charged particles was created at the same point, moving out in opposite directions and with equal but opposite curvature. This corresponded to the earlier prediction by Dirac of a positively charged electron (a positron) based upon an extra solution to the equations of a relativistic invariant form of Schroedinger's Equation. The electron and positron pair (pair production) was produced in a collision of a cosmic ray photon with a heavy nucleus in the vapor.

7. C is correct.

$E = hv$

$E = (6.626 \times 10^{-34}$ J·s$)·(6.43 \times 10^{14}$ Hz$) / (1.60 \times 10^{-19}$ J/eV$)$

$E = 2.66$ eV

8. B is correct. The kinetic energy of the emitted electrons (KE) is the energy of the incident photon minus, at least, the work function of the photocathode surface. Therefore:

$KE = 3.4$ eV $- 2.4$ eV

$KE = (1.0$ eV$)·(1.60 \times 10^{-19}$ J / eV$)$

$KE = 1.60 \times 10^{-19}$ J

9. D is correct.

The energy of each incident photon is transferred to an electron, which must then overcome the material's work function to be ejected. Therefore, to eject an electron:

$hv = hc / \lambda >$ Work function

$\lambda < hc / ($Work function$)$

$\lambda < (6.626 \times 10^{-34}$ J·s$)·(3.00 \times 10^8$ m/s$) / (2.9$ eV · 1.60×10^{-19} J/eV$)$

$\lambda < 428 \times 10^{-9}$ m

The illumination range of 400 nm–700 nm that does not satisfy this requirement is:

$\lambda > 428$ nm

10. A is correct.

Photons move at the speed of light because they are light.

Since the momentum of photon A is twice as great as the momentum of photon B, its energy is twice as great and therefore its wavelength is half as great.

11. A is correct.

The Balmer formula for Hydrogen is:

$1 / \lambda = (1 / 91.2 \text{ nm})(1 / m^2 - 1 / n^2)$

The energy difference of the n = 20 and n = 7 state corresponds to a photon of wavelength:

$1 / \lambda = (1 / 91.2 \text{ nm})(1 / 7^2 - 1 / 20^2)$

$\lambda = (91.2 \text{ nm}) / (1 / 7^2 - 1 / 20^2)$

$\lambda = 5092 \text{ nm}$

The energy of a photon with wavelength λ is:

$E = hc / \lambda$

$E = (6.626 \times 10^{-34} \text{ J·s})·(3.00 \times 10^8 \text{ m/s}) / (5092 \times 10^{-9} \text{ m})$

$E = (3.93 \times 10^{-20} \text{ J}) / (1.60 \times 10^{-19} \text{ J/eV})$

$E = 0.244 \text{ eV}$

12. D is correct.

The de Broglie wavelength is given by:

$\lambda = h / p$

When the energy ($E = p^2 / 2m$ for a non-relativistic proton) is doubled, the momentum is increased by $\sqrt{2}$, and therefore its de Broglie wavelength decreases by $\sqrt{2}$.

13. E is correct.

(Trivially, it is known that the incoming photon must lose energy to the electron in the scattering and therefore its wavelength must increase. There is only one answer with a longer wavelength.)

Using the Compton equation at 120°:

$\Delta\lambda = \lambda_{Compton} (1 - \cos \theta)$, where $\lambda_{Compton} = 2.43 \times 10^{-12} \text{ m}$

$\Delta\lambda = .00243 \text{ nm } (1.5)$

$\Delta\lambda = 0.00365 \text{ nm}$

$\lambda = 0.591 \text{ nm} + 0.00365 \text{ nm}$

$\lambda = 0.595 \text{ nm}$

14. C is correct.

The brightness of a beam of light is linearly proportional to the energy of the photons in the beam and the number of photons in the beam. If the color of the light beam, which is dependent on its frequency distribution or energy distribution, is unchanged, then the frequency and energy distribution of the light beam must be unchanged.

15. E is correct.

The Balmer formula for Hydrogen is:

$$1 / \lambda = (1 / 91.2 \text{ nm})(1 / m^2 - 1 / n^2)$$

$$1 / \lambda = (1 / 91.2 \text{ nm})(1 / 4^2 - 1 / 9^2)$$

$$1 / \lambda = (1 / 91.2 \text{ nm})(1 / m^2 - 1 / n^2)$$

$$1 / \lambda = (1 / 1818 \text{ nm})$$

The frequency of light is given by:

$$v = c / \lambda$$

$$v = (3.00 \times 10^8 \text{ m/s}) / (1818 \times 10^{-9} \text{ m})$$

$$v = 1.65 \times 10^{14} / \text{s} = 1.65 \times 10^{14} \text{ Hz}$$

16. D is correct.

The Balmer formula for Hydrogen for the emission of radiation from the nth level down to the mth (i.e. $n > m$) is:

$$1 / \lambda = (1 / 91.2 \text{ nm})(1 / m^2 - 1 / n^2)$$

Therefore:

$$(1 / m^2 - 1 / n^2) = 91.2 \text{ nm} / 377 \text{ nm}$$

$$(1 / m^2 - 1 / n^2) = .2419$$

$$1 / n^2 = 1 / m^2 - .2419$$

In order for n to be real, it must be either m = 1 or m = 2. If m = 1:

$$1 / n^2 = 1 - .2419 = .7581$$

n is not an integer (i.e. the photon has less energy than the emission photon expected in a transition from n = 2 to m = 1). Therefore, m must be 2 (i.e. the emission is from the n level down to the m = 2 level) and:

$$1 / n^2 = 1 / 4 - .2419 = .0081$$

$$n = 11$$

17. E is correct.

Wein's displacement law describes the wavelength of maximum emission of radiation of a black body at temperature T. It is:

$$\lambda_{max} \cdot T = \text{constant} = 0.00290 \text{ m·K}$$

At T = 5000K:

λ_{max} = 0.00290 m·K / 5000 K

λ_{max} = 580 nm

18. E is correct.

Dirac factored the Schrödinger equation into a simpler equation that had two solutions; one solution described the electron and the other solution described an identical particle with an opposite electric charge. Four years later, such a "positively charged" electron was found in cloud chamber pictures of cosmic rays.

19. B is correct.

The electron absorbs the full energy of the photon and loses the work function energy as it escapes from the material. Therefore, it has a maximum kinetic energy of:

Max KE = E – Work function

Max KE = 3.4 eV – 2.4 eV = 1.0 eV · (1.60 × 10^{-19} J/eV)

Max KE = 1.60 × 10^{-19} J

20. D is correct.

Consider the problem from the center of mass frame, a frame that is moving in the same direction as the incident photon. In this frame, the electron starts moving with the speed of the center of mass frame and in the opposite direction of the center of mass frame. In the center of mass frame, the electron is scattered with the same speed into one direction, and the photon is scattered in the opposite direction, the scattering angle.

Transforming back into the laboratory frame, the electron has a final velocity equal to the vector sum of its scattered velocity in the center of mass frame and the velocity of the center of mass. This sum is greatest when the scattering angle of the electron is in the same direction as the velocity of the center of mass frame, the direction of the incident photon. The photon is then scattered in the opposite direction of the center of mass frame at a scattering angle of 180°. If the velocity of the electron is maximal at that scattering angle, then the energy of the photon is minimal at that scattering angle. Since wavelength is inversely proportional to energy, the maximal change in wavelength occurs when the photon is scattered at 180°.

21. C is correct. This is a trick question that has nothing to do with the photocathode or the work function. If the radiation has energy 3.5 eV, then its wavelength is given by:

E = hv = hc / λ = 3.5 eV

λ = hc / (3.5 eV)

λ = (6.626 × 10^{-34} J·s)·(3.00 × 10^{8} m/s) / (3.5 eV)

λ = (6.626 × 10^{-34} J·s)·(3.00 × 10^{8} m/s) / (3.5 eV)

λ = (5.679 × 10^{-26} J·m /eV) / (1.6 × 10^{-19} J/eV)

λ = 355 nm

22. A is correct.

The energy of a photon is given by:

$$E = h\nu = hc \,/\, \lambda$$

Therefore, if the wavelength is doubled, the energy is halved.

23. D is correct.

The energy of each incident photon is transferred to an electron, which must then overcome the material's work function to be ejected. Therefore:

$$h\nu > \text{Work function}$$

$$\nu > (2.8 \text{ eV} \cdot 1.60 \times 10^{-19} \text{ J/eV}) \,/\, (6.626 \times 10^{-34} \text{ J·s})$$

$$\nu > 6.8 \times 10^{-14} /\text{s}$$

24. B is correct.

The de Broglie wavelength of a matter wave is:

$$\lambda = h \,/\, p = h \,/\, mv$$

$$v = h \,/\, (m\lambda)$$

$$v = (6.626 \times 10^{-34} \text{ J·s}) \,/\, [(9.11 \times 10^{-31} \text{ kg}) \cdot (380 \times 10^{-9} \text{ m})]$$

$$v = 1.91 \times 10^{3} \text{ m/s}$$

25. B is correct.

Using the Compton Equation:

$$\Delta\lambda = \lambda_{\text{Compton}} \, (1 - \cos\theta), \text{ where } \lambda_{\text{Compton}} = 2.43 \times 10^{-12} \text{ m}$$

For $\theta = 90°$:

$$\Delta\lambda = 2.43 \times 10^{-12} \text{ m}$$

and

$$\lambda_{\text{scattered}} = \lambda_{\text{incident}} + \Delta\lambda$$

$$\lambda_{\text{scattered}} = (1.50 \times 10^{-10} \text{ m}) + (2.43 \times 10^{-12} \text{ m})$$

$$\lambda_{\text{scattered}} = 1.5243 \times 10^{-10} \text{ m}$$

26. B is correct. As the intensity of light increases, the photon flux increases but not the energy of the photons. The kinetic energy of the ejected electrons depends solely on the energy of the incident photons and the work function of the metal. Since the energy of the incident photons is unchanged, the kinetic energy of the ejected electrons does not change. On the other hand, the probability of an electron being ejected, and therefore the number of electrons ejected per second, depends on the flux of incident photons. It increases as the intensity of the light increases. The electron is ejected at the same instant as the light is absorbed, independent of the intensity of the light, therefore the time lag does not change.

Note: the time lag between the illumination of the surface (not the absorption of light) and the ejection of the first electron depends on the probability of ejection, which depends on the intensity of the incident light.

27. D is correct. The de Broglie wavelength of a matter wave is:

$\lambda = h / p$

$\lambda = h / (mv)$

The energy of a photon with this wavelength is:

$E = hv = hc / \lambda$

Substituting in for λ:

$E = hc / [h / (mv)]$

$E = mcv$

$E = (1.67 \times 10^{-27} \text{ kg}) \cdot (3.00 \times 10^8 \text{ m/s}) \cdot (7.2 \times 10^4 \text{ m/s})$

$E = 36.1 \times 10^{-15} \text{ J}$

$E = (36.1 \times 10^{-15} \text{ J}) / (1.60 \times 10^{-19} \text{ J/eV})$

$E = 225 \times 10^3 \text{ eV}$

28. B is correct. The Compton effect measures the change in energy as an x-ray scatters off of an electron. Both the total momentum and total energy of the x-ray and the electron, initially at rest, must be conserved. As the scattering angle of the x-ray increases monotonically, its change in momentum increases and therefore the momentum imparted to the electron must increase. If the momentum of the electron increases, then its energy must increase and the energy of the X-ray decreases. If the energy of the X-ray decreases, then the frequency, which is proportional to its energy, must decrease.

29. A is correct. The Rydberg formula for Hydrogen for the emission of radiation from the nth level down to the mth (i.e. n > m) is:

$1 / \lambda = (1 / 91.2 \text{ nm}) \cdot (1 / m^2 - 1 / n^2)$

If n = 16 (since the first spectral line is from n = 2) and m = 1, then:

$1 / \lambda = (1 / 91.2 \text{ nm}) \cdot (1 / 1^2 - 1 / 16^2)$

$\lambda = 91.2 \text{ nm} / (1 - 0.004)$

$\lambda = 91.6 \text{ nm}$

30. D is correct.

If the frequency of light in a laser beam is doubled, the energy of each photon in that laser beam doubles, since each photon has energy $E = hv$. The wavelength of each photon is divided by 2, since $\lambda = c / v$. The intensity of the laser beam is the power per unit area. The power is the energy delivered per unit time. The energy delivered is proportional to the energy of each photon times the number of photons. If the energy of each photon is doubled and the number of photons remains unchanged (assuming the area of the laser beam is unchanged), then the intensity doubles. Therefore, I and III are correct.

31. B is correct.

Order diffraction occurs when the incident and scattered beams hit the crystal at the same angle (i.e. in this case the crystal planes are oriented at 58° / 2 to the normal). The neutron matter waves add coherently if the extra distance that the neutrons must travel as they scatter off the next plane of the crystal is equal to an integer number of de Broglie wavelengths. At 58°, the extra distance is:

$$2 \cdot 159.0 \text{ pm} \cdot \cos(58° / 2) = 278 \text{ pm}$$

The de Broglie wavelength of a matter wave is:

$$\lambda = h / p$$

Therefore:

$$p = h / \lambda$$

and

$$E = p^2 / 2m = (6.626 \times 10^{-34} \text{ J·s} / 278 \times 10^{-12} \text{ m})^2 / (2 \cdot 1.67 \times 10^{-27} \text{ kg})$$

$$E = (1.70 \times 10^{-21} \text{ J}) / (1.6 \times 10^{-19} \text{ J/eV})$$

$$E = 0.0106 \text{ eV}$$

32. A is correct.

The energy of each incident photon is transferred to an electron. The electron's energy goes into overcoming the photocathode's 2.5 eV work function. The remaining energy is then stopped by the stopping potential. The greatest amount of energy an electron can have comes from a photon with a wavelength of 360 nm. The remaining energy is then:

$$\text{remaining energy} = h\nu - 2.5 \text{ eV}$$

$$\text{remaining energy} = hc / \lambda - 2.5 \text{ eV}$$

$$\text{remaining energy} = (6.626 \times 10^{-34} \text{ J·s}) \cdot (3.00 \times 10^8 \text{ m/s}) / (360 \times 10^{-9} \text{ m}) - 2.5\text{eV}$$

$$\text{remaining energy} = [(5.52 \times 10^{-19} \text{ J}) / (1.6 \times 10^{-19} \text{ J/eV})] - 2.5 \text{ eV}$$

$$\text{remaining energy} = 3.45 \text{ eV} - 2.5 \text{ eV} = 0.95 \text{ eV}$$

The electron has a charge of e. Therefore, this energy can be stopped by a voltage of 0.95 volts.

33. D is correct.

The de Broglie wavelength is given by:

$$\lambda = h / p$$

$$\lambda = (6.626 \times 10^{-34} \text{ J·s}) / (1.95 \times 10^{-27} \text{ kg·m/s})$$

$$\lambda = 340 \text{ nm}$$

34. C is correct.

The Balmer formula for Hydrogen for the emission of radiation from the nth level down to the mth (i.e. n > m) is:

$$1 / \lambda = (1 / 91.2 \text{ nm}) \cdot (1 / m^2 - 1 / n^2)$$

If n = 9 and m = 6, then:

$$1 / \lambda = (1 / 91.2 \text{ nm}) \cdot (1 / 6^2 - 1 / 9^2)$$

$$1 / \lambda = (1 / 91.2 \text{ nm}) \cdot (0.01543)$$

Thus:

$$v = c / \lambda$$

$$v = (3.00 \times 10^8 \text{ m/s}) \cdot (1 / 91.2 \text{ nm}) \cdot (0.01543)$$

$$v = 5.08 \times 10^{13} \text{ /s}$$

$$v = 5.08 \times 10^{13} \text{ Hz}$$

35. A is correct.

$$E = hv$$

$$E = (6.626 \times 10^{-34} \text{ J·s}) \cdot (110 \text{ GHz})$$

$$E = (6.626 \times 10^{-34} \text{ J·s}) \cdot (110 \times 10^9 \text{ / s})$$

$$E = 7.29 \times 10^{-23} \text{ J}$$

36. C is correct.

The visible spectrum ranges from 400 nm to 700 nm.

The Balmer formula for Hydrogen for the emission of radiation from the nth level down to the mth (i.e., n > m) is:

$$1 / \lambda = (1 / 91.2 \text{ nm}) \cdot (1 / m^2 - 1 / n^2)$$

Consider emission from any level down to the m = 1 level. The lowest energy is from the n = 2 level and its wavelength is:

$$91.2 \text{ nm} \cdot (4 / 3) = 121 \text{ nm, which is not visible.}$$

Therefore, there are no visible lines radiating down to the m = 1 level.

Consider emission from any level down to the m = 3 level.

The highest energy comes from n = ∞ and its wavelength is:

$$91.2 \text{ nm} \cdot 9 = 820 \text{ nm, which is not visible.}$$

Therefore, there are no visible lines radiating down to the m = 3 level, nor are there any visible lines radiating down to any m level higher than 3.

Consider radiation from various levels down to the m = 2 level.

From n = 3, the wavelength is:

$$91.2 \text{ nm} / (1 / 4 - 1 / 9) = 91.2 \text{ nm} \cdot 7.2 = 656.6 \text{ nm}$$

From n = 4, the wavelength is:

91.2 nm / (1 / 4 − 1 / 16) = 91.2 nm · 5.333 = 486.4 nm

From n = 5, the wavelength is:

91.2 nm / (1 / 4 − 1 / 25) = 91.2 nm · 4.762 = 434.3 nm

From n = 6, the wavelength is:

91.2 nm / (1 / 4 − 1 / 36) = 91.2 nm · 4.5 = 410.4 nm

From n = 7, the wavelength is:

91.2 nm / (1 / 4 − 1 / 49) = 91.2 nm · 4.355 = 397.2 nm, which is not visible.

Therefore, there are 4 visible lines:

m = 2 to n = 3   656.6 nm

m = 2 to n = 4   486.4 nm

m = 2 to n = 5   434.3 nm

m = 2 to n = 6   410.4 nm

37. B is correct.

$E = h\nu = hc / \lambda$

$\lambda = hc / E$

$\lambda = (6.626 \times 10^{-34} \text{ J·s}) \cdot (3.00 \times 10^{8} \text{ m/s}) / (4.20 \text{ eV})$

$\lambda = (4.73 \times 10^{-26} \text{ J·m/eV}) / (1.60 \times 10^{-19} \text{ J/eV})$

$\lambda = 2.96 \times 10^{-7} \text{ m}$

$\lambda = 296 \text{ nm}$

38. C is correct.

The energy of each incident photon is transferred to an electron, which must then overcome the material's work function to be ejected. Therefore, if a wavelength of light is just able to eject an electron, then:

$h\nu = hc / \lambda = \text{Work function}$

$(6.626 \times 10^{-34} \text{ J·s}) \cdot (3.00 \times 10^{8} \text{ m/s}) / (500 \times 10^{-9} \text{ m}) = \text{Work function}$

$(3.98 \times 10^{-19} \text{ J}) / (1.6 \times 10^{-19} \text{ J/eV}) = \text{Work function}$

$2.48 \text{ eV} = \text{Work function}$

39. C is correct.

In the Bohr theory, there is a fixed number of de Broglie wavelengths of the electron in an orbit. This number is the principle quantum number:

$n = 2\pi r / \lambda$

The de Broglie wavelength is given by:

$\lambda = h / p$

Therefore:

$$n = (2\pi / h)rp$$

or:

$$n^2 = (2\pi / h)^2 r^2 p^2$$

The attractive force of the proton keeps the electron in a circular orbit. The attractive force is proportional to $1 / r^2$, and if that force keeps the electron in orbit, $1 / r^2$ must be proportional to v^2 / r. Therefore, v^2 (or p^2) is proportional to $1 / r$. Since $r^2 p^2$ is proportional to n^2, and p^2 is proportional to $1 / r$, then r (i.e. $r^2 \cdot 1 / r$) is proportional to n^2.

40. B is correct.

Heisenberg's Uncertainty Principle states that:

$$\Delta p \Delta x \geq h / 2\pi$$

Therefore:

$$m \Delta v \Delta x \geq h / 2\pi$$

$$\Delta v \geq (6.626 \times 10^{-34} \text{ J·s}) / (2\pi \cdot 0.053 \text{ nm} \cdot 1.67 \times 10^{-27} \text{ kg})$$

$$\Delta v \geq 1.19 \times 10^3 \text{ m/s}$$

41. C is correct.
The Balmer formula for Hydrogen for the emission of radiation from the nth level down to the mth (i.e., n > m) is:

$$1 / \lambda = (1 / 91.2 \text{ nm}) \cdot (1 / m^2 - 1 / n^2)$$

$$1 / \lambda = (1 / 91.2 \text{ nm}) \cdot (1 / 9^2 - 1 / 11^2)$$

$$\lambda = (91.2 \text{ nm}) / (0.00408)$$

$$\lambda = 22{,}300 \text{ nm}$$

42. E is correct.
Heisenberg's Uncertainty Principle states that:

$$\Delta E \Delta t \geq h/2\pi$$

Therefore:

$$\Delta t \geq (h / 2\pi) / \Delta E$$

$$\Delta t \geq (6.626 \times 10^{-34} \text{ J·s} / 2\pi) / (10^{-18} \text{ J})$$

$$\Delta t \geq 1.05 \times 10^{-16} \text{ s}$$

43. C is correct.
The energy of each incident photon is transferred to an electron, which must then overcome the material's work function to be ejected. Therefore, if a wavelength of light is able to eject an electron with energy 2.58 eV, then:

$$h\nu = hc / \lambda = \text{Work function} + 2.58 \text{ eV}$$

$$(6.626 \times 10^{-34} \text{ J·s}) \cdot (3.00 \times 10^8 \text{ m/s}) / (240 \times 10^{-9} \text{ m}) = \text{Work function} + 2.58 \text{ eV}$$

$$\text{Work function} = [(8.28 \times 10^{-19} \text{ J}) / (1.6 \times 10^{-19} \text{ J/eV})] - 2.58 \text{eV}$$

$$\text{Work function} = 2.60 \text{ eV}$$

Atomic and Nuclear Structure – Explanations

1. A is correct.

Though alpha particles have low penetrating power and high ionizing power, they are not harmless. All forms of radiation present risks and cannot be thought of as completely harmless.

2. C is correct.

A beta particle (β) is a high-energy, high-speed electron (β^-) or positron (β^+) emitted in the radioactive decay of an atomic nucleus.

Electron emission (β^- decay) occurs in an unstable atomic nucleus with an excess of neutrons, whereby a neutron is converted into a proton, an electron and an electron antineutrino.

Positron emission (β^+ decay) occurs in an unstable atomic nucleus with an excess of protons, whereby a proton is converted into a neutron, a positron and an electron neutrino.

3. E is correct.

The de Broglie wavelength is given as:

$\lambda = h / p$

where h is Planck's constant and p is momentum

$p = mv$

$\lambda_1 = h / mv$

$\lambda_2 = h / m(2v)$

$\lambda_2 = \frac{1}{2}h / mv$

$\lambda_2 = \frac{1}{2} \lambda_1$

λ decreases by factor of 2

4. B is correct.

The Bohr model places electrons around the nucleus of the atom at discrete energy levels. The Balmer series line spectra agreed with the Bohr model because the energy of the observed photons in each spectra matched the transition energy of electrons within these discrete predicted states.

5. C is correct.

Nuclear reaction:

$$^{55}_{28}\text{Ni} \rightarrow {}^{55}_{27}\text{Co} + \text{e}^+ + v_e$$

where Co = product, e^+ = positron and v_e = electron neutrino

In positron emission (β^+ decay), a proton in the nucleus converts to a neutron while releasing a positron and an electron neutrino.

The atomic number decreases by one, but the mass number stays constant.

6. D is correct. This is an example of an electron capture nuclear reaction.

When this happens, the atomic number decreases by one, but the mass number stays the same.

$$^{100}_{44}Ru + {}^{0}_{-1}e^- \rightarrow {}^{100}_{43}Tc$$

Ru: 100 = mass number (# protons + # neutrons)

Ru: 44 = atomic number (# protons)

From the periodic table, Tc is the element with 1 less proton than Ru.

7. B is correct.

By the Born Rule, the probability of obtaining any possible measurement outcome is equal to the square of the wave function.

8. E is correct.

An alpha particle is composed of two neutrons and two protons, and is identical to the nucleus of a ^{4}He atom.

Total mass of two alpha particles:

$2 \times (2 \text{ neutrons} + 2 \text{ protons}) = 8$

Mass of a ^{9}Be atom:

5 neutrons + 4 protons = 9

Mass of a ^{9}Be atom > total mass of two alpha particles

The mass of a ^{9}Be atom is greater than the mass of two alpha particles, so its mass is also greater than twice the mass of a ^{4}He atom.

9. C is correct.

The superscript is the mass number (atomic weight), which is both neutrons and protons.

The subscript is the atomic number, which is the number of protons.

Therefore, the number of neutrons is equal to the superscript minus the subscript.

$181 - 86 = 95$, which is the greatest number of neutrons among the choices.

10. A is correct. The number of neutrons and protons must be equal after the reaction.

Thus the sum of the atomic number before and mass number before should be equal to after the reaction.

Mass number (superscript):

$(1 + 235) - (131 + 3) = 102$

Atomic number (subscript):

$92 - (53) = 39$

$^{102}_{39}X$ properly balances the reaction.

11. E is correct.

Balmer's equation is given by:

$$\lambda = B[(n^2) / (n^2 - 2^2)]$$
$$\lambda = (3.6 \times 10^{-7}) \cdot [(12^2) / (12^2 - 2^2)]$$
$$\lambda = 3.7 \times 10^{-7} \text{ m}$$

Where c is the speed of light:

$$c = \lambda f$$

Convert wavelength to frequency:

$$f = c / \lambda$$
$$f = (3 \times 10^8 \text{ m/s}) / (3.7 \times 10^{-7} \text{ m})$$
$$f = 8.1 \times 10^{14} \text{ s}^{-1} = 8.1 \times 10^{14} \text{ Hz}$$

12. D is correct. Gamma rays are the most penetrating form of radiation because they are the highest energy and least ionizing. A gamma ray passes through a given amount of material without imparting as much of its energy into removing electrons from atoms and ionizing them as other forms of radiation do. Gamma rays retain more of their energy passing through matter and are able to penetrate further.

13. A is correct.

Use the Rydberg Formula:

$$E = hf$$
$$f = c / \lambda$$
$$E = (hc) \cdot (1 / \lambda)$$
$$1 / \lambda = R(1 / n_1^2 - 1 / n_2^2), \text{ where } n_1 = 1 \text{ and } n_2 = 2$$
$$E = hcR[(1 / n_1^2) - (1 / n_2^2)]$$
$$E = (4.14 \times 10^{-15} \text{ eV·s}) \cdot (3 \times 10^8 \text{ m/s}) \cdot (1.097 \times 10^7 \text{ m}^{-1}) \cdot [(1 / 1^2) - (1 / 2^2)]$$
$$E = 13.6[1 - (1 / 4)]$$
$$E = 10.2 \text{ eV}$$

The positive energy indicates that a photon was absorbed and not emitted.

14. C is correct.

In β^- (beta minus) decay, the atomic number (subscript) increases by 1 but the atomic mass stays constant.

$$^{87}_{37}\text{Rb} \rightarrow {}^{87}_{38}\text{Sr} + {}^{0}_{-1}e + {}^{0}_{0}v$$

Sr is the element with 1 more proton (subscript) than Rb.

${}^{0}_{0}v$ represents an electron antineutrino.

15. C is correct.

The nucleus of an atom is bound together by the strong nuclear force from the nucleons within it. The strong nuclear force must overcome the Coulomb repulsion of the protons (due to their like charges).

Neutrons help stabilize and bind the nucleus together by contributing to the strong nuclear force, so that it is greater than the Coulomb repulsion experienced by the protons.

16. A is correct.

Geiger-Muller counters operate using a Geiger-Muller tube, which consists of a high voltage shell and small rod in the center, filled with low pressure inert gas (e.g. argon). When exposed to radiation (specifically particle radiation), the radiation particles ionize atoms of the argon allowing for a brief charge to be conducted between the high voltage rod and outer shell. The electric pulse is then displayed visually or via audio to indicate radioactivity.

17. A is correct.

Find energy needed to ionize the electron:

$E_n = -13.6$ eV $(1 / n^2 - 1 / \infty)$

$E_n = -13.6$ eV $/ n^2$

$E_2 = (-13.6$ eV$) / 2^2$

$E_2 = -3.4$ eV

The electron must absorb a photon of 3.4 eV to ionize it:

$E = hc / \lambda$

$\lambda = hc / E$

$\lambda = (4.135 \times 10^{-15}$ eV·s$)·(3 \times 10^8$ m/s$) / (3.4$ eV$)$

$\lambda = 365$ nm

18. D is correct.

In the Lyman series, electron transitions always go from $n \geq 2$ to $n = 1$.

19. B is correct.

20. E is correct.

All statements are correct. Nucleons are protons and neutrons, and their mass is different outside the nucleus versus within it. Nucleons in the nucleus change mass slightly due to some mass being converted to bond energy. When nuclei are broken apart, the energy released is from the mass of the nucleons and is converted into the bond energy.

21. B is correct.

$^{36}_{17}\text{Cl}$ has 19 neutrons and 17 protons, thus it has an excess of neutrons. It will probably not undergo β^+ decay because this would convert a proton to a neutron and increase the neutron-to-proton ratio.

Because it is a smaller nucleus (atomic number less than 83), it will probably not undergo alpha decay because this form of decay is most often found in larger nuclei that exceed the bounds of the strong nuclear force. Most likely it will undergo β^- decay, because this converts an excess neutron to a proton and decreases the neutron-to-proton ratio.

22. C is correct.

The Curie is a non-SI unit of radioactivity equivalent to 3.7×10^{10} decays (disintegrations) per second. It is named after the early radioactivity researchers Marie and Pierre Curie.

23. B is correct.

The atomic numbers: $^{235}_{92}\text{U} \rightarrow {}^{141}_{56}\text{Ba} + {}^{92}_{36}\text{Kr}$

The subscripts on each side of the expression sum to 92, so adding a proton ($^{1}_{1}\text{H}$) to the right side would not balance.

The superscripts sum to 235 on the left and sum to 233 on the right.

Add two neutrons ($^{1}_{0}\text{n} + {}^{1}_{0}\text{n}$) to the right side to balance both sides of the equation.

24. C is correct.

The reactants are $^{3}_{2}\text{He} + {}^{3}_{2}\text{He}$, so the superscripts must sum to 6 while the subscripts must sum to 4.

25. A is correct.

^{56}Fe has the highest binding energy because its nucleus is "in the middle" in terms of nuclear size.

Thus, the strong nuclear force and the electromagnetic repulsion are most balanced and the nucleus is at the lowest energy configuration.

Note: all nuclei are most stable at the lowest energy configuration.

26. C is correct.

An alpha particle consists of two protons and two neutrons, and is identical to a helium nucleus, so it can be written as $^{4}_{2}\text{He}$

For a nuclear reaction to be written correctly it must be balanced, and the sum of superscripts and subscripts must be equal on both sides of the reaction. The superscripts add to 238, and the subscripts add to 92 on both sides, therefore it is the only balanced answer.

27. E is correct.

The question is asking for the λ of the emitted photon so use the Rydberg Formula:

$$1 / \lambda = R(1 / n_1{}^2 - 1 / n_2{}^2)$$

$$\lambda = 1 / [R(1 / n_1{}^2 - 1 / n_2{}^2)]$$

Use $n_1 = 5$ and $n_2 = 20$ because we are solving for λ of an emitted (not absorbed) photon.

$$\lambda = 1 / [(1.097 \times 10^7\,\text{m}^{-1}) \cdot (1 / 5^2 - 1 / 20^2)]$$

$$\lambda = 2.43\ \mu m$$

28. D is correct.

When writing a nuclear reaction, the superscript represents the mass number, while the subscript represents the atomic number. A correct nuclear reaction is balanced when the sum of superscripts (mass number) and subscripts (atomic number) is equal on both sides of the reaction.

29. C is correct.

A blackbody is an ideal system that absorbs 100% of all light incident upon it and reflects none. It also emits 100% of the radiation it generates, therefore it has perfect absorption and emissivity.

30. D is correct.

Carbon dating relies upon a steady creation of ^{14}C and knowledge of the rate of creation at various points in time to determine the approximate age of objects.

If a future archeologist is unaware of nuclear bomb testing and the higher levels of ^{14}C created, then the dates they calculate for an object would be too young. This is because a higher amount of ^{14}C would be present in samples and make them seem as if they had not had time to decay and thus appear to be younger.

31. A is correct. Gamma radiation is an electromagnetic wave and is not a particle. Thus, when gamma radiation is emitted, the atomic number and mass number remain the same.

32. C is correct.

In β⁻ decay a neutron is converted to a proton and an electron and electron antineutrino are emitted. In β⁺ decay a proton is converted to a neutron and a positron and an electron neutrino are emitted.

$$^{14}_{6}\text{C} \rightarrow\ ^{14}_{7}\text{N} + e^- + v_e$$

33. E is correct.

In a nuclear equation the number of nucleons must be conserved.

The sum of mass numbers and atomic numbers must be equal on both sides of the equation.

The product (i.e. daughter nuclei) should be on the right side of the equation.

34. A is correct. Photoelectric effect is when increasing the intensity of light upon a metal increases the electron ejection rate, but does not increase their kinetic energy.

35. C is correct.

The Balmer series is the name of the emission spectrum of hydrogen when electrons transition from a higher state to the n = 2 state.

Within the Balmer series, there are four visible spectral lines with colors ranging from red to violet (i.e. ROY G BIV)

36. D is correct. Electrons were discovered through early experiments with electricity, specifically in high voltage vacuum tubes (cathode ray tubes). Beams of electrons were observed traveling through these tubes when high voltage was applied between the anode and cathode, and the electrons struck fluorescent material at the back of the tube.

37. B is correct.

Beams a and c both deflect when an electric field is applied, indicating they have a net charge and therefore must be particles.

Beam b is undisturbed by the applied electric field, indicating it has no net charge and must be a high energy electromagnetic wave, since all other forms of radioactivity (alpha and beta radiation) are charged particles.

38. E is correct. Beam a is composed of negatively charged particles, while beam c is composed of positively charged particles; therefore both beams are deflected by the electric field.

Beam b is also composed of particles; however, these particles are neutral because they are not deflected by the electric field. An example of this kind of radiation would be a gamma ray, which consists of neutral photons.

39. C is correct. A helium nucleus is positively charged, so it is deflected away from the top plate and attracted toward the negative plate.

40. B is correct.

5.37 eV is the amount of energy required to excite the electron from the ground state to the zero energy state.

Calculate the wavelength of a photon with this energy:

$E = hf$

$f = c / \lambda$

$E = hc / \lambda$

$\lambda = hc / E$

$\lambda = (4.14 \times 10^{-15} \text{ eV·s})·(3 \times 10^8 \text{ m/s}) / (5.37 \text{ eV})$

$\lambda = 2.3 \times 10^{-7}$ m

41. D is correct. Elements with atomic numbers of 84 and higher are radioactive because the strong nuclear force binding the nucleus together cannot overcome the Coulomb repulsion from the high number of protons within the atom. Thus, these nuclei are unstable and emit alpha radiation to decrease the number of protons within the nucleus.

42. E is correct. Beta particles, like all forms of ionizing radiation, cannot be considered harmless.

43. A is correct. The Pauli Exclusion Principle states that in an atom no two electrons can have the same set of quantum numbers. Thus, every electron in an atom has a unique set of quantum numbers and a particular set belongs to only one electron.

44. B is correct. Planck's constant quantizes the amount of energy that can be absorbed or emitted. Therefore, it sets a discrete lowest amount of energy for energy transfer.

45. E is correct. The decay rate of any radioactive isotope or element is constant and independent of temperature, pressure, or surface area.

46. B is correct.

Larger nuclei (atomic number above 83) tend to decay because the attractive force of the nucleons (strong nuclear force) has a limited range and the nucleus is larger than this range. Therefore, these nuclei tend to emit alpha particles to decrease the size of the nucleus.

Smaller nuclei are not large enough to encounter this problem, but some isotopes have an irregular ratio of neutrons to protons and become unstable. ^{14}Carbon has 8 neutrons and 6 protons, and its neutron to proton ratio is too large, therefore it is unstable and radioactive.

47. C is correct.

Positron emission occurs during β^+ decay. In β^+ decay a proton converts to a neutron and emits a positron and electron neutrino.

The decay can be expressed as: $^{44}_{21}\text{Sc} \rightarrow {}^{44}_{20}\text{Ca} + e^+ + v_e$

48. C is correct. A scintillation counter operates by detecting light flashes from the scintillator material. When radiation strikes the scintillator crystal (often NaI), a light flash is emitted and detected by a photomultiplier tube, which then passes an electronic signal to audio or visual identification equipment.

49. B is correct. When a Geiger counter clicks, it indicates that it has detected the radiation from one nucleus decaying. The click could be from an alpha, beta, or even gamma ray source, but cannot be determined without other information.

Special Relativity – Explanations

1. A is correct. Alpha sees Beta moving away at +0.7*c*, and Beta sees Gamma moving away at +0.7*c*. To find the speed that Alpha sees Gamma moving at, apply the relativistic velocity addition expression:

$$\beta = (\beta_1 + \beta_2) / (1 + \beta_1\beta_2)$$

$$\beta = (0.7 + 0.7) / [1 + (0.7)(0.70)]$$

$$\beta = 0.94$$

$$v = 0.94c$$

2. E is correct. The train is not moving in the vertical direction, therefore there is no Lorentz Contraction of lengths in that direction.

3. D is correct. As measured in the frame of Earth, the total distance is:

$$d = 2 \cdot (4.367 \text{ years}) \cdot c$$

The time is therefore:

$$t = d / v$$

$$t = (2 \cdot 4.367 \text{ years} \cdot c) / (0.5c)$$

$$t = 17.468 \text{ years}$$

4. E is correct. From the point of view of an observer in the lab, the muon's time appears to be slowed down by relativistic time dilation. The lifetime for the muon in a frame in which it is at rest ($\Delta x = 0$), is $\Delta t = 2.2\mu s$. The Lorentz transformation to the frame in which the muon is moving is:

$$\Delta t' = \gamma (\Delta t - v \Delta x / c^2),$$

where $\gamma = 1 / \sqrt{(1 - \beta^2)}$ and $\beta = v / c$

$$\Delta t' = \gamma \Delta x$$

$$\gamma = 1 / \sqrt{(1 - 0.99^2)} = 7.09$$

$$\Delta t' = 15.6 \text{ } \mu s$$

5. D is correct.

The speed of the scout as measured by the asteroid is the relativistic addition of the speed of the spaceship as measured from the asteroid, plus the speed of the scout as measured from the spaceship.

$$\beta = (\beta_1 + \beta_2) / (1 + \beta_1\beta_2)$$

$$\beta = (0.6 + 0.4) / [1 + (0.6)(0.4)]$$

$$\beta = 0.81$$

$$v = 0.81c$$

6. D is correct.

The angle depends on the ratio of the elevation of the bed to the length of the bed along the floor. The elevation of the bed does not appear different because the motion of the spaceship is zero in that direction. However, the length along the floor appears to be shorter due to Lorentz Contraction when viewed from the observer's frame. Therefore, the ratio appears to be larger and the angle appears to have increased.

7. A is correct.

In the frame of the spaceship, the separation of the two events, Δx, is zero, and the time is dilated according to the Lorentz transformation:

$$\Delta t' = \gamma\, \Delta t$$

$$\gamma = 1 / \sqrt{(1 - \beta^2)}$$

$$\beta = v / c$$

If $v = 0.9640c$:

$$\gamma = 1 / \sqrt{(1 - 0.964^2)}$$

$$\gamma = 3.76$$

$$\Delta t = (10.5 \text{ years}) / (3.76) = 2.79 \text{ years}$$

8. C is correct.

Conservation of energy requires:

$$E_p + E_n = E_{\text{final}}$$

In the center of mass frame, the proton and neutron start out with insignificant kinetic energy, so their initial energies are approximately their rest energies. The final energy is the rest energy of the deuterium plus the released energy:

$$m_p c^2 + m_n c^2 = m_d c^2 + E_{\text{released}}$$

So:

$$m_d c^2 = m_p c^2 + m_n c^2 - E_{\text{released}}$$

The proton rest mass energy is $m_p c^2 = 938.28$ MeV and the neutron rest mass energy is $m_n c^2 = 939.57$ MeV. The rest energy of the deuterium is then:

$$m_d c^2 = [(938.28 \text{ MeV}) + (939.57 \text{ MeV}) - (3.6 \times 10^{-13} \text{ J})] / [(1.6 \times 10^{-19} \text{ J/eV}) \cdot (10^6 \text{ eV/MeV})]$$

$$m_d c^2 = (1877.85 \text{ MeV}) - (2.25 \text{ MeV})$$

$$m_d c^2 = 1875.6 \text{ MeV}$$

Converting to SI units:

$$m_d = (1875.6 \text{ MeV}) \cdot (1.6 \times 10^{-19} \text{ J/eV}) / c^2$$

$$m_d = [(1875.6 \text{ MeV}) \cdot (1.6 \times 10^{-19} \text{ J/eV}) \cdot (10^6 \text{ eV/MeV})] / (3.0 \times 10^8 \text{ m/s})^2$$

$$m_d = 3.3 \times 10^{-27} \text{ kg}.$$

9. B is correct.

In the moving frame, the time interval between events is increased from the value measured in the rest frame because of time dilation. Let primed variables represent quantities measured in the moving frame, and unprimed variables represent quantities measured in the rest frame. Then, the expression for time dilation is:

$$\Delta t' = \gamma \Delta t,$$

where $\gamma = 1 / \sqrt{(1 - \beta^2)}$ and $\beta = v^2 / c^2$.

If time intervals are increased by some factor, rates are decreased by the same factor. Let r be the heart rate measured in the rest frame, and r' be the heart rate as measured in the moving frame. Because of time dilation, the rate in the moving frame is reduced according to:

$$r' = r / \gamma$$

If $v = 0.99c$, then $\gamma = 7.09$.

Thus:

$$r' = 12 \text{ beats/min}$$

10. C is correct.

The speed of Earth as measured by the first spaceship is $0.31c$, and the speed of the second spaceship as measured by the earth is also $0.31c$. The speed of the second spaceship as measured by the first is the relativistic sum of the two speeds.

$$\beta = (\beta_1 + \beta_2) / (1 + \beta_1\beta_2)$$

$$\beta = (0.31 + 0.31) / [1 + (0.31)\cdot(0.31)]$$

$$\beta = 0.566$$

$$v = 0.57 \, c$$

11. E is correct.

The kinetic energy, total energy and linear momentum have no limit. They all increase monotonically with increasing γ. Although the speed of a particle has an upper limit of c, the value of γ goes to infinity as v approaches c.

12. B is correct.

This problem can be solved using Lorentz transformation, time dilation, or length contraction. Using length contraction, the distance between the beacons as measured by the spaceship is contracted:

$$l' = l / \gamma,$$

where $\beta = v / c$ and $\gamma = 1 / \sqrt{(1 - \beta^2)}$.

$$\gamma = 1 / \sqrt{[1 - (0.5)^2]} = 1.155$$

$$l' = (49 \times 10^6 \text{ m}) / 1.155$$

$$l' = 42.42 \times 10^6 \text{ m}$$

The time interval for passage across this distance as measured in the spaceship frame is:

$t' = l' / v = l' / (0.5\ c)$

$t' = (42.42 \times 10^6\ \text{m}) / [(0.5)\cdot(3 \times 10^8\ \text{m/s})]$

$t' = 283\ \text{ms}$

13. A is correct.

The lifetime of the pion is greater as measured by clocks on Earth due to time dilation. The lifetime measured on Earth is:

$\Delta t' = \gamma \Delta t$,

where $\gamma = 1 / \sqrt{(1 - \beta^2)}$ and $\beta = v^2 / c^2$.

If $\beta = 0.23$, then $\gamma = 1.028$, so the lifetime as measured on Earth is $\Delta t' = 2.62 \times 10^{-8}\ \text{s}$.

The distance traveled in that time interval is:

$d' = v\Delta t'$

$d' = 0.23(3 \times 10^8\ \text{m/s})\cdot(2.62 \times 10^{-8}\ \text{s})$

$d' = 1.81\ \text{m}$

14. B is correct.

The problem can be solved in the rest frame of the planets or in the rest frame of the astronaut.

In the rest frame of the planets, the light from the nuclear explosion from planet Y arrives at the astronaut when:

$c\Delta t = (1\ \text{hour})\ c + v\Delta t$

$\Delta t = (1\ \text{hour})\ c / (c - v)$

If $v = 0.6c$, then:

$\Delta t = 2.5\ \text{hours}$

From planet Z, the light arrives to the astronaut at:

$c\Delta t = (1\ \text{hour})\ c - v\Delta t$

$\Delta t = (1\ \text{hour})\ c / (c + v)$

$\Delta t = 0.625\ \text{hours}$

This is 1.875 hours sooner as measured in the frame of the planets. In the planets' frame, the astronaut's clock appears to be moving slower because of time dilation. Therefore, the time interval measured by the astronaut is:

$\Delta t' = (1.875\ \text{hours}) / \gamma$

$\gamma = 1 / \sqrt{(1 - \beta^2)}$

$\gamma = 1.25$

$\Delta t' = 1.5\ \text{hours} = 90\ \text{minutes}$

Alternatively, consider the problem in the rest frame of the astronaut. In that frame, the two explosions do not occur simultaneously but rather at a time interval given by:

$$\Delta t = \gamma \, (\Delta t' + v \, \Delta x' / c^2)$$

where $\Delta t'$, the time interval as measured in the frame of the planets, is 0 and $\Delta x'$ is 2 light-hours. Therefore:

$$\Delta t = 1.25 \cdot (0.6c) \, (2 \text{ hours} \cdot c) / c^2$$

$$\Delta t = 1.5 \text{ hours} = 90 \text{ minutes}$$

15. D is correct. The speed of the Klingon ship as measured by the Enterprise is the relativistic addition of the speed of the Klingon ship as measured from Earth, plus the speed of Earth as measured from the Enterprise. The formula for the relativistic addition of speeds is:

$$\beta = (\beta_1 + \beta_2) / (1 + \beta_1\beta_2)$$

$$\beta = (0.9 + 0.8) / [1 + (0.9)(0.8)]$$

$$\beta = 0.988$$

$$v = 0.988 \, c$$

16. E is correct. In Sofia's inertial frames of reference, one before the spaceship increased its speed and one after, the spaceship is at rest. Therefore, the measurements of time and length must give the same result. Otherwise the laws of physics would be different in these two inertial frames of reference. During the acceleration of the spaceship, there are some unusual effects caused by the acceleration. Those effects are the subject of General Relativity.

17. C is correct.

In the frame of the beacons:

$$t = d / v$$

$$t = (40 \times 10^6 \text{ m}) / [(0.30)(3 \times 10^8 \text{ m/s})]$$

$$t = 44.4 \times 10^{-2} \text{ s}$$

$$t = 444 \text{ ms}$$

18. B is correct. Kinetic energy is total energy minus rest energy:

$$K = E - mc^2 = \gamma mc^2 - mc^2 = (\gamma - 1)mc^2,$$

where $\gamma = 1 / \sqrt{(1 - \beta^2)}$ and $\beta = v / c$.

$$\gamma = 1 / (\sqrt{[1 - (0.737)^2]}$$

$$\gamma = 1.480$$

So:

$$K = (1 - 1.480)(511 \text{ keV})$$

$$K = 245 \text{ keV}$$

19. D is correct.

The space time interval, Δs, is given by:

$$(\Delta s)^2 = (c\Delta t)^2 - (\Delta x)^2$$

For these events, $\Delta s = 90c$ years and $\Delta t = 100$ years. Solving for Δx:

$$(\Delta x)^2 = (100c \text{ years})^2 - (90c \text{ years})^2$$

$$(\Delta x)^2 = 1900c^2 \text{ years}^2$$

$$\Delta x = 44 \text{ light-years}$$

20. A is correct. Lorentz contraction and time dilation are proportional to:

$$\gamma = 1 / \sqrt{(1 - \beta^2)} \qquad \beta = v / c$$

Therefore, if $\gamma = 2$:

$$\beta^2 = 0.75$$

$$\beta = .866$$

$$v = 0.866c$$

21. A is correct. As measured from the inertial frame of Earth, time on the spaceship is dilated and a clock on the moving spaceship moves slower than a stationary clock on the earth. This is true when the spaceship is traveling away from Earth and when it is traveling towards the Earth. Therefore, the elapsed time on the spaceship, and the consequential advance of the age of the twin on the spaceship, is less than the elapsed time and age of the twin on Earth.

What is the difference between the two inertial frames? As viewed from the frame of Earth, nothing unusual happens while the spaceship is decelerating and re-accelerating as it changes directions and heads back to Earth. As viewed from the frame of the spaceship, time on Earth advances quickly while the spaceship is changing directions. It is during this short period that the spaceship-bound twin observes the Earth-bound twin aging rapidly.

If the apparent rate of change of time on Earth is calculated as measured by the twin on the decelerating and then accelerating spaceship, the result reflects the General Relativistic effect of a differing gravitational potential on time. After all, during the deceleration and acceleration, the twin on the spaceship is in a frame that is equivalent to a stationary frame with a uniform gravitational field. In that frame, the Earth, situated at a very different gravitational potential than the spaceship, is experiencing time moving very quickly due to the perceived gravitational potential difference, according to the weak equivalence principle.

22. E is correct.

Using subscript 1 and 2 for the two initial masses and subscript 3 for the final combined mass, conservation of momentum gives:

$$\gamma_1 m v_1 - \gamma_2 m v_2 = \gamma_3 m_3 v_3$$

Conservation of energy gives:

$$\gamma_1 m c^2 + \gamma_2 m c^2 = \gamma_3 m_3 c^2$$

Using these two equations to solve for $v_{\sqcap}$:

$$v_3 = (\gamma_1 v_1 - \gamma_2 v_2) / (\gamma_1 + \gamma_2)$$

$$\gamma_1 = 1 / \sqrt{(1 - 0.650^2)} = 1.316$$

$$\gamma_2 = 1 / \sqrt{(1 - 0.850^2)} = 1.898$$

$$v_3 = [(1.316 \cdot 0.650c) - (1.898 \cdot 0.850c)] / (1.316 + 1.898)$$

$$v_3 = -0.234c$$

$$\gamma_3 = 1 / \sqrt{(1 - 0.277^2)} = 1.029$$

Using the conservation of energy to solve for m_3:

$$m_3 = m(\gamma_1 + \gamma_2) / \gamma_3$$

$$m_3 = (100 \text{ kg}) \cdot (1.316 + 1.898) / 1.029$$

$$m_3 = 312 \text{ kg}$$

23. D is correct. The relativistic expression for momentum is:

$$p = \gamma m v = \gamma m \beta c,$$

where $\beta = v / c$ and $\gamma = 1 / \sqrt{(1 - \beta^2)}$.

Therefore:

$$\beta = 0.60$$

$$\gamma = 1 / \sqrt{(1 - 0.60^2)}$$

$$\gamma = 1.25$$

$$p = (1.25) \cdot (1.67 \times 10^{-27} \text{ kg}) \cdot (0.60) \cdot (3 \times 10^8)$$

$$p = 3.8 \times 10^{-19} \text{ kg·m/s}$$

24. B is correct. The total energy of the rock, γmc^2, is the sum of its rest mass plus the added energy:

$$E_{\text{Total}} = \gamma mc^2$$

$$E_{\text{Total}} = mc^2 + E_{\text{Added}}$$

$$E_{\text{Added}} = (\gamma - 1) mc^2$$

$$\gamma = 1 / \sqrt{(1 - \beta^2)}$$

$$\beta = v / c$$

Given that $v = 0.866c$,

$$\beta = 0.866$$

$$\gamma = 2.00$$

$$E_{\text{Added}} = (2.00 - 1) \cdot (1.0 \text{ kg}) \cdot (3.0 \times 10^8 \text{ m/s})^2$$

$$E_{\text{Added}} = 9.00 \times 10^{16} \text{ kg·m/s}$$

$$E_{\text{Added}} = 9.00 \times 10^{16} \text{ J}$$

25. C is correct.

The speed of the secondary rocket as measured in the frame of Earth is the relativistic addition of the speed of the secondary rocket as measured from the spaceship, plus the speed of the spaceship as measured from Earth. The formula for the relativistic addition of speeds is:

$$\beta = (\beta_1 + \beta_2) / (1 + \beta_1\beta_2)$$

$$\beta = (0.5 + 0.5) / [1 + (0.5){\cdot}(0.5)]$$

$$\beta = 0.80$$

$$v = 0.80\ c$$

26. A is correct.

The observer moving with the rocket is making the time measurements at the same location, i.e., $\Delta x_B = 0$. The Lorentz transformation is therefore simply:

$$T_A = \gamma\ T_B$$

Since γ is greater than one,

$$T_A > T_B$$

This is time dilation— the shortest time interval for two events occurs in the frame in which the two events take place at the same location, a frame stationary with respect to the two events. If those events are the clicking of a clock, then the clock appears to move the fastest in its rest frame.

27. B is correct.

As measured by an observer on Earth, the spaceship will have traveled for:

$$t = d\,/\,v$$

$$t = (4.367\ c\ \text{years}) / 0.50c$$

$$t = 8.734\ \text{years}$$

To an observer on the spaceship, $\Delta x' = 0$, and the time $\Delta t'$ is dilated by the Lorentz transformation:

$$\Delta t = \gamma\ \Delta t'$$

$$\gamma = 1 / \sqrt{(1 - \beta^2)}$$

$$\beta = v\,/\,c$$

$$\gamma = 1 / \sqrt{(1 - 0.50^2)}$$

$$\gamma = 1.15$$

$$\Delta t' = (8.734\ \text{years}) / 1.15$$

$$\Delta t' = 7.6\ \text{years}$$

28. D is correct. The decay time Δt in the rest frame of the particle (where $\Delta x = 0$) is dilated to a shorter elapsed time. Since $\Delta x = 0$, the Lorentz transformation for the two events is:

$$\Delta t' = \gamma \Delta t$$

$$\gamma = 1 / \sqrt{(1 - \beta^2)}$$

$$\beta = v / c = .997$$

$$\gamma = 12.9$$

$$\Delta t = 37.0 \ \mu s / 12.9$$

$$\Delta t = 2.9 \ \mu s$$

29. C is correct.

The total energy of a particle is:

$$E_{Total} = \gamma \ mc^2$$

When the kinetic energy is correctly defined as the difference between the total energy and the rest mass energy, then:

$$E_{Total} = mc^2 + E_{Kinetic}$$

$$E_{Kinetic} = (\gamma - 1) \ mc^2$$

$$\gamma = 1 / \sqrt{(1 - \beta^2)}$$

$$\beta = v / c$$

Given that $v = 0.5c$,

$$\beta = 0.5$$

$$\gamma = 1.1547$$

$$E_{Kinetic} = 0.1547 \ mc^2$$

$$E_{Kinetic} = (mv^2 / 2) \cdot (0.1547 \cdot 2) \cdot (c / v)^2$$

$$E_{Kinetic} = (mv^2 / 2) \cdot (1.24)$$

Therefore, by using $mv^2 / 2$ as the kinetic energy, the calculation will be off by:

$$mv^2 / 2 = 0.81 \times E_{Kinetic}, \text{ which is a 19\% error.}$$

30. B is correct.

The separation $\Delta x'$ of the two stars in a frame moving with respect to the two stars is affected by Lorentz Contraction. In the spaceship's frame, the measurement of $\Delta x'$ was made with $\Delta t' = 0$. The Lorentz transformation is therefore:

$$\Delta x = \gamma \ \Delta x'$$

$$\Delta x' = \Delta x / \gamma$$

$$\gamma = 1 / \sqrt{(1 - \beta^2)} \qquad \beta = v / c$$

Since $\Delta x = 90$ light-years and $\Delta x' = 68.7$ light-years:

$$\gamma = 90 / 68.7$$

Solving for β:

$$\beta = \sqrt{[1 - (1 / \gamma^2)]}$$

$$\beta = 0.646$$

Therefore:

$$v = 0.646c$$

31. D is correct. One of the postulates of Special Relativity is that the laws of physics are the same in all inertial frames. If the laws of physics are the same in all inertial frames, there is no way to differentiate one frame from another.

32. D is correct. Using subscript 1 and 2 for the two initial masses and subscript 3 for the final combined mass, conservation of momentum gives:

$$\gamma_1 m v_1 - \gamma_2 m v_2 = \gamma_3 m_3 v_3$$

Conservation of energy gives:

$$\gamma_1 m c^2 + \gamma_2 m c^2 = \gamma_3 m_3 c^2$$

Using these two equations to solve for v_3:

$$v_3 = (\gamma_1 v_1 - \gamma_2 v_2) / (\gamma_1 + \gamma_2)$$

$$\gamma_1 = 1 / \sqrt{(1 - 0.550^2)} = 1.197$$

$$\gamma_2 = 1 / \sqrt{(1 - 0.750^2)} = 1.512$$

$$v_3 = [(1.197 \cdot 0.550c) - (1.512 \cdot 0.750c)] / (1.197 + 1.512)$$

$$v_3 = -0.1756c$$

(The direction is in the opposite direction of the first satellite.)

33. A is correct. In the moving frame, the time interval between events is increased from the value measured in the rest frame because of time dilation. Consider two heartbeats as two events on the spaceship. They have a value of $\Delta x = 0$ and $\Delta t = (1 / 70)$ minutes. In the frame of Earth, because Δx on the spaceship is 0, the Lorentz transformation for $\Delta t'$ is simply:

$$\Delta t' = \gamma \, \Delta t,$$

where:

$$\gamma = 1 / \sqrt{(1 - \beta^2)}$$

$$\beta = v / c$$

$$\gamma = 1 / \sqrt{(1 - 0.50^2)}$$

$$\gamma = 1.15$$

$$\Delta t' = 1.15 \cdot (1 / 70) \text{ minutes}$$

$$\Delta t' = 0.0164 \text{ minutes}$$

The heart rate is therefore the inverse of this interval, 61 beats per minute.

34. B is correct.

The accelerator's length is contracted as measured in the frame of the particle:

$l' = l / \gamma,$

where $\beta = v / c$ and $\gamma = 1 / \sqrt{(1 - \beta^2)}$.

$l' = (453 \text{ m}) [\sqrt{(1 - (0.875)^2)}]$

$l' = 219 \text{ m}$

35. C is correct.

In the spaceship's frame, the two events have a value of $\Delta x = 0$. The time difference in the spaceship's frame appears to be dilated, so that the time difference in the frame of Earth is given by:

$\Delta t' = \gamma \, \Delta t$

$\gamma = 1 / \sqrt{(1 - \beta^2)}$ $\beta = v / c$

Since $\Delta t = 5.78$ years and $\Delta t' = 10$ years:

$\gamma = 10 / 5.78$

Solving for β:

$\beta = \sqrt{(1 - 1 / \gamma^2)}$

$\beta = 0.816$

Therefore:

$v = 0.816c$

36. C is correct. The length of a moving object appears to be shortened by Lorentz contraction.

In the frame of the stationary observer on the ground, the length measurement involves two events with $\Delta t' = 0$ and $\Delta x'$ being the length of the moving train as measured by the stationary observer. In the frame of the moving train, those two events have an Δx value equal to the length of the train as measured in the rest frame of the train. (Note that the value of Δt is not zero.) Since $\Delta t'$ is zero, the Lorentz transformation for Δx is simply:

$\Delta x = \gamma \, \Delta x'$

Since γ is greater than 1, $\Delta x'$, the length as measured by the stationary observer on the ground, is less than Δx, the length as measured in the rest frame of the train.

37. C is correct.

At first glance this is a complicated problem, since the velocity of the spaceship is not known and cannot be easily determined. However, the space-time interval, Δs^2, of the two events (i.e. the spaceship crossing the orbit of Jupiter and Mars) can be determined. The space-time interval is the same in all frames.

$\Delta s^2 = (c\Delta t)^2 + (\Delta x)^2$

$\Delta s'^2 = (c\Delta t')^2 + (\Delta x')^2$

In the spaceship's frame, the distance between the two measurements is $\Delta x = 0$ and the time between the two measurements is Δt. In the earth's frame:

$$\Delta x' = (778 \times 10^9 \text{ m}) - (228 \times 10^9 \text{ m})$$

$$\Delta x' = 550 \times 10^9 \text{ m}$$

It is given that:

$$\Delta t' = 50.0 \text{ minutes}$$

Solving for Δt by equating the space-time interval in the two frames:

$$(c\Delta t)^2 = (c\Delta t')^2 + (\Delta x')^2$$

$$\Delta t^2 = \Delta t'^2 + (\Delta x'/c)^2$$

$$\Delta t^2 = (50 \text{ minutes} \cdot 60 \text{ s/minute})^2 + (550 \times 10^9 \text{ m}) / (3.0 \times 10^8 \text{ m/s})$$

$$\Delta t^2 = (3000 \text{ s})^2 + (1833 \text{ s})^2$$

$$\Delta t^2 = (3515 \text{ s})^2$$

$$\Delta t = 58.6 \text{ minutes}$$

38. D is correct.

In the frame of the two beacons, in a time Δt, a radar signal goes from one beacon to the other beacon and then back to the moving spaceship, while the moving spaceship travels from the first beacon towards the second beacon. So, the total distance traveled by the spaceship plus the radar signal in Δt is exactly twice the distance between the two beacons:

$$2 \cdot (65 \times 10^6 \text{ m}) = (0.90c + c)\Delta t$$

$$\Delta t = (68.4 \times 10^6 \text{ m}) / (3 \times 10^8 \text{ m})$$

$$\Delta t = 228 \text{ ms}$$

$$\Delta t = 228 \text{ ms}$$

The time interval as measured in the frame of the moving spaceship is this time interval transformed into the spaceship's frame for which a stationary clock has $\Delta x' = 0$ (note that Δx is not zero). Therefore, the Lorentz transformation is:

$$\Delta t = \gamma \, \Delta t'$$

$$\Delta t' = \Delta t / \gamma$$

$$\gamma = 1 / \sqrt{(1 - \beta^2)}$$

$$\beta = v/c = 0.9$$

$$\gamma = 2.29$$

$$\Delta t' = 228 \text{ ms} / 2.29$$

$$\Delta t' = 100 \text{ ms}$$

39. B is correct. The total energy of the electron, γmc^2, is the sum of its rest mass plus the potential difference through which it is accelerated, V, times its charge, e:

$$\gamma mc^2 = mc^2 + eX$$

$$V = mc \, (\gamma - 1)$$

where $\gamma = 1 / \sqrt{(1 - \beta^2)}$ and $\beta = v / c$.

$$\gamma = 1 / \sqrt{[1 - (0.648)^2]}$$

$$\gamma = 1.313$$

$$V = 511 \text{ keV} \cdot 0.313$$

$$V = 160 \text{ keV}$$

40. C is correct. In the particle's frame, the two events (creation and annihilation) have a value of $\Delta x = 0$. The time difference in the laboratory's frame appears to be dilated by:

$$\Delta t' = \gamma \, \Delta t$$

$$\gamma = 1 / \sqrt{(1 - \beta^2)} \qquad \beta = v / c$$

and:

$$\Delta x' = v\Delta t'$$

Since $\Delta t = 1.52 \times 10^{-6}$ s and $\Delta x' = 342$m:

$$342 \text{ m} = v\gamma \, (1.52 \times 10^{-6} \text{ s})$$

Dividing both sides by c:

$$(342 \text{ m}) / (3.00 \times 10^8 \text{ m/s}) = (v/c) \, \gamma \, (1.52 \times 10^{-6} \text{ s})$$

$$0.75 = \beta \, \gamma$$

$$0.75 = \sqrt{[\beta^2 / (1 - \beta^2)]}$$

$$0.75 = \sqrt{[1 / \beta^2 - 1)]}$$

Solving for B:

$$\beta = 0.6$$

$$v = 0.6c$$

41. C is correct. The relativistic kinetic energy formula is derived from the conservation of energy:

$$E_{\text{total}} = \gamma \, mc^2$$

This is true for all values of γ (or velocity). The kinetic energy formula acts as a definition of kinetic energy by dividing the total energy into a rest mass component and a kinetic component:

$$E_{\text{total}} = mc^2 + E_{\text{kinetic}}$$

$$E_{\text{kinetic}} = (\gamma - 1)mc^2$$

For $v < c$, a Taylor expansion for $(\gamma - 1)$ gives the Newtonian formula for kinetic energy:

$$E_{\text{kinetic}} = mv^2 / 2, \quad \text{which will be true only for non-relativistic velocities.}$$

42. B is correct. The separation $\Delta x'$ of Earth and the star in a frame moving with respect to the spaceship is affected by Lorentz contraction. Since the separation $\Delta x'$ is measured when $\Delta t'$ is zero, the Lorentz transformation is simply:

$\Delta x = \gamma \Delta x'$

$\gamma = 1 / \sqrt{(1 - \beta^2)}$ $\beta = v / c$

With $v = 0.800c$ and $\Delta x = 4.30$ light-years:

$\gamma = 1.67$

$\Delta x' = 2.58$ light-years

43. B is correct. The speed of the missile as measured in the frame of the asteroid is the relativistic addition of the speed of the spaceship as measured from the asteroid, plus the speed of the missile as measured from the spaceship. The two velocities are in opposite direction. The formula for the relativistic addition of two speeds in the same directions is:

$\beta = (\beta_1 + \beta_2) / (1 + \beta_1 \beta_2)$

$\beta = (0.8 + 0.5) / [1 + (0.8) \cdot (0.5)]$

$\beta = 0.93$

$v = 0.93c$

44. A is correct. The total energy of a particle of mass m moving with velocity v is given by:

$E = \gamma\, mc^2$

$\gamma = 1 / \sqrt{(1 - \beta^2)}$

$\gamma = v / c$

$\gamma = 0.950$

$\gamma = 1 / \sqrt{(1 - 0.950^2)}$

$\gamma = 3.20$

$E = (3.20) \cdot (9.11 \times 10^{-31}\ \text{kg}) \cdot (3.0 \times 10^8\ \text{m/s})^2$

$E = 2.6 \times 10^{-13}\ \text{J}$

45. D is correct.

In the spaceship's frame, the two events (two time measurements on the same clock) have a value of $\Delta x = 0$. The time difference in the spaceship's frame appears to be dilated, so that the time difference in the frame of Earth is given by:

$\Delta t' = \gamma\, \Delta t$

$\gamma = 1 / \sqrt{(1 - \beta^2)}$ $\beta = v / c$

Since $\Delta t = 1.0$ s and $v = 0.960c$:

$\gamma = 3.6$

$\Delta t = 3.6$ s

46. A is correct.

In the frame of the first particle, the speed of the second particle is the relativistic sum of the speed of Earth (as measured from the frame of the first particle - note that Earth appears to be moving to the right), plus the speed of the second particle (as measured from the frame of Earth – note that it appears to be moving to the right). The formula for the relativistic addition of two speeds in the same directions is:

$$\beta = (\beta_1 + \beta_2) / (1 + \beta_1\beta_2)$$

$$\beta = (0.741 + 0.543) / [1 + (0.741)(0.543)]$$

$$\beta = 0.916$$

$$v = 0.916c$$

47. A is correct.

Relativistic momentum is given by:

$$p = \gamma mv = \gamma m\beta c, \text{ where } \beta = v / c \text{ and } \gamma = 1 / \sqrt{(1 - \beta^2)}$$

Newtonian momentum is given by:

$$p = mv$$

The percentage difference is:

$$(\gamma mv - mv) / \gamma mv = [(1 - (1 / \gamma)]$$

For $v = 0.86c$:

$$\gamma = 1 / \sqrt{(1 - .86^2)}$$

$$\gamma = 1.96$$

$$1 - (1 / \gamma) = .49 = 49\%$$

48. B is correct.

The speed of the secondary rocket as measured in the frame of the space platform is the relativistic addition of the speed of the secondary rocket as measured in the frame of the spaceship, plus the speed of the spaceship as measured in the frame of the space platform. The two velocities are in opposite direction. The formula for the relativistic addition of two speeds in opposite directions is:

$$\beta = (\beta_1 - \beta_2) / (1 - \beta_1\beta_2)$$

$$\beta = (0.1 - 0.56) / [1 - (0.1)(0.56)]$$

$$\beta = 0.487$$

$$v = 0.487c$$

49. D is correct.

The relativistic expression for momentum is $p = \gamma mv = \gamma m\beta c$, where $\beta = v / c$ and $\gamma = 1 / \sqrt{(1 - \beta^2)}$. Therefore:

$$\Delta p = \gamma_1 v_1 m - \gamma_2 v_2 m,$$

where subscript 1 refers to before the slowing and subscript 2 refers to after the slowing.

$\Delta p = [(\gamma_1 v_1 / c) - (\gamma_2 v_2 / c)]mc^2/c$

$v_1 = 0.998c$

$\beta_1 = 0.998$

$\gamma_1 = 1 / \sqrt{(1 - 0.998^2)}$

$\gamma_1 = 15.82$

$v_2 = 0.500c$

$\beta_2 = 0.500$

$\gamma_2 = 1 / \sqrt{(1 - 0.500^2)}$

$\gamma_2 = 1.155$

$\Delta p = [(15.82 \cdot 0.998) - (1.155 \cdot 0.500)] \cdot (511 \text{ keV}) / c$

$\Delta p = (7772 / c \text{ keV})$

$\Delta p = 7.77 \text{ MeV}/c$

50. D is correct.

The speed of light has the same value for any observer, regardless of the state of motion of the source or the observer. This is a fundamental principle of Special Relativity.

Made in the USA
Middletown, DE
03 January 2019